# Frameworks and Cases on Evolutional Supply Chain

Toru Higuchi
*Tokyo Seitoku University, Japan*

IGI Global
PUBLISHER of TIMELY KNOWLEDGE

A volume in the Advances in Logistics, Operations, and Management Science (ALOMS) Book Series

Published in the United States of America by
IGI Global
Business Science Reference (an imprint of IGI Global)
701 E. Chocolate Avenue
Hershey PA, USA 17033
Tel: 717-533-8845
Fax: 717-533-8661
E-mail: cust@igi-global.com
Web site: http://www.igi-global.com



Library of Congress Cataloging-in-Publication Data

Names: Higuchi, Toru, editor.
Title: Frameworks and cases on evolutional supply chain / Toru Higuchi, editor.
Description: Hershey, PA : Business Science Reference, [2022] | Includes bibliographical references and index. | Summary: "This book gives readers the frameworks of evolutional supply chain through symbolic case studies helping more people understand the dynamic aspects of the supply chain, such as changes in the suppliers, factory and storage locations, production processes, distribution structures and more"-- Provided by publisher.
Identifiers: LCCN 2022970042 (print) | LCCN 2022970043 (ebook) | ISBN 9781799898009 (hardcover) | ISBN 9781799898016 (paperback) | ISBN 9781799898023 (ebook)
Subjects: LCSH: Business logistics.
Classification: LCC HD38.5 .F723 2022 (print) | LCC HD38.5 (ebook) | DDC 658.5--dc23/eng/20220223
LC record available at https://lccn.loc.gov/2022970042
LC ebook record available at https://lccn.loc.gov/2022970043

This book is published in the IGI Global book series Advances in Logistics, Operations, and Management Science (ALOMS) (ISSN: 2327-350X; eISSN: 2327-3518)

British Cataloguing in Publication Data
A Cataloguing in Publication record for this book is available from the British Library.

# Advances in Logistics, Operations, and Management Science (ALOMS) Book Series

John Wang
Montclair State University, USA

ISSN:2327-350X
EISSN:2327-3518

## Mission

Operations research and management science continue to influence business processes, administration, and management information systems, particularly in covering the application methods for decision-making processes. New case studies and applications on management science, operations management, social sciences, and other behavioral sciences have been incorporated into business and organizations real-world objectives.

The **Advances in Logistics, Operations, and Management Science** (ALOMS) Book Series provides a collection of reference publications on the current trends, applications, theories, and practices in the management science field. Providing relevant and current research, this series and its individual publications would be useful for academics, researchers, scholars, and practitioners interested in improving decision making models and business functions.

## Coverage

- Computing and information technologies
- Marketing engineering
- Information Management
- Production Management
- Risk Management
- Services management
- Operations Management
- Organizational Behavior
- Decision analysis and decision support
- Political Science

IGI Global is currently accepting manuscripts for publication within this series. To submit a proposal for a volume in this series, please contact our Acquisition Editors at Acquisitions@igi-global.com or visit: http://www.igi-global.com/publish/.

The Advances in Logistics, Operations, and Management Science (ALOMS) Book Series (ISSN 2327-350X) is published by IGI Global, 701 E. Chocolate Avenue, Hershey, PA 17033-1240, USA, www.igi-global.com. This series is composed of titles available for purchase individually; each title is edited to be contextually exclusive from any other title within the series. For pricing and ordering information please visit http://www.igi-global.com/book-series/advances-logistics-operations-management-science/37170. Postmaster: Send all address changes to above address. 

## Titles in this Series

*For a list of additional titles in this series, please visit: www.igi-global.com/book-series/advances-logistics-operations-management-science/37170*

***Empowering Sustainable Industrial 4.0 Systems With Machine Intelligence***
Muneer Ahmad (University of Malaya, Malaysia) and Noor Zaman (Taylor's University, Malaysia)
Business Science Reference • © 2022 • 315pp • H/C (ISBN: 9781799892014) • US $225.00

***Interdisciplinary and Practical Approaches to Managerial Education and Training***
Luísa Cagica Carvalho (Polytechnic Institute of Setúbal, Portugal & CEFAGE, University of Évora, Portugal) Nuno Teixeira (Polytechnic Institute of Setúbal, Portugal) and Pedro Pardal (Polytechnic Institute of Setúbal, Portugal)
Business Science Reference • © 2022 • 353pp • H/C (ISBN: 9781799882398) • US $195.00

***Handbook of Research on the Future of the Maritime Industry***
Nihan Senbursa (University of Ordu, Turkey)
Business Science Reference • © 2022 • 465pp • H/C (ISBN: 9781799890393) • US $395.00

***Handbook of Research on Museum Management in the Digital Era***
Francesco Bifulco (University of Naples Federico II, Italy) and Marco Tregua (University of Naples Federico II, Italy)
Information Science Reference • © 2022 • 412pp • H/C (ISBN: 9781799896562) • US $245.00

***Management Strategies for Sustainability, New Knowledge Innovation, and Personalized Products and Services***
Mirjana Pejic-Bach (University of Zagreb, Croatia) and Çağlar Doğru (Ufuk University, Turkey)
Business Science Reference • © 2022 • 365pp • H/C (ISBN: 9781799877936) • US $215.00

***Cases on Supply Chain Management and Lessons Learned From COVID-19***
Ana Paula Lopes (Polytechnic of Porto, Portugal)
Business Science Reference • © 2022 • 238pp • H/C (ISBN: 9781799891406) • US $225.00

***Key Factors and Use Cases of Servant Leadership Driving Organizational Performance***
Maria Pressentin (International School of Management, France)
Business Science Reference • © 2022 • 368pp • H/C (ISBN: 9781799888208) • US $215.00

***Handbook of Research on Innovative Management Using AI in Industry 5.0***
Vikas Garg (Amity University, Greater Noida, India) and Richa Goel (Amity University, Noida, India)
Business Science Reference • © 2022 • 351pp • H/C (ISBN: 9781799884972) • US $295.00

IGI Global
PUBLISHER of TIMELY KNOWLEDGE

701 East Chocolate Avenue, Hershey, PA 17033, USA
Tel: 717-533-8845 x100 • Fax: 717-533-8661
E-Mail: cust@igi-global.com • www.igi-global.com

# Table of Contents

**Preface** .......... xiv

**Acknowledgment** .......... xix

**Section 1**
**Frameworks and Cases on Evolutional Supply Chain**

**Chapter 1**
Evolutional Supply Chain Management and Strategy: Pencil Supply Chain Case .......... 1
*Toru Higuchi, Tokyo Seitoku University, Japan*

**Chapter 2**
Cost Management of Logistics and Supply Chain Costs .......... 24
*Hiroyuki Nakajima, Meisei University, Japan*

**Section 2**
**Automotive Cases**

**Chapter 3**
Progress of Electric Vehicles and Transformation of Supply Chain in the Japanese Automobile Industry .......... 46
*Kimito Nasuno, Sakushin Gakuin University, Japan*

**Chapter 4**
An Evaluation Model for Supplier Selection for European, American, and Japanese Automotive Companies .......... 68
*Yu-Shan Su, National Taiwan Normal University, Taiwan*
*Tien-Shou Wang, National Taiwan Normal University, Taiwan*

**Chapter 5**
CSR Initiatives in the Supply Chain of the Japanese Automotive Industry: The Role of Parts Industry Association .......... 95
*Hiromu Hatakeyama, Sakushin Gakuin University, Japan*

**Section 3**
**Retailing Cases**


**Chapter 6**
Controlling Bullwhip Effect in Supply Chain by BANDAI Co: Lessons From the Tamagotchi™ Case ........ 115
*Toru Higuchi, Tokyo Seitoku University, Japan*

**Chapter 7**
Supply Chain Management of Seven-Eleven Japan ........ 133
*Nobuaki Ishikawa, Sakushin Gakuin University, Japan*

**Chapter 8**
Driving Forces and Factors of Amazon Effects: From Online Bookstores to Cloud Services ........ 148
*Yang Zhengguang, Sakushin Gakuin University, Japan*


**Section 4**
**Food and Beverage Cases**


**Chapter 9**
Product and Process Innovation in Coffee Supply Chain: From Seed to Cup ........ 169
*Linh Dieu Nguyen, Sakushin Gakuin University, Japan*
*Yukun Huang, Sakushin Gakuin University, Japan*
*Zhengguang Yang, Sakushin Gakuin University, Japan*
*Gary Mason, Independent Researcher, USA*

**Chapter 10**
Supply Chain Models and Functions of Food Service Chains in Japan: The Food SPA at Saizeriya 194
*Hitomi Nakagawa, Sakushin Gakuin University, Japan*

**Chapter 11**
Agri-Food Logistics as a Dynamic Actor in Managing Food Loss and Waste: A Bump-Start by COVID-19 ........ 215
*Erika Quendler, Federal Institute of Agricultural Economics, Rural and Mountain Research, Vienna, Austria*
*Matthew James Lamb, LKT-TGM Polymer and Environmental Centre, Vienna, Austria*
*Noureddin Driouech, International Centre for Advanced Mediterranean Agronomic Studies – CIHEAM, Bari, Italy*


**Section 5**
**Global Issues**


**Chapter 12**
The Global Supply Chain Management System Involving the ASEAN Industrial Clusters ........ 240
*Tetsuro Saisho, Former Gunma University, Japan*

**Chapter 13**
Relocation Strategy of Production, Global Supply, and Value Chains ............ 259
*José G. Vargas-Hernández, Tecnológico Mario Molina Unidad Zapopan, Mexico*

**Chapter 14**
Evolutional Characteristics of the Global Supply Chain in Various Industries ............ 278
*Yanghua Zhou, Edogawa University, Japan*

**Compilation of References** ............ 301

**About the Contributors** ............ 325

**Index** ............ 328

# Detailed Table of Contents

**Preface**............................................................................................................................................. xiv

**Acknowledgment**................................................................................................................................ xix

**Section 1**
**Frameworks and Cases on Evolutional Supply Chain**

*Section 1 clarifies the outline of the entire book by presenting the frameworks for evolutional, variable, and diverse supply chains. This section summarizes the evolution of supply chain structures and activities and discusses supply chain profitability from the view of managerial and logistics costs.*

**Chapter 1**
Evolutional Supply Chain Management and Strategy: Pencil Supply Chain Case................................. 1
*Toru Higuchi, Tokyo Seitoku University, Japan*

At the beginning of this chapter, SCM and related concepts such as physical distribution, business logistics, and company groups are explained, and the areas of difference among them are clarified. In the middle of this chapter, the framework of a supply chain and SCM are described. Important factors about SCM and drivers changing the supply chain management and strategy are proposed. At the end of this chapter, the case of the pencil supply chain is introduced to illustrate the evolutional SCM and supply chain strategy. The pencil supply chain has a long history and has experienced dramatic changes due to product and process innovations.

**Chapter 2**
Cost Management of Logistics and Supply Chain Costs..................................................................... 24
*Hiroyuki Nakajima, Meisei University, Japan*

In order for a supply chain to thrive, it must be evaluated from a financial perspective. In particular, supply chain profits and profitability are important performance measures. However, since it is very difficult to evaluate the profit side of the supply chain, this chapter focuses on the cost management of logistics and supply chain costs. The premise of supply chain cost management is that each company participating in the supply chain is able to manage logistics costs appropriately. Therefore, the authors discuss the management of logistics costs by utilizing management accounting methods such as activity-based costing, total cost of ownership, and life cycle cost. Then, after clarifying what exactly is meant by supply chain costs, supply chain cost management is discussed. The management of costs incurred across multiple companies is much more difficult than the cost management of a single company, and the issues that must be overcome are clarified. Finally, directions for future research are presented.

## Section 2
## Automotive Cases

*Section 2 goes deep into studying the automotive supply chain and its SCM. Automotive companies and their suppliers have formed the most advanced, efficient, and effective supply chains. While the automotive industry's supply chain has constantly improved, they sometimes need to make significant changes.*

**Chapter 3**
Progress of Electric Vehicles and Transformation of Supply Chain in the Japanese Automobile Industry ........ 46
*Kimito Nasuno, Sakushin Gakuin University, Japan*

This chapter looks back on changes in the supply chain of the Japanese automobile industry and then examines its future. In the wake of Volkswagen's diesel fraud, the global automobile industry is moving toward abolishing internal combustion engine vehicles and switching to EVs (electric vehicles) as the environmental policies of each country join the battle for the initiative over next-generation cars. Industry members are in a hurry to gain the initiative. In EV, there is a belief that the horizontal division of labor in the supply chain will be promoted by eliminating complicated engines. Therefore, in this chapter, the author examined whether the vertical "KEIRETSU" or "KEIRETSU transaction," a characteristic of the supply chain of the Japanese automobile industry, would be swallowed up by the wave of horizontal division of labor.

**Chapter 4**
An Evaluation Model for Supplier Selection for European, American, and Japanese Automotive Companies........ 68
*Yu-Shan Su, National Taiwan Normal University, Taiwan*
*Tien-Shou Wang, National Taiwan Normal University, Taiwan*

Taiwanese suppliers lead the world in the fastener market. In 2014, exported fasteners from Taiwan amounted to USD 4.25 billion, ranking third behind Germany and China. Taiwan is an important location for the international procurement of fasteners. This chapter has three objectives. The first is to explore the evaluation criteria and their weights for fastener supplier selection for automotive companies and develop an evaluation model for fastener supplier selection. The second is to explore investment priorities and improvement for fastener suppliers for automotive companies to become qualified fastener suppliers. The third is to explore the differences in the supplier evaluation between European, American, and Japanese automotive companies and the differences in the investment and improvement priorities of being a supplier for the European, American, and Japanese automotive companies. This chapter fills the research gap for fastener supplier selection for European, American, and Japanese automotive companies.

**Chapter 5**
CSR Initiatives in the Supply Chain of the Japanese Automotive Industry: The Role of Parts Industry Association ........ 95
*Hiromu Hatakeyama, Sakushin Gakuin University, Japan*

An automobile product is made up of tens of thousands of parts, many of which are procured from suppliers rather than manufactured by the automaker itself. Therefore, for automakers to steadily implement CSR initiatives, not only automakers but also all companies that make up the supply chain must promote such initiatives. Until now, existing studies have focused only on the efforts of companies such as automakers and suppliers and have not examined the efforts of industry associations, which play an extremely important role in the steady development of CSR initiatives in the supply chain. Therefore, this chapter examines the role and importance of the supplier-side industry association (JAPIA) in the development of CSR initiatives in the supply chain of the Japanese automotive industry. About CSR initiatives in the Japanese automotive industry, JAPIA's efforts have been extremely important in facilitating and ensuring supply chain initiatives. Thanks to the efforts of JAPIA, the Japanese automotive industry has been able to realize supply chain management in terms of CSR.

**Section 3**
**Retailing Cases**

*Section 3 analyzes the transition in the retailing sector, including distribution, from the view of SCM. The retailing sector is much more flexible and variable than the manufacturing sector due to the less fixed assets. Retailing section is more susceptible to market and technology influences than manufacturers.*

**Chapter 6**
Controlling Bullwhip Effect in Supply Chain by BANDAI Co: Lessons From the Tamagotchi™ Case .......... 115
*Toru Higuchi, Tokyo Seitoku University, Japan*

This chapter illustrates how the bullwhip effect is exacerbated in the supply chain through the Tamagotchi™ case. BANDAI first introduced Tamagotchi™ to the market on November 23, 1996. It became tremendously popular throughout the world in 1997, touching the hearts of children and young adults globally. While BANDAI sold 40 million of the first Tamagotchi™ worldwide by March 1999, this effort ended in tragedy. BANDAI suffered from the tragic boom and bust. The causes can be summarized as follows: a demand forecast failure and an immature SCM including a wrong response which created an excessive boom and sudden bust. BANDAI learned from this severe lesson in launching new series and managing the company and supply chain. Instant and substantial ways to cope with the bullwhip effect exaggerated in a supply chain will be proposed.

**Chapter 7**
Supply Chain Management of Seven-Eleven Japan .......... 133
*Nobuaki Ishikawa, Sakushin Gakuin University, Japan*

In this chapter, the supply chain management of Seven-Eleven Japan, the most successful convenience store in Japan, will be taken as a case study. First, the establishment and development of the convenience store industry in Japan (which has always been led by Seven-Eleven) will be described. Next, the characteristics of Seven-Eleven Japan and how it has been accepted by customers will be discussed. Finally, the future prospects of the convenience store industry and Seven-Eleven will be discussed.

**Chapter 8**
Driving Forces and Factors of Amazon Effects: From Online Bookstores to Cloud Services .......... 148
*Yang Zhengguang, Sakushin Gakuin University, Japan*

The development of Amazon so far is mainly due to Jeff Bezos's leadership. By sticking to a customer-focused policy and starting an online bookstore, he changed how retailers handle a wide range of books and everything, breaking Pareto's law and achieving a long tail. What's more, he politely responded to customer demands and devised a Fly Wheel strategy. By providing an effective product lineup at a low cost, Amazon has accelerated the virtuous cycle of increasing the ability to attract customers and has grown sales exponentially. On the other hand, Amazon invested the profits it earned in technology development and conducted research and development of cutting-edge digital technology. In addition, Amazon has been active in business models such as 1-click, FBA, Amazon Prime, and Marketplace. As a platformer, it has expanded its business to its own B2C and the B2B area for other companies' platforms.

## Section 4
## Food and Beverage Cases

*Section 4 provides new perspectives and approaches along with food and beverage cases. Freshness plays a vital role in the taste and hygiene of food and beverages. Individual companies and supply chains take various measures to ensure prompt delivery and freshness.*

**Chapter 9**
Product and Process Innovation in Coffee Supply Chain: From Seed to Cup .................................... 169
*Linh Dieu Nguyen, Sakushin Gakuin University, Japan*
*Yukun Huang, Sakushin Gakuin University, Japan*
*Zhengguang Yang, Sakushin Gakuin University, Japan*
*Gary Mason, Independent Researcher, USA*

In this chapter, the framework of the evolutional supply chain and supply chain strategy is illustrated through the case of the coffee supply chain. Billions of people drink coffee daily throughout the world. The coffee supply chain has a long history that has frequently experienced dramatic changes. The method and instruments for making coffee have changed, and the plantation system has long been used. Today, the world is full of various coffee products and coffee supply chains. It is imperative to refine not only SCM but also to formulate a successful supply chain strategy.

**Chapter 10**
Supply Chain Models and Functions of Food Service Chains in Japan: The Food SPA at Saizeriya 194
*Hitomi Nakagawa, Sakushin Gakuin University, Japan*

This chapter discusses the supply chain management (SCM) of the foodservice industry in Japan. For a restaurant to grow by developing a chain and opening multiple stores, it needs a supply chain that links the central kitchen, manufacture and direct sales, and cold chain. Therefore, using Saizeriya, a major restaurant chain in Japan, as a case study, the authors identify Saizeriya's management strategy, supply chain model, and its functions. Although Saizeriya is in the restaurant industry, it has adopted the business model of speciality store retailer of private label apparel (SPA), which is prevalent in the apparel industry. In this study, the authors clarify how the company has improved the efficiency of its supply chain while controlling the effects of the rising costs of raw materials and logistics.

**Chapter 11**
Agri-Food Logistics as a Dynamic Actor in Managing Food Loss and Waste: A Bump-Start by COVID-19 ..... 215
*Erika Quendler, Federal Institute of Agricultural Economics, Rural and Mountain Research, Vienna, Austria*
*Matthew James Lamb, LKT-TGM Polymer and Environmental Centre, Vienna, Austria*
*Noureddin Driouech, International Centre for Advanced Mediterranean Agronomic Studies – CIHEAM, Bari, Italy*

Perhaps no phenomenon has so quickly and radically challenged agri-food logistics as the onset of the COVID-19 pandemic. This chapter postulates on the short- to longer-term implications of this public health crisis on food loss and waste (FLW) throughout the whole supply chain and the role of agri-food logistics. This chapter outlines examples of several logistic solutions deployed for dealing with FLW as the pandemic has unfolded. Furthermore, since COVID-19 has opened a window of opportunity, this chapter indicates the potential of agri-food logistics to help manage FLW from farm to bin and beyond. In fact, the pandemic and its aftermath may improve agri-food logistics skills, practices, and innovation in a manner that mitigates day-to-day FLW. Moreover, this chapter advocates a rethinking of the opportunities arising from COVID-19 for the transformation of agri-food logistics in alignment with the UN's SDGs. This forms a practical framework for future research and application.

**Section 5**
**Global Issues**

*Section 5 discusses the changes in and evolution of global supply chains from a macro perspective. The supply chain exists everywhere consumers are in the world, and the supply chains are evolving daily to meet consumer needs by changing their structure and management.*

**Chapter 12**
The Global Supply Chain Management System Involving the ASEAN Industrial Clusters ..... 240
*Tetsuro Saisho, Former Gunma University, Japan*

In the ASEAN, as a national industrial policy, many industrial clusters, such as industrial parks, have been established, and the region is experiencing dynamic growth through foreign direct investment. In the industrial clusters of the ASEAN, attracting foreign companies has had a great economic spillover effect, including increased employment of workers and creation of demand in the region. In addition, among the ASEAN countries, especially Thailand and the neighboring CLMV nations, the construction of a global supply chain, with distribution systems such as the East-West Economic Corridor, North-South Economic Corridor, and Southern Economic Corridor, is increasing the countries' connectivity. The regional GSC with neighboring countries is an international business system based on collaboration between cross-border industrial clusters and other business entities, here involving the logistics systems of the ASEAN countries. In this study, the authors consider the current situation and issues regarding the cross-border GSC that Thailand is developing with its neighbors in the ASEAN.

**Chapter 13**
Relocation Strategy of Production, Global Supply, and Value Chains ............................................. 259
*José G. Vargas-Hernández, Tecnológico Mario Molina Unidad Zapopan, Mexico*

This chapter aims to critically analyze the implications that the national protectionist policies have on the global supply and value chains and the relocation of production. The analysis is based on the assumptions that the global economy is facing the possibility of decoupling of many trade connections and this trend favors deglobalization processes have long been promoted by populism, nationalism, and economic protectionism. It is concluded that global supply, production, and value chains, although being economically efficient, are no longer any more secure under national protectionist policies, and therefore, the relocation of production processes is mainly due to the increase in the level of income and wages of the developing countries that are the destination and which reduce the advantages to relocate.

**Chapter 14**
Evolutional Characteristics of the Global Supply Chain in Various Industries ................................. 278
*Yanghua Zhou, Edogawa University, Japan*

In this chapter, a literature review and abstract analysis is conducted on the evolutional characteristics of the global supply chain in various industries of the developed country of Japan and the emerging economy of China, respectively. It finds that in both countries, with the advancement of Industry 4.0, high-tech approaches, such as big data, AI, and DX, are gradually being utilized in the GSC. These approaches greatly contribute to its improvement in terms of efficiency, performance, and anti-risk capabilities. In addition, reducing costs and raising efficiency are effective measures for optimizing the GSC. Specifically, warehouse integration, positioning of warehouses, matching and sharing consumers' needs with both suppliers and agencies, further informatization and visualization of goods, innovative packing methods, reducing container numbers, and storage points are worth considering. A common SC platform and better SC resilience are expected. Other specific measures are also discussed.

**Compilation of References** ........................................................................................................ 301

**About the Contributors** ............................................................................................................. 325

**Index** ........................................................................................................................................... 328

# Preface

*Frameworks and Cases on Evolutional Supply Chain* is designed to explain to readers such as practitioners, students, and supply chain researchers how, why, and when supply chains change. Modern life survives through products that pass through many supply chains. In other words, any product that is not handmade or gathered from the wilderness utilizes a supply chain. The structure and activities of the supply chain are rather diverse and have a significant impact on the quality of goods, prices, and service levels. Properly managing the supply chain will lead to better quality, lower costs, superior service levels, and higher supply chain profitability. Therefore, SCM (Supply Chain Management) is absolutely vital.

Several chapters in this book track the long-term changes in supply chains. Nonetheless, this book is unique because it presents the SCM framework and explains recent trends in the supply chain through various existing cases as well as broader socio-cultural changes like COVID-19 and the environment (Electric Vehicles and food loss). Environmental topics such as EVs and food loss are highlighted in Chapters 3, 5, and 11, while Chapters 1 and 12 address SCM post-COVID-19. Chapters 8 and 14 focus on changes in business and SCM due to ICT (Information and Communication Technologies).

*Frameworks and Cases on Evolutional Supply Chain* consists of 14 chapters divided into five sections. Section 1, "Frameworks of Evolutional Supply Chain," outlines the frameworks for evolutionary, variable, and diverse supply chains. This section attempts to capture the evolution of supply chain frameworks from a long-term and by-stage perspective. Rapidly advancing technology and changing social conditions have created a wide variety of products, widening the range of choices for consumers and increasing competition. The supply chain also continues to undergo significant shifts in response to these changes. This section encapsulates the evolution of supply chain structures and activities and thereby discusses supply chain profitability.

Chapter 1, "Evolutional Supply Chain Management and Strategy: Pencil Supply Chain Case," proposes the definition and framework of the supply chain, SCM, and supply chain strategy. How supply chains and SCM are perceived as well as their scope varies greatly depending on the person and their individual perspective. This chapter clarifies the differences between the supply chain and its comparable terms. It also details the factors that have caused varying views of the supply chain and highlights the drivers that have changed the supply chain and SCM over a long time. Finally, the pencil case serves as a concrete example structured to allow the reader to understand the broader landscape of the supply chain while tracing the process of its birth, product innovation, and popularization. This chapter provides a theoretical basis for discussing the issues covered in this book.

Chapter 2, "Cost Management of Logistics and Supply Chain Costs," examines transactions in the supply chain from a management accounting perspective and discusses supply chain profitability. It is challenging to grasp logistical costs based on inter-company transactions rather than internal management accounting. A company's internal accounting should be appropriately subdivided, accurately measured, and then analyzed as a whole or in its entirety. However, logistics costs must be aimed at total optimization based on transactions between companies. Furthermore, the theory and measurement methods for supply chain profitability are not established in either academic or practical fields because of the large number of companies involved and the need for multifaceted consideration. This chapter organizes the path to this supply chain profitability. It plays a vital role in examining the cases treated in this book from the perspective of profitability.

Sections 2 to 5 are case studies from various industries and their global impact. Since each economic sector has different products, market characteristics, and development stages, its supply chain's structure and visibility vary greatly. All industries have innovative and devising products which constantly form and change their supply chains and SCM. Using the frameworks in Section 1, readers will develop a better understanding of Section 2 and 5 of how to recognize the differences and commonalities of supply chains. It is most critical for readers to understand the whole picture of the supply chain. From the raw material to products or from the gathering/harvesting to consumption, this recognition is crucial to develop an awareness of recognizing the existing and emerging critical contrivances that industries, supply chains, companies, and products bear.

Section 2, "The Automotive Industry," has superb research value and excellent illustrations of the significance of the supply chain. An automobile is composed of tens of thousands of parts, and a single defect has a tremendous impact on the performance and safety of the vehicle. Section 2 consists of three chapters about automotive supply chains. Automotive companies have formed the most advanced, efficient, and effective supply chains that are extensive but responsive. Various parts and multistage manufacturers have operated in collaboration with assembly companies. The automotive supply chain has been engaged in fierce competition in terms of performance, quality, and cost. The automotive industry continues to explore product development in the pursuit of efficiency. While the automotive industry's supply chain has constantly been improving, significant changes are essential to keep their competitive advantage.

Chapter 3, "Progress of Electric Vehicles and Transformation of Supply Chain in Japanese Automobile Industry," discusses structural changes in the Japanese automotive industry. Japan's automotive industry has formed a unique and robust supply chain based on 'keiretsu' and has continued to be cost-competitive and responsive to the market. With the shift from internal combustion engines to electric motor vehicles, Japan's unique supply chain is under constant change to remain competitive. This chapter examines whether the keiretsu will persist and discusses the future of the Japanese auto industry. Through the discussion in this chapter, the reader will realize the shift from a fixed supply chain focused on efficiency and certainty to a flexible supply chain focused on market responsiveness.

Chapter 4, "An Evaluation Model for Supplier Selection for European, American, and Japanese Automotive Companies," examines and confirms the essential factors used to select suppliers through the fastener industry case by comparing European, American, and Japanese automotive companies. Fasteners play a crucial role in the automobile, which has a large number of parts and requires high safety standards. Fastener suppliers also play an indispensable part in keeping other companies together in automobile manufacturing. This chapter highlights the differences in the selection of fastener suppliers and investment policies among European, American, and Japanese automotive companies. Finally, this chapter develops an evaluation model for fastener supplier selection and investment priorities by exploring the evaluation criteria and their respective importance.

Chapter 5, "CSR Initiatives in the Supply Chain of the Japanese Automotive Industry: The Role of Parts Industry Association," discusses CSR in the supply chain. This chapter is a theoretical and practical summary of the supply chain from the perspective of CSR. Contributing to an environmentally friendly company or CSR is essential in increasing corporate and product value. The number of parts and their related companies in an automobile is substantial, making it difficult to grasp and manage the activities of the entire supply chain. This chapter focuses on the function and importance of a supplier-side industry association, JAPIA (Japan Auto Parts Industries Association). JAPIA has contributed to raising CSR initiatives in the Japanese auto parts industry by fostering a shared understanding of CSR throughout the supply chain and enabling each member company to clarify problems in the status of its CSR initiatives.

Section 3, "Retailing Cases," is very practical. The retailing sector, including distribution, should be flexible and variable because it is more susceptible to market and technological influences than manufacturers. Section 3 consists of three chapters that illustrate how market and technology influence change supply chains.

Chapter 6, "Controlling Bullwhip Effect in Supply Chain by BANDAI Co.: Lessons from the Tamagotchi™ Case," illustrates the typical phenomenon that arises from the supply chain features. Supply chains consist of members at different vertical stages who may have conflicting interests. Movements of the supply chain are called chaotic. Adverse effects of unexpected events that are likely to occur in the supply chain can be amplified by the supply chain itself. Through the Tamagotchi™ case, this chapter illustrates how the bullwhip effect is exacerbated in the supply chain. Although Tamagotchi™ became tremendously popular throughout the world, it ended in tragedy. BANDAI suffered from a tragic boom and bust due to a demand forecast failure and an immature SCM, including the wrong response to inflated demand that created an excessive boom and sudden bust. After learning from this severe lesson, BANDAI changed its policy regarding new products and SCM.

Chapter 7, "Supply Chain Management of Seven-Eleven Japan," discusses the SCM of convenience stores through the Seven-Eleven Japan case. Seven-Eleven Japan is the company that turned the US-born convenience store into a modern-day giant. They achieved an effective and efficient product assortment by developing information and distribution systems. Seven-Eleven Japan has dramatically increased the sales and profitability of the convenience store industry. It has created a product development, production, and distribution system in collaboration with its affiliates which enables Seven-Eleven Japan's supply chain to quickly satisfy market demand with items or services consumers desire. Seven-Eleven Japan was one of the first to introduce a full-scale POS (Point of Sale) system in 1982 to instantly identify hot-selling items, improve speed and accuracy of the checkout process, help store managers make decisions about orders, and significantly shorten the lead time from order to delivery.

Chapter 8, "Driving Forces and Factors of Amazon Effects: From Online Bookstores to Cloud Services," tracks Amazon's accomplishments and evolution of its investments in digitals, such as ICT, DX, and analogs, such as warehousing and delivery. Amazon is a leader in boosting online sales, carving out a click-and-mortar business, and efficiently creating a long-tail assortment. While Amazon doesn't necessarily take ownership of the products sold on its site, Amazon is heavily involved in the inventory, shipping, and delivery processes. On the other hand, Amazon has a cutting-edge information platform that seems to conflict with its retailer side as an online marketplace. The prodigious company has grown significantly through digital investments, but the analog aspect of the business emerged as a bottleneck each time. The company has invested in the analog domain to solve these problems while utilizing cutting-edge technology.

Section 4, "Food and Beverage Cases," provides a unique way of looking at supply chains and the new approaches taken in them. Freshness plays a vital role in the taste and hygiene of food and beverages.

Individual companies and supply chains take various measures to ensure prompt delivery and freshness. Section 4 consists of three chapters.

Chapter 9, "Product and Process Innovation in Coffee Supply Chain: From Seed to Cup," explores how the supply chain has changed considering the divergence between production and consumption areas, between producers and consumers, and between harvesting and processing times and consumption times. Coffee has been consumed worldwide for centuries, with the process and products evolving over a long time. The evolutions of coffee processing and brewing, as well as the emergence of instant coffee and coffee beverages, have broadened the range of ways to drink coffee, expanding the consumer base. Although coffee is a simple product, it is an excellent example of how a global supply chain has been formed, overcoming the problem of freshness through processing and drinking methods. This chapter looks back at the history of coffee diffusion in the United States, Japan, Vietnam, and China. Additionally, it highlights the cultural factors behind the spread of coffee and the maturation of the coffee industry.

Chapter 10, "Supply Chain Models and Functions of Food Service Chains in Japan: The Food SPA at Saizeriya," explains the operations of Saizeriya, a highly successful company in Japan. Saizeriya is the largest restaurant chain in the world based on the number of outlets and sales. Saizeriya has introduced the SPA (Specialty store retailer of Private label Apparel) method to the restaurant business and has achieved significant cost-cutting while maintaining an appetizing menu. Saizeriya started systematically producing standardized ingredients for its delicious food items by acquiring farmland. The upstream integration helped ensure that sufficient quantities of high-quality fresh materials were consistently available at low prices. Saizeriya introduced a central kitchen system so that Saizeriya can guarantee the same taste experience in all its outlets. Saizeriya has so thoroughly standardized and systemized operations that there are no knives in the restaurants' kitchens. Only one non-professional cook is needed to oversee cooking at each of its venues.

Chapter 11, "Agri-Food Logistics as a Dynamic Actor in Managing Food Loss and Waste: A Bump-Start by COVID-19," raises important academic and practical FLW (Food Loss Waste) issues and offers logistical solutions to them. This chapter is quite significant because it focuses on FLW, which has not received much attention in the supply chain research field. The chapter presents solutions from the perspective of the entire supply chain, from farm to bin and beyond. With the sudden outbreak of COVID-19, human behavior has changed drastically due to regulations and self-restraint. In the face of this rapid change, a considerable amount of waste was generated globally within the supply chain. Lastly, this chapter proposes a practical framework for future research and application to manage FLW from farm to bin and beyond. This proposed framework would be implemented by transforming agri-food logistics in alignment with the UN's SDGs and considering the advancement of agri-food logistics skills, practices, and innovation post-COVID-19.

Section 5, "Global Issues," discusses the changes and evolution of global supply chains from a macro perspective. Section 5 also consists of three chapters.

Chapter 12, "The Global Supply Chain Management System Involving the ASEAN Industrial Clusters," ponders the future potential of ASEAN in global supply chains. ASEAN countries have established industrial parks as a national industrial policy. The development of industrial infrastructure and the improvement of educational standards in ASEAN countries are increasing their importance in the supply chain and making them more attractive as investment destinations. Thailand has made a significant contribution to developing a noteworthy position in the global supply chain in collaboration with ASEAN countries. In particular, the development of transportation networks among ASEAN countries has enabled activities within the supply chain to become coordinated and efficient. Thailand

and the neighboring CLMV nations are increasing these countries' connectivity and constructing the East-West Economic Corridor, North-South Economic Corridor, and Southern Economic Corridor as a part of global supply chains.

Chapter 13, "Relocation Strategy of Production, Global Supply, and Value Chains," examines the relocation of the global supply chain based on historical events around globalization and de-globalization. Many studies have been done on supply chain globalization, but few have focused on deglobalization. Historically, deglobalization has occurred many times. In the past few years, developed countries with sluggish economies have become much more protectionist due to COVID-19. Domestic supply chains tend to be increasingly separated from global supply chains in the name of protecting domestic industries and increasing self-sufficiency in food. This chapter concludes that today's deglobalization in the reallocation of the supply chain is due to rising wages in developing countries in the face of spreading protectionism in developed countries.

Chapter 14, "Evolutional Characteristics of the Global Supply Chain in Various Industries," reviews the characteristics of global supply chains based on a literature review and examples from Asia. In this chapter, a literature review is conducted on the evolutionary attributes of the worldwide supply chain in various industries of the developed country of Japan and the emerging economy of China, respectively. The characteristics of supply chains vary significantly by industry, goods, services, and region. This chapter compares the supply chains of diverse sectors considering the recent trend toward ICT. In both Japan and China, it has been confirmed that there is a movement in various industries to cut costs further and avoid risks through the supply chain by using the most advanced ICT technologies, such as big data, AI, and DX.

We hope that through this book you will learn the basics and reality of supply chain and SCM, become familiar with them, and be able to apply them to your business and daily lives.

# Acknowledgment

I would like to thank A. Nakamoto for helpful information and discussion.

# Section 1
# Frameworks and Cases on Evolutional Supply Chain

*Section 1 clarifies the outline of the entire book by presenting the frameworks for evolutional, variable, and diverse supply chains. This section summarizes the evolution of supply chain structures and activities and discusses supply chain profitability from the view of managerial and logistics costs.*

# Chapter 1
# Evolutional Supply Chain Management and Strategy:
## Pencil Supply Chain Case

**Toru Higuchi**
*Tokyo Seitoku University, Japan*


## ABSTRACT

*At the beginning of this chapter, SCM and related concepts such as physical distribution, business logistics, and company groups are explained, and the areas of difference among them are clarified. In the middle of this chapter, the framework of a supply chain and SCM are described. Important factors about SCM and drivers changing the supply chain management and strategy are proposed. At the end of this chapter, the case of the pencil supply chain is introduced to illustrate the evolutional SCM and supply chain strategy. The pencil supply chain has a long history and has experienced dramatic changes due to product and process innovations.*


## INTRODUCTION

Supply chains are ubiquitous. Every product has its supply chain. The cost, performance, and availability of products are all determined by the activities of a supply chain. Therefore, competent supply chain management is crucial. In addition, under the conditions of cutthroat competition, supply chain strategy has become vital.

SCM is a relatively new concept adopted in 1983 by Booz Allen Hamilton Inc., a management and information technology consulting firm in the United States. From the structure of the flow and stocking of goods, SCM is a concept that has evolved and incorporated fundamental business logistics and advanced the practice of physical distribution. Furthermore, SCM is the series of transactions among companies related to a product, the advanced concept of a company group. Sometimes, supply chain and SCM are confused with business logistics and a company group.

In this chapter, the framework of the evolutional supply chain is proposed and illustrated through the case of the pencil supply chain while paying attention to the difference between SCM and similar

DOI: 10.4018/978-1-7998-9800-9.ch001

*Figure 1. Image of physical distribution*

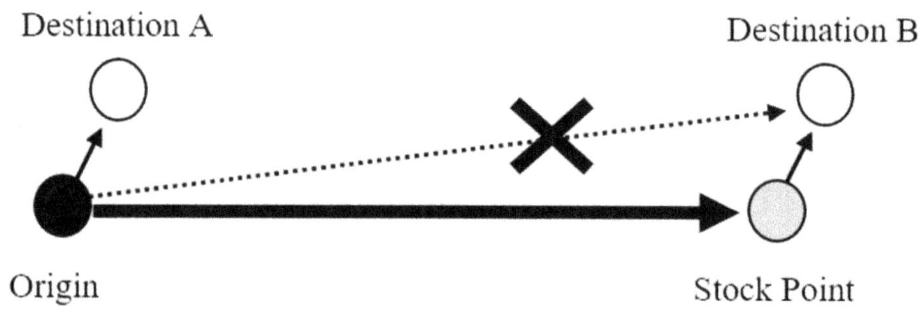


concepts. Billions of people use pencils throughout the world. The pencil chain has a long history that experienced dramatic changes through its inception. The method and instruments for making pencils have changed dramatically. In this day and age, pencil products and their respective supply chains are omnipresent.

## BACKGROUND

Physical distribution is an operation transporting or delivering a product to a location or person/persons. Usually, it includes activities related to transportation or delivery, such as the storage, picking, and packing of products. Sometimes it consists of some finishing work at a distribution center according to client orders or the owners of parcels. However, it does not include conversion or processing work.

Physical distribution bridges the various gaps. Under the division of labor, people consume products at other places and times of production. In addition, harvest or production times and consumption times are different. Workers should store the products somewhere until receiving the orders. Given the time constraints, it is crucial to make plans about the flow and stocking of parcels to maintain related costs reasonably and ensure timely product delivery. Figure 1 illustrates two simple cases. Destination A is very close to the point of product origin. It is reasonable to deliver each time an order is received from Destination A. On the other hand, Destination B is very far from the point of origin. The orders from Destination B are frequent and under severe time constraints. In this case, it is not practical to make deliveries each time. Instead, it would be more reasonable to establish a stock point near Destination B and maintain a sizable inventory before deliveries.

The purpose of physical distribution is to deliver certainty and efficiency based on delivery instructions. Physical distribution by itself tends to achieve only partial optimization because its scope is narrower than logistics and the supply chain.

Business logistics is a civilian application of military logistics. Military logistics has evolved through wars. The word logistics comes from the ancient Greek *λογιστικός* or *logistikós*, meaning calculation or rationality. There is a need to calculate the necessary supplies and secure the transportation modes for those supplies to win a war. In military logistics, the provisioning of weapons and necessities of life are just as important as the allocation of soldiers. The purpose is to transport or deliver these items with certainty and efficiency. The grand purpose of military logistics is to win or not lose a war. After the Cold War, the technology and concept of military logistics were used in the private sector.

The Council of Supply Chain Management Professionals (CSCMP) defines and explains Logistics Management as follows in the Definitions and Glossary <https://cscmp.org/ > (Aug 15, 2021):

*Logistics management is that part of supply chain management that plans, implements, and controls the efficient, practical forward and reverses flow and storage of goods, services and related information between the point of origin and the point of consumption in order to meet customers' requirements.*

*Logistics management activities typically include inbound and outbound transportation management, fleet management, warehousing, materials handling, order fulfillment, logistics network design, inventory management, supply/demand planning, and management of third-party logistics services providers. To varying degrees, the logistics function also includes sourcing and procurement, production planning and scheduling, packaging and assembly, and customer service. It is involved in all levels of planning and execution--strategic, operational and tactical. Logistics management is an integrating function, which coordinates and optimizes all logistics activities, as well as integrates logistics activities with other functions including marketing, sales manufacturing, finance, and information technology.*

Ballou (1991, p.3) pointed out the newness of logistics results from the concept of coordinated management of the related activities rather than from the historical practice of managing them separately. Ballou (1991, pp.6-10) also listed customer service standards, transportation, inventory management, and order processing as key activities in logistics, warehousing, material handling, purchasing, protective packaging, cooperation with production, and information maintenance as to support activities. Ballou (1991, pp.25-26) mentions logisticians' desire to develop a logistics activity mix that will result in the highest possible return on investment over time. Logisticians should have two dimensions to improve the logistics system: the revenue contribution and cost reduction design. Bowersox and Closs (1996, p.8) mentioned that logistical competency is a relative assessment of a firm's capability to provide competitively superior customer service at the lowest possible total cost.

Companies want to maximize their profit which is about equal to sales minus costs, as mentioned by the Council of Logistical Management, the predecessor of the Council of Supply Chain Professionals. To do so, they want to increase sales, decrease costs, or both simultaneously. Although business logistics cannot generate product innovations, it can increase sales through a high level of service and decreased costs such as transportation, inventory, and handling.

The mission of business logistics is to make it possible to maintain a productive line of products at a reasonable cost. The main beneficiary of business logistics is the consumers, not competitors. The support or supplementary activities such as sourcing, manufacturing, and stocking, are critical to maximizing sales, avoiding out-of-stock and unsold products. This is similar to military logistics managing an efficient allocation of soldiers and weapons and replenishing them as needed.

No company can fulfill all their business activities on their own from the production and process of all raw materials to the sale for the end consumers. Finished goods manufacturers, suppliers, and retailers all have a different perspective of logistics, as Figure 2 shows. The shaded area at the top of Figure 2 corresponds to the manufacturers of the finished goods. The finished goods manufacturers prepare for procurement, production, and distribution using their facilities and transactions with other companies to respond to consumer demand directly and indirectly. The transaction terms such as price and delivery

*Figure 2. Image of business logistics*

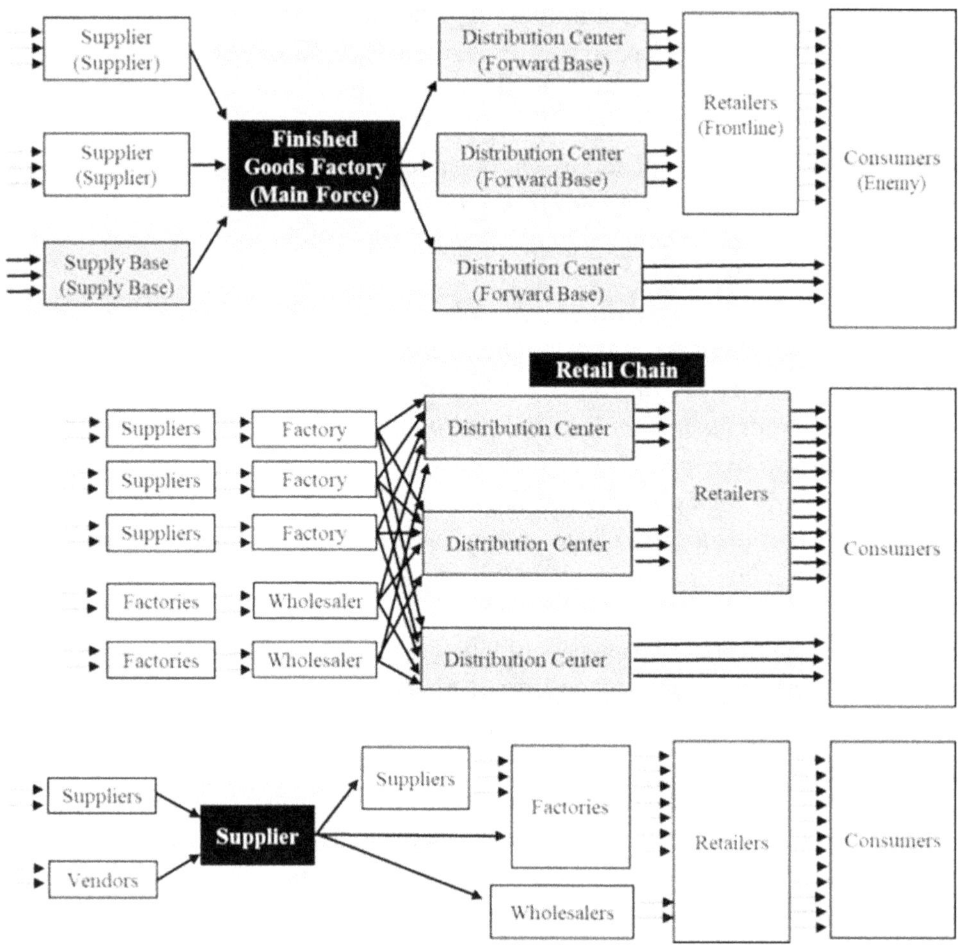


frequency have a significant influence on profitability and risk. Parentheses on top of Figure 2 are listed to compare military logistics and business logistics.

The middle flowchart in Figure 2 shows the scope of retail chains. Although some retailers sell their PB (Private Brand) products, they do not independently produce them. They carry an extensive line of profitable products for capricious and unpredictable consumers. They procure products from factories and wholesalers and keep them at distribution centers and retail stores to purchase them promptly.

The bottom flowchart in Figure 2 shows the scope of suppliers for parts and materials. Suppliers can't conduct their business without interacting with other companies. They also need materials and machines. Although their scope looks small in the figure, their parts may be used widely.

Chopra & Meindl (2001, p.3) defined and explained the supply chain as follows:

*A supply chain consists of all stages involved, directly or indirectly, in fulfilling a customer request. The supply chain can not only include the manufacture and suppliers, but also transporters, warehouse, retailers, and customers themselves. Within each organization, such as a manufacturer, the supply chain*

*Figure 3. Image of supply chain*

| | Materials (→) | Parts & Products | (→) Products |
|---|---|---|---|
| Primary<br>Industry<br>(↓) | **[Ground Surface]**<br>**Agricultural products**<br>**(Farmers)**<br>**Forestry resources**<br>**(Forestry workers)**<br>**[Sea, River, Lake]**<br>**Fishery resources**<br>**(Fishers)** | | |
| (↓)<br>Secondary<br>Industry<br>(↓) | **[Underground]**<br>**Mineral resources**<br>**(Miners)** | **[Factories]**<br>**(Manufacturers)** | |
| (↓)<br>Tertiary<br>Industry | | | **[Distribution Channel]**<br>**(Wholesalers and Retailers)** |
| | **[Related Industries] (Transporters, Bankers, Internet Providers, etc.)** | | |

*includes all functions involved in filling a customer request. These functions include, but are not limited to, new product development, marketing, operations, distribution, finance, and customer service.*

Supply chains have been around far and wide throughout history, except in self-sufficient societies in a state of autarchy or limited outside trade. However, the supply chain concept is relatively new. Every product has its supply chain, which transcends the boundaries of company groups and industries (Figure 3). For example, there are infinite combinations of the sources and types of trees, manufacturers, and distribution channels with wooden tables. The cost, performance, and availability of a product are determined by the collective activities of its supply chain and corresponding SCM. Booz Allen Hamilton Inc., a consulting firm in the United States, introduced this SCM concept in 1983.

From the flow and stock of goods, the supply chain integrated the business logistics concept. This concept encompasses all logistics activities of related companies to a product. In the long term, the supply chain has a strong influence on product development. From an organizational viewpoint, a supply chain is a group of companies that conduct transactions related to a product. Members of a supply chain

*Table. 1 Comparison of resembling concepts*

| | Physical Distribution | Business Logistics | Company Group | Supply Chain |
|---|---|---|---|---|
| Unit | Parcel or transportation order | Company | Group company | All related companies or a product |
| Purpose | Certain and efficient transportation | Maximize individual company's profit | Maximize the profit of whole group companies | Stabilize supply chain profitability and customer satisfaction |
| Scope | Origin to destination | Company and its suppliers | Affiliated companies | All companies related with a certain product |
| Priority | Client or owner of a parcel | Company and customers | Holding companies | Customers |
| Remarks | Partial optimization (operational) | Total optimization (static) | Tightly coupled (strict control) | Loosely coupled (dynamic or chaotic) |

Source: (Higuchi & Troutt 2008, p.4)

are carefully vetted and chosen for their flexibility and ability to contribute to the overall success of the supply chain. Members of these company groups have fixed costs and capital relationships. (Table 1).

## FRAMEWORK OF SUPPLY CHAIN MANAGEMENT AND STRATEGY

### Chain Action in Supply Chain

According to Oxford Advanced Learner's Dictionary, a chain has the following meanings:

1. a series of connected metal rings used for pulling or fastening things; a length of chain used for a particular purpose.
2. a series of connected things or people.
3. a group of shops/ stores, or hotels owned by the same company.
4. a thing that restricts somebody's freedom or ability to do something.
5. a situation in which a number of people selling and buying houses must each complete the sale of their house before buying from the next person.

In light of the above definitions, a supply chain is a series of companies and their transactions predicated on consumer demand, which happens sequentially. In other words, a supply chain is a group of companies related to a product, in which those companies independently conduct merchandising cycles. Chopra and Meindl (2001, pp.7-15) proposed a process view of the supply chain: cycle view and push/pull view. Figure 4 illustrates the cycle view and the push/pull view or the chain actions in the supply chain. It is a simple example of a 5-echelon model whose shape is linear, and chain actions happen one after another. It is assumed that every echelon has its necessary relevant inventory, such as raw materials, parts, or finished products.

This whole chain of events starts with consumer demand. Consumers visit a store or place an order on the internet. At this stage, usually, consumers buy products on display or from in-store inventory. Retailers place orders as needed to wholesalers to maintain adequate inventory levels. If wholesalers

*Figure 4. Chain action in supply chain*

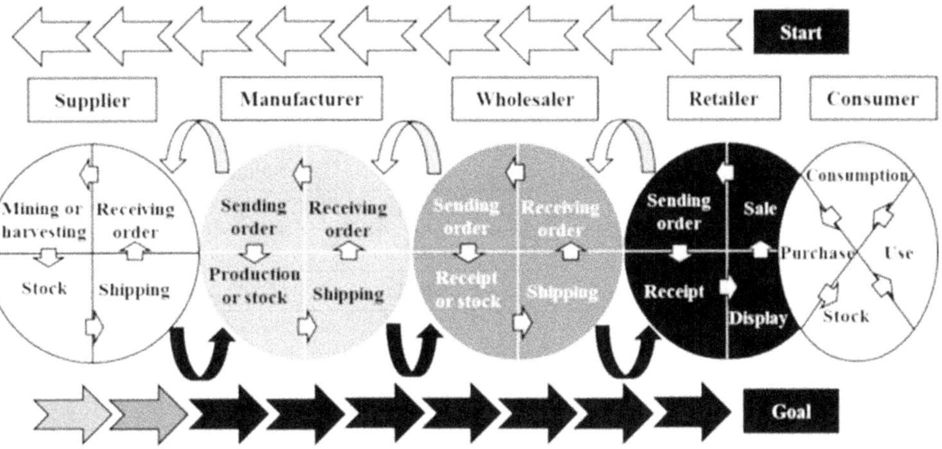


have enough stock on hand, they ship products on order in a timely manner. If they do not have enough stock, they must also place orders to a manufacturer.

A manufacturer has an inventory of finished products, as well as parts and materials for ongoing production. If they have enough finished products on hand, they can ship them to wholesalers to fill their orders. Having enough products on hand, they need to increase production, assuming they have the necessary parts and labor force. If either is lacking, they will place orders to their suppliers of the parts needed. Their suppliers also maintain inventories of parts or materials for their production. If they have enough parts or raw materials available, they ship them to manufacturers. If there are missing parts or raw materials, they need to mine, harvest, or otherwise procure the required items in response to orders.

In summary, the activities in a supply chain start and end at the interface between a retailer and a consumer who makes a purchase in a retail store or on an internet site. All entities have their original business cycle whose triggers exist at the interfaces between adjacent echelons, such as supplier/manufacturer, manufacturer/wholesaler, wholesaler/retailer, and retailer/consumer.

In the real world, stores of products, parts, and materials have far-reaching implications. Without them, chain actions are disjointed and smooth cooperation among supply chain members is impossible. On the other hand, excessive inventories have the inherent risk of unsold merchandise and lowered prices. There are push/pull boundaries in a supply chain (Table 2). The push operations are predicated on demand forecasts and start before receiving orders. In this case, having stock on hand guarantees a smooth and cooperative operation. On the other hand, the pull operations wait for orders. There is almost no unsold product because companies prepare only for what is actually ordered.

Table 2 illustrates the push and pull boundaries in a supply chain based on the type of products. Ready-Made (I) are ordinary products sold at existing stores and which consumers buy and take. Ready-Made (II) and Ready-Made (III) are products with less demand that consumers need to order and which a wholesaler or manufacturer might have in stock.

MTO (I) is a made-to-order product such as made-to-order clothes and food at a restaurant. The manufacturers have the necessary material and parts on hand, and they can start fulfilling an order quickly. MTO (II) consists of products whose materials and parts are so uncommon or rarely ordered that parts suppliers do not want to maintain their relevant stock. MTO (III) is composed of products

*Table 2. Boundaries between push and pull operations*

| | Supplier (materials) | Supplier (parts) | Manufacturer | Wholesaler | Retailer | Consumer |
|---|---|---|---|---|---|---|
| **Ready-Made (I)** | Push | Push | Push | Push | **Push** | **Pull** |
| **Ready-Made (II)** | Push | Push | Push | **Push** | **Pull** | Pull |
| **Ready-Made (III)** | Push | Push | **Push** | **Pull** | Pull | Pull |
| **MTO (I)** | Push | **Push** | **Pull** | Pull | Pull | Pull |
| **MTO (II)** | **Push** | **Pull** | Pull | Pull | Pull | Pull |
| **MTO (III)** | **Pull** | Pull | Pull | Pull | Pull | Pull |

whose materials and parts are even more uncommon or infrequently ordered than MTO (II) or need vast quantities of materials such as iron ore for large shipbuilding.

## Structure of Supply Chain

The supply chain literally looks like a chain. However, its typical structure is a network composed of procurement and distribution elements. Figure 5 shows an example of a finished goods manufacturer, a manufacturer that completes a product.

Many materials and parts are needed to complete a product and its respective parts. Materials are scattered and transported worldwide to become a component of a product and parts eventually. A finished goods manufacturer is a confluence point of materials and parts, apparent when viewing the merging activity shown on the left side of Figure 5.

Consumers are also located all over the world and within individual countries. A distribution network is needed to sell to them. Recently, many manufacturers have increased their direct sales because online sales and home delivery have become increasingly accessible and convenient. The right side of Figure 5 is suggestive of a shipping or trucking container. Finished goods manufacturers are confluence points where procured materials and parts are fabricated or assembled to completed products.

Individually, supply chain members have their perspective and strategy because it is challenging to understand an entire supply chain in detail and easy to lose focus quickly. The typical case of suppliers is shown at the top of Figure 6. Their materials and parts are incorporated into products at various locations. The primary function of suppliers is shunting or divergence. The typical case of finished goods manufacturers is shown in the middle of Figure 6. Finished goods manufacturers tend to procure their necessary parts and materials from widely dispersed yet strategically located suppliers. However, most of them only understand well their direct suppliers, with whom they experience direct contact and collaboration. Their ongoing interaction develops a synergistic and cooperative relationship. They do not have the same level of understanding and relationship with the suppliers of their suppliers. Consumers are located worldwide, so it is not easy to sell to them directly. A typical example of chain stores is shown at the bottom of Figure 6. The store collects various products and sells them directly to customers.

*Figure 5. Structure of supply chain*

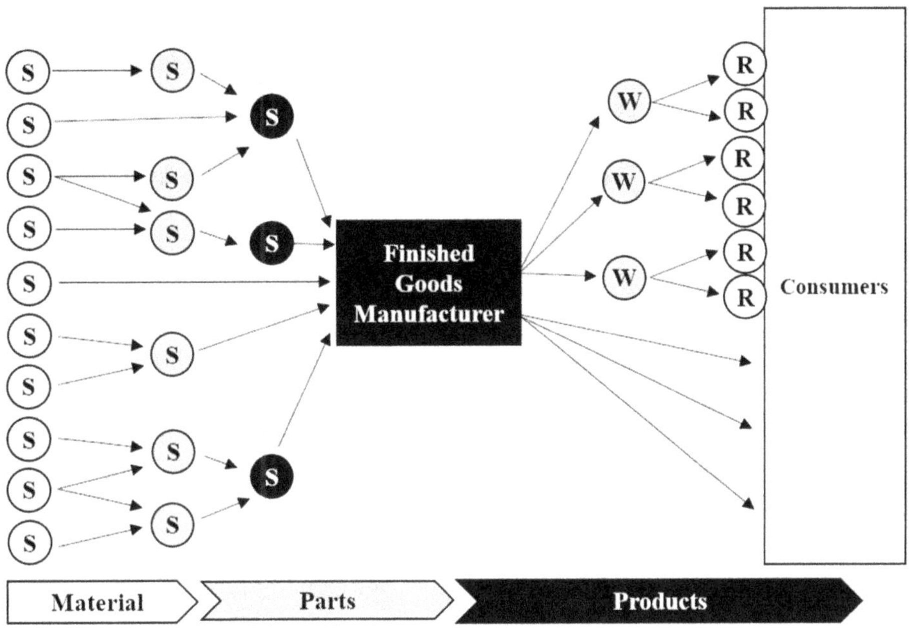


*Figure 6. Coverage of supply chain by individual company*

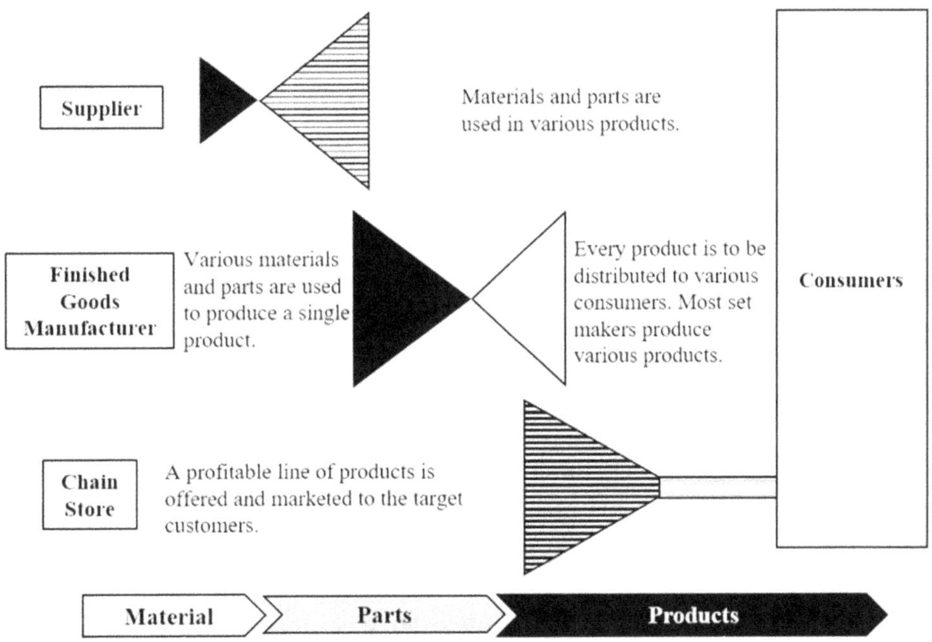

## Supply Chain Management

The Council of Supply Chain Management Professionals (CSCMP's) defines and describes Supply Chain Management as follows in their Definitions and Glossary <https://cscmp.org/ > (Aug 15, 2021):

*Supply chain management encompasses the planning and management of all activities involved in sourcing and procurement, conversion, and all logistics management activities. Importantly, it also includes coordination and collaboration with channel partners, which can be suppliers, intermediaries, third party service providers, and customers. In essence, supply chain management integrates supply and demand management within and across companies.*

*Supply chain management is an integrating function with primary responsibility for linking major business functions and business processes within and across companies into a cohesive and high-performing business model. It includes all of the logistics management activities noted above and manufacturing operations. It drives coordination of processes and activities with and across marketing, sales, product design, finance, and information technology.*

From a consumer's viewpoint, there are many differences among products in the same category. The brand, product name, price, etc., are different on the surface. At the store, consumers recognize these differences and make their purchasing choices accordingly. In reality, the materials, designs, manufacturing methods, manufacturing locations, storage locations, quality, etc., may also differ in many ways (Figure 7). In particular, the distribution channel varies depending on the location of the customer. Sometimes products of the same brand have quite different supply chains. Therefore, SCM is an essential activity, and under cutthroat competition, the supply chain strategy has become critical.

## Supply Chain Strategy

It is only natural that the question arises as to who determines a particular supply chain strategy, given that supply chains are comprised of many companies. Nowadays, companies that decide entire supply chain strategies are generally manufacturers responsible for completing products and choosing target customers, or large retail chains that sell products to customers directly and that have strong bargaining power. These types of companies select the members of their supply chains. Other companies have the option of taking part in a supply chain or not.

Fisher (1997) proposed a simple framework for choosing the right supply chain strategy. His central premise is that the most appropriate supply chain strategy depends on whether the product is functional or innovative. Functional products are solidly established staple items whose demands are predictable and sold by a wide range of retailers. Although they have a long lifecycle, their stability invites competition, leading to low-profit margins. On the other hand, innovative products give customers an additional reason to buy them, leading to high-profit margins. However, their newness makes demand unpredictable. The answer to this dilemma is that physically efficient supply chains are suitable for functional products, and market-responsive supply chains are ideal for innovative products.

Chopra & Meindl (2001, p 27) state that a supply chain strategy determines the nature of procurement of raw materials, the transportation of materials to and from companies, the manufacture of products or the operations to provide service, and the distribution of products to customers, along with any follow-

*Figure 7. Supply chains from consumer's viewpoint*

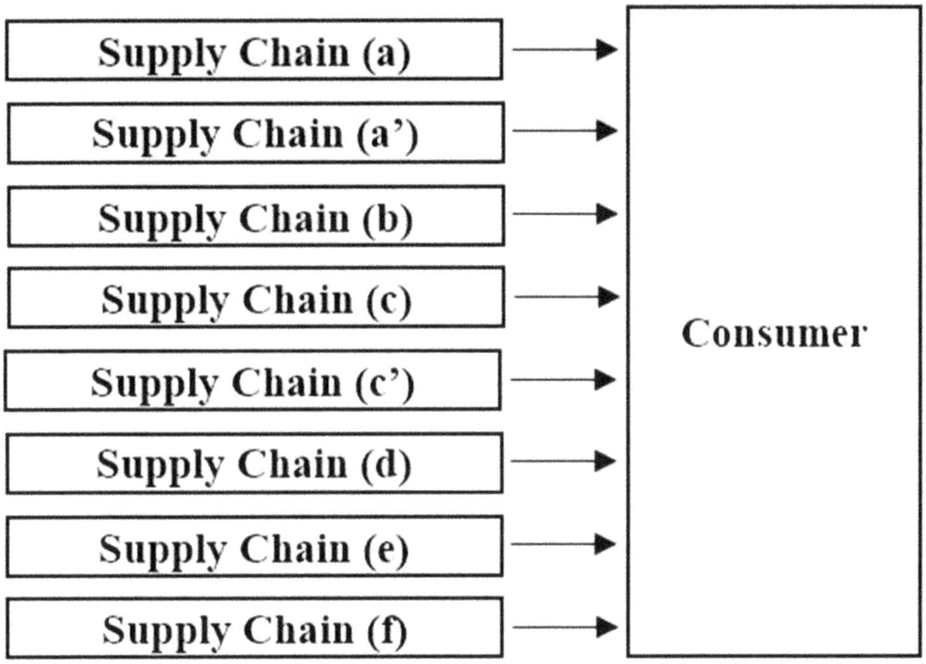


up service. They emphasize the importance of a strategic fit for competitive and supply chain strategies with the same goal.

According to Chopra & Meindl (2001, pp. 49-63), there are the following four drivers that determine the performance of any supply chain:

1. Inventory:
   Changing inventory policies can dramatically alter the supply chain's efficiency and responsiveness.
2. Transportation:
   Transportation can take the form of many combinations of modes and routes, each with its own performance characteristics. Transportation choices have a substantial impact on the supply chain's effectiveness and efficiency.
3. Facilities:
   Two major types of facilities are production sites and storage sites. Whatever the function of the facility, decisions regarding the location, capacity, and flexibility of facilities have a significant impact on the supply chain's performance.
4. Information:
   Information consists of data and analysis regarding inventory, transportation, facilities, and customers throughout the supply chain. It is potentially the preeminent driver of performance in the supply chain as it directly affects all of the other drivers. Timely and accurate information allows management to make their supply chain more responsive and efficient.

*Figure 8. Overall image of supply chain strategy*

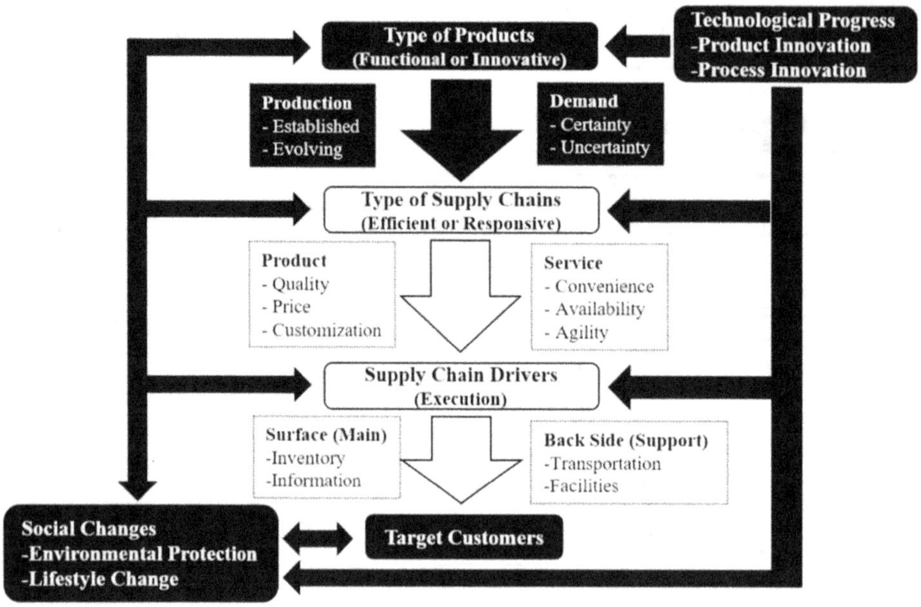


Supply Chain Strategy is a choice of the type of supply chain and the level of supply chain drivers most appropriate for a particular product and target customers (Figure 8). In addition, supply chains are also a part of society. Technological advancements and social changes impact significant influence not only on products and customers but also on supply chains.

## INNOVATION IN SUPPLY CHAIN

Schumpeter (1949, pp.65-74) classified innovations, spontaneous and sporadic changes or new combinations, into the following five categories:

1. The introduction of a new product with which consumers are not familiar or of a new quality or feature of a product.
2. The introduction of a new method of production, i.e., one not yet tested by experience in the relevant branch of manufacturing, which needs by no means to be founded upon a new scientific discovery, and which can also consist of a new way of the commercial handling of commodities.
3. The opening of a new market, that is, a market which the particular branch of the manufacturer of the country in question has not previously targeted, whether or not this market existed before.
4. The acquisition of a new source of raw materials or work-in-progress goods, irrespective of whether this source existed before or not.
5. The implementation of the new organization of any industry, like the creation of a monopoly position or the breaking up of a monopoly position.

*Figure 9. Innovations from supply chain perspective*

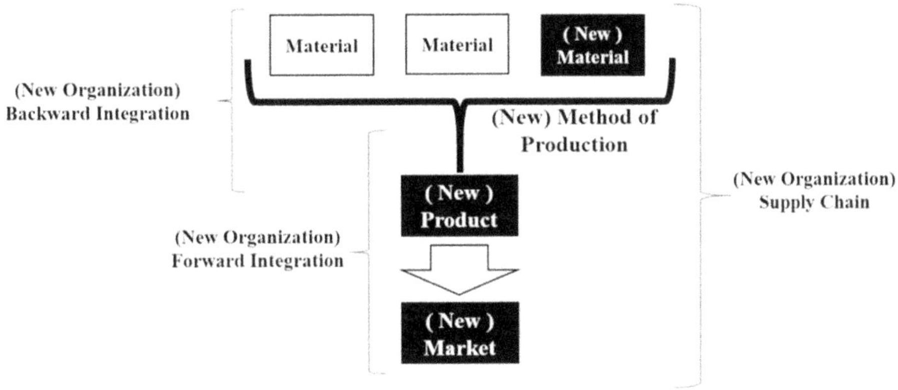


The introduction of a new product is typical product innovation. The question remains whether opening a new market is product innovation or not because some products introduced in a new market are technologically new. Others are the result of process innovation. Figure 9 illustrates the supply chain perspective of innovations.

## Product Innovation

In the long term, new products are introduced to the market, and old products disappear. Some new products are so innovative that consumer reaction is unpredictable, and the materials and product designs may change significantly. Examples of product innovations are creating a new category of products, a change of their basic design or materials, or the addition of an innovative function. According to Abernathy (1978, pp.3-49.), at the beginning of innovative product development, developers might face various technical challenges and overcome them to improve product performance. The situation changes entirely with the emergence of Dominant Design, a superior design of products that seems to mark a turning point in developing their respective productive units (Abernathy 1978, p 75). Before the emergence of Dominant Design, developers might require dramatic and significant revisions in product design several times due to changes in basic product performance, functions, materials, etc. After Dominant Design, the basic product performance, functions, and design are fixed. Then, the product performance progresses cumulatively, and the production system evolves and becomes established (Figure 10).

In the past, when basic functions and designs were fluid, manufacturers would locate facilities near their customers to respond quickly to their needs and prepare for mass production. Nowadays, with the aid of experience, manufacturers can localize the impact of design and material changes. In addition, information technology has advanced so much that it can respond efficiently even to the needs of far-away customers.

Nevertheless, producing and selling innovative products is precarious because the demand is uncertain and the production system may change. When innovative products are first introduced to the market, although they may be far from sophisticated, the impracticability of early mass production makes them expensive and is a constraint on increased production.

*Figure 10. Transition of production performance and fluidness of production system*

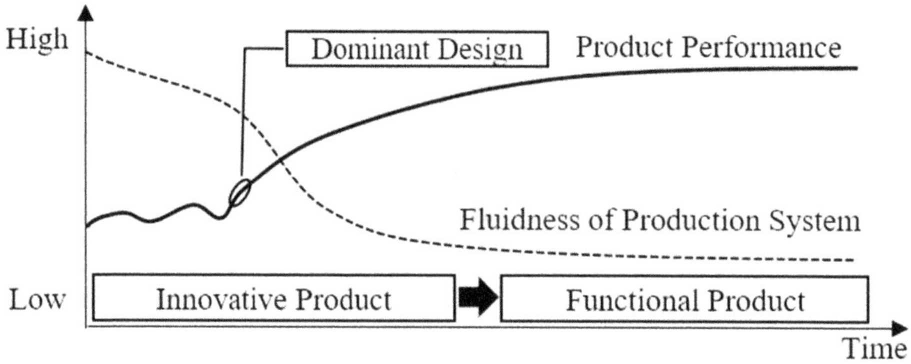


If a supply chain deals with an innovative product, it should be flexible to changes in many different ways. Also, manufacturers in these supply chains should be prepared for significant variances of demand, change of product design, materials, and production system. Accordingly, the supply chains need to choose the most appropriate suppliers capable of responding to increased consumer needs at a reasonable cost.

## Process Innovation

After product innovation, process innovations progress. Typical process innovations are the introduction of mass production and a flexible manufacturing system. Abernathy (1978, pp.54-55) mentioned that process innovations could generally be grouped according to four functions: introducing new process capabilities, organizing the process, integrating an existing process, and improving the overall process as a system. These process innovations significantly affect the cost and quality of the product and contribute to expanding the range of customers. The product performance/cost ratio increases steadily with Dominant Design (Figure 11). Standardization plays a vital role in the manufacturing process. Standardization of the work procedures and parts is an essential factor in mass production. Once high-quality products can be mass-produced efficiently, distribution channels need to be developed or expanded.

Process innovations enable consumers to buy a product from a wide range of products at a reasonable price at their convenience. They take place at every stage and between stages of the supply chain. Process innovations in manufacturing make it possible to mass-produce high-quality products. These innovations cannot be achieved without suppliers. Suppliers are also making progress in building an integrated supply chain. Process innovations in the distribution channel are also progressing. CRM (Customer Relationship Management) has seen significant advances due to electronic money payment and POS (Point of Sales) systems. Nowadays, a combination of online shopping and rapid delivery accelerates process innovations in the distribution channel.

It is difficult to avoid either excessive inventory or a stockout. Supply chains need to be responsive to customer needs regarding volume, quality, wide assortment, service, etc. In addition to the process innovations in manufacturing, process innovations in the distribution channels are also necessary. Some process innovations in the supply chains can contribute to strengthening the unification of the entire supply

*Figure 11. Transition of performance/cost ratio and uncertainty of demand*

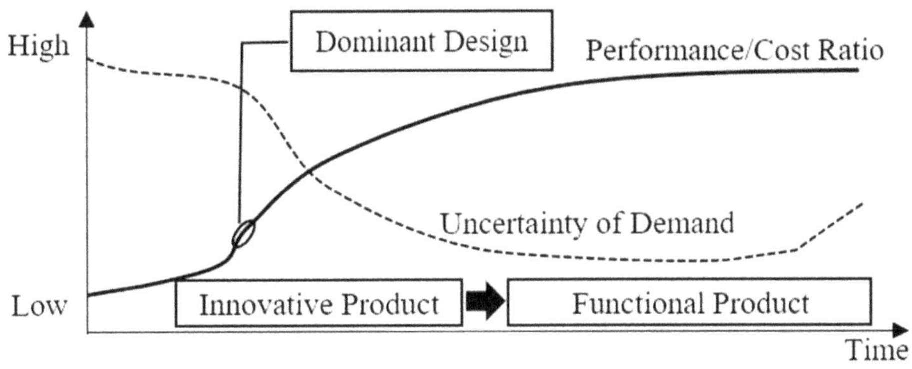


chain process. As a result, supply chains can offer a wide range of products at reasonable costs because they moderate stockouts and excessive inventories by sharing information and shortening lead times.

Process innovations inspire other newcomers or industry competitors to enter the market because it may be easy to imitate those products in which process innovations have occurred. Often such entrants have strength in cost-cutting, or they serve a niche market. A wide range of products is offered to the consumers. To have products chosen by consumers, companies should develop products from the consumer's point of view.

Gradually, the impact of novel process innovations is weakened. Most companies might have difficulty differentiating their products from others in product performance and price. This may be a sign that their product has matured and is no longer growing. Although it achieves excellent productivity and high quality at a low cost, the product's opportunities for improvements and innovations have diminished. Abernathy (1978, p 3) called this phenomenon the productivity dilemma and mentioned that instead of achieving gains in productivity, products lost innovative capabilities.

Abernathy called this situation a Productivity Dilemma. Every product has the intrinsic risk that another product may replace it or consumers may stop buying it. Although functional products might have a high performance/cost ratio, there is little opportunity for those products to increase their performance. Under this situation, consumers might want something else, and more new entrants from a different industry might satisfy their preferences. Uncertainty of demand might increase, as Figure 8 shows.

## Social Change

Society and innovation are interdependent. Innovations take place in society. Some innovations are desired by society for convenience, environmental protection, and other reasons. At their introduction, other innovations are not recognized as being that necessary by society. Both types of innovation are widely adopted and make significant changes to society and lifestyle.

Society has longed for the appearance of some kinds of concrete dream-like products and services. The accumulation of innovations materially enriches modern life. For example, the refrigerator was developed to be able to store food for a long time, and the microwave oven was invented to easily and quickly warm and cook food. Public utilities such as electricity, gas, water, and sewerage are also a collection of innovations. Nowadays, material innovations have become so ubiquitous and expected that environmental protection, added convenience, and even spiritual enrichment such as SDGs is desired.

It is inevitable that society thought that some of the newly introduced innovative products and services were unnecessary or questionable. At the time, most people could live an ordinary life without these innovations because people did not consider or appreciate the value of the added convenience or enhanced performance. For example, 30 years ago, it was assumed that car navigation systems were unnecessary because of good maps. Social Networking Service was not initially thought to be necessary either because of the availability of letters, phone calls, TV, and magazines. Most people thought that electronic money was unnecessary and suspect compared to banknotes, credit cards, and checks. However, all these innovations became an indispensable part of everyday life. They also contributed to raising the level of the economy significantly.

## THE CASE OF THE PENCIL SUPPLY CHAIN

Let us consider a simple example, the pencil, to understand the proposed frameworks. In this section, for the sake of simplicity, a pencil is defined as a writing instrument using graphite. Pencils are specific products that are mainly made of graphite, clay, and wood. Pencil writing is erasable.

### Beginning of Pencil: Finest Graphite Mine

Letters have been written and left behind since ancient times. During the Mesopotamian civilization, clay tablets were marked with sticks. Later, ink by way of pen and brush was used on papyrus, bamboo slips, and leather paper. Until recently, letter writing on paper with a ballpoint pen, fountain pen, or pencil was mainstream. Currently, PCs and smartphones are used to convey information, including letters.

The history of the pencil began at England's Borrowdale mine in the middle of the 16th century. Residents found part of a lump of the finest graphite on the surface. Cumberland graphite, the type of graphite produced from the mine, was so high quality that people could use it in its unprocessed natural state. Some used graphite lumps to mark sheep, while others cut them and used them as writing instruments. Some people wrapped graphite in sheepskin or cloth, tied it with a string, or put it in a mold. Some people started using the solid core from liquid ink, which enhanced a more extended storage period and more accessible transportation. Flemish traders spread Cumberland graphite all over the world. Italian art schools were very influential in increasing their fame. A small cottage industry for making pencils was started in Keswick, close to the Borrowdale mine.

### The First Product Innovation: Wooden Holder

The European people who obtained the finest Cumberland graphite from the Borrowdale mine were clever in using it. The first wooden holder was developed in Europe, possibly in Italy. In the middle of the 17th century, the German Friedrich Staedtler developed a method for fitting cut graphite into a wooden holder - the birth of the pencil. His descendant, Johann Sebastian Staedtler, started STAEDTLER Mars GmbH & Co. KG in 1835.

Early pencils were made by hand as follows:

*Figure 12. Cross section of the early pencil*

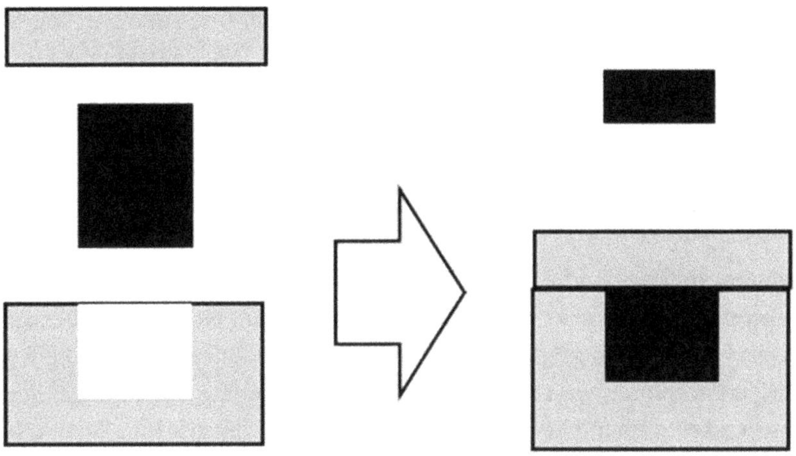

1. Acquiring and cutting Cumberland graphite.
2. Routing out a groove in the wood for graphite core.
3. Insert cut graphite into the groove.
4. Leveling out the protruding part of the cut graphite.
5. Covering it with another piece of wood glued in place (Figure 12).

Craftsmanship became an essential factor for making pencils.

Wooden mold was the first significant product innovation of the pencil, and it remains the dominant design in pencil production to this day. The pencil became a mass-produced product and a necessary implement of painting in Europe. This product innovation produced the following effects:

1. Delicate Touch

People were able to write letters without getting their hands dirty. Not only was it easier to write, but it was also possible to draw with a delicate touch.

2. Improved Durability and Efficiency During Transportation

Damages and stains during transportation were reduced, and consequently, the trade area could be expanded.

3. Market Expansion to a Certain Area

Although the price of pencils was high, art people all over Europe wanted to buy them.

Pencil makers imitated the wooden holder and improved it. Wood seemed to be the critical factor in terms of weight, volume, and comfort. Wood for pencils needs to have a moderate hardness that facilitates easy processing and comfortable holding. Woods that were suitable for pencils were imported from South America.

Keswick was still an excellent place to make pencils because of its proximity to the Borrowdale mine, which had a sufficient labor force. The most vital constraint at that time was the most refined quality graphite from Borrowdale mine. Although the finest graphite was extremely rare, it had many uses, such as fabricating the molds manufacturing cannonballs. Most of them were transported to London by armed stagecoaches.

## The Second Product Innovation: Synthetic Graphite Core

Graphite has excellent thermal and electric conductivity qualities, as well as outstanding lubrication and intercalation properties. It is also very resistant to oxidation. Because of these attributes, it offers a wide variety of uses. Cumberland graphite is the most refined. Unfortunately, the Borrowdale mine, the source of Cumberland graphite, was closed in the late 19th century due to the exhaustion of the graphite deposits and decreased demand because of second product innovation. Britain banned Cumberland graphite exports to France in the wake of the French Revolution. The French needed an alternative to Cumberland graphite.

Nicolas-Jacques Conté, a French painter, succeeded in making an artificial pencil lead, substituting synthetic graphite for natural graphite. He devised a method of crushing graphite, mixing it with clay and water, and baking it. This new process was the prototype of today's pencils. His clever innovation generated the following benefits:

1. Crushed or inferior quality graphite could be used as material, thus eliminating the severe constraint of Cumberland graphite. It became possible to utilize powdered graphite. The problems of graphite deficiency and waste were resolved.
2. Mass production became a reality.

Natural pencil leads must be handled delicately because they are fragile. On the other hand, artificial pencil leads are sturdy and easy to form. It is now possible to supply a vast amount of inexpensive and reliable quality products.

3. It became possible to offer a wider variety of products

By changing the product composition to graphite and clay, the hardness of the core could be altered for various purposes. In addition, by mixing in dyes, core color variations became richer. Pencil variations for many different applications have emerged.

## Production Process of Modern Pencil

Many process innovations have taken place since the first and second product innovations. Here we briefly describe modern pencil manufacturing and sales. Graphite from Sri Lanka, Brazil, and China is mainly used. It is necessary that the graphite used must be of somewhat good quality and that it can be reliably supplied. Graphite lumps are crushed and refined many times near the mine. After it becomes

*Figure 13. From graphite mining to shipping*
*Source: (Bogala Graphite Lanka PLC)*

a high purity powder, it is shipped. The refining process differs depending on the required purity. These conditions require that mining and refining be done according to the customer company's production plan.

Here is an example of Bogala Graphite Lanka PLC, a Sri Lankan company started in 1965. Graphite Kropfmuehl, one of the oldest group companies operating in the Republic of Germany for over 150 years, became the major shareholder of Bogala Graphite Lanka PLC in 2000. They do not store any finished products in stock. They maintain a limited inventory of raw material that is sorted according to carbon%. They usually accept only large orders over 2000 tons. After the confirmation of orders, they can be shipped in 2-3 weeks. If they do not have sufficient raw material on hand, they start mining at the Bogara Graphite Mine (left side of Picture 1). They can hire temporary workers on short notice and quickly train them because of a prearranged training program. Temporary workers can be assigned within two weeks to increase production yield. They then start processing the raw material at the factory adjacent to the Bogara Graphite mine. The finished product is shown in the middle of figure. 13 below. On the right side of the figure below, we see the finished product packaged, palletized, and ready for shipment.

For wood to be suitable for the fabrication of pencils, it needs to meet certain conditions. First, the wood must be light, smooth, and durable for ease of holding. For mass production, the wood must be reliably supplied in large quantities at a commercially reasonable cost. Based on these requirements, it is essential to decide which type of tree to use and from which area to procure it. This decision is of the most important secrets of pencil manufacturing.

Transporting logs as raw material is inefficient and expensive. Instead, the fallen trees are shredded into slats 70 mm wide, 185 mm long, and 5 mm thick at a nearby sawmill. The shredding process is rigorous and requires hard work and accuracy. The cut slats are then packed in cardboard, loaded on pallets and containers, and then exported.

Clay and oil are also used in the production of pencils. The suppliers of clay and oil are also chosen to consider quality, price, output, and other concerns. Material suppliers conduct logging and mining operations according to order requirements.

The factories that fulfill pencil orders tend to locate near their customers. Graphite, clay, and oil are mixed and baked to form a cylindrical pencil lead in the factory. Grooves are routed on the slats to fit the pencil lead. Pencil leads are then sandwiched between two matching slats that are glued together.

*Figure 14. Cross section of pencil assembly*

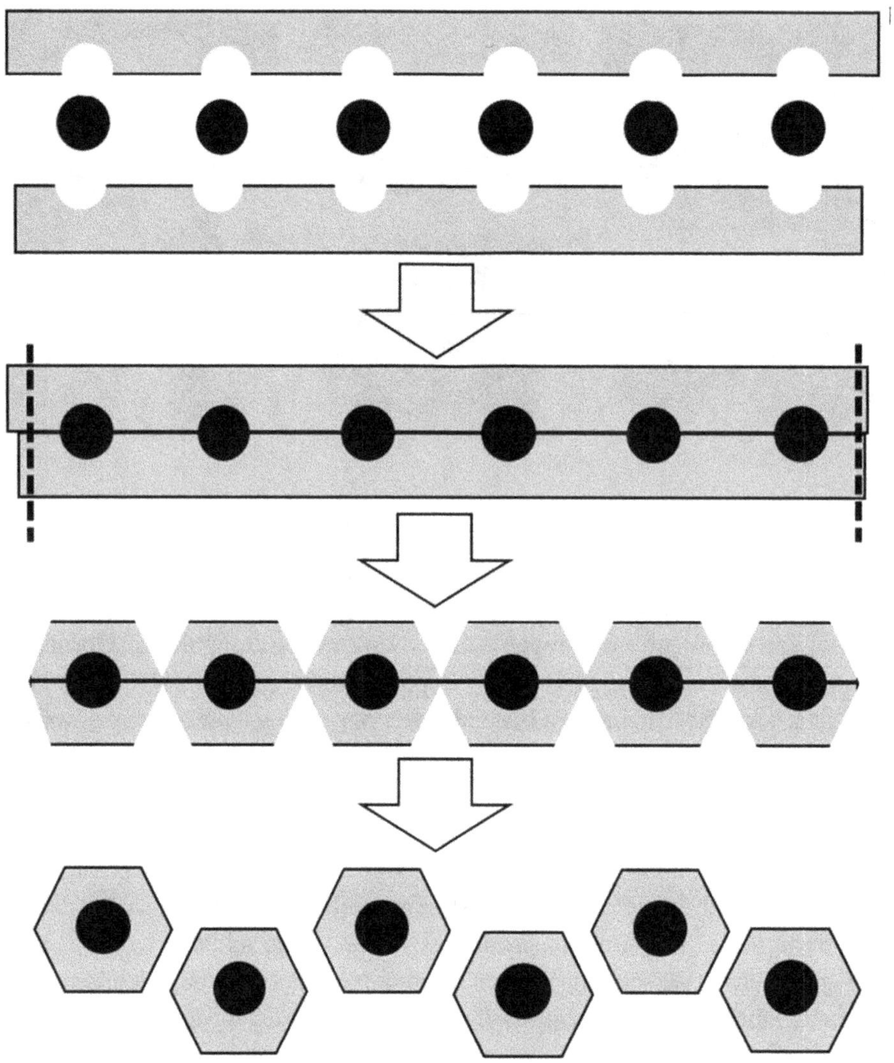

Generally, the glued piece is cut into separate, hexagonal-shaped pencils (Figure 14). Paint is applied, and the pencils are completed.

## Distribution of Pencil

Pencils are mainly used in schools and are indispensable for marking papers. There are numerous pencil makers, from small, to medium-sized, to large scale-manufacturers. A distribution channel needs to be established to sell pencils widely to domestic and foreign markets. Small lot sizes are suitable for making customized pencils with logos, company names, and other such imprints.

Consider Mitsubishi Pencil Co. Ltd. as an example. Until 1980, the company manufactured and sold more than about one billion pencils a year. (Figure 15). The sales volume included international sales

*Figure 15. Sales volume of Mitsubishi Pencil Co., Ltd.*
*(Data Source: Mitsubishi Pencil Co., Ltd.)*

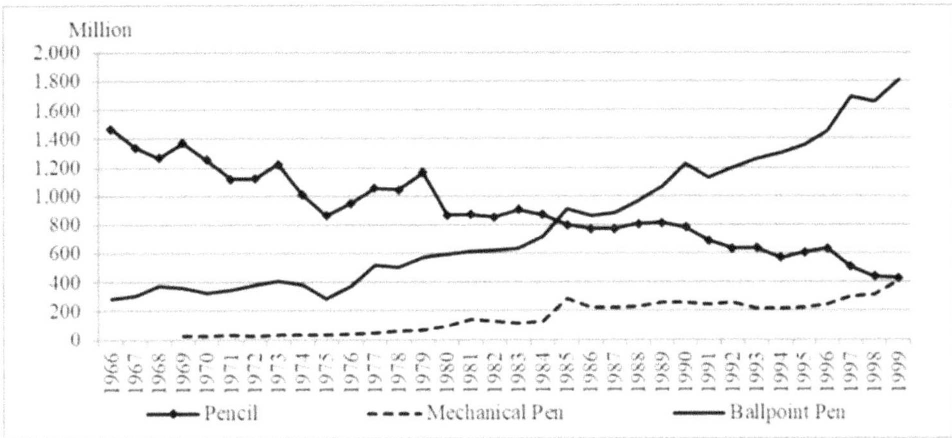


that constitute 20-30% of the total. The company specializes in luxury goods, but even a simple product such as a pencil is needed by consumers worldwide. However, the number of pencils manufactured and sold by Mitsubishi Pencil is declining (Figure 15). This is primarily due to the increased popularity of mechanical pencils and a declining birthrate. Even with the declining demand for pencils, they continue to evolve writing instruments. Their company philosophy consists of guaranteed quality, "focus on safety and security," and "consideration for the environment." While rival pencil makers are launching direct sales sites, a hallmark of the Mitsubishi Pencil Co. is how they value their enduring relationship with traditional stationery stores. Nonetheless, the company goes beyond writing instruments and extends its activities to industrial materials and cosmetics.

## SOLUTIONS AND RECOMMENDATIONS

The supply chain must be viewed from an objective and subjective perspective. First, with an overall view of a supply chain, analyze its strengths and weaknesses objectively. Next, it is necessary to confirm the standpoint in a supply chain and take concrete measures from a subjective perspective. While supply chains must value continuity as a whole, it is supported mainly by individual efforts.

## FUTURE RESEARCH DIRECTIONS

SCM has gained experience and has matured to some extent, but it will be more important to respond to changes in the external environment. COVID-19 and environmental protection will continue to be significant challenges for the supply chain. To be sustainable, SCM must become more sophisticated and diverse in response to changing conditions. An appropriate and timely response will allow SCM to adapt to a wide variety of supply chains predicated on different products, industries, countries, business practices, and other issues. In addition, it is necessary to study various perspectives to achieve more holistic supply chain strategies.

## CONCLUSION

This chapter clarifies the differences between supply chains and similar concepts, such as physical distribution, business logistics, and company group. The supply chain is a broader concept than physical distribution and business logistics. It includes all companies and activities related to goods and services. Supply chains transcend companies, industries, and countries, and their members are more operationally flexible than those of a company group.

The purpose of this chapter is to propose frameworks for supply chains, SCM, and supply chain strategies. This chapter also describes the drivers that increase supply performance immediately and factors that evolve supply chain and SCM in the long term. These frameworks will be examined and substantiated in subsequent chapters.

## REFERENCES

Abernathy, W. J., Clark, K. B., & Kantrow, A. M. (1983). *Industrial renaissance*. Basic Books.

Ballou, R. H. (1992). *Business logistics management*. Prentice-Hall.

Bowersox, J., & Closs, D. J. (1996). *Logistical management*. McGraw-Hill.

Corbett, C. J., Blackbum, J. D., & Van Wassenhove, N. (1999). Partnerships to improve supply chains. *Sloan Management Review*, *40*(4), 71–82.

Fisher, M. L. (1997). What is the right supply chain for your product? *Harvard Business Review*, *1997*(March-April), 105–1156.

Higuchi, T, & Troutt, M. D. (2008). *Life cycle management in Supply Chains*. Idea Group.

Schumpeter, J. A. (1949). *The theory of economic development. Harvard University Press*. Translated by Redvers Opie from Germany.

## ADDITIONAL READING

Abernathy, W. J., Clark, K. B., & Kantrow, A. M. (1983). *Industrial renaissance*. Basic Books.

## KEY TERMS AND DEFINITIONS

**Business Logistics:** A part of the supply chain. It is a broader concept than physical distribution. Its main activity is backup and supplement. It contributes to a company's financial performance directly through increased sales and lower costs.

**Company Group:** A group of companies with a capital relationship. A holding or headquarter company tightly controls the group. The members are not flexible.

**Physical Distribution:** The flow and stock of goods between an origin and a destination. It is required to ensure delivery as requested and to keep costs down. Partial optimization under constraints is also needed.

**Process Innovation:** A process change that increases the productivity or production capacity in manufacturing, distribution channels, and other areas. It does not contribute to improved product performance directly; rather, it enhances availability and convenience.

**Product Innovation:** The creation of a brand-new category of products with added innovative functions. It changes basic design, materials, production system, use, and other features.

**Push Operation:** An act on expectations. Inventory makes it possible to respond to orders quickly. For example, retailers maintain an inventory of products in anticipation of customer demand. Factories also keep an inventory of products and parts to respond to orders quickly.

**Pull Operation:** An act on actual orders. In other words, it is "build-to-order manufacturing" or "made-to-order." If the manufacturer does not have enough inventory of material and parts to fulfill its orders, it will also have to place orders with its suppliers.

**Supply Chain:** A group of companies and activities related to a product. Every product has its supply chain.

**Supply Chain Management:** An activity to reinforce the interlock in a supply chain. It contributes to increased supply chain performance and profitability.

**Supply Chain Strategy:** The choice of the type of supply chain and the level of supply chain drivers appropriate for a product and target customers. Supply chains are also a part of society. Technological advances and social changes greatly influence not only products and customers but also supply chains.

# Chapter 2
# Cost Management of Logistics and Supply Chain Costs

**Hiroyuki Nakajima**
*Meisei University, Japan*

## ABSTRACT

*In order for a supply chain to thrive, it must be evaluated from a financial perspective. In particular, supply chain profits and profitability are important performance measures. However, since it is very difficult to evaluate the profit side of the supply chain, this chapter focuses on the cost management of logistics and supply chain costs. The premise of supply chain cost management is that each company participating in the supply chain is able to manage logistics costs appropriately. Therefore, the authors discuss the management of logistics costs by utilizing management accounting methods such as activity-based costing, total cost of ownership, and life cycle cost. Then, after clarifying what exactly is meant by supply chain costs, supply chain cost management is discussed. The management of costs incurred across multiple companies is much more difficult than the cost management of a single company, and the issues that must be overcome are clarified. Finally, directions for future research are presented.*

## INTRODUCTION

This chapter examines supply chain management from the perspective of cost management. Various possible measures are used to evaluate the performance of a supply chain, including financial and non-financial indicators. For example, shortening lead time, optimizing inventory, and determining whether related data is managed centrally are non-financial measures to evaluate supply chains.

However, for a supply chain to be maintained and developed over time, it is essential to evaluate it financially. In particular, the profit and supply chain profitability, backed by financial indicators, is an essential evaluation measure. The following formula expresses the profit of a supply chain.

Profit = Sales obtained from end consumers in the supply chain

- All costs paid by the supply chain members to obtain the sales.

DOI: 10.4018/978-1-7998-9800-9.ch002

While a supply chain needs to earn as much profit as possible, measuring whether it efficiently earns profit is also important. Therefore, it is necessary to measure the supply chain profitability; there are several possible ways to do this, but the simplest way is to evaluate the ratio obtained by dividing the supply chain's profits by the sales. By expressing the profit as a ratio to the sales amount instead of an absolute amount, it is possible to compare the profitability of supply chains of different sizes. The higher the ratio, the more profit is earned with fewer sales, and the higher the profitability.

It is necessary to consider both the revenue and cost sides to evaluate a supply chain's profitability; however, it is challenging to evaluate the revenue side in practice. Since sales, which account for the majority of revenue, are easily influenced by external factors such as trends of rival companies and market conditions, it is essential to consider these factors in the evaluation. For the reasons mentioned above, it is difficult to evaluate sales, even for individual companies, but it becomes even more complicated when evaluating a supply chain's sales because of the organization's complexity.

Conversely, it is easier to evaluate the cost side than the revenue side because the incidence of costs is less affected by external factors; even if it is affected by external factors, the impact is limited. This is also because most cost-related factors depend on the supply chain's internal environment, and the costs incurred can be predicted with some accuracy.

Nevertheless, inherent difficulties arise when evaluating the costs of a supply chain. Since multiple companies participate in supply chains and the chain members are often replaced, evaluating the costs incurred in a supply chain is much more complex than evaluating the costs of individual companies. The question arises of allocating manufacturing overhead and various common expenses incurred in the supply chain to the participating companies.

It is not enough to simply evaluate its performance to make a supply chain financially successful and develop it further. Financial management is required to achieve better performance. Improving a supply chain's performance requires increasing revenue, reducing costs, or both. As mentioned earlier, management on the revenue side is difficult, so this chapter focuses on the supply chain's cost management and management of logistics costs in individual companies, which is the premise of management.

## BACKGROUND

The Japan Institute of Logistics Systems has been continuously surveying the ratio of logistics costs (the sum of transportation, storage, packaging, cargo handling, and logistics management costs) to sales. According to the Japan Institute of Logistics System's survey, the logistics costs to sales ratio in FY2020 is 5.70% (average for all industries) among the Japanese companies that responded to the survey. Figure 1 shows the logistics costs to sales ratio over the past 20 years. The ratio has hovered around the 4% range since the early 2000s but has increased rapidly in recent years. Reasons for this include an overall increase in the volume of cargo, a workforce shortage, and requests from logistics companies to raise freight rates.

As corporate activities become increasingly globalized and imports and exports proliferate, logistics costs are expected to rise even more in the future. The ratio of logistics costs to sales is 5%, which is not a low number. Higher logistics costs lead to lower profits for companies, leading to higher product prices, forcing consumers to pay more. Therefore, managing logistics costs is an essential theme in business administration.

According to Ballou (1992, pp.78-79), traditional cost accounting methods are not suitable for calculating logistics costs because they aim to calculate manufacturing costs accurately. He also pointed

*Figure 1. Trends in the ratio of logistics cost to sales (all industries)*
*Source: (Japan Institute of Logistics Systems 2021, p. 2)*

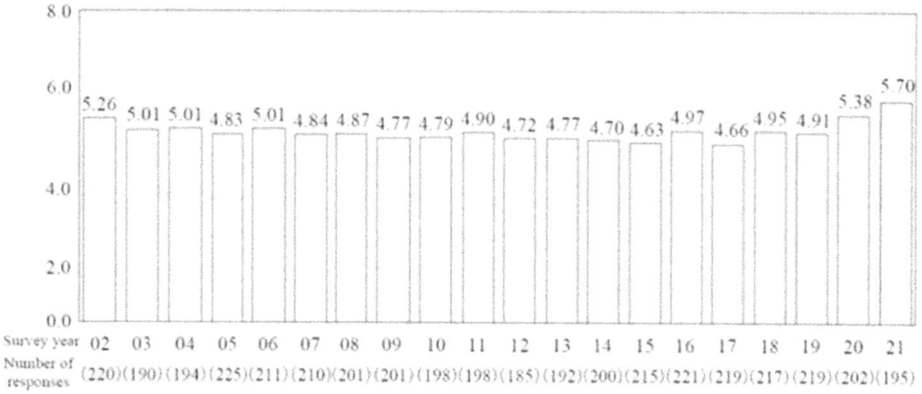


out that the arbitrariness in calculating the allocation of common and indirect costs distorts the true profitability of customers and markets.

Against this background, the research fields of costing of physical distribution costs or management accounting of physical distribution costs were established for accurate calculation and management. Their purpose is to calculate the total amount of physical distribution costs incurred by individual companies and reduce them. Specifically, physical distribution costs include transportation, storage, packaging, cargo handling, and logistics management costs.

Abo and Yazawa (2000, p.13, pp.16-17) pointed out two problems in costing physical distribution costs or management accounting for physical distribution costs. First, such costing cannot deal with complex logistics activities and supply chains across companies because they are based on discussions within a single company's physical distribution division. Second, costing physical distribution costs or management accounting of physical distribution costs can not accurately grasp the actual situation of logistics activities and supply chains because they are too focused on reducing physical distribution costs, an accounting-driven approach.

It is not easy to improve the performance of individual companies and supply chains by only managing physical distribution costs. Therefore, the concept of logistics management, which integrates physical distribution and manufacturing, sales, and other activities within a company, becomes essential. The Council of Supply Chain Management Professionals (CSCMP), presented in Chapter 1, defines logistics management as follows:

*Logistics management is that part of supply chain management that plans, implements, and controls the efficient, practical forward and reverses flow and storage of goods, services and related information between the point of origin and the point of consumption in order to meet customers' requirements.*

Logistics management aims at overall optimization, i.e., maximization of profits, at the individual company level by integrating the manufacturing and sales functions within the company. After setting a target service level, the division of labor among companies and work processes within companies are adjusted to meet the target level, aiming to achieve overall optimization.

*Figure 2. Logistics cost classification*
*Source: (Nishizawa 1999, p.27)*

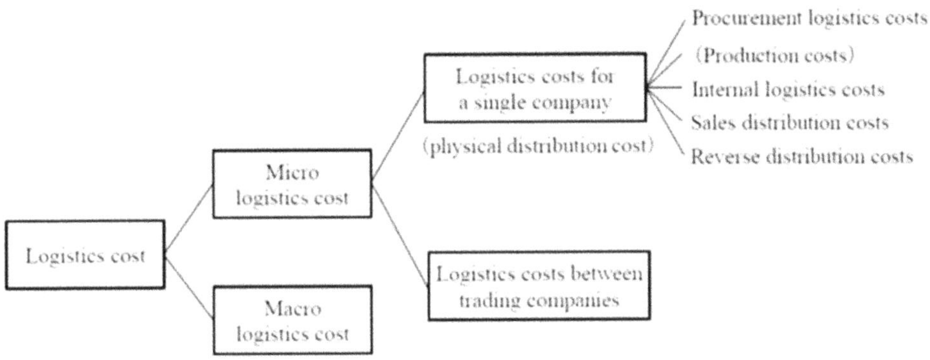


## LOGISTICS COST MANAGEMENT

### What are Logistics Costs?

The cost concept important in logistics management is not physical distribution cost, but logistics cost. According to Nishizawa (1999, p.27), logistics costs can be classified as shown in Figure 2. This chapter focuses on micro logistics cost, classified into logistics cost for a single company and between trading companies.

According to Ballou (1992, pp.7-8), business logistics represents a series of procedures from the supply of raw materials through the manufacturing plant to the supply of products to customers; the process consists of key activities and support activities listed as follows.

#### Key Activities

1. Customer service standards
   Cooperate with marketing to
   a. Determine customer needs and wants for logistics customer service)
   b. Determine customer response to service
   c. Set customer service levels
2. Transportation
   a. Mode and transport service selection
   b. Freight consolidation
   c. Carrier routing
   d. Vehicle Scheduling
   e. Equipment selection
   f. Claims processing
   g. Rate auditing
3. Inventory management
   a. Raw materials and finished goods stocking policies

   b. Short-term sales forecasting
   c. Product mix at stocking points
   d. Number, size, and location of stocking points
   e. Just-in-time, push, and pull strategies
4. Order processing
   a. Sales order-inventory interface procedures
   b. Order information transmittal methods
   c. Ordering rules

Support Activities

1. Warehousing
   a. Space determination
   b. Stock layout and dock design
   c. Warehouse configuration
   d. Stock placement
2. Materials handling
   a. Equipment selection
   b. Equipment replacement policies
   c. Order-picking procedures
   d. Stock storage and retrieval
3. Purchasing
   a. Supply source selection
   b. Purchase timing
   c. Purchase quantities
4. Protective packaging
   Design for
      a. Handling
      b. Storage
      c. Protection from loss and damage
5. Cooperate with production to
   a. Specify aggregate quantities
   b. Sequence and time production output
6. Information maintenance
   a. Information collection, storage, and manipulation
   b. Data analysis
   c. Control procedures

Ballou (1992, p.8) cites activities that occur in all logistics activities within a particular company and activities that occur depending on the situation as the necessity of categorizing activities into key activities and support activities, as described above. Ballou then points out a "critical loop," a sequence of customer orders, order processing, shipment from the warehouse, and delivery to the customer, as shown in Figure 3. According to Ballou, activities related to the critical loop account for most logistics costs. In

*Figure 3. Critical loop*
*Source: (Ballou 1992, p.9)*

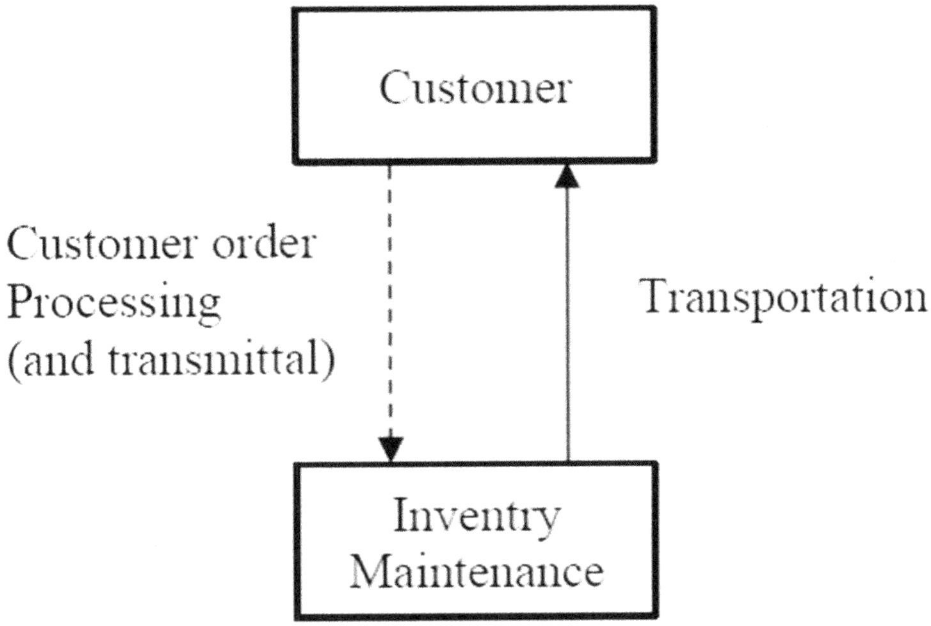


particular, the costs associated with transportation activities account for 1/2 to 2/3 of the total logistics costs. Therefore, properly managing the logistics activities on the critical loop also reduces logistics costs.

As corporate activities become more widespread and complex, and supply chains are expanding beyond national borders, there is a limit to what can be achieved by simply managing the logistics costs of individual companies. It is necessary to expand the scope of cost management to include logistics costs. In addition, cost management methods are inevitably required to calculate and manage logistics costs for each company and each supply chain.

## Managing Logistics Costs with Activity-Based Costing (ABC) and Activity-Based Management (ABM)

As mentioned earlier, logistics costs are characterized as activities along with a series of distribution channels from suppliers to customers; Christopher (2016, p.79) specifically characterizes this as a "flow-oriented concept." Therefore, it is necessary to measure costs and performance while being aware of the consumption of resources along the distribution channel; accounting for logistics costs must be flow-oriented.

In contrast, Christopher (2016, p.79) points out that the traditional costing method was devised to measure manufacturing costs on a product basis and is unsuitable for logistics cost management. In other words, traditional cost accounting is not a flow-oriented calculation process; it aggregates the various cost items generated into direct material costs, direct labor costs, direct expenses, and manufacturing overhead costs, and then directly charges or allocates them to the cost accounting target (product). In addition, Christopher criticizes traditional costing methods for distorting the true profitability of each

*Figure 4. CAM-I cross*
*Source: (CAM-I 1990, https://www.cam-i.org/docs/Toolkit_CAM-I_Cross.pdf (2022.2.14 access))*

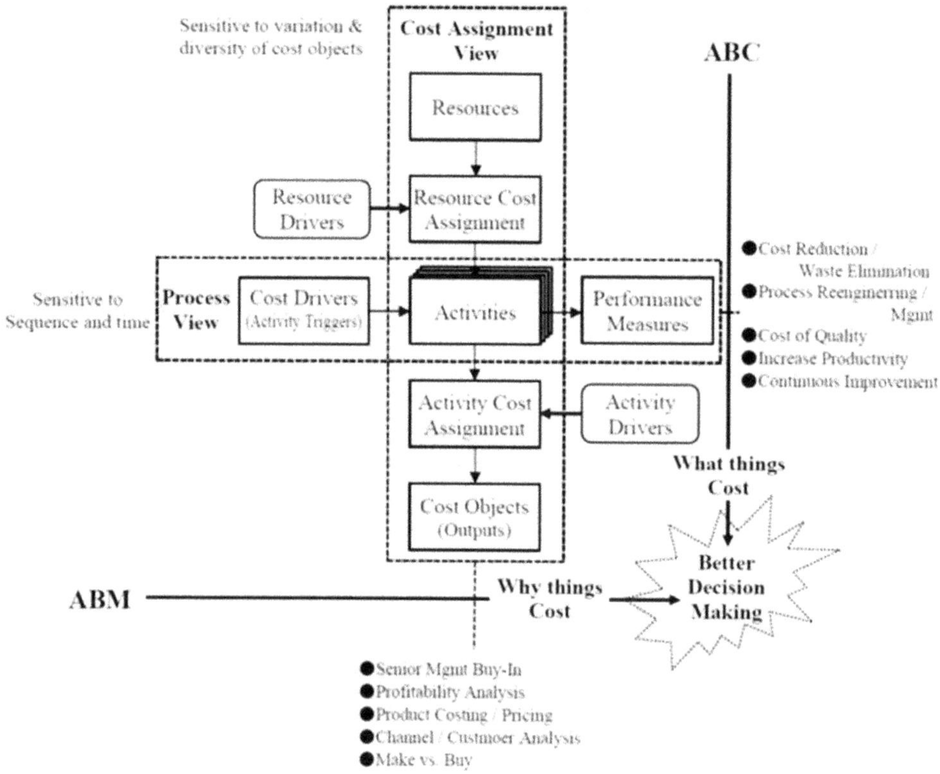


product or customer by lumping together manufacturing overhead costs and then allocating them to costing objects according to allocation standards that are not necessarily appropriate. Bowersox and Closs (1996, p.12) argue that ABC and ABM, developed by R. S. Caplan and R. Cooper in the late 1980s, are helpful for logistics cost calculation and management.

The Consortium for Advanced Management International (CAM-I), a non-profit international consortium, presents a model diagram of ABC and ABM, known as the "CAM-I cross" (see Figure 4). The vertical arrows in Fig. 4 show the calculation structure of ABC from the perspective of cost allocation, and the purpose is to understand "how much cost is involved." The horizontal arrows in Fig. 4 show cost reduction by ABM from the perspective of process, and the purpose is to understand "why costs are incurred." The key concept common to both ABC and ABM is "activity;" the two cross through activity in the center of the diagram, and such crossing is the CAM-I cross.

A two-step calculation process characterizes ABC. The two-step calculation process can indeed be achieved by performing departmental costing in traditional costing. However, by placing activities at the center of the calculation process, ABC enables a more accurate calculation of manufacturing overhead allocation, resulting in more accurate costing.

The area above the activities in Figure 4 is the first stage of the calculation process, based on the concept that activities consume resources. Here, resources are direct material, direct labor, and manufacturing overhead costs in traditional costing. In addition, activities include, for example, material orders, acceptance inspection activities, and setups. Resource drivers allocate resources to each activity; for example, the number of times an order is placed and the number of times a setup is performed are examples of resource drivers. In the first stage of the calculation process, the cost is calculated for each activity.

The lower part of the activity in Figure 4 is the second stage of the calculation process, where the cost aggregated for each activity is allocated to the costing target (e.g., products). The allocation standard at this time is the activity driver, for example, the number of setup activities. The cost aggregated to the "setup activity" activity is allocated to the product, the object of cost calculation, according to the number of setup activities. In this way, manufacturing overhead costs can be allocated more accurately than traditional cost accounting by focusing on activities and performing a two-step allocation calculation.

ABM is unique because it focuses on cost drivers, the factors that generate activities, and reviews the activities themselves. If an activity does not bring added value, the activity itself may be deleted. Alternatively, cost drivers may be reviewed to make activities more efficient. ABM aims to reduce the cost aggregated to activities through these efforts.

ABC can be used for manufacturing costs and calculating logistics costs. As mentioned earlier, Christopher pointed out that flow orientation is important in calculating logistics costs. Using ABC to aggregate costs in units of various activities that occur in logistics is precisely in line with flow orientation. Therefore, ABC and ABM are very effective means of managing logistics costs.

## An Actual Example of Logistics Cost Calculation by ABC

This section discusses ABC's calculation of logistics cost by examining the calculation example of SPC-Logic, a Portuguese global logistics company, presented by Themido et al. (2000, pp. 1151-1156).

SPC-Logic provides third-party logistics, including collecting, warehousing, packing, loading, and distribution of goods.

Figure 5 shows the structure of the ABC calculation performed by SPC-Logic. This case study divides Portugal into four regions (Centre, B.A. & Alg., T.M. & B.I., and Alto Minho). Furthermore, transport to the Centre region, including the capital Lisbon, is divided into Transport_1 and Distribution_1; transport to B.A. & Alg. is divided into Transport_2 and Distribution_2; transport to T.M. & B.I. is divided into Transport_3 and Distribution_3; transportation to Alto Minho region is divided into Transport_4 and Distribution_4. These divisions are based on the two-stage calculation model shown in Figure 4, where the ten measured resources (costs) are assigned to the seven activities by resource drivers, and the costs aggregated to the activities are finally allocated to the seven costing objects based on the activity drivers.

Table 1 provides June 1998 data on resource volumes (costs) for the ten resources measured. According to Table 1, transportation to the Centre region and indirect costs account for nearly 70% of the total. Table 1 also shows the resource drivers that were determined to be optimal for assigning each resource to an activity. The resource drivers are set individually, considering the nature of the resource. For example, the floor space is set as the resource driver for a warehouse.

Table 2 shows that for each of the seven predefined activities, the amount of resources (cost) is assigned to each activity by the resource driver. For example, in the case of warehousing, the resource quantity (cost) of 3437428 (no currency units are given in Themido et al. [2000]) is allocated to the three activities of the Stock entrance, Storage, and Dispatching, in the ratio of 126:380:294, according to the resource driver, floor space. Similarly, overheads are allocated in the ratio shown in Table 2. As a result, for example, 1632778 is allocated from Warehouse and 987525 is allocated from Overheads to Storage activities, resulting in a total cost of 2620303 for Storage activities (see Table 3). Table 3 shows

*Figure 5. Structure of ABC calculations in SPC-Logic*
*Source: (Themido et al. 2000, p.1153)*

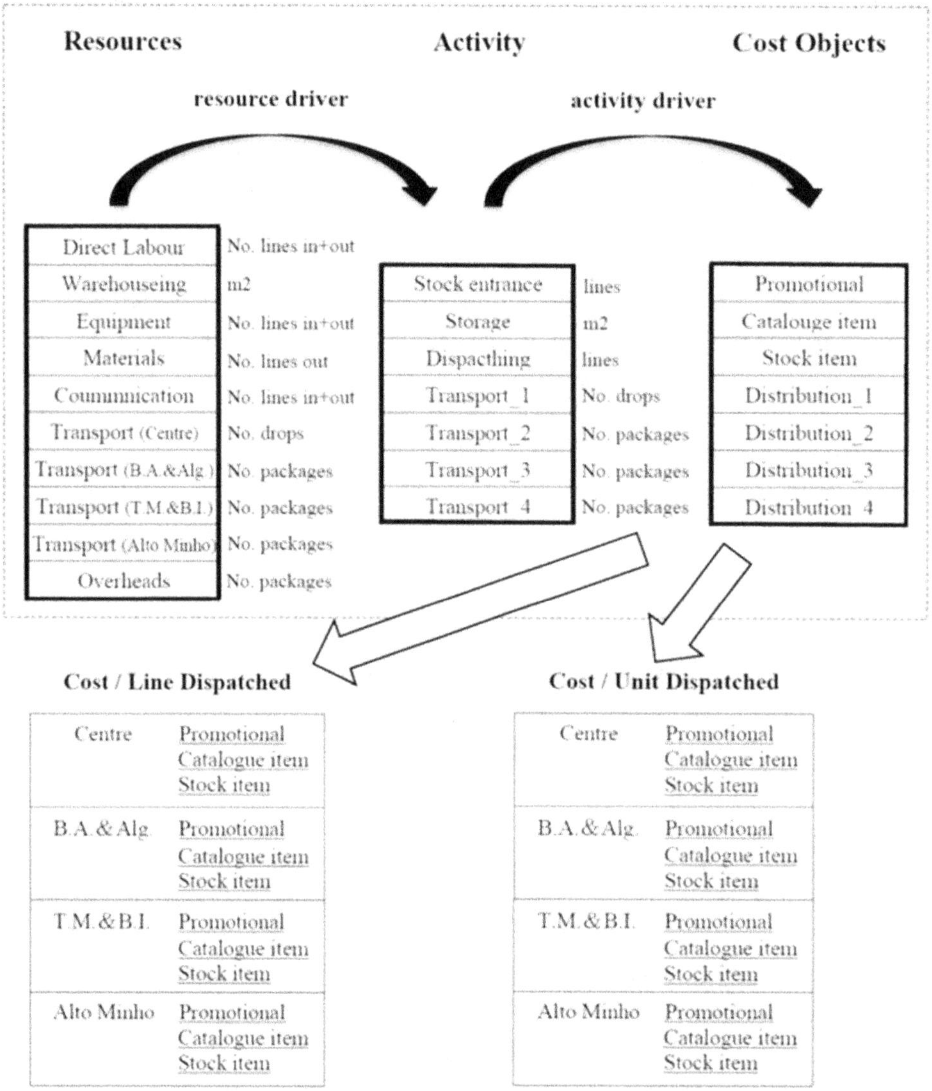


the activity costs allocated to each activity by the first stage of the ABC calculation process, consisting of Tables 1 and 2, and the associated activity drivers, respectively.

As ABC's second step, the activity costs aggregated in Table 3 are finally allocated to the seven costing objects by the activity drivers. The process is shown in Table 4, and Table 5 provides the results. Taking Storage activity as an example, the cost calculated in Table 3, 2620303, is allocated to three costing objects, Promotional, Catalog item, and Stock item, in the ratio of 97:22:261, using floor space as the activity driver. After performing such allocation calculation for each activity cost, the Table 5 results can be obtained by aggregating the results for each costing object.

Based on Table 5, Table 6 shows the total cost by region. By contrasting Table 6 with regional sales, we can understand profitability by region. Based on the cost information obtained from ABC, ABM can

*Table 1. Amount of resource (cost) and resource driver*

| **Resource** | *Cost June 98* | % | *Resource driver* |
|---|---|---|---|
| Direct labour | 3788919 | 10.2% | Number of order lines handled (in + out) |
| Warehouse | 3437428 | 9.2% | Square meters of floor space |
| Equipment | 681537 | 1.8% | Number of order lines handled (in + out) |
| Materials | 849980 | 2.3% | Number of order lines handled (out) |
| Communication | 99935 | 0.3% | Number of order lines handled (in + out) |
| Transport (Centre) | 11149609 | 30.0% | Number of drops |
| Transport (B.A.& Alg.) | 533482 | 1.4% | Number of packages dispatched |
| Transport (T.M.& B.I.) | 1535960 | 4.1% | Number of packages dispatched |
| Transport (Alto Minho) | 1006707 | 2.7% | Number of packages dispatched |
| Overheads | 14107500 | 37.9% | % management time consumed by activity |
| Total | 37191058 | 100.0% | |

Source: (Themido et al. 2000, p.1154)

be used to make various management decisions, such as improving profitability by reviewing activities, strengthening services in highly profitable regions, and suspending services in unprofitable regions.

Abo and Yazawa (2000, p.107) point out that it is impossible to apply the ABC to logistics activities whose situation changes drastically at each point in time. In other words, even if cost drivers and activity drivers are set and an elaborate cost accounting system is established, the cost drivers and activity drivers must be reviewed each time the situation changes. It is essential to consider building an optimal ABC/ABM system by considering the overall logistics activities.

*Table 2. Resource driver and amount of activity*

| **Resource** | *Resource driver* | *Activity* | | | | | | | |
|---|---|---|---|---|---|---|---|---|---|
| | | *Stock entrance* | *Storage* | *Dispatching* | *Transport* | | | | *Total* |
| | | | | | *1* | *2* | *3* | *4* | |
| Direct labour | No. lines in + out | 60 | 0 | 5470 | | | | | 5530 |
| Warehouse | $m^2$ | 126 | 380 | 294 | | | | | 800 |
| Equipment | No. lines in + out | 60 | 0 | 5470 | | | | | 5530 |
| Materials | No. lines out | 0 | 0 | 5470 | | | | | 5470 |
| Communication | No. lines in + out | 60 | 0 | 5470 | | | | | 5530 |
| Transport (Centre) | No. drops | | | | 677 | 0 | 0 | 0 | 677 |
| Transport(B.A.& Alg.) | No. packages | | | | 0 | 172 | 0 | 0 | 172 |
| Transport (T.M.& B.I.) | No. packages | | | | 0 | 0 | 408 | 0 | 408 |
| Transport (Alto Minho) | No. packages | | | | 0 | 0 | 0 | 310 | 310 |
| Overheads | % time | 13 | 7 | 35 | 15 | 10 | 10 | 10 | 100 |

Source: (Themido et al. 2000, p.1154)

*Table 3. Activity cost and activity driver*

| Activity | Cost June 98 | % | Resource driver |
|---|---|---|---|
| Stock entrance | 2424958 | 6.5% | Number of order lines handled (in) |
| Storage | 2620303 | 7.0% | Square meters of floor space |
| Dispatching | 11571663 | 31.1% | Number of order lines handled (out) |
| Transport_1 | 13265734 | 35.7% | Number of drops |
| Transport_2 | 1944232 | 5.2% | Number of packages dispatched |
| Transport_3 | 2946710 | 7.9% | Number of packages dispatched |
| Transport_4 | 2417457 | 6.5% | Number of packages dispatched |
| Total | 37191058 | 100.0% | |

Source: (Themido et al. 2000, p.1155)

*Table 4. Calculation of allocations to costing objects by activity drivers*

| Activity | Activity driver | Cost Objects | | | | | | | |
|---|---|---|---|---|---|---|---|---|---|
| | | Promotional | Catalogue item | Stock item | Distribution | | | | Total |
| | | | | | 1 | 2 | 3 | 4 | |
| Stock entrance | Lines | 13 | 28 | 19 | | | | | 60 |
| Storage | $m^2$ | 97 | 22 | 261 | | | | | 380 |
| Dispatching | Lines | 1575 | 2819 | 1076 | | | | | 5470 |
| Transport_1 | No. drops | | | | 677 | 0 | 0 | 0 | 677 |
| Transport_2 | No. packages | | | | 0 | 172 | 0 | 0 | 172 |
| Transport_3 | No. packages | | | | 0 | 0 | 408 | 0 | 408 |
| Transport_4 | No. packages | | | | 0 | 0 | 0 | 310 | 310 |

Source: (Themido et al. 2000, p.1155)

*Table 5. Costs aggregated and allocated for each cost accounting object*

| Cost object | Cost June 98 | % |
|---|---|---|
| Promotional | 4523720 | 6.5% |
| Catalogue item | 7246641 | 7.0% |
| Stock item | 4846563 | 31.1% |
| Distribution_1 | 13265734 | 35.7% |
| Distribution_2 | 1944232 | 5.2% |
| Distribution_3 | 2946710 | 7.9% |
| Distribution_4 | 2417457 | 6.5% |
| Total | 37191058 | 100.0% |

Source: (Themido et al. 2000, p.1155)

*Table 6. Final calculation results based on ABC*

| Cost objects | Centre | | B.A. & Alg. | | T.M. & B.I. | | Alto Minho | |
|---|---|---|---|---|---|---|---|---|
| Promotional | 3213996 | 12.8% | 252754 | 8.8% | 600291 | 11.7% | 456680 | 11.2% |
| Catalogue item | 5151568 | 20.5% | 406162 | 14.1% | 958850 | 18.6% | 730062 | 17.8% |
| Stock item | 3445744 | 13.7% | 270254 | 9.4% | 644106 | 12.5% | 486458 | 11.9% |
| Distribution | 13265734 | 52.9% | 1944232 | 67.7% | 2946710 | 57.2% | 2417457 | 59.1% |
| Total Cost | 25077041 | 100.0% | 2873402 | 100.0% | 5149957 | 100.0% | 4090658 | 100.0% |

Source: (Themido et al. 2000, p.1156)

## Logistics Cost Management by Total Cost

In addition to ABC and ABM, Total Cost is another analytical perspective when considering the management of logistics costs. The total cost is the sum of the two cost elements at each level indicated by the horizontal axis in examining the trade-off between the two cost elements (see Figure 6). Therefore, Total Cost cannot be clearly defined, as it varies depending on the cost elements to be considered for a trade-off.

According to Iwata (2003, pp.90-91), ABC relies on arbitrary cost allocation because it does not consider the organization a single system, while ABM focuses on eliminating partial non-value added activities. He points out that ABC and ABM are oriented toward partial optimization. Conversely, Bowersox and Closs (1996, pp.11-12) point out that the main objective of trade-off analysis is to find the optimal level of logistics costs that can achieve the performance of logistics services demanded by customers. Since the key goal is to provide the performance demanded by the customer, minimizing the total cost is not necessarily the best option. Instead, it is important to strike a balance between logistics performance and cost from the perspective of total optimization.

It is clear from these remarks that partial optimization, i.e., lowering logistics costs, can be achieved by accurately calculating logistics costs and reviewing activities using ABC and ABM; however, ABC and ABM are insufficient for total optimization and trade-off analysis based on total costs is necessary.

The central concept of the total cost is trade-off analysis. After looking at the overall logistics cost, we consider a trade-off analysis between the cost of providing logistics services and non-cost factors.

Bowersox and Closs (1996, p.79) emphasize that in considering trade-offs, it is necessary to consider two points: how it affects the total cost and the impact on sales. Figure 6 shows an example of a trade-off analysis. For example, as shown in (a), improving customer service results in higher transportation costs, order fulfillment costs, and storage costs for inventory items to provide a higher level of service. Conversely, the opportunity loss in sales reduces because the improved service results in higher customer satisfaction. However, improving customer service to the utmost limit decreases the opportunity loss in sales, but transportation, order processing, and storage costs increase significantly. If the other costs that make up the logistics cost remain constant, the total cost also increases to the limit. Figure 6 (a) illustrates this point. Therefore, in (a) of Figure 6, we consider that the optimal total cost is at the intersection of the curve of transportation, order processing, and inventory costs, and the cost of lost sales, which is also the optimal level of customer service. In Figure 6, graphs of (b), (c), and (d) are also determined in the same way to determine the optimal level of the total cost.

*Figure 6. Models with various trade-offs*
*Source: (Bowersox and Closs 1996, p.79)*

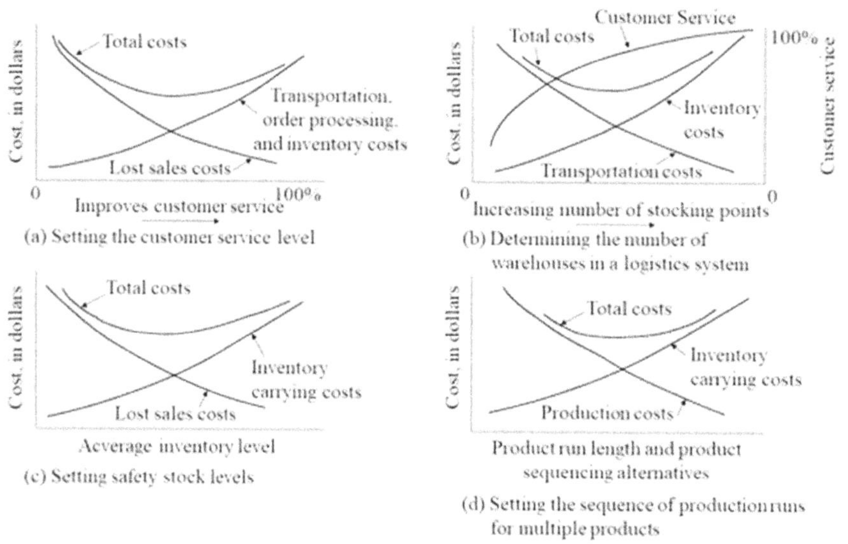


When making decisions through trade-off analysis, the impact of a particular decision, on the whole, must also be considered. Bowersox and Closs (1996, p.80) point out that even when decisions are made after determining the optimal level through trade-off analysis, they directly or indirectly impact various parts of the company. These impacts may not be visible in Figure 6. A typical example is a case where a change in service level affects variable costs, while the impact will not necessarily be felt in fixed costs. Therefore, trade-off analysis must also consider the impact on fixed costs inherent in logistics costs.

## USEFUL COST INFORMATION FOR LOGISTICS DECISION MAKING

### Total Cost of OWNERSHIP

ABC/ABM is useful for obtaining accurate cost information and making cost reduction measures and decisions by precisely aggregating costs based on "activities." Therefore, the information obtained from ABC/ABM is helpful for decision making, which is true even if the ABC/ABM's target is logistics costs, not manufacturing costs.

However, the cost information obtained from ABC/ABM is already incurred. The actual information is important when considering managerial decision-making, but forecast information is also important. In particular, when the impact of a decision is long-term, it is necessary to consider the actual information and the forecast information. In the case of decisions related to logistics, such as the launch of an information system or the establishment of a new warehouse or relay base, the amount of capital investment is large, and the impact of the decision making once made remains for a long time. Therefore, it is necessary to make decisions based on actual and the most accurate forecast information possible. Total Cost of Ownership (TCO) is useful for organizations to optimize through logistics management.

*Figure 7. Relationship between TCO and LCC*
*Source: (ISO 20400 2017, p.26)*

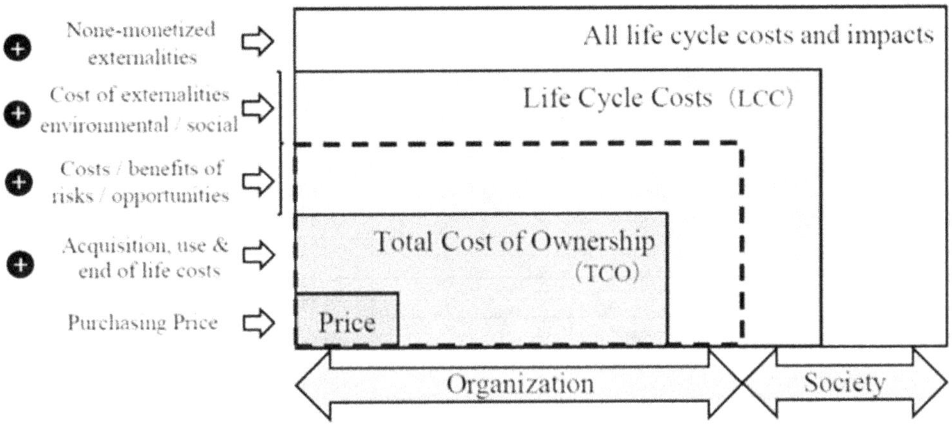


According to Christopher (2016, pp.29-30), TCO is useful in making purchasing decisions, and specifically, it includes the acquisition cost or purchase price and the inventory carrying, maintenance, running, and discrete costs that occur after the purchase. In cases where such cost is larger than the acquisition cost or purchase price, it is more meaningful to consider TCO. In this case, TCO plays an important role in the purchasing decision. In other words, deciding to lower the acquisition cost or purchase price leads to increasing inventory carrying, maintenance, running, and disposition costs. As a result, the TCO increases, leading to inappropriate decision-making.

The concept of TCO is not always uniformly settled. Coniato et al. (2015, pp.427-430) show that there are diverse models of TCO depending on the theorist. Coniato et al. extract common elements from various models presented in the past and attempt to present a new TCO model. Specifically, they aggregate the costs associated with the supply chain along the life cycle of the target products and services. They present and verify a TCO model that contributes to decision-making, using the supply chain of the painting industry as a case study.

## Extension from TCO to Life Cycle Cost (LCC)

It is useful to extend the cost concept used in decision-making from TCO to LCC to make decisions about logistics more valuable. Blanchard and Fabrycky (1998, p.560) define LCC as:

*All costs associated with a product or system that is used over a predetermined life cycle period.*

As is evident from the above definition, LCC appears to be similar to TCO; however, they are different concepts, as illustrated in Figure 7, which indicates that LCC covers more costs than TCO. TCO includes the costs associated with the acquisition, use, and disposal of goods in individual organizations. In contrast, LCC includes opportunity losses, environmental measures, and social costs in addition to the costs considered by TCO. LCC is characterized by including costs borne by individual organizations and some of the costs borne by society.

*Table 7. Examples of cost elements that make up Life Cycle Costs*

| | Explicit costs | Hidden costs |
|---|---|---|
| Installation | Purchasing Cost | Installation and training |
| | Installation and training cost | Late deliveries |
| Yearly use | Preventive maintenance cost | Dispensing labour cost |
| | Interventions cost | Daily maintenance |
| | Spare parts cost | Refilling |
| | Energy cost | Training |
| | Training cost | Cost of floor space at POS |
| | Service contract | Lost sales due to queues |
| | Cost of floor space at POS | Lost sales due to interventions |
| End of life | Transportation cost | Labour cost |
| | Disposal cost | |

Source: (Caniato et al. 2015, p.431)

Caniato et al. (2015) use a case study of a painting contractor, and they present Table 7 as a model that extends the TCO of logistics costs to life cycle costs. In Table 7, the life cycle is divided into three stages: Installation, Yearly use, and End of life. The nature of costs is classified into two categories: Explicit costs and Hidden costs. Explicit costs are incurred whenever logistics activities are conducted and are included in TCO. Hidden costs include costs incurred only when specific events transpire, such as delivery delays or opportunity losses that occur when there is a concentration of orders or stock-outs. However, some of the hidden costs are difficult to estimate reasonably.

By considering LCC instead of TCO in making decisions about logistics, it is possible to make decisions from more diverse perspectives. If the cost factors included in LCCs extend to environmental and social costs, decision-making based on more judgment factors is possible, but not easy to estimate environmental and social costs rationally. As with TCO, there are various interpretations of the cost components of LCC. Therefore, when using LCC, it is essential to select the most appropriate range of cost elements for decision making, depending on the type of decision.

## SUPPLY CHAIN PROFITABILITY

### Revenue of Supply Chain

Supply chain profitability is the profitability of the entire supply chain. Supply chain revenues are only those derived from external sources and exclude those arising from transactions within the supply chain. A major source of them is the sales to end consumers. Supply chain profitability can be defined as the sales of goods and services to end consumers minus the cost of the whole supply chain. The allocation of revenues, costs, and risks among members of the supply chain is a major issue. While increasing supply chain sales requires collaboration and information sharing among supply chain members, the distribution of revenues, costs, and risks among supply chain members is a significant issue.

In order to increase sales, it is necessary to sell attractive products at the right price point in the right place. While market research and advertising by retailers and manufacturers play an essential role in appealing to consumers, the role of the supply chain is to ensure that quality products are offered at affordable prices and with high service standards. If a product is out of stock, it cannot be sold. Defective products are costly to collect and dispose of and damage the product's reputation. Good SCM based on collaboration and information sharing among supply chain members is essential for the supply chain to provide the products demanded by the market in a timely and stable manner. A poor SCM will not allow the supply chain to develop, produce, and distribute products effectively and efficiently.

## Components of Supply Chain Costs

As discussed in Chapter 1, the supply chain is a concept that integrates business logistics. Therefore, cost information aids logistics cost management and logistics-related decision-making, which can be utilized in various ways. However, since supply chain management is conducted across multiple companies, it is even more difficult than when considering logistics cost management and decision-making for a single company.

It is necessary to clarify supply chain costs to consider supply chain cost management. In general, supply chain costs are understood as all the costs borne by the supply chain participants to obtain sales in the supply chain, but there are indeed various debates on what specific elements should be included.

For example, according to Shapiro (2000, p.8), the following are listed as components of supply chain costs.

- · Raw materials and other acquisition costs
- · Inbound transportation costs from material suppliers to the company
- · Cost of capital investment
- · Direct manufacturing costs and indirect manufacturing costs
- · Direct and indirect costs associated with distribution centers
- · Inventory management costs
- · Transportation costs to relay points
- · Cost of delivery to customers

In addition, according to Pettersson et al. (2013, p.360), the components of supply chain costs are shown in Figure 8. While there are similarities with Shapiro's approach described above, costs that Shapiro excludes, such as capital alliance costs, are also included, and the components comprise a more comprehensive range of costs.

## The Necessity of Open-Book Accounting and Challenges to its Realization

The ABC/ABM, total cost, TCO, and LCC discussed are useful in supply chain cost management and decision making. However, although these methods are effective in logistics cost management and decision making related to logistics for a single company, it is complicated to apply these methods to a supply chain consisting of multiple companies and in which members are frequently replaced.

Abo and Yazawa (2000, p.245) suggest that this is because the accounting standards adopted by each company are not necessarily the same. Therefore, meaningful cost information cannot be obtained by

*Figure 8. An example of supply chain cost components*
*Source: (Pettersson et al. 2013, p.360)*

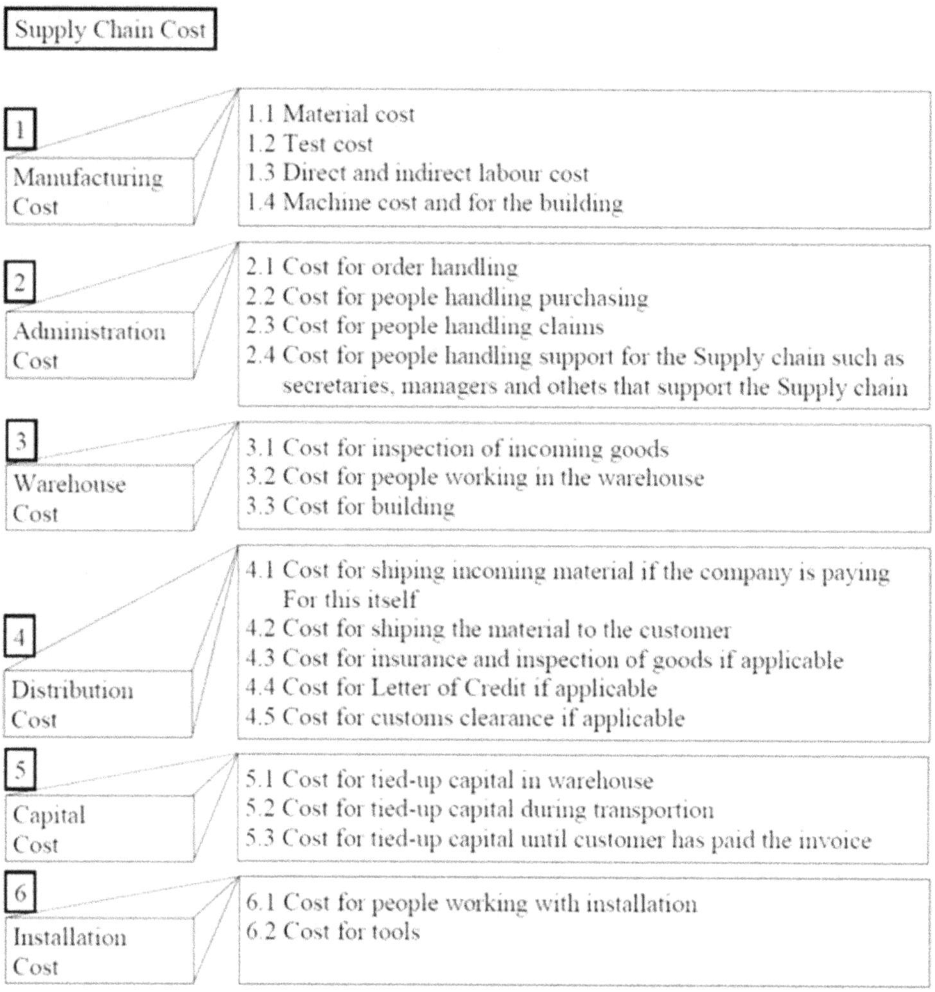


directly summing the calculated cost under different standards. In addition, not all products manufactured by a company are in the same supply chain, and products manufactured by the same company may belong to multiple supply chains, which raises the question of how to allocate manufacturing overhead and common expenses throughout the supply chain.

According to Cullen (2009, pp.24-25), open-book accounting is a method to obtain useful accounting information for cost management and decision making in supply chain management. Cullen (2009, pp.24-25) points out that open-book accounting is the sharing of information across the supply chain, and the purpose of this method is to identify and eliminate non-value-added processes inherent in the supply chain, i.e., processes that do not add value to the end customer, thus contributing to improving the supply chain profitability. Conversely, he said that companies are reluctant to open book accounting in reality. As for the reasons for reluctance to open book accounting, Cullen cites the lack of trust in supply chain participants in sharing cost information, concerns about loss of competitive advantage, and the technical difficulty of unifying accounting standards and methods.

Companies participating in supply chains vary in size, and their management resources of people, money, facilities, and information, often differ significantly. Therefore, even if contributing companies agree to participate in open-book accounting, it is not easy to provide information at the same level. If the quality of the provided information is not at a certain level, the effectiveness of open-book accounting itself is questionable. In addition, supply chains are not permanent, and members change frequently, so there is a risk that companies leaving the supply chain may misuse the previously shared cost information. Currently, the disadvantages outweigh the advantages of open-book accounting, so it is not making much progress.

## FUTURE RESEARCH DIRECTIONS

Appropriately managing costs incurred in the supply chain and their use in decision making are essential for promoting the overall optimization of the supply chain; however, as we have already seen, there are inherent difficulties compared to the cost management of a single company. Therefore, it is not easy to manage the costs occurring in the supply chain at present, and it is necessary to deepen the research on management methods to optimize the costs of current supply chains, using the results of research in the field of inter-organizational management accounting.

From the perspective of total optimization, it is essential to manage current and future costs in the supply chain. This is because the total optimization of costs occurring does not necessarily contribute to the total optimization of costs anticipated in the future. Therefore, supply chain cost management that considers the time axis while focusing on life cycle costs is also necessary.

Future research directions can be illustrated in Figure 9. The triangle in Figure 9 shows supply chain management spreading around Company A. From a cost management perspective, the first step would be to start with appropriate management of logistics costs for company A, and gradually expand the scope of logistics costs to include costs incurred among multiple companies that make up the supply chain. At present, specific methods have been established for logistics cost management for a single company, but no firm method has yet been established for the management of logistics costs that are incurred across multiple companies, and further research is needed. Therefore, further research on this point is one of the future directions of research on supply chain cost management.

On the other hand, to make supply chain cost management more effective, it is necessary not only to optimize the costs incurred in the current supply chain but also to optimize the costs that will be incurred in the future. In order for the supply chain to develop over time, it is essential to properly manage future costs at the present time. However, this is a very difficult study. It can be said that this research should be undertaken as the next challenge after the establishment of a method to appropriately manage the costs of the supply chain that are currently being incurred. Therefore, the supply chain triangle in Figure 9 is expected to become a three-dimensional figure by extending from the present to the future, but at this point, we do not yet know what kind of three-dimensional figure it will become. It is expected that Figure 9 will be completed by accumulating the results of many supply chain case studies in the future, but this will require some time yet.

*Figure 9. Research directions in supply chain cost management*

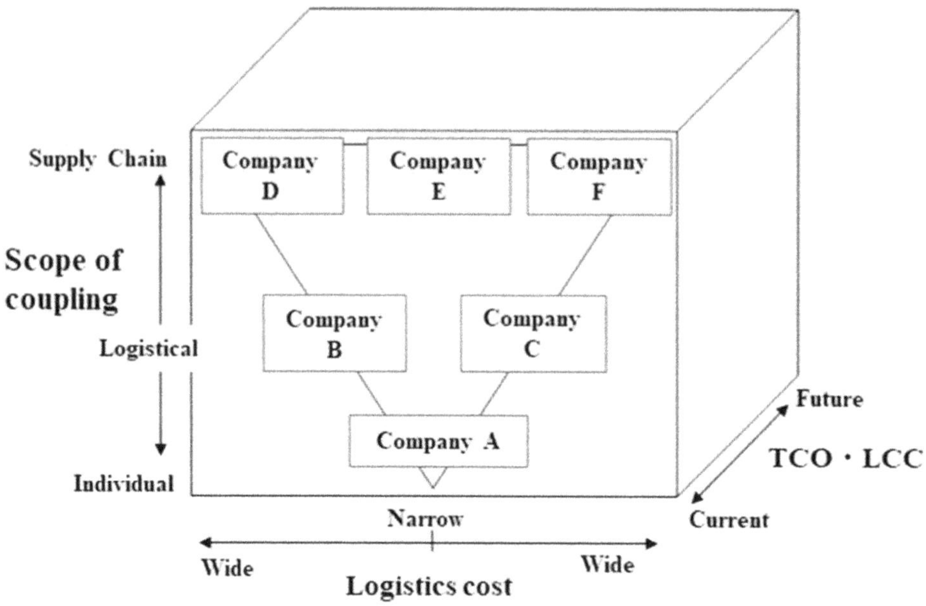


## CONCLUSION

This chapter focuses on evaluating the supply chain profitability, especially on the cost aspect, and discusses, in particular, the management of logistics costs and the management of the supply chain. It is practical to utilize ABC/ABM, total cost, TCO, and LCC to manage the logistics cost of a single company. Optimization of logistics costs needs to be considered in two-time horizons: the currently incurred cost and the cost incurred in the future.

In the case of supply chain cost management, a significant issue is how to aggregate the costs across multiple organizations and allocate overhead and common expenses. Theoretically, this can be solved by unifying the accounting standards of each company participating in the supply chain and adopting open book accounting; however, this is not an easy task due to the differences in each company's management resources, the quality of the information provided, and the problem of securing trust among companies. Therefore, management accounting methods for improving supply chain profitability are still unexplored, and further research is required in the future.

## REFERENCES

Ballou, R. H. (1992). *Business Logistics Management*. Prentice-Hall.

Blanchard, B. S., & Fabrycky, W. J. (1998). *Systems Engineering and Analysis* (3rd ed.). Prentice-Hall.

Bowersox, J., & Cioss, D. J. (1996). *Logistical management*. McGraw-Hill.

Christopher, M. (2016). *Logistics and supply chain management* (5th ed.). Financial Times Publishing.

Coniato, F., Ronchi, F., Luzzini, D., & Brivio, O. (2015). Total cost of ownership along the supply chain: A model applied to the tinting industry. *Production Planning and Control*, *26*(6), 427–437. doi:10.1080/09537287.2014.918285

Consortium for Advanced Management International (CAM-I). (1990). *The CAM-I ABC model-AKA The CAM-I cross*. https://www.cam-i.org/docs/Toolkit_CAM-I_Cross.pdf

Cullen, J. (2009). *Supply Chain Management Accounting*. The Society of Management Accountants of Canada, the American Institute of Certified Public Accountants and The Chartered Institute of Management Accountants. http://www.cimaglobal.com/documents/importeddocuments/cid_mag_supply_chain_aug09.pdf

International Organization for Standardization. (2017). *ISO 20400 Sustainable Procurement*. Author.

Iwata, H. (2003). The Relationship between Activity-Based Costing and Theory of Constraints. *The Journal of Cost Accounting Research*, *27*(2), 89–98.

Japan Institute of Logistics Systems. (2021). *FY2021 Logistics Cost Survey Report (Preliminary Version) (Japanese only)*. https://www1.logistics.or.jp/(2022.2.14 access)

Nishizawa, O. (1999). *Logistics Cost*. Hakuto shobo.

Pettersson, A. I., & Segerstedt, A. (2013). Measuring Supply Chain Cost. *International Journal of Production Economics*, *143*(2), 357–363. doi:10.1016/j.ijpe.2012.03.012

Shapiro, J.F. (2000). *Modeling the Supply Chain*. Duxbury Thomson Learning.

Themido, I., Arantes, A., Fernandes, C., & Guedes, A. P. (2000). Logistics Costs Case Study-An ABC Approach. *The Journal of the Operational Research Society*, *51*(10), 1148–1157.

## ADDITIONAL READING

Coniato, F., Ronchi, F., Luzzini, D., & Brivio, O. (2015). Total cost of ownership along the supply chain: A model applied to the tinting industry. *Production Planning and Control*, *26*(6), 427–437. doi:10.1080/09537287.2014.918285

## KEY TERMS AND DEFINITIONS

**Activity-Based Costing (ABC):** A costing method that is intended to allocate manufacturing overhead costs accurately. ABC aggregates costs by activity unit and performs two-step allocation calculations using resource drivers and activity drivers.

**Activity-Based Management (ABM):** A management method to review activities themselves by focusing on the cost drivers that cause activities to occur. ABM makes it possible to remove activities that do not bring added value and review cost drivers to improve the efficiency of activities, aiming to reduce the aggregate cost of activities.

**Life Cycle Cost (LCC):** The sum of all costs incurred over a product's entire life cycle, from purchase and use to disposal. LCC is similar in concept to Total Cost of Ownership (TCO), but LCC includes a broader range of costs in its calculation.

**Logistic Cost:** The sum of the costs of each activity related to logistics management, such as order fulfillment, distribution, inventory management, and sales. Logistic cost includes a broader range of costs than physical distribution cost. It is essential to optimize, rather than minimize, logistics costs by conducting a trade-off analysis.

**Supply Chain Profitability:** A profitability of the entire supply chain. Supply chain profitability is defined as the sales of goods and services to end consumers minus the cost of the whole supply chain. The allocation of revenues, costs, and risks among members of the supply chain is a major issue. While increasing supply chain sales requires collaboration and information sharing among supply chain members, the distribution of revenues, costs, and risks among supply chain members is a significant issue.

**Total Cost of Ownership (TCO):** The sum of all costs incurred over a product's entire life cycle, from purchase and use to disposal. TCO is a concept similar to Life Cycle Cost (LCC), but the range of costs to be calculated is narrower than LCC.

# Section 2
# Automotive Cases

*Section 2 goes deep into studying the automotive supply chain and its SCM. Automotive companies and their suppliers have formed the most advanced, efficient, and effective supply chains. While the automotive industry's supply chain has constantly improved, they sometimes need to make significant changes.*

# Chapter 3
# Progress of Electric Vehicles and Transformation of Supply Chain in the Japanese Automobile Industry

**Kimito Nasuno**
*Sakushin Gakuin University, Japan*

## ABSTRACT

*This chapter looks back on changes in the supply chain of the Japanese automobile industry and then examines its future. In the wake of Volkswagen's diesel fraud, the global automobile industry is moving toward abolishing internal combustion engine vehicles and switching to EVs (electric vehicles) as the environmental policies of each country join the battle for the initiative over next-generation cars. Industry members are in a hurry to gain the initiative. In EV, there is a belief that the horizontal division of labor in the supply chain will be promoted by eliminating complicated engines. Therefore, in this chapter, the author examined whether the vertical "KEIRETSU" or "KEIRETSU transaction," a characteristic of the supply chain of the Japanese automobile industry, would be swallowed up by the wave of horizontal division of labor.*

## INTRODUCTION

This chapter discusses a structural change in the Japanese automotive industry. The strength of Japanese automotive companies has come from a framework for cooperation among group companies called "KEIRETSU." Capital relationships and long-term transactions tie together group companies. Today, changes in the social and technological environment have become so rapid that it can be a burden to maintain strictly coupled keiretsu. It makes sense to change to a more flexible supply chain, loosely coupled, to reduce risks and costs and speed up product development.

DOI: 10.4018/978-1-7998-9800-9.ch003

Looking back at the origin of the supply chain, we can see that the Toyota Production System, representative of the Japanese automobile industry, was a harbinger to the formation of supply chain management in the United States.

The concept of "supply chain management" was triggered by the US apparel industry feeling threatened by imported clothing and asking consultancy Kurt Salmon to investigate to strengthen their competitiveness. The company's 1985 report states that only 11 of the 66 weeks from manufacture to sale generate added value, with the remaining 55 weeks remaining in stock(Honma,et al.,1998).

Therefore, the apparel industry started to work on QR (Quick Response) activities with the cooperation of Kurt Salmon. This system shifts the supply chain from a manufacturer-led push method to a consumer-led pull method which quickly reflects the response (purchasing information) from the market in inventory management, production management, and procurement management in the supply chain. It was something the industry was trying to do. To that end, industry companies organized committees to standardize information technology. QR activities quickly spread to many industries with such great success, and by the mid-1990s, today's SCM concept was formed(Honma,et al.,1998).

Incidentally, the QR system was based on the just-in-time (JIT) method, which is one of the two pillars of the Toyota Production System. JIT utilizes "KANBAN" (a vinyl encased card with the type and quantity of products written on it) as a means of transmitting information to reduce inventory and level production (change in production). The idea was to decrease or eliminate equipment and people waste and realize cost reduction as much as possible. However, QR added the utilization of information systems, a new element not found in JIT(Teramae,2010)

In this way, the formation of supply chain management and the system of the Japanese automobile industry are closely related.

## BACKGROUND

The evaluation of "KEIRETSU" has fluctuated dramatically with the times. Until around 1960, the aspect of dominance by automobile manufacturers was emphasized. However, with the development of the Japanese automobile industry, the economic efficiency of KEIRETSU was evaluated, and the view that this is the basis of the competitiveness of the Japanese automobile industry became influential. Later, the Nissan Motor Co., Ltd., under economic pressure, launched its management reconstruction plan, "Nissan Revival Plan," in response to the collapse of the bubble economy of the 1990s. "The collapse of KEIRETSU" was whispered, but it prevailed. Nonetheless, with the rapid progress of EV, the continuation of KEIRETSU is now being questioned.

## JAPANESE AUTOMOBILE INDUSTRY SUPPLY CHAIN "KEIRETSU"

The characteristics of the supply chain of the Japanese automobile industry can be expressed by the words "KEIRETSU" or "KEIRETSU transaction." In Keiretsu, an automobile manufacturer produces some of the main parts while different manufacturers make the other components to provide the needed parts and assemblies. It is a method or network of cooperative manufacturing.

According to popular wisdom, KEIRETSU was gradually formed from 1950 to 1970(Fujimoto,1995). The premise of KEIRETSU formation is that various companies tend to cooperate through division of labor based on the characteristics of the many products that machines are composed of (especially automobile parts amounting to tens of thousands). In addition, in Japan, when trying to promote industrialization after the war, individual automobile manufacturers had scant capital. So there were times when they tried to utilize conventional small and medium-sized enterprises in a cooperative endeavor along with their low-wage labor force(Chushoukigyo cho,1969). As a result, a pyramid-shaped KEIRETSU was completed, with the automobile manufacturer at the top and the primary, secondary, and tertiary parts manufacturers below it.

The primary parts maker often orders parts or a portion of the parts ordered by the automobile maker to an external parts maker (secondary parts maker). Similarly, secondary parts maker places an order for a portion of the orders to the tertiary parts maker. Primary parts manufacturers grow into large companies, but secondary parts manufacturers are often small and medium-sized enterprises, and tertiary parts manufacturers are often micro-enterprise companies. Therefore, this pyramid-shaped KEIRETSU and the KEIRETSU transaction based on it were once seen as the structure of control and exploitation of SMEs by large companies, and some considered this to be the source of the strength of Japanese automobile manufacturers(Chushoukigyo cho,1969).

However, *The1969 (Showa 44) White Paper on Small and Medium Enterprises* stated that this system had merits on both sides and listed the following as merits of allied parts manufacturers: (1) By connecting with a specific automobile manufacturer, it is possible for parts manufacturers to secure relatively stable orders and credit, and it is not always necessary for them to have sales ability, product planning ability, and design ability (later, parts manufacturers with planning and design ability emerge), (2) It is possible to receive management/technical guidance and financial support from an automobile manufacturer, and (3) It is possible for parts manufacturers having limited technology and equipment to connect with any automobile manufacturer(Chushoukigyo cho,1969).

*The 1980 White Paper on Small and Medium Enterprises* shows the differences in supply chains between the Japanese and American automobile industries, as shown in Figure 1. In the case of Japanese automobile manufacturer A, a multi-layered pyramid structure has been formed by parts manufacturers with the company at the top. The division of labor by outsourcing has progressed remarkably, with the outsourcing ratio as of 1978 at about 75%. On the other hand, in the case of American automobile manufacturer B, many parts are manufactured in-house by its parts production division (outsourcing ratio is 52%). In the case of Company B, the outsourced parts manufacturers are not fixed, and there is no multi-layered division of labor structure as in Japan. The white paper also highly evaluated the efficiency of KEIRETSU's pyramid-type supply chain, with Japanese automobile manufacturers at the top and their parts manufacturers below them.

"In the Japanese automobile industry, under a highly developed subcontracting division of labor structure, subcontractors (parts manufacturers [author]) are in charge of parts production and processing departments that require expertise and diversity, and production technology, quality control, etc. In addition to demonstrating excellent production capacity in terms of production, finished vehicle manufacturers have realized an extremely efficient production system by organically organizing these subcontractors in terms of production and technology through technical guidance and financial assistance." (Chushoukigyo cho,1980)

In periods of high economic growth, primary parts manufacturers, in particular, gradually reduced their dependence on KEIRETSU automobile manufacturers to take advantage of mass production effects and specialization, diversified transactions, and specialized production systems. In the past, automobile manufacturers sometimes prohibited KEIRETSU parts manufacturers from accepting orders from other

*Figure 1. Comparison of automobile production structure*
*Note 1. In primary subcontractors, etc., the parent company is not always just one.*
*Note 2. The figure above is partially simplified.*
*(Source: Chushoukigyo cho (1980).1980nenban Chushoukigyo Hakusyo.[1980 SME White Paper]. Chapter 4.)*

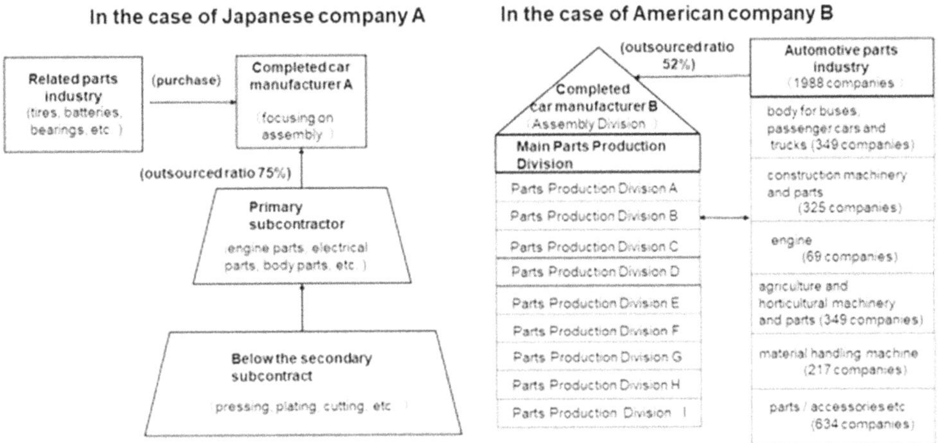


automobile manufacturers for reasons such as “leaking corporate secrets” and “delaying delivery to the company.” However, the need for cost reductions associated with internationalization has even welcomed orders from other automakers (Chushoukigyo cho,1980).

Therefore, it comes to be said that the supply chain of Japanese automobile manufacturers is not a pyramid type, but an “Alps type” or “mountain range type” with multiple vertices because parts manufacturers deliver parts to various automobile manufacturers(Konno,2004a).

## CONVERSION OF EVALUATION OF KEIRETSU

The evaluation of the Japanese automobile industry supplier system, KEIRETSU or KEIRETSU transaction, has changed significantly historically. Until around 1960, the mainstream view was that KEIRETSU was a symbol of the backwardness of the Japanese economy. This view emphasized the aspects of dominance by automobile manufacturers and subordination of parts manufacturers. However, in the 1970s, especially many primary parts manufacturers grew into large companies, and the concept of “subcontracting” no longer applied. The international competitiveness of the Japanese automobile industry increased, so KEIRETSU, rather than being seen as a dominance/subordination relationship, emerged with a positive evaluation because of its economic efficiency. Later, in the 1980s, low-priced, high-quality Japanese products swept the world market. The economic rationality of KEIRETSU transactions began to be evaluated worldwide, and even Western manufacturers that adopted the mechanism began to appear(Konno,2004a).

Despite a positive evaluation, when numerous fuel-efficient, high-quality Japanese cars flowed into the United States and “Japan-US automobile friction” occurred, criticism came out that the Japanese

KEIRETSU was anticompetitive. Indeed, there may be cultural barriers, but in reality, KEIRETSU was not permanently exclusionary. For example, in Fujimoto and Takeishi's (1994) writing, they analyze the "cooperation associations" of parts manufacturers organized by each automobile manufacturer and find that more than 60 parts manufacturers belong to five or more cooperative associations. They point out that 20 parts makers received capital participation from a particular automaker(Fjimoto,Takeishi,1994).

By the way, when the bubble economy collapsed in 1990, domestic demand stagnated. The international competitiveness of Japanese automobile manufacturers declined due to the significant appreciation of the yen, and the disadvantages of KEIRETSU that had been hidden until then began to make themselves known. For example, parts manufacturers have insufficient competition when parts transactions are concentrated in a specific company. Sometimes, it is difficult to break old business relationships due to human relationships such as seconded/transferred persons from automobile manufacturers. It became clear that circumstances hindered the rational pursuit of economic gains. Some parts manufacturers lacked independence and submitted to the management of the KEIRETSU automobile manufacturers. Subsequently, KEIRETSU is suffering from situational friction and administrative/bureaucratic fatigue, and it has begun to be argued that dismantling is unavoidable(Konno,2004a).

## "NISSAN REVIVAL PLAN" AND PROGRESS IN OPEN PARTS TRADING

### Nissan Revival Plan

In the 1990s, Nissan Motor Co., Ltd.'s management deteriorated due to the collapse of the bubble economy and the rapid appreciation of the yen that followed this event. At the end of the 1990s, the company was in danger of going bankrupt. Then, in 1999, Nissan initiated their management reconstruction plan, "Nissan Revival Plan," after drastically reviewing their business relationship with parts manufacturers and aiming to reduce procurement costs significantly. This new plan provided an opportunity to promote open parts trading in the automobile industry(Konno,2004a Kimura,2011).

With the decline of Nissan's business situation, their global market share fell from 6.6% in 1991, when the bubble burst began, to 4.9% in 1998, and their domestic market share also fell from 17.8% to 14.7%. Net income fell into the red from 1992, and it was only in 1996 that it was in the black until 1998. Interest-bearing debt (excluding sales finance) also increased, and although it decreased slightly later, it did not fall below 2 trillion yen until 1998. On the verge of bankruptcy in March 1999, Nissan secured a capital tie-up with Renault and received support. On September 17th, Renault managers visited Japan. Under the leadership of Carlos Ghosn, who was appointed as COO, in October of the same year, Nissan's reconstruction plan, "Nissan Revival Plan," was announced(Nissan Jidosha,1999a,1999b).

The plan was bold and revolutionary. The core of the revival plan was cost reduction to the tune of 1 trillion yen in four areas: purchasing, production, selling, and general and administrative expenses. However, the focus was on reducing purchasing costs, which account for 60% of the total cost. The new purchasing strategy initiated a policy of reducing costs by 20% in three years, decreasing the number of parts and material suppliers from 1,145 companies currently doing business to 600 or less, and lowering purchase prices through centralized purchasing. Carlos Ghosn was confident he would achieve his goal. In addition, a strategic cancellation of stock holdings was also announced, with the objective being to reduce the number of stock holding companies from 1,394 to just four in the end. This was precisely the dismantling of "KEIRETSU itself(Konno,2004b). Behind this was the fact that the KEIRETSU company became an *amakudari* destination for senior Nissan employees and was a breeding ground for corruption. Carlos Ghosn stated that "Nissan's KEIRETSU is not working."(Inoue,2018)

In the end, the sift in Nissan's purchasing strategy was half-backed. Although the number of suppliers was halved, mainly small and medium-sized parts manufacturers reduced transactions. Ultimately, KEIRETSU suppliers that once held shares still support Nissan's parts procurement(*Nihon Keizai Shimbun*,2019a).

## Progress in Openness of Parts Trading

As we have seen, the supply chain of the Japanese automobile industry was once depicted as a pyramid-shaped vertical chain. However, as production volume increases and vehicle types diversify during high economic growth, one parts manufacturer has come to deliver parts to multiple automobile manufacturers. Each automobile manufacturer also accepted parts from various parts manufacturers. In this way, the opening of parts trading began to progress gradually. This tendency will continue to develop and should be confirmed by the following factual analysis.

Goko (2015) first analyzed the business relationships between eight major Japanese passenger car manufacturers and primary parts manufacturers from 1989 to 2010. Their analysis reveals that 2/3rds or 160 types of the 245 different parts whose transactions were confirmed in 2010 have already been traded since 1989. New parts appeared one after another due to computerization and other reasons during the analysis period. Most parts have been traded for many years as measured by the number of parts and money. In this way, long-term business relationships, characteristic of KEIRETSU, were maintained for the Japanese automobile industry overall. However, the duration of transactions with primary parts manufacturers of each automobile manufacturer is significantly different. For example, Toyota tends to maintain long-term business relationships, while Nissan tends to have short transaction durations. There are, in essence, two types of transaction durations. In cases where the transaction duration is short, automobile manufacturers have an increasing tendency to frequently reorganize their trading partners (at both the company level and the parts level)(Goko,2015).

The early part of the analysis period (until the mid-1990s) was when computerization progressed in earnest and new electrical manufacturers entered the market. At the end of the analysis period (after the mid-2000s), a movement to break away from intra-KEIRETSU transactions occurred due to the full-scale progress of standardization and the dissolution of capital relations. However, when looking at parts transactions as a whole, they are becoming more open(Goko,2015). In particular, the openness of parts trading in the 2000s is thought to be due to the influence of Nissan's intention to centralize purchasing through the "Revival Plan" on other automobile manufacturers, and each parts manufacturer was forced to respond accordingly.

Ikeuchi et al. (2015) described the status and causes of the opening of 11 automobile manufacturers in Japan, the primary parts manufacturers that supplied parts from 1989 to 2010. And they analyzed the impact of openness on R&D, export, productivity, etc(Ikeuchi,et al.,2015).

According to Ikeuchi et al., the average annual number of automobile manufacturers to which each primary parts manufacturer delivers gradually increases from 4.4 in 1989 to 5.2 in 2010. In addition, when they divided the parts by type and considered the average value per company of the number of automobile manufacturers they delivered during the same period, that number of manufacturers increased for all parts. The opening of transactions occurs for all items (see Figure 2). Others say that in the early 1990s, one primary parts manufacturer handled about ten types of parts, but in the latter half of the

*Figure 2. Changes in the average number of automobile manufacturers to which primary parts manufacturers are delivered (by parts)*
*Note: Average number of automobile manufacturers to which primary parts manufacturers are delivered (by parts).*
*Source: (Ikeuchi et al., 2015, .p.7. https://www.rieti.go.jp/jp/publications/dp/15j017.pdf)*

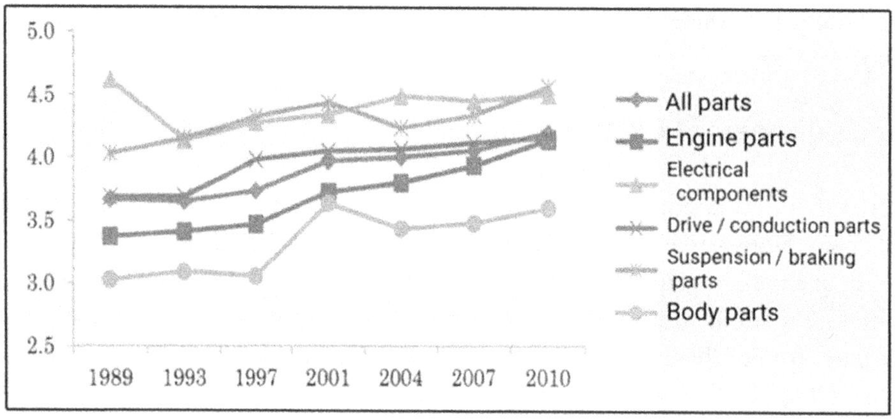


2000s, it increased to about 14 items. They also see that the productivity of companies that do business with more than one automaker has increased since 2000, while the productivity of companies that do business with only one automaker shows little change. It is said that the productivity gap between the two is widening(Ikeuchi,et al.,2015).

As the number of automobile manufacturers increases in the delivery of parts, productivity tends to decrease. Still, in Ikeuchi et al., the importance of "matching" parts has been reduced due to modularization and standardization progress, which has led to the openness of parts transactions. Therefore they suggested that it widened the gap between companies that actively respond to openness and those that do not(Ikeuchi,et al.,2015).

However, earlier in Konno(2004a) analyzed that as the time for new car development is becoming shorter and shorter, the engineers of parts makers are transferred to the development center of the KEIRETSU automobile makers at the initial stage of development. He points out an increase in the "guest engineer" system or "design-in," in which guest engineers become temporary residents of the development center and perform close information sharing and work coordination. He further examined how to understand such a movement of "closeness," contrary to openness, and concluded that automakers clearly distinguish between projects involving the development of new technologies and projects that do not. The former project collaborates with parts manufacturers with long-term, continuous, cooperative, and close business relationships. For the latter project, automakers are promoting the opening of transactions. Therefore, it is thought that KEIRETSU will not be dismantled in the future, but the essence of KEIRETSU, "coexistence of competition and cooperation," will be further refined and strengthened(Konno,2004a).

The "Nissan Revival Plan" mentioned "disassembly of KEIRETSU" in parts trading. Although openness is continuously progressing, we can infer that it is not necessarily "disassembly of KEIRETSU." That stage has not been reached.

## ADVANCES IN ELECTRIFICATION OF AUTOMOBILES AND POSSIBILITY OF DISMANTLING KEIRETSU

### Rapid Turn to EV Due to Diesel Fraud

Recently, the movement toward EVs to reduce CO2 has intensified, and the "dismantling of KEIRETSU" has been dealt with again. Therefore, here, I would like to consider the possibility of EV conversion and "disassembly of KEIRETSU."

Today, the automobile industry is said to be in a period of revolution once every 100 years. Four factors are pressing the automobile industry to make a significant change, expressed by the acronym "CASE." In CASE, "C" means Connected, "A" signifies Autonomous, "S" represents Shared / Service, and "E" denotes Electric. The recent rapid shift to EVs is partly because electricity has a high affinity with other elements of CASE. Still, the direct cause of the brisk progress toward EVs was a fraudulent exhaust gas incident in the diesel car.

In September 2015, the US Environmental Protection Agency announced that the German carmaker Volkswagen was guilty of fraud regarding their diesel engine car. Volkswagen had incorporated fraudulent software to prevent the exhaust gas reduction device from working during bench testing, but not during actual driving. Since the exhaust gas reduction device does not work in the diesel vehicle during actual driving, fuel efficiency, acceleration performance, and the like are better than when the device is working. However, 30 to 40 times the regulated value of NOx was dispersed when the device was not engaged. The number of vehicles subject to fraud reached approximately 11 million(Kato,2015).

As a measure against CO2, Japanese automobile manufacturers have put hybrid cars into practical use and popularized them. However, European manufacturers did not follow Japan's environmental standards, partly because Japanese manufacturers had patented hybrid vehicles and tried to compete with their own "clean diesel." Diesel vehicles have the advantages of better fuel efficiency and lower CO2 emissions than gasoline vehicles. On the other hand, they also have the disadvantage of generating a large amount of soot (PM) and NOx. Therefore, it has been said that "clean diesel" was developed to control this demerit with an exhaust gas reduction device(Kato,2015). However, it became clear that "clean diesel" was a ruse, and its trustworthiness quickly dissipated.

Therefore, in October 2015, Volkswagen announced shifting focus on environmental measures to EVs. The medium-term management plan announced in November 2016 states that it will strengthen the SUV lineup and convert it to EV to become the top brand for mass-market vehicles and allocate 2.5 billion euros for EV. The company plans to design a dedicated module and launch about 1 million EVs and 30 models annually by 2025. Some believe that the reason for this abrupt announcement was their intention to divert attention from the unpleasant diesel issue and change the game's rules to position itself as a leader in the new EV era and establish an image of a new Volkswagen(Wada,2015 Saito,2016). Following the drop in diesel vehicle sales due to the fraud incident, EU countries have helped their manufacturers increase sales of electric vehicles and plug-in hybrid vehicles through bailouts, including increased subsidies(Fujimura,2021). In July 2021, the EU announced a policy to ban the sale of new passenger cars with internal combustion engines in the region by 2035. This ban also includes hybrid vehicles. The final decision requires the approval of the member states and the European Parliament, but the EU's commitment to such a policy was a shocking move. Behind this was that European countries had already promoted rapid EV conversion. Norway has announced a ban on the sale of vehicles with internal combustion engines in 2025, Germany and the United Kingdom in 2030, and France in 2040(JI.

JI.COM,2021). However, there are different views on whether to allow hybrid vehicles, and Germany and France have a policy of accepting them.

In the United States, California has already announced a policy to ban the sale of vehicles with internal combustion engines by 2035. In August 2021, President Biden signed an executive order to raise the percentage of EVs in US sales to 50% by 2030. This action is a sign of his determination to promote EVs, but his goal is less than that of the EU and other countries because he was concerned about his order's effect on the midterm elections.

While promoting the growth of its automobile manufacturers, China focused on EVs in their guidelines announced in 2016 and initiated NEV (New Energy Vehicle) regulations in 2019. However, China switched to preferential treatment for hybrid vehicles in 2020, considering that thermal power generation accounts for 70%(*Nihon Keizai Shimbun*,2021e).

CO2 reduction should be considered throughout the life cycle of automobile manufacturing, sales, disposal, and recycling, and for EVs, how that electricity is generated must also be considered. China and the United States (excluding California) have taken relatively realistic steps to ban the sale of vehicles with internal combustion engines, but European policies are incredibly radical. The reality is that the global automobile policy does not objectively consider CO2 reduction. Still, the guidelines are mixed over the hegemony of automobile manufacturers and the automobile industry, and as a result, the shift to EV is rapidly promoted.

## Progress of Internal Combustion Engine Vehicle Ban Policy and Trends of Japanese Automobile Manufacturers

The wave of EVs that originated in Europe is rapidly covering the world. Some of the policies of some countries ban the hybrid cars that Japanese automakers are good at, so Japanese automakers are forced to decide how to deal with this situation with specific measures.

Before looking at the response of Japanese automobile manufacturers, I would like to cite the policies of the Japanese government. The Ministry of Economy, Trade, and Industry summarized the government's response to next-generation vehicles at the "New Era Strategy Conference for Automobiles" in 2018. In 2030, gasoline and diesel vehicles will account for 30-50% of the total market. It set a goal of increasing the number of generation cars to 50-70%. A specific breakdown of next-generation vehicles is as follows: HV (hybrid vehicle) is 30-40%, EV (electric vehicle) and PHV (plug-in hybrid vehicle) is about 3%, and clean diesel vehicle is 5-10%(Momota,2020).

However, in October 2020, Prime Minister Suga issued a "2050 Carbon Neutral Declaration" in his statement of belief that he would achieve carbon neutrality by 2050. In response to this, in December of the same year, the Ministry of Economy, Trade, and Industry formulated a "green growth strategy" to connect the challenge of carbon neutrality to a virtuous cycle of economy and environment. In the strategy, recognizing that Europe and China are strategically promoting EVs and PHVs, the Japanese government has revealed that 100% of electric vehicles will be sold for new passenger cars by the mid-2030s. We will take comprehensive measures that can be achieved(Naikakufu Kanbo,et al.,2021). Although, the goal of the Japanese government is to include HVs as "electricity."

How are Japanese automakers responding to the increasing pressure on EVs worldwide and the government raising its electrification target? Toyota is developing an omnidirectional strategy of "electricity." Omnidirectional refers to promoting four technologies: EV (electric vehicle), FCV (fuel cell vehicle), PHV (plug-in hybrid vehicle), and HV (hybrid vehicle). With this strategy, Toyota recognizes that various powertrains should be prepared to fully respond to the energy situation and market needs of developed, emerging, and developing countries(Kikawa,2021a,2021b).

A characteristic of Toyota's electrification plan is its focus on FCVs. FCVs that run on hydrogen fuel by hydrogen reacting with oxygen in the air are also called "ultimate eco-cars" because they only emit water when running. In addition, FCVs have a short hydrogen filling time of about 3 minutes, and the new model "MIRAI" announced in December 2020 has an extended cruising range of 850 km. These advantages in general exceed those of EVs. However, FCVs have high initial purchase prices (the second generation "MIRAI" starts from 7.1 million yen including tax), and the construction of a hydrogen station costs 300 to 400 million yen (excluding land costs) just for fixed costs. An operating cost of about 30 million yen is required annually. In addition, since the number of FCV owners is still small, recovery of those costs is expected to be challenging even if more hydrogen stations are constructed in the future, though presently, new construction is not progressing as desired(Kikawa,2021a Yokoyama,2021e).

Toyota has created a highly flexible FC system based on several assumptions in developing the second-generation MIRAI. The FC system, unsuitable for EVs due to its weight, will be installed on heavy-duty trucks and sold in other fields. By doing so, Toyota has tried to reduce the cost through the mass production effect and increase the demand for hydrogen by expanding FCVs and FC systems and promoting the spread of hydrogen stations(Kikawa,2021c).

Toyota focuses on FCVs because they have an overwhelming advantage in the number of worldwide hydrogen-related patents. In addition, FCVs have more parts than EVs, and the structure of the FC system is complicated, so those things lead to Toyota's strength. In other words, Toyota wants to maintain its competitiveness by making the most of its strong technological capabilities(Kikawa,2021a).

On the other hand, in the reconstruction process under the "Revival Plan," Nissan selected and concentrated on developing next-generation vehicles, narrowing down R&D investment to EVs at an early stage in 2010. They launched the "LEAF," the world's first mass-produced electric vehicle.

Unlike Nissan but similar to Toyota, Honda has been focusing on FCVs. However, Honda announced in June 2021 that it would end production of the FCV "CLARITY" in August 2021. In April 2021, Honda had just set a goal of making all new cars sold EVs and FCVs by 2040 due to the sense of crisis about the globally accelerating "de-engined cars." Despite FCV research continuing, it seems that Honda has, in reality, turned to EV because there are no concrete plans to launch a new FCV car. Honda's automobile business has been sluggish in recent years, and in FY03/19, the automobile business finally fell into the red. People say that Honda has become a two-wheeled company, not a four-wheeled company, both in terms of the absolute amount of operating profit and the rate of return. Predicament also seems to influence their judgment(Kikawa,2021a Yokoyama,2021c).

As mentioned above, major Japanese automakers are also turning to EVs except for Toyota. Therefore, the omnidirectional strategy can only be taken by Toyota, which alone is in a state of winning and is a highly profitable company.

## Horizontal Division of Labor in EV Production and Upset of KEIRETSU

How will the structure of automobiles change due to the shift to EVs? As shown in Fig. 3, the shift to EV eliminates the need for gasoline-only parts and replaces them with EV-only parts. Passenger car manufacturers have formed a large supply chain around the engine, producing the engine in-house(Kikawa,2020d). For passenger car makers, the loss of the engine, which is the most significant source of competitiveness,

*Figure 3. Cost comparison of gasoline car and EV components*
*Source: (Kikawa, 2012. https://premium.toyokeizai.net/articles/-/25737)*

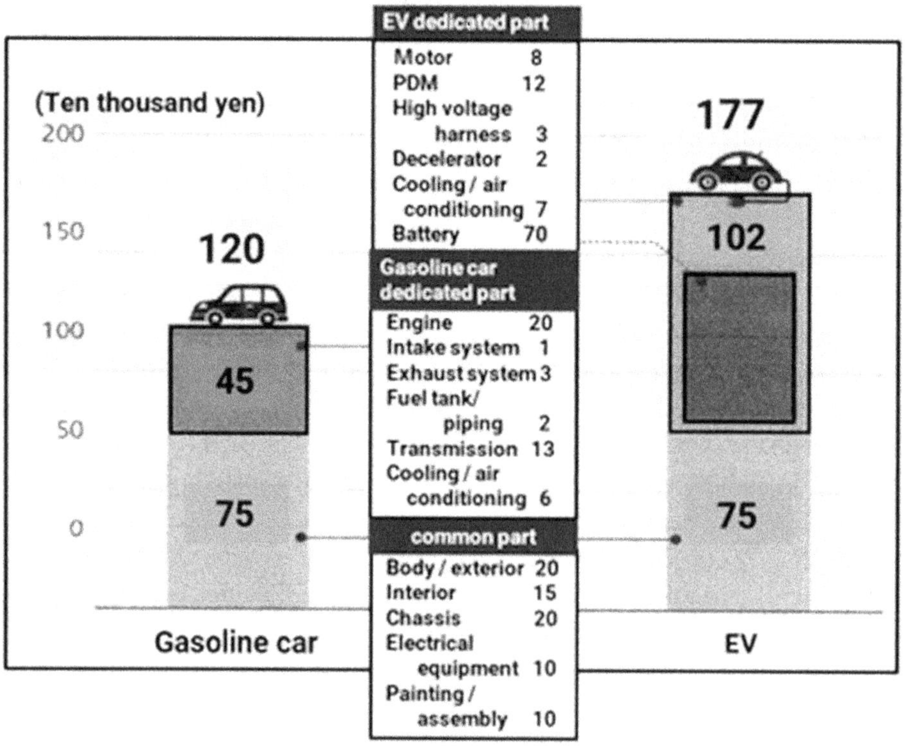


is a big blow. In addition, engine parts manufacturers urgently need to formulate survival measures for the EV era.

The number of parts for EVs would decrease by 30 to 50%. When motors and batteries play a leading role in engines, it is no longer necessary to match pieces that have previously been a barrier to entry mechanically. It is relatively easy to purchase and combine modularized and commoditized system parts, making it possible to produce passenger cars. As a result, new entrants will have more access, and entry from different industries is expected to increase(Kikawa,2020d). This can also be expressed as the conversion of automobiles into "home appliances." As a result, hardware production becomes relatively easy, and the focus of competition would shift from hardware to software. However, high battery costs are a bottleneck for EVs (see Fig. 3).

How will the shift to EVs change KEIRETSU? As for Apple, it is rumored that an "Apple car" will appear. However, when Apple enters the EV market, their product will be planned, designed, and developed like smartphones, but they will outsource production. EV fabless and contract manufacturing companies are already beginning to emerge. Among EVs' horizontal division of labor, the most notable one is Hon Hai Precision Industry Co., Ltd. of Taiwan, the world's largest contract manufacturing company for electronic devices and contract manufacturer of Apple's iPhone. The company has already made concrete moves toward EV production, intending to contract Apple cars.

In October 2020, Hon Hai launched the "MIH (Mobility in Harmony) Consortium," which is said to be an "open EV alliance." The consortium aims to set industry standards and develop kits that significantly reduce EV development time and costs. More than 1800 companies have already participated in the consortium, including leading companies such as Qualcomm, Microsoft, and China's Ningde Age New Energy Technology (CATL), the world's largest battery maker. Nidec and Murata Manufacturing Co., Ltd. are participating Japanese electrical and electronic parts manufacturers, respectively. Hon Hai's chairman, Liu, said he would win 10% of the world's EV sales share in 2027, which means it will be comparable to Toyota and Volkswagen. There is a view that automobile assembly is different from standardized smartphone assembly. Despite that view, in January 2021, Hon Hai scouted Mr. Chung Ken Satoshi, with extensive experience in the automobile industry, to be the CEO of their EV business. In addition, to acquire automotive know-how, it has established a joint venture with Stellantis and Geely Holding Group. It is also in joint venture negotiations with Nidec. Hon Hai has announced plans to build finished vehicle assembly plants in the United States and Thailand and is also looking for manufacturing bases in Europe(*Nihon Keizai Shimbun*,2021c,2021f Shimizu,2021).

## JAPANESE AUTOMAKER'S STRATEGY FOR EV

In response to the tightening of global environmental regulations for CO2 and the EV wave, Toyota has advanced its electrification plan and increased the projected number of EVs and FCVs that do not emit CO2. The original plan for 2017 was to sell 5.5 million electric vehicles worldwide by 2030 (including 1 million EVs and FCVs). However, in 2019, the achievement year was changed to 2025, five years sooner. Furthermore, in the plan for May 2021, the total number of partially or fully electric vehicles sold in 2030 would be increased to 8 million units, and EVs and FCVs would also be increased to 2 million units. However, immediately after Toyota's plan, the EU announced July 2021 to ban the sale of new internal combustion engines by 2035. The ban also includes hybrid vehicles, Toyota's forte, forcing Toyota to reconsider its options(Endo,2021).

As we saw earlier, automobile manufacturers worldwide are pushing toward the EV amid heightened environmental regulations. Different industries, fabless and contract manufacturing companies, have entered the automobile industry to shift to EVs. New electrical and electronic parts manufacturers aim to enter the automobile industry. Horizontal parts trading, which differs from the vertical KEIRETSU, is also beginning to occur.

What kind of strategy are Japanese automakers responding to such challenges to the conventional KEIRETSU? Toyota is adopting an approach that rather strengthens its KEIRETSU. To cooperate in developing next-generation vehicles, they have decided to form a capital tie-up with Suzuki, Mazda, Daihatsu, and Hino Motors and strengthen their previously existing capital relationship with Subaru. This capital strategy is indicative of "expanding the Toyota Group." As a result, the total sales volume of the Toyota Group exceeded 160 million units(Shukan Daiyamondo Henshubu,2019a). Because the development of EVs and FCVs is exceedingly costly, the vehicle prices of EVs and FCVs are still excessively high. However, high-income earners finally purchase them with government subsidies that promote environmental policies. That is the reality. Therefore, if the Toyota Group expands to standardize chassis and other components, it will reduce costs through mass production.

Toyota is also selecting KEIRETSU parts manufacturers based on its capital strategy. While lowering the investment ratios of Aisan Industry and Trinity Industrial Corp., it is raising the investment ratios of Aisin Seiki and Denso. Several personnel changes were carried out for DENSO, which has become the world's second-largest parts manufacturer. Mr. Koji Kobayashi, who had been transferred from

Toyota to Denso and served as vice president, had an unusual appointment back to Toyota as first vice president. Then Toyota's president Toyoda himself, became a director of Denso(Shukan Daiyamondo Henshubu,2019a).

Regarding the reorganization of KEIRETSU parts manufacturers, Aisin Seiki decided to merge with Aisin AW, a subsidiary, and the world's largest automatic transmission company. These changes demonstrate that Toyota's strategy is working. On the other hand, Denso handed over a portion of their internal combustion engine business to Aisan Industry. Denso and Aisin have established a joint venture with Toyota to research and develop drive modules that integrate EV motors, inverters, gearboxes, autonomous driving control software, and next-generation semiconductors. They are essential companies in the EV strategy(Shukan Daiyamondo Henshubu,2019a). Toyota will strengthen relationships with parts manufacturers to play a central role in electrification by investing and dispatching officers. On the other hand, they will exclude other parts manufacturers. In this way, Toyota is reorganizing the KEIRETSU in a sense.

Next, I would like to examine Honda's EV strategy. In April 2021, Honda's first ambitious goal of a major Japanese automaker was to limit new car sales in 2040 to only non-CO2 emitting EVs and FCVs to cope with the global wave of EV conversion. However, in July of the same year, the EU announced a policy going beyond Honda's drastic decision, saying that it would ban the sale of new internal combustion engines by 2035(*Nihon Keizai Shimbun*,2021d).

Up to now, Honda has consistently been on an independent route. Still, in the onslaught of EV conversion, it plans to proceed with the electrification strategy in the future in collaboration with GM in the United States and with CATL, a primary battery company in China. Honda is currently developing a chassis called "e-architecture" for small and medium-sized EVs. In the latter half of the 2020s, EVs that adopt this application will be introduced to the market. GM will also be provided with design information for this platform. Honda and GM strive to reduce procurement costs by unifying the chassis and sharing motors, batteries, and inverters (power converters) and ordering large quantities of the same parts(Yokoyama,2021c *Nihon Keizai Shimbun*,2021g).

Honda has also begun to work on the reorganization of parts manufacturers. In October 2019, Honda and Hitachi announced the integration of Hitachi Automotive Systems, a subsidiary of Hitachi, with Keihin, Showa, and Nissin Kogyo, which are leading Honda-KEIRETSU parts manufacturers. Keihin handles power trains, Showa deals with steering, and Nissin Kogyo fabricates critical parts such as brakes. The integration will create the manufacturer of the third-largest part in Japan after Denso and Aisin. Hitachi will have a 66.6% stake, and Honda will have a 33.4% stake. The integration supports CASE and reduces costs by expanding the production scale. CASE is a weakness of automakers, which might be why the merger led by Hitachi-KEIRETSU parts makers. In addition, automobile manufacturers are now provided with equipment such as safety products as standard options. Still, the price is kept down due to competition with other companies, and the scale is expanded to deal with such a problematic cost situation. They have no choice(Tomioka,2019 Yasui,2020 M&A Online,2020).

Nissan has already terminated its capital ties with many KEIRETSU parts manufacturers through its "revival plan" and has promoted "optimal global procurement" by buying from any manufacturer of low-cost parts, regardless of the substance. On the other hand, Honda is trying to acquire low-priced CASE-compatible parts while maintaining a capital relationship. However, it has passed the initiative of the manufacturer of the parts through the reorganization of the KEIRETSU. Honda must have chosen a path that goes between Toyota and Nissan(M&A Online,2020).

With the overwhelming upsurge of EVs and the progress of CASE, such as in autonomous driving, the response of major Japanese automobile manufacturers was divided. Toyota, self-sufficient and having abundant financial resources, adhere to the "omnidirectional" strategy for next-generation vehicles. Nissan has received Renault's support due to the deterioration of management, so it squeezed into EVs at an early stage. Honda has stopped selling FCVs, on which it has been focusing up to now. President Mibe says he will release a new FCV, but no concrete plan exists. It seems that he has turned to EV, and he is strengthening cooperation with GM in the EV field. On the supply chain side, Toyota is trying to respond to new situations by improving the reorganization of parts manufacturers within its KEIRETSU. On the other hand, Nissan, which has fallen into financial difficulty, and Honda, whose automobile business is not always in good shape, are moving in a slightly different direction that may lead to the dismantling of the KEIRETSU.

Therefore, with the progress of CASE relating to EVs and autonomous driving, the supply chain support of Japanese automobile manufacturers has become differentiated, and there are situations where it cannot be collectively expressed as a "KEIRETSU."

## JAPAN'S EV CONVERSION AND SUPPLY CHAIN TRANSFORMATION AS SEEN FROM CHINA AS A LEADING INDICATOR OF EV

In China, EV makers have emerged early and are anticipating global trends. EVs are selling well in China, and the horizontal division of labor in parts trading is progressing. However, EVs do not sell well in all price ranges, and the ones that do sell well are the high and low-end models. The polarization of EVs continues. A major US EV is the high-priced Tesla "Model 3", which will become the top EV passenger car sold in 2020. EVs tend to be expensive due to the high cost of batteries, but sales of the "Model 3" are increasing due to the advancements of EVs and the attractiveness of luxury cars. Tesla built "Gigafactory 3" with a maximum production capacity of 500,000 units in Shanghai, and they started shipping in December 2019. The increase in sales is primarily due to cost reduction efforts. However, the "Model 3" price is still relatively high, starting at about 250,000 yuan, but high-income earners are beginning to reach out with the aid of government subsidiesTan,2021).

On the other hand, the best-selling low-priced product is the "Hong Guang MINI," an EV launched in the summer of 2020 by SAIC-GM-Wuling Motor Co., Ltd. (Headquarters, Liuzhou City, Guangxi Zhuang Autonomous Region). The state-owned SAIC Motor has a majority stake. As the name above implies, GM is also a shareholder. Although it is smaller than a Japanese light vehicle, it seats four people and costs 28,000 yuan. The vehicle's capability is limited: the cruising range is 120km, the maximum speed is 100km/h, safety equipment is limited, and air conditioning is an extra option. However, it is convenient for daily use; it can be charged with a household power supply. SAIC-GM-Wuling Motor has expanded models such as women's cars and convertibles. "Hong Guang MINI" is gaining popularity mainly in local cities because of its affordability and design. During the January-June period of 2021, the number of "Hong Guang MINI" sold was 157,939 units, almost double the number of Tesla's "Model 3", and it ranked first. However, the mid-price range for significant sales of EVs is an "impregnable" area(*Nihon Keizai Shimbun*,2021b).

There is also a movement in Japan to utilize low-priced EVs. In April 2021, Sagawa Express announced its policy to replace all 7200 mini-vehicles for delivery with EVs. Tokyo venture company ASF will design this EV, and SAIC-GM-Wuling Automobile will manufacture it in China. The cruising range is more than 200km, covering the daily mileage of typical light delivery vehicles. The manufacturing cost is estimated to be less than 1 million yen. The newly designed EV is undergoing a driving test and is scheduled for delivery in September 2022 after a formal contract. In this way, the same horizontal division of labor as in the electrical industry, such as fabless design and overseas manufacturing consignment, has already begun in Japan(Nakano,2021).

ASF President Iizuka (former Yamada Denki Vice President) explained why the new company, which was just established in June 2020, was selected by Sagawa Express. When major manufacturers design from scratch, including parts, an order of 7200 units would normally be considered too small. Yet, ASF furnished a design with a combination of existing parts, which was possible because it was an EV. The production location is in China because it provides the lowest cost, and ASF is proceeding with development in cooperation with SAIC-GM-Wuling Motor. Of course, the car's design and construction should reflect the culture of its intended market. Therefore, even though the new EV will be built in China, its Japanese design will be appropriate for the Japanese market and taste. ASF has received inquiries from other industries, but it would like to develop cars for B2C in the future(Nakano,2021).

In February 2021, Idemitsu Kosan, a significant oil wholesaler, announced entering the EV business. Their reason is that the demand for fuel oil is gradually decreasing due to the declining population and fuel efficiency of automobiles. They thought it was essential to create new businesses. In addition to EV sales, Idemitsu gas stations plan to handle after-sales services such as maintenance and insurance. Tajima Motor Corporation, which develops racing vehicles, oversees development. The EV to be launched this time is a model called "ultra-compact mobility," which is smaller than a light vehicle. They plan to launch a four-seater passenger car and a one-seater commercial vehicle. These EVs have a top speed of 60km/h and a cruising range of about 120km. The maximum speed and cruising range are lower than a typical light vehicle, and the price is expected to be about 1 to 1.5 million yen. Charging is also possible with a household power supply. The performance was suppressed, and the expected price was lower than a light vehicle. After a demonstration experiment, it became clear that enhanced performance in a light vehicle is not required for everyday shopping, transportation of children, sales, and local commuting(Yokoyama,2021d).

On the other hand, the rise in the price of light vehicles has become problematic in recent years. The average price as of December 2020 was about 1.55 million yen, an increase of 470,000 yen, or 43%, from 10 years ago. The cause is the installation of safety devices such as automatic braking. In addition, all light hybrid vehicles are equipped as a simple "mild hybrid" that is inexpensive and reduces cost. Still, the improvement in fuel economy is minimal (about 10%). Electrification to reduce CO2 facilitates further improvements in fuel efficiency in light vehicles. However, if a full-scale "strong hybrid" is introduced, the cost may rise, with the price possibly reaching nearly 2 million yen. In addition, because both the drive motor and battery are larger in strong hybrids than in mild hybrids, providing ample interior space in the vehicle is much more challenging(Yokoyama,2021a,2021b). In that case, the ultra-compact EVs we saw earlier may erode the light vehicle market.

In May 2021, Toyota announced a new electrification plan to sell 8 million electric vehicles (including HVs) in 2030. Then, in September 2021, in response to the plan, Toyota announced that they will invest 1.5 trillion yen in in-vehicle batteries by 2030 (of which 1 trillion yen will expand production capacity, and 500 billion yen will be allocated for research expenses). It set a goal of halving the battery cost per electric vehicle(*Nihon Keizai Shimbun*,2021h). Currently, the middle price range of the volume zone is regarded as an "impregnable" area for EVs because the high cost of in-vehicle batteries is an impediment. Even if Toyota can cut battery costs in half quickly, other automakers and battery makers will likely follow suit soon after. Therefore, EVs are expected to eventually expand into the “impregnable” volume zone of the mid-price range. However, the aggressive response of automakers to EVs can potentially undermine the accomplishments of existing automakers.

## SOLUTIONS AND RECOMMENDATIONS

A major change that is said to occur once every 100 years is about to happen in the automobile industry. It is a powertrain shift from the gasoline engine to an electric motor. Behind this is the “CASE” phenomenon, based on the technological innovation of batteries and ICT development. Furthermore, the speculations of governments worldwide and automobile manufacturers are intricately intertwined as a rapid shift to EVs occurs. As a result, an important shift in the supply chain is about to transpire. It is necessary to analyze this radical change from a broad perspective and comprehend this transformation.

## FUTURE RESEARCH DIRECTIONS

Because EVs are analogous to smartphones for automobiles, an analysis of the phenomena that have already occurred in the electrical industry will help consider the future of the automobile industry. Digitization has shifted the mainstream supply chain from vertically integrated to horizontally divided labor in the electrical sector, and commoditized products have made the Japanese electrical industry less competitive. The electrical industry experience is a valuable reference when examining the transformation of the supply chain of the automobile industry.

## CONCLUSION

There is a traditional vertical “KEIRETSU” in the supply chain of the Japanese automobile industry, although some of them have already begun to collapse. As we have already seen, the specific content of the KEIRETSU is quite different between the winners Toyota and Nissan / Honda. Furthermore, Nissan and Honda also have different relationships with KEIRETSU parts manufacturers. Therefore, today, it is no longer accurate to define the characteristics of the supply chain of the Japanese automobile industry as a simple “KEIRETSU.” On the other hand, in Japan as well, in the field of ultra-compact EVs, a horizontal division of labor has begun, in which fabless companies manage design development and outsource production to overseas companies. The contractor produces EVs by combining the optimum parts. In other words, in the supply chain of the Japanese automobile industry, the coexistence of vertical “KEIRETSU” and horizontal division of labor, though still only minimal, has begun. However, this is expected to eventually erode the light-vehicle field and gradually expand to the volume zone in the middle price range. For the time being, the supply chain of the Japanese automobile industry is expected to have both vertical “series” and horizontal division of labor (see Fig. 4). Nevertheless, unless there are epoch-making technological innovations such as FCV, including infrastructure, there is a possibility that the horizontal division of labor will eventually overwhelm the vertical “KEIRETSU” due to EV progress.

*Figure 4. Coexistence of vertical integration and horizontal division of labor*
*Note: This figure is an excerpt from the original figure.*
*Source: (Nihon Keizai Shimbun, 2021, August 7)*

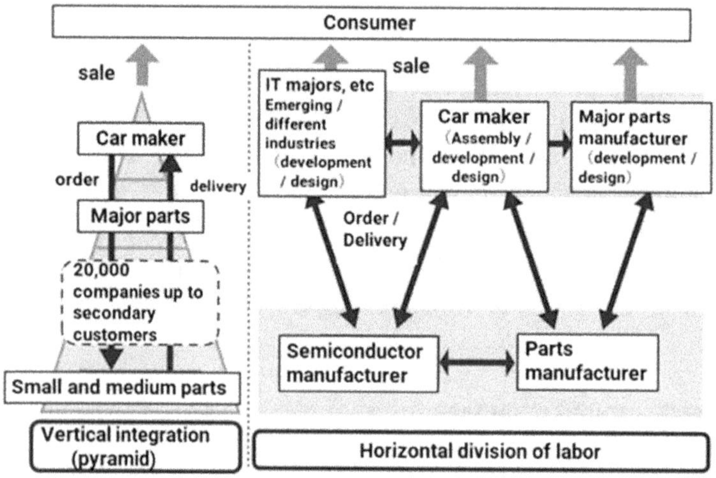


## REFERENCES


Chushoukigyo cho (1969). *1969nenban Chushoukigyo Hakusyo*. [1969 SME White Paper]. Chapter 2.

Chushoukigyo cho (1980).*1980nenban Chushoukigyo Hakusyo*.[1980 SME White Paper]. Chapter 4.

Endo, K. (2021, Sept. 7). Toyota no seizo joken. Mada tarinai EV hanbai mokuhyo. 30-nen ni Obei-muke 250 man-dai hitsuyo [Toyota's manufacturing conditions. Still insufficient. EV sales target 2.5 million units required for Europe and the United States in 30 years]. *Shukan Economist*, p. 30.

Fujimoto, T. (1995). Buhin torihiki to kigyo-kan kankei: jidosha sangyo no jirei o chushin ni [Parts Transactions and Business-to-Business Relationships: Focusing on Cases of the Automotive Industry]. In Nihon no sangyo soshiki: riron to jissho no furontia [Japanese Industrial Organization: Frontier of Theory and Demonstration]. Yuhikaku.

Fujimoto, T., & Takeishi, A. (1994). *Jidosha sangyo 21 seiki e no shinario: seicho-gata shisutemu kara baransu-gata shisutemu e no tenkan* [Automotive Industry 21st Century Scenario: Transition from Growth System to Balanced System]. Seisansei Syuppan.

Fujimura, T. (2021). *Machigaidarake no CO2 senryaku. Naze kakukoku seifu wa enjin-sha haishi ni keichu suru no ka. Sono ura o yomu* [CO2 Strategy Full of Mistakes. Why Governments Focus on Abolishing Engine Vehicles. Read Behind the Scenes]. Nikkei XTECH. https://xtech.nikkei.com/atcl/nxt/column/18/01721/00003/

Goko, H. (2015). *Nihon jidosha sangyo ni okeru kansei-sha meika to 1-ji sapuraiya no torihiki kozo to sono henka* [Transaction structure and changes of finished vehicle manufacturers and primary suppliers in the Japanese automobile industry]. April, RIEIT Discussion Paper Series 15-J-014, Dokuritsu-Gyoseihojin Keizai Sangyo Kenkyujo. https://www.rieti.go.jp/jp/publications/dp/15j014.pdf

Honma, M., Nakamura, M., Sato, T., & Sakata, K. (1998). *Sapuraichen manejimento ga wakaru hon* [The book which understands supply chain management]. JMA Management Center.

Ikeuchi, K., Fukao, K., Goko, H., Kin, E., & Gon, K. (2015). *Torihiki kankei no opun-ka ga Nihon no jidosha buhin sangyo no seisansei ni ataeta eikyo no bunseki* [Analysis of the impact of open business relationships on the productivity of the Japanese automobile parts industry]. April, RIEIT Discussion Paper Series 15-J-017, Dokuritsu-Gyoseihojin Keizai Sangyo Kenkyujo. https://www.rieti.go.jp/jp/publications/dp/15j017.pdf

Inoue, H. (2018). *Nissan ni Tuiho sareta "ratsuwan keieisya" Gon no kozai. Kiki kara fukkatsu togetaga shanai ni wa fuman mo tsunotta* [The merits and demerits of Ghosn, who was banished by Nissan. Resurrected from the crisis, but also raised dissatisfaction within the company]. Toyo Keizai Online. https://toyokeizai.net/articles/-/250620

Jidosha, N. (1999a). *Nissan jidosha, "Nissan ribaibaru puran" o happyo* [Nissan Motor announces "Nissan Revival Plan"]. Nissan Motor News Room. https://global.nissannews.com/ja-JP/releases/release-d151058c73d721dcf6d0cc853f0088bb-nissan-unveils-revival-plan-j

Jidosha, N. (1999b). *Nissan ribaibaru puran* [Nissan Revival Plan]. Nissan-Global. https://www.nissan-global.com/JP/DOCUMENT/PDF/ FINANCIAL/REVIVAL/DETAIL/1999/fs_re_detail1999h.pdf

JI.JI.COM. (2021). *Oshu, EV shifuto kasoku. Haiburiddo "kieru shukumei"* [Europe, EV shift acceleration. Hybrid "disappearing fate"]. JI.JI.COM. https://www.jiji.com/jc/article?k=2021071500757&g=int

Kanbo, N. (2021). *2025-Nen kabon nyutoraru ni tomonau gurin seicho senryaku* [2025 Carbon Neutral Green Growth Strategy]. Ministry of Economy, Trade and Industry. https://www.meti.go.jp/press/2021/06/20210618005/20210618005-3.pdf

Kato, J. (2015). *VW dizeru fusei, "jujitsu, haikei, kongo" o "jikan-jiku" de seiri* [VW diesel fraud, "facts, background, future" organized by "time axis"]. SPEEDA. https://jp.ub-speeda.com/ex/analysis/archive/vwディーゼル不正、事実・背景・今後を時間で整理

Kikawa, Y. (2020d). *EV fukyu hayamareba noriokure no risuku mo. Haiburiddo gijutsu ni tsuyoi nihonzei no muzukashi tachi ichi* [If EVs become widespread, there is a risk of missed rides. Difficult position of Japanese automaker strong in hybrid technology]. Shukan Toyo Keizai Plus. https://premium.toyokeizai.net/articles/-/25737

Kikawa, Y. (2021a). *Toyota ga egakaku "nenryo denchi-sha" senryaku no seihi. ① 6-nen-buri no sasshin, shingata "MIRI" ga miseta gijutsu shinka* [Success or failure of Toyota's "fuel cell vehicle" strategy. ① Renewal for the first time in 6 years, technological evolution shown by the new "MIRI"]. Shukan Toyo Keizai Plus. https://premium.toyokeizai.net/articles/-/25889/

Kikawa, Y. (2021b). *Dendo-ka no kyoso o uranau "juyo shihyo". Toyota no kabuka josho, Tesla no atamauchi o yomitoku* [An"important index" that predicts the competition for electrification. Toyota's stock price rise and Tesla's peak]. Shukan Toyo Keizai Plus. https://premium.toyokeizai.net/articles/-/27315

Kikawa, Y. (2021c). *Toyota ga egakaku "nenryo denchi-sha" senryaku no seihi. ② Suiso infura fukyu o unagasu "Toyota no hisaku"* [Success or failure of Toyota's "fuel cell vehicle" strategy. ② "Toyota's secret policy" to promote the spread of hydrogen infrastructure]. Shukan Toyo keizai Plus. https://premium.toyokeizai.net/articles/-/25890/

Kimura, T. (2011). Jidosha meika no sapuraiya kankei ni kansuru riron-teki kento [Theoretical study on supplier relations of automobile manufacturers]. Yokohama kokusai shakai kagaku kenkyu, 16(3), 56.

Konno, Y. (2004a). Nihon-gata sangyo kozo no tenkan: Nihon no jidōsha buhin sapuraiya shisutemu no henka ni tsuite [Transformation of Japanese-style industrial structure: Changes in Japanese automobile parts supplier system]. *Kuotari Seikatsu Fukushi kenkyu, 13*(1).

Konno, Y. (2004b). Nissan ribaibaru puran iko no sapuraiya shisutemu no kozo henka [Structural changes in the supplier system since the Nissan Revival Plan]. *Keiei Shirin, 41*(3).

M&A Online. (2020). *[Honda] Toyota tomo Nissan tomo chigau, dokuji "keiretsu saihen" no yukue wa?* [[Honda] What is the whereabouts of the original "series reorganization" that is different from Toyota and Nissan?]. M&A Online. https://maonline.jp/articles/archives_honda_200709

Momota, K. (2020). *Seifu ga "2030-nen gasorin-sya kinshi" o uchidashitawake. Hoshi tankan de meika no senryaku shuseiwa hissi ni* [The reason why the government has announced "2030 gasoline car ban":Manufacturer's strategy revision is essential due to sudden policy change]. Toyokeizai Online. https://toyokeizai.net/articles/-/394007

Nakano, D. (2021). *Sagawa-kyubin ga haiso-yo kei ban o 7200-dai so tokkae e. Nipponhatsu, "kojo ga nai" EV meka tanjo no shogeki-do* [Sagawa Express to replace 7200 light vans for delivery. Total impact of the birth of Japan's first "factoryless" EV maker]. Shukan Toyo keizai Plus. https://premium.toyokeizai.net/articles/-/26947/

Nihon Keizai Shimbun. (2019a). *Nissan ribaibaru puran 20-nen. Gekiteki kaikaku, Seiko to kashin* [Nissan Revival Plan 20 Years. Dramatic Reform, Success and Overconfidence]. Nihon Keizai Shimbun. https://www.nikkei.com/article/DGXMZO51045710W9A011C1X11000/

Nihon Keizai Shimbun. (2021b). *50 Man-en EV, Chugoku de kyu kasoku* [ 500,000 yen EV, rapid acceleration in China]. Author.

Nihon Keizai Shimbun. (2021c). *Honhai EV, 1200-sha to renkei. Nihondensan nado buhin/sofuto ote* [Hon Hai EV collaborates with 1200 companies, major parts and software companies such as Nidec]. Nihon Keizai Shimbun. https://www.nikkei.com/article/DGXZQOGM2556X0V20C21A3000000/

Nihon Keizai Shimbun. (2021d). *Honda, EV-ka maedaoshi kento* [Honda considers EV conversion ahead of schedule]. Author.

Nihon Keizai Shimbun. (2021e). *Amerika seiken no kankyo kisei, Oshu to sa. Kuruma meika/roso ni hairyo* [Environmental regulations of the US administration, consideration for car manufacturers and labor unions that differ from Europe]. Nihon Keizai Shimbun. https://www.nikkei.com/article/DGXZQOG-N062VT0W1A800C2000000/

Nihon Keizai Shimbun. (2021f). *Sumaho kara kuruma e. Honhai no yabo* [From smartphone to car. Hon Hai's ambition]. Author.

Nihon Keizai Shimbun. (2021g). *Honda / GM, EV kyotsu-ka. Ikinokori e kibo kakuho* [Honda / GM, EV commonization. Securing scale for survival]. Author.

Nihon Keizai Shimbun. (2021h). *Toyota, Shasai denchi 1.5 Cho-en toshi. Kosuto hangen mokuhyo* [Toyota invests 1.5 trillion yen in in-vehicle battery, cost halving target]. Author.

Saito, Y. (2016). *VW no 2025-nen made no keiei keikaku wa SUV kakuju to denki jidosha 100 man-dai ga kagi, 2 man-nin-cho no kaiko mo* [VW's management plan by 2025 is key to expanding SUVs and 1 million electric vehicles and dismissing more than 20,000 people]. MONOist. https://monoist.atmarkit.co.jp/mn/articles/1611/29/news039.html

Shimizu, N. (2021). *Honhai EV kaihatsu, bakusoku no 800-sha sanka. Nihon no teki ka mikata ka* [Hon Hai EV development, 800 companies are participating in detonation velocity. Japanese enemy or ally?"]. Nikki XTECH. https://xtech.nikkei.com/atcl/nxt/column/18/00138/030800747/

Shukan Daiyamondo Henshubu. (2019a, Nov. 23). Toyota tendosetsu [Toyota Ptolemaic theory]. Shukan Daiyamondo, pp. 28-31.

Shukan Daiyamondo Henshubu. (2019b, Nov. 23). Tokushu, Jidosha saishu ketsudan Part 3. Honda no gyakushu [Special Feature, Final Decision on automobiles Part 3. Honda's Counterattack]. Shukan Daiyamondo, p. 41.

Tan, J. (2021, Sept. 7). Chugoku no shijo shihai. Kokyu to kakuyasu no ni kyoku-ka ka. 25-nen iko wa taishusha mo EV ni [China's market power. IS it a Polarization of high-class and low-grade? After 2025, popular car will be EVs]. *Shukan Economist*, p. 28.

Teramae, T. (2010, November). SCM no rutsu kara mita sai teigi [Redefinition from the roots of SCM]. *Meijo Ronso*, *11*(3), 46–47.

Tomioka, K. (2019). *Hitachi ga Honda-kei buhin 3-sha o sanka ni (osameru wake. Jido unten jidai ni haken o nigiru koto ga dekiru ka* [The reason why Hitachi puts three Honda parts manufacturers under its umbrella. Can it take the hegemony in the era of autonomous driving?]. Toyo Keizai Online. https://toyokeizai.net/articles/-/311672

Wada, K. (2015). *Forukusuwagen no haigasu fusei kara hajimaru, jidosha meika no EV sabaibaru* [EV survival of automakers starting from Volkswagen's exhaust gas fraud]. https://monoist.atmarkit.co.jp/mn/articles/1510/26/news008.html

Yasui, I. (2020). *Honda-kei buhin meika togo, erabareru joken* [Honda-based parts manufacturer integration, conditions to be selected]. Nikkei XTECH. https://xtech.nikkei.com/atcl/nxt/column/18/01193/00001/

Yokoyama, J. (2021a). *Datsu gasorin-sha ni yureru Nihon no "kei". ① keijidosha no dendo-ka, tachi-hadakaru "2tsu no nandai"* [Japan's "light vehicles" swaying by gasoline-free vehicles. ① "Two challenges" that confront the electrification of light vehicles]. Shukan Toyo Keizai Plus. https://premium.toyokeizai.net/articles/-/26064

Yokoyama, J. (2021b). *Datsu gasorin-sha ni yureru Nihon no "kei". ② EV jidai ga tou keijidosha no "sonzai igi"* [Japan's "light vehicles" swaying with gasoline cars. ② "Significance of existence" of light vehicles questioned by the EV era]. Shukan Toyo Keizai Plus. https://premium.toyokeizai.net/articles/-/26071

Yokoyama, J. (2021c). *Honda "datsu enjin" no shogeki ① EV ni zen shuchu, daitan sugiru "seizon sen-ryaku"* [Impact of Honda's "de-engine" ① Fully focused on EV, too bold "survival strategy"]. Shukan Toyo Keizai Plus. https://premium.toyokeizai.net/articles/-/26878

Yokoyama, J. (2021d). *Jidosha meika no shu senjo wa ganchuninai Idemitsu, aete "tei supekku no EV" de misueru shosan* [Idemitsu, the main battlefield of automobile manufacturers, is not in sight, dare to look at "low-spec EV"]. Shukan Toyo Keizai Plus. https://premium.toyokeizai.net/articles/-/27002

Yokoyama, J. (2021e). *Honda "datsu enjin" no shogeki ⑤ Honda, nenryo denchi-sha no "syubai" de towa reru honki-do* [Impact of Honda's "de-engine" ⑤ Honda, seriousness questioned by "sold out" of fuel cell vehicles]. Shukan Toyo Keizai Plus. https://premium.toyokeizai.net/articles/-/27312

## ADDITIONAL READING

Clark, K. B., & Fujimoto, T. (1991). *Product Development Performance: Strategy, Organization, and Management in the World Auto Industry*. Harvard Business School.

Fujiki, K. (2002). Kawaru jidosha buhin torihiki: Keiretsu kaitai [Changing Auto Parts Trading: Series Dismantling]. *Economist.*

Hino, N. (Ed.). (2018). *Nikkei BP mukku, Maru wakari EV* [Nikkei BP Mook, Fully understand EV. car]. Nikkei BP.

Nakanishi, T. (2018). *CASE kakumei 2030-nen no jidosha sangyo* [CASE revolution: Automotive industry in 2030]. Nikkei Publishing Co., Ltd.

Nakaoka, S., Takeishi, A., & Noro, Y. (2008). Determinants of Firm Boundaries: Empirical Analysis of the Japanese Auto Industry from 1984 to 2002. *Journal of the Japanese and International Economies*, *22*(2), 22. doi:10.1016/j.jjie.2008.03.002

Okamuro, H. (2001). Risk Sharing in the Supplier Relationship: New Evidence from the Japanese Automotive Industry. *Journal of Economic Behavior & Organization*, *45*(4), 361–381. doi:10.1016/S0167-2681(01)00152-4

## KEY TERMS AND DEFINITIONS

**CASE:** Abbreviation for the latest trends in the automobile industry: internet connection, autonomous driving, sharing & services, and electrification.

**Just-in-TIME (JIT):** A method that aims to reduce costs by reducing inventory by utilizing KANBN (a card with the written type & quantity of products and enclosed in a vinyl case).

**KEIRETSU:** In a narrow sense, KEIRETSU refers to the case where there is a capital relationship or personal relationship (dispatch of officers, etc.) between an automobile manufacturer and a parts manufacturer. In a broader sense, even if there is no capital or personal relationship, but a long-term business relationship is maintained, it is considered a KEIRETSU relationship. This chapter deals with the latter position.

**Light Vehicle:** A standard unique to Japan based on the Road Transport Vehicle Law and which refers to a vehicle with a total length of 3.4 m or less, a total width of 1.48 m or less, a total height of 2.0 m or less, and a displacement of 660cc or less. It is suitable for narrow Japanese roads, has a good fuel economy, and has tax benefits.

**Opening up Parts Trading:** This means that the delivery destinations of parts suppliers expand beyond the framework of the KEIRETSU.

**QR (Quick Response):** This is a method to reduce excess inventory, etc., by converting the supply chain to a consumer-led pull method and quickly reflecting the response (purchasing information) from the market in inventory management, production management, and procurement management.

**Ultra-Compact Mobility:** A vehicle standard newly established by Japan's Ministry of Land, Infrastructure, Transport, and Tourism in 2020. The new standard specifies that the vehicles have a maximum speed of 60 km/h or less, do not exceed 2.5 m in length, 1.3 m in width, and 2 m in height, and do not operate on national expressways.

# Chapter 4
# An Evaluation Model for Supplier Selection for European, American, and Japanese Automotive Companies

**Yu-Shan Su**
*National Taiwan Normal University, Taiwan*

**Tien-Shou Wang**
*National Taiwan Normal University, Taiwan*

## ABSTRACT

*Taiwanese suppliers lead the world in the fastener market. In 2014, exported fasteners from Taiwan amounted to USD 4.25 billion, ranking third behind Germany and China. Taiwan is an important location for the international procurement of fasteners. This chapter has three objectives. The first is to explore the evaluation criteria and their weights for fastener supplier selection for automotive companies and develop an evaluation model for fastener supplier selection. The second is to explore investment priorities and improvement for fastener suppliers for automotive companies to become qualified fastener suppliers. The third is to explore the differences in the supplier evaluation between European, American, and Japanese automotive companies and the differences in the investment and improvement priorities of being a supplier for the European, American, and Japanese automotive companies. This chapter fills the research gap for fastener supplier selection for European, American, and Japanese automotive companies.*

## INTRODUCTION

This chapter discusses the essential factors to select suppliers through the fastener industry case by comparing European, American, and Japanese Automotive Companies. Fasteners are devices to fix parts such as buttons and pins and are widely used in automobiles. The poor functioning of fasteners directly

DOI: 10.4018/978-1-7998-9800-9.ch004

affects the performance and safety of automobiles. The fastener industry connects the automotive parts industries as fasteners connect automotive parts.

The automotive manufacturers are known as Original Equipment Manufacturers (OEMs) (Jacobides, MacDuffie, & Tae, 2015). According to IHS Automotive (2017), the global sales volume of automobiles was 88.74 million vehicles in 2015 and 92.68 million vehicles in 2016. The projected volume is 93.54 million vehicles in 2017, 95.58 million vehicles in 2018, 98.56 million vehicles in 2019, and it is expected to exceed the hundred million milestones and reach 101.12 million vehicles in 2020. China and India will become major consumer markets for the automobile industry in the future.

Pai (2015) compiled a list of the top 10 automotive companies (as shown in Table 1) in Tharawat Magazine according to the total sales volume of each automotive company in 2014. Apart from Hyundai, a South Korean company that was ranked fifth on the list, the remaining 9 companies are based in Europe, the USA, and Japan, and their total sales volume was 59.94 million vehicles, accounting for 84.22% of total global automotive sales in 2014. The top 3 automotive companies: Toyota from Japan, Volkswagen (VW) from Germany, and General Motors (GM) from the United States. The total sales volume of the top 3 companies was 30.22 million vehicles, accounting for 42.46% of total sales. We reached two key points:

1. The automotive industry is mostly composed of European, American, and Japanese automotive companies.
2. When studying European, American, and Japanese automotive companies, three major companies of Volkswagen (VW), General Motors (GM), and Toyota represent the respective markets significantly.

*Table 1. Rankings of the top 10 automotive companies in 2015*

| Ranking | Name of automotive company | Country | Total sales volume in 2014 (million vehicles) | Global market share (%) | Number of employees (people) |
|---|---|---|---|---|---|
| 1 | Toyota | Japan | 10.20 | 14.33% | 330,000 |
| 2 | VW | Germany | 10.10 | 14.19% | 592,586 |
| 3 | GM | United States | 9.92 | 13.94% | 216,000 |
| 4 | Renault-Nissan | France- Japan | 8.47 | 11.90% | 450,000 |
| 5 | Hyundai | South Korea | 7.71 | 10.83% | 249,366 |
| 6 | Ford | United States | 6.32 | 8.88% | 224,000 |
| 7 | Fiat-Chrysler | Italy- United States | 4.75 | 6.67% | 228,690 |
| 8 | Honda | Japan | 4.36 | 6.13% | 199,368 |
| 9 | PSA | France | 2.94 | 4.13% | 184,804 |
| 10 | Suzuki | Japan | 2.88 | 4.05% | 14,571 |

Source: (Pai, 2015)

Taiwanese suppliers lead the world in the fastener market. According to the import/export statistics published by the Taiwan Industrial Fasteners Institute, the total value of exported fasteners from Taiwan reached USD 4.25 billion in 2014. This allowed Taiwan, a small island, to become the third biggest supplier in the world, following Germany and China. The Taiwan fastener industry is mainly composed of small and medium enterprises. There are overall 1,200 companies in the Institute, but the actual number of companies is over 2,000. From the standpoint of automotive fastener tier-1 procurers, finding partners among the more than 2,000 fastener suppliers which will comply with the strict requirements of automotive companies together with the tier-1 companies is a difficult task. Being able to systematically and effectively evaluate suppliers has become an important issue for international automotive companies, Tier-1 international automotive suppliers, or procurement offices in Taiwan purchasing fasteners for international automotive companies.

The study conducts actual interviews (face to face or through telephone and email) with 12 experts from tier-1 fastener suppliers for automotive companies (1 from Germany, 2 from the United States, 4 from Japan, 1 from China, and 4 from Taiwan) to induce the major dimensions and criteria of an evaluation model for supplier selection. The study uses the AHP method to calculate the weights between the different dimensions (and different criteria). Additionally, although the AHP method can be used to calculate the weights between the different dimensions (and different criteria), the different dimensions (and different criteria) also influence each other in the real world. For example, quality and price may be contradictory to each other. We usually ask the suppliers to provide high-quality products at low prices, which is impossible. Moreover, when we ask a supplier to lower their price, the supplier may simplify or even eliminate a production process or testing process related to quality in order to lower their costs. Hence, quality usually affects price and vice versa. In order to supplement AHP and illustrate the criteria that have an influence on each other (such as the price-quality relationship described above), the study also adopted the DEMATEL method to calculate the causal relationships between each dimension (and each criterion). The aim of DEMATEL is to calculate the prominence and causal relationships. Prominence can show us the total sum of the level of "influence" and "effect" of all 18 criteria and the causal relationships can be presented in causal diagrams. After which, the causal diagrams can be used to understand the importance of the 18 criteria and help manage the priority of different resource investments of the company. The study uses two methods, AHP and DEMATEL. AHP can calculate the weights of each criterion but cannot calculate the correlation between each criterion. DEMATEL can calculate the correlation between each criterion; it cannot calculate the weights of dimensions (or criteria). Therefore, we combine to use the two methods of AHP and DEMATEL. Lastly, the study integrates the results of expert questionnaires from different automotive companies in Europe, the United States, and Japan. We explore the differences between the views of the Tier-1 suppliers of European, American, and Japanese automotive companies. And we compare the views in order to find out if the different automotive companies of Europe, the United States, and Japan have different opinions on the requirements for tier-1 suppliers, which will also affect the weight and ranking of tier-2 suppliers selected by the tier-1 suppliers.

There are three objectives of the study:

1. Explore the evaluating dimensions and criteria, and their weights for automotive fastener suppliers. And develop an evaluation model for supplier selection for automotive companies.
2. Explore the investment and improvement priorities for fastener suppliers to become a qualified automotive fastener supplier according to the evaluation dimensions and criteria.
3. Explore the differences between the supplier selection of European, American, and Japanese car companies. And explore the investment and improvement priorities of automotive fastener suppliers in becoming a qualified supplier to the three major automotive companies of Europe, the United States, and Japan.

## BACKGROUND

### Global Supply Chain Management

Christopher (2005) once stated that a so-called supply chain represents "a network within an organization that includes upstream and downstream connections. It supplies products and services to the end customer through different production processes and activities." A broader description of a supply chain would be a network that includes two or more organizations connected through the material, informational and financial flow. These organizations can be companies that manufacture parts, components, finished products, logistics companies, and even the end customer. Therefore, the definition of a supply chain includes the target group, which is the end customer. Supply chain management creates value through the interactions between the companies, customers, and stakeholders in the supply chain (Estampe, Paris, & Brahim-Djelloul, 2013). However, some scholars have said that the global supply chain management is much more challenging than managing domestic supply chains (Dornier, Ernst, Fender, & Kouvelis, 2008; MacCarthy & Atthirawong 2003). The geographical distance not only increases transportation costs, but delayed deliveries, increased inventory, and other factors must be considered, which increases the complexity of decision making. Furthermore, different local cultures, languages, and work habits will diminish the effectiveness of demand forecasting and material planning during the process. In other words, the global supply chain includes unique risks that will affect performance. These include fluctuating and uncertain exchange rates, economic factors, unstable political factors, and changes to related environmental laws and regulations. The study conducted by Wu, Huang, Goh, and Hsieh (2013) found that when dealing with globalization, logistics personnel must be able to integrate, communicate, and analyze financial information on an international scale, maintain good relationships between the industry and customers, build connections, maintain health, and understand laws and regulations. However, there are significant disagreements between the industry and scholars related to this issue. The industry believes that cross-functional capabilities in the market are critical and they emphasize the importance of risk and financial management. On the other hand, scholars believe that traditional logistical management capabilities, such as predicting needs, contracting, planning, and system integration, are important items.

### Supplier Selection

Numerous criteria related to supplier selection have been listed in past literature. The study has induced the 6 dimensions and 18 criteria of supplier selections in Table 2.

### Supplier Relationships and Procurement Strategies of European, American, and Japanese Automotive Companies

In 1994, Ford, GM, and Chrysler, the Big Three automotive companies in the United States, formulated the shared QS-9000 standard together based on the quality standards defined in ISO-9000 and QS-9000. QS-9000 has influenced over 14,000 tier-1 suppliers in the automotive industry, including the fastener industry, and global services. QS-9000 is also the predecessor of the current ISO/TS-16949 system. The study conducted by Ming-Wen Gao (2007) pointed out that ISO/TS-16949 was formulated between 1999 to 2002 by the International Automotive Task Force (IATF) and International Organization for Standardization (ISO). The members include the BMW Group, Daimler Chrysler, Fiat, Ford, GM, Peugeot,

*Table 2. Six dimensions of criteria in supplier selections*

| Dimension | Title | ⊕ Criteria of the Study | Researchers:<br>A: Weber, Current, & Benton(1993)<br>B: Chao, Scheuing, & Ruch(1993)<br>C: Wei, Zhang, & Li(1997)<br>D: Ghodsypour & O'Brien (1998)<br>E: SCOR(2010)<br>F: Cheraghi, Dadashzadeh, & Subramanian(2011)<br>G: Baležentis, A., & Baležentis, T.(2011)<br>H: Huang & Hu (2013)<br>I: Sultana, Ahmed & Azeem(2015)<br>J: Azadnia, Saman, & Wong(2015)<br>K: Keskin(2015)<br>L: Dweiri, Kumar, Khan & Jain(2016)<br>M: Cieśla(2016) | | | | | | | | | | | | |
|---|---|---|---|---|---|---|---|---|---|---|---|---|---|---|---|
| | | | A | B | C | D | E | F | G | H | I | J | K | L | M |
| Cost | Cost (or price competitiveness) | ⊕ | ✓ | | ✓ | ✓ | ✓ | ✓ | ✓ | ✓ | ✓ | ✓ | ✓ | ✓ | ✓ |
| | Long-term relationship | ⊕ | | | | | ✓ | ✓ | | | | | ✓ | | |
| | Payment terms | ⊕ | | | | | | | ✓ | | | | | | ✓ |
| Quality | Quality (or quality system) | ⊕ | ✓ | ✓ | ✓ | ✓ | | ✓ | ✓ | ✓ | ✓ | ✓ | ✓ | ✓ | ✓ |
| | Quality assurance | | | | | | | | | | | | ✓ | | |
| | Problem solving and improvements | ⊕ | | | | | | ✓ | | | | | ✓ | | |
| | Defect rates | ⊕ | | | | ✓ | | | | | | | ✓ | | |
| Delivery | On-time supply (or delivery) | ⊕ | ✓ | ✓ | | ✓ | ✓ | ✓ | ✓ | ✓ | ✓ | ✓ | ✓ | ✓ | ✓ |
| | Preparation or completion time | ⊕ | | | | | | | ✓ | | ✓ | | | | ✓ |
| | Flexible and immediate | ⊕ | | ✓ | | ✓ | ✓ | ✓ | | | ✓ | | ✓ | | |
| | Geographical location | | | | ✓ | | | | ✓ | | ✓ | | | | ✓ |
| | Supply chain management | | | | | | | ✓ | | | | | | | |
| Technology | Engineering technological capabilities | ⊕ | | | | | | | | | | ✓ | ✓ | | |
| | Manufacturing capabilities | ⊕ | | | | ✓ | | | | | | | | | |
| | Research and development capabilities | ⊕ | | | | | | | | | ✓ | | | | |
| Service | Service and response | ⊕ | | | | ✓ | ✓ | ✓ | | ✓ | | | | ✓ | |
| | Responsibilities | | | | | ✓ | | | | | | | | | |
| | Convenient communications | ⊕ | | | | ✓ | | ✓ | | | | | ✓ | | |
| | Integrity and attitude | ⊕ | | | | | | | | | | | ✓ | | |
| Reputation | Finances and assets | ⊕ | | | | | ✓ | ✓ | ✓ | | | | ✓ | | |
| | Reputation (past performance) | ⊕ | | | ✓ | | | | | | | ✓ | ✓ | | ✓ |
| | Environmental and social responsibilities | ⊕ | | | | | | | | | | ✓ | | | |

Renault, and VW, together with the AIAG (America), VDA (Germany), SMMT (UK), ANFIA (Italy), and FIEV (France). Therefore, ISO/TS-16949 is equivalent to QS-9000 in the United States, VDA 6.1 in Germany, ACSQ in Italy, and EAQF in France. Additionally, the Japan Automobile Manufacturers Association (JAMA) also became an official member of ISO/TS-16949 later. So, ISO/TS-16949 has become a common standard for automotive OEM companies and parts and component suppliers.

The top 3 automotive companies (Toyota, VW & GM) account for a large portion of the market share and the companies are from different continents. Florea and Corbos, R.A. (2015) focused on the 3 major automotive companies to analyze their supplier management and relationship maintenance developed from cultural differences. Supplier relationships and procurement strategies of European, American, and Japanese automotive companies are as follows.

## European Model: Using Volkswagen (VW) as an Example

The study found that the VW group faces more difficulty because VW operates 12 different automotive brands: VW Passenger Cars, Audi, Seat, Skoda, Bentley, Bugatti, Lamborghini, Porsche, Ducati, VW Commercial Vehicles, Scania, and Man. Although the VW group owns the 12 automotive brands, they maintain their corporate cultures. McElroy (2012) stated that VW chooses to produce their components and products through vertically integrated companies. In 2006, the overall procurement amounted to EUR60 billion, among which 60% to 70% was continued procurement from original suppliers. Although the procurement strategy is implemented equally in every factory of VW, the relationships with suppliers are different for the different brands. According to the IHS study conducted in 2014, the relationship between suppliers and the sports-car brand, Porsche, and the high-end brand, Audi, ranked first and second among the 12 brands. VW and Skoda were ranked in the middle and Seat was ranked last. The study results showed that: Although the procurement strategies were the same, there were differences due to the different corporate cultures of the brands.

Even though the 12 brands of the VW group are independently operated, VW adopts unified procurement strategies. According to VW's official website, the four procurement strategies are as follows:

1. In order to ensure competitive quality and innovations in the independent markets, the companies shall implement technical and environmental innovations.
2. During the entire lifecycle of products, the target cost shall be met and the product must be profitable.
3. Long-term supply of consistently high-quality products shall be ensured to maintain stable and efficient products and safe manufacturing processes to satisfy the needs for future market growth.
4. Utilize optimal product innovations to improve customer satisfaction and appeal for the procurement team.

In 2014, VW started the Future Automotive Supply Track (FAST) strategy to strengthen relationships with suppliers. The strategy includes 7 basic concepts: Future, innovation, globalization, transparency, commitment, dialog, and speed. At the start of 2015, 44 suppliers stood out among the selection results. The 44 companies were given the opportunity to participate in projects related to product innovation and improvement. The time at which the companies started participating in the projects was earlier than previous projects. Recently, VW has further implemented a project called optimization and standardization of procurement processes. This project aims to maximize procurement transparency and to allow suppliers to seek technical guidance and integration with the parent company within the shortest possible time.

## American Model: Using General Motors (GM) as an Example

Although GM was the third largest automotive company in the world in 2014 and 2015, its relationships with suppliers have not been excellent. GM has tried to improve these relationships, but internal forces prevent it from becoming comparable to the top two companies (Toyota and VW). In 2005, the procurement director of GM, Bo Anderson, launched a campaign to improve supplier relationships. The investigation commissioned to SupplyBusiness.com in 2007 showed that GM performed well in static indicators, such as delivery, quality, program launches, and productivity. However, GM did not perform well in dynamic indicators, such as communication, teamwork, availability, and visits to suppliers' plants. In the past, GM wanted to improve its supplier relationships and help the suppliers. However, a major supplier for GM, Delphi, suffered a financial crisis in 2006. Delphi was a company owned by GM but became independent from GM in 1999. During the transformation, Delphi lost several thousand contracts with GM and asked GM to give it other contract opportunities. GM responded by including terms such as renegotiating prices and demanded price reductions.

Another senior procurement executive of GM, Grace Lieblein, introduced a new strategy called "Supplier Engagement Program" in 2014 to deepen its supplier relationships. Firstly, GM used several selection criteria, such as cost, open communication, and technology sharing of the cultural dimension, to select excellent suppliers. GM then provided the excellent suppliers with guidance, training, and several opportunities in the numerous GM procurement projects. GM hoped that the suppliers could contribute to the technological fields of safety and fuel efficiency. However, these improvement strategies did not yield success. Lieblein pointed out that it is not easy to change the habits of the more than 6,000 GM procurement personnel.

## Japanese Model: Using Toyota as an Example

According to Toyota's official website, its procurement process is based on 3 major directions: Open and fair competition, mutual trust leading to mutual profits, and localized procurement. Toyota uses the milk-run method to collect parts from suppliers to achieve Just In Time deliveries to the factories for manufacturing. For the UK plant alone, Toyota has over 800 suppliers, most of which are located near the parent plant. The long-term development of mutually beneficial relationships with suppliers is not just a slogan for Toyota. In fact, the strategy has been relatively successful. According to the supplier survey conducted by Automotive News in the US in 2015, 48% of Toyota's suppliers felt good or very good about their partnership with Toyota. Only 19% of GM's suppliers reported the same, and VW's score was even lower. Toyota also cares about environmental and social responsibility. The points have been converted into guidelines and are included in Toyota's supplier's manual.

Due to the close relationship with the parent company, Toyota's suppliers are more willing to invest in new technologies and share them with Toyota. They are willing to go beyond the terms stipulated in the contract, communicate more openly and with more integrity, and make bigger concessions related to their prices. Even though Toyota has become a multi-national company today, it still adopts these long-term relationships with its suppliers. New suppliers must undergo a long observation period and will only receive smaller orders initially. The supplier must prove their determination and capabilities by satisfying the high standards related to quality, cost, and delivery stipulated by Toyota. Toyota does not replace suppliers when a cheaper source is found. Instead, it works with and helps suppliers to improve and lower their costs.

Liker (2016) stated that The Toyota Way began with enthusiasm towards solving problems for customers and society. In order to achieve this goal, Toyota had to highly respect "people" and their ability to adopt suitable and innovative ways to solve problems to create a good environment and avoid using oppressive methods. By consistently implementing this method over several decades, Toyota's employees deeply believe in and continue to carry out the ideal of continuous improvements. Toyota has put this into practice through practical actions and achieved this goal.

## The Supplier Selection for European, American, and Japanese Automotive Companies

A summary of the supplier selection criteria for European, American, and Japanese automotive companies:

1. *The global automotive industry* continues to grow. By 2020, global automotive sales will exceed 100 million vehicles per year and China and India will become major markets due to their large populations. However, in terms of global automotive manufacturing, the market is still dominated by American, and Japanese automotive companies, with the 3 major companies of VW, GM, and Toyota representing the respective markets.
2. *Taiwan is the world leader in fasteners.* Many high-precision automotive fasteners produced by Taiwan's subcontractors are sold to automotive by foreign tier-1 fastener companies. Because Taiwan is a major manufacturer of automotive fasteners, the foreign tier-1 fastener companies will often establish an international procurement office in Taiwan. However, the fastener industry in Taiwan is mainly composed of small and medium enterprises, which makes stipulating evaluation factors and using scientific methods to evaluate the fastener suppliers with the stipulated factors a difficult issue.
3. *There are many factors in supplier selections.* The evaluation factors in the early years 1993-1998 are explored in the literature. The evaluation is mainly based on economic factors, with quality, cost, and delivery acting as the 3 major evaluation dimensions. Service and technology were then gradually included in the important evaluation factors. After entering the 21st century, the concept of sustainable procurement must be considered. When selecting suppliers, besides considering economic factors, the supplier's environmental systems (such as ISO-14001), pollution prevention, labor health and safety, and good interactions with the community must also be considered. Therefore, reputation is becoming more important.
4. *European, American, and Japanese automotive companies:* Although the quality requirements of European, American, and Japanese automotive companies are based on the common standards of TS-16949, their development strategies for suppliers still differ due to their conditions and developmental histories. The differences are classified as below:
    a. *European automotive companies* focus on modularization. They consider the manufacturing capabilities and technological innovations of suppliers to be important. To become a tier-1 company, the supplier's scale, technology, and capability for innovation must reach high standards, in order to engage in product development and manufacturing with the automotive companies.
    b. *American automotive companies* focus on static and quantifiable items, such as cost, quality, and delivery. They are less focused on dynamic items, such as communication, supplier visits, history, and technological capabilities.

c. *Japanese automotive companies* focus on long-term relationships with suppliers and are more willing to observe and cultivate suppliers over a longer period. They will not replace suppliers for short-term price factors. Japanese companies favor localization, Just In Time (JIT) deliveries, and working with suppliers to implement long-term improvements and lower costs. They focus on manufacturing capabilities, cooperation, capital relationships, supplier visits, and history.

d. *For the top 3 automotive groups in the world (Toyota, VW, and GM)*, although their procurement strategies may have differed in the past, the thinking of their executives have become very similar today. However, due to the past experiences of their basic procurement personnel and differences in corporate culture, the execution is very different. Therefore, their relationships with their suppliers are also very different. Despite the differences, the annual sales volumes of the 3 major automotive companies are very similar (around 10 million vehicles). According to the study conducted by Laing (2016), in 2015, Toyota group's total sales was 15 million vehicles, VW group's total sales was 99 million vehicles, and GM group's total sales was 98 million vehicles. This shows that the different management models and supplier strategies can still achieve the same results and are examples of success.

## METHODOLOGY

The study has reviewed literature and interviewed experts of the domestic and foreign automotive fastener supply chains. It was identified 6 major dimensions and 18 criteria. We designed two questionnaires based on AHP and DEMATEL. We surveyed 12 experts of top managers whose companies are the Tier-1 fastener suppliers to European, American, and Japanese car companies. The questionnaires were sent to 4 experts from the European, American, and Japanese supply chains respectively, totaling 12 experts. We used physical visits or telephone calls to explain the meaning of the dimensions and each evaluation criterion, and asked the 12 experts to complete and return the questionnaire. The evaluation model consists of 6 dimensions of cost, quality, delivery, technology, service, and reputation, and 18 criteria.

The returned data for the study was used to calculate the weight of the dimensions and criteria with the AHP method. The DEMATEL method calculated the causal relationship between each criterion and the other 17 criteria, resulting in a causal diagram. In the causal diagram, the quadrants in which the 18 criteria reside can be found to assess the type of criterion (core, driving, independent, affected), which can be used as a reference for prioritizing resource investments and improvements.

In order to further explore the discrepancies in how European, American, and Japanese automotive companies view fastener supplier selection, we independently analyzed and compared the questionnaires from the European, American, and Japanese automotive companies (4 experts from each country), in order to identify differences in weight and causal relationships of fastener supplier evaluation dimensions and criteria between European, American, and Japanese automotive companies.

We used two methods, AHP and DEMATEL. AHP is used to evaluate the weight of the 6 dimensions and 18 criteria for European, American, and Japanese automotive companies. DEMATEL causal diagrams are used to determine the relationships between the 18 criteria. AHP can calculate the weights of each criterion but cannot calculate the correlation between the criteria. DEMATEL can calculate the correlation between the criteria but cannot calculate the weights of each criterion. The two methods were chosen to be "supplementary."

## Study Subjects

The study subjects are the personnel responsible for tier 1 fastener supply chains for automotive companies. First, we interviewed 12 top managers of Tier-1 American, European and Japanese fastener suppliers to induce an evaluation model for supplier selection. 12 experts from around the world were interviewed through two types of questionnaires based on AHP and DEMATEL (1 from Germany, 2 from the United States, 4 from Japan, 1 from China, and 4 from Taiwan) to ascertain the weights and rankings of the 6 major dimensions and 18 evaluation criteria for supplier selection.

## Analytic Hierarchy Process (AHP)

The Analytical Hierarchical Process (AHP) was proposed by Professor Saaty of the University of Pittsburgh, USA, in 1971. It is mainly used for decision-making problems related to uncertain conditions with multiple evaluation standards. AHP is simple and easy to implement. It is mainly used for decision-making problems related to uncertain conditions with multiple evaluation standards, and is widely used as a decision-making support system. Every AHP problem can be deconstructed into evaluated types or components, forming a directional hierarchy structure. The relationships between each layer and the standards between each layer are independent. The AHP method can calculate the weights of each independent criterion. The AHP research diagram is shown in Figure 1.

*Figure 1. AHP research diagram*

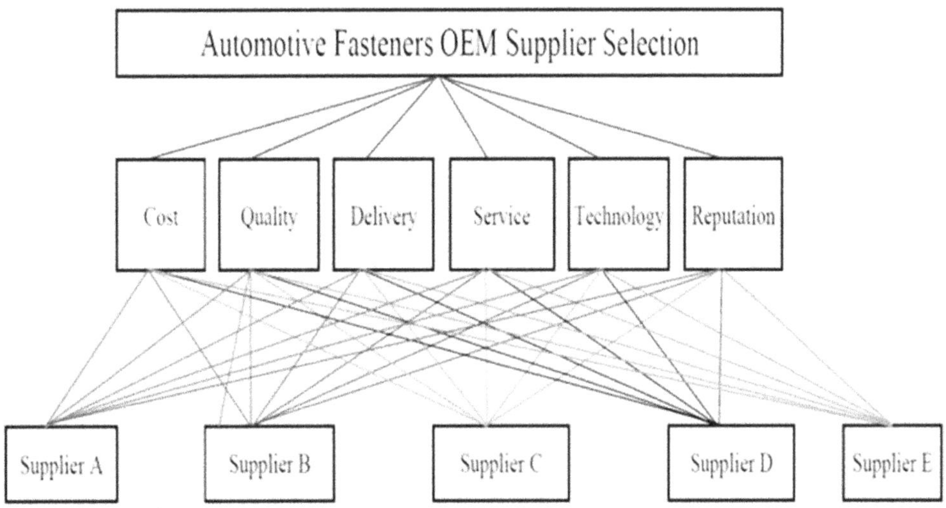


## Decision Making Trial and Evaluation Laboratory (DEMATEL)

The Decision Making Trial and Evaluation Laboratory (DEMATEL) was developed in the Battelle Memorial Institute of the Geneva Research Center. At the time, the DEMATEL method was used in complex study problems, such as race, hunger, environmental protection, energy, etc. (Fontela & Gabus, 1976) DEMATEL is used to inspect the correlation between variables in a decision-making system.

Compared to the AHP system, which considers each variable as independent, DEMATEL considers each variable as dependent on the others, and the level of influence between each variable is different. The DEMATEL research diagram is as shown in Figure 2.

*Figure 2. DEMATEL research diagram*

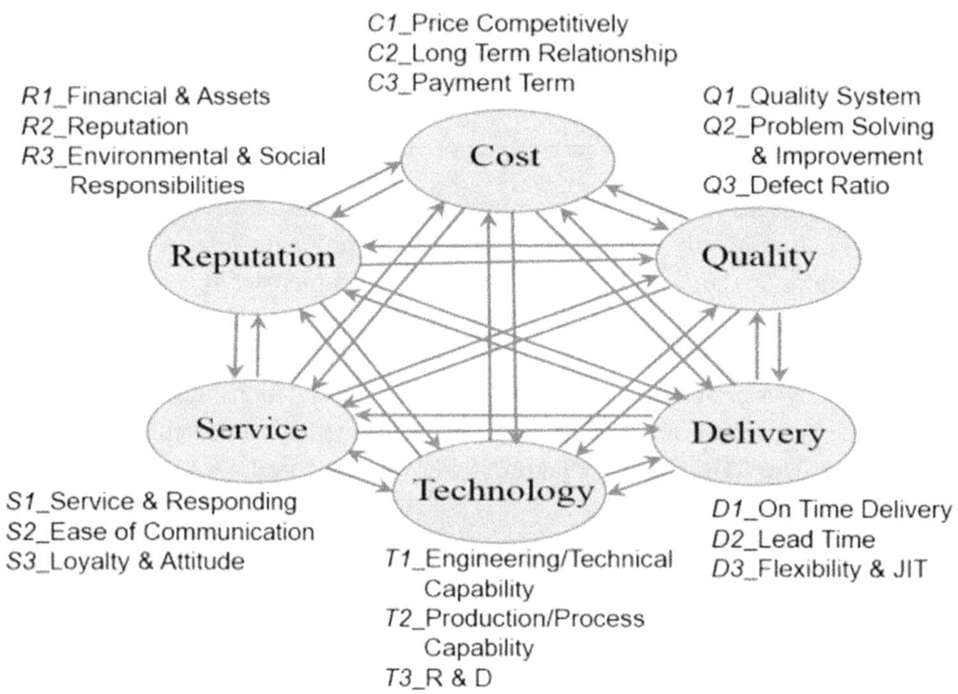


## Six Dimensions for Supplier Selection for European, American, and Japanese Automotive Company

The 6 major dimensions and criteria of the study are described in Table 3.

# RESULTS

## AHP Results

The study aims to understand the differences in tier-1 fastener supplier requirements of European, American, and Japanese automotive companies. We interviewed different experts from European, American, and Japanese automotive companies, totaling 4 experts from each region. The data we collected from surveying the 12 experts was named the Global Supply Chain, or Global SC. The data collected from the 4 experts in Europe was named the European Automotive Supply Chain, or European SC. The data collected from the 4 experts in the United States was named the American Automotive Supply Chain, or American SC. The data collected from the 4 experts in Japan was named the Japanese Automotive

*Table 3. Six Dimensions for supplier selection for automotive companies*

| Criterion | Description | Literature |
|---|---|---|
| **(1) Cost** | | |
| ***C1*_Competitive Price** | The supplier is maintaining a competitive price level to support our company. Also, the supplier is willing to accommodate cost reduction requests in line with customers'''' requests in some special cases. | • Weber, Current, & Benton (1993)<br>• Wei, Zhang, & Li (1997)<br>• Ghodsypour & O'Brien (1998)<br>• SCOR (2010)<br>• Cheraghi, Dadashzadeh, & Subramanian (2011)<br>• Baležentis & Baležentis (2011)<br>• Huang & Hu (2013)<br>• Sultana, Ahmed & Azeem (2015)<br>• Azadnia, Saman, & Wong (2015)<br>• Keskin (2015)<br>• Dweiri, Kumar, Khan & Jain (2016)<br>• Cieśla (2016) |
| ***C2*_Long Term Relationship** | The supplier is willing to maintain a long term relationship and follow the pricing model developed by our company and/or the pricing agreement between the supplier and our company. | • SCOR (2010)<br>• Cheraghi, Dadashzadeh, & Subramanian (2011)<br>• Keskin (2015) |
| ***C3*_Payment Terms** | The supplier is willing to follow the payment terms (CIF, FOB, etc.) and also the days for payment received as established by the Maclean-Fogg payment term policy. | • Baležentis & Baležentis (2011)<br>• Cieśla (2016) |
| **(2) Quality** | | |
| ***Q1*_Quality System** | The supplier has acquired the required quality certificates (TS-16949 / ISO-9001 / ISO-17025) and has rigorously followed up on non-conformances (NCs) and/or the findings from audits by third parties and/or customers. | • Weber, Current, & Benton (1993)<br>• Chao, Scheuing, & Ruch (1993)<br>• Wei, Zhang, & Li (1997)<br>• Ghodsypour & O'Brien (1998)<br>• Cheraghi, Dadashzadeh, & Subramanian (2011)<br>• Baležentis & Baležentis (2011)<br>• Huang & Hu (2013)<br>• Sultana, Ahmed, & Azeem (2015)<br>• Azadnia, Saman, & Wong (2015)<br>• Keskin (2015)<br>• Dweiri, Kumar, Khan & Jain (2016)<br>• Cieśla (2016) |
| ***Q2*_Problem Solving & Improvement** | The supplier can solve problems from our company and/or our customers. Concern documents (e.g., the 8D report) are rigorously retained. The supplier makes continuous improvement day to day and trains their employees. | • Cheraghi, Dadashzadeh, & Subramanian (2011)<br>• Keskin (2015) |
| ***Q3*_Defect Ratio** | The supplier has a meager defect ratio (no higher than 50 PPM). The current standard for automotive parts is 0 PPM. As a best practice, the supplier should also set 0 PPM as one of the items in their quality improvement goals/objectives. | • Ghodsypour & O'Brien (1998)<br>• Keskin (2015) |
| **(3) Delivery** | | |
| ***D1*_On Time Delivery** | The supplier can use an adequate schedule control tool/system (e.g. EDI, MRP, ERP, etc.) and ship, the parts by the PO shipping date. | • Weber, Current, & Benton (1993)<br>• Chao, Scheuing, & Ruch (1993)<br>• Ghodsypour & O'Brien (1998)<br>• SCOR (2010)<br>• Cheraghi, Dadashzadeh, & Subramanian (2011)<br>• Baležentis & Baležentis (2011)<br>• Huang & Hu (2013)<br>• Sultana, Ahmed & Azeem (2015)<br>• Azadnia, Saman, & Wong (2015)<br>• Keskin (2015)<br>• Dweiri, Kumar, Khan & Jain (2016)<br>• Cieśla(2016) |
| ***D2*_Lead Time** | The supplier has an acceptable lead time per customer requirements and is willing to shorten the lead time for continuous improvement projects. | • Baležentis, & Baležentis (2011)<br>• Sultana, Ahmed & Azeem (2015)<br>• Cieśla (2016) |
| ***D3*_Flexibility & JIT** | The supplier follows the PO release/change/withdrawal setup with Maclean-Fogg per the timing identified by the Maclean-Fogg PO release/change/withdrawal policy. However, the supplier also could reserve flexibility for Maclean-Fogg regarding PO changes for special cases (emergency customer demand, concerns, inventory adjustments, weather/transportation issues, etc.).<br>The supplier also supports the just in time (JIT) policy of supplying products based on customer demand. | • Cieśla (2016)<br>• Ghodsypour & O'Brien (1998)<br>• SCOR (2010)<br>• Cheraghi, Dadashzadeh, & Subramanian (2011)<br>• Sultana, Ahmed & Azeem (2015)<br>• Keskin (2015) |
| **(4) Technology** | | |
| ***T1*_ Engineering & Technical Capability** | The supplier has qualified engineers that handle all engineering tasks such as drawing/specification reviews and product/tooling designs. Also, it is recommended to have the requisite computer-aided design (CAD) software. | • Azadnia, Saman, & Wong (2015)<br>• Keskin (2015) |
| ***T2*_Production & Process Capability** | The supplier has facilities/machines/tooling/equipment of the requisite quality and qualified employees to handle production and meet customer demand. | • Ghodsypour & O'Brien (1998) |
| ***T3*_Research & Development** | The supplier is focusing on new technology development, innovation, and product improvement. | • Sultana, Ahmed & Azeem (2015) |
| **(5) Service** | | |
| ***S1*_Service & Responding** | The supplier is responsible for providing good services with a fast response time to acquire after-sales service, customer/product concerns, delivery changes, etc. | • Ghodsypour & O'Brien (1998)<br>• SCOR (2010)<br>• Cheraghi, Dadashzadeh, & Subramanian (2011)<br>• Huang & Hu (2013)<br>• Dweiri, Kumar, Khan & Jain (2016) |
| ***S2*_Ease of Communication** | The supplier can easily handle global communications. Such communication includes personnel fluent in English for written or verbal communications with global customers. Also, they have the capability to use modern communication tools such as email, e-conference calls, EDI, etc. | • Ghodsypour & O'Brien (1998)<br>• Cheraghi, Dadashzadeh, & Subramanian (2011)<br>• Keskin (2015) |
| ***S3*_Loyalty & Attitude** | The supplier is honest when providing information. They consider our company as important and they are looking for a business with our company. | • Keskin (2015) |
| **(6) Reputation** | | |
| ***R1*_Financial & Assets** | The supplier is financially secure. Also, the company is independent, with good enough assets for long term business. | • Ghodsypour & O'Brien (1998)<br>• SCOR (2010)<br>• Cheraghi, Dadashzadeh, & Subramanian (2011)<br>• Keskin (2015) |
| ***R2*_Reputation** | The supplier has had a good reputation. The company also has a good performance history of supplying products to customers over the long term. | • Wei, Zhang, & Li (1997)<br>• Azadnia, Saman, & Wong (2015)<br>• Keskin (2015)<br>• Cieśla (2016) |
| ***R3*_Environmental & Social Responsibilities** | The supplier takes responsibility for environmental protection (green product/production deployment), has employee health and safety programs, and enjoys good relationships and communications with the community. | • Azadnia, Saman, & Wong (2015) |

*Table 4. Global supply chain criteria: weights & ranking*

| Dimension | Criteria | Weights | Ranking |
|---|---|---|---|
| Cost | *C1*_Price Competitively | 0.0547 | 8 |
| | *C2*_Long Term Relationship | 0.0485 | 11 |
| | *C3*_Payment Term | 0.0363 | 15 |
| Quality | *Q1*_Quality System | 0.0962 | 1 |
| | *Q2*_Problem Solving & Improvement | 0.0898 | 2 |
| | *Q3*_Defect Ratio | 0.0843 | 3 |
| Delivery | *D1*_On Time Delivery | 0.0814 | 4 |
| | *D2*_Lead Time | 0.0649 | 6 |
| | *D3*_Flexibility & JIT | 0.0526 | 9 |
| Technology | *T1*_ Engineering/Technical Capability | 0.0607 | 7 |
| | *T2*_Production/Process Capability | 0.0699 | 5 |
| | *T3*_R & D | 0.0439 | 12 |
| Service | *S1*_Service & Responding | 0.0497 | 10 |
| | *S2*_Ease of Communication | 0.0393 | 13 |
| | *S3*_Loyalty & Attitude | 0.0313 | 17 |
| Reputation | *R1*_Financial & Assets | 0.0384 | 14 |
| | *R2*_Reputation | 0.0247 | 18 |
| | *R3*_Environmental & Social Responsibilities | 0.0333 | 16 |
| *Total==>* | | 1.0000 | |

*Table 5. European supply chain criteria: weights and ranking*

| Dimension | Criteria | Weights | Ranking |
|---|---|---|---|
| Cost | *C1*_Price Competitively | 0.0406 | 12 |
| | *C2*_Long Term Relationship | 0.0552 | 9 |
| | *C3*_Payment Term | 0.0308 | 18 |
| Quality | *Q1*_Quality System | 0.0975 | 1 |
| | *Q2*_Problem Solving & Improvement | 0.0820 | 3 |
| | *Q3*_Defect Ratio | 0.0892 | 2 |
| Delivery | *D1*_On Time Delivery | 0.0793 | 4 |
| | *D2*_Lead Time | 0.0637 | 6 |
| | *D3*_Flexibility & JIT | 0.0561 | 7 |
| Technology | *T1*_ Engineering/Technical Capability | 0.0540 | 10 |
| | *T2*_Production/Process Capability | 0.0752 | 5 |
| | *T3*_R & D | 0.0378 | 15 |
| Service | *S1*_Service & Responding | 0.0557 | 8 |
| | *S2*_Ease of Communication | 0.0384 | 14 |
| | *S3*_Loyalty & Attitude | 0.0387 | 13 |
| Reputation | *R1*_Financial & Assets | 0.0419 | 11 |
| | *R2*_Reputation | 0.0322 | 16 |
| | *R3*_Environmental & Social Responsibilities | 0.0317 | 17 |
| *Total==>* | | 1.0000 | |

*Table 6. American supply chain criteria: weights & ranking*

| Dimension | Criteria | Weights | Ranking |
|---|---|---|---|
| Cost | *C1*_Price Competitively | 0.0660 | 6 |
| | *C2*_Long Term Relationship | 0.0389 | 13 |
| | *C3*_Payment Term | 0.0436 | 12 |
| Quality | *Q1*_Quality System | 0.0868 | 4 |
| | *Q2*_Problem Solving & Improvement | 0.0897 | 2 |
| | *Q3*_Defect Ratio | 0.0883 | 3 |
| Delivery | *D1*_On Time Delivery | 0.0902 | 1 |
| | *D2*_Lead Time | 0.0808 | 5 |
| | *D3*_Flexibility & JIT | 0.0501 | 10 |
| Technology | *T1*_ Engineering/Technical Capability | 0.0539 | 9 |
| | *T2*_Production/Process Capability | 0.0586 | 7 |
| | *T3*_R & D | 0.0320 | 16 |
| Service | *S1*_Service & Responding | 0.0549 | 8 |
| | *S2*_Ease of Communication | 0.0459 | 11 |
| | *S3*_Loyalty & Attitude | 0.0343 | 15 |
| Reputation | *R1*_Financial & Assets | 0.0378 | 14 |
| | *R2*_Reputation | 0.0249 | 17 |
| | *R3*_Environmental & Social Responsibilities | 0.0233 | 18 |
| *Total==>* | | 1.0000 | |

*Table 7. Japanese supply chain criteria: weights and ranking*

| Dimension | Criteria | Weights | Ranking |
|---|---|---|---|
| Cost | *C1*_Price Competitively | 0.04885 | 10 |
| | *C2*_Long Term Relationship | 0.0443 | 12 |
| | *C3*_Payment Term | 0.0297 | 16 |
| Quality | *Q1*_Quality System | 0.0987 | 1 |
| | *Q2*_Problem Solving & Improvement | 0.0938 | 2 |
| | *Q3*_Defect Ratio | 0.0752 | 4 |
| Delivery | *D1*_On Time Delivery | 0.0733 | 5 |
| | *D2*_Lead Time | 0.0488 | 11 |
| | *D3*_Flexibility & JIT | 0.0492 | 9 |
| Technology | *T1*_ Engineering/Technical Capability | 0.0723 | 6 |
| | *T2*_Production/Process Capability | 0.0778 | 3 |
| | *T3*_R & D | 0.0622 | 8 |
| Service | *S1*_Service & Responding | 0.0428 | 13 |
| | *S2*_Ease of Communication | 0.0354 | 15 |
| | *S3*_Loyalty & Attitude | 0.0240 | 17 |
| Reputation | *R1*_Financial & Assets | 0.0373 | 14 |
| | *R2*_Reputation | 0.0191 | 18 |
| | *R3*_Environmental & Social Responsibilities | 0.0680 | 7 |
| *Total==>* | | 1.0000 | |

Supply Chain, or Japanese SC. The data from the different groups of experts in Europe, the United States, and Japan were analyzed independently to understand differences in the requirements of European, American, and Japanese automotive companies, which cause the experts in different regions to select different tier-1 fastener suppliers. The study results are shown in Table 4 to Table 7.

## DEMATEL Results

The DEMATEL causal diagrams are shown in Figure 3 to Figure 6.

*Figure 3. Global supply chain causal diagram*

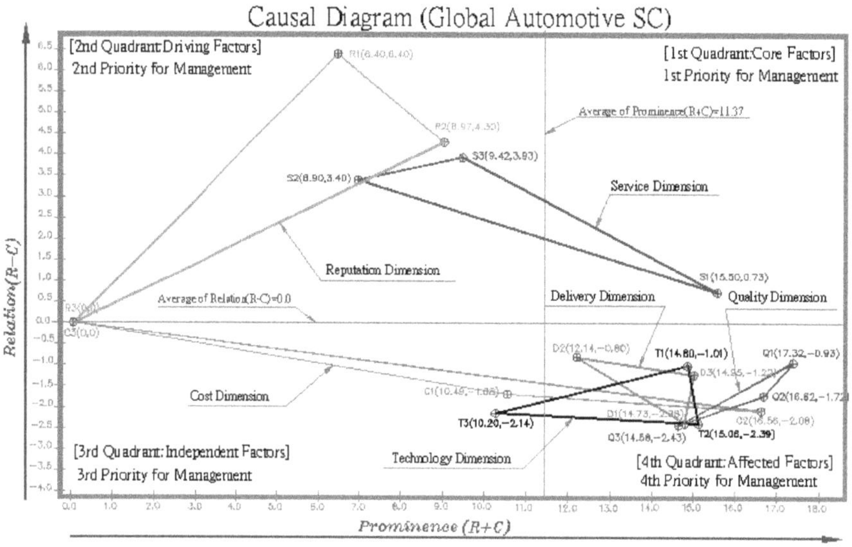


*Figure 4. European supply chain causal diagram*

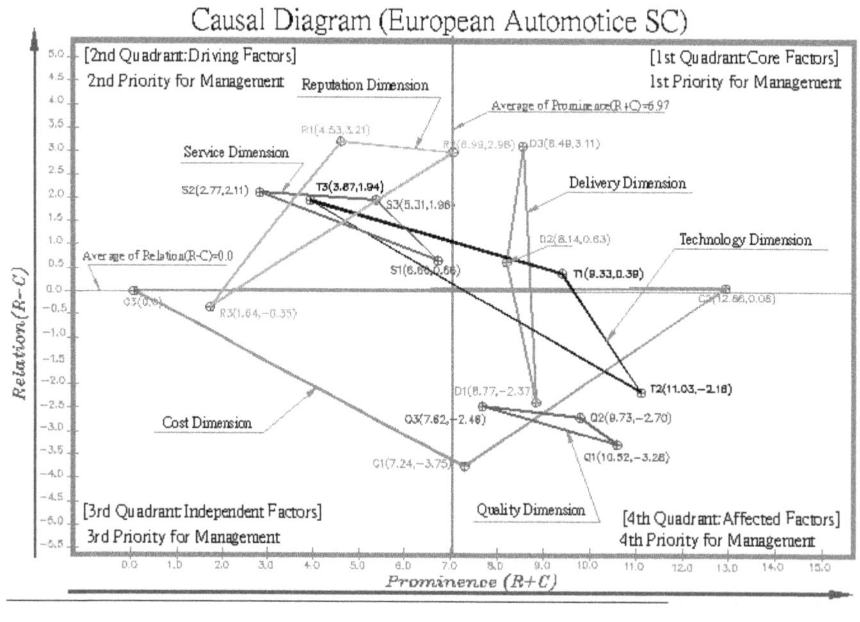

*Figure 5. American supply chain causal diagram*

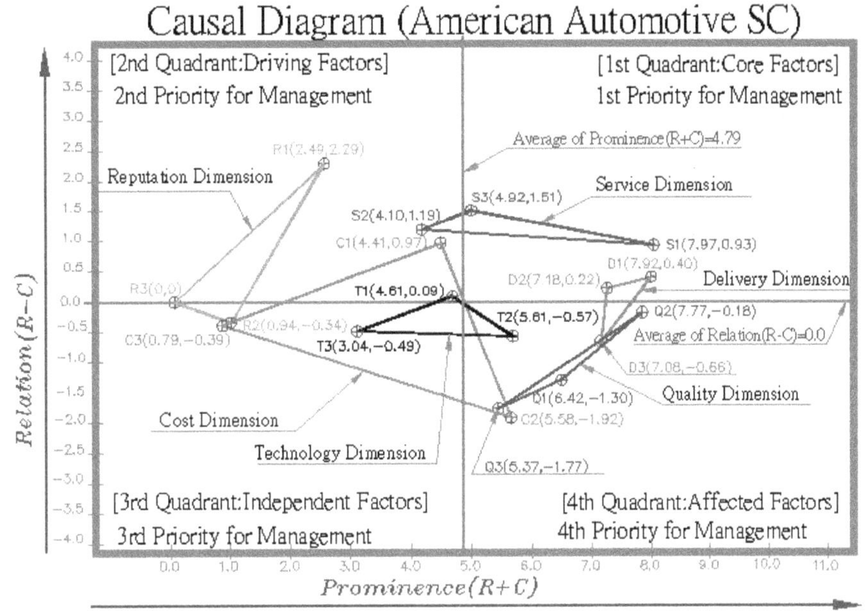


*Figure 6. Japanese supply chain causal diagram*

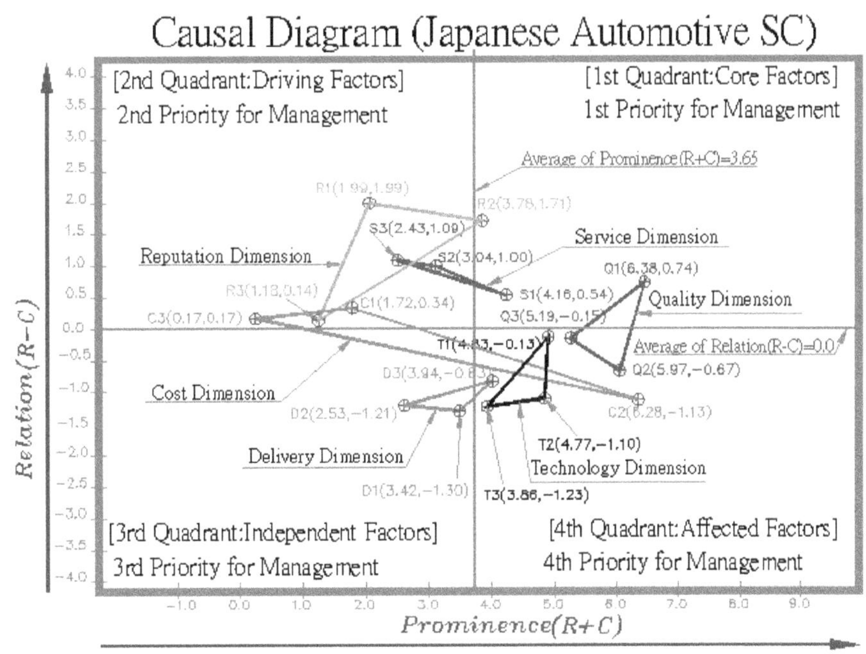

# DISCUSSION

## Discussion on AHP

### AHP Weights and Ranking of 18 Criteria

We have sorted the 18 criteria for supplier selection in the 4 supply chains, the Global Supply Chain, European Supply Chain, American Supply Chain, and Japanese Supply Chain, by order of importance. We have ordered the 18 criteria in each supply chain by importance and classified them into 3 groups: criteria ranked 1st to 6th are classified as a high priority, which are shown in bold, criteria ranked 7th to 12th are classified as medium priority, and criteria ranked 13th to 18th are classified as low priority, as shown in Table 8.

*Table 8. AHP weights and ranking of criteria for global and top 3 automotive supply chain*

| Criterion | Global Automotive SC | | Top 3 Automotive SCs | | | | | |
|---|---|---|---|---|---|---|---|---|
| | | | European SC | | American SC | | Japanese SC | |
| | *Weights* | *Ranking* | *Weights* | *Ranking* | *Weights* | *Ranking* | *Weights* | *Ranking* |
| *Q1*_Quality System | **0.0962** | **1** | **0.0975** | **1** | **0.0868** | **4** | **0.0987** | **1** |
| *Q2*_Problem Solving & Improvement | **0.0898** | **2** | **0.0820** | **3** | **0.0897** | **2** | **0.0938** | **2** |
| *Q3*_Defect Ratio | **0.0843** | **3** | **0.0892** | **2** | **0.0883** | **3** | **0.0752** | **4** |
| *D1*_On Time Delivery | **0.0814** | **4** | **0.0793** | **4** | **0.0902** | **1** | **0.0733** | **5** |
| *T2*_Production/Process Capability | **0.0699** | **5** | **0.0752** | **5** | 0.0586 | 7 | **0.0778** | **3** |
| *D2*_Lead Time | **0.0649** | **6** | **0.0637** | **6** | **0.0808** | **5** | 0.0488 | 11 |
| *T1*_Engineering/Technical Capability | 0.0607 | 7 | 0.0540 | 10 | 0.0539 | 9 | **0.0723** | **6** |
| *C1*_Price Competitively | 0.0547 | 8 | 0.0406 | 12 | **0.0660** | **6** | 0.0488 | 10 |
| *D3*_Flexibility & JIT | 0.0526 | 9 | 0.0561 | 7 | 0.0501 | 10 | 0.0492 | 9 |
| *S1*_Service & Responding | 0.0497 | 10 | 0.0557 | 8 | 0.0549 | 8 | 0.0428 | 13 |
| *C2*_Long Term Relationship | 0.0485 | 11 | 0.0552 | 9 | 0.0389 | 13 | 0.0433 | 12 |
| *T3*_R & D | 0.0439 | 12 | 0.0378 | 15 | 0.0320 | 16 | 0.0622 | 8 |
| *S2*_Ease of Communication | 0.0393 | 13 | 0.0384 | 14 | 0.0459 | 11 | 0.0354 | 15 |
| *R1*_Financial & Assets | 0.0384 | 14 | 0.0419 | 11 | 0.0378 | 14 | 0.0373 | 14 |
| *C3*_Payment Term | 0.0363 | 15 | 0.0308 | 18 | 0.0436 | 12 | 0.0297 | 16 |
| *R3*_Environmental & Social Responsibilities | 0.0333 | 16 | 0.0317 | 17 | 0.0233 | 18 | 0.0680 | 7 |
| *S3*_Loyalty & Attitude | 0.0313 | 17 | 0.0387 | 13 | 0.0343 | 15 | 0.0240 | 17 |
| *R2*_Reputation | 0.0247 | 18 | 0.0322 | 16 | 0.0249 | 17 | 0.0191 | 18 |
| Total=> | 1.000 | | 1.000 | | 1.000 | | 1.000 | |

The AHP results are shown in Table 8. It can be seen from the order of importance and the classification of high, medium, and low priority. Although there are differences in the views on and ranking of detailed evaluation criteria, the distribution of the high, medium, and low priorities are relatively consistent.

1. Quality:
   The 3 criteria of the quality dimension (Q1_Quality System, Q2_Problem Solving & Improvement, Q3_Defect Ratio) have been ranked as highly important in all 4 supply chains (Global SC, European SC, American SC, Japanese SC). The criteria have been ranked as the top 3 criteria in the Global SC and European SC.
2. D1_On Time Delivery:
   D1_On Time Delivery was ranked as the most important in the American automotive industry. Its priority was higher than the 3 criteria of quality, which means that the American Supply Chain places great importance on on-time deliveries.
3. T2_Production/Process Capability:
   T2_Production/Process Capability was ranked as a high priority in the Global SC, European SC, and Japanese SC. This criterion was ranked fifth for its importance in the Global SC and European SC. It was ranked third in the Japanese SC, placing it higher than Q3_Defect Ratio in the rankings. However, the American SC considers the criterion as a medium priority.
4. D2_Lead Time:
   The Global SC, European SC, and American SC all attach great importance to D2_Lead Time. The 3 supply chains classified the criterion as high priority (ranked fifth to sixth). However, the Japanese SC considers the criterion to be of medium priority, ranking it eleventh.
5. T1_Engineering Technical Capability:
   The Japanese SC is relatively focused on T1_Engineering Technical Capability, classifying it as a high priority and ranking it sixth among the criteria. However, the other 3 supply chains consider it as medium priority, ranking it between seventh to tenth.
6. C1_Price Competitively:
   The American SC attaches importance to C1_Price Competitively, classifying it as a high priority and ranking it sixth. However, the other 3 supply chains consider it as medium priority, ranking it between eighth to twelfth.
7. D3_Flexibility & JIT:
   The Global SC, European SC, and American SC consider D3_Flexibility & JIT as medium priority, ranking it seventh to tenth.
8. S1_Service & Responding:
   The Global SC, European SC, and American SC consider S1_Service & Responding as a medium priority (ranking it eighth to tenth). However, the Japanese SC considers the criterion to be a low priority, ranking it thirteenth.
9. C2_Long Term Relationship:
   The Global SC, European SC, and Japanese SC consider C2_Long Term Relationship as a medium priority (ranking it ninth to twelfth). However, the American SC considers the criterion to be a low priority, ranking it thirteenth.
10. C3_Payment Term:
    The American SC considers C3_Payment Term as a medium priority (ranking it twelfth). However, the Global SC, European SC, and Japanese SC consider the criterion to be of low priority, ranking it between fifteenth to eighteenth.

11. R3_Environment & Social Responsibilities:
    The Japanese SC considers R3_Environment & Social Responsibilities as a medium priority (ranking it seventh). However, the Global SC, European SC, and American SC consider the criterion to be of low priority, ranking it between sixteenth to eighteenth. This shows that the Japanese SC emphasizes environmental protection and social responsibility more than the other supply chains. This verifies Toyota's care for environmental and social responsibility in the supplier survey conducted by Automotive News in the United States in 2015.
12. S3_Royalty and Attitude and R2_Reputation:
    S3_Royalty and Attitude and R2_Reputation were uniformly deemed as low priority, ranking between thirteenth to eighteenth.

## AHP Weights and Ranking of Six Dimensions

We analyzed the order of importance if the 6 major dimensions were ranked. Are the views of the 4 supply chains (Global SC, European SC, American SC, Japanese SC) the same? We analyzed the "Dim. Weights" and "Dim. Ranking" of the 6 major dimensions, as shown in Table 9.

*Table 9. AHP ranking of six dimensions for global and top 3 automotive supply chain*

| Dimension | Criterion | Global Automotive SC | | | Top 3 Automotive SCs | | | | | | | | |
|---|---|---|---|---|---|---|---|---|---|---|---|---|---|
| | | | | | European SC | | | American SC | | | Japanese SC | | |
| | | *Weights* | *Dim. Weights* | *Dim. Rank* | *Weights* | *Dim. Weights* | *Dim. Rank* | *Weights* | *Dim. Weights* | *Dim. Rank* | *Weights* | *Dim. Weights* | *Dim. Rank* |
| (1) Cost | *C1*_Price Competitively | 0.0547 | | | 0.0406 | | | **0.0660** | | | 0.0488 | | |
| | *C2*_Long Term Relationship | 0.0485 | 0.1396 | 4 | 0.0552 | 0.1266 | 5 | 0.0389 | 0.1486 | 3 | 0.0433 | 0.1218 | 5 |
| | *C3*_Payment Term | 0.0363 | | | 0.0308 | | | 0.0436 | | | 0.0297 | | |
| (2) Quality | *Q1*_Quality System | **0.0962** | | | **0.0975** | | | **0.0868** | | | **0.0987** | | |
| | *Q2*_Problem Solving & Improvement | **0.0898** | 0.2703 | 1 | **0.0820** | 0.2686 | 1 | **0.0897** | 0.2648 | 1 | **0.0938** | 0.2677 | 1 |
| | *Q3*_Defect Ratio | **0.0843** | | | **0.0892** | | | **0.0883** | | | **0.0752** | | |
| (3) Delivery | *D1*_On Time Delivery | **0.0814** | | | **0.0793** | | | **0.0902** | | | **0.0733** | | |
| | *D2*_Lead Time | **0.0649** | 0.1989 | 2 | **0.0637** | 0.1991 | 2 | **0.0808** | 0.2210 | 2 | 0.0488 | 0.1713 | 3 |
| | *D3*_Flexibility & JIT | 0.0526 | | | 0.0561 | | | 0.0501 | | | 0.0492 | | |
| (4) Technology | *T1*_Engineering/ Technical Capability | 0.0607 | | | 0.0540 | | | 0.0539 | | | **0.0723** | | |
| | *T2*_Production/Process Capability | **0.0699** | 0.1746 | 3 | **0.0752** | 0.1670 | 3 | 0.0586 | 0.1445 | 4 | **0.0778** | 0.2124 | 2 |
| | *T3*_R & D | 0.0439 | | | 0.0378 | | | 0.0320 | | | 0.0622 | | |
| (5) Service | *S1*_Service & Responding | 0.0497 | | | 0.0557 | | | 0.0549 | | | 0.0428 | | |
| | *S2*_Ease of Communication | 0.0393 | 0.1203 | 5 | 0.0384 | 0.1328 | 4 | 0.0459 | 0.1351 | 5 | 0.0354 | 0.1023 | 6 |
| | *S3*_Loyalty & Attitude | 0.0313 | | | 0.0387 | | | 0.0343 | | | 0.0240 | | |
| (6) Reputation | *R1*_Financial & Assets | 0.0384 | | | 0.0419 | | | 0.0378 | | | 0.0373 | | |
| | *R2*_Reputation | 0.0247 | 0.0963 | 6 | 0.0322 | 0.1059 | 6 | 0.0249 | 0.0860 | 6 | 0.0191 | 0.1244 | 4 |
| | *R3*_Environmental & Social Responsibilities | 0.0333 | | | 0.0317 | | | 0.0233 | | | 0.0680 | | |
| Total=> | | 1.000 | 1.000 | | 1.000 | 1.000 | | 1.000 | 1.000 | | 1.000 | 1.000 | |

## Discussion on DEMATEL

In order to further observe the distribution of the 18 criteria of the 6 major dimensions in the 4 supply chains in the causal diagram, we have organized the distribution patterns in the 4 quadrants of the criteria for the Global SC, European SC, American SC, and Japanese SC in Table 10.

The results of DEMATEL in Table 10 showed that:

*Table 10. Criterion distributions in DEMATEL causal diagram for global and top 3 automotive supply chain*

| Dimension | Criteria | Criterion Distributions (Quadrants) in Causal Diagram | | | |
|---|---|---|---|---|---|
| | | Global Automotive SC | Top 3 Automotive SC | | |
| | | | European SC | American SC | Japanese SC |
| (1) Cost | *C1*_Price Competitively | 3 | 4 | 2 | 2 |
| | *C2*_Long Term Relationship | 4 | 1 | 4 | 4 |
| | *C3*_Payment Term | 2 | 2 | 3 | 2 |
| (2) Quality | *Q1*_Quality System | 4 | 4 | 4 | 1 |
| | *Q2*_Problem Solving & Improvement | 4 | 4 | 4 | 4 |
| | *Q3*_Defect Ratio | 4 | 4 | 4 | 4 |
| (3) Delivery | *D1*_On Time Delivery | 4 | 4 | 1 | 3 |
| | *D2*_Lead Time | 4 | 1 | 1 | 3 |
| | *D3*_Flexibility & JIT | 4 | 1 | 4 | 4 |
| (4) Technology | *T1*_ Engineering/Technical Capability | 4 | 1 | 2 | 4 |
| | *T2*_Production/Process Capability | 4 | 4 | 4 | 4 |
| | *T3*_R & D | 3 | 2 | 3 | 4 |
| (5) Service | *S1*_Service & Responding | 1 | 2 | 1 | 1 |
| | *S2*_Ease of Communication | 2 | 2 | 2 | 2 |
| | *S3*_Loyalty & Attitude | 2 | 2 | 1 | 2 |
| (6) Reputation | *R1*_Financial & Assets | 2 | 2 | 2 | 2 |
| | *R2*_Reputation | 2 | 1 | 3 | 1 |
| | *R3*_Environmental & Social Responsibilities | 2 | 3 | 2 | 2 |

1. Cost dimension

   The views on the cost dimension of the 3 major automotive industries are relatively more inconsistent.

   a. European automotive companies prefer long-term co-development with suppliers. Due to the need for long-term co-development, long-term relationships must be maintained.
   b. American automotive companies consider "C1_Price Competitively" as an independent cause that requires active improvements. This verifies the importance the American SC places on cost and price criteria.
   c. Japanese automotive companies consider "C1_Price Competitively" and "C3_Payment Term" as causes that require active improvements. Although the Japanese SC does not consider the cost dimension as a high priority in the AHP analysis, it affects the criteria of the other dimensions, so it must be actively improved.

2. Quality dimension

   To improve quality, quality control methods (such as inspections or testing) are not sufficient. It can only be achieved by implementing methods related to multiple aspects.

   a. Besides the different views held by the Japanese SC regarding "Q1_Quality System", the 3 major automotive industries all consider the quality dimension as the most important in the AHP analysis. However, its evaluation criteria have been classified as affected criteria.
   b. The European SC, American SC, and Japanese SC consider "Q2_Problem Solving & Improvement" and "Q3_Defect Ratio" as results within the affected criteria, which do not require active improvements.
   c. The Japanese SC was the first to invest resources to improve the quality system. Therefore, it will have more activities related to quality control systems, such as quality control diagrams and improvement proposals and systems.

3. Delivery dimension

   a. Regarding the 3 criteria of the delivery dimension, the European SC considers "D2_Lead Time" and "D3_Flexibility & JIT" as very important and has classified them as causes in the core criterion quadrant, which require active improvements. Regarding the "D1_On Time Delivery" criterion, the European SC considers it to be a result in the affected criteria quadrant, and it does not require active improvements.
   b. This shows that the European SC is focused on co-developments with suppliers. Because of the co-development model, it considers the flexibility, immediacy and shortening of delivery deadlines of the co-development as very important. Since the delivery deadline may require flexible adjustments, the criterion has been classified as an affected criterion and does not require active management.
   c. Regarding the 3 criteria of the delivery dimension, the American SC considers "D1_On Time Delivery" and "D2_Lead Time" as very important and has classified them as causes in the core criterion quadrant, which require active improvements. Regarding the "D3_Flexibility & JIT" criterion, the American SC considers it to be a result in the affected criteria quadrant, and it does not require active improvements.
   d. This shows the importance the American SC places on static management items, such as lead time and on time deliveries. Dynamic criteria related to flexibility and immediate deliveries are considered to be criteria that do not require active management.

4. Technology dimension
    a. Regarding the 2 criteria of the technology dimension, the European SC considers "T1_Engineering/Technical Capability" and "T3_R & D" as very important and has classified them as causes in the core criterion and driving criterion quadrants, which require active improvements. Regarding the "T2_Production/Process Capability" criterion related to manufacturing, the European SC considers it to be a result in the affected criteria quadrant, and it does not require active improvements.
    b. The Japanese SC considers that 3 criteria as results in the affected criteria quadrant, and it does not require active improvements.
    c. The views of the American SC fall between the two.
    d. It shows that the European SC more actively invests in engineering, technology, and research and development.
5. Service dimension
    a. Regarding the 3 evaluation criteria of the service dimension, the European, American, and Japanese automotive companies consider them to be causes in the core criterion and driving criterion quadrants, which require active improvements and management.
    b. For automotive fastener suppliers, the service criteria are the top priority for investments and improvements. This view is shared by all automotive companies.
6. Reputation dimension
    a. Regarding the 3 evaluation criteria of the reputation dimension, the Japanese SC considers them to be causes in the core criterion and driving criterion quadrants, which require active improvements and management.
    b. The European SC considers "R3_Environmental & Social Responsibilities" as an independent criterion
    c. The American SC considers "R2_Reputation" as an independent criterion. For the other criteria, the American SC shares views similar to that of the Japanese SC.
    d. Compared to other supply chains, the Japanese SC focuses more on reputation, and will prioritize investments in improving the environment and social responsibility.

## CONCLUSION

This research used two methods, AHP and DEMATEL, to verify the results. The study used interviews with experts and questionnaires to explore the selection criterion weights and the causal relationship between the selection criteria of automotive fastener supplier selection. Therefore, the AHP method and DEMATEL method were used.

**AHP Method in This Study:** The AHP method can organize complex selection criteria into quantified weights, allowing us to easily order the results and add the weights to the total score during evaluations. However, AHP assumes the dimensions and selection criteria are independent from each other, which is incorrect. For example, price (or cost) affects quality. Higher quality products generally have a higher price. When a customer forces a supplier to reduce their price, the supplier may reduce the product functions or quality to reduce cost to survive. In this case, the quality of the product is lowered. In other words, if a customer asks the supplier to improve their product quality to a new level (such as automotive fasteners to aeronautics fasteners), the supplier will increase their product prices due to the additional costs. This relationship where the price affects quality and vice versa is called correlation.

**DEMATEL Method in This Study:** We used the DEMATEL method to calculate the correlations between the selection criteria and presented the attributes of each criterion (core criterion, driving criterion, independent criterion, affected criterion) within the entire group in causal diagrams. This was done to provide references for resource investments and improvements. This method is closer to reality and more acceptable for managers, because one, every dollar must be used wisely, and two, the root causes of problems must be solved to eradicate the issues.

**Research Contributions:** According to the study, we found that in the AHP study, the quality dimension was the most important. The importance of the dimension was ranked first and the 3 selection criteria (Q1, Q2, Q3) of the dimension were ranked first among the 18 selection criteria. This was not surprising because automotive fasteners are mostly parts for safety. The price for customer complaints or even recalls due to poor-quality products is very high. Therefore, it was expected that the automotive companies considered the quality dimension as the most important. However, after conducting the DEMATEL analysis, we learned that besides the "Q1_Quality System" criterion in the Japanese SC, the 3 selection criteria in the quality dimension were classified as "affected" criteria in the "result" quadrant of the causal relationships, which is to say that although the quality is very important, improving quality must be accomplished through the other aspects. Through the DEMATEL analysis, we found that active resource investments in and improvements of service will also improve the other dimensions, including quality. Therefore, the study found that in the AHP results, the quality dimensions should be ranked first. But in the DEMATEL study results, the primary dimension for resource investments is service. Quality was actually ranked least important for resource investments. Because of this, we can see that conducting AHP and DEMATEL studies on the same sample can show us the rankings by importance to the customer (procurer) and the level of priority of investments and improvements for each criterion from the standpoint of the suppliers. The rankings of the selection criteria from the two different points of view are different.

**Managerial Implications:** Our study found that "quality" is the most important dimension in evaluations for fastener supplier selection for automotive companies. For the suppliers, they must improve "service" and "reputation" first to become excellent fastener suppliers for the automotive industry. Our practical contributions provide a multi-criteria decision evaluation model for fastener supplier selection for automotive companies. And we also provide an evaluation model for fastener suppliers to prioritize their resource investments and improvements to become a qualified supplier. The study mainly explored the criteria for automotive fastener supplier selection of European, American, and Japanese automotive companies, and the weights of the 18 criteria were calculated. Evaluations of multiple suppliers can be conducted by different people according to these 18 criteria. The ideal supplier can be found by using the method provided by the study and calculating scores according to the weights.

**Directions of Future Research:** For the auditor, how can they score individual criteria? For example, if an auditor scores the "Q3_Defect Ratio" of Supplier A as "87", how did he or she find out the defect rate of Supplier A during manufacturing and give it a score of 87? Furthermore, for evaluating "T2_Production/Process Capability", if the auditor does not fully understand the type, quantity, usage, and maintenance status of the machinery and equipment, how can he or she provide a score? In fact, the procurer can generally send an information form to the supplier to be filled out (such as a supplier information form). After which, the procurer can visit the supplier's factory and conduct interviews and detailed audits to acquire the necessary information. The auditor can then score each criterion. During this process, different procurers can use different forms, called "worksheets" in general. We suggest that future researchers conduct further studies on the worksheets of automotive fastener procurers to understand the main types and timings for use. The researchers can learn how to use the work sheets to help the automotive fastener procurers in evaluating supplier selection.

## REFERENCES


Azadnia, A. H., Saman, M. Z. M., & Wong, K. Y. (2015). Sustainable supplier selection and order lot-sizing: An integrated multi-objective decision-making process. *International Journal of Production Research*, *53*(2), 383–408. doi:10.1080/00207543.2014.935827

Baležentis, A., & Baležentis, T. (2011). An innovative multi-criteria supplier selection based on two-tuple MULTIMOORA and hybrid data. *Economic Computation and Economic Cybernetics Studies and Research*, *45*(2), 37–56.

Chao, C., Scheuing, E.E., & Ruch, W.A. (1993). Purchasing performance evaluation: An investigation of different perspectives. *International Journal of Purchasing and Materials Management Summer, 29*(3), 33–39.

Cheraghi, S. H., Dadashzadeh, M., & Subramanian, M. (2011). Critical success factors for supplier selection: An update. *Journal of Applied Business Research*, *20*(2). doi:10.19030/jabr.v20i2.2209

Christopher, M. (2005), *Logistics and Supply Chain Management: Creating Value-Adding Networks* (3rd ed.). Financial Times Prentice Hall.

Cieśla, M. (2016). Aluminium supplier selection for the automotive parts manufacturer. *Metalurgija*, *55*(2), 237–240.

Council, S. C. (2010). Supply-chain operations reference-model. *Overview of SCOR Version*, *10*, 7-8.

Dornier, P. P., Ernst, R., Fender, M., & Kouvelis, P. (2008). *Global operations and logistics: Text and cases*. John Wiley & Sons.

Dweiri, F., Kumar, S., Khan, S. A., & Jain, V. (2016). Designing an integrated AHP based decision support system for supplier selection in automotive industry. *Expert Systems with Applications*, *62*, 273–283. doi:10.1016/j.eswa.2016.06.030

Estampe, D., Lamouri, S., Paris, J. L., & Brahim-Djelloul, S. (2013). A framework for analysing supply chain performance evaluation models. *International Journal of Production Economics*, *142*(2), 247–258. doi:10.1016/j.ijpe.2010.11.024

Fontela, E., & Gabus, A. (1976). Current perceptions of the world problematique. In *World Modeling: A Dialogue*. North-Holland Publishing Company.

Ghodsypour, S. H., & O'Brien, C. (1998). A decision support system for supplier selection using an integrated analytic hierarchy process and linear programming. *International Journal of Production Economics*, *56*, 199–212. doi:10.1016/S0925-5273(97)00009-1

Govindan, K., Rajendran, S., Sarkis, J., & Murugesan, P. (2015). Multi criteria decision making approaches for green supplier evaluation and selection: A literature review. *Journal of Cleaner Production*, *98*, 66–83. doi:10.1016/j.jclepro.2013.06.046

Huang, J. D., & Hu, M. H. (2013). Two-stage solution approach for supplier selection: A case study in a Taiwan automotive industry. *International Journal of Computer Integrated Manufacturing*, *26*(3), 237–251. doi:10.1080/0951192X.2012.685762

IHS Automotive Data Center. (2017). Global light vehicle production summary. *IHS Automotive*. Available at https://www.ihs.com/pdf/IHS-Automotive-Global-Summary-Production-LVP-12-16_222719110913052132.pdf

Jacobides, M. G., MacDuffie, J. P., & Tae, C. J. (2015). Agency, structure, and the dominance of OEMs: Change and stability in the automotive sector. *Strategic Management Journal.*

Keskin, G. A. (2015). Using integrated fuzzy DEMATEL and fuzzy C: Means algorithm for supplier evaluation and selection. *International Journal of Production Research*, *53*(12), 3586–3602. doi:10.1080/00207543.2014.980461

Li, C. W., & Tzeng, G. H. (2009). Identification of a threshold value for the DEMATEL method using the maximum mean de-entropy algorithm to find critical services provided by a semiconductor intellectual property mall. *Expert Systems with Applications*, *36*(6), 9891–9898. doi:10.1016/j.eswa.2009.01.073

Liker, J. K. (2016). Striving for Excellence. *The Routledge Companion to Lean Management, 9.* Available at https://books.google.com.tw/books?hl=zh-TW&lr=&id=kDolDwAAQBAJ&oi=fnd&pg=PA9&dq=Liker,+J.+K.+(2016).+Striving+for+Excellence.+The+Routledge+Companion+to+Lean+Management,+9.+&ots=w92Z0Wq7AE&sig=cZHL0JX2ZI6zYo2swMey7LGYwag&redir_esc=y#v=onepage&q&f=true

Pai, P. (2015). Top 10 largest car companies in the world. *Tharawat Magazine.* Available at http://www.tharawat-magazine.com/facts/10-largest-car-companies/#gs.PbvLurI

Rahman, S., & Wu, Y. C. J. (2011). Logistics outsourcing in China: The manufacturer-cum-supplier perspective. *Supply Chain Management*, *16*(6), 462–473. doi:10.1108/13598541111171156

Rajesh, G., & Malliga, P. (2013). Supplier selection based on AHP QFD methodology. *Procedia Engineering*, *64*, 1283–1292. doi:10.1016/j.proeng.2013.09.209

Rattanavijit, S., Somboonwiwat, T., & Khompatraporn, C. (2015). Analysis of Causal Competitive Factors of Thai Iron and Steel Supply Chain by DEMATEL Method. In *Industrial Engineering* (pp. 541–550). Management Science and Applications. Available at https://link.springer.com/content/pdf/10.1007%2F978-3-662-47200-2.pdf

Saaty, T. L. (1980). The Analytic Hierarchy Process. McGraw-Hill.

Stadtler, H. (2015). Supply chain management: An overview. *Supply chain management and advanced planning*, 3-28. Available at https://link.springer.com/content/pdf/10.1007%2F978-3-642-55309-7.pdf

Sultana, I., Ahmed, I., & Azeem, A. (2015). An integrated approach for multiple criteria supplier selection combining Fuzzy Delphi, Fuzzy AHP & Fuzzy TOPSIS. *Journal of Intelligent & Fuzzy Systems*, *29*(4), 1273–1287.

Sumrit, D., & Anuntavoranich, P. (2013). Using DEMATEL method to analyze the causal relations on technological innovation capability evaluation factors in Thai technology-based firms. *Int Trans J Eng Manag Appl Sci Technol*, *4*(2), 81-103.

Taiwan Industrial Fastener Institute. (2016). *The Republic of China (Taiwan) Import/Export Statistical Data.* Available at http://www.fasteners.org.tw/Default.aspx?tabindex=8&tabid=11

Vujanović, D., Momčilović, V., Bojović, N., & Papić, V. (2012). Evaluation of vehicle fleet maintenance management indicators by application of DEMATEL and ANP. *Expert Systems with Applications*, *39*(12), 10552–10563. doi:10.1016/j.eswa.2012.02.159

Weber, C. A., & Current, J. R. (1993). A multiobjective approach to vendor selection. *European Journal of Operational Research*, *68*(2), 173–184. doi:10.1016/0377-2217(93)90301-3

Wei, S., Zhang, J., & Li, Z. (1997). A supplier-selecting system using a neural network. In *Intelligent Processing Systems, 1997. ICIPS'97. 1997 IEEE International Conference on Intelligent Processing Systems*. IEEE.

Wu, W. W. (2008). Choosing knowledge management strategies by using a combined ANP and DEMATEL approach. *Expert Systems with Applications*, *35*(3), 828–835. doi:10.1016/j.eswa.2007.07.025

Wu, Y. C., Lin, B. W., Shih, C., & Chen, C. J. (2013). Communicating and prioritizing science and technology policy using AHP. *Innovation*, *15*(4), 437–451. doi:10.5172/impp.2013.15.4.437

Wu, Y. C. J., Huang, S. K., Goh, M., & Hsieh, Y. J. (2013). Global logistics management curriculum: Perspective from practitioners in Taiwan. *Supply Chain Management*, *18*(4), 376–388. doi:10.1108/SCM-04-2012-0145

Yang, Y. P. O., Shieh, H. M., Leu, J. D., & Tzeng, G. H. (2008). A novel hybrid MCDM model combined with DEMATEL and ANP with applications. *International Journal of Operations Research*, *5*(3), 160-168.

Yang, Y. P. O., Shieh, H. M., & Tzeng, G. H. (2013). A VIKOR technique based on DEMATEL and ANP for information security risk control assessment. *Information Sciences*, *232*, 482–500. doi:10.1016/j.ins.2011.09.012

## KEY TERMS AND DEFINITIONS

**American Automotive Companies:** The companies which involved in the design, development, manufacturing, marketing, and selling of American brand motor vehicles.

**Automotive Companies:** A wide range of companies involved in the design, development, manufacturing, marketing, and selling of motor vehicles.

**Automotive Industry:** An industry which comprises a wide range of companies and organizations which involve in the design, development, manufacturing, marketing, and selling of motor vehicles. It is one of the world's largest industries by revenue. The automotive industry does not include the industries which are dedicated to the maintenance of automobiles following delivery to the end-user, such as automobile repair shops and motor fuel filling stations.

**Automotive OEM Company:** A company that makes and sells automobiles. It's also called "Auto OEM Companies" which is the same as car companies. The Automotive OEM Companies are the top level for the automotive parts supply chain.

**Car Company:** A company that makes and sells automobiles. For example, the Volkswagen Group (Germany), Toyota Motor (Japan), and Daimler AG (Germany) are the top 3 car companies ranking by revenue in 2021.

**European Automotive Companies:** The companies which involve in the design, development, manufacturing, marketing, and selling of European brand motor vehicles.

**Japanese Automotive Companies:** The companies which involve in the design, development, manufacturing, marketing, and selling of Japanese brand motor vehicles.

**OEM:** Original Equipment Manufacturer (OEM). It traditionally is defined as a company whose goods are used as components in the products of another company, which then sells the finished items to users.

**Tier-1 Fasteners Suppliers:** The fasteners companies which supply the fasteners products to the car companies directly.

**Tier-2 Fasteners Suppliers:** The fasteners companies which supply the fasteners products to the tier-1 companies. Their customers (The tier-1 companies) include not just the tier-1 fasteners companies but also the other tier-1 companies (e.g., the tier-1 suspension companies).

# Chapter 5
# CSR Initiatives in the Supply Chain of the Japanese Automotive Industry:
## The Role of Parts Industry Association

**Hiromu Hatakeyama**
*Sakushin Gakuin University, Japan*

## ABSTRACT

*An automobile product is made up of tens of thousands of parts, many of which are procured from suppliers rather than manufactured by the automaker itself. Therefore, for automakers to steadily implement CSR initiatives, not only automakers but also all companies that make up the supply chain must promote such initiatives. Until now, existing studies have focused only on the efforts of companies such as automakers and suppliers and have not examined the efforts of industry associations, which play an extremely important role in the steady development of CSR initiatives in the supply chain. Therefore, this chapter examines the role and importance of the supplier-side industry association (JAPIA) in the development of CSR initiatives in the supply chain of the Japanese automotive industry. About CSR initiatives in the Japanese automotive industry, JAPIA's efforts have been extremely important in facilitating and ensuring supply chain initiatives. Thanks to the efforts of JAPIA, the Japanese automotive industry has been able to realize supply chain management in terms of CSR.*

## INTRODUCTION

This chapter discusses Corporate Social Responsibility (hereinafter, this is called "CSR ") in the supply chain. CSR is not only a problem for large corporations, but also for the supply chain associated with the manufacture and sale of materials, parts, and products. This chapter examines CSR in the supply chain from the perspective of the parts industry.

DOI: 10.4018/978-1-7998-9800-9.ch005

Currently, companies are required to address CSR. It is essential to address various items such as global environmental issues, human rights issues such as discrimination and illegal labor, and product safety, and to enhance responses to achieve sustainability.

The benefits of proactively addressing CSR include not only achieving social and environmental sustainability, but also corporate sustainability.

Failing to comply with CSR-related risks and regulations is not only illegal, but also increases reputational risks and may lead to boycotts. In other words, not only social and environmental sustainability, but also corporate sustainability will be degraded. This is true for both large and small companies.

Furthermore, building a sustainable supply chain is an extremely important issue for companies. If a CSR-related problem arises in one company in the supply chain, it will affect the sustainability of the entire supply chain. Therefore, not only the company itself, but all companies in the supply chain need to work on CSR.

An automobile product is made up of tens of thousands of parts, many of which are procured from suppliers rather than manufactured by the automaker itself. Therefore, for automakers to steadily implement CSR initiatives, not only automakers but also all companies that make up the supply chain must promote such initiatives.

The Japan Auto Parts Industries Association (hereinafter, this is called "JAPIA"), an industry association of parts suppliers, is important when developing initiatives in the supply chain. When implementing various CSR-related initiatives in the supply chain, such as measures against chemical substances in products, other environmental measures, and conflict minerals, JAPIA first implements various initiatives before the suppliers do. Then, based on the initiatives taken by JAPIA, the suppliers implement their own initiatives.

Therefore, the purpose of this chapter is to clarify the role and importance of industry associations, which play an extremely important role in the development of CSR initiatives in the supply chain of the Japanese automotive industry. The target industry organization is JAPIA, which is a supplier-side industry association.

## BACKGROUND

Prior research dealing with CSR in the Japanese automotive industry includes discussions of the realization of the SDGs (Negishi, 2019), ESG strategies in the auto industry (Kurokawa, 2017), and CSR strategies of auto manufacturers (Sakuma, 2006, 2008; Suga and Ishida, 2008). In addition, Hatakeyama (2011, 2014) examines the development of CSR in the supply chain of the Japanese automotive industry. Through these previous studies, we have been able to understand the actual status of various CSR initiatives in the Japanese automotive industry, and we have also obtained valuable implications.

However, one of the issues that remains in these previous studies is that they focus only on the efforts of companies such as automobile manufacturers and suppliers, and do not consider the efforts of industry associations of parts suppliers, which play an extremely important role in ensuring the steady development of CSR initiatives in the supply chain.

When various CSR-related initiatives are undertaken in the supply chain, JAPIA conducts a variety of initiatives before the suppliers that make up the supply chain do. Thanks to the efforts of JAPIA, suppliers can implement CSR-related initiatives smoothly. Therefore, to clarify the CSR initiatives in the supply chain of the Japanese automotive industry, it is inevitable to consider the industry associations of parts suppliers.

In this chapter, the author will examine the role and importance of industry associations in the development of CSR initiatives in the supply chain of the Japanese automotive industry.

## WHAT TO DO IN THE SUPPLY CHAIN

In this section, the author will review the following three main items that need to be addressed in the supply chain of the automotive industry. ISO 26000, an international standard for CSR, Laws and regulations related to chemical substances in products and conflict minerals related to human rights issues.

The first is about ISO 26000. As the social situation changes, expectations of corporations from their stakeholders such as business partners and consumers are increasing. Under these circumstances, ISO 26000, an international standard for social responsibility, was published in 2010. The objectives, definitions, and action items related to CSR have been standardized globally, and companies around the world are now expected to proceed with their initiatives based on this standard.

The objective of CSR in ISO 26000 is to contribute to sustainable development, including health and the welfare of society. The definition of CSR is the responsibility of an organization for the impacts of its decisions and activities on society and the environment, through transparent and ethical behavior (ISO SR Domestic Committee, 2011).

ISO26000 outlines seven principles, which are important perspectives that each organization should base on to fulfill its social responsibility, and based on these principles, organizations should address the seven core subjects. The seven core subjects are organizational governance, human rights, labor practices, the environment, fair operating practices, consumer issues, and community involvement and development. Organizations are not required to address all seven core subjects. They should review their own efforts and focus on areas where they are lacking or where problems are occurring.

The second is about chemical substances in products. Two European regulations have had a major impact on the management of chemical substances in products in the supply chain. The European ELV Directive refers to the End-of-Life Vehicle (ELV) Recycling Directive (2000/53/EC), which came into effect in 2000. The European ELV Directive aims to prevent the generation of waste from vehicles, to promote the reuse and recycling of ELVs, and to improve the environmental protection capabilities of ELV processors. The objectives of the Directive are to achieve high recycling rates, to establish a collection network and to reduce the use of environmentally hazardous substances. In terms of the recycling rate, the recyclability rate has been made a requirement for type certification of new vehicles. As for the reduction of environmentally hazardous substances, the use of lead, cadmium, mercury, and hexavalent chromium is prohibited in principle (EUR-Lex, 2000).

The European REACH Regulation is the "Regulation on the Registration, Evaluation, Authorization and Restriction of Chemicals (EC No 1907/2006)", which came into force in 2007 and aims to minimize the impact of chemical substances on humans and the environment and to clarify corporate responsibility for chemical substance management. In addition to the designation and restriction of use of chemical substances by the government, companies themselves are required to identify the chemical substances they use or contain, conduct risk assessments, register, and report them to the government, and disclose information. As a result, substances manufactured or imported into the European Union and substances in preparations must be registered, and products and parts must be notified of substances of very high concern and information must be disclosed. The European REACH Regulation clearly requires corporate responsibility for the management of chemical substances, and companies are obliged to identify, and risk assess the chemical substances used and contained in their products and to manage them throughout the supply chain (EUR-Lex, 2006).

These European regulations have triggered the management of chemical substances in products throughout the supply chain and have had a significant impact. To comply with these regulations, not only automobile manufacturers but also all companies in the supply chain must act.

The third is about conflict minerals. In the Democratic Republic of the Congo (DRC), many people died in the conflict in the 1990s due to massacres and other causes. Although the conflict is believed to have ended, armed groups have taken effective control of mines and continue to use the minerals they extract as a source of funds by forcing residents to work. In response to these events, measures are being taken in various countries.

In the United States, The Dodd Frank Wall Street Reform and Consumer Protection Act (Dodd-Frank Act) was passed (adopted in August 2012, effective in 2013). It includes a "conflict mineral resources provision" that requires companies that use minerals (tin, tantalum, tungsten, and gold) produced in the Democratic Republic of Congo and surrounding areas to register and report to the US Securities and Exchange Commission (SEC) (Japan Electronics and Information Technology Industries Association, 2018).

Also in the EU, the Regulation 2017/821 on Conflict Mineral Resources became applicable on 1 January 2021. This regulation requires due diligence to ensure that the procurement of mineral resources does not contribute to human rights abuses. It applies to EU smelters and importers of tin, tantalum, tungsten and gold from "conflict and high risk areas", which is a different area of application from the US. These conflict minerals laws require companies to clarify how they relate to human rights issues and to act responsibly (EUR-Lex, 2017).

Minerals such as tin, tantalum, tungsten, and gold are used in a variety of products, including automobiles. Therefore, it is essential for the automotive industry to act on a global scale, and companies that make up the supply chain must act, respect human rights, and pay attention not to be complicit in human rights violations and conflicts.

## MANAGEMENT METHODS OF AUTOMOBILE MANUFACTURERS

In this section, the author will confirm the management methods used by Japanese automobile manufacturers in addressing CSR-related items throughout their supply chains.

Green purchasing is a method used by automobile manufacturers to promote environmental initiatives in their supply chains. Green purchasing means adding environmental initiatives to the terms and conditions of transactions, evaluating suppliers based on QCD+E (Quality, Cost, Delivery, and Environment), and selecting suppliers. To understand the specific matters that automobile manufacturers are working on, this chapter will look at Nissan's green purchasing efforts as an example (Figure 1).

In the current situation where various environmental problems such as climate change, environmental pollution, and depletion of materials and energy resources are expanding, Nissan believes that it is necessary to share its purchasing policy and environmental philosophy with suppliers of parts and materials that make up automobiles, and to promote activities to reduce environmental load such as quality control and material management throughout the supply chain. It also states that the requirements of the

*Figure 1. Requirements in Nissan's green purchasing.*
*Source: (Nissan Motor Co., Ltd, 2021)*

| NISSAN GREEN PURCHASING GUIDELINE |
|---|
| · Climate change |
| $CO_2$ emissions reduction throughout the value chain |
| · Resource dependency |
| Proactive efforts by suppliers in individual recycling activities and the use of recycled materials |
| · Air quality |
| Development on VOC, Odor reduction and compliance with standard |
| · Water scarcity |
| Water reduction throughout the value chain |
| · Enhancement of business foundation |
| Enhancement of Environmental Impacting Substance Control for Environmental Compliance |
| Establishment and Use of an Environmental Management System |
| Management of Environment-Impacting Substances |
| Management of environmental impacts through vehicle life cycle and proactively propose environmentally efficient solutions |
| Environment impact reduction with supplier |

"Nissan Green Purchasing Guidelines" are essential for the realization of a sustainable mobility society and sustainable corporate management. Nissan believes that by working with suppliers to reduce the environmental impact of their products, Nissan and its suppliers will be able to build a growing win-win relationship and increase their competitiveness in the global market(Nissan Motor Co., Ltd, 2021).

Suppliers doing business with Nissan are required to address five environmental requirements (climate change, resource dependency, air quality, water resources, and enhancement of business foundation) and to report to Nissan.

1. In the area of "climate change", suppliers are required to promote efforts to reduce $CO_2$ emissions from products, services, and corporate activities in order to achieve carbon neutrality. Companies are required to promote the reduction of $CO_2$ emissions through the supply chain by using technologies that lead to weight reduction of parts and improvement of fuel efficiency of vehicles, and energy-saving facilities in production.
2. In the area of "resource dependence", suppliers are required to actively promote their own recycling activities and the use of recycled materials. Nissan is promoting "closed-loop recycling" activities in which scrap materials generated from production activities and materials collected from end-of-life vehicles are reused during production. Therefore, the company considers the recycling activities and use of recycled materials independently implemented by suppliers to be important. By doing so, we aim to reduce our dependence on newly mined resources and minimize the negative environmental impact of resource extraction. In addition, they are expected to give priority

to the use of recycled materials in all materials, promote the development and adoption of new recycled materials, and continue to cooperate on proposals to promote the use of recycled parts in after-sales services.

3. In the area of "air quality", there is a need to reduce vehicle emissions and create a comfortable air environment in the cabin to protect human health and reduce the impact on the ecosystem. There is a need to promote the development of technologies to improve the air quality environment inside the cabin, and to reduce VOC (Volatile Organic Compounds & Carbonyl Compounds) generated in the production of vehicles.
4. In the area of "water resources", efforts to reduce water consumption are required. To promote the reduction of water consumption in the entire supply chain, companies are required to reduce water consumption by installing facilities that lead to the reduction of water consumption, such as recycling of wastewater in factories.
5. "Enhancement of business foundation" requires further enhancement of environmental management. The three specific requirements are as follows (a: Enhancement of Environmental Impacting Substance management for Environmental Compliance, b: Management of environmental impacts through vehicle life cycle and proactively propose environmentally efficient solutions, and c: Environment impact reduction with supplier).
    a. "Enhancement of Environmental Impacting Substance management for Environmental Compliance" includes the establishment of an environmental management system, such as obtaining ISO14001 or equivalent external certification, the appointment of an environmental manager, the management of tier2 and tier3 suppliers to ensure that products are delivered in compliance with all requirements of the guidelines, the provision of information on LCA, and the reduction of environmental issues in cooperation with suppliers. Suppliers are also required to respond to audits, manage chemical substances in accordance with the laws and regulations of each country, and deliver products and materials in compliance with the laws and regulations of each country and Renault-Nissan technical standards for chemical substance reduction.
    b. "Management of environmental impacts through vehicle life cycle and proactively propose environmentally efficient solutions" requires the provision of environmental data during manufacturing. Nissan uses LCA as a method to quantitatively evaluate not only fuel consumption and exhaust emissions during driving, but also the environmental impact at all stages of the life cycle, from the mining of raw materials necessary for manufacturing to manufacturing, transportation, and disposal. The company is required to cooperate in submitting the necessary data for this purpose.
    c. "Environment impact reduction with supplier" requires suppliers to cooperate with surveys on climate change and water, and to provide data and other information to understand the status of their environmental management and the results of their activities, and to promote improvements. The suppliers are also required to reduce $CO_2$ emissions and water consumption through their own supply chains.

In this way, suppliers doing business with Nissan are required to comply with a variety of environmental requirements and report the status of their efforts to Nissan. Since many of the requirements are not something that each supplier can address on its own, they work together with tier2 and tier3 suppliers to deliver products that comply with all the requirements of the guidelines. Suppliers are evaluated based on their performance, and if any violation of the guidelines occurs, strict action is taken in accordance with internal rules.

To meet the requirements of the automobile manufacturers, the tier1 suppliers need to implement the same initiatives with their tier2 and tier3 suppliers. Therefore, tier1 suppliers, as well as automakers, will develop their initiatives upstream of the supply chain by making it a condition of doing business with tier2 and tier3 suppliers, and as a result, the entire supply chain will be able to respond. The tier1 supplier, not the automaker, is responsible for the management of the tier2 and tier3 upstream suppliers.

The automakers are extending this method of developing environmental initiatives to other CSR-related items. Next, the author will check the supply chain management methods of CSR-related items of the three major Japanese automakers.

Honda has issued "Honda Supplier Sustainability Guidelines", "Honda Green Purchasing Guidelines", and "Honda Product Chemical Substance Management Standards" to promote sustainability with its suppliers. Through these guidelines, Honda is expanding its CSR-related initiatives, such as reducing environmental impact, throughout its supply chain. Honda selects the most appropriate suppliers for parts and raw materials based on QCDDE (Quality, Cost, Delivery, Development, and Environment) as well as human rights, labor, safety, compliance, risk, and information protection. The company selects the most appropriate suppliers. Suppliers whose improvement plans and other efforts are judged to be insufficient are considered for continuation of business (Honda Motor Co., Ltd, 2018a, 2018b).

Toyota has issued "Supplier CSR Guidelines" and "Green Purchasing Guidelines" to work with its suppliers. Based on these guidelines, suppliers are expected to steadily implement their own initiatives, and then expand these initiatives to tier2 and subsequent suppliers, so that the guidelines will permeate the entire supply chain and be put into practice. It is also assumed that there may be a review of the business relationship if events that violate the guidelines are discovered, and no improvement is seen (TOYOTA MOTOR CORPORATION, 2012, 2016).

Nissan has issued "Renault-Nissan Supplier CSR Guidelines" and "Nissan Green Purchasing Guidelines" in order to build a sustainable supply chain. The company has also formulated a "Global Mineral Sourcing Policy" to address conflict mineral purchasing and requires suppliers to thoroughly manage all minerals procured from conflict areas and high-risk areas. Based on these guidelines, Nissan is working with all its suppliers to promote sustainability initiatives. In the event of a violation of the guidelines, strict action is taken in accordance with internal rules, and efforts are made to prevent recurrence. In addition, tier1 suppliers are responsible for the management of tier2, tier3, and subsequent upstream suppliers, and are required to work with tier2, tier3, and subsequent upstream suppliers to ensure that delivered products comply with all requirements of the Guidelines (Renault Nissan PURCHASING ORGANIZATION, 2015; Nissan Motor Co., Ltd, 2020, 2021).

In this way, Japanese automobile manufacturers' supply chain management in terms of CSR uses the following methods: (1) create guidelines and communicate the items and contents of initiatives, (2) make the status of initiatives a condition and evaluation item for transactions, and (3) require management responsibility on the upstream side.

## THE JAPAN AUTO PARTS INDUSTRIES ASSOCIATION (JAPIA)

The Japan Auto Parts Industries Association (JAPIA) is an organization dedicated to addressing various issues related to auto parts, developing the auto parts industry, and contributing to economic develop-

*Figure 2. Organization of JAPIA's committees*
*Source: (Japan Auto Parts Industries Association, 2021a)*

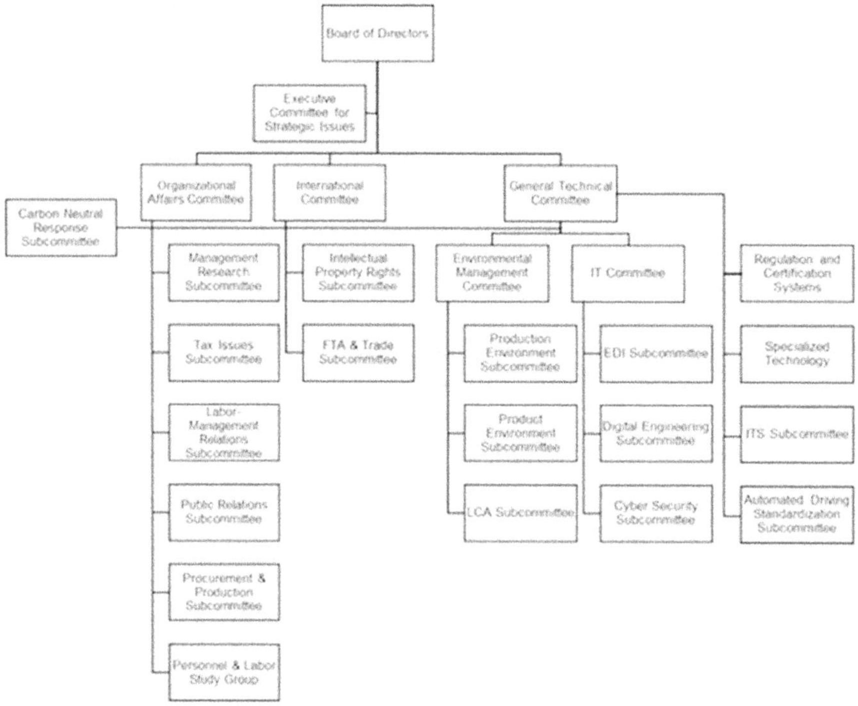


ment and the improvement of the lives of the people. The main activities of JAPIA are the production, distribution, import and export of auto parts, and various other surveys, research, and publications of statistical research materials related to auto parts. Its members consist of corporations engaged in the development, manufacture, or processing of automotive parts (including software and other important components) and corporations engaged in other businesses closely related to the manufacture of automotive parts and the automotive parts industry.

Figure 2 shows the organization of the committees of JAPIA. A committee is an organization for investigating and researching the matters it aims to address. Under each committee are subcommittees, and under each subcommittee are subcommittees. The following is a list of committees and their contents that are responsible for CSR-related items, the subject of this paper's research (Japan Auto Parts Industries Association, 2021a).

1. The Management Research Subcommittee of the Organizational Affairs Committee holds seminars on corporate initiatives and experts on ESG management and plays a role in promoting understanding among member companies. In addition, the working group compiles case studies on compliance issues and shares the results with member companies to raise the level of compliance.
2. The Procurement and Production Subcommittee of the Organizational Affairs Committee collects information on regulatory trends in various countries with the aim of reducing the burden on parts suppliers in the Conflict Minerals Survey and works with related organizations to improve survey methods (entry procedures, tabulation tools, etc.).

3. The Production Environment Subcommittee of the Environmental Management Committee is responsible for responding to the strengthening of environmental regulations related to production activities by periodically collecting and analyzing information on laws and regulations and collecting and developing examples of waste and water resource improvements to promote the Voluntary Environmental Action Plan and respond to the strengthening of environmental regulations in each country.
4. The Product Environment Subcommittee of the Environmental Management Committee has been collecting information and analyzing the impact on the industry to respond to the strengthening of chemical substance regulations, to grasp the trend of global strengthening of chemical substance regulations, and to submit requests as an industry in cooperation with related organizations. In addition, we are operating a substance survey tool to respond to the survey and management of chemical substances in products.
5. The Life Cycle Assessment (LCA) Subcommittee of the General Technical Committee is working to add functions, integrate, and update standard data for calculation tools to assess the environmental impact of products and services, and to standardize assessment methods using LCA.
6. The Carbon Neutral Response Subcommittee works to understand the actual situation and needs of member companies to support their efforts to achieve carbon neutrality, and works in cooperation with the government, the Japan Automobile Manufacturers Association (hereinafter, this is called " JAMA"), and other related organizations.

The members of these committees and their sub-committees mainly consist of employees of member companies. In this way, JAPIA is making various efforts in its committees and subcommittees for the benefit of its member companies.

## RESPONSE TO CSR-RELATED ITEMS IN JAPIA

This section will check for compliance with JAPIA's CSR-related items (CSR, conflict minerals, chemical substance management, and data sheet support).

The first is JAPIA's support for CSR. Compared to automobile manufacturers, many suppliers, especially tier2 and tier3 suppliers, are small in scale and lack management resources such as personnel, technology, funds, and knowledge, making it difficult for them to promote environmental measures and CSR-related initiatives.

Considering this situation, to support its member companies, JAPIA has been working to achieve a total of three objectives: (1) to foster a common understanding of CSR, which is essential for promoting CSR throughout the supply chain, (2) to enable each member company to clarify problems in the status of its own CSR initiatives, and (3) to make improvements in the future. "CSR Guidebook" and "CSR Check Sheet" were developed in 2008. These were improved and revised in 2010 as tools for expanding CSR into the supply chain.

JAPIA's "CSR Guidebook" is intended to be used as a guideline for each company's CSR activities and to help raise the level of the entire auto parts industry. In addition, "CSR Check Sheet" is designed to visualize the current status of CSR activities and to be used by each company for improvement activities.

The target fields and contents of the "CSR Guidebook" are based on the current trends in CSR promotion in Japan and overseas, and the guidebook identifies 30 items in 8 fields where member companies are expected to clarify and improve problems. The contents are based on ISO26000, and furthermore, it considers the characteristic of the industry as JAPIA. The ideal state of each field is presented, and the items and contents of efforts are further described(Japan Auto Parts Industries Association,2010a).

1. In the area of "safety and quality", the ideal is to produce and provide safe and high-quality products and services in a safe manner, and to continue to earn the trust and satisfaction of customers. The items are a) providing products that meet customer needs, b) providing appropriate information on products, c) ensuring product safety, and d) ensuring product quality.
2. In the area of "Human Rights and Labor" is to respect the human rights of employees and to continue to value each and every one of them. The items to be addressed are a) elimination of discrimination, b) respect for human rights, c) prohibition of child labor, d) prohibition of forced labor, e) wages, f) working hours, g) dialogue and consultation with employees, h) safe and healthy working environment, and i) human resource development.
3. In the area of "Environment" is to continue activities in consideration of the global environment in order to grow in harmony with the environment. The items are a) environmental management, b) reduction of greenhouse gas emissions, c) prevention of environmental pollution of air, water, soil, etc., d) resource conservation and waste reduction, and e) chemical substance management.
4. In the area of "compliance" is to comply with the laws and regulations of each country and region, and to strive to act in a socially sensible manner. The items are a) compliance with laws and regulations, b) compliance with competition laws, c) anti-corruption, d) management and protection of confidential information, e) export transaction control, and f) protection of intellectual property.
5. In the area of "information disclosure" is to continue to disclose corporate information in a fair and proactive manner. The item is disclosure of information to stakeholders.
6. In the area of "risk management" is to strive to prevent risks before they occur, and to take prompt and appropriate action when they do occur. The items are risk management system, and formulation of business continuity plan.
7. In the area of "social contribution" is to continue contributing to society in order to coexist with society. The item is Contribution to the local community.
8. In the area of "Development of the company and business partners" is that the company correctly understands the importance of CSR, and develops and confirms CSR within the company and with business partners. The items are the structure and development of CSR activities within the company, and the structure and development of CSR activities from the company to its business partners.

The "CSR Check Sheet" is a self-diagnostic tool to help companies understand their strengths and weaknesses. For each of the eight areas of the "CSR Guidebook", questions are asked from the following five perspectives: (1) legal and regulatory requirements, (2) systems, (3) prevention, (4) awareness-raising, and (5) actual conditions. The questions were not response-oriented, i.e., do you have a system to deal with problems when they occur, but proactive, i.e., do you have policies, systems, rules, and procedures in place to ensure thorough implementation within the company? The results of each company's self-diagnosis are tabulated and visualized on a radar chart, and for each item, the following priorities are set for improvement: (1) top priority reform, (2) upgrading, and (3) maintaining the status quo (Japan Auto Parts Industries Association, 2010b).

In this way, JAPIA is helping suppliers to develop a common understanding of CSR, clarify problems, and guide improvements through the development of the "CSR Guidebook" and "CSR Check Sheet".

The second is to address conflict minerals. In response to conflict minerals, automakers are working to develop company management system to conduct due diligence processes, strive to identify and assess risks in the supply chain, manage risks by implementing risk management plan, monitor and track progress, and report on supply chain due diligence.

To ensure that the human rights measures implemented by automobile manufacturers, especially those related to the investigation of conflict minerals, cooperation, and efforts on the part of suppliers that make up the supply chain are indispensable on a global scale.

In response to this situation, JAPIA has been working with JAMA and other related organizations to develop and improve survey methods (entry procedures, tabulation tools, etc.), collect information on regulatory trends in each country, and provide information to member companies to achieve the following two objectives: (1) to reduce the burden on suppliers with respect to the Conflict Minerals Survey, and (2) to promote the survey with efficiency and transparency.

The Conflict Minerals Survey materials and tools currently available to suppliers include (1) questionnaires, (2) the social significance and necessity of the survey, (3) survey implementation manuals (summary and detailed versions), (4) tabulation tools, (5) tabulation tool operation manuals, and (6) FAQs (Japan Auto Parts Industries Association. 2021b).

The third is chemical substance management initiatives. Laws and regulations for the management of chemical substances contained in products have begun to be formulated and enforced in various countries around the world. Therefore, companies are required to comply with the laws and regulations of each country.

JAPIA established the Environmentally Hazardous Substance Working Group in 2003 to respond to the European ELV Directive, and the Subcommittee for Chemical Substance Management in 2007 and the Subcommittee for REACH Regulation in 2009 as an organization to respond to the European REACH Regulation. In 2010, the Subcommittee for Chemical Substance Control was established under the Product Environment Subcommittee with the aim of responding to global regulations on chemical substances. The following four tasks are handled by the Subcommittee for Chemical Substance Management of JAPIA (Japan Auto Parts Industries Association, 2017b).

1. Grasping the trend of laws and regulations in each country. Each member company of the Executive Committee shares information on chemical-related laws and regulations in each country that may have an impact on the automotive industry, including Japan (Chemical Substances Control Law), North America (U.S. TSCA, U.S. state laws, Canadian laws), Europe (REACH, ELV, RoHS), China (ELV, RoHS, VOC, etc.), India (ELV), and South Korea (ELV). Each member company is investigating and analyzing the impact of these laws and regulations.
2. This is the scrutiny of regulated substances. For chemical substances that are about to be regulated by the laws and regulations of various countries, we analyze the degree of their impact on the automotive industry at an early stage to disseminate information and reduce unnecessary surveys on their inclusion. These impact analysis activities also serve the purpose of checking requests for surveys from automobile manufacturers, and by disseminating information to JAMA companies, we aim to reduce the burden of survey work throughout the supply chain.
3. Information gathering and liaison activities through participation in external organizations. We participate in the activities of ACEA (European Automobile Manufacturers Association) and

CLEPA (European Auto Parts Association) in Europe to understand the laws and regulations and the stance of the industry, and to reflect the opinions of JAPIA.

4. Holding briefing sessions for JAPIA members. In addition to explaining the new regulations at the briefing sessions, specific methods of responding to the regulations are shared and information is disseminated to the entire supply chain so that the automotive parts industry can take a unified response (Japan Auto Parts Industries Association, 2017b).

The fourth is data sheet support. Surveys in the supply chain for the management of chemical substances in products started with the response to the European ELV Directive enforced in 2000. The European ELV Directive requires the reduction of lead, mercury, cadmium, and hexavalent chromium and the calculation of recycling rates, and substance survey operations became necessary to respond to the directive.

Initially, each automaker and supplier were responsible for complying with the European ELV Directive, but with the development of the International Material Data System (IMDS) in Europe, the Japanese automotive industry recognized the need to discuss substance surveys. The IMDS system response time was very slow, and it took a whole day to input data for a single small part, and there were many small and medium-sized suppliers at that time who could not support IMDS due to problems with the Internet environment.

In addition, in 2003, there were a wide variety of data sheets, and suppliers were required to respond to multiple data sheets, which meant that many different types of data had to be created for the same part. In addition, upstream in the supply chain, suppliers had to respond to their own requirements, resulting in an enormous number of man-hours. At that time, the response rate for material surveys was only about 50% over a two-year period, even for automakers with significant purchasing power (Japan Auto Parts Industries Association, 2017a).

Under these circumstances, JAPIA started to work on the standardization of substance survey operations, especially the promotion of survey methods using Excel format. Standardization of Material Data Sheet (MDS) was carried out in three areas: (1) standardization of MDS format, (2) standardization of substances to be controlled, and (3) standardization of entry rules. To achieve this, JAPIA conducted many coordination negotiations with JAMA and IMDS officials. As a result, the "JAMA/JAPIA Unified Data Sheet" was completed in 2006, which enabled the search and selection of materials and chemical substances in Japanese, even for those who had difficulty in dealing with English, and greatly contributed to the promotion of the survey work. In the following year, 2007, an automatic input function of ingredients was added to many JIS metal materials. The "JAMA/JAPIA Unified Data Sheet" has greatly contributed to the standardization of internal systems and operations of each company in the supply chain, and this has enabled smooth material investigation operations in the supply chain (Japan Auto Parts Industries Association, 2020).

As a result, it was found that IMDS and "JAMA/JAPIA Unified Data Sheet" were sufficient for the investigation of substances in the supply chain as before. The only function added in response to REACH was to display substances of very high concern in italics.

It is expected that China ELV will be issued not only in Europe but also in China, and a substance survey tool for confirming non-inclusion of banned substances and calculating recycling rates has become necessary. In China, the CAMDS (China Automotive Material Data System) was developed as an original tool for this purpose, and it was expected that a huge amount of data re-input work would occur when the demand for compliance with CAMDS became full-scale. However, suppliers were unable to take effective measures individually due to the unclear timing of the start of regulations and system specifications.

JAPIA thought that it was essential to draw information from CATARC (China Automotive Technology and Research Center Co., Ltd.) and to obtain its cooperation to deal with this problem. In June 2015, China's ELVs were promulgated, and automakers and other suppliers have increased their demands for CAMDS compliance. In response to this, JAPIA provided a variety of user support services, including the provision of a Japanese version of the CAMDS manual, guidance on the use of CAMDS, the establishment of a help desk to provide support on how to correct errors after running the conversion tool, and the launch of a special support site on the JAPIA website. JAPIA has been actively involved in the development of CAMDS since its inception, setting up a conversion tool between the "JAMA/JAPIA Unified Data Sheet" and CAMDS, and has greatly contributed to the streamlining and standardization of substance investigation operations at Japanese suppliers(Japan Auto Parts Industries Association, 2018).

After several years of transition work, the "JAMA/JAPIA Unified Data Sheet" became the "JAPIA Sheet" (successor to the JAMA/JAPIA Unified Data sheet) in 2020. In 2015, JAMA and JAPIA started to discuss the future of substance investigation in the Japanese automotive industry based on the advantages and disadvantages of the "JAMA/JAPIA unified Data Sheet" and IMDS. Automakers have decided to switch to IMDS. However, Japanese suppliers have decided not to make a sudden switch to IMDS as a component industry. This is because the "JAMA/JAPIA Unified Data Sheet" is well-established, and the tier1 supplier can modify it to meet slightly different requirements for the same product. In order to prevent confusion in the substance investigation work, it was decided that suppliers could choose between IMDS and "JAPIA sheets".

In order to reduce the number of man-hours required to resolve errors in the JAPIA Sheet, (1) liaison with JAMA (agreement to significantly improve the basic functions of the JAMA Sheet/JAPIA Unified Data Sheet) and (2) liaison with the IMDS Steering Committee (improvement of the IMDS rules and system) were conducted to improve data interchangeability between the "JAPIA Sheet" and IMDS. On the supplier's internal IT system, the EXCEL-based "JAPIA Sheet" is often more cost effective and efficient for data handling than the web-based IMDS, and it is also easier to learn. The "JAPIA Sheet" prevents missing information, delays in delivery, and the generation of original forms, and maintains order in the investigation of substances in the supply chain (Japan Auto Parts Industries Association, 2020).

As a result, the three standards essential for maintaining order in the survey of chemical substances in products ("format", "substances to be controlled", and "entry and operation rules") have been realized. And the accuracy of surveys and the efficiency of survey operations throughout the supply chain have been improved.

As a result, unlike other industries, the supply chain of the Japanese automotive industry is currently able to complete surveys for the management of chemical substances in products using only two tools: the interchangeable IMDS and the "JAPIA Sheet".

## IMPLICATION

Due to CSR and the enforcement of various laws and regulations, the companies that make up the supply chain of the automotive industry have been required to take various measures. In addition, automobiles are made up of tens of thousands of parts, many of which are procured from suppliers rather than manu-

*Figure 3. Process of initiatives*

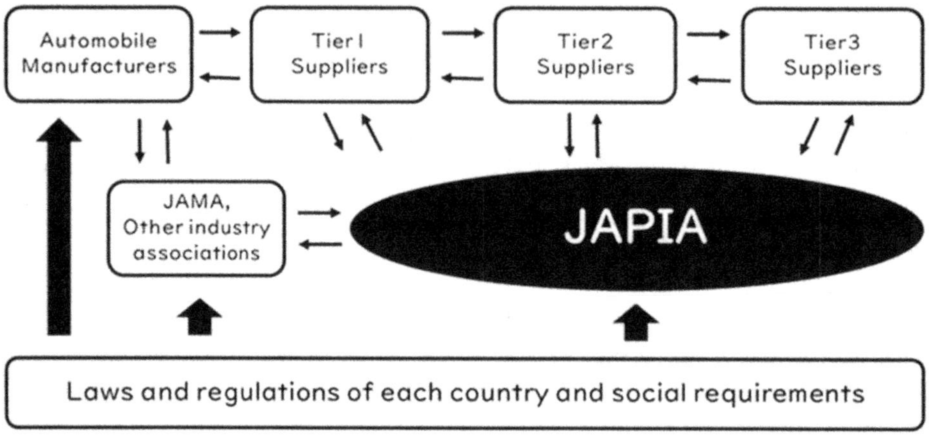


factured by the automakers themselves. Therefore, many CSR-related issues could not be completed only by the efforts of each company but were essential to be addressed by the entire supply chain.

As a way of dealing with this issue, automakers located downstream in the supply chain adopted a method of spreading their efforts throughout the supply chain by making the status of their efforts a condition of doing business. Suppliers, on the other hand, did not respond individually, but rather JAPIA first addressed the underlying issues. The suppliers then acted based on JAPIA's initiatives (Figure 3).

JAPIA played an extremely important role in implementing a variety of CSR-related initiatives in the supply chain. To promote overall CSR initiatives, JAPIA formulated the "CSR Guidebook" and the "CSR Check Sheet", which are indispensable for promoting CSR throughout the supply chain, and fostered a common understanding of CSR, thereby raising the level of initiatives throughout the automotive parts industry.

About conflict minerals, the company collaborated with related organizations, created, and improved survey methods (entry procedures, tabulation tools, etc.), collected information on regulatory trends in each country, and provided information to member companies to reduce the burden on suppliers regarding surveys and ensure efficiency and transparency.

About the substances to be controlled, the company grasped the trend of laws and regulations in each country, carefully examined the regulated substances, collected information, and conducted liaison activities by participating in external organizations, and held briefing sessions for member companies.

As for the data collection for the management of chemical substances in products, the company created a data sheet and standardized the substance survey work of each supply chain company in three ways: (1) unification of the format of the data sheet, (2) unification of the substances to be managed, and (3) unification of the entry rules. They also provided user support to member companies. By these means, the accuracy of the survey and the efficiency of the survey work in the entire supply chain were improved.

Thanks to the efforts of JAPIA, suppliers can respond to various requests from automakers, and as a result, the entire supply chain is able to respond. JAPIA's initiatives are indispensable and extremely important in ensuring that supply chain initiatives are carried out properly.

## CONCLUSION

This chapter has discussed the role and importance of the supplier-side industry association (JAPIA) in developing CSR initiatives in the supply chain in the Japanese automobile industry.

The establishment of a sustainable supply chain is an extremely important issue for companies. If a CSR-related problem arises in one company in the supply chain, it will affect the sustainability of the entire supply chain. Therefore, not only the company itself but all companies in the supply chain need to work on CSR.

When undertaking any kind of initiatives in the supply chain, it is fundamental that each company in the supply chain makes its own efforts, and that the companies with which it has business relationships cooperate and collaborate with each other.

However, when it comes to CSR initiatives in the Japanese automotive industry, JAPIA's initiatives come before those of its suppliers, and thanks to JAPIA's various CSR-related initiatives, suppliers can respond smoothly and reliably to the demands of automakers. JAPIA's efforts are playing a pivotal role in building a sustainable supply chain.

## FUTURE RESEARCH DIRECTIONS

It is important to build a sustainable supply chain and achieve corporate sustainability as well as social and environmental sustainability. In this chapter, we have looked at CSR initiatives in the supply chain of the Japanese automotive industry. There are two possible research directions that will be important for future CSR initiatives in the supply chain of the automotive industry.

The first is the importance of international comparison. Global procurement has been progressing in the automotive industry. Procurement is conducted under different inter-firm relationships, such as keiretsu relationships in Japan and competitive purchasing in Europe and the United States. Comparing how supply chains are managed in terms of CSR under such different intercorporate relationships may lead to new insights.

Second is the importance of responding to changes in industrial structure. In the automotive industry, electrification such as electric vehicles is being promoted. As a result of electrification, product architecture will shift from integral to modular, and the industrial structure is expected to change from a vertical to a horizontal division of labor. It is necessary to consider what kind of CSR-related supply chain management methods are suitable for the changing industrial structure.

By conducting research from the above two points of view, we can obtain knowledge that will be important for the construction of a sustainable supply chain in the automotive industry.

## REFERENCES

EUR-Lex. (2000). *End-of life vehicles Directive 2000/53/EC.* Retrieved April 5, 2022, from https://eur-lex.europa.eu/legal-content/EN/TXT/?uri=celex%3A32000L0053

EUR-Lex. (2006). *Reach Regulation (EC) No 1907/2006.* Retrieved April 5, 2022, from https://eur-lex.europa.eu/legal-content/en/ALL/?uri=CELEX%3A32006R1907

EUR-Lex. (2017). *EU Regulation, 2017*(821). Retrieved April 5, 2022, from https://eur-lex.europa.eu/legal-content/EN/TXT/?uri=celex%3A32017R0821

Hatakeyama, H. (2011). Jidoshasangyo niokeru sapuraiya tono kankyotorikumi – Nissan jidosha wo chushin ni [The environmental action with the supplier in the Japanese automotive industry: Case study on Nissan Motor]. *Journal of Sustainable Management, 11*(1).

Hatakeyama, H. (2014). Nihon jidoshasangyo niokeru seihinganyukagakubusshitsukanri – unyomen deno torikumi nitsuite [The management of chemical substances in products in the Japanese automotive industry: Focusing on the operational aspect]. In Hiroshima Papers on Society and Culture (Vol. 13). Hiroshima University Graduate School of Integrated Arts and Sciences.

Honda Motor Co. Ltd. (2018a). *Honda gurin purchasing gaidorain* [Honda Green Purchasing Guidelines]. https://www.honda.co.jp/sustainability/supply-chain/pdf/green-guideline.pdf

Honda Motor Co. Ltd. (2018b). *Honda sapuraiya sasutenabiriti gaidorain* [Honda Supplier Sustainability Guidelines]. https://www.honda.co.jp/sustainability/supply-chain/pdf/supplier-sustainability-guidelines.pdf

ISO SR Domestic Committee. (2011). *Nihongoyaku ISO26000:2010 - shakaitekisekinin ni kansuru tebiki* [ISO26000:2010—Guidance on social responsibility]. Japanese Standards Association.

Japan Auto Parts Industries Association. (2010a). *CSR gaidobukku* [CSR Guidebook]. https://www.japia.or.jp/files/user/japia/work/csrbcp/csr/CSR_H22guidebook.pdf

Japan Auto Parts Industries Association. (2010b). *CSR chiekkushito* [CSR Check Sheet]. https://www.japia.or.jp/files/user/japia/work/csrbcp/csr/CSR_H22check.pdf

Japan Auto Parts Industries Association. (2017a). *JAPIA kankyojohoshi* [Activity of Environmental Management Committee] (Vol. 1). https://www.japia.or.jp/files/user/japia/work/kankyo/EMC_vol1_20170926.pdf

Japan Auto Parts Industries Association. (2017b). *JAPIA kankyojohoshi* [Activity of Environmental Management Committee] (Vol. 2). https://www.japia.or.jp/files/user/japia/work/kankyo/EMC_vol2_20180206.pdf

Japan Auto Parts Industries Association. (2018). *JAPIA kankyojohoshi* [Activity of Environmental Management Committee] (Vol. 3). https://www.japia.or.jp/files/user/japia/work/kankyo/EMC_vol3_20180928.pdf

Japan Auto Parts Industries Association. (2020). *JAPIA kankyojohoshi* [Activity of Environmental Management Committee] (Vol. 7). https://www.japia.or.jp/files/user/japia/work/kankyo/EMC_vol7_20210216.pdf

Japan Auto Parts Industries Association. (2021a). *Jigyokeikakusho* [Business Plan FY2021]. https://www.japia.or.jp/files/user/japia/japia/R3keikaku.pdf

Japan Auto Parts Industries Association. (2021b). *Konfurikutomineraru chosashiryo* [Conflict Minerals Survey Data]. https://www.jama.or.jp/c_minerals/index.html

Japan Electronics and Information Technology Industries Association. (2018). *Study Group on Conflict Minerals Purchasing*. Retrieved November 19, 2021, from https://www.jeita.or.jp/japanese/pickup/category/180802-02.html

Kurokawa, F. (2017). *Jidoshasangyono ESGsenryaku* [ESG Strategies for the Automotive Industry]. Chuokeizai-Sha Holdings, Inc.

Negishi, K. (2019). Nihon jidoshamekano CSR to jizokukanonakaihatsumokuhyo ni kansuru yobiteki kosatsu [Japanese Automobile Manufacturer's Corporate Responsibility and Sustainable Development Goals]. In Corporate Research Reports, (34). Chuo University Institute of Business Research.

Nissan Motor Co. Ltd. (2020). *Gurobarukobutsuchotatsunikansuru hoshin* [Nissan Minerals Sourcing Policy]. https://www.nissanglobal.com/JP/DOCUMENT/PDF/SR/Minerals_Sourcing_Policy_j.pdf

Nissan Motor Co. Ltd. (2021). *Nissan gurinchotatsu gaidorain* [Nissan Green Purchasing Guidelines]. https://www.nissanglobal.com/JP/DOCUMENT/PDF/SR/Nissan_Green_Purchasing_Guildeline_2021_j.pdf

Renault Nissan Purchasing Organization. (2015). *Runo Nissan sapuraiya CSR gaidorain* [Renault Nissan Corporate Social Responsibility Guidelines for Suppliers]. https://www.nissanglobal.com/JP/DOCUMENT/PDF/SR/CSR_Alliance_Guidelines.pdf

Sakuma, T. (2006). *Toyota no CSRsenryaku - sekaikara sonkeisareru kigyono keiei* [Toyota CSR Strategy]. Japan Productivity Center.

Sakuma, T. (2008). *CSRsenryaku no hoteishiki - hondato rikcohno chidosetsu keiei* [Copernican CSR Management]. Japan Productivity Center.

Suga, K., & Ishida, H. (2008). *Nissanno CSRsenryaku - seichoto shinraini motozuku jizokukanoseino keiei* [Nissan CSR Strategy]. Japan Productivity Center.

Toyota Motor Corporation. (2012). *Shiiresaki CSR gaidorain* [Toyota Supplier CSR Guidelines]. https://global.toyota/pages/global_toyota/sustainability/csr/gri/supplier_csr_jp.pdf

Toyota Motor Corporation. (2016). *Gurinchotatsu gaidorain* [Toyota Green Purchasing Guidelines]. https://global.toyota/pages/global_toyota/sustainability/esg/toyota_green_purchasing_guidelines_jp.pdf

## ADDITIONAL READING

Fujii, T., & Mizue, U. (Eds.). (2006). *Gurobaru CSR chotatsu – sapuraichenmanejimento to kigyono shakaitekisekinin* [Global CSR Purchasing - Supply Chain Management and Corporate Social Responsibility]. JUSE Press, Ltd.

Hatakeyama, H. (2010). Gurobaruchotatsuni okeru kankyotaisaku [Environmental measures in global purchasing]. In Chinese Automotive Industry. Maruzen Publishing Co., Ltd.

Hatakeyama, H. (2012). *Nihonjidoshasangyo ni okeru sapuraichen deno kankyotorikumi* [Environmental Initiatives in the Supply Chain of the Japanese Automotive Industry]. Hiroshima University.

Hatakeyama, H. (2015). Gurupukigyokanni okeru kankyomendeno soshikikangakushu – hondano kesu [Inter-organizational learning in environmental aspects among group companies - The case of Honda]. *Journal of Sustainable Management, 14*.

Hatakeyama, H. (2017). Sapuraichenniokeru CSRkanren itotekifuseieno taisaku – mitsubishijidoshakabushikikaisha nempifuseimondai wo jireitoshite [Countermeasures against CSR-Related Intentional Fraud in Supply Chains - A Case Study of falsifying fuel economy tests in Mitsubishi Motors Corporation]. *Bulletin of Institute for Interdisciplinary Studies of Culture, 34.*

Hatakeyama, H. (2019). Fushojino genin haikeini taisuru ninshikino henka – kabushikikaishaSUBARU niokeru ichirenno kanseikensamondai wo jireini [Changing Perceptions of the Causes and Context of Scandals - A Case Study of a Series of Completion Inspection Problems at SUBARU Corporation]. *Bulletin of Institute for Interdisciplinary Studies of Culture, 36.*

Honda Motor Co. Ltd. (2013). *Sapuraiya CSR gaidorain* [Honda Supplier CSR Guidelines]. https://www.honda.co.jp/sustainability/supply-chain/pdf/csr-guideline.pdf

Ichikawa, Y. (2004). *Aratanakisei wo bijinesuchansuni kaeru kankyokeiei senryaku* [Strategies of Environmental Corporate Management for Business Globalization]. Chuohoki Publishing CO., Ltd.

ISO 26000:2010. (n.d.). *Guidance on social responsibility.* Retrieved November 19, 2021, from https://www.iso.org/iso-26000-social-html

Japan Auto Parts Industries Association. (2018). *JAPIA kankyojohoshi* [Activity of Environmental Management Committee] (Vol. 4). https://www.japia.or.jp/files/user/japia/work/kankyo/EMC_vol4_20190215.pdf

Japan Auto Parts Industries Association. (2019a). *JAPIA kankyojohoshi* [Activity of Environmental Management Committee] (Vol. 5). https://www.japia.or.jp/files/user/japia/work/kankyo/EMC_vol5_20191009.pdf

Japan Auto Parts Industries Association. (2019b). *JAPIA kankyojohoshi* [Activity of Environmental Management Committee] (Vol. 6). https://www.japia.or.jp/files/user/japia/work/kankyo/EMC_vol6_20200210.pdf

Japan External Trade Organization. (n.d.a). *European Parliament Adopts Draft Regulation on Conflict Mineral Resources.* Retrieved November 19, 2021, from https://www.jetro.go.jp/biznews/2017/03/3f59b092ac45a22e.html

Japan External Trade Organization. (n.d.b). *Supply Chains and Human Rights.* Retrieved November 19, 2021, from https://www.jetro.go.jp/biz/areareports/2021/7d71c95432ad0c76.html

Kasagi, K. (2010). *Yokuwakaru seizogyono kagakubusshitsukanri - kagakubusshitsukisei wo seizogyono tsuyomini kaeru* [Understanding Chemical Substance Management in the Manufacturing Industry]. OHMSHA, Ltd.

Kawamura,M.(2015). *CSR keiei pafekuto gaido* [CSR Management Perfect Guide]. Wis Works, Inc.

Nissan Motor Co. Ltd. (2021). *Kobutsuchotatsuheno torikumi* [Action for Minerals Sourcing]. https://www.nissan-global.com/JP/DOCUMENT/PDF/SR/Minerals_j.pdf

Seki, M. (2011). *ISO26000 wo yomu* [Read ISO26000]. JUSE Press, Ltd.

Sera, K. (2021). CSR niokeru shakaiseito keizaisei no tsuikyuni kansuru jireibunseki - nihon no jidoshameka wo taishotoshita yobitekikosatsu [Case Study to Pursue Social Performance and Financial Performance in CSR: A Preliminary Consideration for Japanese Automobile Manufacturers]. *The Journal of Contemporary Social Sciences*, (18).

Toyota Motor Corporation. (2021). *Shiiresaki sasutenabiritei gaidorain* [Toyota Supplier Sustainability Guidelines]. https://global.toyota/pages/global_toyota/sustainability/esg/supplier_csr_jp.pdf

## KEY TERMS AND DEFINITIONS

**Chemical Substances in Products:** A chemical substance contained in a product. In the past, the term used to refer to the four substances required to be addressed by the European ELV Directive in the automotive industry, but now it refers to all chemical substances.

**Conflict Minerals:** Refers to mineral resources where human rights violations may be taking place during the mining and refining stages.

**Green Purchasing:** Green purchasing is the evaluation and selection of suppliers based on their environmental measures. The requirements are presented as guidelines, and suppliers are required to comply with them.

**IMDS:** A standardized system for collecting data on materials and substances contained in products. It is the standard material data collection system used worldwide in the automotive industry.

**ISO 26000:** ISO 26000 is an international standard on social responsibility, published in November 2010, which outlines seven principles for fulfilling social responsibility. The seven core subjects are: Organizational Governance, Human Rights, Labor Practices, Environment, Fair Business Practices, Consumer Affairs, Community Involvement and Community Development.

**LCA (Life Cycle Assessment):** A method for measuring and evaluating the environmental impact of a product throughout its life cycle, from procurement of raw materials through production, distribution, use, disposal, and recycling.

**Life Cycle:** Refers to the life cycle of a product, from procurement of raw materials to production, distribution, use, disposal, and recycling.

**Supplier:** A company that manufactures parts or raw materials for automobiles. It does not include automobile manufacturers.

**Supply Chain:** Refers to both the upstream and downstream operations of the target company, and is defined differently from ISO26000.

# Section 3
# Retailing Cases

*Section 3 analyzes the transition in the retailing sector, including distribution, from the view of SCM. The retailing sector is much more flexible and variable than the manufacturing sector due to the less fixed assets. Retailing section is more susceptible to market and technology influences than manufacturers.*

# Chapter 6
# Controlling Bullwhip Effect in Supply Chain by BANDAI Co: Lessons From the Tamagotchi™ Case

**Toru Higuchi**
*Tokyo Seitoku University, Japan*

## ABSTRACT

*This chapter illustrates how the bullwhip effect is exacerbated in the supply chain through the Tamagotchi™ case. BANDAI first introduced Tamagotchi™ to the market on November 23, 1996. It became tremendously popular throughout the world in 1997, touching the hearts of children and young adults globally. While BANDAI sold 40 million of the first Tamagotchi™ worldwide by March 1999, this effort ended in tragedy. BANDAI suffered from the tragic boom and bust. The causes can be summarized as follows: a demand forecast failure and an immature SCM including a wrong response which created an excessive boom and sudden bust. BANDAI learned from this severe lesson in launching new series and managing the company and supply chain. Instant and substantial ways to cope with the bullwhip effect exaggerated in a supply chain will be proposed.*

## INTRODUCTION

This chapter illustrates the typical phenomenon that arises from the supply chain features. Supply chains consist of members at different stages in the supply chain. Therefore, the movements of the supply chain are chaotic. Supply chains often face unexpected results.

BANDAI Co. was founded in 1950 by Naohara Yamashita. From the beginning, BANDAI has been in the business of *Dreams and Creation*. BANDAI is famous for products featuring popular characters, such as POWER RANGERS™, GUNDAM™, and DIGIMON™. They call themselves the *Happy Moment Creator*. In the 2020 fiscal year, their global sales were 118.8 billion Japanese yen (US$ 1.1 billion at US$ 1 = 110 yen), and their ordinary profit to sales ratio was 8.8%. BANDAI classifies its products into six divisions: character goods for kids, vending machine products, tabletop and computer game cards, foods and snacks, apparel, and others.

DOI: 10.4018/978-1-7998-9800-9.ch006

*Figure 1. Picture of Tamagotchi™*
*Source: (BANDAI Co. https://www.bandai.co.jp/corporate/history/)*

BANDAI introduced *Tamagotchi™* to the market on November 23, 1996, in Japan. *Tamagotchi™* is a compound word derived from *Tamago*, egg, and Watch. It was a handheld egg-shaped computer game that was the first simulation game of the digital pet class (Figure 1). This game aims to *raise Tamagotchi™* through several distinct phases of its life cycle. The interface is straightforward and involves taking care of the *Tamagotchi™* by feeding, providing medical care and attention, and other treatment activities.

*BANDAI* forecast their initial target sales volume for the *Tamagotchi™* at 300,000 units by the end of 1996 (the first six weeks of its release) in the domestic market. *Tamagotchi™* became so rapidly and widely popular that *BANDAI* sold about 450,000 units and abruptly ran out of stock. Immediately, BANDAI expanded its manufacturing facilities tremendously and broadened its sales territory worldwide on May 1, 1997. BANDAI won the Ig Nobel Prize for Economics in 1997. Although BANDAI's sales increased sharply in 1997, the operating profit to sales ratio was not sustainable (Figure 2). Furthermore, after the *Tamagotchi™* boom, their sales volume declined sharply. BANDAI announced they had 16 billion yen (US$ 123 million at US$ 1 = 130 yen) in after-tax losses between the fiscal year 1998 and 1999.

BANDAI's damage was so severe that they were hesitant to launch a new *Tamagotchi™* product until 2004. It took about five years to recover from the bust. However, BANDAI learned valuable lessons from their misfortune, and they adopted appropriate measures to ensure the success of future product releases. The *Tamagotchi™* series has regained its former status as a top product in BANDAI today.

*Figure 2. Financial performance of BANDAI during 1993-2000*
*Source: (Annual report of BANDAI Co.)*

## BACKGROUND

*Tamagotchi*™ was a typical example of a supply chain member crippled by an exaggerated short-term bullwhip effect. The bullwhip is a short whip used to control cows. The tip moves much faster than the handle because the tip is lighter and more supple than the handle. The bullwhip effect is the exaggerated negative effect within the supply chain, which slight variations in customer demand may cause. The upstream members, such as manufacturers, might experience much more damage than the downstream members from these variations.

Lee et al. (1997a) explained the cause of this phenomenon as the result of successive decision-making with various lags at each stage of a multi-echelon system that might amplify the order swings. The downstream activities can respond to the demand change much more quickly than the upstream activities, such as assembly and production. Retailers and wholesalers can respond to the demand change through the placement of orders and by altering the shelf and reserve spaces. On the other hand, manufacturers need to plan for production facilities and prepare for steady operations, and their batch sizes are much bigger than those of retailers. Sometimes, it takes a long time to build assembly lines, hire and train employees, and secure materials and parts. The upstream members are more inflexible regarding quantity and less responsive to the market than the downstream members.

*The information transferred in the form of orders tends to be distorted and can misguide upstream members in their inventory and production decisions. In particular, the variance of orders may be larger than that of sales, and the distortion lends to increase as one moves upstream. (Lee et al. 1997a).*

Supply chains need dynamic interactions and coordination between adjacent layers, as mentioned by the Council of Supply Chain Management Professionals (CSCMP). However, successive decision-making at each stage might create *a* severe information distortion within a supply chain. Lee et al. (1997b) illustrate how information distortion is created and aggravated in a supply chain. The various lags such as decision time and lead time and the tricks or deceptive practices might reduce the reliability of the information and distort it (explained further below). Under severe information distortion, it is impossible to forecast demand accurately.

Ballou (1992) holds that successful supply chains must be very responsive to customer needs and requirements. However, very short life cycles, such as the boom and bust, generate another problem, as exemplified by the *Tamagotchi*™ case. Paich & Sterman (1993) built a System Dynamics model to simulate a case of the boom and bust and demonstrated that word of mouth, marketing, and learning curve effects can fuel rapid growth, often leading to overcapacity, price war, and bankruptcy. In the boom phase, the demand for a product overgrows so that the supply cannot keep up with it. This disparity leads to the shortage game. The shortage game is one of the significant causes of the bullwhip effect being more powerful and inducing the boom and bust. It starts when a top-rated product runs out of stock. This stock shortage enforces consumers to go to multiple retailers to check their inventory. In this situation, it is typical for consumers to place multiple orders with various retailers. Retailers and wholesalers see a spike surge in demand and, therefore, misjudge the situation because of the phantom or inflated demand.

Higuchi & Troutt (2004) made a simulation model analyzing the short-term bullwhip effect exaggerated in a supply chain based on the first *Tamagotchi*™, from 1997 to 1999. The model consisted of three echelons: the market, retailer, and factory, expressed as the result of the interactions between them. After the *Tamagotchi*™ boom and bust, BANDAI changed its strategy and operations.

## PRODUCT DEVELOPMENT OF *TAMAGOTCHI*™

Akihiro Yokoi created the concept of Tamagotchi™. He was a former employee of BANDAI, and in 1986 he established a planning company, WiZ CO., LTD. He brought the *Tamagotchi*™ project to BANDAI. It approved the project and appointed Aki Maita as the point person. Akihiro Yokoi and Aki Maita jointly promoted the project and were later called the father and mother of *Tamagotchi*™.

The concept of *Tamagotchi*™ was very innovative and original. It was developed and produced in accordance with the following Japanese toy industry's five formulas for success *(Tanaka 1997):*

1. Ride the Boom;

During a boom, a large number of products can be sold without the usual need for advertising. It might be even easier to ride the boom with celebrities, food, and pets. In this case, BANDAI chose a pet and introduced the virtual pet, *Tamagotchi*™.

2. Narrow Down Target Segmentation;

The target should be narrowed down to acquire stable customers through advertising efficiency first. After initial success, companies spread product popularity beyond their first target segmentation. BANDAI narrowed down the target to high school girls initially and then extended it to other segments beyond age and gender.

3. Listen to Customer Feedback;

It is essential to understand customer needs and expectations. *Tamagotchi*™ developers surveyed the impressions and perceptions of high school girls on the street. With this knowledge, they were able to develop an excellent product.

4. Choose the Proper Advertising Media;

The Tamagotchi™ case demonstrated the power of word-of-mouth and social media. Advertisements on mass media such as television and newspapers were costly but were mainstream in the mid-1990s. BANDAI instead chose word-of-mouth and social media because they were confident in Tamagotchi™'s ability to attract buyers even in a distressed financial situation, despite a budget too small to advertise on mass media.

5. Do not Overproduce;

It is essential to avoid excessive unsold inventory and thereby maintain product value. Out of stock is an indication of product popularity and that product becomes trendy and in demand. On the other hand, unsold products convey a bad image and have a negative financial impact. BANDAI made a production plan of about 80% of the demand forecast.

The concept of *Tamagotchi*™ was unique in the mid-1990s. It was the first simulation game of the virtual pet class that pioneered its market. The purpose of the *Tamagotchi*™ game is to raise a virtual chick through its life cycle in a dedicated machine. Contrary to their counterparts, *Tamagotchi*™ was not a high-tech machine. It was a 4-bit small, handheld machine, while other mainstream home video games were 64-bit machines (Yamagata 1998).

The game of *Tamagotchi*™ *was* well planned and user intuitive. The interface is straightforward and interactive. In the game, one earth day was equal to about one year for *Tamagotchi*™. *Tamagotchi*™ would change its appearance several times before it reached its adult form. If *Tamagotchi*™ could survive more than ten gam*e* years, players were considered to have done an excellent job.

The official instructions for *Tamagotchi*™ from BANDAI can be summarized as follows. *Tamagotchi*™ was said to have come from space. *Tamagotchi*™ would wake up from its year-long sleep by removing the insulating sheet from the side of the machine. Then, a pulsating egg would appear after setting the communication screen to adjust the time difference between Tamagotchi's planet and earth. Finally, *Tamagotchi*™ would hatch in about 5 minutes.

*Tamagotchi*™ needs to be taken care of by its players. If they can take proper care of *Tamagotchi*™, it will be on a path to good growth. Players need to diligently feed and play with *Tamagotchi*™, control the lighting, and address issues of health and excretion by monitoring a health meter and pressing the appropriate buttons. If *Tamagotchi*™ is treated very well, it will become adorable and live long. Lacking the proper care, *Tamagotchi*™ will quickly die or grow into an unattractive alien.

*Tamagotchi*™ games have an egg shape and a *c*onvenient portable size. They composed a Large-Scale Integration (LSI) chip and a Liquid Crystal Display (LCD) with a sound function. The majority of them run on two small LR44 batteries.

According to Nemoto (2000), the original plan was to sell 60,000 units at 2,980 yen (US$ 22.9 at US$ 1 = 130 yen). *Tamagotchi*™ was much more advanced than similar products; keyholder-type portable game machines priced at about 1,500 yen (US$ 11.5 at US$ 1 = *130 yen). BANDAI* was concerned that their planned price for *Tamagotchi*™ might be twice as high as other similar products. Therefore, they decided to price the *Tamagotchi*™ at 1,980 yen (US$ 15.2 at US$ 1 = 130 yen), which was just a little higher than competitive products. To reduce the price, they realized they should increase the initial target volume to 300,000 units, considering the experience curve effect of the Large-Scale Integration (LSI) chip (Yokoi, 1997, pp. 96-101). The experience curve effect implies that additional production costs will be reduced in conformity with cumulative production. In the Japanese toy market, 300,000 units were considered a high initial sales target.

## BOOM AND BUST

### Beginning of the Boom

BANDAI started selling *Tamagotchi*™ on November 23, 1996, in Japan. As previously stated, BANDAI did not advertise *Tamagotchi*™ on TV (Anonymous, 1997) because they wanted to save on advertising costs. Furthermore, they were expecting a word-of-mouth effect. The mid-1990s was just before the Internet became widespread. BANDAI hoped that *Tamagotchi*™ would become a hot topic among high school girls and that *Tamagotchi*™ would be a hit.

The initial target sales volume for the *Tamagotchi*™ was 300,000 by the end of 1996 (for the first six weeks). It was very difficult to accurately predict demand for *Tamagotchi*™ because it was the first simulation game of the virtual pet class. The Word-of-mouth effect is also difficult to predict. In addition, although the price difference with other keyholder-type portable game machines was small, *Tamagotchi*™ had a considerable potential to become an epoch-making product.

Tie-in with magazines starting before the sale of *Tamagotchi*™ on November 23, 1996, BANDAI distributed numerous *Tamagotchi*™ to the editors of teen magazines, resulting in more than 20 magazines featuring *Tamagotchi*™. Around the same time, some young people became active on SNS and acted as influencers, popularizing the products to others. *Tamagotchi*™ became a big topic before the sales even began.

On November 23, 1996, *Tamagotchi*™'s sales were so strong that inventories were quickly depleted. It was featured on TV numerous times and posted heavily on homepages by users or buyers of *Tamagotchi*™. The *Tamagotchi*™ boom thus began in November 1996.

BANDAI initiated many measures to deal with out-of-stock events promptly. They released product inventory to retailers in a timely manner, and *t*hey quickly increased production through overtime work. *Tamagotchi*™ was manufactured in China and was typically transported to Japan by ship. BANDAI switched transportation modes from ship to air. Their transportation costs increased by 100 million yen (US$ 769.2 thousand at US$ 1 = 130 yen) over budget (Nihon Keizai Shimbun, 1997, May 13). BANDAI sold 450,000 units of *Tamagotchi*™ by the end of 1996. They succeeded in selling 150% of their initial target of 300,000.

Despite the costly measures undertaken by BANDAI, a terrible out-of-stock condition persisted. From the SCM view, the adjustment ability of manufacturing departments is much slower and smaller than that of sales departments because the former may have many physical constraints, especially regarding their facilities, raw material, and assembly components. It is true that the manufacturing department needs to react quickly when the need arises, but sometimes they are reluctant to expand manufacturing ability because they might have an excessive ability. It takes months or even years to adjust manufacturing ability either for expansion or reduction.

## Acceleration of the Boom

*Tamagotchi*™ became popular so widely and rapidly that BANDAI sold about 450,000 units in 1996 and unexpectedly suffered inventory depletion. BANDAI made two fatal mistakes in its demand forecasting. First, *Tamagotchi*™ became a hot topic beyond the target audience immediately after the product release and subsequent sales. Although BANDAI had narrowed down their target audience to high school girls, other segments outside of the predetermined age and gender parameters were interested in *Tamagotchi*™.

To make matters worse, many consumers wanted to buy more than one *Tamagotchi*™ because it was available in various assortments of colors (Figure 1). Nonetheless, specific colors such as gold and silver products were scarce and created a fandom of exclusivity. Tamagotchi™ was so simple and cheap that players could buy and play two or more at the same time. Repeat buyers and multiple-unit owners appeared in the very early stage of sales.

The second mistake in demand forecasting was that the word-of-mouth effect was far more than expected. Tamagotchi™ might be the first case to illustrate the power of social media. The novelty and commentaries of *Tamagotchi*™ quickly spread within and across generations and genders. This meant that Tamagotchi™ was significantly undervalued and that the production system was woefully insufficient.

Hundreds of people endured long lines all night long in the middle of winter at toy stores that had much smaller inventories than the demand required. BANDAI was worried that stories of people freezing to death might start appearing. At the boom's peak, Bandai received about five thousand customer complaints by phone a day regarding the shortages (Yokoi, 1997, pp. 122-126.). It is natural that those who could not find a *Tamagotchi*™ at one store then tried to purchase it at another store. Some customers visited a few stores or made phone inquiries to check the availability and arrival dates of inventory on order. The severe shortages of *Tamagotchi*™ created *a* vast number of duplicate phantom demands.

This was not just a consumer issue but rather an entire supply chain issue. Store clerks had to deal with people waiting in long lines and customer complaints in-store and by phone. Store personnel dealt with the massive actual demand as well as the phantom demand. Following customary store policy, all they could do was to place an order equal to the sum of the sizable actual need and the enormous phantom demand. However, they could only obtain a fraction of their order because the overall manufacturing capacity was seriously incapable of fulfilling the actual demand, much less the additional enormous phantom demand.

Stores that sold *Tamagotchi*™ vigorously complained to the sales staff in charge and management of BANDAI. In the 1990s, small and medium-sized toy stores were the leading players in distribution. The sales staff needed to remain on good terms with those stores. The sales staff demanded impossible increases in production. However, increased production was not feasible at that time because it was very difficult to procure liquid crystal parts. It was hopeless to expect increased production, especially in a short time. BANDAI asked some suppliers to increase their manufacturing facilities immediately.

Meanwhile, stores decided to order quantities that were significantly inflated to get more and sell more. They were only mildly concerned about the risk of accumulating excess inventory because they could simply stop ordering and then sell excess inventory over a more extended period. BANDAI sales department began receiving inordinately large orders and demanded a significant expansion of manufacturing capacity.

*Figure 3. Summary of boom phase*

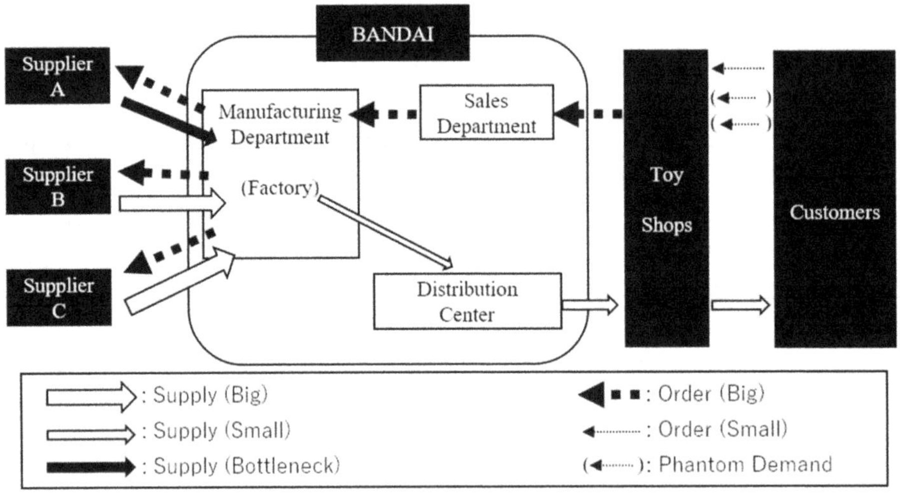


The main points of the boom phase are illustrated in Figure 3. Most customers could not easily purchase *Tamagotchi*™. To get it, they had to visit many toy stores or call them to inquire about availability. Toy shops could not ascertain demand accurately and were receiving smaller numbers of *Tamagotchi*™ than what they had ordered. Subsequently, they decided to place unrealistically large orders greater than the actual demand they perceived to be true or accurate because their customers were overly eager to obtain the product. The sales department tried to fulfill these inflated orders as much as possible because they wanted to remain on good terms with the toy shops and because, of course, they wanted to maximize their sales. As a result, they asked the manufacturing department to fulfill orders through overtime work. The overtime work was limited and expensive. In addition, as can be seen in Figure 3, supplier A was the cause of a paralyzing bottleneck. The weakest part of the supplier chain determined the overall supply speed and efficiency. To improve turnaround time, the manufacturing department reluctantly asked suppliers to expand their facilities. NEC (Nippon Electric Company, Limited.) decided to increase the microcontroller price for the 4-bit machines. The manufacturing department and the suppliers wanted to keep costs low and avoid the possible risk of the manufacturing facilities becoming too burdensome. The shortage continued until the expansion of facilities was completed.

This demand boom, which outpaced BANDAI's fulfillment ability, reduced the number of potential customers. Some of the original target customers were frustrated by *Tamagotchi™'s* extreme popularity and resultant shortages and decided to forego any purchase. Some bought products at exorbitantly high prices at auction. *Others* bought poor quality and expensive knockoffs. These imitations harmed the reputation of the product and brand as well as future demand. However, at that time, BANDAI could not afford to deal with these problems.

## End of the Boom

While Tamagotchi™ was in short supply, they gradually yet tremendously upgraded their manufacturing facilities. BANDAI sold 4 million Tamagotchi™ by the end of March 1997. To add to this accomplishment, they planned to expand their sales worldwide on May 1, 1997. Finally, they decided to expand their manufacturing facilities to produce 2 to 3 million units per month by July 1997, knowing the high risk of overstocking and excess capacity could be an issue.

BANDAI started selling *Tamagotchi*™ in North America, Europe, and Asia in May 1997. The total overseas sales volume of *Tamagotchi*™ exceeded 2.4 million by the end of October 1997. BANDAI won the Ig Nobel Prize for Economics in 1997. Despite these grand feats, however, they began to suffer from oversupply.

A critical turning point for BANDAI was the decision to expand their manufacturing facilities to produce *2-3* million units per month by July 1997. They made the decision when they were experiencing severe shortages. They needed several months to significantly expand their manufacturing capacity because of the construction period, increasing their operations to hire and train. These issues were substantial constraints over the long term. There was also an alarming plan to increase production capacity to 10 million units per month in September 1997 by establishing a new factory in Indonesia.

Soon after BANDAI expanded their manufacturing capability to 2-3 million units per month in July 1997, they, unfortunately, encountered a sharp decline in demand for some reasons. The first and main reason was the enormous phantom demand disappeared as the persistent shortage of the product was resolved. In the late 1990s, very few companies had started using a POS System (Point of Sales System) to forecast demand. The phantom demand was identified after all prospective customers were able to buy the desired quantity of *Tamagotchi*™. It became clear that BANDAI had made a colossal mistake in demand forecasting, including the overseas market.

Secondly, *Tamagotchi*™ quickly lost its novelty and cachet after it became overly saturated in the market. The game was so simple that it became monotonous to play for months. Even if some players briefly owned multiple units, very few would replace them. Some people owned multiple units even when the product was out of stock, but the number of such people had decreased sharply since its availability became widespread. Originally, *Tamagotchi*™ was not something that inspired repeat buying.

Third, BANDAI lost some of its target customers. Although they narrowed down the target of *Tamagotchi*™ to high school girls, it also became trendy in other segments outside of the original targeted age and sex. Once the boom waned, some of them were left behind, and they lost interest in *Tamagotchi*™. After the shortage of the product was resolved, BANDAI started advertising in newspapers and TV directed toward high school girls in November 1997. They used the pretext of commemorating the 1st anniversary of the release of *Tamagotchi*™ as the reason for their advertising. Their advertising campaign had little effect because their market was already saturated, and there remained little interest in *Tamagotchi*™ among other prospective buyers.

Finally, swayed by the *Tamagotchi*™ boom, BANDAI became complacent and failed to protect the reputation of *Tamagotchi*™. They worked diligently to increase production and mollify complaints about the shortages. Still, due to financial constraints, they could not take measures against pirated products and the resale of genuine products at exorbitant prices. After the *Tamagotchi*™ boom and bust, even BANDAI no longer mentioned *Tamagotchi*™ for many years.

After the *Tamagotchi*™ boom, its sales volume declined sharply. BANDAI announced they had 16 billion yen (US$ 123 million at US$ 1 = 130 yen) in after-tax losses in fiscal 1998 ending March 1999. This was mainly because a monumental number of *Tamagotchi*™ were left unsold. This case illustrates how BANDAI was overly influenced by the bullwhip effects exaggerated by information distortion in the supply chain. BANDAI incurred damages so severe that they remained apprehensive about launching a new *Tamagotchi*™ product until 2004.

## CAUSES OF TRAGIC BOOM AND BUST

BANDAI succeeded in producing a blockbuster product, *Tamagotchi*™. However, they suffered from a tragic boom and bust. The genesis of their misfortune was an unreliable demand forecast and the erroneous SCM such as the wrong responses that created an excessive boom and sudden bust. The causes for their boom and bust are summarized here.

BANDAI made a mistake in forecasting the shift of the demand. They expected *Tamagotchi*™ to be a big hit before its release, but their demand forecast was seriously inaccurate in the demand increase and decline phase. In the increase phase, BANDAI misunderstood the range of their customer base and diffusion speed. Although BANDAI chose high school girls as the initial target of *Tamagotchi*™, it became trendy beyond the selected age and sex parameters right after its release. It meant that the number of potential customers had increased many times over. Figure 4 shows the Japanese population pyramid in 1998. For example, if a company chose teen girls as their target customer, the number of potential users would be 7.3 million, represented as two horizontal bars with vertical stripes. Suppose the target group is expanded up to age 24 and includes both females and males, indicated by the black areas with white dots. In that case, the number of potential users increases to 24.3 million, 3.3 times the original number. At this point, BANDAI should have reassessed its plan of action.

Initially, BANDAI decided not to advertise via mass media. They induced customers to buy it through word-of-mouth. The late 1990s was the transition period during which the Internet had become more prevalent. The younger generation started sending and receiving information on SNS and homepages. The effect of word-of-mouth was much stronger and more pervasive than BANDAI had expected. If the diffusion speed were faster, the resultant peak demand would be larger and more acute. Consequently, *Tamagotchi*™ unexpectedly ran out of stock, which triggered a severe shortage game.

Let's examine the simple example that follows. A company formulates a plan to produce and sell 200,000 products every month, part of an entire life cycle of 12 months[1]. They start production one month before the product release because the stores and wholesalers need an initial inventory. Figure 5 shows the result of the initial plan. They produce 200,000 pieces, but they do not sell them in month 0. Therefore, they have 200,000 pieces in stock at the beginning of month 1. During months 1-11, they produce and sell 200,000 pieces each month. They have 200,000 units in stock at the beginning of each of the months 1-12. The 12th month's production is sold and not replenished, so there remains no stock at the end of that month or at the beginning of the 13th month. This means that the product is finished, and preparation for the following product begins.

In the real world, plans often do not happen as intended. Figure 6 shows the results of a case where the diffusion speed is three months shorter than the initial plan and where the company involved is able to increase production by 25%. It is a very fortunate situation where the spread speed has remained uniform, and a 25% increase in production is possible without capital investment or time lag. Assuming the total demand is constant, monthly demand would increase to 266,667 pieces. Inventory is steadily decreasing due to the difference between sales and production. Fortunately, they would not have any backlog and lost sales avoided through overtime, which would raise costs. Although the amount of total sales is the same as the initial plan, *the profit might be smaller.*

Sometimes, companies cannot increase their manufacturing ability because of a bottleneck. Employees, parts, facilities, contacts with suppliers, and regulations can all cause a bottleneck. Figure 7 shows a situation where inventory runs out at month 4. Backlog then occurs in month 5. The maximum cumulative backlog is 400,000 at month 10. By this time, the backlog might be beyond the possibility of

*Figure 4. Japanese population pyramid in 1998*
*Source: (e-Stat. https://www.e-stat.go.jp/)*

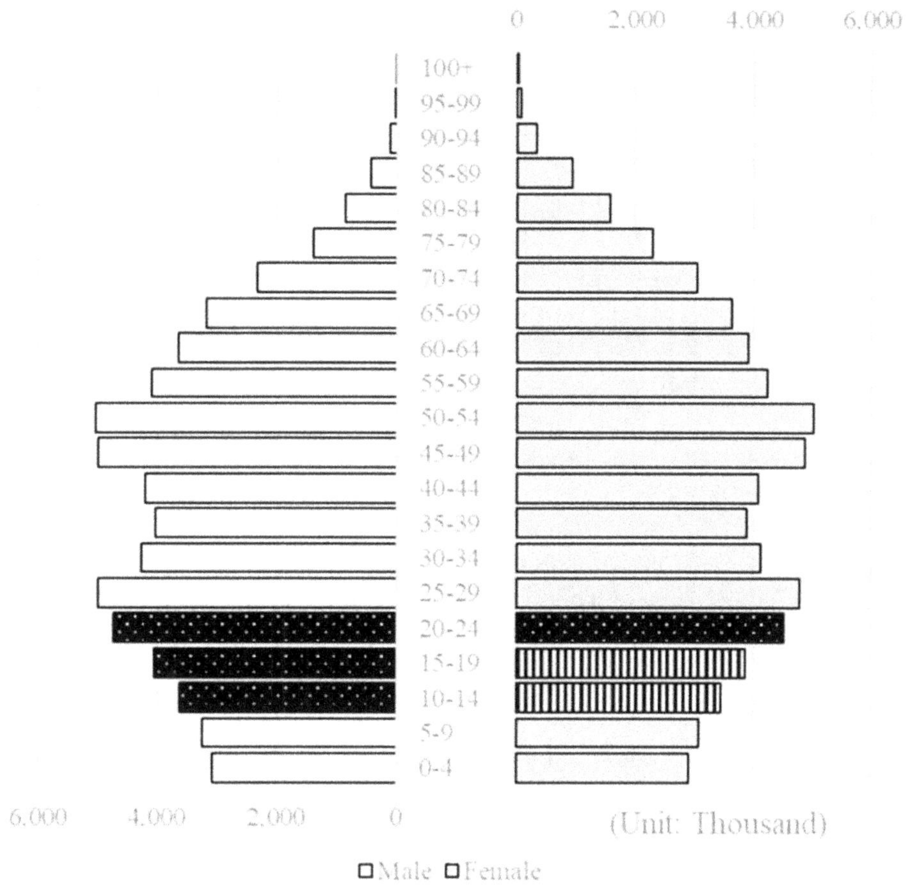


being resolved in a timely manner. Delayed fulfillment of the backlog might not satisfy actual purchase orders because of the long wait time. In addition, this backlog might create a phantom demand. A company might decide to make a major investment in their facilities. It would be essential for companies to manage this type of backlog. Although a company might still lose some customers, they would incur considerable costs, including phantom demand.

From the SCM viewpoint, supply chains are multi-echelon systems composed of many companies and departments from upstream to downstream. Conflicts of interest often arise in supply chains because the situation of each company, department, or employee is different. For example, while sales departments want to maximize sales, manufacturing departments tend to pursue efficiency. As the direct point-of-contact for their business, sales departments are concerned with building valuable relationships with current customers. On the other hand, manufacturing departments tend to make decisions considering their long-term effects and economy of scale because they are working with huge batch sizes. In addition, each company in a supply chain wants to maximize its profit by selling at a high price and buying at a low cost.

*Figure 5. Initial plan*

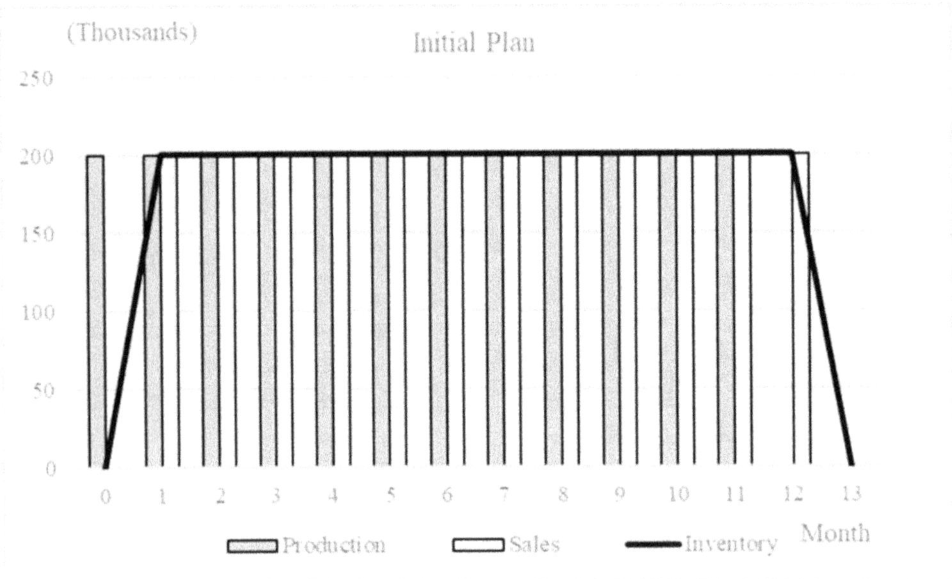


An undeveloped SCM made the situation worse. Under a situation where supply was completely incapable of keeping up with demand. However, they took every possible measure to produce as much as possible. The sales department wanted to sell as much as possible and remain on good terms with toy stores and customers. On the other hand, it took several months to expand manufacturing facilities and purchase a great number of various vital parts. This meant that the severe shortages continued for many months and threatened to cause a variety of problems, including instances of the shortage game, coun-

*Figure 6. 25% increase in production (9 months)*

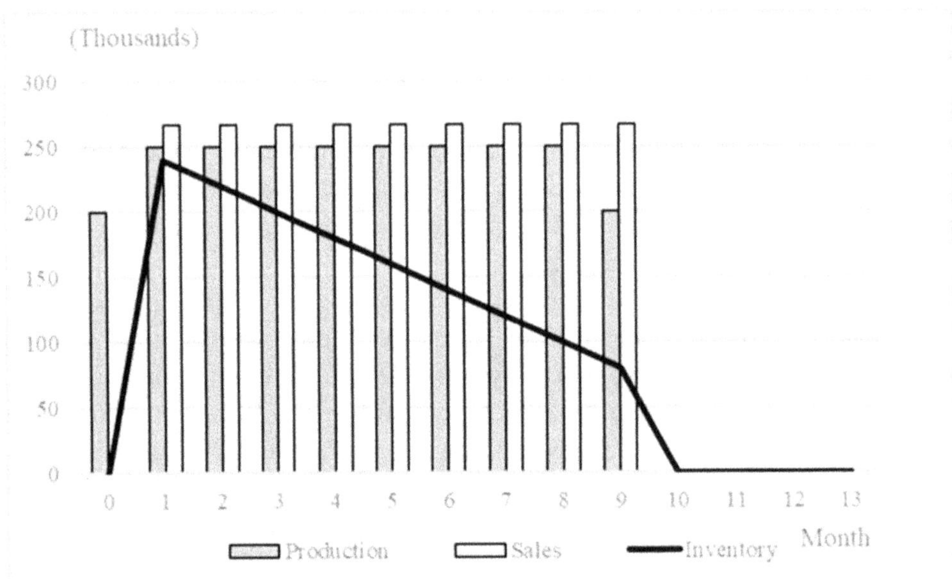

*Figure 7. No increase in production (9 months)*

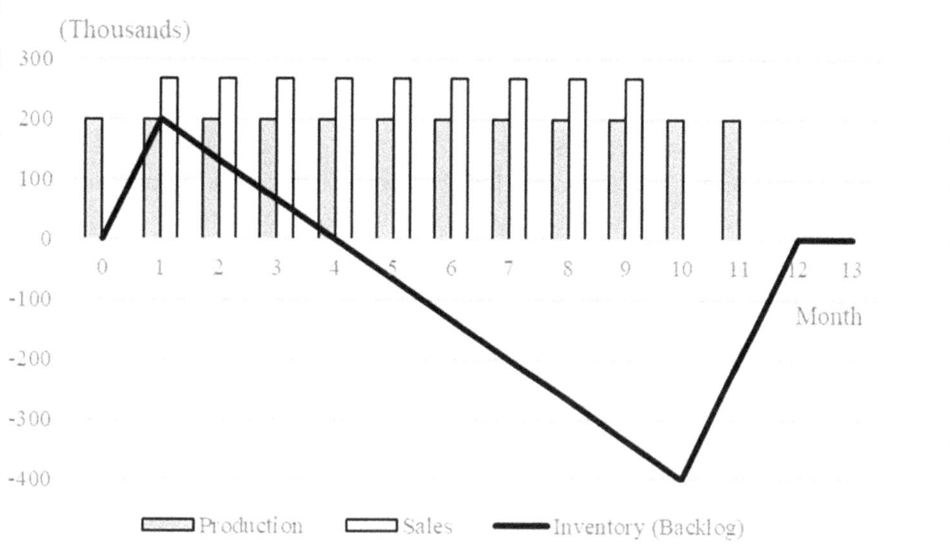


terfeit issues, and even actual crimes like theft. Numerous robberies and aggravated assaults committed in order to acquire the toy were reported to the police. BANDAI could not take robust measures to stop the shortage game by suspending sales or controlling demand until they had produced enough stock.

In addition, multi-echelon systems might create time lags in knowing about the latest market demand and extreme phantom demand order swings in the supply chain. In the late 1990s, BANDAI did not have an effective information system to share sales data and orders among its suppliers and stores. This exacerbated the distortion of information and the shortage game. As a result, BANDAI had increased their manufacturing capacity too much; 2 - 3 million units per month in July 1997. They also made a fatal mistake in predicting the maximum demand.

BANDAI posted an extraordinary loss of 6 billion yen (US$ 462 million at US$ 1 = 130 yen) due to the disposal of unsold *Tamagotchi*™, and in total had 16 billion yen (US$ 123 million at US$ 1 = 130 yen) in after-tax losses in fiscal 1998 ending March 31, 1999. BANDAI and some of its suppliers made a considerable capital investment in factory facilities in 1997. They had to stop and dispose of the product line and a massive number of unsold *Tamagotchi*™ due to oversupply in fiscal 1998. BANDAI and other supply chain members of *Tamagotchi*™ were at the mercy of the boom and bust.

Besides an undeveloped SCM, there were other reasons for this boom and bust. Consumers were capricious, their newfound interest shifting quickly from hot to cold. The product features of *Tamagotchi*™ provoked the consumer's erratic behavior even more. The speed of the Internet's viral spread of *Tamagotchi*™ was much faster than expected and much wider than the intended target. With a more developed SCM, this tragedy could have been avoided.

## SOLUTIONS AND RECOMMENDATIONS

After *Tamagotchi*™'s boom and bust, BANDAI became disaffected with *Tamagotchi*™. The lesson learned at this point was that excessive booms were very alarming, and they soon realized that strong measures needed to be taken to avoid being swayed by them.

There are good examples of a short-term solution for excessive product booms in Japan. The PASMO Card is an IC Card for transportation. The name *PASMO* derives from *pass net* and *more*. This contactless stored value card was launched on March 18, 2007, and it was estimated that 5 million cards would be sold in its first year. However, 3 million were sold in the first month, and inventory was quickly depleted. It took several months to acquire additional IC chips, and the sales of the PASMO Card were suspended from April to September of 2007. This helped to avoid unnecessary confusion. Now, PASMO can be used at about 30 railway companies and close to 80 bus companies.

Another good example is the 100th anniversary of the Tokyo station SUICA Card, which launched December 20, 2014. The SUICA Card was introduced by the East Japan Railway Company in 1994 and is a major IC Card for transportation in Japan. The design of the card was exceptionally beautiful. The East Japan Railway company limited the number of cards to 15 thousand units, the sales location to Tokyo Station only, and the number of tickets that could be purchased to just three per person. A vast number of people flooded Tokyo station on the day of the sale, which resulted in the sale of the card stopping within a few hours of its release before stock ran out. Instead, East Japan Railway Company switched to pre-order sales through the Internet or mail. Finally, East Japan Railway Company sold 4.3 million units *for* 8.6 billion yen (US$ 71.3 million at US$ 1 = 120 yen) and sent them out by mail.

Six years had passed since the *Tamagotchi*™ bust, and people began to experience a feeling of nostalgia for the iconic virtual pet. BANDAI had finally decided to release a new series of *Tamagotchi*™ Plus / Connection on March 20, 2004. Subsequently, BANDAI launched a new series of *Tamagotchi*™ every two to three years. BANDAI used the lessons learned from the *Tamagotchi*™ boom as follows:

1. Introduction of Information System

BANDAI was severely damaged by the exaggerated information distortion that persisted in their supply chain during the *Tamagotchi*™ Boom. In 2000, BANDAI introduced an information system that connected about one hundred toy stores and managed POS (Point of Sales) data. As a result, they quickly determined the exact product inventory status and accurate reservation order information. Later, BANDAI selected 20 stores to analyze market trends in detail. The sharing of information in the supply chain is critical in estimating accurate damage and quickly understanding prevailing market trends.

2. Downsizing Lot Size

Lot sizes in the manufacturing sector are often in the hundreds of thousands. BANDAI has significantly reduced its lot sizes. This results in products being produced more frequently or as required based on current market demand. BANDAI now formulates a shorter-term production plan than before. BANDAI functions better with a more accurate demand picture with the added benefit of introducing an information system.

3. Establishment of Chief Tamagotchi Officer

Prior to launching their new series, BANDAI established the position of Chief Tamagotchi Officer. One of the responsibilities of the Chief Tamagotchi Officer is to make all critical decisions regarding *Tamagotchi*™. Erratic in-house communication and lack of cooperation were known problems during the *Tamagotchi*™ boom. A board member, Takeichi Hongo, was appointed as BANDAI's first Chief Tamagotchi Officer. His duties were to manage product development, the manufacturing process, and sales promotion and promote information sharing inside and outside the company.

4. Narrowing Down Target

BANDAI has now rigorously targeted girls aged 6 to 15 years for the *Tamagotchi*™. They have tried to rein in their aspirations for too large a target area. Instead, they have begun to focus more on planning and stability. They hope that all girls will purchase *Tamagotchi*™ at least once. BANDAI expects *Tamagotchi*™ to become one of their standard products and a staple of their business, rather than a big, short-lived one-hit-wonder. However, BANDAI has intermittently launched new series featuring superheroes that targeted young boys.

5. High Functionality

BANDAI has added various features to keep new *Tamagotchi*™ products fresh and exciting. Previously the way to play the game had become too complicated. Additionally, the game's communication function has been enhanced, connecting game consoles and the Internet. BANDAI introduced new series several times with collaborating cartoon characters and existing chain stores and restaurant chains.

6. Emphasis on Planning

BANDAI began to focus on systematic production and sales. They set the production run of each machine to 1 - 2 years. They also strived to ensure stable and planned sales. As a result, the cost of production and the risk of unsold inventory could be decreased.

However, consumers did not buy as Bandai had planned. After 1996, Tamagotchi sales peaked starting in 2004, 2012, and 2020. The results suggest that Tamagotchi sales will peak every eight years. These peaks were much smaller than the ones that started in 1996 because Bandai has narrowed down its target customers. Few consumers continue to purchase Tamagotchi on a regular basis for a long period of time. For many consumers, buying a Tamagotchi once will be enough. Furthermore, many consumers purchase Tamagotchi because their friends have one, rather than voluntarily. Although Tamagotchi's temporary network externalities have led to Tamagotchi's periodic peaks, Bandai is no longer being swayed by the boom because it has taken the appropriate measures.

## FUTURE RESEARCH DIRECTIONS

Information distortion occurring and then being further exaggerated throughout a supply chain can cause tragedy. To prevent it, information sharing is vital for a collaborative relationship among all supply chain members. It is essential to maintain supply chain profitability and share it among the supply chain members for a collaborative relationship.

It is often difficult for individual companies to respond to unexpected events. In addition, it can be extremely difficult or impossible for a supply chain to respond to unexpected events. Supply chain members are loosely coupled, unlike the Japanese concept of *keiretsu,* where various companies may be linked together as suppliers to each other. They do not have to have a capital or equity relationship. Instead, each member has the core competence to take part in a designated supply chain. The most favorable situation for some companies may not always be the same for others. Future research must create a system to equitably share profits and risks among all members of a supply chain.

## CONCLUSION

A supply chain might not have enough time to make critical adjustments and prosper under a short life cycle, such as experienced with a boom and bust. *Tamagotchi*™''s initial release is a story of tragedy in a supply chain, but BANDAI learned great lessons about SCM through this incident.

A fast or faster product diffusion is not always beneficial. In the product introduction period, steadily diffusion is indeed important. Rapid diffusion might lead to exaggerated peak demand. It is equally important to stabilize demand variations in order to minimize shortages and phantom demands. Sometimes, under solid manufacturing and distribution constraints, adoption and repeat purchases cannot be accurately estimated. In this situation, control of diffusion speed is highly desirable. Without proper management, the supply chain might experience a sizable loss after a boom and bust, as Paich & Sterman (1993) demonstrated.

Phantom demands amplify the peak and intensity of the observable demand. If it takes a long time to detect phantom demands, they tend to grow exponentially. If the information is processed without recognizing the phantom demands at each stage and then used for forecasting actual or future demands, the expected demand will have a greater discrepancy. Lowson et al. (1999) assert that timely and accurate information flows enable a quick and precise response. Corbett et al. (1999) concluded that companies could eliminate the bullwhip effect altogether and ensure ongoing improvement through the more open, frequent, and accurate exchange of information.

Finally, information distortion in a supply chain can start from and be amplified by independent decision-making. Multi-echelon systems tend to create time lags in knowing the latest market demand and recognizing gratuitous yet avoidable phantom demand order fluctuations in the supply chain. A coordinated process is vital to the effective and efficient sharing of information using an appropriate information system to minimize information distortion. Bowersox and Closs have noted that "Coordination is the backbone of overall information system architecture among value chain participants." (Bowersox & Closs, 1996, p.37).

## REFERENCES

Anonymous. (1997). Tamagotchi koukoku senndennhi zero de suta-to sita Tamagotchi ga kokomade ureta riyuu [Tamagotchi The reason why Tamagotchi was sold a lot Without advertising]. *Senden Kaigi, 44*(6), 28–32.

Anonymous. (1997). Salaried man dai 439 wa boom no urade [Salaried worker episode 439, Behind the boom]. *Nihon Keizai Shimbun.*

Ballow, R. H. (1992). *Business logistics management.* Prentice-Hall.

Bowersox, J., & Closs, D. J. (1996). *Logistical management.* McGraw-Hill.

Corbett, C. J., Blackbum, J. D., & Van Wassenhove, N. (1999). Partnerships to improve supply chains. *Sloan Management Review, 40*(4), 71–82.

Higuchi, T., & Troutt, M. D. (2004). Dynamic simulation of the supply chain for a short life cycle product - Lessons from the Tamagotchi case. *Computers & Operations Research, 3*(7), 1097–1114. doi:10.1016/S0305-0548(03)00067-4

Lee, H., Padmanabhan, V., & Whang, S. (1997a). The bullwhip effect in supply chains. *Sloan Management Review, 38*(3), 93–102.

Lee, H., Padmanabhan, V., & Whang, S. (1997b). Information distortion in a supply chain: *The bullwhip effect. Management Science, 73*(4), 546–558. doi:10.1287/mnsc.43.4.546

Lowson, B., King, R., & Hunter, A. (1999). *Quick response.* Wiley.

Nemoto, T. (2000). Dejitaru jidai ni okeru hikari to kage (jou) [Light and shadow of a big Hit product in the digital era]. *Chushou Kigyou to Kumiai, 55*(8), 4–8.

Paich, M., & Sterman, J. D. (1993). Boom, bust, and failures to learn in experimental markets. *Management Science, 39*(12), 1439–1458. doi:10.1287/mnsc.39.12.1439

Tanaka, M. (1997). Tamagotchi kaihatsu no kiseki wo ou [Following the development process of Tamagotchi]. *Nikkei Electronics, 686*, 131–134.

Yamagata, M. (1998). Keiki teimei no genzai, AM sanngyou no genntenn ni tachimodori, aratana asobi no kouchiku wo Pokemon ya Tamagotchi nado no dai boom wo kanngaeru [Under the economic downturn, review the big boom of Pokemon, Tamagotchi, et al. to create new entertainment in the amusement industry]. *Amusement Industry, 27*(1), 204–205.

Yokoi, A. (1997). *Tamagotchi no tannjouki* [Birth record of Tamagotchi™]. KK Best Sellers.

## ADDITIONAL READING

Higuchi, T., & Troutt, M. D. (2004). Dynamic simulation of the supply chain for a short life cycle product - Lessons from the Tamagotchi case. *Computers & Operations Research, 3*(7), 1097–1114. doi:10.1016/S0305-0548(03)00067-4

Lee, H., Padmanabhan, V., & Whang, S. (1997a). The bullwhip effect in supply chains. *Sloan Management Review, 38*(3), 93–102.

Lee, H., Padmanabhan, V., & Whang, S. (1997b). Information distortion in a supply chain: The bullwhip effect. *Management Science, 73*(4), 546–558. doi:10.1287/mnsc.43.4.546

Paich, M., & Sterman, J. D. (1993). Boom, bust, and failures to learn in experimental markets. *Management Science*, *39*(12), 1439–1458. doi:10.1287/mnsc.39.12.1439

## KEY TERMS AND DEFINITIONS

**BANDAI:** A Japanese corporation established in 1950 in the toy industry. BANDAI is famous for products featuring popular characters, such as POWER RANGERS™, GUNDAM™, and DIGIMON™.

**Boom and Bust:** A tragic phenomenon in which a collapse occurs right after the end of a boom. The more enthusiastic the boom over a short period, the greater the damage.

**Bullwhip Effect:** A phenomenon in which upstream members of a supply chain might experience much more damage than the downstream members because of demand variation in the market. The term derives from the bullwhip whose tip moves much more than the handle.

**Information Distortion:** An alteration of information due to multiple interactions within a supply chain. Messages are enhanced or impaired during the interactions between people in different positions with corresponding time lags.

**Multi-Echelon System:** A system that is composed of plural positions. A supply chain is composed of a manufacturer, suppliers, distributors, and others.

**Shortage Game:** An activity whereby people and companies want and order more than they actually need when there is a perceived or real shortage of stock.

*Tamagotchi*™**:** A virtual pet game BANDAI introduced. The first series was introduced in November 1996.

## ENDNOTE

1 This example case is so simple that the result is understandable. In the diffusion model, the logistics curve and Weibull distribution are often used to estimate the demand. Higuchi & Troutt (2004) simulated *Tamagotchi*™ demand and sales based on the logistics curve, in which the information distortion had occurred and become amplified within a supply chain.

# Chapter 7
# Supply Chain Management of Seven-Eleven Japan

**Nobuaki Ishikawa**
*Sakushin Gakuin University, Japan*

## ABSTRACT

*In this chapter, the supply chain management of Seven-Eleven Japan, the most successful convenience store in Japan, will be taken as a case study. First, the establishment and development of the convenience store industry in Japan (which has always been led by Seven-Eleven) will be described. Next, the characteristics of Seven-Eleven Japan and how it has been accepted by customers will be discussed. Finally, the future prospects of the convenience store industry and Seven-Eleven will be discussed.*

## INTRODUCTION

This chapter focuses on convenience stores, which were born in the United States and have made great strides in Japan. The key success factor for convenience stores is to their product lineups that focus on consumer needs and the development of logistics and information systems, which can be achieved through excellent SCM strategies. In Japan's convenience store market, Seven-Eleven Japan has always been a leader, and the systems developed by Seven-Eleven Japan have often become the industry standard. 7-Eleven stores have expanded into Asia, North America, and Europe. Therefore, this chapter discusses SCM in convenience stores, using Seven-Eleven Japan as a case study.

## BACKGROUND

A convenience store is a relatively small store (about 100 square meters) that sells a wide range of daily food products, including lunchboxes and side dishes, processed foods, and daily sundries, mainly through a self-service system, located in residential areas or along roads, and characterized by long hours of operation, such as 24 hours a day, seven days a week (Kakeda and Sumiya, 2009). The Ministry of Economy, Trade and Industry (METI) defines a convenience store as "a store that sells food and bever-

DOI: 10.4018/978-1-7998-9800-9.ch007

ages, has a sales floor area of at least 30 square meters but less than 250 square meters, and is open at least 14 hours a day, using a self-service system" (METI, 2014).

Convenience stores were originally established and developed in the United States. In 1927, J. J. Green, who was in charge of Southland Ice Company's ice sales office in Texas sold 12 items including milk, bread, and eggs along with ice cubes from his home refrigerator. This was the origin of the convenience store (Kakeda and Sumiya, 2009). While grocery stores of the time closed in the evenings and were not open on Sundays, Green's store was open 16 hours a day, 7 days a week. A totem pole was set up in the storefront, and the store was named Totem Store. The Southland Ice Company developed this type of business and changed the name to 7-Eleven in 1946, establishing the convenience store as a retail format that offered convenience to consumers.

The first convenience store in Japan was Mamy Toyonaka opened by My Shop chain in Toyonaka City in 1969 (Umezawa, 2020; . Kmart, Cocostore, Seicomart and other voluntary chains followed, then major general merchandise stores entered the market. It is well known that many citizens of the country lead busy lives, and the convenience of long opening hours have been well appreciated. In 2020, there were over 56 thousand convenience stores operating in Japan (Diep, 2021).

## FEATURES OF CONVENIENCE STORES

As mentioned earlier, convenience stores are small grocery stores characterized by long hours of operation. This section provides a more detailed explanation of the characteristics and systems of convenience stores.

### High-Mix, Low-Volume Inventory

While food supermarkets cater to household demands in daily life, convenience stores are characterized by their product lineups that cater to urgent individual demands. In order to achieve this under the constraint of a small store, a new type of product assortment was established that was not seen in the conventional retailing format of high-mix, low-volume inventory.

A standard convenience store has 3,000 items on a sales floor of about 100 square meters, which is more than three times the number of items displayed per sales floor area than the processed food section of a standard general supermarket (Yahagi, 1994).

The backyard area is also small in addition to the small sales floor, making it difficult for a convenience store to hold a large amount of inventory with many different products. As a result, convenience stores need to reduce the amount of inventory, but this increases the risk of product shortages. An empty shelf leads to missed sales opportunity, which accumulates to a huge loss for the store. In order to solve this problem, the following systems were developed.

### Small-Lot, High-Frequency Delivery System

In this "small-lot, high-frequency delivery," small quantities are delivered many times a day. This method can supplement the disadvantages of small stores, but it is not easy to implement this system.

Generally, transporting a large amount of goods at one time is less expensive, and transporting a small variety of goods is easier to manage. Doing a lot of small deliveries of a wide variety of products is naturally more costly.

In the beginning, many convenience stores did not have their own distribution centers, but used the systems of wholesalers. This means that each manufacturer or wholesaler delivered to the stores separately. The demand for small-lot, high-frequency delivery increased costs for manufacturers and wholesalers. Convenience stores were a costly delivery destination for them and not an important customer. Numerous problems occurred, such as delayed deliveries, missed deliveries, and refusal of frequent deliveries.

Seven-Eleven Japan was the first company to address these problems, and its supply system almost became the industry standard for convenience store chains. In 1976, Seven-Eleven Japan's first attempt was to consolidate its suppliers and establish a system of bulk delivery, instead of purchasing by product type or by agents or distributors of specific manufacturers.

At the same time, the efficiency of the order and receiving system was also improved. Previously, each store had placed orders with suppliers by phone every day. Wholesalers had to process the order information manually, and as the number of stores increased and the deal unit became smaller, the order processing cost increased significantly.

In 1978, 7-Eleven developed its own ordering terminal, enabling online processing of order data between franchisees and headquarters. In addition, from 1982, it became possible to process order data online between stores, headquarters, and business partners, thereby improving the efficiency of operations related to the purchase and supply of products.

## POS System

In order to select items from a group of products and reduce the amount of inventory for each item, sales data for each individual item is necessary. It was impossible to get sales data for all 3,000 single items quickly, and a new approach was needed for this purpose. In the United States, the introduction of POS systems, in which barcodes affixed to products are optically read by the cashier, began in the 1970s. While POS systems were introduced in the U.S. to improve the efficiency of cashier operations in supermarkets, it took time for them to spread in Japan, where cashier operations were highly productive. In convenience stores in Japan, Seven-Eleven Japan started to introduce the system in October 1982, and completed the installation in all stores in February of the following year.

## Expansion of Service Products

Convenience stores have become a place where many people visit every day (or several times a day) due to their long hours of operation and wide variety of products. Taking advantage of this familiarity, convenience stores began to offer a wide variety of services.

After Seven-Eleven launched its parcel delivery service in 1981, many convenience store chains expanded their services to include photocopying, faxing, photo developing, ticket sales, and utilities payment. In 2001, Seven-Eleven began operating Seven Bank through ATMs installed in each of its stores.

## Franchise Chains

Most of the convenience stores in Japan are operated by small independent retailers organized in voluntary or franchise chains. Major convenience stores such as 7-Eleven, Lawson, and FamilyMart are operated under the franchise system.

In the franchise system, franchisees are granted the right to use the chain's brand, logo, distribution system, equipments, and management advice under a contract. In return, the franchisees pay joining fees and royalties to the headquarters. This structure would also allow stores to focus on doing business without being busy with cash flow and purchasing.

In the case of 7-Eleven, most of its stores in Japan are operated under the franchise system, while in Southland they are directly managed (Yahagi, 1994). The main source of income for Seven-Eleven Japan is royalties from franchisees. 7-Eleven franchisees pay royalties based on the amount of merchandise delivered to their stores (Higuchi, 2016).

## 7-ELEVEN'S DISTRIBUTION STRATEGY

So far, the systems of convenience stores have been discussed. In many cases, 7-Eleven has created advanced structures. From here, 7-Eleven's unique strategies will be explained. First, a brief history of Seven-Eleven Japan will be reviewed.

In 1973, Ito-Yokado formed a business alliance with Southland Corporation, which at the time had 4,000 stores in the United States, to establish York Seven (now 7-Eleven Japan), and the following year opened its first 7-Eleven store in Koto-ku, Tokyo on a franchise basis. In the next two years, York Seven opened 100 7-Eleven stores and established a leading position in the convenience stores in Japan. In 1991, 7-Eleven Japan acquired Southland Corporation, which had been in financial trouble. In 2007, the company achieved the largest number of retail stores in the world.

### Dominant Strategy (Dominant Store Opening)

7-Eleven's success can be attributed to its superior distribution strategy. One of them is the dominant strategy. The dominant strategy is also known as the high-density concentrated store opening strategy. The dominant strategy is to open a large number of stores in a short period of time within a certain area. In addition to gaining market share in a certain area by increasing the chain's recognition and the frequency of store visits, the dominant strategy also has efficiency advantages, such as improved logistics efficiency, advertising efficiency, and efficiency in management advice.

On the other hand, the dominant strategy has the following disadvantages. Neighboring stores compete with each other for sales, which causes difficulties for store owners at 7-Eleven, which operates a franchise chain. In addition, when the local environment changes, all stores in a concentrated area are affected by the change. As a result, the company may be forced to close all stores in the area.

Seven-Eleven Japan has emphasized a dominant strategy from the beginning, opening its first store, the Toyosu Store, in Toyosu, Koto-ku, Tokyo in 1974 and remaining within the 42.99 square kilometers area of Koto-ku until it opened 10 stores.

As of the end of December 2021, Seven-Eleven Japan had 21,227 domestic stores, but it was in 2020 that it opened stores in all prefectures. In 2003, 7-Eleven opened a store in Aichi Prefecture, which includes Nagoya, one of Japan's three largest cities; in 2013, it opened a store in the Shikoku region; and in 2020, it opened a store in Okinawa Prefecture.

Even in the prefectures where stores have been opened, they may not have opened stores throughout the prefecture. Due to the high density of store openings, the area of stores opened is small in contrast to the number of stores.

Seven-Eleven Japan's decision-making process for opening new stores is also unique. Many products in the 7-Eleven lineup are manufactured in dedicated factories and delivered to stores in dedicated vehicles. The quality and expiration dates are controlled so that customers can buy the same quality products no matter where they are located in Tokyo, Hokkaido, or Kyushu. Onigiri (rice balls), bento boxes, sandwiches, etc., have expiration dates that are determined by the hour, and the time available for delivery from the distribution center to the stores is limited. For this reason, 7-Eleven only opens stores if it can ensure the same quality from the dedicated rice factory to the store.

At the beginning of each fiscal year, Seven-Eleven Japan formulates an annual plan for each distribution center. At this stage, product mix, store opening plans, and display plans for the following year are thoroughly discussed. If the sales department is allowed to freely expand the opening area, it will immediately affect the logistics cost, which will increase the cost and hinder efficiency. For this reason, Seven-Eleven Japan decides on store opening areas from the logistics department.

In this way, the same services can be provided to all stores nationwide and delivered with the same frequency, leading to store owners being able to focus on their business with peace of mind (Shinoda, 2013).

## Delivery Frequency

At Seven-Eleven, the frequency of product delivery is determined by the product's sales characteristics and sales amount. For example, rice products such as lunchboxes and hand-rolled rice balls, prepared foods, cooked noodles, sandwiches, chilled products such as milk, and beverages such as soft drinks and beer account for 75% of total sales. Therefore, for product groups such as these, which account for a very high percentage of sales, the frequency of delivery is high as Table 1 shows. Rice-related products are selling well. In addition to this, due to their product characteristics, shelf life is controlled by time and the sales period is short. For these reasons, they are delivered three times a day. Chilled products have a higher sales volume, but their shelf life is set longer than that of rice-related products because they are managed at a low temperature of 5 degrees Celsius. For these products, deliveries are made twice a day. For beverages, such as drinks and beer, which account for a high percentage of sales, we use one delivery per day. For other products, the number of items to be checked per day is reduced by placing orders three times a week, thereby increasing the time available for placing orders per item. Also, in logistics, the number of stores in charge per day is reduced to improve the sorting productivity of the center.

## Just-in-Time

Rice and chilled products are delivered according to the hours when their needs are highest. For example, lunch is usually taken around noon, breakfast around 7:00 a.m., and dinner around 7:00 p.m. If the fresh product is delivered just before each meal time, customers will feel "fresh" and "ready-made" and will be more loyal to the store. Especially for rice-related products, which are deeply familiar to Japanese people, eating while the " rice " has not lost its flavor is the key to its taste.

To cope with this, 7-Eleven has established a distribution system that delivers three times a day, and has set up a timetable where each meal is fully inspected and displayed before the peak.

In the case of lunch, the approximate peak time is from around noon to 2 pm. In order not to miss this peak time, the trucks strictly deliver to the last store on the delivery route by 11 am. After that time, they never go to the stores so as not to disturb the increased number of customers during the lunch peak. This

*Table 1. Frequency of delivery according to sales characteristics (2007)*

| | Frequency of delivery |
|---|---|
| Rice Products | 3/day |
| Chilled Foods | 2/day |
| Soft drinks, Beer | 7/week |
| Snacks | 3/week |
| Processed foods | 3/week |
| General Goods | 3/week |
| Liquors | 3/week |
| Frozen Foods | 3-7/week |

Prepared by the author, Source: (Shinoda, 2013)

delivery deadline is also in anticipation of the end of the store's inspection and display process. Similarly, evening deliveries are to be completed by 5:00 p.m., late night, early morning, and breakfast rice deliveries are to be completed by midnight. This means that the delivery time is determined according to the meal time of each customer. Therefore, Seven-Eleven's own products, such as boxed lunches, hand-rolled rice balls, sandwiches, and prepared foods, will be manufactured according to the delivery time.

On the other hand, the cutoff time for orders from stores, which determines the number of units produced, is determined for each delivery service so that the lead time from order to delivery is minimized.

For example, the delivery time for lunch is from 8:00 to 11:00 a.m., and the cut-off time for orders for this delivery is 6:00 p.m. the day before. During the previous day's business, the staff confirms the product trends for that day and also checks the latest weather forecast for the next day (delivery day) released by the Japan Meteorological Agency at 5:00 p.m. to see if there will be any sudden changes in the weather or sudden rise or fall in temperature. In addition, taking into account information on nearby events and changes in trends, 6:00 p.m. is set as the final deadline for ordering quantities for the next day's noon delivery. Thanks to this system, the store is able to respond to sudden changes in temperature.

Also, when there is a major event such as a fireworks display or field day, they check the weather forecast right up until the last minute to determine whether or not the event will be held, and reflect this in the number of orders placed to reduce lost opportunities and unnecessary losses. In this way, the business conditions and ordering activities of the stores and the manufacturing and distribution activities of the manufacturers work in unison to deliver the products to the stores.

## Delivery by Temperature Zone

Seven-Eleven Japan strictly controls the temperature of its products. In order to maintain quality, the products are managed in multiple temperature zones depending on the product category.

Temperature control is set at -20°C for frozen products, +20°C for rice products, and +25°C for room temperature products such as chocolates and gummies in the summer. The controlled temperature for each product in joint delivery is shown in Table 2.

For example, once rice products such as boxed lunches and hand-rolled rice balls are cooled in a temperature range of 5°C, the flavor of the rice disappears and they become dry and irreversible even when heated in a microwave oven. On the other hand, if the temperature exceeds 25°C, bacteria will

*Table 2. Temperature control by products*

| | |
|---|---|
| Ice creams, Frozen foods | -20°C |
| Milk, Milk beverages, Processed Meat, Deli Foods | +5°C |
| Cooked rice, Fresh-baked Bread | +20°C |
| Gummies, Chocolates | +25°C |
| Processed Foods, Liquors, Snacks, General Goods | Room temperature |

Prepared by the author

thrive and the risk of food poisoning will increase. Therefore, the product control temperature for rice is set at 20°C plus or minus 2°C. This temperature is set to preserve the eating quality of rice, which deteriorates over time, and is maintained through the use of refrigeration in spring, summer, and fall.

In Northern Japan, however, it is not uncommon for the outside temperature to drop below freezing from late at night to early in the morning during the severe cold season of winter. In such cases, in order to control the delivery temperature inside the container to 20°C, it is necessary to install a heater and maintain the temperature at 20°C while delivering.

In addition, the interior temperature of room temperature vehicles in the summer often exceeds 40°C, which is very damaging to products that melt easily, such as chocolates and gummies. Therefore, from the time the outside temperature exceeds a certain level in the summer, these products are placed in a cold box filled with dry ice at the delivery.

The temperature inside the containers from departure to arrival at the distribution center is recorded by the on-board terminals installed in all vehicles. If the temperature deviates from the set temperature, a notification is sent to the driver so that any changes in the temperature inside the container during delivery will not be overlooked. Considering the fact that stores are clustered together and cargo doors are opened frequently due to the dominant strategy, double curtains have been installed to keep cool air inside the cargo space.

In the consistent temperature control from manufacturing to the point of sale, the delivery process is the one with the highest risk. It is therefore necessary to use freezing and refrigeration equipment installed in the vehicles to deliver the products safely to the stores. To ensure that each delivery vehicle complies with temperature control, Seven-Eleven Japan has developed specialized vehicles in collaboration with car body manufacturers and container manufacturers.

## Preventive Maintenance

If a problem occurs with the vehicle during delivery, it will not be able to deliver the goods safely. To prevent this from happening, Seven-Eleven, through the company that operates the center, requires delivery companies to perform regular “preventive maintenance. Preventive maintenance means that every few months or so, the entire vehicle is checked in advance for problems, and containers are checked for cooling and heating problems. With this kind of system, they are striving to maintain their business advantage by putting the safety of their products first and keeping them in good condition during delivery.

## Improving Efficiency of Store Operations

Seven-Eleven Japan operates deliveries during its 24-hour business hours. Stores need to receive deliveries while handling cash register operations and customer inquiries. In addition, 7-Eleven's main products, such as rice and prepared foods, have strict expiration dates and temperatures, so if they are left in the aisles or backyards for a long time after arriving from the distribution center, sales opportunities may be greatly reduced.

To prevent this, Seven-Eleven Japan has devised ways to make it easier for stores to receive the products. For example, if the shape of the cardboard or other packaging is different for each product, work efficiency will be reduced. Therefore, as much as possible, each product is sorted into crates before being delivered. In addition, for room temperature products, only the necessary amount of products are delivered in small portions. As a result, the backroom inventory is reduced as much as possible, and only the delivered products are displayed, thereby improving work efficiency. (Shinoda, 2013)

## Necessity of Joint Delivery

The most important policy in Seven-Eleven Japan's logistics is joint delivery. When Seven-Eleven Japan was founded in 1974, the majority of products were delivered to retailers either by route sales conducted by sales staff at points designated by the manufacturer for each region, or by special agents. Each region had a specific company and salesperson in charge, and it was impossible for stores to freely request a change in the person in charge.

Products ranged from soft drinks, milk and dairy beverages, ice cream, frozen foods, processed meats, and delicacies. The salespersons in charge were also in charge of displaying the products, so they displayed their own products in the best position regardless of whether they were selling well or not. As a result, there were various negative effects such as the loss of sales of hot-selling products.

When a salesperson had a sales quota for his or her own product, the delivery of that product became the top priority, leaving no room for the products that the store and its customers wanted, and the store could not place orders as it does now.

However, this method is not a good idea for manufacturers either. This is because they will have to sell their own excess inventory in the stores, while the best-selling products will be out of stock or not displayed in sufficient quantities. In addition, stores know more about the characteristics of their business areas and the needs of their customers than their route salespersons.

At the time, Seven-Eleven Japan took opportunity loss very seriously. If opportunity loss continues, customers' trust in the store will be lost, leading to sluggish sales.

In the past, when stores placed orders, the quantities ordered were rarely delivered. Manufacturers, wholesalers, and distributors did not give priority to 7-Eleven because they also wholesaled their products to retailers other than 7-Eleven. Manufacturers' inventory, wholesalers' inventory, and distributors' inventory were all managed as joint inventory with other stores, not exclusively for 7-Eleven.

In addition, even when orders were placed, they were not delivered to stores in time for delivery. Seven-Eleven has been promoting 24-hour business from a relatively early period and had a system in place to accept deliveries around the clock. However, delivery times varied due to the mix of deliveries to other stores.

The stores became frustrated with the situation that the manufacturers and wholesalers were setting delivery times while the stores were open 24 hours a day and customers could visit the stores at any time. Finally, as a result of repeated negotiations, deliveries were made based on orders from the stores, rather than based on the decisions of the route sales staff.

## Current Delivery Types

Deliveries to 7-Eleven stores can be broadly categorized into joint deliveries in each of the four temperature zones and some company-specific deliveries. In the case of joint delivery, the controlled temperature and delivery frequency are determined according to product needs and the product temperature determined by each manufacturer. The product with the highest delivery frequency is "rice-related products & original freshly baked bread" at a controlled temperature of 20°C, which is delivered to stores 3 to 4 times a day. Chilled products (sandwiches and other prepared breads, salads, prepared foods, milk, milk beverages, etc.) are delivered three times a day at a controlled temperature of 5°C. The third temperature zone, "room temperature products," is delivered seven times a week (daily), but the contents of the loads vary greatly depending on the day of the week. Sundries, confectionery, and processed food" and "sundries and processed food" sets are delivered three times a week, alternating daily.

The fourth type of delivery, "frozen" (delivery control temperature: -20°C), consists mainly of ice cream, frozen foods, and fast foods served over the counter (fried foods, steamed buns, oden, etc.). In 7-Eleven's business, the majority of frozen deliveries are ice cream, which sells extremely well in the summer and hardly at all in the winter, depending on the outside temperature. As a result, the delivery frequency to stores varies greatly by season: six deliveries per week starting in late April, seven deliveries per week starting in early June, six deliveries per week starting in mid-August, and three deliveries per week starting in mid-September. Naturally, the fixed costs associated with frozen deliveries are much higher than for deliveries in other temperature zones, as frozen deliveries require freezers at distribution centers and freezer trucks. Therefore, it is essential to adjust delivery frequency in order to streamline logistics and reduce costs. The delivery frequency is changed by season for this reason. In recent years, however, sales of fried foods as over-the-counter fast food have grown significantly throughout the year. Since these are delivered frozen, seasonal fluctuations are decreasing.

The fifth type of delivery, Yamazaki Baking, magazines, and cigarettes are not delivered jointly, but each company delivers on its own. Yamazaki Baking has strictly zoned delivery areas for its baking plants, which is not consistent with 7-Eleven's distribution network. Yamazaki Baking consolidates deliveries with other retailers, but each retailer strictly adheres to delivery deadlines for business reasons and there are few delays or missing products. There is therefore no need to put Yamazaki's bread on the 7-Eleven joint delivery system.

Magazines are a difficult delivery item to include in shared delivery. Magazines have a well-established traditional business practice of "sending books" in Japan. Unlike normal products, the publisher decides the number of copies of magazines to be published, and the distributor decides the number to be sent to each retailer. Magazines cannot be ordered by retailers, so the entire product assortment and quantity is left to the distributors. One of the reasons is that it is very difficult for stores to place orders for magazines, since their contents are not known until they are published. All unsold products are guaranteed through a "book return system."

Lastly, for cigarettes, legal and tax regulations do not allow for joint delivery. Sales of cigarettes by convenience stores have recently increased due to the operation of "taspo" cards, which has led to the closure of cigarette shops.

## Joint Distribution Centers

As of the end of February 2017, there were 150 distribution centers for joint delivery nationwide. In the Tokyo metropolitan area, which has high store sales, chilled products are delivered to stores from dedicated chilled distribution centers, and rice products are delivered to stores from dedicated rice distribution centers, each with dedicated vehicles. In other areas, a dedicated sorting room for chilled products has been set up at the rice distribution center to improve logistics efficiency.

An important factor is the location of distribution centers and major factories. Rice products, the mainstay of Seven-Eleven Japan, have the most stringent time management from production to sales. Rice products have the shortest time from production to sales, and are sold in stores within 24 hours of production. In principle, the expiration period is two hours after the end of sales, and the standard time to eat is within 26 hours after production. Chilled factories and rice factories are located near the distribution center to reduce distribution time and ensure production time.

Seven-Eleven Japan has established criteria for locating a joint distribution center. When opening a store in a new area, the company thoroughly confirms that the store will not be isolated, including administrative divisions, distance from existing centers, tolls and other costs, road conditions, track record of road closures during stormy weather, and availability of bypass roads.

For example, there were several reasons why store openings in the four prefectures of Shikoku and the outlying islands were postponed until 2012. These reasons include the extremely high risk of the Honshu-Shikoku Bridges being closed due to strong winds, bridge tolls driving up logistics costs, and the small scale of store openings due to the small population.

Vehicles delivering to stores have partition walls inside to separate loads. The partitions can be moved back and forth to change the size of the room according to the amount of cargo. Each cargo compartment is equipped with a temperature sensor, which alerts delivery staff if an abnormality is detected.

The dominant strategy makes the delivery route flexible. The ideal delivery route would be a "petal-shaped" radial route centered on the distribution center. In addition, since traffic in Japan drives on the left side of the road, it is necessary to cross the oncoming lane when turning right. Therefore, a counterclockwise delivery route would reduce the risk of traffic accidents. Seven-Eleven stores are often renovated, closed, or newly opened, so delivery routes will be revised as needed.

## Supply and Demand Management

Seven-Eleven Japan places great importance on supply and demand management: even though the number of orders per store is small, the number of products required from all stores is huge: if one store orders 10 items per day, that would be 210,000 items for 21,000 stores in Japan.

In the case of a grilled mackerel bento, which uses 0.5 mackerel per serving, 105,000 mackerel would be required per day in Japan. However, Seven-Eleven Japan selects the source of the mackerel to ensure that there is no variation in taste or quality, and also has strict regulations on the size of the mackerel, so if it is too large or too small, it cannot be used. Therefore, a stable supply of even a single ingredient is not easy to maintain. Bento consists of rice and several kinds of ingredients, but a shortage of just one ingredient is enough to make it impossible to ship.

Therefore, a meeting called "Team MD" was established to facilitate the planning and execution of merchandising. Accumulated store POS data and data on sales of similar products are checked by three parties: the daily-delivery manufacturer, the ingredient manufacturer, and the 7-Eleven Merchandise Department (Shinoda, 2013).

Order data for daily-delivery products is shared with manufacturers not only finalized data after the order is closed, but also provisional closing data every few hours. This allows the manufacturer to predict the closing figures for the day and prepare them in advance.

As described above, Seven-Eleven Japan strives to ensure a stable supply of products by thoroughly managing supply and demand.

## NEW INITIATIVES BY SEVEN-ELEVEN JAPAN

### 'Premium' Private Brand

Private brands (private labels) are products developed originally by retailers or distributors, who are involved from production to sales and branding (Sato, 2008, et al.). In contrast, national brands are those developed by manufacturers.

Private brands are characterized by low prices for consumers and high profit margins for stores. In many cases, national brand manufacturers produce private brand products, and although they have to produce them in response to orders from retailers, they have the advantage of securing long-term and stable business (Sato, 2008).

Retailers and distributors are sometimes asked to raise prices on food products and commodities produced by major manufacturers due to strong supplier power. Private brands are well introduced for such products.

Major convenience store chains have traditionally sold their products at fixed prices, but competition from discount stores, drugstores, and other formats that sell products at lower prices is intensifying. Therefore, they are increasing the variety of low-priced private-brand products to create a sense of affordability and prevent customers from leaving the store due to price hikes. Seven-Eleven Japan launched "Seven Premium" in 2007, Lawson launched "Lawson Select" in 2010, and FamilyMart launched "Famima Collection" in 2012.

Behind the emergence of private brands is the increasing complexity of competition in the retail industry. While product differentiation is becoming more difficult, private brand products are 20-30% less expensive than national brand products, and their quality is maintained. Private brands can gain an advantage over national brands because they can keep prices low while maintaining quality.

However, Seven-Eleven Japan's private brand Seven Premium has a completely different philosophy than its predecessors. Seven Premium was introduced in 2007 as a brand common to the Seven & i Group. Unlike conventional private brands, Seven Premium is a higher quality product at the same price as national brands. It was sold at the same price across retail formats, including 7-Eleven, supermarkets Ito-Yokado and York-Benimaru, and department store Sogo. This has been a success and sales continue to grow.

For national brand manufacturers, cooperating with private brands that sell at lower prices may lower the value of their brands. However, because Seven Premium is a high-quality product, manufacturers were cooperative in product development (Asanaga, 2013).

Another feature of Seven Premium is that the name of the national brand manufacturer that produced the product is always displayed to gain customer trust. This also overturns the common practice of conventional private brands, which only display the name of the seller.

*Figure 1. Channel variation*
*Prepared by the author*

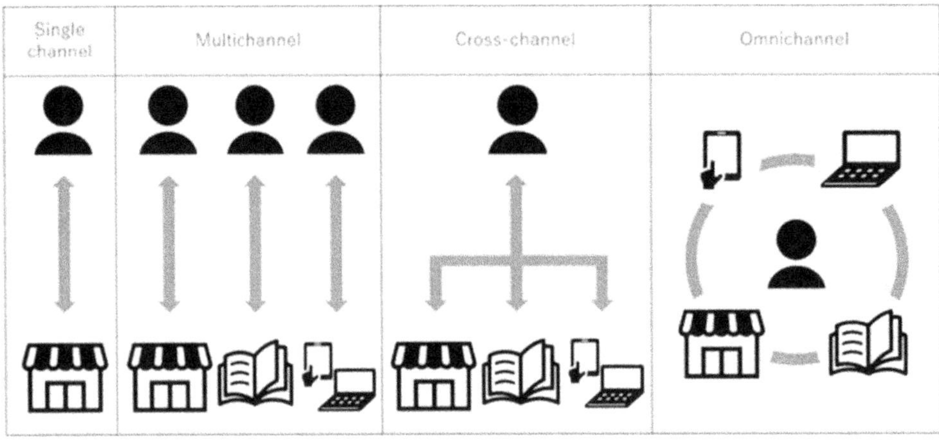


Traditionally, it has been taken for granted to make products at lower prices, but private brands are not defined as such. The low price method is often chosen by chance as a way to maintain superiority over national brands. However, Toshifumi Suzuki (1932-), Chairman of Seven & i Holdings Co., Ltd. insisted, "It is important to continue pursuing quality.'' The company has continued to develop products accordingly, and has developed even higher quality products such as Seven Gold.

## Omnichannelization

Figure 1 illustrates the evolution of customer contact points in purchasing. The most basic point of contact with customers in retailing is the one-on-one contact between the store and the customer. Eventually, other points of contact will emerge, such as catalog and online shopping. This is called multi-channel. Although multiple purchasing options have been created for customers, each channel of contact between the retailer and the customer remains a single relationship. As this multi-channel relationship evolves, customers will be able to make purchases such as ordering online and picking up the order at the store. This type of purchasing is called cross-channel because the customer makes purchases at his or her convenience while crossing multiple channels. Omni-channel is a further evolution of cross-channel. Omni-channel aims to maximize the customer experience by observing customer purchasing behavior and restructuring the flow so that customers can move back and forth between the real world and the Internet without discomfort. By linking all channels together and centrally managing customer information, an infrastructure will be in place that can respond to individual preferences and emotions. The proliferation of smartphones will play an important role in this.

Seven-Eleven Japan is trying to support omni-channel. In 1999, Softbank, Seven-Eleven Japan, Tohan, and Yahoo invested to establish e-Shopping Books Co. The company began as an online bookstore, but expanded its services to include CDs, DVDs, and BDs in 2004. It has now been merged into Seven & i Net Media Co., Ltd, which was established by Seven & i Holdings. In 2015, Seven & i Net Media opened Omni7, the group's comprehensive shopping site. Omni7 sells products from the Seven & i Group and its partner companies online. Users can pay for and pick up their orders at participating stores. By utilizing a network of physical stores, the company seeks to eliminate the hassle and anxiety of picking up items at home (Higuchi, 2018).

Stores in the omni-channel era are not necessarily designed solely to bring customers to the store, so other factors must be added to conventional metrics such as traffic volume and population. Therefore, all the store networks and infrastructure that have been built so far may become legacy costs. For example, if an increasing percentage of customers purchase from their smartphones, stores along high rent boulevards may no longer be needed.

Seven-Eleven Japan has the potential to become the world's strongest omni-retailer. Retailers with a high volume and density of customer contact points will be able to build an advantage over others through omnichannelization. Seven & i Holdings has an overwhelmingly well-known and trusted brand, a broad product lineup, strong product development capabilities, robust customer service, infrastructure, and a network of stores, including 7-Eleven stores. No other retailer in the world can match these conditions. Specifically, first, there are more than 20,000 7-Eleven stores in Japan. In addition, there are nine temperature-controlled delivery services per day that support 7-Eleven's operations. Recently, 7-Eleven has also launched a new service in which 7-Eleven store staff delivers products from the stores to customers' homes. Along with the rice balls, boxed lunches, and prepared foods sold at 7-Eleven stores, there are also proprietary products such as Seven Premium, a private brand that aims to exceed the quality of national brands.

The key to overcoming various difficulties and achieving further growth will be whether the company can leverage these elements to create ever more innovation while developing the entire supply chain over the long term.

## CONCLUSION

In this chapter, SCM strategies of convenience stores have been discussed using Seven-Eleven Japan as a case study. Convenience store innovations can be summarized as follows: at the retail level, such as high-mix low-volume sales and long hours of operation 24 hours a day, 365 days a year; at the distribution level, such as short delivery times, small lots, integrated production and sales, and joint product development; and at the management level, such as information networks, alliances, and franchising (Yahagi, 1994). Seven-Eleven Japan, in particular, achieved success in Japan by adapting the established know-how and systems of convenience store management in the U.S. to Japan's unique distribution environment and culture, rather than simply adopting them. And they have continued to create innovations that are important to the convenience store industry, offering new convenience to customers.

On the other hand, convenience store sales peaked in FY1982 with a 28.8% increase over the previous year, but the growth rate has declined, and the high-growth convenience stores have entered a period of maturity. In addition, with the increasing penetration of smartphones, customers will be able to access a great deal of information. Under these circumstances, it is necessary to accurately determine and realize what individuals need.

Seven-Eleven Japan is a successful example of building a new business model through SCM strategy. The key to overcoming various difficulties and achieving further growth will be the ability to create ever more innovation while developing the entire supply chain over the long term. It will be interesting to see what Seven-Eleven Japan will do in the future.

## REFERENCES

Asanaga, M. (2013). *Seven & I HLDGS. 9 chou en kigyou no himitsu - sekai saikyou omnichannel heno chousen* [Seven & i HLDGS. The secret of a 9 trillion yen company - Challenge to the World's Strongest Omnichannel]. Nikkei Business Publications.

Chopra, S., & Meindl, P. (2007). *Supply Chain Management: Strategy, Planning & Operations* (3rd ed.). Pearson Education.

Diep, C. (2021). *Convenience store numbers in Japan 2011-2020*. Retrieved November 23, 2021, from https://www.statista.com/statistics/810901/japan-convenience-store-numbers/

Higuchi, T. (2016). Fusion of Short-term and Long-term SCM Strategies -The Case of Seven Eleven Japan. *Third International Workshop on Successful Supply Chain Management*.

Higuchi, T. (2018). *Supply Chain ga umidasu kyousou yuui* [Competitive Advantage Created by Supply Chain]. Chuokeizai-sha.

Kakeda, Y., & Sumiya, H. (2009). *Gendai no kouri ryuutsuu* [Modern Retail Distribution]. Chuokeizai-sha.

Kawabe, N. (2003). *Sebun-irebun no Keieishi* [A Business History of Seven-Eleven]. Yuhikaku Publishing. Retrieved October 11, 2021, from https://www.city.koto.lg.jp/

Lowson, B., King, R., & Hunter, A. (2010). *Quick Response: Managing the Supply Chain to Meet Consumer Demand*. John Wiley & Sons.

Sato, T. (2008). *Building Private Brand in Retail Marketing: Cooperation and specialization of The Hassyakai, Journal of Nippon-Keiei-Shindan-Gakkai*. Seven-Eleven Japan Co., Ltd. Retrieved October 27, 2021, from https://www.sej.co.jp/company/

Seven-i HLDGs. Co., Ltd. (2016). *Corporate outline*. Retrieved November 27, 2021, from https://www.7andi.com/library/dbps_data/_template_/_res/ir/library/co/pdf/2017_05.pdf

Seven Bank. (n.d.). Retrieved November 8, 2021, from https://www.sevenbank.co.jp/

Shapiro. (2006). *Modeling the Supply Chain*. Brooks/Cole.

Shinoda, Y. (2013). *Sebun-irebun no Butsuryuu kenkyuu kokunai saidai no tenpomou wo musubu sekai saikyou rojisuthikusu no subete* [A Study of Seven-Eleven's Logistics -All about the World's Strongest Logistics Connecting Japan's Largest Store Network]. The Shogyokai Publishing.

Shinoda, Y. (2015). *Sebun-irebun no Hacchuuryoku* [Seven-Eleven's Ordering Capability]. The Shogyokai Publishing.

Umezawa, S. (2020). *Konbini Chain Shinka Shi* [History of Convenience Store Chains]. Eastpress.

Yahagi, T. (1994). *Konbiniensu sutoa shisutemu no kakushinsei* [Innovations in Convenience Store Systems]. Nikkei.

## KEY TERMS AND DEFINITIONS

**Book Return System:** Under the Japanese bookstore distribution system, retailers can return books that have not sold for a certain period of time to the publishers through wholesalers.

**Fixed Cost:** Fixed amount of costs that are incurred regardless of sales amount, even if no manufacturing, sales, or other operations are conducted, including labor costs, ground rent, utilities, leases, advertising, depreciation, etc.

**Just-in-Time:** A system of production activities that thoroughly reduces inventory by supplying each process with only the necessary items when they are needed, well known as the production system introduced by Kiichiro Toyota of Toyota Motor Corporation.

**Oden:** Japanese fish cake stew. At convenience stores, consumers purchase it over the counter choosing the ingredients.

**Opportunity Loss:** Loss of sales caused by the absence of products that should have been sold.

**POS:** Point-of-sale is the recording of information such as product name, price, and time of sale on a per-item basis at the point when a product is sold in the retail business. The information is often maintained online and used to manage purchasing, inventory, and other business operations.

**Supplier Power:** In Porter's Five Forces, suppliers have the power to influence resource availability and prices. Suppliers exert the most power when a company is dependent on a supplier and cannot switch to another supplier because of high costs or lack of alternative sources of supply.

**Taspo Card:** An adult identification card required to purchase cigarettes from vending machines in Japan, introduced to prevent underage smoking.

**Voluntary Chain:** A voluntary association of independent retailers working together to achieve economies of scale in buying, advertising, etc.

# Chapter 8
# Driving Forces and Factors of Amazon Effects:
## From Online Bookstores to Cloud Services

**Yang Zhengguang**
*Sakushin Gakuin University, Japan*

## ABSTRACT

*The development of Amazon so far is mainly due to Jeff Bezos's leadership. By sticking to a customer-focused policy and starting an online bookstore, he changed how retailers handle a wide range of books and everything, breaking Pareto's law and achieving a long tail. What's more, he politely responded to customer demands and devised a Fly Wheel strategy. By providing an effective product lineup at a low cost, Amazon has accelerated the virtuous cycle of increasing the ability to attract customers and has grown sales exponentially. On the other hand, Amazon invested the profits it earned in technology development and conducted research and development of cutting-edge digital technology. In addition, Amazon has been active in business models such as 1-click, FBA, Amazon Prime, and Marketplace. As a platformer, it has expanded its business to its own B2C and the B2B area for other companies' platforms.*

## INTRODUCTION

This chapter discusses the changes in distribution structure and business along with the case of Amazon. Since the 1990s, the Internet has become exceptionally widespread. With the growth of the Internet as a tailwind, Amazon has actively introduced computer technology into the distribution area. It has significantly changed the distribution structure so far in a different way from the traditional business model of physical stores. Since the founding of Amazon, it has continued to grow explosively. Amazon's stock price has risen more than 1,000 times since its listing. Thus far, people have witnessed various innovations not only in distribution but also in cloud services. This chapter will explain how Amazon has achieved various innovations and transformed society in its roughly quarter-century history.

DOI: 10.4018/978-1-7998-9800-9.ch008

## BACKGROUND

Countless books and articles have been written on Amazon. Their primary focus is on transforming store sales to Internet shopping and its impact on consumers and society. In recent years, there has been a growing number of articles that view Amazon as an IT company. However, it is believed that this change is inevitable or consistent. In order to increase profit and sales volume, Amazon has been increasing its contact with consumers and gathering more information. Either the digital or the analog part, or both, have been the bottlenecks. In order to solve these bottlenecks that have emerged, Amazon has made significant improvements to the analog side of its business by effectively using digital technology. Outstanding digital technology and its effective use have solidified Amazon's high-profit margins and stable position. This chapter aims to illustrate the transition between analog and digital through the case of Amazon.

Goods flow from producers to consumers through distributors. Distribution plays an integral role as part of the supply chain. Producers and consumers are connected through distributors who may or may not have physical stores. In recent years, the Internet has developed, and this connection method has changed significantly. Consumers can now order online and shop without going to a physical store. In this way, distribution innovation is progressing, and business models and people's lifestyles have changed.

It was customary for people to only shop at physical stores in the old days. Now that we have entered an era in which physical and online stores coexist due to the spread of the Internet, people have begun to consider multiple options when shopping. They select an online shopping site such as Amazon when they want to shop quickly and efficiently, and they choose a traditional brick and mortar store when they wish to enjoy hands-on shopping with an up-close experience as in real life. With the development of cloud computing and drones, innovation occurs in various fields of life and business. In addition, more and more distributors are moving to platforms that handle both the Internet and the real world simultaneously.

This chapter explains distribution innovation by analyzing Amazon (Amazon.com), which has significantly influenced the distribution part of the supply chain. On that basis, Amazon's competitive advantage will be clarified, as we also consider the future direction of distribution innovation.

## ONLINE BOOKSTORE (1994-2001)

### Establishment

Jeff Bezos was born in 1964 in Albuquerque, New Mexico, USA. He worked with his grandfather on a Texas ranch every summer when he was young. After earning a degree in computer science from Princeton University, Bezos declined a job from semiconductor giant Intel and the well-known AT & T research arm at Nokia Bell Labs. He decided to get his first job at FITEL. FITEL's main customers were Wall Street investors, and it was a company that connected various computers owned by securities companies, investment banks, and ordinary banks to enable stock trading. After that, he changed jobs and finally got a job at the hedge fund company D.E. Shaw in New York. Two years later, he was quickly promoted to senior vice president of the company.

In 1991, some specialized bookstores opened online shops such as Computer Literacy Bookstore (clbooks.com), O'Reilly & Associates (ora.com), and Stanford University Books Department. Many retailers had started to check their sites where people had online accounts. These sites in which people could order books by email were still scarce at the time. In 1992, a startup named Books.com began offering a similar service, and the following year it launched an online database with about 40,000 titles. With a better system, they could increase the number of book titles offered. They were the pioneer of the online bookstore.

In 1994, the Internet grew at an astounding annual rate of 2,300%. The booming internet business inspired Bezos in the mid-1990s. His first motivation was to establish Amazon as the world's largest internet retailer. Bezos also decided to focus on one market to understand its needs and match them with the supplier's capabilities via the Internet. At first, he listed just 20 products to be sold online. They included computer software, office supplies, apparel, and music CDs. Later, he decided also to sell books online.

There are several reasons why books were selected for sale. First, books are familiar products to everyone in terms of target products. Customers can order and purchase online with peace of mind. Next, although the competition was fierce, the book market was huge. As of 1994, North American retailers sold nearly $7 billion in PC software, according to the US Census Bureau data. By comparison, the total number of books sold in the United States in the same year was $19 billion. Finally, book titles are too numerous to stock at a single physical store. While about 300,000 CD titles were sold, 3 million book titles were sold worldwide. The physical bookstores had limited space and could not manage such an overwhelming inventory.

Jeff Bezos spent $300,000 from his parents to set up a company in a garage in Seattle. He chose Seattle because of nearby University of Washington and Microsoft headquarters, both of which attracted an abundance of high-tech talent. Washington has a smaller population than California, New York, and Texas. In addition, retail sales tax was lower in the state of Washington. The initial company name was Cadabra.com. This company name was far from being a well-chosen company name. In 1995, it was renamed Amazon.com to have a better alphabetical hierarchy and, therefore, easier to find in a search. The new name embodied its goal, the world's largest online shopping site. Amazon offers a wide range of products as the world's largest retailer. Immediately after its founding, Amazon sold books online to customers in all 50 US states and 45 countries. Just three years later, Amazon went public on May 15, 1997 (Stone, 2013, pp. 30-59).

## Merit of Online Bookstore

It isn't easy for physical bookstores to make a profit because of the rent, labor costs, inventory costs, and other expenses. These costs are an enormous and unavoidable burden for a physical store. Some online bookstores do not have physical shops or warehouses but still sell titles that they do not have. This type of shop has an advantage in terms of cost. Besides, books are easy to mail in the form of booklets. Online bookstores need to spend less on management and personnel expenses to earn a profit compared to physical bookstores (Figure 1). Bezos instead used the power of the Internet. Amazon had 1,600 employees at the time, with annual sales of $375,000 per employee. In contrast, the brick-and-mortar stores of Barnes & Noble employ 27,000 people, with per capita sales less than one-third that of Amazon.

Book sales were the central part of Amazon's overall sales from 1997 to 2008. Amazon was able to save on otherwise massive management and labor costs. They used this saved money to invest in marketing and technology. Amazon could efficiently sell a massive number of book titles throughout the USA and worldwide (Figure 2). Barnes & Noble Booksellers was at the time the most prominent bookstore in the physical book market in the United States. Amazon took only ten years to surpass Barnes & Noble Bookstore.

*Figure 1. Net sales and general and administrative costs*
** GANS = General and Administrative Costs / Net Sales*
*Source: (Annual Reports of Amazon and Barnes & Nobel from 1997 to 2008)*

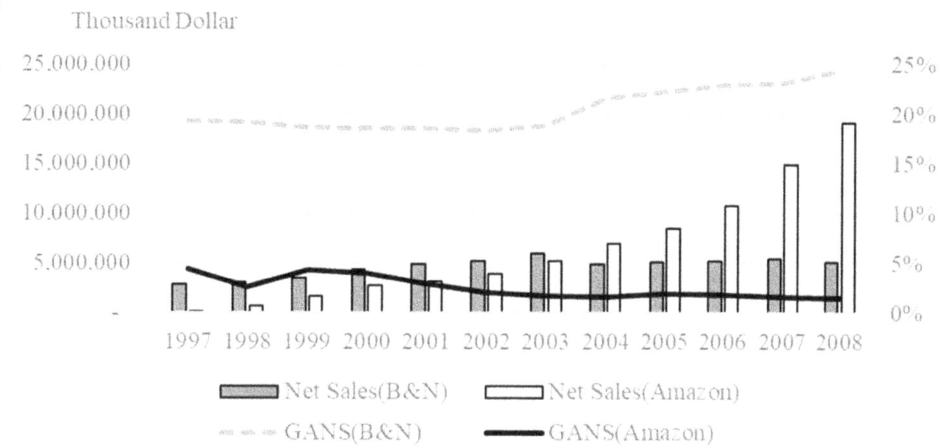


Amazon has changed the book business model, shifting from physical stores to online sites. Online sales can overcome physical distance barriers and reduce general and administrative expenses and inventory costs much more than physical stores. Furthermore, online shops can offer a much broader lineup more economically than physical stores.

## Outstanding Services

In 1996, Bezos launched an Associates Program (performance rewards for referrals) that allowed non-Amazon businesses to link to books recorded in Amazon's database. Clicking on this link to buy a book on Amazon resulted in a 5% - 15% referral fee being credited to the sites participating in the Associates Program, depending on what was purchased.

Not only did this mechanism increase sales for Amazon, but it also contributed to the growing reputation that Amazon could find books in any field. In 1998, Bezos declared the program "a breakthrough in the top class." Amazon has applied for a patent on the idea of the Associates Program(Brant, 2011, pp. 121-122).

Two years after launching Amazon, Bezos set out to leverage technology to provide outstanding service to its users. The patented technology "1-Click order" was born from this policy. The 1-Click software was developed by Perry Hartmann, a programmer who joined Amazon in 1997. One day behind the scenes, Bezos said, "We need to devise ways to eliminate friction in the ordering system. We need to be able to order products with a minimum of effort. I think." Hartmann realized his idea and developed a program that allows customers to order products with just 1-Click.

When Amazon started 1-Click, consumers were still apprehensive about buying online. Therefore, when purchasing, it takes many steps to complete the order in the system. People often stop purchasing after putting the product in the shopping cart. The industry average "cart abandonment rate" exceeded 65%. It was thought that buying with a single click would further increase consumer anxiety, but as a result, Amazon's customers grew dramatically after adopting 1-Click.

*Figure 2. Expansion of marketing area*

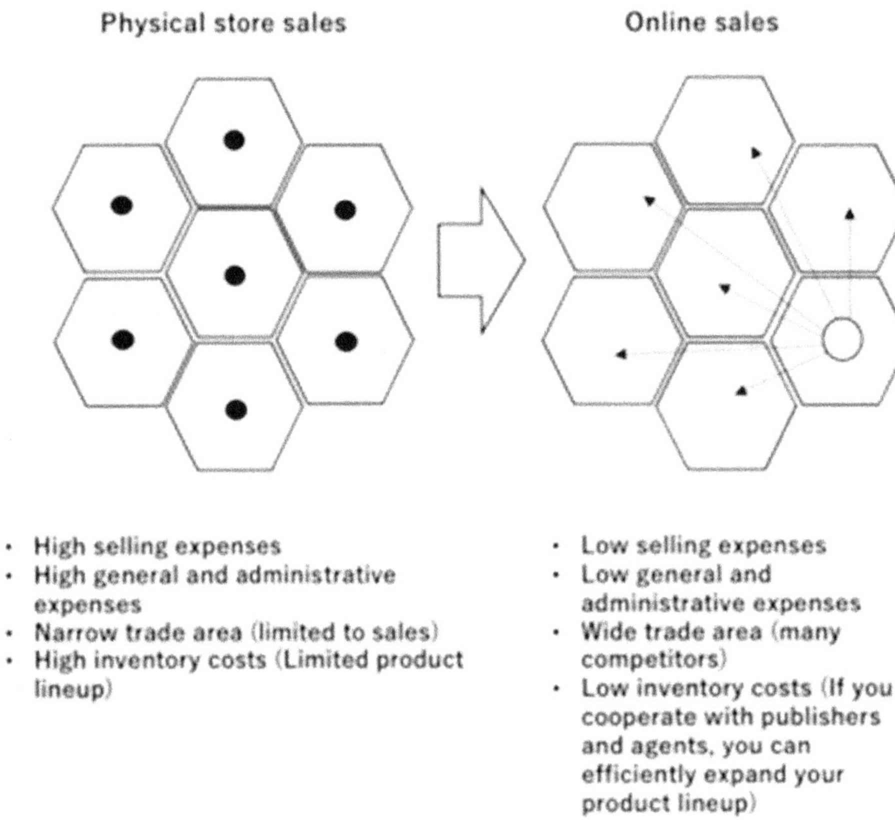


Consumers living near physical stores can visit them and browse through books in stock. If they like them, they can buy them on the spot. However, Amazon utilizes a program it has developed to change the lifestyles of its customers, allowing them to order the books they are looking for from a wide selection of books while at home. Some customers may regret receiving a book far from what they expected, and they regret their purchase. It was necessary to reduce the anxiety of consumers who could not buy the books they wanted on the spot and inform them of the estimated delivery date as soon as possible. Easy search and order indeed lead to more sales. People can conveniently place an order with just 1-Click, and Amazon can provide recommendations and advice by analyzing their purchase history. The Associates Program enriched the book review functions and preemptively decreased customer anxiety (Figure 3).

## New Economy (Click and Mortar)

Amazon eventually acquired so many book titles it became the largest bookstore on earth, the goal at its founding. However, most of the inventory of these books was owned by publishing agencies (distributors who mediate between publishers and bookstores, sell on consignment, and earn commission income) and publishers. Currently, Amazon carries inventories mainly of trendy books that sell well and require prompt response. Amazon keeps its list as small as possible while maintaining a large selection. When Amazon receives an order for a product not in stock, they order it with a publishing agency or publisher.

*Figure 3. Flows of book order and deliver*

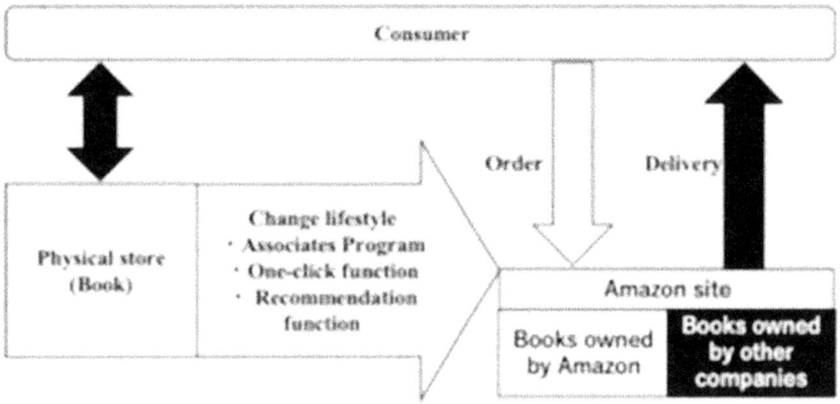


The advantage program introduced in 1998 became the basis of the intermediary platform mail-order business. Amazon made it possible to amass a rich assortment of titles without holding a considerable inventory in-house. This new program has made it easier for other bookstores and publishing agencies to sell on Amazon. By fulfilling its role as a consignment seller, Amazon has been able to offer customers a vast number of products owned by other companies on its site. According to Pareto's law, about 20% of the best-selling book inventories will earn 80% of sales. However, in Amazon, the remaining minor book sales account for the majority of sales. The product lineup focuses on top-selling products considering restrictions such as storage space and the risk of unsold products in a physical store. Nevertheless, in the case of Amazon, their site mainly constitutes consignment sales, so it can differentiate itself from competitors by offering an overwhelming product lineup (long-tail).

Amazon makes it possible to smoothly collaborate with sellers and affiliates on the information system to provide a multitude of products to fulfill customer orders through an efficient 1-Click function. They have succeeded in improving customer convenience through product recommendation functions that utilize big data. In the world of book and CD sales, which was previously dominated by physical stores (brick & mortar type), Amazon created a flow to the mail-order business via the Internet (click & mortar type) (Figure. 4).

## ONLINE SHOPPING SITE (2002-2014)

### Diversification of Product Categories

In 1997, Amazon leveraged its first book-selling assets, such as brands and customers, and extended its management know-how to non-book products. In the same year, Amazon began selling music CDs online as well as books. This venture into music CDs was the first sale of anything other than books for Amazon. At the same time, it acquired IMDb (Internet Movie Database), a site that exchanges informa-

*Figure 4. Flows order and delivery*

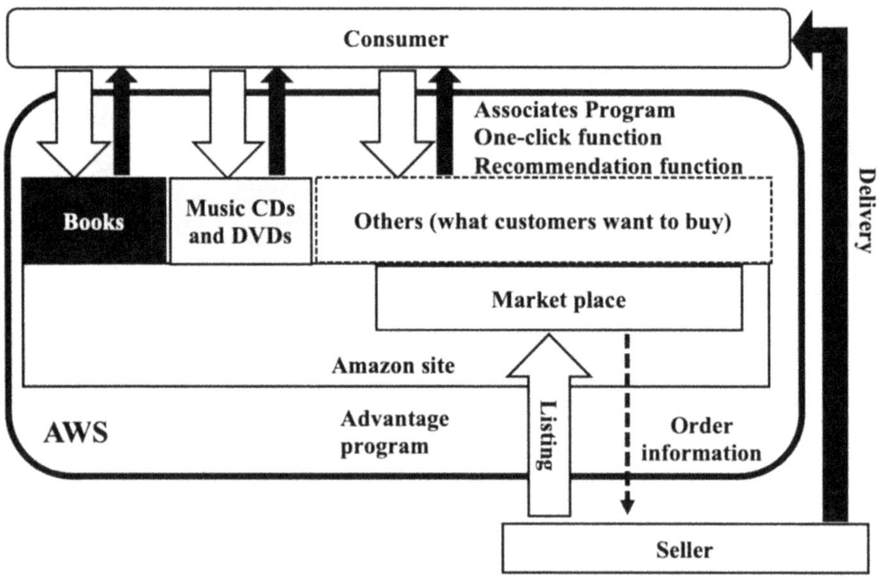


tion on movies, television, and actors, and began preparing for DVD sales. Amazon hopes to achieve long-tail success in a wide variety of categories (Higuchi, 2018 p. 133).

In 1998, Amazon started its first wave of expansions into new categories such as music, video, and gifts, and into other countries, such as the UK and Germany. After that, the company accelerated its further expansions into toys, consumer electronics, home improvement, software, video games, and many more. These expansions were representative of the essence of Bezos's vision.

Amazon has a mission statement that "we strive to offer our customers the lowest possible prices, the best available selection, and the utmost convenience." Amazon also has a vision statement that "to be Earth's most customer-centric company, where customers can find and discover anything they might want to buy online." Amazon's goal was to become a company where customers bought everything online at the lowest prices through digital technology. Moreover, Amazon remembers their original intention when first established and always competes as if it is Day One. Even if initially they provided good service, they know their rivals would soon catch up with them. Amazon needed to offer discounts, free delivery, construction of distribution network, improvement of academic affairs, and research. It is also a characteristic of Amazon's management to invest aggressively in development and generate inspiration. Rather than pursuing short-term profits, the emphasis is on long-term strategies to increase future corporate value.

Amazon has robust analytical and management tools. They can make the most of this advantage. However, Amazon lists search results of first-party and third-party seller products on the same page. They empower third-party sellers and share Amazon's customer base and core competencies with them.

Amazon's famous flywheel (Figure.5) visually and vividly illustrates the inner logic of how their platform works. Amazon can offer many items, serve many customers, and essentially grow linearly as a standalone online store. The platform business model opens everything up for third-party sellers, who

*Figure 5. FlyWheel*
*Source: (https://www.amazon.jobs/jp/landing_pages/about-amazon)*

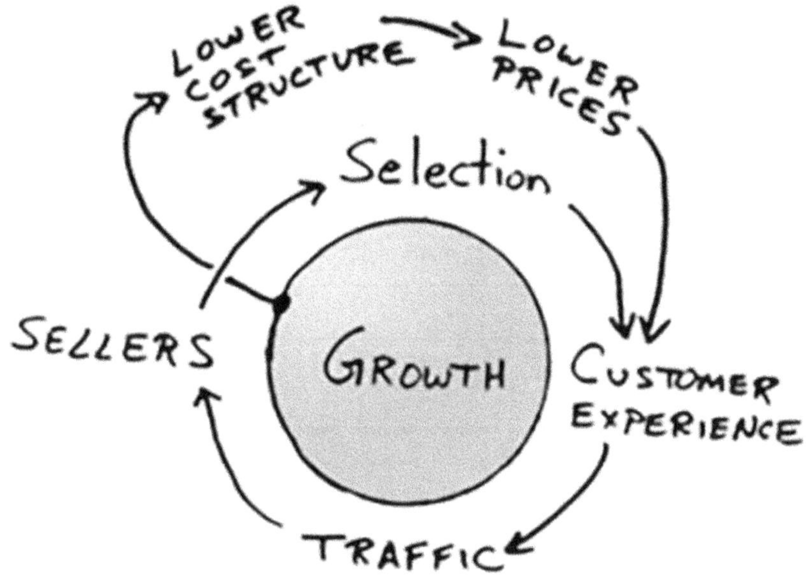


trigger the growth of a higher order. More sellers will bring in more selection, attract more customers, and thus increase scale. Increased scale will further reduce cost structure and translate into even lower prices. The expanded selection, decreased price, and improvement in the convenience (another side benefit of increased scale), will enhance the overall customer experience. Subsequently, this enhanced customer experience will generate more traffic by growing a powerful flywheel (Charan & Yang, 2019, p. 19).

Amazon became a magnificent everything store at a dazzling speed. During this rapid growth in products, categories, and working areas, Bezos kept acquiring companies with a focus on customer needs. He articulated Amazon's "pillars of customer experiences" in 2001 and reinforced the durability of these pillars in his 2008 Shareholder Letter:

1. Selection: already 45,000 items and millions of book titles on sale in 2001.
2. Convenience: a combination of 1-click ordering, recommendations, wish lists, instant order update, Look Inside the Book on the Internet, and fast delivery.
3. Low price: not simply by the scale of economy, but more so by Moores's Law and its variants (price performance of bandwidth, disk space, and processing power are doubling about every 9, 12, and 18 months, respectively).

## Securing Third-Party Sellers

Amazon ventures Amazon Auction and zShops failed to attract third-party sellers (both launched in 1999). Amazon abandoned Amazon Auctions in 2000 and zShops in 2007. They then audaciously launched the

*Figure 6. Fulfillment by Amazon*

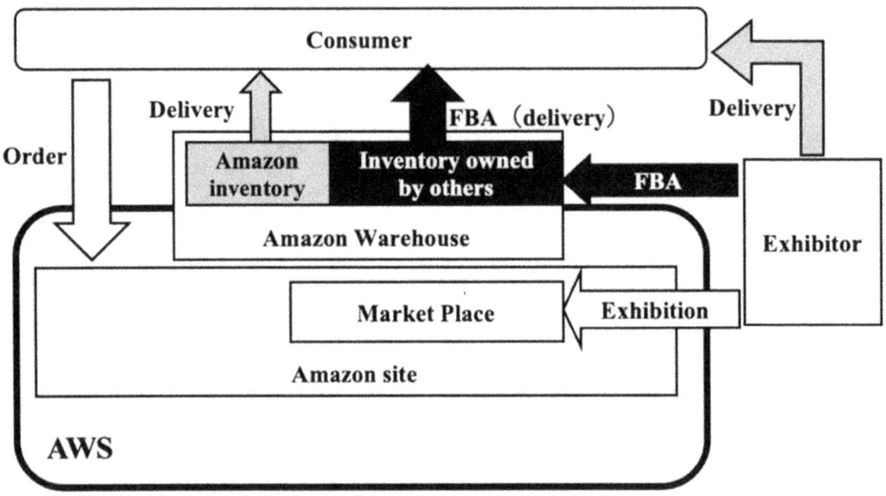


Marketplace, an e-commerce platform owned and operated by Amazon that enables third-party sellers to sell new or used products alongside Amazon's regular offerings (Armstrong and Associates Inc., 2020).

zShops converted to the Marketplace in 2000, providing a service listed by external businesses outside Amazon. The Marketplace has enabled Amazon to offer a more comprehensive selection of products. For customers, the range of products that can be selected on the Amazon site has expanded. In addition, Amazon has enhanced its Fulfillment by Amazon (FBA) to take advantage of the Marketplace logistics. Besides sales support services for sellers, Amazon manages inventory, arranges delivery, and provides after-sales service. It has the advantage of ensuring and facilitating commercial transactions on the Amazon site. When a customer places an order in Amazon's warehouse, it will be quickly picked up, packed, and shipped. Amazon fulfills the order instead of third-party sellers. Amazon executes orders more swiftly and efficiently than them. (Figure 6).

The Marketplace makes it possible for customers to quickly get what they want at a low price through the Amazon site. The platform also supports sellers and users, small and medium-sized domestic and foreign businesses. The Marketplace also had a practical impact on Amazon's range of products offered. Suppose Amazon has a variety of products that it has never handled before. In that case, it would be handled in-house by referring to the sales methods and assortments of products dealt with by other experienced retailers in the Marketplace. Amazon does not offer as much commission as other selling sites on the Marketplace. However, consumers know the Amazon site is the best-selling site. Many third-party sellers decide to sell their products there.

## Customer Acquisition

Since 2005, Amazon has been offering customers a membership program called Amazon Prime that offers various benefits such as free shipping and the fastest same-day delivery services. It has announced a free policy for members to eliminate customers' resistance to online shopping costs that may be higher than purchasing at a physical store. This policy has made it possible to improve customer support and promote bulk purchases. Free shipping has made it easier for customers to make frequent purchases on Amazon, even in small quantities, and customers are now shopping in new categories as well. In addition, Prime Day started in 2015, and Prime members could purchase members-only products at a discounted price. As a market positioning strategy, Prime Day remains to this day an effective way to acquire and retain Prime members (Taguchi, 2019).

Amazon Prime provides exclusive services. For Prime's paid membership, Amazon has a mechanism to encourage members to continue to purchase products and services by providing free shipping services and offering discounts (Berman, 2019). For example, Amazon recommends various members buy Kindle, an Amazon-only device for reading e-books, Fire TV sticks for watching TV, Fire tablets for videos other than reading, unlimited video viewing service, and unlimited music listening service.

Amazon has completed their ecosystem with a legion of customers and sellers. Amazon explored new businesses that leveraged the ecosystem. In 2009, Amazon announced its private brand *Amazon Basics* which offers home goods, office supplies, and tech accessories. Amazon Basics products are designed to be high-quality at low prices. As of December 2017, Amazon Basics is the best-selling private label brand on Amazon.com. Amazon Basics gives Amazon several advantages:

1. Amazon can advertise effectively and efficiently because it knows its customers very well.
2. Amazon has the advantage of enticing targeted customers to purchase Amazon Basics products by displaying them without promoting other competitive products.
3. Amazon can cut its cost of sales because it can procure products more economically by exerting its Amazon brand influence on manufacturers.

Amazon controls the supply chain from its lower end.

## Killing Two Birds with One Stone

Amazon has a marketplace that provides a platform for other sellers to market their products and services. Amazon has enriched its product lineup by adding other companies' products and has helped customers broaden their product selection range. Amazon had suffered from various problems between sellers and customers, and it could not guarantee the multitude of products sold on its site.

Amazon charges sellers a fee to list their products and receives a sales commission percentage based on the total amount of sales. Additionally, Amazon wanted another revenue from third-party sellers. It has enhanced its Fulfillment by Amazon (FBA) to capture marketplace logistics. Charges for the use of FBA services are reasonable. There is no fixed monthly fee. Only an inventory storage fee according to the required area and number of days of the product and a delivery agency fee based on the price and weight of the product are incurred, which is also a big attraction for small business sellers (MWPVL International, 2021).

The fulfillment center is a large-scale distribution facility, and it plays an essential function in online shopping distribution. Many products stored in the fulfillment center are picked up and shipped according to the orders received. The fulfillment center sends them to a transport company such as UPS, which outsources delivery to other distribution facilities. Deliveries from the seller incur more cost and time. By storing and delivering other companies' products, economies of scale in logistics are achieved, and various costs are reduced.

Data shows that in the ten years from 2010 to 2020, Amazon's fulfillment space has increased by 14 times, and it has always accounted for about 90% of Amazon's total space. In 2017, as Amazon started to operate its own physical stores, the proportion of fulfillment space decreased by 10%, but it remained the highest proportion of total space.

Amazon has expanded online shopping rapidly so far. Such a rapid expansion of sales will significantly increase the number of products that must be processed, which will necessitate an expansion of fulfillment centers accordingly. Amazon has opened new fulfillment centers at an accelerating pace worldwide since 2015 due to the expansion of e-commerce (Rodrigue, 2020). The installation status of Amazon's fulfillment centers is shown in figure 7.

The FBA service is a convenient service for small business sellers. FBA and advertising services are benefits of using the Marketplace. Businesses that sell on Amazon can place product advertisements there. It's a pay-per-click ad called a "sponsored product." This feature is displayed at the bottom of the screen and is linked to the keywords Amazon customers search. When combined with FBA, everything from product promotion to shipping can be completed by asking Amazon. Amazon will suffice to secure stores and logistics for companies with limited staffing.

Amazon improved the quality and speed of distribution by reforming the distribution network software. Even if the customer simultaneously orders multiple products, it may sometimes be possible to ship them together, provided the fulfillment center near that customer has those items in stock. Products can be shipped in the shortest time and at a lower cost (Saito, 2021).

## AMAZON WEB SERVICES (2015-)

### Overview

Amazon has been promoting further business expansion based on online shopping. At its core is AWS, a cloud service provider business released in 2006. Cloud services gather and send large amounts of data to external data centers via the Internet and use various ICT resources such as networks, server processing, storage, computing, databases, applications, and AI on demand. With AWS, many companies can process and analyze vast amounts of data such as big data, helping them comprehend, utilize more accurate forecasts, create new models, operate sites, and develop Internet businesses.

In 2000, Amazon began developing the merchant.com site to encourage major retailers to sell on the Amazon site. Amazon also recognized the need for Infrastructure as a Service (IaaS), allowing significant retailers to customize their platforms. IaaS is a service that provides computing resources such as CPU, memory, storage, and network. The user can freely select and use their desired resource configuration and build any application on IaaS. Initially, Amazon began using cloud services rather than physical consolidation to reduce the number of servers in its data centers. IaaS is highly customizable and allows flexible configuration selection. IaaS development was an important event during the birth of AWS.

In 2006, AWS officially released a cloud service that allowed corporate users to use Amazon's open infrastructure to build their own applications. Later, Amazon launched storage services (S3: Simple Strong Service), server leasing, and hosting services (EC2: Elastic Compute Cloud) one after another. These services have been highly acclaimed since their introduction to the market.

Over the next decade, AWS offered more than 100 services, including storage, computing, developer tools, IoT, security, and more. In 2012, the first AWS Developers Conference (RE: Invent) was held in

*Figure 7. Space of fulfillment, data center, and other*
*(Data Source: Amazon Annual Report, 2005-2020)*

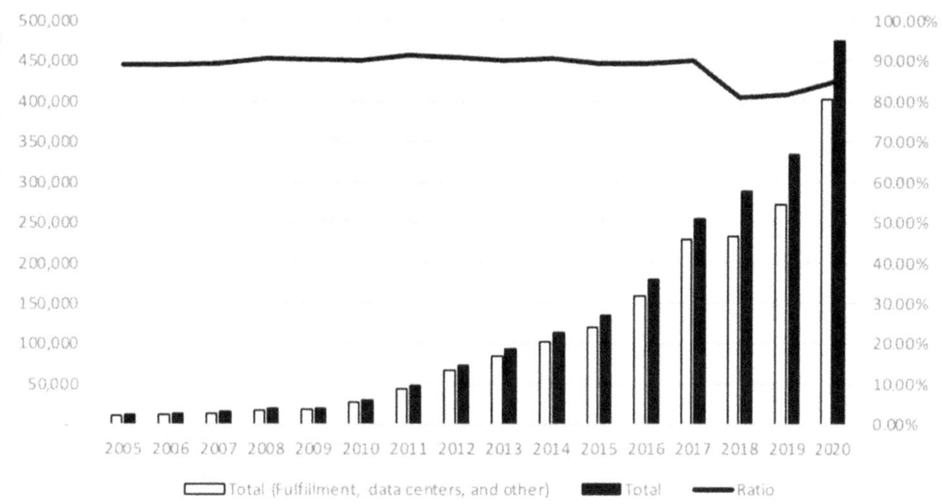


Las Vegas. Even today, more than 30,000 people register for the RE: Invent conference each year. In 2013, AWS beat a strong competitor, IBM, to win a US $ 600 million cloud deal from the Central Intelligence Agency (CIA) (Naruke, 2018, p. 134).

To flexibly provide the data that corporate users want, AWS has enhanced the ability to link multiple data sources easily. Amazon focuses on a data lake strategy that collects data in the object storage "Amazon S3" on AWS. The basic pattern of data utilization on AWS is as follows:

Step 1: Load all the data into S3.

Step 2: Build a data lake.

Step 3: Arrange the data format with AWS Glue.

Step 4: Proceed to data analysis using various tools.

The cloud provides many services to collect, store, and analyze data. Corporate users can utilize the information obtained from it to enhance customer service. With S3, it is possible to create buckets to store and download data and save data. In addition, authentication mechanisms can protect data sources from unauthorized access. Corporate users can easily use functions that are indispensable for data utilization, such as object storage, various databases, data warehouse (DWH), ETL (extract, exchange, load) tools, BI (business intelligence) tools, and AI (artificial intelligence).

AWS has become a more strategic tool and a competitive platform. Currently, Amazon holds the top share of the industry in the cloud services business (Figure 8). AWS contributes to creating many Internet-related startups and transitioning Amazon from the Everything Store to a Technology Company (Berg & Knights, 2019, pp. 280-281).

Amazon sales (consolidated basis) have increased more than nine times between 2007 and 2016. Meanwhile, the cost of sales to sales ratio has fallen, and gross profit has risen from 24% to 35%. Figure 9 shows the breakdown of operating expenses in 2003, 2010, and 2020. Due to rationalization and economies of scale, the portion of fulfillment costs (total of inventory and shipping costs) and general management costs to sales have decreased. In contrast, the technology, content-related, and marketing

*Figure 8. 2021 AWS first quarter market share*
*Source: (Canalys estimates, April 2021)*

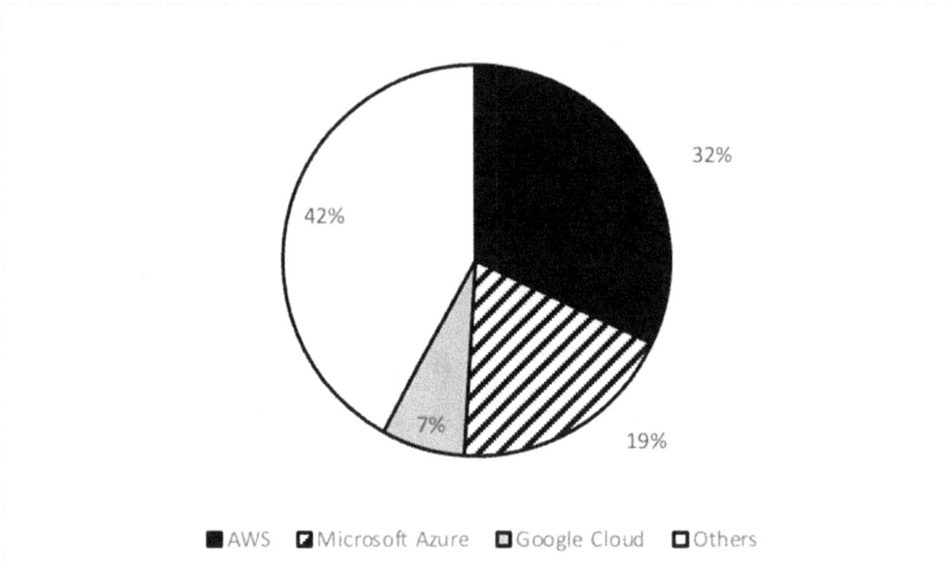


costs have increased. From the above, it is obvious that Amazon is actively investing in the future. Amazon is focusing on developing cutting-edge technologies for cloud services and AI and realizing drone delivery to connect Last One Mile.

*Figure 9. Trend of Amazon operating expenses*
*(Data Source: Amazon Annual Report, 2002, 2010, and 2020)*

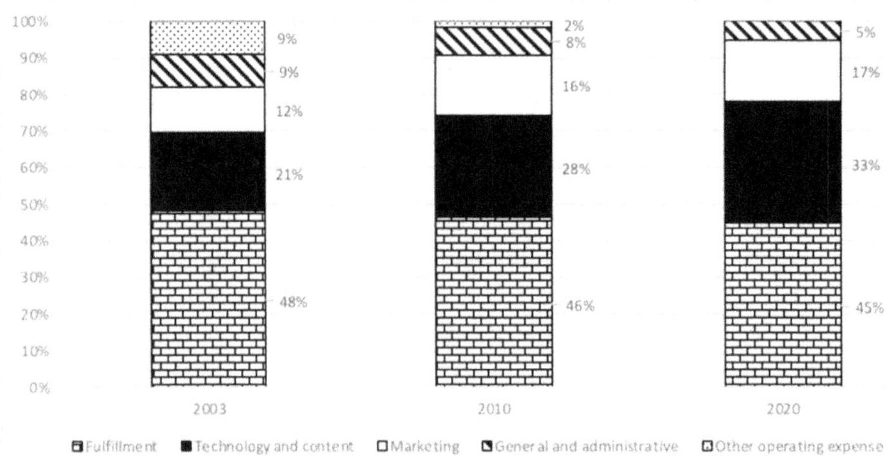


The sales of AWS launched in 2006 have grown at a rate of over 20% in the last few years (Figure 10). AWS accounts for only about 10% of Amazon's total sales, but the operating profit it generates accounts for more than half of the company's operating profit (Figures 10~12). In 2020, Amazon's overall operating profit was $22.9 billion, while AWS's operating profit was $13.5 billion. AWS supports Amazon as its top earner.

*Figure 10. AWS sales trends*
*(Data Source: Amazon Annual Report, 2016-2020)*

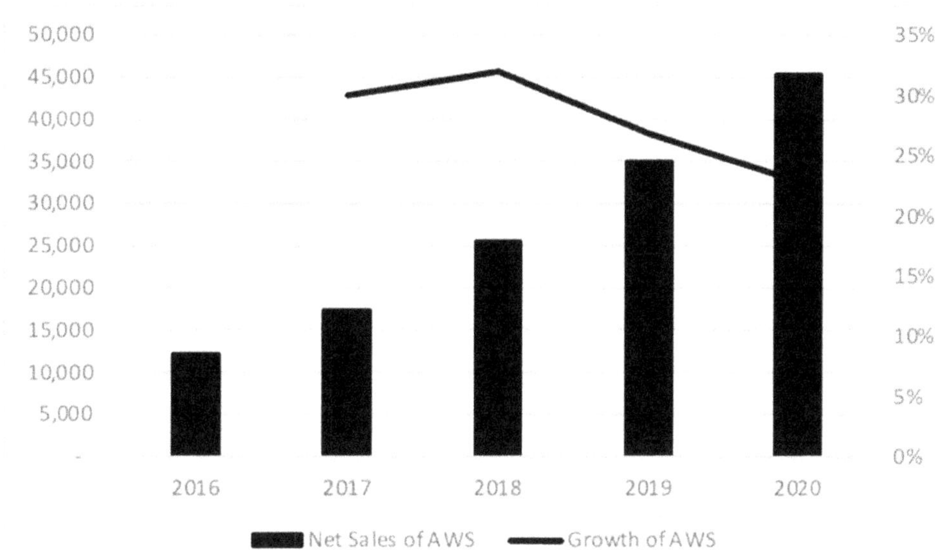


*Figure 11. AWS sales percentage*
*(Data Source: Amazon Annual Report, 2016-2020)*

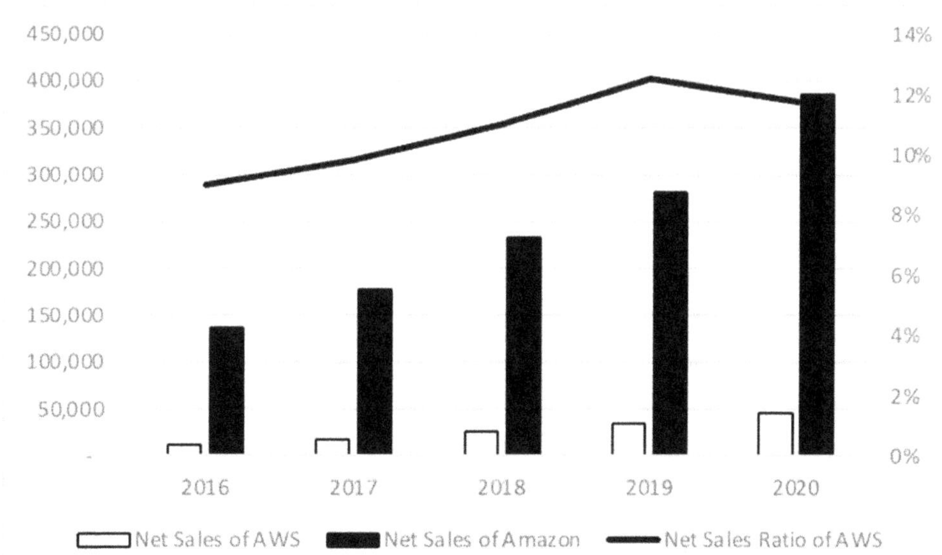

*Figure 12. AWS net income percentage*
*(Data Source: Amazon Annual Report, 2016-2020)*

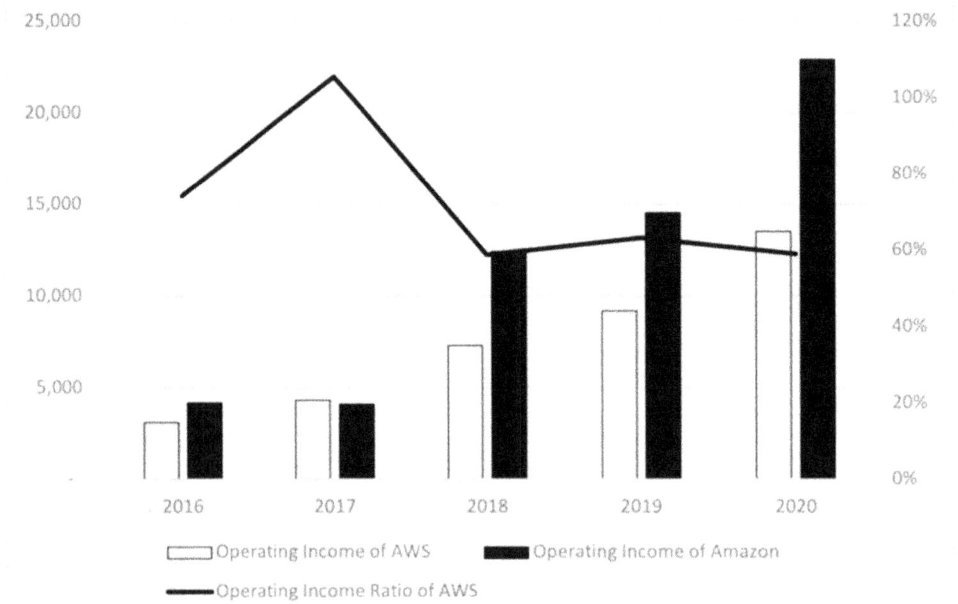


The Gartner site expects the global public cloud services market to grow from $257.5 billion in 2020 to $304.9 billion in 2021. Also, Gartner says IaaS will be the second segment in the market to reach more than $50 billion in 2020 (high growth rate of 24%) (Table 1). It has the highest growth rate in the market, and AWS will create more value as the primary provider of IaaS.

Amazon has created a new Flywheel strategic concept centered on AWS (Figure 13). This new strategy focuses on deep learning and machine learning. The artificial intelligence Echo smart equipment development team and the Alexa smart voice platform development team have an essential role in this

*Table 1. Global public cloud service market size (In millions of dollars)*

| | 2019 | 2020 | 2021 | 2022 |
|---|---|---|---|---|
| Cloud Business Process Service(BPaaS) | 45,212 | 44,741 | 47,521 | 50,336 |
| Cloud Application Infrastructure Service(PaaS) | 37,512 | 43,823 | 55,486 | 68,964 |
| Cloud Application Service(SaaS) | 102,064 | 101,480 | 117,773 | 138,261 |
| Cloud Management and Security | 12,836 | 14,880 | 17,001 | 19,934 |
| Cloud System Infrastructure Service(IaaS) | 44,457 | 51,421 | 65,264 | 82,225 |
| Desktop as a Service(DaaS) | 616 | 1,204 | 1,945 | 2,542 |
| Total Market | 242,696 | 257,549 | 304,990 | 362,263 |

Source: (https://www.gartner.com/en/newsroom/press-releases/2020-11-17-gartner-forecasts-worldwide-public-cloud-end-user-spending-to-grow-18-percent-in-2021)

*Figure 13. Flywheel strategy concept diagram centered on AWS*
*Source: (https://pages.awscloud.com/EMEA-Data-Flywheel.html?nc1=f_ls)*

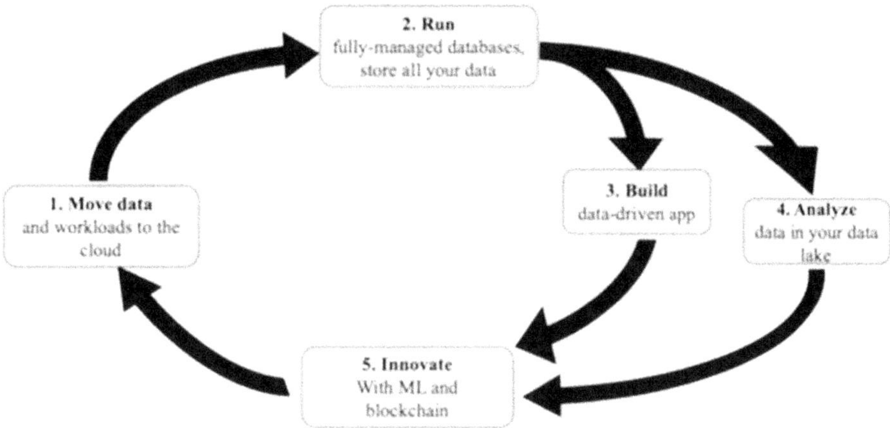


strategy. These teams can also be used directly by other Amazon development teams. While improving existing products and services in-house, it is also influencing Amazon's internal engineering team in artificial intelligence and encouraging the accumulation of related technologies for internal R & D personnel (Bishop, 2017).

Companies that hold the de facto standard in the IT industry tend to dominate, and such companies generally accelerate technology development. Until now, IBM has established an overwhelming position in host computers, Microsoft in personal computer operating systems, and Intel in semiconductors. In the cloud world, Amazon has the de facto standard.

On February 2, 2021, Amazon announced that Jeff Bezos, CEO, would retire, and Andy Jassy, CEO of Cloud Services Division (AWS), succeeded him. With the former AWS department personnel at the helm of the current Amazon, Amazon will focus on AWS dissemination and further feature development (Stone, 2021, p. 405).

## CONCLUSION

Bezos decided on his goal of selling everything in the world from the very beginning when he established an "internet bookstore" in 1994. Amazon developed a customer review function in 1995 and introduced the Associate Program the following year. Then, it created a 1-click order function and, in 1997, was listed on NASDAQ. With these programs, Amazon has converted the world from "brick and mortar" to "click and mortar."

In 1998, Amazon began to sell CDs, DVDs, and other items. After more than 20 years, Amazon has grown into a vast company with sales of 386 billion dollars. Meanwhile, the business domain expanded quickly to become an "everything store." Amazon took a critical step in breaking down the limitations of Pareto's Law and demonstrated the effectiveness of the "long-tail." In 2005, it introduced a prime membership system, adding various benefits such as free delivery and same-day delivery services to further retain customers. Amazon became indispensable to consumers.

In 2003, Amazon started reinforcing its relationship with corporate users through the Marketplace and by supporting B2C businesses as a "platformer." The "marketplace" where other retailers sell on Amazon's site accounts for more than half of the total sales volume, and it boasts an overwhelming position with a market share of over 40% in the US e-commerce market. Amazon also launched the "Amazon Basics" private label in 2005, even reaching out to the manufacturing sector of the supply chain. In 2006, Amazon expanded its FBA fulfillment center to stabilize service and generate new revenues. That same year, it unveiled AWS. Amazon continues to lead the cloud world by identifying future development opportunities, developing AWS's state-of-the-art cloud service, and growing it into a huge market. Before the advent of AWS, companies had to buy servers and build their own systems, so Amazon started a service that rents the system's in-house functions to other companies. Corporate users don't have to have servers and data centers. Finally, Amazon has established its self-expandable "ecosystem."

## FUTURE RESEARCH DIRECTION

Amazon has been aggressively investing in technology development to advance into various cutting-edge areas. Among them are "Blue Origin," a business aimed at manned space flight, "Alexa," a voice recognition technology, and others. However, Amazon has a significant problem: securing the user interface or Last One Mile. Consumers are scattered throughout the world, and fulfilling their purchases is the goal of most companies' activity and supply chain. Amazon has exceptional attention to the companies and systems, threatening the advantage Amazon acquired by securing consumer interface and Last One Mile delivery. Amazon has been strengthening these areas.

Last One Mile is a term initially used in the telecommunications industry to mean the last section of providing telecommunications connections to end-users and businesses. It is often used in the logistics industry and refers to the last part of goods and services arriving in customers' hands.

The actual customer interface and Last One Mile remain a bottleneck even in a digital world. In 2017, Amazon finally utilized its Amazon Go technology in a physical store by acquiring Whole Foods. Apart from the register, there are sundry IoT tools throughout the store, and Amazon Go, an almost unmanned store, proposes new user experiences through convenience and an excellent product lineup. Amazon caused a direct consumer interface to gather information about patrons and their behavior and analyze it to improve customer satisfaction and present new products and services to them. Amazon can connect more deeply with customers, understand their needs, and provide a better customer experience. In addition, this system is adaptable and useful for other retailers, and Amazon might obtain much more revenue and information in the near future (Satou, 2021, pp. 54-55).

The most stringent constraint for online shopping operators is the Last One Mile delivery. Keeping costs down and delivering products to consumers as quickly and reliably as possible with Last One Mile delivery, which has high logistics costs, has a significant impact on the success of the online shopping business. In the United States, Amazon has outsourced Last One Mile delivery to UPS, FedEx, and USPS. However, the oligopoly system of three major companies in the United States is well established, and major courier companies such as UPS and FedEx have strong control over the fare. Delivery charges have been raised almost every year. Increasing delivery cost is a heavy burden on online sales.

Covering the Last One Mile is one of the most significant issues in logistics. Amazon addressed this issue by developing Last One Mile and launching various other measures. Since 2015, crowdsourced delivery has been expanding in the United States. This business model provides a transportation service whereby a contractor allows individuals to carry cargo in their own private vehicles using mobile phone or tablet apps. To this end, Amazon launched Amazon Flex and Amazon Delivery Service Partner (Taylor, 2018). Amazon makes a contract with a truck company and personnel to conduct flexible Last One Mile deliveries at a lower cost. This program helps a transportation company specialize in delivering Amazon freight and recruits managers to create a new transportation company.

In March 2017, Amazon unveiled Prime Air at a conference in California. A video was also released on YouTube. A drone with four rotors landed on a sheet laid out on the lawn. This drone was developed in-house by Amazon and was capable of fully autonomous flight. There are no initial investments compared to ground delivery, and labor and operating costs are reduced. In addition, drones are a part of IoT, which transmits diverse information and executes orders. Amazon may also be able to control deliveries and their costs, another benefit. However, there are strict regulations about drone flight (Sudbury & Hutchinson, 2016). For example, in the United States and Japan, commercial drones can only fly within a limited area in operators' visual line of sight. Since this requires many drivers, commercial drones are not profitable. On August 29, 2020, Amazon received approval from the Federal Aviation Administration (FAA) under Part 135 of FAA regulations to deliver customer packages via drone "beyond the visual line of sight" of the drone operator. The acquisition of this certification was also an important step for "Prime Air." It is no exaggeration to say that Amazon has changed global distribution.

## REFERENCES

Amazon Annual Report 1997-2020. (n.d.). https://ir.aboutamazon.com/annual-reports-proxies-and-shareholder-letters/default.aspx

Amazon Web Services Inc. (2021). https://pages.awscloud.com/EMEA-Data- Flywheel.html?nc1=f_ls

Armstrong & Associates Inc. (2020). *Rising Tide: The Rapid Growth of E-Commerce Logistics, 3PL Solutions, Last-Mile Delivery, and the Dominance of Amazon.* Armstrong and Associates Inc. https://www.prnewswire.com/news-releases/rising-tide-the-rapid-growth-of-e-commerce-logistics-3pl-solutions-last-mile-delivery-and-the-dominance-of-amazon-301137811.html

Berg, N., & Knights, M. (2019). *Amazon: How the world's most relentless retailer will continue to revolutionize commerce*. Kogan Page.

Berman, J. (2019, Dec.). Amazon's shipping and logistics spend remains in lockstep with expectations. *Logistics Management,* 12-13. https://www.logisticsmgmt.com/article/amazons_shipping_and_logistics_spend_remains_in_lockstep_with_expectations

Bishop, T. (2017). Amazon Bringing Echo and Alexa to 80 Additional Countries in Major Global Expansion. *GeekWire.* https://www.geekwire.com/2017/amazon-bringing-echo-alexa-80-additional-countries-major-global-expansion/

Brant, R. (2011). *One Click: Jeff Bezos and the Rise of Amazon.com.* Portfolio.

Canalys. (2021). *United States cloud services market Q1 2021.* https://www.canalys.com/newsroom/united-states-cloud-infrastructure-q1-2021

Charan, R., & Yang, J. (2019). *The Amazon Management System.* Ideapress.

Gartner, Inc. (2020). *Worldwide Public Cloud Services End-User Spending Forecast.* https://www.gartner.com/en/newsroom/press-releases/2020-11-17-gartner-forecasts-worldwide-public-cloud-end-user-spending-to-grow-18-percent-in-2021

MWPVL International. (2021). *Amazon Global Supply Chain and Fulfillment Center. Network.* MWPVL International. https://www.mwpvl.com/html/amazon_com.html

Naruke, M. (2018). *Amazon sekai saisendan no senryaku ga wakaru.* Daiyamondosya.

Rodrigue, J. (2020, October). The distribution network of Amazon and the footprint of freight digitalization. *Journal of Transport Geography, 88*, 1–28. doi:10.1016/j.jtrangeo.2020.102825 PMID:32834678

Saito, M. (2021). *Amazon's Logistics Strategy in the E-Commerce Era* (Vol. 47). The Studies. In Economics and Trade.

Satou, M. (2021). *Amazon siki kawaritudukeru tikara* [Continuous Improvement by Amazon]. Daiwasyobou.

Stone, B. (2013). *The Everything Store.* Back Bay Books Press.

Stone, B. (2021). *Amazon Unbound.* Simon & Schuster Inc.

Sudbury, A. W., & Hutchinson, E. B. (2016). A Cost Analysis of Amazon Prime Air (Drone Delivery). *The Journal of Economic Education, 16*, 1–12.

Taguchi, F. (2019). Ryutsu inobesyon kenkyu amazon no seityoukatei to kyousouyuui no gensen [A Study on Innovation in the Distribution: The Secret of Growth of Amazon]. *Business Review of the Senshu University., 108*, 41–76.

Taylor, R. (2018) Amazon Embraces the Gig Economy: Small Business Risk or Game-Changing Opportunity? *Forbes.* https://www.forbes.com/sites/forbestechcouncil/2018/09/04/amazon-embraces-the-gig-economy-small-business-risk-or-game-changing-opportunity/?sh=18c5d0897e63

## KEY TERMS AND DEFINITIONS

**1-Click:** A technology that enables the online purchase of products with a single click. The 1-Click purchase requires the user to enter payment information in advance. Amazon.com filed a 1-Click patent application in 1997, and it is used on the company's website worldwide.

**Amazon Marketplace:** An e-commerce platform owned and operated by Amazon.com. Along with regular Amazon sales, third-party sellers can sell new or used items at fixed prices online. The Amazon Marketplace gives sellers access to Amazon's customer base and allows Amazon to expand its on-site sales without additional inventory investment.

**Amazon S3 (Amazon Simple Storage Service):** An object storage service offering industry-leading scalability, data availability, security, and performance. Customers of all sizes and industries can store and protect any amount of data for virtually any use case, such as data lakes, cloud-native applications, and mobile apps. With cost-effective storage classes and easy-to-use management features, customers can optimize costs, organize data, and configure fine-tuned access controls to meet specific business, organizational, and compliance requirements.

**AWS:** A cloud computing service provided by Amazon.com since 2006. Amazon provides a wide variety of infrastructures, not limited to web services. It gathers and sends large amounts of data to external data centers via the Internet and uses various ICT resources such as networks, server processing, storage, computing, databases, applications, and AI on demand.

**Click and Mortar:** A business model with both online and offline operations. Brick and mortar indicates old-style transactions at physical stores. On the other hand, click and mortar indicates new-style transactions on the web.

**Ecosystem:** A self-expandable network of organizations composed of suppliers, distributors, customers, competitors, government agencies, and others, and engaged in mutual competition and cooperation. Within the ecosystem, members are flexible and adaptable and are affected by others.

**FBA (Fulfillment by Amazon):** A fulfillment service Amazon offers to third-party sellers on the Amazon site. Amazon stores their stock at Amazon fulfillment centers. When customers order these products, Amazon fulfills these orders quickly and efficiently by picking, packing, and shipping. Amazon provides customer service on behalf of third-party sellers.

**IaaS (Infrastructure as a Service):** A service that provides computing resources such as CPU, memory, storage, and network. It allows significant retailers to customize their platforms. Users can select and use the resource configuration and build any application on IaaS.

**Last One Mile:** A term initially used in the telecommunications industry to mean the last section of providing telecommunications connections to end-users and businesses. It is also called the "last mile" and is mainly used in the logistics and transportation industries for customers.

# Section 4
# Food and Beverage Cases

*Section 4 provides new perspectives and approaches along with food and beverage cases. Freshness plays a vital role in the taste and hygiene of food and beverages. Individual companies and supply chains take various measures to ensure prompt delivery and freshness.*

# Chapter 9
# Product and Process Innovation in Coffee Supply Chain:
## From Seed to Cup

**Linh Dieu Nguyen**
*Sakushin Gakuin University, Japan*

**Yukun Huang**
*Sakushin Gakuin University, Japan*

**Zhengguang Yang**
*Sakushin Gakuin University, Japan*

**Gary Mason**
*Independent Researcher, USA*

## ABSTRACT

*In this chapter, the framework of the evolutional supply chain and supply chain strategy is illustrated through the case of the coffee supply chain. Billions of people drink coffee daily throughout the world. The coffee supply chain has a long history that has frequently experienced dramatic changes. The method and instruments for making coffee have changed, and the plantation system has long been used. Today, the world is full of various coffee products and coffee supply chains. It is imperative to refine not only SCM but also to formulate a successful supply chain strategy.*

## INTRODUCTION

This chapter illustrates the relationship between the transition of products and the structure of supply chains through the case of coffee beverages. During the long history of coffee, the coffee beverage has evolved many times and been drunken worldwide. According to the evolvement and development of coffee beverages, the coffee business and its supply chain changed dramatically.

DOI: 10.4018/978-1-7998-9800-9.ch009

An untold number of people drink coffee all over the world. The coffee they consume and the places where they drink are all different. In addition, the time and reason for drinking coffee are varied. These facts are evidence that there are countless coffee supply chains throughout the globe. To survive, supply chain members need to consistently improve their supply chain process and develop their appropriate strategy together as a whole unit to implement that strategy accordingly.

Regarding the origin of coffee, there is a legend about ancestors of the Oromo tribe in Ethiopia being the first to eat coffee beans and then cultivate coffee plants a long time ago. Around the 15th century, drinking coffee during Islamic religious ceremonies was introduced to prevent drowsiness and hunger during long periods of prayer and meditation. Later, people began to drink the liquid of boiled coffee beans. The Yemeni port of Mocha, located on the opposite bank of the Red Sea across from Ethiopia, quickly became famous as a coffee bean exporter.

Today's coffee goes through the following steps before drinking:

Step 1: Plant coffee trees (Coffea genus plants)
Step 2: Harvest coffee cherries from coffee trees (cherry).
Step 3: Remove the exodermis and pulp of coffee cherries (parchment).
Step 4: Remove the inner pericarps (green bean).
Step 5: Roast coffee beans (roast bean).
Step 6: Grind coffee beans (ground coffee).
Step 7: Pour boiling water over the ground coffee and filter (drip method).
Step 8: Drink coffee.

From steps 1 to 4, the first half of making green beans is conducted near the production area to prevent decay. The taste and flavor differ depending on whether cherries and parchments are dried or washed with water. A green bean covered by silver skin can preserve the freshness longer. Temperature is the most critical parameter of storage. At a warm temperature, green beans lose aroma due to the oxidation process. An excellent way to keep the coffee fresh is to freeze the beans during transportation and storage.

From steps 5 to 8, the second half is mainly conducted near the consumption area. The silver skin is removed from the green beans during the roasting process. Roast beans lose their freshness quickly. When roast beans are ground outside of their consumption area, they need to be stored in an inert atmosphere (i.e., nitrogen) or in a vacuum to prevent the degradation of aroma and flavor through oxidation. Ground coffee is more susceptible to aging than whole roast beans. Sometimes, different kinds of coffee beans are blended to adjust the taste and flavor of the finished coffee. There are numerous options for drinking coffee. After dripping, step 7, some dripped coffee is packaged in bottles or cans or processed into instant coffee.

Nowadays, people can choose their roasting and grinding preferences, brewing method, hot or cold, and drinking venue, starting with selecting coffee beans. Most consumers have their likes and choose one from the broad types of products and places. Companies strategically define their consumer needs to meet and manage their supply chains.

## BACKGROUND

Coffee research has been conducted mainly by enthusiasts of coffee or coffee companies and associations. Coffee enthusiasts tend to make emphasize the history and taste of coffee. On the other hand, the coffee companies and associations tend to highlight the status of coffee and their contribution. Recent research related to SCM has been conducted from a specific region, product, period, etc. Nguyen & Sarker (2018) discussed sustainable coffee supply chain management through the case of Vietnam, in which the production of green beans and instant coffee has been increasing. Wong et al. (2020) analyzed the cost structure and illustrated the profit of instant coffee compared to regular coffee. Bashiri et al. (2021) simulated the risk of the coffee supply chain from Indonesia to the UK. Kittichotsatsawat et al. (2021) exploited modern agricultural technologies that reduce the supply chain's cost and time. This chapter discusses the coffee supply chain from a more comprehensive and long-term point of view to propose the basis to analyze and classify the type of coffee business and supply chain.

Worldwide, three main types of coffee trees (coffea) are cultivated for drinking coffee. Cultivation conditions for all coffee trees are so stringent that they can only grow in a limited area near the equator. The fact that coffee is consumed worldwide means that coffee producers and consumers are very diverse socially and widely separated physically. The coffee supply chains consist of many members from different tiers, covering the global market.

Arabica Coffee Bean (Coffea arabica) is the most popular coffee bean. It originated many centuries ago in the highlands of Ethiopia and is tasty and expensive. However, Coffea arabica has a disadvantage in that they dry out quickly. All coffee beans grow in the so-called Bean Belt, and Coffea Arabica requires extra shade, water, and high altitude to develop correctly. These plants are more susceptible to plant diseases and must be cultivated at an elevation of at least 2,000 feet.

Robusta Coffee Bean (Coffea canephora), the second most popular type of coffee, originated in sub-Saharan Africa. It is also prevalent in Indonesia and Vietnam. The Robusta bean has such a strong bitter taste that it is often added to coffee blends. Its price is much lower than Arabica beans, and robusta beans are larger and more rounded than the others. In addition, Robusta plants are much larger than Arabica plants so planting them is a real-time-saver. Robusta trees are generally considered more profitable because they can grow at lower altitudes, resist diseases, and produce 2-3 times more berries than Arabica trees (Urban Bean Coffee, 2021).

Liberica Coffee Bean (Coffea liberica) is the third primary type of coffee tree. These trees are so tolerant of hot, humid climates that they grow as much larger plants than Arabica or Robusta, mainly in Indonesia, Malaysia, and the Philippines. Most Liberica cherries tend to be irregular in shape and closer to Robusta in size and general appearance. Despite the tree's tolerance to heat, it accounts for only a few percent of the world's coffee production because it is so scarce that farmers cannot scale it to satisfy a global market (District Roasters, 2019). This rare coffee has a pleasant piquant, floral aroma, and smoky flavor. Sometimes it is mixed with other varieties to add volume and complexity.

Taste, flavor, and price are essential considerations in the production of coffee. Many factors determine the final product at the raw material stage before the roast. The types of coffee trees, the place of origin, and the method and duration of processing are all sources of significant difference. The degree of roasting and grinding needs to be adjusted to suit the consumer. Finally, coffee is processed for the drip method of making coffee, one of the most common methods used by consumers. The coffee supply chains are very diverse due to the numerous combinations of available options in production.

The diversification of coffee products is ongoing such as freshly brewed coffees, canned coffees, instant coffees, and others. People enjoy various coffees in different situations. Therefore, each coffee supply chain must target and satisfy the needs of specific consumer groups accordingly. Coffee supply chains are evolving at a rapid pace.

Figure 1 illustrates the evolution of the coffee industry. Demand and supply have grown due to product and process innovations. Turkish coffee was one of the earliest product innovations, which used finely ground roast beans and was brewed with boiling water without filters. Green coffee beans remain after their parchment (hull) and pericarp (outer skin) have been removed. The beans are stored for a long time, then efficiently transported over long distances. Roasting green beans improves their taste and flavor. Finely ground beans allow easy passage of the boiling water to produce the liquid coffee. The drip method and espresso method are two popular brewing methods.

Around 1960, the popularity of a quick cup of coffee at a reasonable price arose. In other words, coffee became an industrialized or manufactured product or commodity. Packed roast and ground beans and coffee sets had previously been sold under various brand names. Instant coffee and canned coffee emerged in the market, and mass production made mass consumption possible. Greater consumption led to more demand for Robusta varieties of coffee because of their lower cost and ability to blend well with other coffees, especially iced coffee.

Starbucks, established in 1971, led the second wave where people could buy and drink a wide variety of quality coffee products. They helped the coffee industry contribute significantly to the tertiary sector of the economy. Serving a wide variety of uniform, quality products at many chain stores is a complicated operation. Currently, a third wave arising may emphasize coffee's place of origin.

For the production of these coffees, small farmers, for example in Brazil or Colombia, are more suitable than huge plantations. The small farmers have a unique experience and expertise in selecting and picking the best beans with a singular focus on quality. On the other hand, the large commercial brands are interested mainly in keeping their costs low. In addition, a small farm's limited production has the advantage of creating and strengthening its brand. This prevailing third wave deals with officially graded high-quality specialty coffees.

*Figure 1. Evolution of coffee industry*

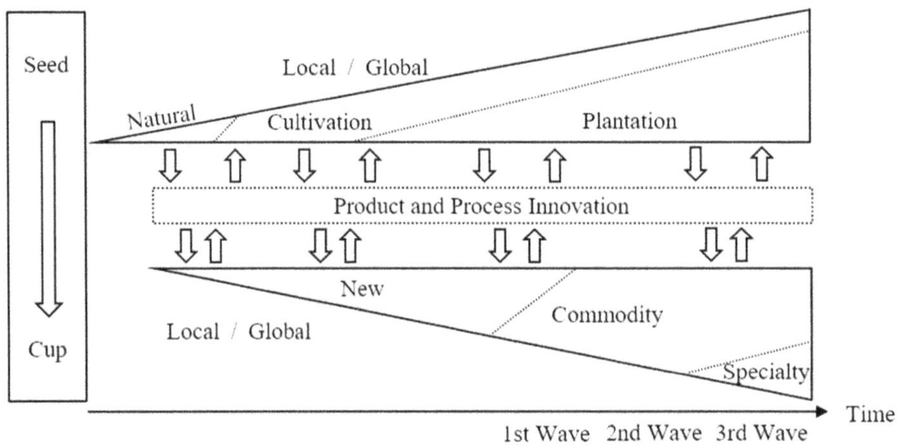

## MAJOR PRODUCT AND PROCESS INNOVATIONS IN COFFEE

### Processing of Green Beans

Coffee cherries deteriorate quickly. Removing the exodermis and pulp of coffee cherries and the inner pericarps should be done soon after harvesting. This procedure includes cleaning and drying. The beans become smaller, lighter, and more easily transported through these processes than before. In addition, the taste and flavor of the resulting coffee are enhanced because almost all inferior beans are eliminated. After this stage, green beans have become a tradable product due to the expansion of the trading area.

### Drip Method and Coffee

The establishment of the drip method was a significant process innovation and gave birth to drip coffee. Grinding roast beans and filtering the liquid coffee during the drip method process provides a better coffee taste and flavor. Drip coffee has been the mainstream in the coffee industry for a few centuries. Espresso is made somewhat similar to the drip method, i.e., hot water passes through coffee grounds to develop a coffee-flavored liquid. However, the very robust espresso coffee is usually made in a signature espresso machine that forces high-pressure steam through the ground coffee to shorten the brew time significantly.

### Coffee Houses

Coffee houses were places where drip coffee was served. Early coffee houses in London and Istanbul were elegant meeting places in the 17th and 18th centuries. Coffee houses are restaurants serving coffee, other beverages, and food while listening to music, poetry, or otherwise relaxing. Roasting coffee beans correctly and finely grinding them is labor-intensive without the appropriate equipment or coffee sets. At that time, distribution channels of roast and ground beans were unavailable to ordinary people.

### Cultivation and Plantation

At first, the number of natural coffea for the production of coffee was minimal. Production was minimal and unstable. In addition, the quality was poor due to the lack of quality control. Cultivation started near the natural coffea habitat with subsequent increased production and improved quality. The Dutch East Company established plantations in Ceylon and Java and exported green beans to Europe at lower prices in the 18th century. France and England also started plantations in the Caribbean islands. Brazil has been the most significant export country since the 19th century. Plantations in Brazil are large-scale and very mechanized.

### Distribution Channel and Coffee Sets

It is challenging to make drip coffee without appropriate coffee sets. People can fry green beans in a frying pan and grind roast beans with a mortar and pestle. However, making coffee without suitable equipment or coffee sets is awkward and time-consuming. With this situation in mind, it would be precarious to establish a distribution channel of roast and ground beans. After coffee shops increased their number and companies enhanced and expanded household coffee sets, including roasters, coffee grinders or mills, coffee makers, and coffee pots, people started making and drinking more drip coffee at home and in offices. The demand for home-brewed coffee grew. The distribution channel for roast and ground beans and widespread availability of practical coffee sets popularized drip coffee. In addition, the advancement of transportation mode in the 19th century boosted the establishment and expansion of distribution channels. As a result, people could start drinking drip coffee at home and the office.

## Instant Coffee

In 1988, Satori Kato, a Japanese chemist, invented freeze-dried instant coffee while researching green tea powder. Instant coffee became hugely popular with American soldiers during World War II. It helped them recover from exhaustion and refreshed their minds by simply mixing it with hot water in cups. Although instant coffee is inferior to drip coffee in taste and flavor, it is quite convenient. It has a very long shelf life and is portable. In addition, instant coffee is much cheaper than drip coffee. All these benefits have contributed to expanding the coffee market worldwide.

## Coffee Beverage

In 1969, UCC (Uejima Coffee Company) started selling canned coffee. They developed coffee that stayed delicious for a long time, even if it was thicker than the usual coffee or cold. They brewed drip coffee and canned it at a factory. This process introduced the concept in Japan that coffee didn't always have to be hot to be enjoyed. Some people drink it cold, while others drink it at room temperature. These revolutionary canned coffee beverages were sold at retailers and in vending machines in Japan, and they remain very popular to this day. Shortly afterward, some coffee beverages were packaged in glass bottles or paper cartons. Some vending machines had a warming function.

Many people around the world still have a feeling of resistance to coffee beverages. It took a few decades to spread the habit of drinking coffee beverages internationally. Nowadays, global coffee chains such as Starbucks and Costa Coffee also sell coffee beverages in plastic bottles worldwide.

## Coffee Shop Chains

Starbucks and Costa Coffee are the most famous global coffee shop chains, offering premium coffee with consistent quality. They started as roasters in Seatle and London respectively in the 1970s and later launched into coffee stores in the 1980s. Their new ventures grew into far-reaching coffee shop chains. Buying green beans in bulk reduced the cost of sales and the cost of freight. They spend massive amounts of money on product development and advertisement for their brands and new products. Their brand names are so well-known that they attract new and old customers alike.

A vast number of local coffee shop chains exist around the world. Some started as coffee stores or privately-run coffee houses that expanded their coffee store network, and others entered from the restaurant industry or other enterprises. Global and local coffee shop chains have been replacing privately-run coffee houses.

## WORLD COFFEE PRODUCTION AND CONSUMPTION

### Overview

The origin of coffee is mainly in the highlands near the equator. More than 50 countries harvest and export coffee beans. The top six countries, Brazil, Vietnam, Colombia, Indonesia, Ethiopia, and Honduras, account for 77% of global exports (Figure 2). Nowadays, South America and Southeast Asia are the primary sources of coffee beans. The harvest time is different in the Southern and Northern Hemispheres.

*Figure 2. Export volume of coffee beans*
*(Data Source: International Coffee Organization)*

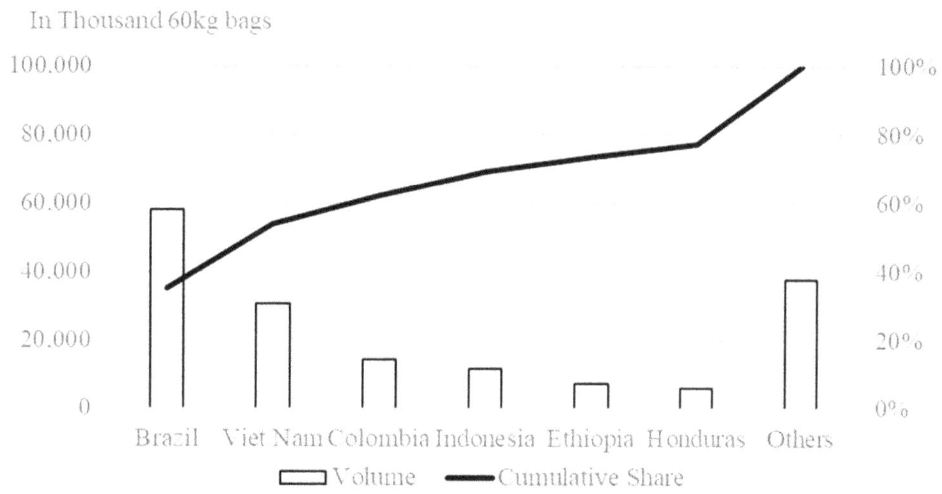


Being able to supply coffee beans to the market throughout the year is beneficial.

World coffee bean exports have increased about 1.8 times in the last 30 years from 1990 to 2020. 84% of this growth comes from Brazil and Vietnam (Figure 3). In Brazil, large-scale, mechanized coffee plantations of Arabica varieties have been developed. In Vietnam, Robusta varieties that are resistant to diseases and can be harvested in large quantities have increased significantly. Coffee is an international product, although it is produced in limited areas. Most coffee is consumed outside its production area. Coffee is drunk a lot in Europe and the United States, and people tend to drink more coffee in cold regions.

Regular coffee was the only type of coffee product available up until 1960. The price of regular coffee tended to decrease due to plantation and process improvements. Companies sold various brands of coffee beans and coffee sets. Around 1960, the first wave took place in the coffee industry. The emergence of instant coffee and canned coffee boosted the diffusion of coffee. Their average price deviated from regular coffee and was lower because their beans were cheaper than those used for drip coffee and espresso (Figure 4). People began to appreciate higher quality, more expensive regular coffee during the second wave. As a result, the average price of coffee is increasing. Nowadays, some coffee companies

*Figure 3. Expansion of export volume of coffee beans*
*(Data Source: International Coffee Organization)*

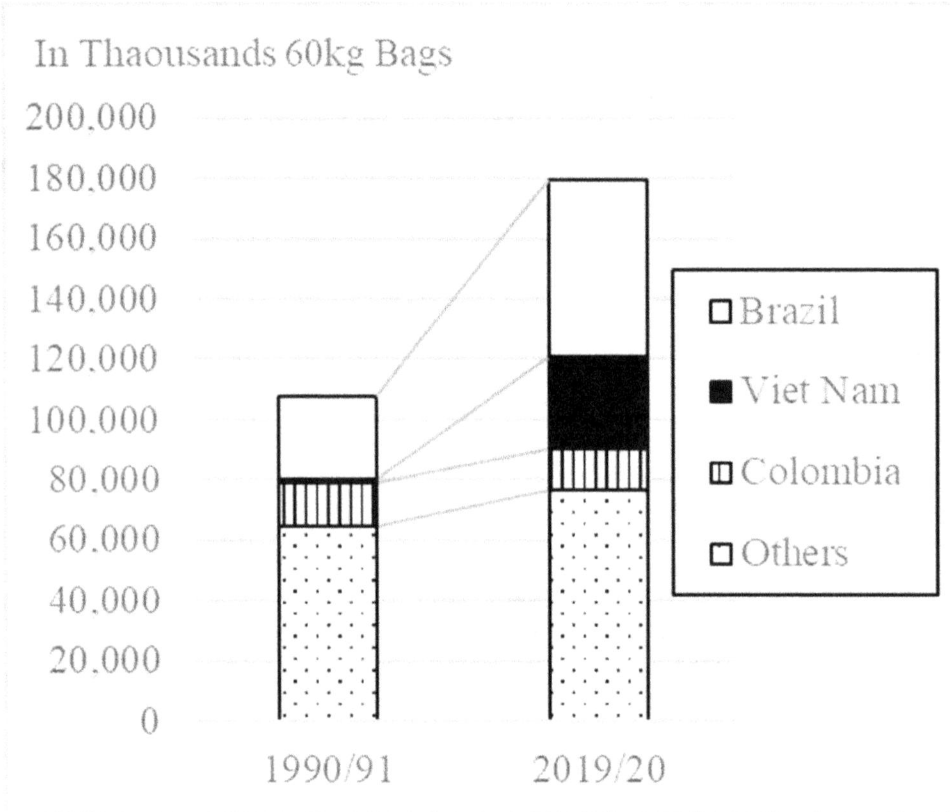


*Figure 4. Image of transition of coffee price*
**Regular coffee includes drip coffee and espresso.*
**Non-regular coffee includes instant coffee and canned or bottled coffee.*
**Average is the weighted average of regular coffee and non-regular coffee.*
**The weighting factor is a market share.*

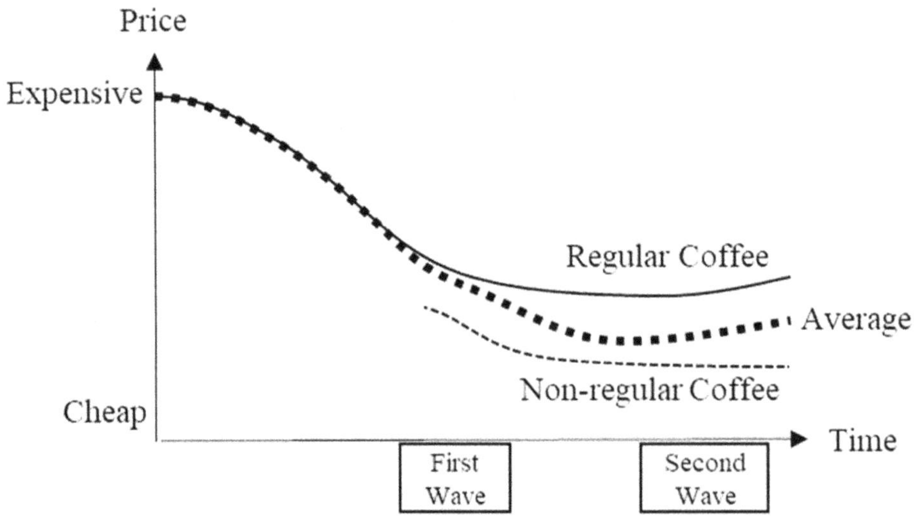

are actualizing the third wave through differentiation from competitors by selecting the highest quality beans certified to be environmentally friendly.

## USA Case (From the Boston Tea Party to Starbucks and Beyond)

Did the coffee boom in the USA emanate from an excessive tax on tea? Apparently so. In 1773, King George III of England and his vindictive British parliament enacted the Tea Act of May 1773. It levied an extremely unpopular tax on tea stored on three ships and intended for the American colonists in Boston. In retaliation, the unhappy settlers, disguised as Mohawk Indians, showed their disfavor by emptying 342 crates of tea into the Boston Harbor. They transferred the numerous 90 to 400-pound containers up from the cargo area. A single British officer with his sword drawn was the only opposition the colonizers encountered. Being heavily outnumbered, he simply stepped aside. It remains unclear even to this day which the colonists responsible for this now historic Boston Tea Party were. Yet, it became one of the most iconic events of the American Revolution. It ignited an underdog revolt against British rule that unified a fledgling nation in waiting.

There is little doubt that after the Boston Tea Party, coffee consumption experienced an upsurge because all things British, especially tea, fell into disfavor. However, coffee was indeed consumed before the incident. Historical records show that a coffee trader's license was granted to Dorothy Jones of Boston in 1670. Additionally, some historians reference 1689 in the book History and Antiquities of the City of Boston by Samuel Gardner Drake as evidence that Boston was home to the first American coffee house, named the London Coffee House. Even earlier documents mention the availability of coffee in New York (formerly New Amsterdam) in the mid-1600s.

Coffeehouses thrived throughout New England by the mid-1770s, but tea was still the favored beverage. After the Boston Tea Party, Americans switched their predilection for tea to coffee as part of their patriotic duty. Even George Washington, the first president of the United States, not only liked drinking it, but he also imported it. Records show that he had received more than 200 pounds by 1770. Coincidentally, an American-Belgian inventor named George Constant Louis Washington is credited with inventing the first commercially mass-produced instant coffee. He was purportedly a distant relative of President Washington.

The coffee industry thrived through the end of the 18th century, and coffee became the most widely preferred breakfast drink, with beer as its successor. Fortunately for the U.S. military, coffee replaced rum and brandy rations to their soldiers during battle to preclude misconduct by those who imbibed. With this change in allotments, coffee imports increased from 12 million pounds per year to over 38 million pounds. During the American Civil War of 1861-1865, soldiers relied heavily on a caffeine boost for energy during battle. Some soldiers craving unavailable coffee appraised a concoction of roasted sweet potatoes and corn as a substitute. It was not a suitable replacement.

Coffee drinking continued to thrive, and the first coffee company was founded in San Francisco in 1850. Folgers Coffee, formerly the Pioneer Steam Coffee and Spice Mills, was the first known company to commercialize and mass produce coffee. Founded in 1892, Maxwell House eventually surpassed Folgers in the 1980s and is now the best-selling coffee brand in the United States. It has 14.5% of the ground coffee market share in the U.S. and was one of the top coffee brands worldwide in 2020.

Peet's Coffee became America's first major coffee chain in 1966. Starting as a single, small storefront in Berkeley, California, it now boasts more than 200 locations across 11 states. Their success inspired the three founders of Starbucks. Gordon Bowker, Zev Siegl, and Jerry Baldwin were personally trained by Alfred Peet to make perfect roast coffee. They had long wanted to establish a popular retail chain of their own, so they officially launched Starbucks in 1971 at Seattle's Pike Place Market. Today, Starbucks has grown to become the most extensive worldwide coffeehouse chain.

Coffee trends come and go, but here are some of the latest trends described in the blog of Joe's Garage Coffee (2021), joesgaragecoffee.com › blog › coffee-trends.

1. Dalgona or Whipped Coffee - This trendy drink was popularized by substantial social media presence. Named after a Korean honeycomb toffee because of its similar light texture, this coffee is usually blended in a mixer for 2 to 5 minutes. It combines whipped instant coffee, sugar, and hot water. It's served over milk or ice and occasionally sprinkled with cocoa, coffee powder, or crumbled cookies.
2. Snapchilled TM - This beverage takes advantage of the popularity of cold, premade coffees. It consists of freshly brewed coffee that is "snapchilled" and immediately canned to preserve its flavor and freshness. It competes with cold brew, iced coffees, and nitro coffees below.
3. Nitro Cold Brews - Cold brew coffee, steeped in cold water for 12 to 24 hours, is infused with nitrogen gas using a process previously used by beer homebrewers. The tiny bubbles added with the gas improve the coffee's flavor and texture but don't make it taste carbonated like a soda. This brew costs a dollar or more than your usual iced coffee.
4. Matcha Lattes - This coffee trend doesn't involve coffee. It's a drink made with matcha green tea powder, water, and milk. It may "provide a cleaner caffeine boost than coffee." With less caffeine than coffee, it offers many health benefits, including antioxidants, fiber, and significant vitamin C and other vitamins. Matcha and its lattes are said to "reduce bad cholesterol, protect the liver, improve brain function, and provide other benefits."
5. Ready-to-Drink-Coffee (RTD) - These familiar, ubiquitous 'ready to drink' cold coffee beverages come in bottles or cans. They are found in convenience stores, grocery stores, and even gas stations. The RTD industry anticipates the emergence of new coffee brands and large manufacturers and estimates generated revenue of a whopping 3.1 billion U.S. dollars by 2022.
6. Plant-Based, Non-Dairy Milk - Vegan and lactose intolerant patrons can now add plant-based milk to their coffee. Non-dairy options are available in sweetened and flavored forms. Some options are soy, coconut, almond, hemp, and macadamia nut. This evolving trend accounted for 18.8 billion U.S. dollars of market value in 2020 but is expected to expand to an astronomical 41.06 billion U.S. dollars by 2025.
7. Coffee Drive-Thrus. Some fast-food locations earn as much as 70% of their revenue from drive-up windows, which the coffee industry has noticed. In fact, coffee giant Starbucks plans to relocate many of its mall locations to drive-thru stores between 2021 and 2022. Customers continue to appreciate the convenience of drive-thrus, especially on busy days or in bad weather.
8. Coffee Delivery - Uber Eats and Postmates (owned by Uber with headquarters in San Francisco) have joined coffee shops to offer this service. Consumers are already accustomed to food delivery services, so coffee delivery seems a logical next step. Some people appreciate the convenience and taste of high-quality coffee, whether from a large coffee chain or a local coffee shop.

Other trends include growing demand for high-quality 'specialty' coffees with environmental and social aspects. Their sales increase by 20% every year. Also experiencing 50% growth since 2015 is the market for single-cup coffee brewers, with coffee pods and capsules as the primary drivers. Lastly, though coffee as a subscription model has been around for a few years, Covid-19 lockdowns further prompted consumers to look to suppliers to deliver high-quality blends to their homes or offices. With a return to normalcy Post-Covid-19, this trend may subside, or buyers may choose to continue their self-imposed habit.

Coffee is one of the most valuable legally traded commodities in the world. An estimated 2.25 billion cups of coffee are consumed every day worldwide. America ranks 8th among the top 10 coffee drinking countries, behind Brazil, and ahead of Japan. In the U.S., New Yorkers allegedly drink seven times the amount of any other city. Starbucks is especially ubiquitous in Manhattan.

Overall, Americans consume an average of 400 million cups of coffee per day. Nearly 15,000 Starbucks shops in the U.S. are responsible for much of that amount, with another 24,000 coffee shops across the country contributing their part with an average sell rate of 230 cups per day. However, Starbucks is not the only player in town, as these percentages from the World Coffee Portal show:

Most popular coffee shops in the USA (World Coffee Portal):

- Starbucks - 40% (14,875 stores)
- Dunkin' Donuts - 26% (9,570 stores)
- Caribou Coffee -13% (4,700 stores)
- Other - 21%

According to the National Coffee Association USA, as quoted in Urban Bean Coffee 2020 blog: "the total economic impact of the coffee industry in the United States in 2015 was $225.2 billion". That is an astounding number. However, the Unleashed Software Company October 2020 report "The Key Coffee Industry Trends for 2022 & Beyond" states as follows: "Due to a weakening downstream demand and delays in the supply chain (i.e., trade shipments), coffee revenue has largely flatlined in the U.S. and isn't expected to grow again until after the pandemic. Though to be fair to the U.S., this is happening across markets and isn't isolated to the Americas."

Despite this unpleasant assessment brought about by a pandemic, there is little doubt that what started with the Boston Tea Party will soon regain its previous momentum. The genesis of America's love of coffee may be an 'accident of history' or the result of unintended consequences, but her love of coffee continues unabated to this day and for the foreseeable future.

## Japan Case (Creation of New Categories of Coffee)

Japan has contributed significantly to the development of coffee. Japan isolated itself from other countries from 1639 to 1854. During that period, coffee spread around the world. During World War II, coffee consumption paused in Japan. However, the Japanese market is an excellent example of the evolution of the coffee supply chain because the Japanese government has long-term statistical data on coffee consumption.

Japan's coffee bean imports have grown steadily and are now stable at high levels (Figure 5). Roast beans and instant coffee are calculated by multiplying 1.3 and 3.0, respectively [Roast beans = 1.3, instant coffee = 3.0]. Each manufacturer declares the number of green beans used in the production of coffee extract. Before the 1960s, coffee was a luxury item in Japan, and it was common to enjoy it at a coffee house to relax and share conversations with friends. Few coffee lovers purchased coffee sets and drank drip coffee at home or work.

*Figure 5. Import volume of green beans to Japan*
*(Data Source: Trade Statistics of Japan)*

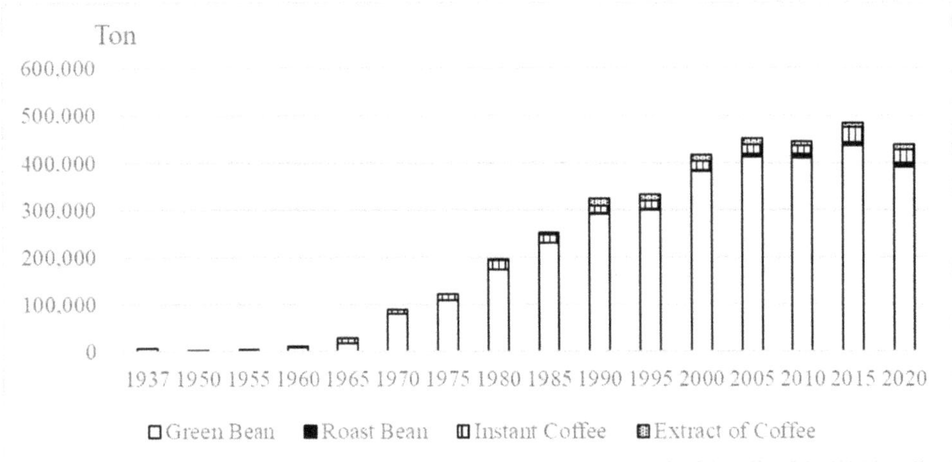


The first coffee wave began in Japan around 1970. According to the Survey of Business Establishment Census conducted by the Ministry of Internal Affairs and Communication, coffee houses increased from 27,000 in 1966 to 155,000 in 1981. Most of them were small private businesses. Many consumers started purchasing ground beans and making drip coffee at home and the office. Instant coffee, prepared quickly and easily by simply adding hot water, further popularized coffee. In 1969, UCC (Uejima Coffee Company) developed the world's first canned coffee beverage and began its manufacture and sales. It has become common for the Japanese to purchase cold canned coffee at vending machines for the past 50 years. According to the Japan Vending System Manufacturers Association, 2.1 million vending machines for bottled and canned drinks, including coffee and other beverages and waters, were operating in Japan at the end of 2019.

*Figure 6. Beverage consumption in Japan in 2019*
*(Source: Survey of Household Economy)*

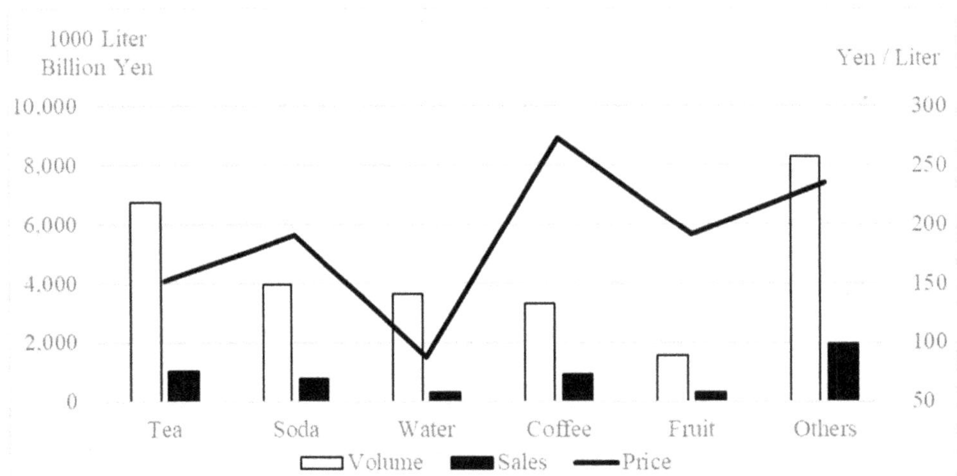

Japan is historically a tea country. Japanese drink various teas such as green tea, oolong tea, red tea, and others, in different ways such as bottled, canned, packaged, leaf, instant, concentrated, and still others. However, bottled and canned soda drinks and bottled mineral waters are now consumed significantly. On the other hand, Japanese sales of coffee products are second only to tea, and coffee is the most expensive individual item among the drinks except for alcoholic beverages (Figure 6).

According to the All Japan Coffee (n.d.) Association, the Japanese drink 11.5 cups of coffee per week. Older consumers drink more coffee than younger consumers, and men drink a little more coffee than women. The Japanese usually drink coffee at home. About 66% of coffees are drunk at home. 20% of coffees are consumed at work and in schools. 10% of coffees are drunk during travel or commute. A few percent are enjoyed in coffee houses, coffee stores, shops, and restaurants.

There have been two significant changes in coffee consumption in Japan over the last few years (Figure 7). First, more people are taking regular coffee to the office and schools. Seattle Coffee, an excellent and expensive coffee, has taken root in Japan. Convenience stores also provide fresh drip coffee at a reasonable price by vending machines. The three major convenience store chains, 7-ELEVEN, FamilyMart, and Lawson, provide machines that grind roast beans that are then brewed and poured into the consumer's cup, all within one minute. Customers can choose blended or premium, dark or light, and hot or cold coffees. These machines are in operation at more than 50 thousand convenience stores in Japan.

Secondly, liquid iced coffee consumption surpassed canned coffee. Liquid coffee is mainly packaged in plastic bottles or paper cartons. Canned coffee containers cannot be closed once opened and are smaller than liquid coffee containers. Consumers can open and close bottled coffee at their leisure, allowing them to enjoy their coffee whenever and wherever they choose. On the other hand, temperature control of bottled coffee is more challenging than canned coffee. Companies have developed coffee that maintains its flavor profile even at room temperature. Most coffee packaged in paper cartons is iced coffee. The paper cartons, which can be refrigerated, are much bigger than the canned coffee containers.

*Figure 7. Coffee consumption in Japan*
*(Source: All Japan Coffee Association, n.d.)*

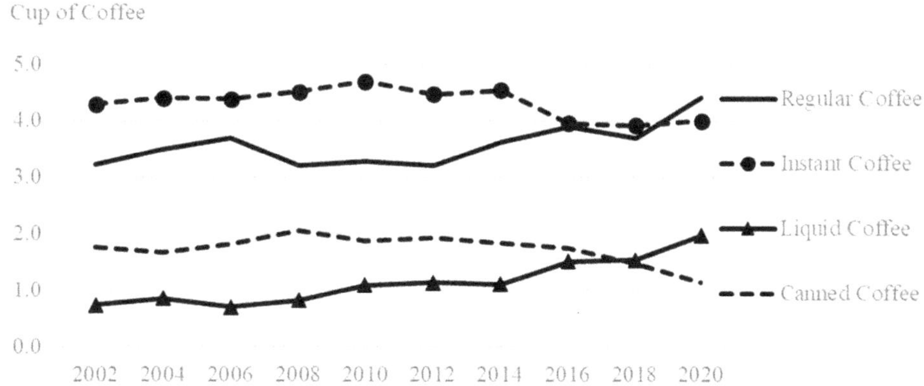

## Vietnam Case (Game Changer)

Arabica (Coffea arabica) was the first coffee variety introduced into Vietnam in 1857 by French missionaries. Trial plantings occurred at Catholic churches in the northern provinces, such as Ninh Binh, Thanh Hoa, Nghe An, and Ha Tinh, and later at some central regions such as Quang Tri and Quang Binh. Finally, coffee beans were brought to the southern provinces of the Central Highlands and the Southeast. Subsequently, people discovered that the Central Highlands was the most suitable place to cultivate coffee.

Later, in 1908, the French brought two other varieties of coffee to Vietnam, namely Robusta (Coffea canephora) and Excelsa (Coffea excelsa). They then introduced various types from the Congo to the Central Highlands. During the Vietnam War and until 1986, the coffee-producing area grew slowly, and output was low. In 1986, the country's total area devoted to coffee production was only about 50,000 hectares, and the volume of production was 18,400 tons (just over 300,000 60-kg bags).

Since 1986, the Government of Vietnam has concentrated its resources on investing in the coffee sector, aiming to make coffee a key agricultural industry. In addition to state-owned farms, the government also encourages individual households to grow coffee. As a result, coffee production in Vietnam has boomed.

The Central Highlands in Vietnam has become the largest Robusta production area in acreage and yield, and it is famous in Vietnam and all over the world. This legendary area of coffee production has produced the well-known Buon Ma Thuot coffee. The coffee regions of Buon Ma Thuot, Cau Dat, Da Lat, and Son La are known for their high-quality coffee with a sweet aroma and intense flavor owing to the soil characteristics.

By the late 1990s, Vietnam became the leading producer of coffee beans in Southeast Asia and the world's second-largest producer and exporter of green coffee beans after Brazil. Production was focused mainly on Robusta beans accounting for 97% of Vietnam's total output volume. While Robusta accounts for 92.9% of the total coffee growing area, Arabica varieties are responsible for only a few percent.

Most Robusta varieties in Vietnam originated from Indonesia's Java Island, and Vietnam now plants two primary types of Robusta. Firstly, the original Robusta variety of high-quality, small-sized beans is grown in some regions but with limited acreage due to low yields and weak resistance to pests and diseases. The second kind is the so-called high-yield varieties.

Since the early 1990s, coffea plants have been widely grown in the Central Highlands provinces, and various agricultural seedling research institutes have studied hybridizing and grafting different Robusta varieties. In particular, the Western Highlands Agriculture & Forestry Science Institute (WASI) participated in this research. They improved coffea by selecting dozens of new Robusta varieties. They succeeded in creating a new coffea from them with much more output and healthy growth achieved without much effort. The new coffea exhibits higher adaptability to soil and climate and high resistance to pests and diseases (especially leaf rust).

From 1986 to 2016, coffee production in Vietnam has increased nearly 100-fold, from 18,400 tons in 1986 to 900,000 tons in 2000, reaching 1.76 million tons in 2016. Between 90% to 95% of that volume has been exported every year. The key to Vietnam's coffee success has been its focus on Robusta varieties, and Vietnamese started drinking Robusta coffee in their style and producing instant coffee.

Vietnam's coffee production is considerably higher than any other coffee-producing country globally because of its highly harvested area compared to the total growth area (Figure 8). Vietnam has created a unique method of high-intensity Robusta cultivation resulting in trees that yield many more beans per hectare than Arabica and making Vietnam the coffee-producing country with the highest production. Cultivating Robusta has boosted profitability for coffee farmers in Vietnam.

*Figure 8. Coffee production in Vietnam*
*(Source: VIETNAM COFFEE – COCOA ASSOCIATION (VICOFA))*

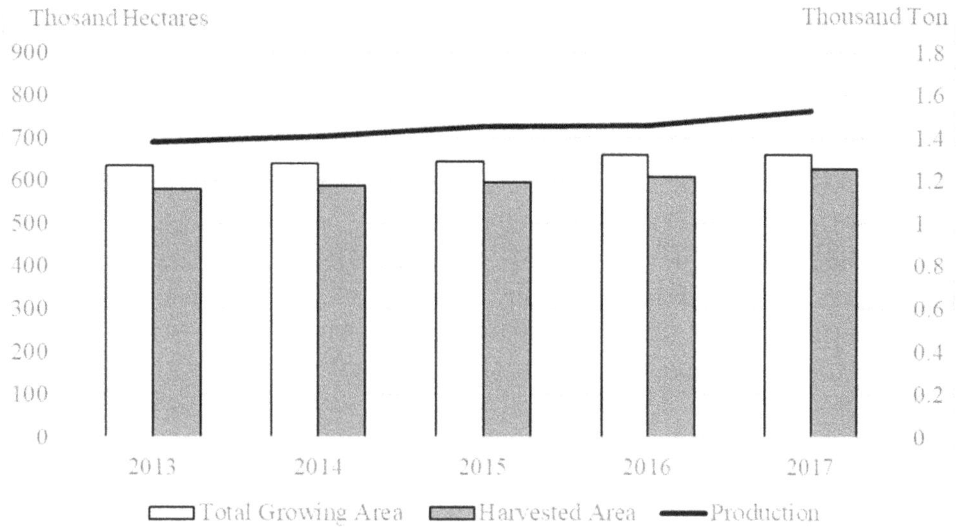


*Figure 9. Sidewalk café in Vietnam*

According to the International Coffee Organization, during the period 2011-2017, the average annual green bean export growth rate was 8.2%, with a turnover of around US$3 billion a year, accounting for over 10% of the country's total agricultural exports. The export price of coffee beans per kilo was about US$2, and green beans accounted for more than 90% of Vietnam's export volume. Recently, exports of highly processed coffee have increased, and in 2016, nearly 63,000 tons of roasted and soluble coffee products were exported.

Nowadays, coffee is a familiar beverage for Vietnamese people. Some cafes have also become famous as tourist destinations, loved by domestic and foreign tourists (Figure 9). In the late 1990s, sidewalk cafes without names or signs began to flourish in Vietnamese cities, and they set chairs and small tables on the sidewalk. Customers mainly drank Vietnam's Robusta coffee, a drip coffee made with condensed milk and sugar. Recently, sidewalk cafes gradually gave way to modern coffee houses with spacious and gorgeous interiors. Customers read books while enjoying background music. Aside from drip coffee, instant coffee with sugar and non-dairy cream is also popular.

## China Case (Potential Market and Producer)

In recent years, the demand for coffee has been rising globally. One of the reasons is the growth of emerging countries, including China. As the country develops, living standards improve, followed by a growing demand for coffee as a luxury item. China may continue to grow as a coffee producer and consumer in the near future.

Previously in China, coffee was an imported product that symbolized Western culture and consumer tastes. While China has a long history of tea culture, they have a short coffee drinking history of only about 200 years. During the Tongji period of the late Qing dynasty, coffee began to appear in the cities on the East Coast of China when it opened its borders. The first documented record of coffee in China was a book called "Zhao Yang Fan Shu," written by the American Mission Society in Shanghai. This book compiled the methods to prepare western foods for the Chinese cooks who would analyze and solve the eating and drinking problems faced by the foreign missionaries in China. Coffee is transliterated into the word "kefei" in the book.

The British first introduced coffea in Taiwan in 1884. Coffee culture became popular in Taiwan when Japan annexed it. In China, French missionaries brought coffea from Vietnam to Yunnan province in 1892. However, very few people drink coffee daily in mainland China.

Yunnan is a province located in southwest China, and it borders Myanmar, Laos, and Vietnam. According to data from China's Ministry of Agriculture and Rural Affairs, Yunnan is the primary producer of coffee beans in China, accounting for more than 98% of China's coffee beans in both cultivated areas and production. Unlike Shanghai or other big cities, it is a secluded region blessed by nature and covered with forests and lush greenery. The coffee grown in Yunnan Province is Arabica. The characteristic taste of Chinese coffee is that of moderate acidity and bitterness.

There are minimal areas of coffee production in the world. However, in recent years the size of coffee cultivation in China has expanded. In addition, the coffee trees are young and highly productive. This combination of expanding cultivation areas and young coffee trees should boost production soon.

China has significant potential to become one of the largest consumption areas due to its population if more people drink more coffee daily. According to 2019 statistics, instant coffee had accounted for more than 70% of China's coffee market. The market share of drip coffee made from freshly ground coffee was only 18%, far less than the average market share of drip coffee globally.

According to a Chinese Academy of Commercial and Industrial Research report, coffee consumption in China has increased by about 2.5 times in eight years. Imports are also growing by about 16% per year. Chinese consumers' demand for coffee continues to grow. Although consumption accounts for only 2.4% of global coffee consumption, the annual growth rate of coffee consumption in China is prodigious. In terms of China's coffee consumption and its share of global coffee consumption, green bean consumption continues to rise in China. Compared to 2012, the annual consumption of coffee beans increased by 250% in 2018.

Currently, China's coffee market might be just before the stage of rapid development. The per capita coffee consumption increased from 3.2 cups in 2013 to 7.2 cups in 2019. Although the per capita consumption of coffee is still small, the market size is growing steadily (Figure 10). The increasing number of coffee houses and stores in China's urban areas is evidence of a growing demand for coffee. However, that number is still low compared to developed countries, and the disparity is considerable. China's coffee consumption will grow over the long term due to rising incomes, improved consumer sentiment, and diversification of the benefits of coffee.

*Figure 10. Coffee consumption per capita in 2018*
*(Source: The International Coffee Organization)*

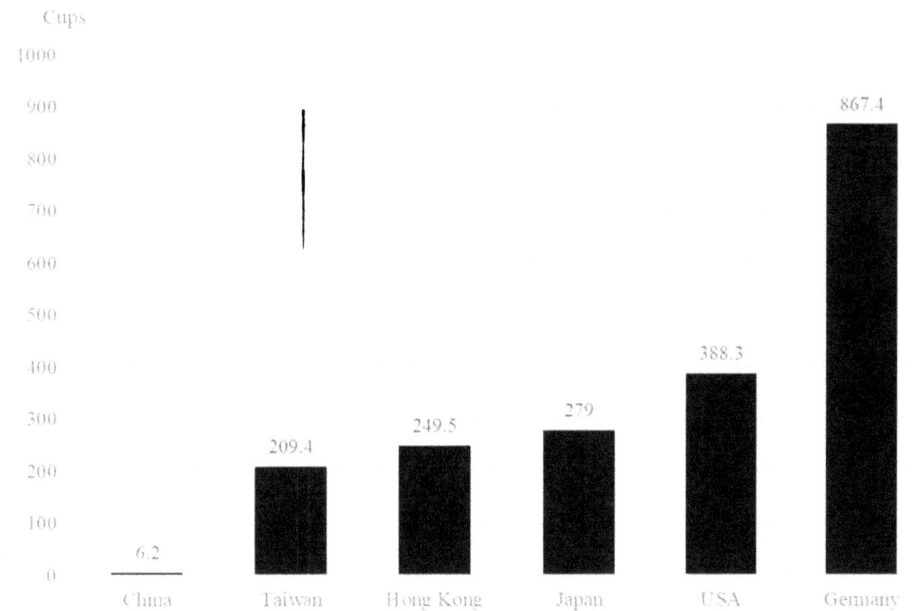


In eight major Chinese cities, the primary consumers of coffee are the young and the middle-aged. Young consumers in their twenties and thirties promote the development of China's coffee market because they are more receptive to foreign food cultures as they pursue fashion and quality of life. Young office workers under tremendous pressure tend to drink instant coffee to concentrate and relax, and they also drink coffee to stay up late at the office or home or on long business trips. Nescafe entered the Chinese market in the 1980s, and instant coffee has become popular because of its convenience and reasonable price.

Middle-aged business people with disposable incomes tend to enjoy their lifestyles. More men than women prefer coffee as a luxury item. After Starbucks launched in China in the 1990s, many consumers liked its elegant atmosphere and quiet environment to socialize with acquaintances. Starbucks is also a symbol of affluent status.

The coffee business is growing with the rise of the Internet and e-commerce platforms. Today, many Chinese use an online service to order takeout coffee and self-service coffee. As coffee choices and features become more diverse and convenient, consumers have a more comprehensive selection of different coffee products. Many coffee merchants are trying to create unique coffees and offer more and more new products to attract consumers. With the spread of the coffee culture, more consumers with disposable incomes and an interest in the coffee culture will lead to more consumption, particularly of drip coffee.

## STRATEGIES AT EACH STAGE INCLUDING A VIEW OF SCM

There are numerous ways to reach customers. Figure 11 illustrates various coffee supply chains from the process view. The goal of the coffee supply chains is to satisfy the different tastes and drinking habits of consumers who then buy and drink their coffee products. This figure helps analyze the current situation and determine the target product and segment. With this information, companies can then decide on labor division and select their partners.

*Figure 11. Various supply chains from process view*

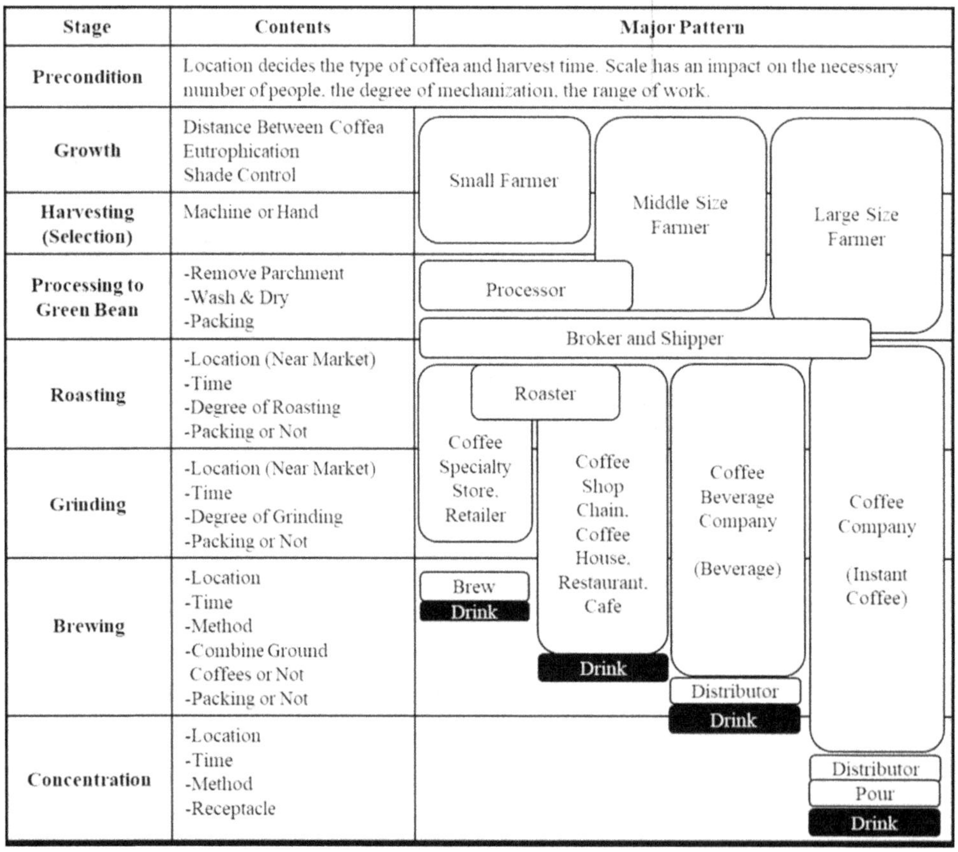

To simplify the discussion, we will review supply chain strategy at each stage from the view of Porter's Generic Competitive Strategies and Ansoff's Growth Vector Matrix in Figure 12. Porter proposed Generic Competitive Strategies from the competitive scope (broad or narrow target) and advantage (lower cost or differentiation). Segments of the Competitive Advantage are cost leadership, differentiation, and focus (cost focus and differentiation focus). On the other hand, Ansoff proposed his Growth Vector Matrix based on the newness and existence of a market and product. It shows four strategic paths: market penetration, product development, market development, and diversification. Combining Generic Competitive Strategies and Growth Vector Matrix is beneficial in analyzing strategies. Generic Competitive Strategies expresses the target market, whereas Growth Vector Matrix demonstrates concrete measures.

*Figure 12. Generic competitive strategy and Ansoff matrix*

| **Generic Competitive Strategy** | | **Competitive Advantage** | |
|---|---|---|---|
| | | **Lower Cost** | **Differentiation** |
| **Competitive Scope** | **Broad Target** | Cost Leadership | Differentiation |
| | **Narrow Target** | Focus (Cost Focus) | (Differentiation Focus) |
| **Ansoff Matrix (Growth)** | | **Products** | |
| | | **Existing** | **New** |
| **Markets** | **Existing** | Market Penetration | Product Development |
| | **New** | Market Development | Diversification |

## Strategy of Farmer

Green Beans can be shipped worldwide and are an international product due to their portableness and long storage life. Farmers have a big chance to select broad targets. It is unreasonable to take a focus strategy unless the extreme freshness reevaluates high or specific coffee has a particular benefit. Farmers should instead pursue a cost leadership or differentiation position. Labor costs are low in most coffee production areas. The primary practical methods to reduce costs are large-scale plantations and mechanization. Revision of the division of labor to expand or narrow the scope of activities might be sufficient to minimize expenses.

Vietnam is an excellent example of conducting a cost leadership strategy. They mainly grow Robusta varieties designed to be more sturdy and to yield a larger crop. The amount of Robusta beans blended has increased due to coffee demand and the pressure to reduce costs (market penetration). They sell instant Robusta coffee with milk and sugar worldwide (product development and market development). For diversification, they can enhance their product mix by incorporating other food products, such as jelly, bread, and similar items.

Providing proper shade and ventilation has a beneficial effect on coffea and cherries. Hand-picking makes it possible to precisely select the best coffee cherries, which improves the overall quality of the harvest. Sun-dried parchment has a unique flavor. These quality details take time and effort but are effective differentiation methods (market penetration).

Premium coffee and Third Wave Coffee are other ways to differentiate (product development). Warranty and traceability are the keywords, and small farms are more suitable to produce these beans than huge plantations. Many countries and companies advertise their coffee beans' uniqueness and premium nature (market development).

Some farms have started offering paid guided farm tours (diversification). This approach may increase brand loyalty, and although it is challenging, it enhances the understanding of coffea and its environment. This type of tourism has become popular (Figure 13).

*Figure 13. UCC's farm in Hawaii*

## Strategy of Coffee Shop Chains

Nowadays, coffee shop chains are a vital part of the coffee industry. Some major coffee shop chains are growing steadily worldwide. They execute differentiation strategies. They advertise extensively to raise their brand recognition and sell drip coffee at relatively higher prices. They buy in bulk to reduce procurement costs. They spend massive amounts of money on product development, stable procurement, and advertising. Expansion of stores directly affects sales under suitable conditions with good brand loyalty and before a saturated market. Some coffee shop chains started selling coffee beverages at their stores and through major channels (market development). Starbucks opened special roasteries that serve unique coffee, food, and alcoholic drinks (diversification).

Minor coffee shop chains are domestic or local chains. They embrace cost focus or differentiation focus strategies. Coffee shop chains with a cost focus strategy sell drip coffee at a much lower price than major coffee shop chains. They tend to open much more than the other minor chains with differentiation focus strategies (market penetration). They reduce their costs by bulk buying and standardizing their service. On the other hand, coffee shop chains with a differentiation focus strategy tend to offer a more elegant or comfortable environment and a more comprehensive range of drip coffees and light meals than the other minor chains. It would be difficult for them to take growth strategies because they might get stuck between the major and minor chains.

## Strategy of Beverage Companies

The coffee beverages are solid against transportation and storage due to canned and bottled. But their marketing areas are limited to domestic or local because they are so heavy due to the water. The Japanese market has been at the leading edge of coffee beverages. It is not easy for beverage companies to take cost leadership because coffee beverages are luxury items. In addition, people can drink instant coffee at a lower price with some adjustments.

Big companies such as Kirin Beverage, Suntory, and Nestle tend to take differentiation strategies. They produce a wide variety of coffee beverages all over Japan, and most of them are sold at almost the same price through the primary distribution channels. They develop their brand for market penetration, and they continuously improve their products to create newness and correspond to market needs. Some of them opened restaurants and bought out coffee shop chains for market research and advancement into new areas (diversification). Coca-Cola acquired Costa in 2019.

Minor beverage companies tend to employ a cost focus strategy. To reduce distribution and advertising costs, they sell their products in a particular area or distribute them through minor channels such as vending machines and drug stores. They advance market penetration through price differentiation in a specific area or secondary channels.

# SOLUTIONS AND RECOMMENDATIONS

Coffee supply chains are a global multi-echelon system. Their goal is customer purchase and customer satisfaction. Potential customers are diverse in nationality, religion, region, gender, generation, lifestyle, preference, and other areas. Nowadays, companies consider first and foremost the customers. Due to product and process innovations, some supply chains can efficiently access fragmented segments by offering various products through different channels.

To survive, each supply chain member should consider its role in a supply chain and its opportunities as necessary. To increase supply chain performance and profitability, each should collaborate with other members because supply chain management is a cooperative activity to reinforce the interlocking of the supply chain. On the other hand, it is difficult for every company to keep participating in a supply chain because it is a loosely coupled merit system.

Each supply chain member should complete a strategy under technological advances and social changes to make the most of their endeavor. It might be risky to pursue only efficiency because average subcontracted workers might be substituted for others. Companies seek their ideal future domain, appropriate products, and target customers by reflecting technological advances and social changes.

## FUTURE RESEARCH DIRECTIONS

Analyzing the value chain process within supply chains is one of the most critical research directions. Coffee is a global product whose value is added step by step globally, and it is challenging for outsiders to grasp the realities beyond company and country borders. Appropriate sharing of supply chain profit among supply chain members is necessary for the sustainable development of coffee.

Another critical research direction is to map out a strategy for the potential market and developing countries. Coffee products are so varied that they might fill the most fragmented market segmentation. Historically, foreigners introduced drip coffee, and coffee cultures developed slowly from the upper class. Nowadays, instant coffee might be most suitable for opening a new market due to its affordability and convenience. The next step might be to shift popular taste to drip coffee gradually. Then, a quest for the finest drip coffee brewed with unique coffee beans or the possibility of bottled coffee through retailers or vending machines might begin.

## CONCLUSION

Coffee is a global product with a long history. The coffee supply chain has been prolonged and has changed its structure dramatically as coffee became widespread. This chapter explains how the coffee supply chain and product and process innovations changed the coffee industry and market globally.

We described four countries' case studies to show how the coffee industry and global market have changed over time. The United States has been the most significant contributor and largest consumption country for drip coffee, and Japan is a country that has created several new coffee categories. Vietnam is a newcomer, but it has already become the world's second-largest producer. China is undeveloped in coffee, but it has enormous potential as a producer and consumer. These four countries have developed their coffee culture differently and adopted different strategies.

There are manifold products and ways to approach fractionalized consumers. From the process view, the model of various supply chains proposed in this chapter helps understand coffee supply chains and their strategies. We hope the proposed coffee supply chain model combining Generic Competitive Strategies and Growth Vector Matrix hints at mapping the supply chain strategy.

## REFERENCES

All Japan Coffee Association. (n.d.). *Monthly data*. https://coffee.ajca.or.jp/english/monthlydata/

All Japan Coffee Association. (n.d.). *World coffee consumption*. https://coffee.ajca.or.jp/english/consumption/

Avey, T. (2013). *The caffeinated history of coffee. History of coffee-the history kitchen-PBS Food*. https://www.pbs.org/food/the-history-kitchen/history-coffee/

Bashiri, M., Tjahjono, B., Lazell, J., Ferreira, J., & Perdana, T. (2021). The dynamics of sustainability risks in the global coffee supply chain: A case of Indonesia–UK. *Sustainability*, *13*(2), 589. doi:10.3390u13020589

BizVibe. (2020). *Top 10 coffee brands in the world 2020, Top coffee brands, Global coffee market factsheet*. https://blog.bizvibe.com/blog/top-10-coffee-brands

Chen, H., & Xiao, X. P. Z. (2011). China's coffee industry situation and development measures. *Tropical Agricultural Engineering*, (23), 42.

Coffee.org tm. (2021). *20 Interesting coffee facts*. https://coffee.org/blogs/news/20-interesting-coffee-facts?

District Roasters. (2019). *Types of coffee beans and what sets them apart*. https://districtroasters.com/blogs/news/types-of-coffee-beans

Espresso & Coffee Guide. (2012). *Coffee history / 1650-1700*. https://espressocoffeeguide.com/all-about-coffee-2/worlds-best-history-of-coffee/coffee-history-1650-1700/

Fratus, M. (2019). *The Boston tea party: How coffee became the official morning beverage of America, Coffee or die magazine*. https://coffeeordie.com/boston-tea-party-history/

History of Beverage. (2014). *George Washington inventor of instant coffee process*. https://www.beveragehistory.com/2014/10/george-washington-inventor-of-instant.html

International Coffee Organization. (n.d.). *Historical data on the global coffee trade*. https://www.ico.org/new_historical.asp?section=Statistics

International Coffee Organization. (n.d.). *Trade statistics tables*. https://www.ico.org/trade_statistics.asp?section=Statistics

Joe's Garage Coffee. (2021). *Coffee trends to watch in 2021*. https://joesgaragecoffee.com/blog/coffee-trends/

Kittichotsatsawat, Y., Jangkrajarng, V., & Tippayawong, K. Y. (2021). Enhancing Coffee Supply Chain towards Sustainable Growth with Big Data and Modern Agricultural Technologies. *Sustainability*, *13*(8), 4593. doi:10.3390u13084593

Koffee Retail. (2021). *Life begins after coffee*. https://koffeeretail.com/

LEHOANGDIEPTHAO. (2021). *Thoi quen uong ca phe cua nguoi Viet thay doi ra sao?* [How have Vietnamese people's coffee-drinking habits changed?]. https://lehoangdiepthao.com/thoi-quen-uong-ca-phe-cua-nguoi-viet-thay-doi-ra-sao/

Morris, J. (2019). *Coffea: A global history*. Reaktion Books.

Nguyen, G. T., & Sarker, T. (2018). Sustainable coffee supply chain management: A case study in Buon Me Thuot City, Daklak, Vietnam. *International Journal of Corporate Social Responsibility*, *3*(1), 1. doi:10.118640991-017-0024-x

Unleashed Software. (2021). *The key coffee industry trends for 2022 & beyond*. https://www.unleashed-software.com/blog/the-key-coffee-industry-trends-for-2021-beyond

Urban Bean Coffee. (2020). *The most interesting coffee statistics*. https://urbanbeancoffee.com/coffee/usa-coffee-statistics/

Urban Bean Coffee. (2021). *Arabica vs. robusta: The ultimate guide - urban bean coffee*. http://urban-beancoffee.com>coffee>arabica-vs-robusta/

Vietnam Coffee Cocoa Association (VICOFA). (n.d.). *Country coffee profile: Vietnam*. http://www.vicofa.org.vn/country-coffee-profile-vietnam-bid385.html

Wang, H., Potter, A., & Naim, M. (2011). Evaluation of postponement in the soluble coffee supply chain: A case study. *International Journal of Production Economics*, *131*(1), 355–3564. doi:10.1016/j.ijpe.2010.08.015

Zhang, J. (2006). The origin, development, spread, and drinking culture of coffee. *Chinese Agricultural History*, (25), 22–29.

## ADDITIONAL READING

Wang, H., Potter, A., & Naim, M. (2011). Evaluation of postponement in the soluble coffee supply chain: A case study. *International Journal of Production Economics*, *131*(1), 355–3564. doi:10.1016/j.ijpe.2010.08.015

## KEY TERMS AND DEFINITIONS

**Cafe:** A small restaurant or shop that sells drinks and light meals. In this chapter, it means a small restaurant serving drip coffee with café terraces on the roadside.

**Coffea:** A coffee tree that grows in the highlands near the equator. Coffea Arabica and Coffea Robusta are the two major types of coffea. Although Coffea Arabica is inferior to Coffea Robusta in productivity and robustness, it is cultivated much more than Coffea Robusta, and arabica beans are higher-grade than Robusta beans.

**Coffee Beverage:** A bottled or canned coffee sold at retailers or through vending machines. The coffee beverage companies make it with a particular manufacturing method to maintain good taste and flavor longer at room temperature.

**Coffee House:** A restaurant serving drip coffee, light meals, and other sundries. The first coffee houses opened in London or Istanbul in the 17th century, and they offered a luxury space to converse with friends while listening to music.

**Coffee Shop:** A restaurant serving drip coffee with light meals or a specialty store selling roast and ground beans, coffee sets, and other items. Global and local coffee shop chains play a lively part in the coffee industry.

**Instant Coffee:** A concentrate made from drip coffee. It is effortless to drink a cup of instant coffee, and the only requirement is to mix instant coffee with boiled water in a cup.

# Chapter 10
# Supply Chain Models and Functions of Food Service Chains in Japan:
## The Food SPA at Saizeriya

**Hitomi Nakagawa**
*Sakushin Gakuin University, Japan*

## ABSTRACT

*This chapter discusses the supply chain management (SCM) of the foodservice industry in Japan. For a restaurant to grow by developing a chain and opening multiple stores, it needs a supply chain that links the central kitchen, manufacture and direct sales, and cold chain. Therefore, using Saizeriya, a major restaurant chain in Japan, as a case study, the authors identify Saizeriya's management strategy, supply chain model, and its functions. Although Saizeriya is in the restaurant industry, it has adopted the business model of speciality store retailer of private label apparel (SPA), which is prevalent in the apparel industry. In this study, the authors clarify how the company has improved the efficiency of its supply chain while controlling the effects of the rising costs of raw materials and logistics.*

## INTRODUCTION

This chapter discusses SCM in the food industry based on the case of Saizeriya, one of the largest restaurant chains in Japan. In restaurants, cost and freshness are so critical that SCM will determine the restaurant's fate. Saizeriya is a company that has fully embraced "Specialty store retailer of Private label Apparel (SPA) " and has an excellent track record in taste and profit.

The Global Supply Chain Forum (GSCF) defines supply chain management (SCM) as follows. Supply Chain Management integrates critical business processes from end users through original suppliers that provide products, services, and information that add value for customers and other stakeholders (Douglas, Martha,2000). The supply chain includes not only the manufacturer and suppliers, but also transporters, warehouses, retailers, and customers themselves (Sunil & Peter, 2014). Mawson & Fearne

DOI: 10.4018/978-1-7998-9800-9.ch010

*Figure 1. Image of SCM*

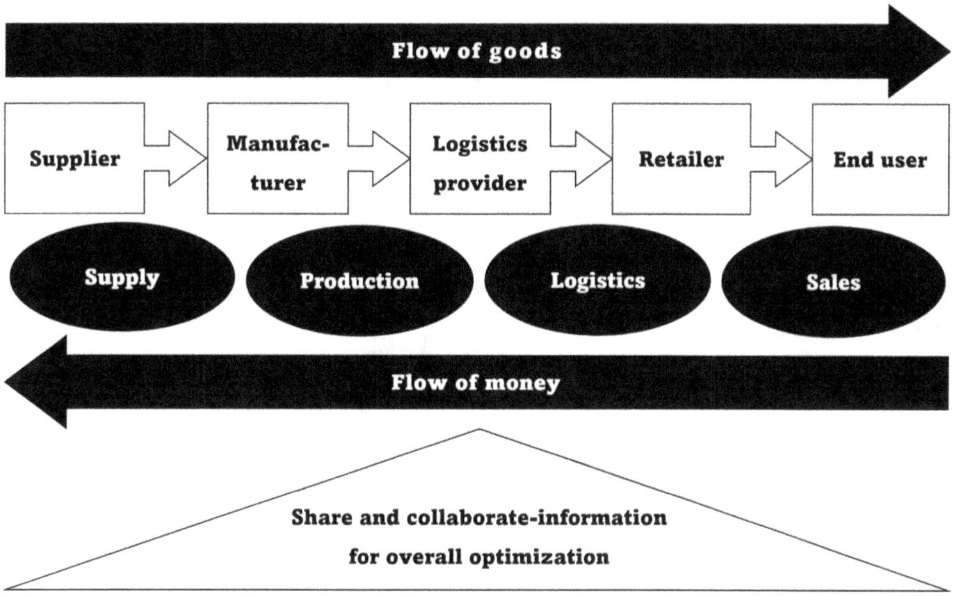


(1996) describes SCM as "It seeks to achieve a relationship of mutual benefit by defining the organizational structures and contractual relationships between buyer and seller, which up until now have been classified as adversarial." A company's supply chain comprises geographically dispersed facilities where raw materials, intermediate products, or finished products are acquired, transformed, stored, or sold and transportation links that connect facilities along which products flow (Jeremy, 2006). The actual activity of a supply chain is often a two-way exchange on a network structure rather than a linear chain activity. In other words, the overall picture of a supply chain is more of a network structure than a chain, and SCM is an activity that comprehensively manages these activities (Higuchi, 2018).

Business management is based on the flow of cash, both incoming and outgoing, and the faster the cash flow, the more stable the business entity. SCM is management that increases the speed of cash flow, and it also aims to increase the rate of cash turnover within a company to improve its health. Therefore, the critical management index of SCM is ROA (return on assets) to evaluate profitability.

In today's world, supply chains are becoming more widespread and internationalized. It is not uncommon for vegetables and other industrial products from overseas to appear in domestic markets and on dinner tables (Higuchi,2018). With that background in mind, this chapter clarifies the models and functions of SCM specific to the food service industry. It presents various distribution models, including food ingredients, to give the reader new insights. As a case study, it explains the business model of Saizeriya and how it functions, revealing the efficiency of the supply chain in the restaurant industry.

Saizeriya Co., Ltd. is an Italian wine and café restaurant chain that started operating in the 1970s, the early days of the family restaurant business in Japan. The company's store development is based on the "regional dominance" method, in which it concentrates on opening stores in a particular area. Unlike the "route dominant" system, in which new stores are opened sequentially along a specific railroad line or highway, the "regional dominant" system is designed to establish superiority as a restaurant company in a particular area. Saizeriya is not just running a restaurant. They import raw materials and wine from

*Figure 2. Impact of SCM on cash flow*
*Source: (John Gattorna,2017)*

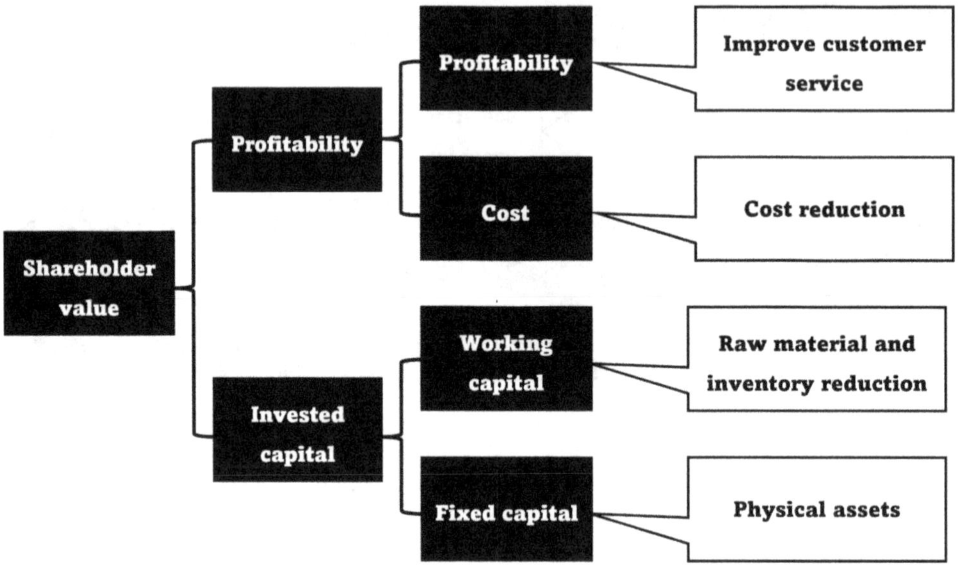


Italy, grow vegetables under contract with farmers, and have Austria's production and processing plant. They import Italian ingredients from Italy without going through a trading company and repeatedly develop their menu, focusing on taste and cutting unnecessary costs to determine the price. In addition, the central kitchen and the kitchen's single operation are outstanding.

*Figure 3. Food and wine served at Saizeriya.*
*Source: (SAIZERIYA Co. https://www.saizeriya.co. jp/corporate/philosophy/price/)*

Saizeriya is one of Japan's leading restaurant chains. Behind Saizeriya's ability to achieve high quality and low prices simultaneously is a characteristics business model that can be called the "Specialty store retailer of Private label Apparel (SPA)" for food service. This is a model in which the company is responsible for all product development, production, processing, distribution, and product delivery. Saizeriya's supply chain consists of cultivation and harvesting, production and processing, and processing and cooking. The company can control the cost ratio and procure desired ingredients by attacking the supply chain upstream. Saizeriya's purchasing department plays a vital role in the direct import and

*Figure 4. Image of SCM in Saizeriya*

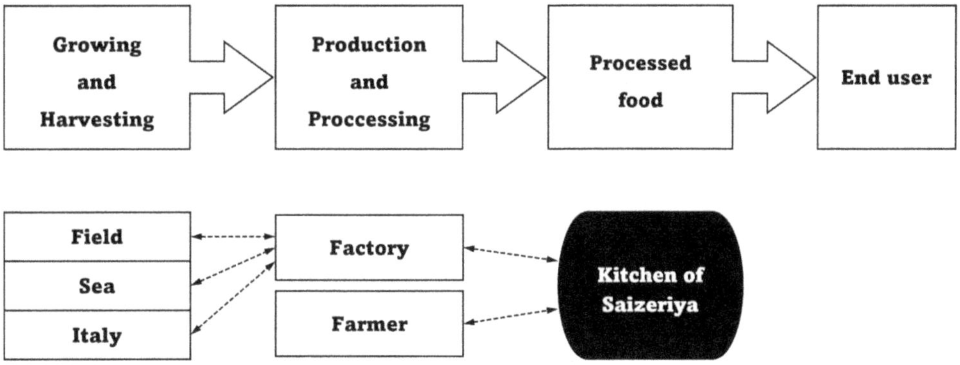


in-house production of elements essential for the SPA. The company's strength lies in the fact that it can unify the taste of its products because it handles everything from development to production and processing in-house. And since there are no intermediate costs involved in each process, Saizeriya can lower its costs and provide food at lower prices.

Figure 4 is an excellent example of the characteristics of Japanese-style SCM in the food service industry, and the model plays an important role. The case of Saizeriya can be an excellent reference for SCM in the food service industry in other countries. Saizeriya has created a new concept called the "SPA model of the restaurant industry. In this study, we call it SPFB (Speciality store retailer of Private label Food and Beverage) and propose to reveal the front and back of the Japanese food service industry to encourage the development of the food service industry in other countries. Therefore, this chapter explains how Saizeriya has improved the efficiency of its supply chain while controlling the impact of the rising costs of raw materials and logistics. Then, Saizeriya's business model and its functions to clarify the efficiency of supply chains in the restaurant industry are discussed.

## BACKGROUND

This section describes the current state of the food service industry in Japan. The size of the restaurant industry market in 2019, before the impact of COVID 19, is estimated to be 26.43 trillion yen, up 1.3% from the previous year, due to increased per capita restaurant spending, increased foreign visitors to Japan, and a consumption tax hike (Japan Food Service Association,2020).

The graph shows that fast food and family restaurants are the most common types of business in the restaurant industry, accounting for 57% of the total market size of 26.04 trillion yen. Restaurants include cafeterias and restaurants, soba and udon noodle stores, sushi restaurants, and other eating establishments. Saizeriya is the leader of an Italian family restaurant and other restaurants.

According to the consolidated data for 2020, Saizeriya has 1,517 stores. The breakdown is 1,089 domestic stores and 428 overseas stores, and this is an increase of 13 stores from the previous year. Sales in 2020 will be 126.8 billion yen, and the average daily sales per store will be about 300,000 yen. In addition, Saizeriya has demonstrated its strength in attracting customers, with approximately 200 million customers visiting its stores annually. After the Great East Japan Earthquake, Saizeriya opened dozens of stores in Miyagi Prefecture as part of its support for the affected areas (Suzuki,2014).

*Figure 5. Market size by food service industry sector in Japan*
*Source: (Food service Industry Research Institute,2019)*

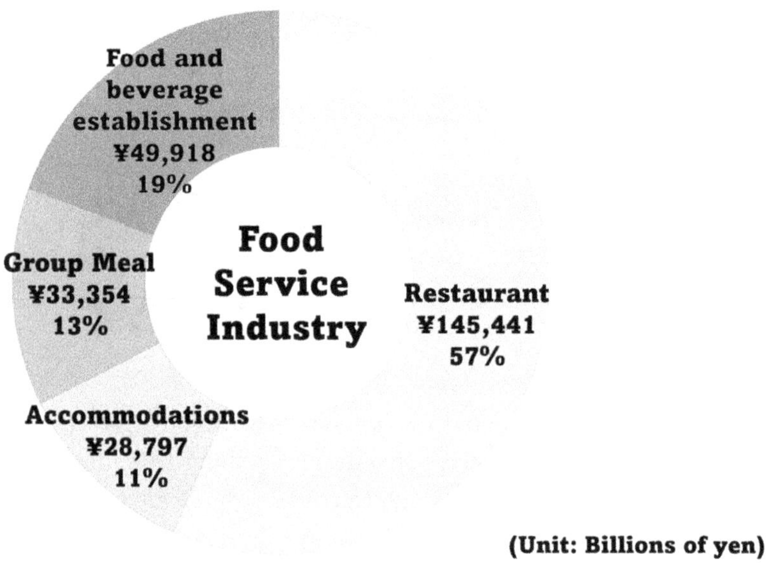


*Table 1. Number of stores and factories in 2020*

| Stores | | Factories | |
|---|---|---|---|
| Japan | 1,089 | Japan | 5 |
| Shanghai | 143 | Australia | 1 |
| Guangzhou | 112 | | |
| Beijing | 83 | | |
| Hong Kong | 45 | | |
| Taiwan | 16 | | |
| Singapore | 29 | | |

Saizeriya has been able to offer products at low prices by thoroughly eliminating waste and digitizing its operations. As a result, the company was able to outperform its peers. Saizeriya's operating profit margin in 2019 was 6.2%. This makes it one of the most successful companies in the restaurant industry.

The graph shows changes in net income attributable to shareholders of the parent company and net sales. Sales continue to grow steadily. Net income has made a V-shaped recovery; we have recovered from the business slump in 2014. The reason for this is the expansion of expenses due to the yen's depreciation.

The average capital adequacy ratio for the entire accommodation and food service industry is 24.8%. Looking at Saizeriya's financial position in 2014, the capital ratio is 78.7%, which is very good. With low debt and a high degree of stability, the company was not dragged down by a temporary deficit.

*Figure 6. Profit and loss statement of Saizeriya*
*Source: (SAIZERIYA Co. https://www.saizeriya.co.jp/corporate/investor/ir/)*

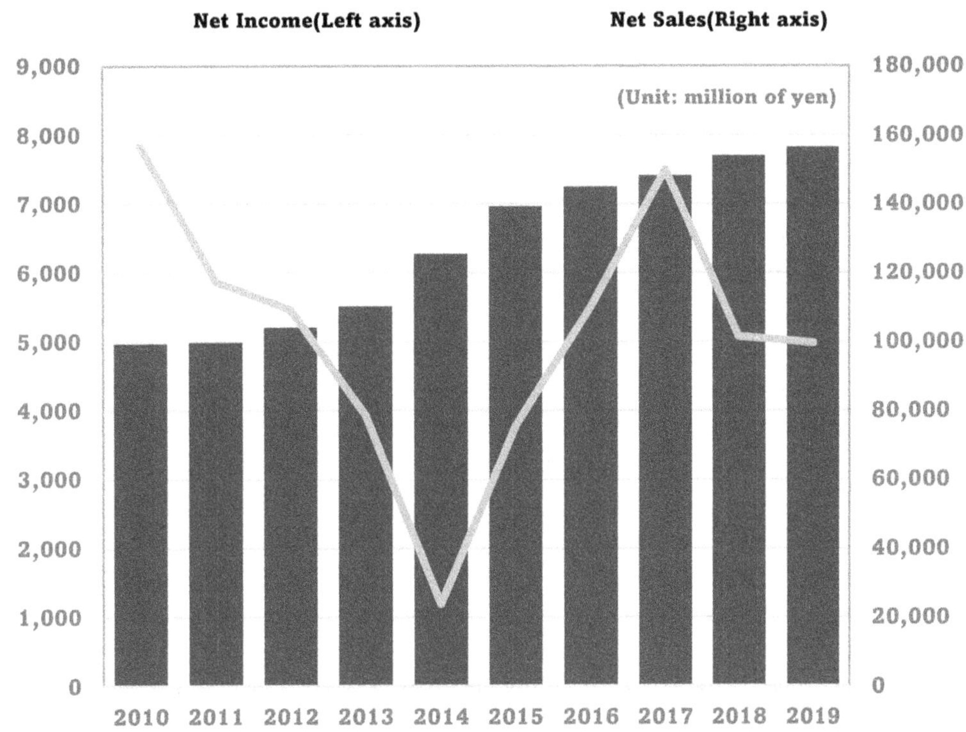


Supply chain strategies include building a competitive business model with a supply chain, building a supply chain to improve customer satisfaction, and improving overall productivity through optimal operations (Shimura,1998). There are many examples of food service chain companies developing pro-

*Table 2. Balance sheet of Saizeriya in 2014*

| (Debit) | (Credit) |
|---|---|
| Asset<br>\87,224,000,000 | Liabilities<br>\18,581,000,000 |
| | Capital<br>\68,643,000,000 |

*** Capital Ratio=(\68,643,000,000÷\87,224,000,000)×100=78.7%**
*Source: (SAIZERIYA Co.* < https://www.saizeriya.co.jp/corporate/investor/ir/>)

*Table 3. Average capital ratio*

| | Whole Scale | Over 1 Billion Yen | 100 Million Yen or More But Less Than 1 Billion Yen | More Than 50 Million But Less Than 100 Million Yen |
|---|---|---|---|---|
| Food & Beverage Industry | 24.5% | **50.9%** | 38.5% | 28.0% |

Source: (Ministry of Finance,2019)

duction areas and contract cultivation. They have been focusing on building supply chains that deepen cooperation with production areas to ensure a stable supply in terms of quality and quantity. With the growing interest in food safety in the past few years, the trend toward contracting and supply chains has become more active (Michihata,2010). Food safety issues have profound ramifications on the design of the supply chain. For instance, proper monitoring and response to food safety problems require the ability to trace back small lots, from retailer to processor or even back to the supplying farm (Dimitrios & Eleftherios,2005). In the regular procurement of food ingredients for restaurants, deliveries are made from food manufacturers to each store from multiple food wholesalers divided by field via food trading companies., there is a limit to the standard method of procuring food ingredients for restaurants to cope with the widespread development of stores. It is necessary to develop a chain and establish a system of procurement from distribution centers, manufacturing plants, and suppliers linked to store delivery (Hara, 2021). Therefore, it is necessary to establish a system for procurement from distribution centers, manufacturing plants, and suppliers linked to store delivery. Thus, Saizeriya has launched a new business model. Specifically, the company has introduced SPA in the apparel industry, even though it is a restaurant industry. It has created a supply chain structure in which it manages everything from upstream to downstream.

The popularity of SPA in the apparel industry is due to the following idea: Sellers have absolute responsibility for the brand and quality of the product. This led to the SPA business model of planning and producing products themselves, going back to the upstream of production. In sales, the company has no hesitation in selling as many products as possible, as it handles products that it can confidently recommend to its customers (Mizoue, 2001). This single-minded retailing has never been seen before.

For this reason, the retail industry was lumped together as a distribution industry for a long time. There was an ingrained belief that the manufacturers made the products they handled and that it was not their responsibility if they did not sell or receive complaints. Since they were not ultimately responsible for the products, there was no comprehensive management or sales process. In contrast, today's apparel companies are accountable for producing and selling their products. This is a pioneer of a new type of retailing. Saizeriya was the first restaurant company to adopt this style, and it has been a great success.

Saizeriya's management philosophy is to propose three types of meals to society and propose ways to enhance value further. Saizeriy is aggressively expanding its chain of stores so that many people can use its services in their daily lives. Saizeriya is tackling the seemingly contradictory issues of "reasonable prices" that allow customers to visit its stores repeatedly in their daily lives and "deliciousness" that satisfies its customers. Saizeriya is working to improve the value of its products by taking full responsibility for the entire process from development to processing to serving to provide healthy and safe food that makes the most of the ingredients.

SCM was born to manage the entire manufacturing, logistics, and sales process. This management philosophy can now be realized efficiently and in earnest through SCM. By utilizing its unique platform, the company is able to provide services that are in line with its vision. The generalization of the concept and theorists has often originated in the West (Imaoka,1998). We will examine Saizeriya's unique SCM, which has been arranged in the Japanese style.

*Figure 7. Distribution in the apparel industry*

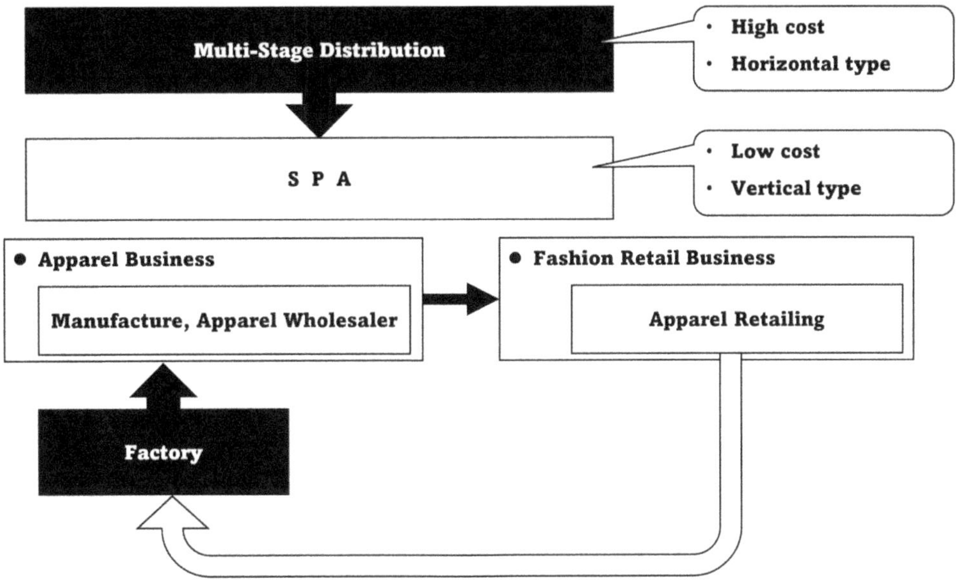


## SUPPLY CHAIN MODEL AND FUNCTION OF SAIZERIYA

A major Italian restaurant chain, Saizeriya, established Mariane Shokai Co. in 1973 and started to expand the chain of "Restaurant Saizeriya" that it had been operating until then. In 1987, the company name was changed to Mariano Co. In 1987, the company changed its name to Mariano's Corporation, and in 1992, it became the current Saizeriya Corporation. Saizeriya is a company headquartered in Yoshikawa City, Saitama Prefecture. The company's founder, Yasuhiko Shogaki, had been running a private restaurant called Restaurant Saizeriya, and in May 1973, he incorporated the company and established Mariane Shokai Co. In 1998, the company's stock was registered with the Japan Securities Dealers Association (JSDA) as over-the-counter stock. It was listed on the Second Section of the Tokyo Stock Exchange the following year. In August 2000, the company was listed on the First Section of the Tokyo Stock Exchange.

### Issues and Analytical Perspectives

The world moves as one, with no borders, distance, or time constraints. Companies that can build open, global supply chains will be more competitive: the world changes to an open and dynamic industrial structure. Under the situation, Japanese companies should engage in a supply chain management revolution to increase their competitiveness (Fukushima, 1998).

This chapter aims to clarify the model and function of supply chain management in the food service industry in today's complex society. Therefore, a case study will be used as a methodology. Using Saizeria, a Japanese restaurant chain restaurant, as a case study, its unique SCM structure is explained, and how it functions is discussed. In doing so, the company's business strategy is linked to its SCM, and its corporate value is examined from multiple perspectives.

*Figure 8. Management principles*
*Source: (SAIZERIYA Co. https://www.saizeriya.co.jp/corporate/idea/idea/)*

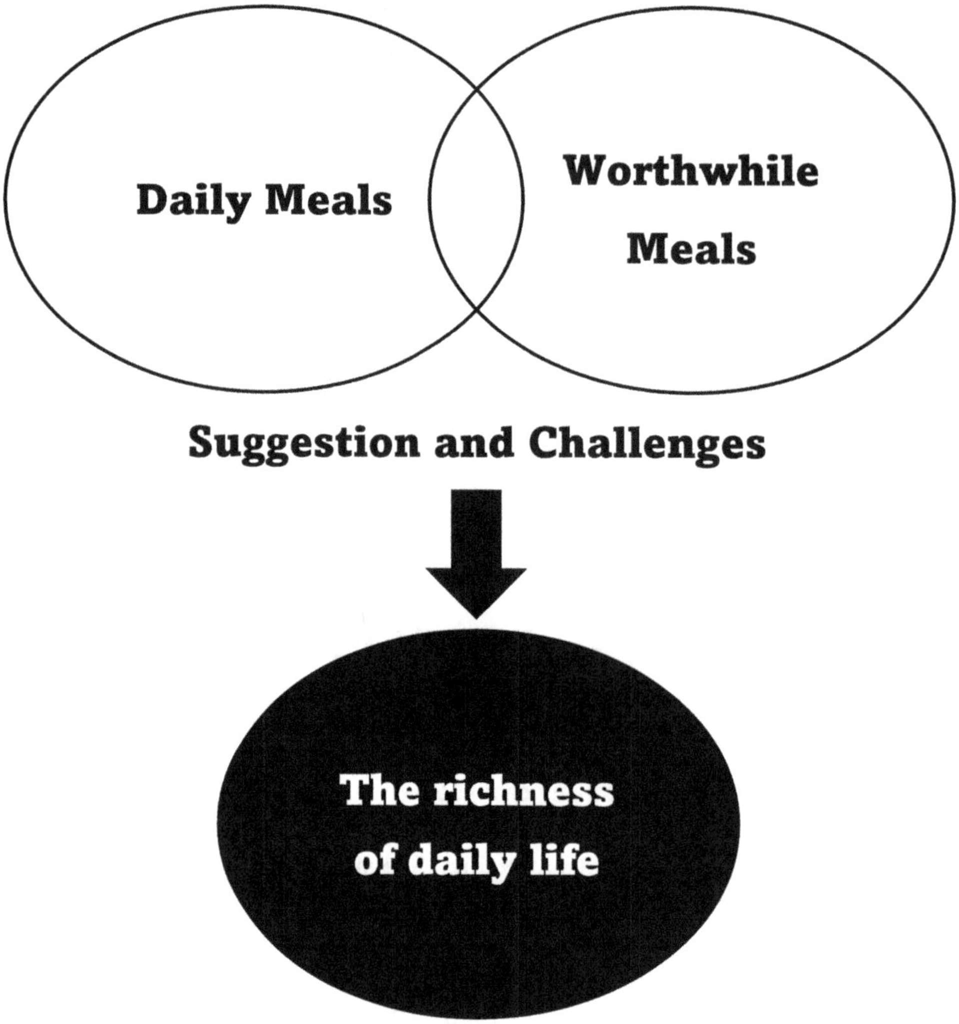


## History of Saizeriya

The origin of Saizeriya is a small western-style restaurant started by Yasuhiko Shogaki, Chairman of the Board, with his friends. Mr. Shogaki solidified his business theory that it needed to be organized to turn the restaurant business into an industry (Shogaki, 2020). By collecting and dividing the work, everyone could work towards a single goal and demonstrate their abilities. As a result, Mr. Shogaki searched for a business model that would not go out of business for 40 years and found that the most popular cuisines in the world are Italian and Chinese. Further research revealed that tomatoes, pasta, and cheese consumption was growing at a high rate, and he was convinced that Italian cuisine was the most sustainable business model. He went on a study tour to Italy and was shocked by the depth of its food culture. Even small restaurants offered healthy and nutritionally balanced dishes with attention to detail. There were so many combinations and choices of dishes that customers never got bored. Impressed, Mr. Shogaki

*Figure 9. Transition of number of stores of Saizeriya*
*Source: (Shogaki,2020)*

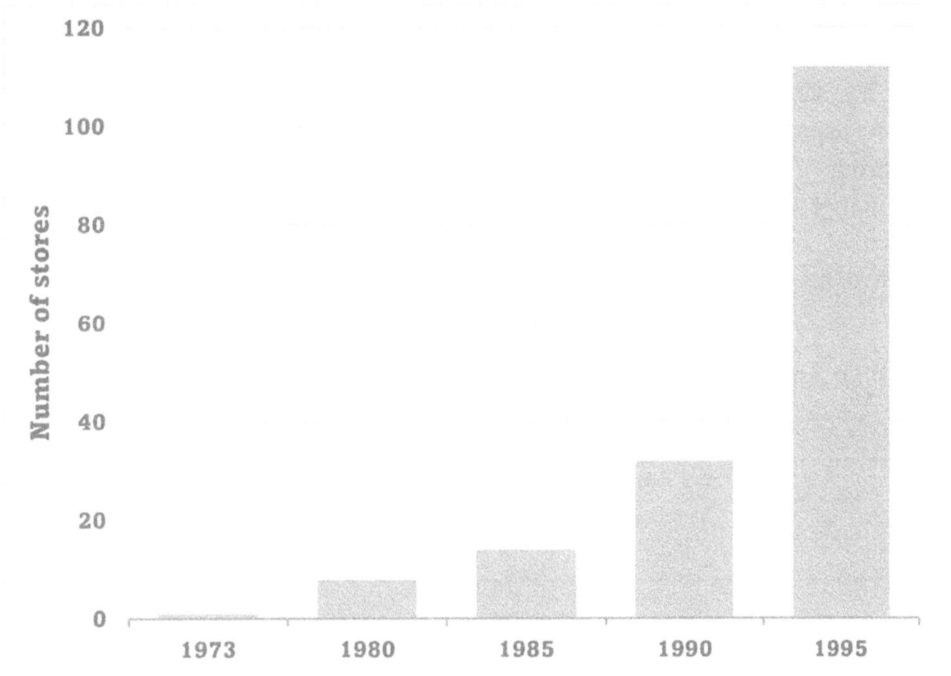


decided to spread Italian cuisine in Japan, which was inexpensive and could be eaten every day. After returning to Japan, he renovated his restaurant and opened it as an Italian specialty restaurant. However, the number of customers did not increase because the price was too high, even though it was less than half the price of a high-end restaurant. The president thought that if the products were worth the price, customers would come to the restaurant even if it was in a bad location, so he reduced the menu price by 70%(Shogaki,2020). By doing this, he succeeded in gaining customers and learned how to expand the chain.

Later, they became a national chain and covered broad processes about their ingredients. They worked with contract farmers such as Saizeriya Farm to develop Saizeriya's vegetables, making their dream a reality. However, the seven discounts did not generate any profit for the company, and they could no longer pay their employees' salaries. Nevertheless, some of Saizeriya's customers were regulars, and the deficit was eliminated when many customers came to the restaurant. Also, in Australia, 17 factories were built on 400,000 square meters of land. With factories in the northern and southern hemispheres, there would be two summers to have a supply system. And they can supply food to poor people all over the world. Saizeriya's management policy is to formulate hypotheses based on objective facts and then verify them by implementing them. This is the method of science, and both scientists and restaurateurs must be humble in the face of facts, knowing their ignorance. This management policy is both scientific and logical.

At Saizeriya, store managers are not given sales targets or quotas. Store sales are greatly influenced by location, menu, and price, but it makes no sense to measure the manager's ability by sales in a chain store. Store managers are evaluated based on person-hour productivity (gross profit divided by the total hours worked). The Saizeriya way is to raise productivity by controlling expenses and efficiently organizing shifts of part-timers even if sales are low. By putting this into practice and creating a direct manufacturing and sales system with consistent quality control, the company has achieved both quality and reasonable prices. As a listed company on the first section of the Tokyo Stock Exchange, Saizeriya strives to create a system that is not bound by common sense. It aims to become a company where employees can be happy by generating productivity comparable to other industries in the restaurant industry where productivity is low.

While many companies in the food service industry are struggling to grow, Saizeriya is succeeding with its low prices. I will now clarify why Saizeriya can offer such low-priced products and explain why it does not lose money.

*Table 4. Surprisingly low wine price in 2021*

| | |
|---|---|
| Glass of wine (red and white) | 100yen |
| Decanter of wine (red and white) | 200yen |
| Margherita | 400yen |
| Pepperoncino | 300yen |
| Milanese doria | 300yen |
| Hamburg steak | 400yen |

*Source: (SAIZERIYA Co.* https://www.saizeriya.co.jp/menu/)

In Japan, the consumption tax was increased from 8% to 10% in October 2019. Saizeriya decided to keep the price unchanged even when the consumption tax was increased. The price was effectively reduced since the menu was labeled with an internal tax. One of the secrets of Saizeriya's low prices is its large scale. Instead of increasing the price per customer, it increases the number of customers by increasing the number of stores. The reason why the company has succeeded in expanding its stores while maintaining low prices is explained below.

## Low-Cost Strategy

### Store Opening Strategy with ROI

Saizeriya has established a discipline of not opening new stores if the return on investment (ROI) does not reach 30%. ROI is calculated by dividing the profit by the capital invested. The higher the number, the higher the return on investment. Saizeriya has arranged this ROI into a unique formula. Considering the necessity of calculating the ROI for each store, the company divided the store's operating profit by the amount of investment required to open the store (Shogaki,2020).

Saizeriya's store-based ROI

=Operating Income of Stores / Amount of Investment Required to Open a Store×100

*Figure 10. Image of kitchen area*

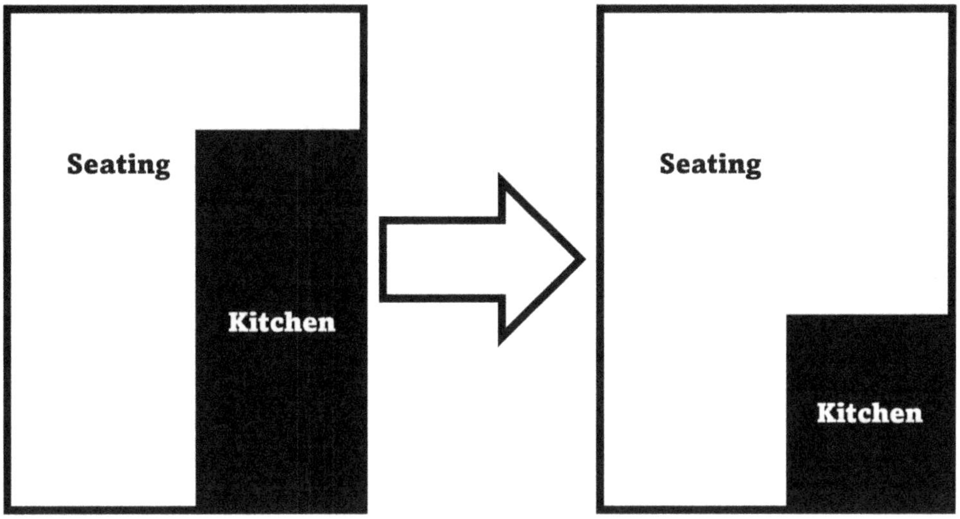


## Stabilization of Quality

In the beginning, Saizeriya built a central kitchen in the backyard and delivered the food cooked in the middle to multiple stores. Then, deterioration in the quality of food due to transportation occurred. It is vital to reduce the following four factors to stabilize the quality.

- ・Temperature while storing food
- ・Humidity while storing food
- ・Time elapsed since harvest
- ・Vibration to the food during transportation

Therefore, Saizeriya asked a factory of a major food manufacturer about the know-how to manufacture sauces and dressings. Finally, Saizeriya made it possible to provide high-quality products stably.

## Menu Development

In pursuit of cost reduction, the ingredients were narrowed down. Instead of abundant ingredients, Saizeriya focused on vegetables and dairy products. The menu was narrowed down, and the core products were thoroughly refined (Shogaki,2020). Some products have been improved more than 1,000 times so far. The products are then scored according to five factors: Look, Flavor, Aroma, Taste, and Price.

## Labor Cost Reduction

One of Saizeriya's strengths is its formulation and implementation of a concept to eliminate waste and unevenness. Saizeriya employs a central kitchen to maintain a consistent quality of taste and freshness. A central kitchen refers to a large in-house factory. The kitchen area can be reduced by using a central kitchen without changing the overall store area. As a result, the number of seats for customers can be increased. In addition, the smaller the kitchen area, the smaller the overall store area, and the lower the tenant fees, land purchase costs, and construction costs. In fact, by reducing the size of the kitchen, Saizeriya has been able to expand into areas where it had not been able to open before, including small areas in the city center.

Saizeriya is trying to improve efficiency by simplifying the cooking process in its stores. There are very few cooking utensils in the kitchen of Saizeriya. There is no gas range in stores. As a result, almost no cooking is done in the stores at all. There are no knives either since there is no need to cut food (with two exceptions: tomatoes and lemons). And since no fire is used, the kitchen is equipped with induction cooktops with high thermal efficiency. Since the food is almost perfectly prepared in the central kitchen and brought to the store, the kitchen can be made smaller. By shrinking the kitchen, a cost zone, they have created a structure that generates profit even at low prices. Also, even though the restaurant is crowded with many customers at lunchtime, each restaurant needs only two kitchen staff. Orders come in one after another, but most of the ingredients are processed in the central kitchen. One person can run the kitchen during the not busy time. Since the number of tasks is small and simplified, training is straightforward. This kind of thorough labor cost reduction is being carried out.

### Various Management Strategy

Saizeriya considers the chain store theory, the “Management Principles,” for restaurant chains to open multiple stores. The company implements the PDCA cycle and carries out scientific management without relying on intuition based on this concept.

The management indicator that Saizeriya focuses on to secure appropriate profits is “man-hour productivity.” Restaurants need to increase person-hour productivity to stabilize their operations. The best way to improve efficiency is to consider whether the time-consuming parts of the operation can be shortened or eliminated (Shogaki,2020). For a single task, Saizeriya has found an efficient method using the concept of IE (Industrial Engineering). Hence, the faster Saizeriya teaches it to new staff, the more efficient the work will be, and the total working hours will decrease.

The key to multiple opening stores lies in “location creation,” Companies that succeed in this have become large chains. Rent and security deposits are cheap before anyone realizes the value of the land. Saizeriya found such locations faster than others and increased the number of stores. This strategy is the reason behind Saizeriya’s decision to open more stores. In this way, Saizeriya is thoroughly building an organization and implementing management strategies in line with its management philosophy to become a restaurant that will thrive for a long time.

## THE FOOD SPA AT SAIZERIYA

Behind Saizeriya’s ability to achieve high quality and low prices simultaneously is a business model that could be called the “SPA of food service.” Saizeriya’s purchasing department plays a vital role in the direct import and in-house production of ingredients essential for the SPA. The company can control the cost ratio and procure desired ingredients by attacking the supply chain upstream. This study is called SPFB (Speciality store retailer of Private label Food and Beverage) and provides a business model for the Japanese food service industry.

## Manufacture and Direct Sales

Saizeriya has established SPFB by directly importing ingredients and producing ingredients in-house. In 1993, the company started importing wine directly from Italy without a trading company. In 1996, the company outsourced the cultivation of arugula to Japanese farmers. Moreover, it is not just an in-house production but a direct manufacturing and sales company that handles the entire process from cultivation and harvesting to processing and cooking. Lettuce, for example, is developed from the seed stage. While a single ball of ordinary lettuce can only be used to make a salad for a few people, Saizeriya has developed highly efficient lettuce that can be used for more than five people by improving the variety. Saizeriya has also built a special factory in Australia, where milk is inexpensive, to produce the white sauce used in its restaurants.

Saizeriya aims to become a "direct manufacturing and sales" company in the restaurant industry. The manufacturing business manufacturing direct sales business is a business form in which the company handles everything from product development to production, processing, and delivery of food ingredients in-house. Saizeriya has been building a direct manufacturing and sales system from having only a dozen stores to opening 1,000 stores in 60 years. The most significant advantage of direct manufacturing is the ability to sell products directly to customers. And Saizeriya can control the quality and price itself.

Even Saizeriya decided to pursue the deliciousness for its customers. It is a tough challenge to set the standard of deliciousness because everyone has different tastes and preferences. It is very difficult for anyone other than themselves to understand the standard of deliciousness. In addition, the more people intervene in the middle, the more difficult it is to communicate and the more costly it is. Saizeriya goes to the production area to develop the ingredients, pick them, and store them. Saizeriya knows the production area to develop materials, how to collect materials, how to store, how to process, and how to transport very well. Saizeriya controls the entire supply chain to improve quality and efficiency while reducing waste.

## Central Kitchen (In-House Factory)

Saizeriya established its first central kitchen in 1997. However, the company was not familiar with the technology related to production and had a series of failures at first. The company was rescued from this predicament by a group of engineers. They had been transferred from the food manufacturers with whom the company did business. After that, Saizeriya built new factories one after another. In this way, Saizeriya is able to produce in-house what had been outsourced to food processing manufacturers. Currently, 90% of its products are procured through direct purchase and in-house production.

Since completing the large food manufacturing plant, Saizeriya no longer has to use knives, and the food is sent to stores in pouches. All store staffs have to do is transfer it to a plate and serve it. This made the work much easier and increased productivity. There is no longer any difference in how the products are cut or seasoned, and all staff can now provide a stable quality menu. The number of stores increased even more as customers began to support the company. With the operation of the large factory, packed ingredients are delivered by the case. By improving the efficiency of logistics sorting, stores now only need to hold the right amount.

The following is an explanation of how Saizeriya effectively utilizes its factories. Domestically, Saizeriya located five factories, and each factory manufactures and processes a batch of each ingredient for each dish, such as sauce, cheese, and vegetables. The company decides what to make at which fac-

*Figure 11. Percentage of food procurement methods*

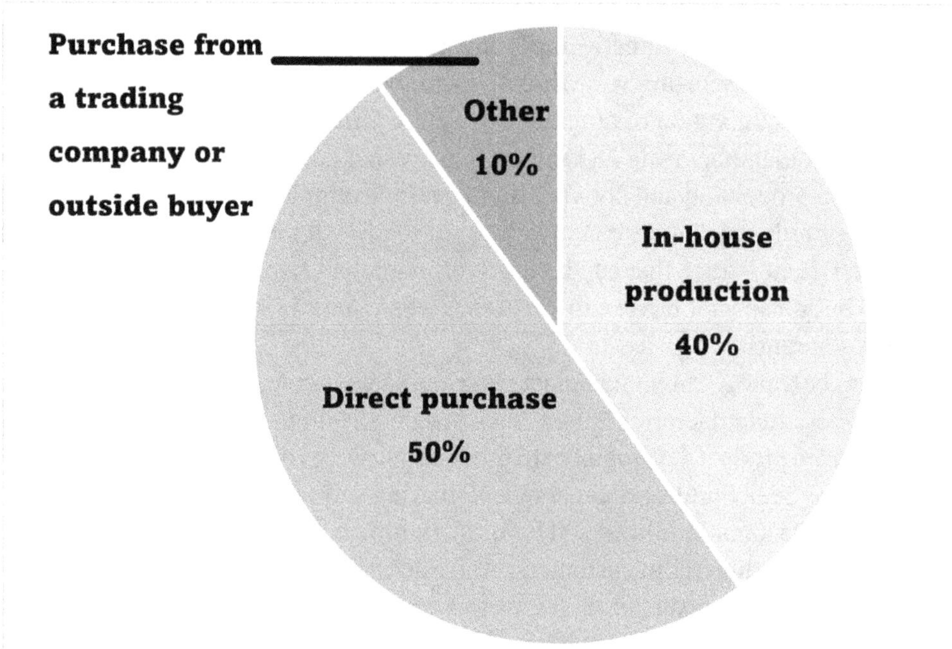


tory, considering the production location of the raw materials. Each of the five locations has its own role in optimizing the process. By doing so, Saizeriya can avoid duplication of production lines. Vegetables lose their freshness very quickly, so Saizeriya has set up bases in the east and west to reduce the time required for transportation because Japan is very long from east to west and north to south. Also, by meeting with the farmers who consign the products to us, Saizeriya can operate the factories more efficiently. Saieriya explains the specifications of the vegetables we want them to deliver to the farmers in detail. For example, Saizeriya asks them to deliver lettuce with the outer leaves removed. It is essential to build a relationship with the farmer to ensure smooth delivery and processing.

In general, the restaurant industry catches the trend, plans the following year's products, and commercializes them within a year. However, Saizeriya is not very good at being agile because Saizeria works from upstream. When creating a new product from scratch often takes three to five years. Therefore, the fundamental stance of Saizeriya is that Saizeriya will not handle current dishes. Saizeriya can avoid being influenced by trends and narrow down the ingredients Saizeriya uses by offering orthodox Italian cuisine.

Explain how the quality of Saizeriya's products is ensured. While pursuing cost reduction, Saizeriya does not use any raw material, no matter how cheap, if it does not meet a certain level of quality. At the stage of raw material procurement, its buyers check the quality of the raw materials. Processed and final products are tasted daily by the factory manager. If there is a problem with the taste, they investigate at what stage of the supply chain the problem occurred and make improvements.

## Business Model of SPA for Food Service

The secret behind Saizeriya's low prices lies in its business model, called the "manufacturing and retailing" of food service. SPA in the apparel industry, where the company handles everything from manufacturing to retailing, is well known. Saizeriya is the first Italian restaurant with a direct manufacturing and retailing system, just like the apparel industry. The entire process is carried out from serving the product to the consumer to upstream operations such as manufacturing and cultivation of raw materials. This is the only business model followed by a restaurant in Japan.

Raising prices can increase sales and profits in the short term, but the number of customers is sure to decrease. The menu's price range probably forms the restaurant market. If there is a high price range and a low price range, naturally, the low price range has a larger market size. The sales amount divided by the price per customer almost equals the number of customers. Lowering the price per customer will increase the number of customers. Anyway, Saizeriya's mission is to create a low-price market, lower the price per customer, and let as many people enjoy authentic Italian cuisine as possible. Of course, Saizeriyae will not lower the quality of its food just because Saizeriya has reduced the various cost by its efforts.

The food at Saizeriya is of super high quality, and the mozzarella cheese used is from a famous brand in Naples. The mozzarella cheese they use is from a renowned brand in Naples, and surprisingly, they sell it at a lower price than in Italy, where it is produced. Saizeriya can sell it at such a low price because Saizeriya buys it in large quantities. And by purchasing and importing raw materials independently without going through trading companies, Saizeriya also saves on intermediate margins.

Saizeriya is also known as the "SPA of food service," planning the menu and serving it to consumers and manufacturing and growing the raw materials. SPA is a business model for apparel companies that carry out the entire process from manufacturing to retailing in a single process. The most famous SPA is Uniqlo in the apparel industry. However, there is a difference between Saizeriya and UNIQLO. UNIQLO does not produce the fibers used to make its clothes, nor does it have its factories. UNIQLO does not have its factories but buys large quantities of products made on dedicated production lines in China, Myanmar, Cambodia, and other countries where labor costs are as low as possible to achieve low prices.

Saizeriya, on the other hand, does everything by itself, from upstream to downstream. They breed some vegetables. That is why they are able to offer good products at low prices. This is truly the establishment of a new business model called "SPFB (Speciality store retailer of Private label Food and Beverage).

Since direct manufacturing and sales have many disadvantages and difficulties, many restaurant chains have not adopted this method. Saizeriya is the only one able to convert to SPFB because it specializes in orthodox Italian cuisine rather than trendy menu items. This makes SPFB possible because of a low risk that predictions will be wrong. SPFB has some benefits. It is less susceptible to the rising cost of goods and logistics costs, easier to control quantity and price, and completely original products. On the other hand, SPFB has some demerits. It requires a significant investment and a prolonged period (five years) from planning to sales, making it difficult to keep up with trends.

## Cold Chain

Saizeriya pays particular intention to the temperature and humidity during food storage, the time elapsed since harvesting, and the vibration to the food during transportation. Vegetables continue to live even after they are harvested. As time passes after harvesting, they consume the nutrients stored in their bodies and lose their deliciousness. When harvested vegetables are stored in a dormant state, their activity stops, and the deliciousness is locked inside the vegetable. This property is utilized in the cold chain system. At saizeriya, the entire process is kept at 4 degrees Celsius until it reaches the store, delivering the freshly picked taste to the customers.

*Figure 12. Model of SPFB*
*Source: (News Picks. https://newspicks.com)*

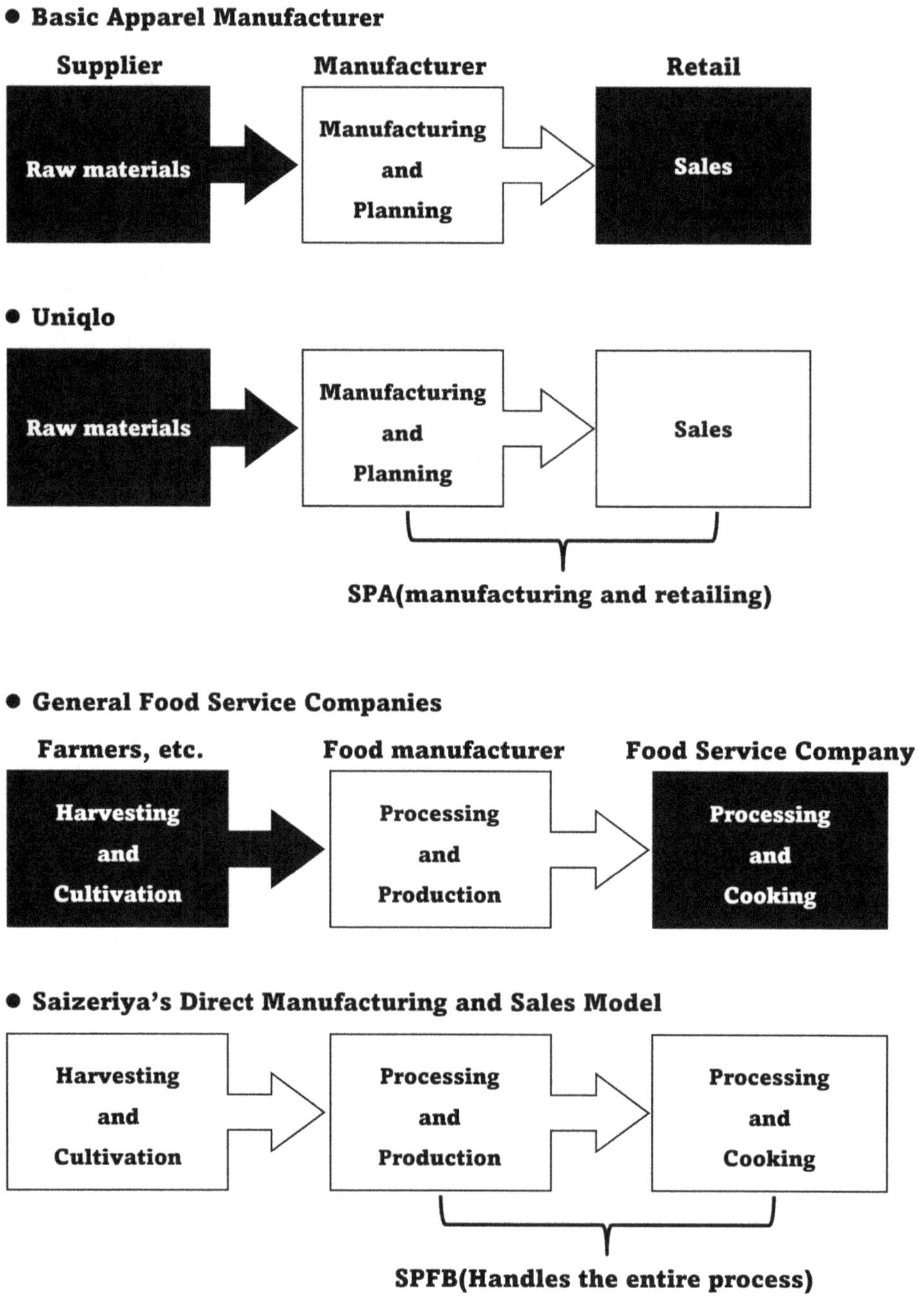


It is inevitable for the restaurant chains pursuing a stable and efficient operation to expand their chains. They need a supply chain connecting farmers, the central kitchen, and stores directly through the cold chain. Saizeriya has built such a business model to improve efficiency, reduce costs, and increase customer satisfaction.

*Figure 13. Cold chain process*

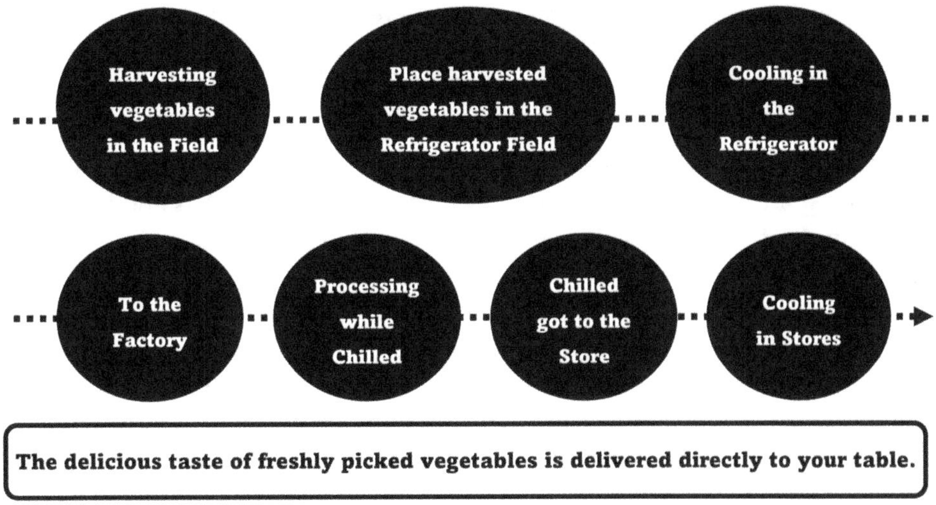


## FUTURE RESEARCH DIRECTIONS

The current restaurant industry is facing the problem of balancing taste and cost including food loss. The current food service industry is a system in which the cook is at the center. However, Saizeriya has succeeded in providing delicious food at a low cost through its own supply chain and standardized single operation. Saizeriya has revolutionized the restaurant industry by improving its supply chain and operations. In the future, freshness and environmentally friendly will become more important. Supply chain and SCM are closely related to the pursuit of freshness and creating an environmentally friendly society. With the development of SCM and information systems in other industries, just-in-time delivery of even small quantities has become the norm. Freshness leads not only to good taste and reduced waste, but also to safer food through the reduction of additives. The food supply chain and its SCM must become more sophisticated in order to deliver good food to customers and reduce food loss efficiently. In particular, reducing food waste and balancing food production efficiency with food miles will be the next challenge in this area.

## CONCLUSION

This chapter describes the Japanese restaurant industry's supply chain management (SCM). David, Philip, and Edith (2000) mention today's companies face fierce competition in international markets, shorter product lifecycles, and more sophisticated consumer demands, making it imperative to invest money and attention in their supply chains. Robert and Ernest (1999) state that the supply chain is essentially a chain from supplier to customer. In other words, every customer company is a supplier to its own upstream company until the product reaches the end consumer. The companies need to build an agile and adaptable supply chain aligned with customer interests.

The food service industry's supply chain has developed in response to socioeconomic factors such as globalization. This chapter deals with Saizeriya as a case study. Saizeriya, the biggest restaurant chain in the world, has developed a model of supply chain management based on its management philosophy of "challenging to deliciousness and affordability." As a direct manufacturing and sales business in the restaurant industry, Saizeriya has adopted a form of integrated in-house operations from product development, production of ingredients, processing to delivery. Saizeriya controls the quality and price itself and reduces unnecessary costs. Saizeriya personally visits production areas and goes into every step of the process, from the development of ingredients, how to pick them, how to store them, how to process them, and how to transport them to improve quality reduce waste. Saizeriya is not limited to restaurants but aims to truly industrialize the food service industry by having its functions from material development to processing and manufacturing.

SPA is an acronym for "Specialty store retailer of Private label Apparel," which was coined by Donald Fisher, chairman of the American clothing retail giant GAP, in 1986. In the 1990s, the concept of SPA became more widespread. Today it is defined as a business model that minimizes waste and losses in the entire supply chain by considering all processes, including material procurement, planning, development, manufacturing, logistics, sales, inventory management, and store planning, as a single flow. Saizeriya has achieved success by adopting this SPA, despite being in the restaurant industry. This can truly prove to be a new model called SPFB (Speciality store retailer of Private label Food and Beverage), which is why we defined it in this study. For the SPFB model to function smoothly, the company has established a central kitchen and adopted a cold chain. For the restaurant industry to grow as a company, such as through chain expansion and multi-store development, it needs a supply chain connecting the central kitchen, manufacturing, direct sales, and the cold chain. As a result, the company is able to provide customers with high-quality products at low prices. In this way, Saizeriya is implementing various management strategies to improve its corporate value and customer satisfaction, the most important part of SCM.

This chapter clarifies the model and functions of SCM in the restaurant industry. The example of Saizeriya can be used in various industries beyond the framework of the restaurant industry. As competition in management intensifies, logistics strategy plays an important role. In recent years, any company in any industry should not overlook the fact that total optimization of the logistics supply chain supports management fundamentals.

## REFERENCES

David, S., Philip, K., & Edith, S. (2000). *Designing and managing the Supply Chain*. McGraw-Hill Companies.

Dimitrios, V., & Eleftherios, I. (2005). A System Dynamics Modeling Framework for the Strategic Supply Chain Management of Food Chains. *Journal of Food Engineering*, *70*(3), 351–364. doi:10.1016/j.jfoodeng.2004.06.030

Douglas, M. L., & Martha, C. C. (2000). Issues in Supply Chain Management. *Industrial Marketing Management*, *29*(1), 65–83. doi:10.1016/S0019-8501(99)00113-3

Fukushima, M. (1998). *Supply Chain keiei kakumei* [Revolution of SCM]. Nihonkeizaishimbumsha.

Hara, T. (2021). Gaishyoku sangyo no Supply Chain Management [Supply chain management in restaurant industry]. *Shogakukenkyusyu*, *54*, 237–256.

Higuchi, T. (2018). *Supply Chain ga umidasu kyosoyuii* [Competetive advantage generated by supply chain]. Tyu-oukeizaisya.

Imaoka, Z. (1998). *Kigyo syu-eki wo ageru shikake supply chain management* [Increasing profit by SCM]. Kogyo-tyousakai.

Japan Food Service Association. (2020). https://jfnet.or.jp

Jeremy, F. S. (2006). *Modeling the supply chain*. Cengage Learning.

John, G. (2017). *Strategic supply chain alignment*. Routledge.

Mawson, E., & Fearne, A. (1996). Purchasing strategies and decision-making processes in the food service industry: A case study of UK restaurant chains. *Supply Chain Management*, *1*(3), 34–41. doi:10.1108/13598549610155305

Michihata, M. (2010). Food service sangyo no syokuzai kaihatsu supply chain no Kochiku [Development of supply chain for foodstuff in food service industry]. *Kanko-gakukennkyu*, *9*, 103–115.

Mizoue, Y. (2001). *Mujirushi syo-hin VS Uniqlo* [Muji vs. Uniqulo]. Paru syuppan.

News Picks. (n.d.). https://newspicks.com

Robert, B. H., & Ernest, L. N. (1999). *Introduction to supply chain management*. Prentice-Hall.

SAIZERIYA Co. (n.d.). https://www.saizeriya.co.jp

Shimura, Y. (1998). *ERP/Supply Chain Seiko no himitsu* [The secret of ERP/supply chain]. Kogyo-tyousakai.

Shogaki, Y. (2020). *Saizeriya oishii kara ureru no de ha nai ureteiruno ga oishisii nda* [Saizeriya is popular and the menu is delicious]. Nikkei BP.

Sunil, C., & Peter, M. (2014). *Supply chain management: Strategy, planning, and operation*. Pearson.

Suzuki, T. (2012). *Zukai Ninki gaisyoku ten no rieki no dashikata* [Profitability of popular restaurant]. Ko-dansya.

## KEY TERMS AND DEFINITIONS

**Central Kitchen:** A central kitchen is a cooking facility that centralizes the food preparation process to achieve efficiency.

**Cold Chain:** A distribution system that keeps perishable foods at low temperatures during the production, transportation, and consumption processes and refers to a low-temperature distribution system.

**Industrial Engineering:** A method of scientifically analyzing processes and work contents to pursue the best production control methods.

**Location Creation:** Finding locations where other companies will not open stores but where you can open your own stores, or creating locations where you can open stores by improving your business model.

**Management Principles:** Considering cause and effect relationships observed in every phenomenon that occurs in a store with numerical or objective data.

**Person-Hour Productivity:** This is calculated by dividing the store's gross profit generated in a day by the total working hours of all employees working that day.

**Platform:** It refers to the corporate management infrastructure for sustainably creating corporate value related to the entire logistics process, including facilities, transportation, and logistics processing.

**ROA:** The ROA shown in this chapter is different from the ROA in accounting. The numerator is the cash flow of the supply chain operations.

**Single Operation:** A single person running the kitchen at a Saizeriya restaurant. In order to allow non-cooks to cook alone, he or she will be primarily responsible for only warming and serving food sent from the central kitchen. There are no knives in the kitchen of Saizeriya.

**SPA:** SPA refers to a business model that eliminates SCM waste by vertically integrating the entire process from planning to manufacturing and sales of fashion products, thereby enabling a quick response to consumer needs.

**SPFB:** SPFB refers to a new model introduced in the food service industry based on the SPA model popularized in the apparel industry and is a business model that integrates upstream activities such as the procurement of raw materials.

# Chapter 11
# Agri-Food Logistics as a Dynamic Actor in Managing Food Loss and Waste:
## A Bump-Start by COVID-19

**Erika Quendler**
https://orcid.org/0000-0002-3573-2266
*Federal Institute of Agricultural Economics, Rural and Mountain Research, Vienna, Austria*

**Matthew James Lamb**
*LKT-TGM Polymer and Environmental Centre, Vienna, Austria*

**Noureddin Driouech**
*International Centre for Advanced Mediterranean Agronomic Studies – CIHEAM, Bari, Italy*

## ABSTRACT

*Perhaps no phenomenon has so quickly and radically challenged agri-food logistics as the onset of the COVID-19 pandemic. This chapter postulates on the short- to longer-term implications of this public health crisis on food loss and waste (FLW) throughout the whole supply chain and the role of agri-food logistics. This chapter outlines examples of several logistic solutions deployed for dealing with FLW as the pandemic has unfolded. Furthermore, since COVID-19 has opened a window of opportunity, this chapter indicates the potential of agri-food logistics to help manage FLW from farm to bin and beyond. In fact, the pandemic and its aftermath may improve agri-food logistics skills, practices, and innovation in a manner that mitigates day-to-day FLW. Moreover, this chapter advocates a rethinking of the opportunities arising from COVID-19 for the transformation of agri-food logistics in alignment with the UN's SDGs. This forms a practical framework for future research and application.*

DOI: 10.4018/978-1-7998-9800-9.ch011

## INTRODUCTION

Growing awareness that food loss and waste (FLW) is a global phenomenon and covers the decrease in mass (quantitative) or nutritional value (qualitative) of food, has prompted a plethora of "solutions" and strategies. This chapter discusses FLW from the view of the supply chain and extends the scope of SCM. Generally, supply chain management (SCM) scope is from raw materials to consumption. However, SCM has a great influence on FLW. The international commitment by the United Nations (2015) includes the issue of FLW in the Sustainable Development Goal (SDG) target 12.3, which aims to "*halve per capita global food waste at the retail and consumer levels and reduce food losses along production and supply chains, including postharvest losses*" by 2030. While FLW occurs throughout the whole supply chain from farm to bin and beyond, Gustavsson et al. (2011) differentiates between food losses occurring during production and processing and food waste occurring at the retail and final consumption stage, i.e., household and foodservice providers. Nevertheless, usually both terms are considered together as FLW.

Before the pandemic, up to 30 to 50% of all food produced — approximately 1.2 to two billion tons —was lost or wasted every year on its way to people's stomachs (Institutions of Mechanical Engineers, 2013). FLW amounts reached roughly US$ 680 billion in industrialized countries and US$ 310 billion in developing countries (FAO, 2013). In low-income countries, more than 40% of the FLW occurs during postharvest (and processing), while in developed countries more than 40% of the FLW occurs at retail and consumer stages (Gustavsson, Dederberg and Sonesson, 2011). Furthermore, FLW also detracts from the resources used to produce food: losses of 250 km3/year of water and 28% of the world's agricultural area (FAO, 2013). Moreover, the carbon footprint of FLW has been estimated at 3.3 billion tons of $CO_2$ equivalent per year. The total greenhouse gas emissions are emitted not only from energy generation and industry as well as transport, but also through FLW decomposition itself (FAO, 2013). In this context, its nutritional, economic, environmental, and social implications have been recognized not only at the highest levels of global governance by the SDGs (United Nations, 2015) and the EU Farm to Fork (F2F) strategy for sustainable food (EC, 2020) but also in the literature (cf., Lemaire & Limbourg, 2019). Indeed, the Covid-19 pandemic has created disruptions (Hobbs, 2020) of varying severity in the supply chain from farm to bin. Around the world, generally, farmers' biggest buyers are the foodservice industry, including food processors, restaurants, universities canteens, etc. COVID-19 social and physical distancing rules and restrictions have forced many of these places to scale or shut down their operations. A shortage of goods and services has been observed and experienced. In others, as many food businesses or retailers close or need to adapt, farmers and food producers are left with more commodities and food than they can market and sell, i.e., food cannot reach end consumers, is processed or ends up in bin. To counteract FLW, logistics is a vital element of the agri-food sector (Fredriksson & Liljestrand, 2015). It includes both cold and ambient agri-food logistics based on precise planning, execution, and efficient monitoring to effectively manage the movement of food products on-time from farm to bin and beyond.

However, the literature shows that FLW from farm to bin during the pandemic and the potential of agri-food logistics have been largely overlooked. New logistic management and business models increasingly using digital technologies and services play a key role (Niewiadomski, 2020). Despite these advances, the "guidance dimension" is still considered one of the most acute knowledge gaps in the transformation, hampering its development (Korhonen et al., 2018a; Hobson, 2020).

It is well recognized that the situation in each country is specific, as there are great differences among them. Yet, there are similarities, and it is believed that useful lessons can be drawn from the implementation of technology, innovation, and new business models in agri-food logistics. The COVID-19 pandemic represents a "stress test" for agri-food logistics and should be seized to make it more efficient and sufficient in a sustainable way. This pandemic is also a good moment to enhance awareness and concern about FLW while increasing resilience to future shocks and crises.

In this context, this chapter, a pathway, aims to provide research guidance for investigating the role of agri-food logistics in reducing or better managing FLW in a post-COVID-19 environment. This chapter reviews issues of FLW for the following actors, 1) farmers, 2) processors, 3) foodservice operators, 4) retailers, 5) consumers in households, and 6) FLW collectors, as well as highlights the potential of agri-food logistics. For each actor, the authors discuss FLW under the COVID-19 pandemic and its emerging changes as referenced in literature. There follows a discussion about FLW mitigation efforts, or "pandemic pivots," by considering classic but also modern logistics that we had seen from farm to bin in 2020 and the beginning of 2021. Drawing on these findings, the authors have proposed a guidance framework that outlines the process and phases of transformation through agri-food logistics in FLW management. In conclusion, this chapter can constitute a basis to promote FLW prevention further, outlasting the COVID-19 crisis.

## BACKGROUND AND DEFINITIONS

Depending on the ambient conditions of agricultural production, commodities, and type of food, there is bound to be some loss or waste on the way from farm to bin. Along this journey, FLW comes in many forms and can be "*removed from the food supply chain to be recovered or disposed (including - composted, crops ploughed in/not harvested, anaerobic digestion, bioenergy production, co-generation, incineration, disposal to sewer, landfill or discarded to sea)*" (Stenmarck et al., 2016). One should also distinguish between the natural inedibility of FLW, such as bones and pits, and inedibility as a consequence of weather conditions or food degradation, such as destroyed or rotten FLW. While the former cannot be avoided, the latter can be avoided to some extent. In neither case can this FLW per se be eaten by the end consumer, but it can be put to other use (i.e., bioeconomy and/or circular economy). This is where circularity comes into play in the form of innovative guidance arrangements, such as the adoption of reverse logistics and take-back systems, design of contracts that facilitate the deployment of new technologies, development of incentives and collaboration schemes aimed at enhancing circular flows along and throughout the supply chain, new service-oriented revenue engines such as pay-per-result and pay-per-use, and new long-term financing mechanisms with longer payback periods (Roos & Agarwal, 2015; Pieroni et al., 2019). As said, some portion of FLW, even if FLW mitigation measures were to be successful, is unavoidable (cf., Schott & Anderson, 2015).

The vision of Figure 1 is to illustrate how FLW is generated and can be reused or recycled at the various stages along and throughout the food supply chain. The food supply chain is a series of stages through which food travels from the farmer to bin (Wunderlich & Martinez, 2018). This comprises a network of actors – basically farmers, processors and retailers, consumers and logistics providers – producing and delivering to the end consumer or bin. By extension, actors from governance, education, and research also impact, mostly an indirect one, on the supply chain. The reason to put food logistics separately is that it plays a role at all stages from farm to bin and beyond, i.e., it is a cross-cutting issue. The same applies to FLW collectors throughout the whole chain. In simple terms, in this chapter, agri-food logistics refers to how agricultural commodities and food are handled and moved along and throughout the supply chain (Verdouw et al., 2013a). Effective agri-food logistics aims to deliver "*the right product,*

*Figure 1. FLW throughout the food supply chain (Adapted from Teigiserova et al., 2019)*

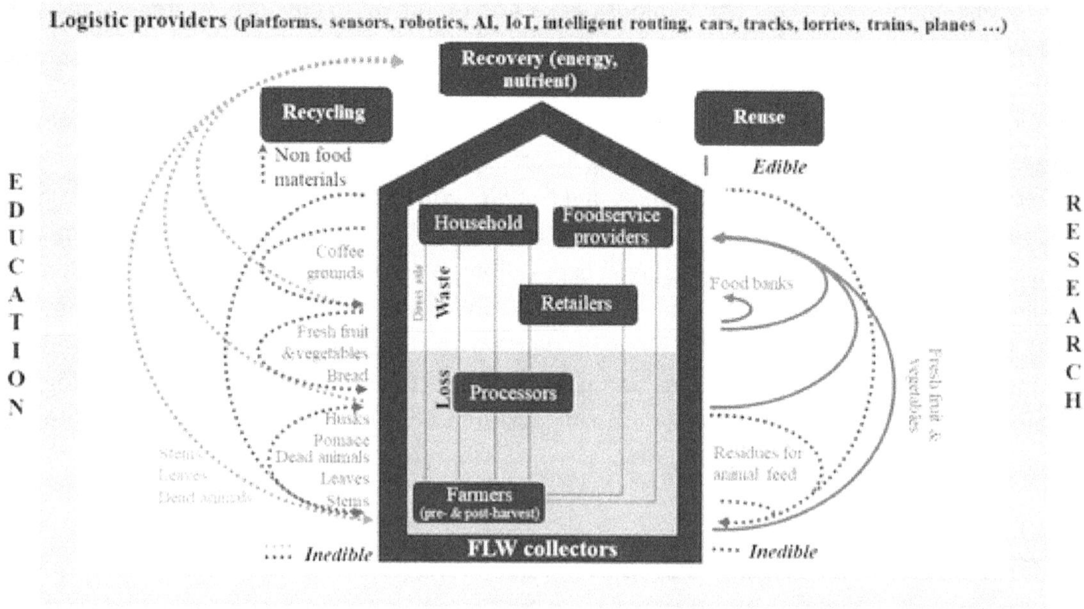


*in the right quantity and the right condition, to the right place at the right time for the right customer at the right price*" (Swamidass, 2000). It is based upon the idea of a smooth supply from farm to bin in the sense of circularity and SDGs. On that note, the authors look at the integration of circular thinking into the management of the FLW throughout the supply chain and its surrounding industrial and natural ecosystems. This approach systematically restores technical materials and regenerates biological materials toward a vision of zero-FLW. This vision also considers innovation in business models and supply chain functions from product/service design to end-of-life, and involves all stakeholders in a product/service lifecycle (parts/product manufacturers, service providers, consumers, and users).

In that sense, logistics mitigate or minimize FLW throughout the supply chain. "Loss" and "waste" are used, as presented in Figure 1, to form the boundaries and scope of the research potential in agri-food logistics. In this context, the principles of recycling, finding further uses for materials previously regarded as FLW, and the concepts of circularity, regenerative practices, and sustainable development are crucial. Figure 1 is one illustration; the results may differ due to the various definitions used, sectors and actors included in studies performed.

## FLW FROM FARM TO BIN AND BEYOND

Within the supply chain research community, the COVID-19 pandemic has brought up the discourse of ensuring food security and mitigating FLW. This section outlines the potential FLW generated by the COVID-19 pandemic and the unique role of agri-food logistics to mitigate FLW from farm to bin and beyond.

## Farmers

At the farm level, FLW is often the result of (i) market factors (such as price volatility, labor costs, or lack of labor, or market access), (ii) a product failing to meet aesthetic standards for a buyer (most common for grocery retail and foodservice buyers), (iii) damage from weather, pests and microbial attack (Minor et al., 2020; Wills et al., 1998). Furthermore, during the COVID-19 pandemic, farmers were also weakened by the restrictions since the international market contains endless numbers of their buyers, and some of them were not available. When restrictive export policies were applied, local farmers or sellers could not find buyers, resulting in excess supply and FLW and economic losses. (Aday & Aday, 2020). Moreover, many farmers, particularly in developing countries, do not have the resources and infrastructure to store food for any length of time (Mitchell, 2020).

The food supply chain is complex and highly specialized. It can be broadly divided into two groups: the staple commodities (e.g., wine, meat, wheat, maize, corn, soybeans, and oilseeds) and the high-value commodities (e.g., milk, fruits, vegetables, and flowers). Farmers who produce perishable products like meat, milk, fruits, and vegetables frequently do so expressly for grocery retail or the foodservice sectors (e.g., restaurants, schools, hospitals, hotels, stadiums, movie theatres). Each industry has its own set of buyer demands. For example, fresh produce (such as heads of lettuce) is usually packaged in bulk for foodservice buyers, but retailers want more individualized packaging (Richards, 2020; Ellison et al., 2020). Further, for field crops, such as wheat or olive trees or grapevines, which are planted long ahead of harvest, farmers do not have the flexibility to change their production mid-season when disruptions in the demand emerge. In the same way, animals do not stop growing (or producing – milk, eggs, etc.) on livestock farms. Thus, for farmers largely dependent on the foodservice sector, increases in FLW due to COVID-19 could be quite significant. Below are some examples:

- High-value commodities: During the lockdown, when borders were closed, the fruit was left to rot in Southern Europe because most pickers come from Romania and North Africa (Burgen, 2020). Also, with restaurants closed and people staying away from markets, tons of tomatoes, avocados, and other fruit and vegetables have been rotting in piles (Mambondiyani, 2020). As the COVID-19 pandemic has cut demand, tons of flowers land in shredders and/or are composted (DW Akademie, 2020). Since quantities bought at a retail level by consumers did not compensate for the loss in the demand of food services (e.g., schools, restaurants, and coffee shops) and the potential processing into other products with longer shelf lives was limited, farmers had no choice but to dispose of, for instance, their raw milk (cf., Appelbaum & Gaby-Biegle, 2020; Clements, 2020).
- Staple commodities: Wine sales have fallen dramatically due to the poor tourist season. The Spanish government offered growers subsidies to destroy part of the year's record grape harvest. Concretely, 26 Mallorcan winegrowers did not harvest their grapes in 2020. This corresponds to more than 124 hectares or 18% of the cultivated area covered by the "Denominación de Origen Binissalem" region. Moreover, some wine-growing regions, such as the Rías Baixas in Galicia, in the northwest, say they are having difficulty recruiting grape pickers as people fear exposure to COVID-19 or the loss of their furlough payments (Burgen, 2020). Other winemakers took part in the grape harvest but had to store the wine until the situation improved again (MM-Redaktion, 2020). For wineries, storage is also an issue because clients do not schedule appointments for winetasting or touristic winery tours (Cervera & Ortiz de Arri, 2020). As many meatpacking firms

had outbreaks, there was reduced labor and slower output. Given the resulting slowdown in meat processing, chicken farmers recognized that it would be too expensive to raise the chickens they had, therefore some euthanized their birds. For further information, go to Parshina-Kottas et al., 2020; Polansek & Huffstutter, 2020; Jeffery & Newburger, 2020; Yaffe-Bellany & Corkery, 2020.

## Processors

In reducing FLW, processors are frequently one of the most efficient nodes in the food supply chain. Food loss or trimmings are typically repurposed for other products at the processor level (e.g., animal feed or bioenergy).

COVID-19 has undoubtedly impacted food processing facilities, particularly meat processors (Taylor et al., 2020). The impact, however, on food loss in processing facilities is likely to be small. Processors are unlikely to be the party to incur food loss when processing capacity is reduced; rather, farmers are more likely to experience the food loss because they cannot move their product off the farm to a processing facility, as previously stated. However, agricultural commodities or foods that are not grown locally but needed for processing were not available due to the restrictions, and the ability of food-manufacturing plants to respond to the change in the demand was also negatively affected (Arianina & Morris, 2020; Ndemezo et al., 2018; Reddy et al., 2016).

## Foodservice Operators

Food waste is generated in both the back-of-house (kitchen waste) and front-of-house (plate waste) operations of the foodservice industry. With careful planning and inventory management, it can, however, exert more control over back-of-house waste. Nevertheless, no planning could prepare foodservice operations for the sudden closing down of businesses during COVID-19. Many countries, including Italy, Spain, France (Rubinstein, 2020), classified restaurants, cafes, canteens, etc., as non-essential in the pandemic, forcing them to close temporarily. This likely increased food waste in these restaurants in the short term as they could no longer use their existing food stocks.

Furthermore, food usually shipped to restaurants is kept in warehouses, while simultaneously retail inventory orders shoot up. (Rubinstein, 2020) As restaurants were re-opened, the uncertainty around demand for dine-in or take-out services may also have contributed to the generation of waste, though likely in a much smaller amount than initially with the closures during the first lockdown (Ellisson & Kalaitzandonakes, 2020).

## Retailers

At the retail-level, food waste in stores is often attributed to (i) over-stocking perishable products such as fruits and vegetables to guarantee that consumers are satisfied with the product assortment and (ii) products that are nearing or have reached the end of their actual shelf life (Gunders, 2012).

When COVID-19 hit Europe as the rest of the world, the media consistently reported on empty shelves at grocery shops. Consumers panic-buying water, rice, beans, pasta, bread, and frozen foods, then there were shortages of meat and eggs, then pasta, bread and flour, and so on (cf., Rubinstein, 2020; Taylor et al., 2020). Such empty store shelves may indicate that food waste decreased for retailers (Rubinstein, 2020). Household stockpiling behavior probably reduced food waste at the retailer-level overall, though it is possible that waste of more expensive products (e.g., cuts of meat) increased at the retailer level. The reason for that is that some households experienced negative income shocks and shifted to lower-cost alternatives (Ellisson & Kalaitzandonakes, 2020).

## Consumers (Household)

Before the COVID-19 pandemic, households were identified as the largest source of food waste along and throughout the supply chain (c.f., Amicarelli & Bux, 2020; Pappalardo et al., 2020). In the European Union, households were responsible for about 53% of the food wasted within the food chain (Stenmarck et al., 2000). Food waste in the Near East and North Africa region was estimated to be 250 kg per year per individual and, at the consumption stage, to be 34% (FAO 2015). Several studies (e.g., Fanelli & Di Florio, 2016; Szabó-Bódi et al., 2018) identified food categories most wasted in households, such as fresh fruits and vegetables, bakery goods as well as leftovers.

Consumer behavior and attitudes to food waste have changed during times of crisis, for instance, during the recessions in Greece and Italy (Abeliotis et al., 2014; Martinengo, 2014; Fanelli & Di Florio, 2016). Because of the economic crisis, Italians have decreased food waste by 57%, according to Coldiretti-SWG (2011). This is a necessary precondition for future behavior modification.

As consumers play a key role, changes in consumer behavior strongly affect food waste. Some consumers will be more careful thereby reducing food waste (Shafiee-Jood & Cai, 2016). Conversely, overbuying perishable items because of panic buying resulted in higher food waste levels (Fleetwood, 2020; Sharma et al., 2020). Changing demands will also bring changes to packaging materials/design, delivery options, and storage conditions at home (Reynold, 2020). All in all, Aldaco et al. (2020) indicated that the COVID-19 pandemic had a minor impact on the overall food waste generation in Spain but resulted in 12% higher generation of food waste at the household level. In contrast, one in three French consumers respondents stated that they waste less food because of the pandemic (Askew, 2020). In Tunisia, 85% of respondents declared that nothing of what they bought was discarded, and most respondents set up a strategy of saving, storing, and eating leftovers (Jribi et al., 2020).

Several factors contribute to food waste in a household, such as poor planning and inventory management and bulk purchasing as well as psycho-social factors (personal choice and lifestyle, food habits, lack of cooking skills) (Aschemann-Witzel et al., 2015; Jörissen et al., 2015; Gunders, 2012). For households, changes in waste during the COVID-19 pandemic will depend on the extent of stockpiling behavior and food inventory management skills. This notwithstanding, other factors could decrease food waste in households. Namely, unemployment has risen sharply during the COVID-19 pandemic. Food waste is positively connected to income, hence households with lower income will likely have less waste (cf., Gustavsson et al., 2011; Aschemann-Witzel et al., 2017). Furthermore, during the pandemic, higher food prices are likely to lower food waste for households at all income levels (Amicarelli & Bux, 2020, Lyndhurst, 2007; Pappalardo et al., 2020; cf., Ellison et al., 2020). Although the net effect on food waste is unknown, there is likely to be significant variation between households.

## Collectors

With all this in mind, the FLW collectors and their management are being challenged by the pandemic and the overall concept of sustainability. FLW accumulation determined by food items getting stuck on the field or road due to restrictions in vehicle movements or lack of workers or closed restaurants, canteens or cafes, etc., has increased. According to Aldaco et al. (2020), there was no significant change in overall waste generation. Generally, organic municipal waste, e.g., food and kitchen waste, decreased with the pandemic in most cities, with a significant decrease in waste generated by commercial activities, e.g., canteens, restaurants, and cafes. However, the latter did not compensate for the increase of household waste linked with lockdown measures such as "stay at home," etc. Touristic areas were also able to experience significant decreases. Nevertheless, the pandemic did not affect waste sorting performances because most respondents reported stabilizing or even increasing performances. There were, however, reductions reported in regions where selective collection and recycling could not be maintained, e.g., collection frequencies of food waste were decreased. (Bel & Marengo, 2020).

### Logistics

It is very difficult to find concrete information on FLW within logistics. Due to poor agri-food logistics, deterioration of harvested products can significantly cause FLW (Kader, 2005). The integrity of food being distributed depends upon a mix of technologies, such as temperature-controlled vehicles[1] and specialist warehousing, which need to be optimized for maximum efficiency (see Figure 2).

The generation of FLW through agri-food logistics is comparatively low along and throughout the supply chain. Nevertheless, agri-food logistics innovation can contribute to the mitigation of FLW at each stage in the chain. However, agri-food logistics are negatively affected, as food transportation is hampered in and across cities, provinces, regions, and countries (Cullen, 2020). Challenges to agri-food logistics, especially air and sea cargo, are also knock-on issues connected with FLW (OECD, 2020). Logistic barriers that disrupt the food supply chains affect the high-value commodities even more because of the latter's perishability (Cullen, 2020).

Due to the surge in demand at food retail locations, agri-food logistics are challenged in getting their agricultural commodities and food to consumers before the latter becomes FLW for various reasons. Some suppliers, e.g., farmers or food service providers, are forced to find new retail channels due to declines in their food orders or related services. For farmers wishing to donate their products to local food banks, challenges exist for bulk donations due to a shortage of labor and disrupted transportation to donation locations. This is more time-consuming, requires certain management skills, and may require adjusting to new retailers' product portion sizing and packaging requirements. (Padilla, 2020). In terms of trade, key staple commodity-exporting countries have to make every effort to deal with logistic disruptions to ensure the movement of major staple commodities across regions and countries. The COVID-19 crisis provides a chance to identify and fix bottlenecks. Multilateral development banks and key donors are responsible for assisting countries that export staple commodities in contributing to and ensuring food security.

## AGRI-FOOD LOGISTICS IN THE 21st CENTURY

Having identified the different stages above, the authors are going to look at logistics "as having its fingers in every pie." On that and relevant literature, a guidance framework is set up. This framework aims to show the transformation for FLW management given by the COVID-19 pandemic and beyond.

## Current and Future Technological Responses in Agri-Food Logistics

Before COVID-19, the main cause for FLW during transit was a result of poor-quality control during last-mile delivery. The pandemic brought to light how fixed and inflexible the supply chain has evolved, so much so that when true disruption occurs, there is little guidance or capacity to adapt. In response to these unprecedented challenges, the agri-food industry is acting through a broad range of logistic solutions to combat the paradox of mounting FLW and rising food insecurity.

Generally, in developing countries, the lack of infrastructure and associated technical and managerial skills in food production and postharvest processing have been identified as key drivers in creating FLW (cf., WFP, 2009). This is in contrast with the developed countries where the majority of FLW continues to be produced post-consumer, driven by the low price of food relative to disposable income, consumers' high expectations of food cosmetic standards, and the increasing disconnection between consumers and producers (cf., Parfitt, Barthel & Macnaughton, 2010). As "*the line between disorder and order lies in logistics*" (Sun Tzu, Chinese military theorist), agri-food logistics with special consideration of innovation and new business models may contribute to in-time food supply, thereby mitigating FLW.

Mitigating LFW means maximizing freshness and selling time by harnessing the power of technology to create smart systems to move agricultural commodities and food efficiently. Solutions include classic and modern logistics, such as intelligent routing and sensors that aid agri-food chain management. These solutions must be within updated management procedures that shorten transit times, so suppliers, consumers, and the environment have much to gain. Figure 2 shows fine examples, some were already present before, and others have become more popular during the pandemic.

These are just some of the many ways logistics can help mitigate and collect FLW. Figure 2 gives examples of innovations that target the negative impacts of FLW by optimizing logistics and mitigating FLW, whereby the authors have to consider as Bocken et al. (2013, p.488) highlights: "This appears distinct from seeking new opportunities for customer-orientated value creation."

Logistics is expected to benefit from digital transformation when dealing with major sustainability challenges, such as FLW, variable harvest, unpredictable supply, and food safety. In its turn, the agri-food chain is expected to benefit from innovations in food chain logistics when dealing with FLW. Furthermore, this development has driven up demand for an omnichannel[2] perspective with new business logistic models along the supply chain (see Figure 2). If we can learn from this pandemic-driven experience of adapting in near-real-time, we can make a true change to combat FLW and fight food insecurity even beyond the pandemic.

## Evolutional Agri-Food Logistic Pathway: From Sustainability and Resilience via Thrivability to Transformation

The commitment to understanding the FLW from farm to bin has contributed to a growing realization that transformation in the agri-food logistic system is necessary. It is widely acknowledged that we are in the midst of a profound societal transformation from a world-view where everything is mechanistic, linear, and deterministic to a world-view where everything is complex, adaptive, dynamic, emergent, interdependent, and never in equilibrium. In this way, agri-food logistics must be imbued with active political and NGO guidance and implemented through prototyping and citizen participation within an enabling guidance framework. This shift reflects trends in the field of FLW studies, where there is a growing emphasis on applying resilience theory to notions of SDGs, especially the SDG 15 (United

*Figure 2. Select food-logistic examples with potential to mitigate FLW from farm to bin and beyond (own elaboration)*

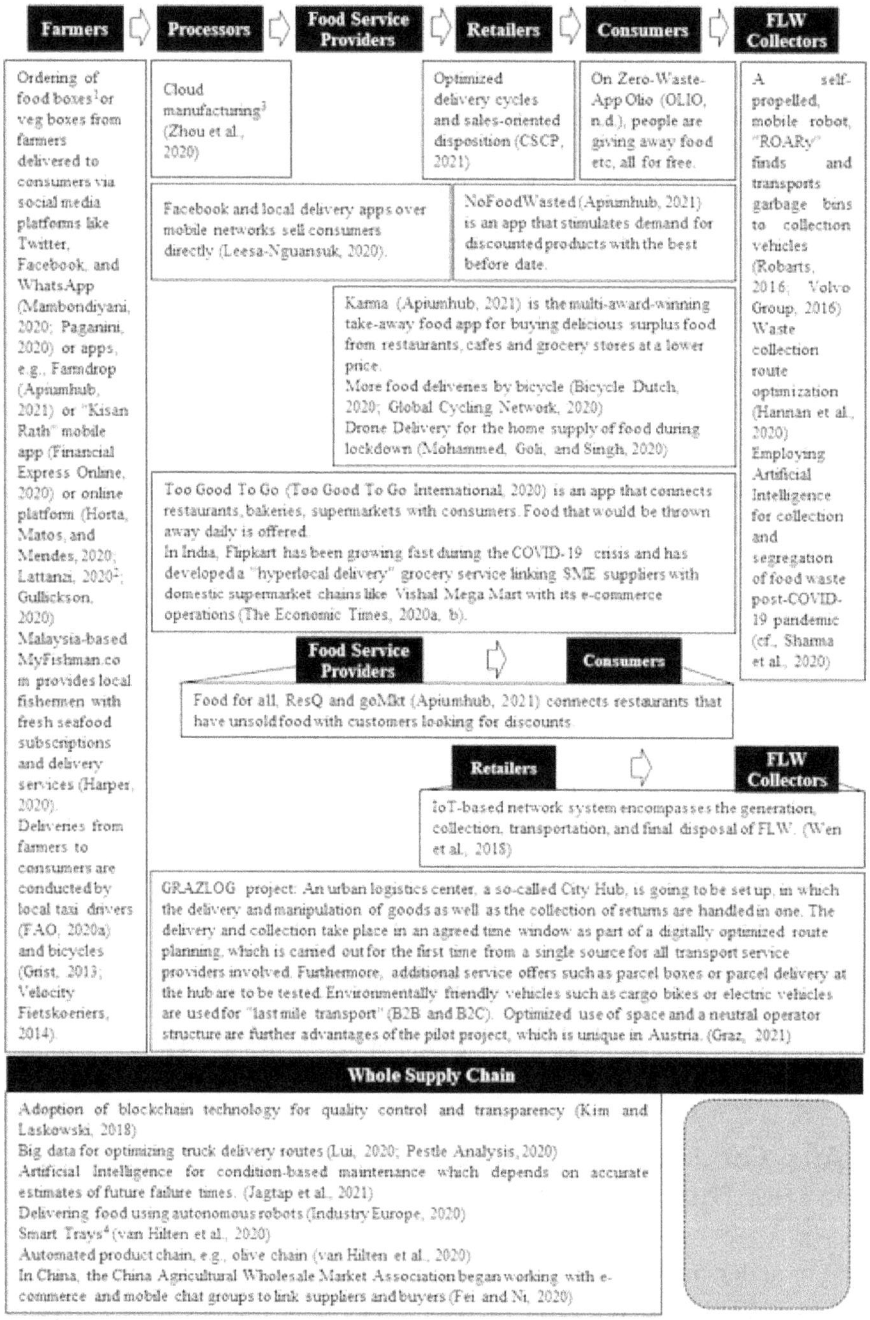


Note: [1] The US Department of Agriculture (USDA) introduced the Farmers to Families Food Box program (USDA, 2020). This box program will likely reduce upstream waste but could increase consumer waste.

[2] For instance, Barn2Door connects farmers to customers through a web platform by integrating online and local sales. La Ruche Qui Dit Oui! is an online platform that links consumers with local producers for the trade of foodstuffs produced within a short distance from the point of distribution in France. The Copia platform links businesses with excess food – such as restaurants – to people in need, with the double aim of fighting against food waste and redistributing food to those who need it.

[3] Cloud manufacturing (CMfg) is a service-oriented manufacturing paradigm that provides customers with diverse on-demand manufacturing services through networks and logistics (Zhang, 2014; Wang, Torngren, and Onori, 2015).

[4] Intelligent logistics for tracking and tracing by Smart Trays (van Hilten et al., 2020) monitors location and analyses freshness. In the first lockdown because of the faster flow from the farmers to consumers and the change in consumer behavior, the reduction of FLW was about 20% (Schmidt, 2021).

Nations Environment Programme, 2015). This is also beginning to be articulated in the sustainable FLW management field, with notions of transformation repeatedly cropping up (O'Brien, 2021; Vincent, 2017).

This new turn has been heralded for decades and in different guises, and is most usefully viewed since 2015 as it is in progress under the guidance of SDGs and the F2F strategy of the EU. Responses to increasing changes in the agri-food logistic system are labeled by ever-shifting terminology, including sustainability, resilience, adaptation, and transformation. Furthermore, the concepts of thrivability, anti-fragility, regenerative design, bio-regionalism—all refer to a new narrative beyond traditional notions of "sustainability" and "resilience" that is gaining popularity in the framing of "transformation" in order also to mitigate FLW (cf. Gillard et al., 2016). The international commitment, aiming to "*halve per capita global food waste at the retail and consumer levels and reduce food losses along production and supply chains, including postharvest losses*" by 2030, has planted the seed of interest into the dynamics of transformative change.

## A Guidance Framework for Analyzing Transformation in the Agri-Food Logistic System

The main question, thus far, is what form does the transformation take that (1) can be brought about by deliberate changes in agri-food logistics after the COVID-19 pandemic, (2) has impacts on the current dominant feedback-loops, and (3) leads to further changes in the structure of and flows within the FLW supply chain. Although transformation is inherently unpredictable and nonlinear (Geels, 2002; Goldstein et al., 2010), some trends do emerge, leading to a set of assumptions about the transformation that has inexorably molded this framework.

Firstly, FLW changes in agri-food logistics towards a more sustainable path are uncommon because current structures are often self-reinforcing and negligible perturbations may be accommodated through adaptation (Park et al., 2012). Influential actors tend to resist transformation pressures and work to keep the habitual practices (cf., Meyer & Staggenborg 1996). Therefore, when a transformation occurs, it is typically caused by a combination of transformational pressures with a multi-stage dimension (Smith et al., 2005). For instance, in the COVID-19 pandemic, digital technologies and services have played a key role in expanding and improving emergency food assistance and social protection programs (FAO, 2020b). In this instance, key actors were able to change multi-stage feedback in such a way as to make transformation possible.

Secondly, when it does occur, transformation is not entirely random; it is determined both by the existing elements and their interactions, such as path dependency as well as deliberate agency from within the agri-food logistic system (Westley et al., 2013) with a clear idea of where they do not want to end up (cf., Olsson et al. 2008, Folke et al. 2011). However, the trajectory of transformation will be determined by the interaction of agency and structure, rather than by either one of them (Westley et al., 2006, Nicholls & Murdock, 2012). As a result, actors do not have complete control over the path of a transformation, but they can steer it in the direction of their goals and affect the transformation's trajectory. (Westley et al., 2013).

These two assumptions form the basis for the authors' analytical framework. On top of this, the authors draw on Moore et al. (2014) to set up an agri-food logistic guidance framework for FLW management. Such a guidance framework refers to how the transition is organized throughout the chain. Supply chain guidance attempts to mitigate conflict and promote cooperation between actors (cf., Williamson, 1999; Lumineau & Henderson, 2012) whereby the features – real-time virtualization, connectivity, and logistics intelligence – play critical roles in the agri-food logistic system. With this in mind, the authors outline the key subprocesses that scholars need to consider in any transformation analysis of the agri-food logistic system (Figure 3). It should be emphasized that, while the authors present the phases and processes sequentially, in any transformation process, the phases may occur simultaneously or in a different order. The guidance framework designed aims to enable new types of efficient and responsive logistics networks with flexible tracking and tracing systems throughout the supply chain and decision support based on that information. These effectively virtualize the logistics flows from farm to bin and beyond, support a timely and error-free exchange of logistics information and provide functionality for intelligent analysis and reporting of exchanged data to enable early warning and advanced forecasting and ensure just-in-time delivery. Four critical features of these systems are distinguished, as derived from Figure 2 and also illustrated in Figure 3:

- Real-time virtualization in the form of decoupling of the physical flows of products and logistics resources (objects), and the information flows for planning, control, and coordination/orchestration;
- Logistics connectivity encompassing timely and error-free exchange of the information about (lots of) products and logistic resources with other organizations and additional services to enable quick response;
- Logistics intelligence as a means of intelligent analysis and reporting of the exchanged data to enable early warning and advanced forecasting;
- Modern logistic technology consists of robots and autonomous vehicles, artificial and augmented intelligence supporting the transport of goods and FLW. (cf., Verdouw et al., 2013a; Verdouw et al., 2013b).

*Figure 3. Framework for analyzing agri-food logistics in the FLW chain based on multiple subprocesses (Adapted from Moore et al., 2014)*

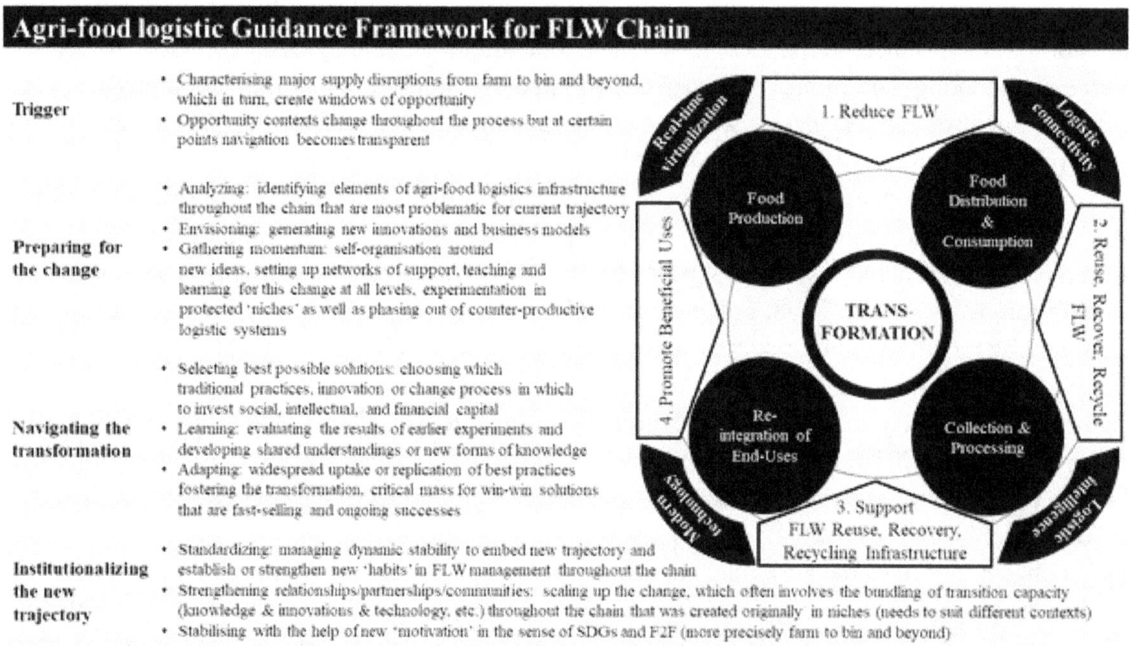

## FURTHER RESEARCH DIRECTIONS

This highlights the transition potential realizable by agri-food logistics. Further research is needed to determine the applicability of these insights since the greater weight of the literature analyzed has a marked theoretical or case study character. Scholars from various disciplines might use the framework to analyze the impact of agri-food logistics on FLW, identify significant hurdles and leverage points, and assess the transformation's outcome. Additionally, such testing will help to refine the guidance framework further. However, the authors believe that this framework can help bridge the understanding of transformation towards more sustainable and resilient food systems to apply a more holistic approach. The chapter presents a framework for analyzing the transition of the agri-food logistics system. However, this proposal needs to be tested in different scenarios. Moreover, currently, no figures about the nutritional, economic, environmental, or social negative or positive chapter to the SDG(s) are available throughout the supply chain as a whole or product-specific; it is a narrative approach. However, further research will investigate the role of agri-food logistics to complete the lack of detailed and reliable data about FLW from farm to bin and beyond. In addition, the authors believe it is essential to investigate further the role of sustainable and resilient agri-food logistics models along the FLW chain.

## CONCLUSION

One of the main scientific statements from the chapter, and in line with the literature researched, is that FLW awareness has increased. The Covid-19 pandemic has pointed out the potential for FLW management from farm to bin and beyond by emphasizing the need for more sustainable and resilient logistic models. A transformation of the agri-food logistics system can be a catalyst to achieve the SDGs and the goals of the F2F strategy.

All in all, it remains to be seen whether these shifts in FLW from farm to bin will continue once the pandemic ends. It is unclear whether short-term changes and responses will result in a new "normal." What is clear is that flexibility, new partnerships, and innovative solutions in agri-food logistics will be key in combating FLW and connecting our food supply with consumers amidst unprecedented challenges. By considering FLW as a resource and the relevant actors as the suppliers of this input, this chapter provides a new way of thinking about logistics services for LFW collection. This involves the reduction, collection, and reuse concepts of circularity, sustainable development, and regenerative practices.

This chapter only starts the discussion on "how logistics can mitigate FLW" and cannot cover everything. On the one hand, agri-food logistics might provoke new thoughts on how to involve all stages along the supply chain in FLW management. On the other hand, this might lead to multiple pathways for sustainable and resilient omnichannel innovation with new business logistics models. The latter may also consider creating a new shared value of FLW towards sustainable development through regeneration and circularity.

Given that humans have actively to transform the current agri-food logistic system, the authors have attempted a clear definition of what a transformation involves. Moreover, this chapter outlines a framework to conceptualize the multiple processes that make up the transformation in an agri-food logistic system. Instead of taking an integrated approach, the authors understand that this covers multiple system perspectives. However, the authors contend that greater analytical specificity can be developed by treating the subprocesses and system elements as linked but not homogenous.

This chapter has implications for managers, entrepreneurs, and consumers in their FLW management throughout the supply chain regarding individual, organizational, and network contributions. It also has implications for policymaking by highlighting barriers to adoption and growth. According to the SDGs, it is clear that institutional frameworks and financial systems need to be redesigned to support the FLW management.

There is a limitation related to the research phase, where the authors limit their search to articles published in the selected journals and skip other journals. The authors have only reviewed publications in English, so research published in different languages has not been analyzed in this study. The chapter presents a guidance framework for analyzing the transformation of the agri-food logistics system. However, this proposal needs to be tested in different scenarios. Further research should investigate the role of agri-food logistics to complete the lack of detailed and reliable data about FLW from farmers to bin and beyond. The authors, therefore, believe that further research about the role of sustainable and resilient agri-food logistics models along the FLW chain is necessary. The future looks bright for creating new sustainable and innovative multi-stage logistic hubs that will support, connect, and enable businesses from farm to bin facing FLW beyond the COVID-19 pandemic.

Finally, given the enormity of the COVID-19 pandemic, this may be the moment people have been anticipating, highlighting the significance of a smart FLW chain within a sustainable and resilient food system. By taking advantage of such a crisis, awareness for more sustainable and resilient agri-food logistics could significantly impact each actor on the FLW issues from the farm to bin and beyond.

## REFERENCES

Abeliotis, K., Lasaridi, K., & Chroni, C. (2014). Attitudes & behaviour of Greek households regarding food waste prevention. *Waste Management & Research, 32*(3), 237–240. doi:10.1177/0734242X14521681 PMID:24525671

Aday, S., & Aday, M. S. (2020). Impact of COVID-19 on the food supply chain. *Food Quality and Safety, 4*(4), 167–180. doi:10.1093/fqsafe/fyaa024

Akademie, D. W. (2020). *Dutch flower industry hit hard by the pandemic*. Retrieved October 14, 2021, from https://www.dw.com/en/dutch-flower-industry-hit-hard-by-the-pandemic/av-55714834

Aldaco, R., Hoehn, D., Laso, J., Margallo, M., Ruiz-Salmón, J., Cristobal, J., Kahhat, R., Villanueva-Rey, P., Bala, A., Batlle-Bayer, L., Fullana-i-Palmer, P., Irabien, A., & Vazquez-Rowe, I. (2020). Food waste management during the COVID-19 outbreak: A holistic climate, economic and nutritional approach. *The Science of the Total Environment, 742*, 140524. Advance online publication. doi:10.1016/j.scitotenv.2020.140524 PMID:32619842

Amicarelli, V., & Bux, C. (2020). Food waste in Italian households during the Covid-19 pandemic: a self-reporting approach. *Food Sec.* doi:10.1007/s12571-020-01121-z

Apiumhub. (2021). *Top 11 Waste Apps Available on IOS and Android*. Retrieved October 13, 2021, from https://apiumhub.com/tech-blog-barcelona/top-food-waste-apps/

Appelbaum, E., & Gaby-Biegle, J. (2020). *Spilt Milk: COVID-19 and the Dangers of Dairy Industry Consolidation*. Working Paper, 134. Retrieved October 15, 2021, from https://www.ineteconomics.org/uploads/papers/WP_134-Appelbaum-and-Gaby-Biegel.pdf

Arianina, K., & Morris, P. (2020). *COVID-19 Export Restrictions Threaten Global Food Supply*. Retrieved October 16, 2021, from https://www.law360.com/articles/1275290/covid-19-export-restrictions-threaten-global-food-supply

Aschemann-Witzel, J., De Hooge, I., Amani, P., Becl-Larsen, T., & Osstindjer, M. (2015). Consumer-Related Food Waste: Causes and Potential for Action. *Sustainability*, *7*(6), 6457–6477. doi:10.3390u7066457

Aschemann-Witzel, J., Haagen Jensen, J., Haagen Jensen, M., & Kulikovskaja, V. (2017). Consumer behaviour towards price-reduced suboptimal foods in the supermarket and the relation to food waste in households. *Appetite*, *116*(1), 246–258. doi:10.1016/j.appet.2017.05.013 PMID:28487247

Askew, K. (2020). *Life in lockdown: Coronavirus prompts half of French consumers to reappraise "value" of food*. Retrieved October 24, 2021, from https://www.foodnavigator.com/Article/2020/05/29/Life-in-lockdown-Coronavirus-prompts-halfof-French-consumers-to-reappraise-value-of-food

Bel, J.-B., & Marengo, P. (2020). *The impact of the COVID-19 pandemic on municipal waste management systems. Results and analysis of a survey carried out by ACR+ between July and October 2021. CR+*. Retrieved October 29, 2021, from https://acrplus.org/images/technical-reports/2021_ACR_Impact_COVID-19_pandemic_on_municipal_waste_management_systems.pdf

Bicycle Dutch. (2020). *More food deliveries by bicycle in the Corona crisis*. Retrieved October 24, 2021, from https://bicycledutch.wordpress.com/2020/05/27/more-food-deliveries-by-bicycle-in-the-corona-crisis/

Bocken, N., Short, S., Rana, P., & Evans, S. (2013). A value mapping tool for sustainable business modelling. *Corporate Governance*, *13*(5), 482–497. doi:10.1108/CG-06-2013-0078

Burgen, S. (2020). *Spain's vineyards destroy record harvest as wine sales crash*. Retrieved October 14, 2021, from https://www.theguardian.com/food/2020/aug/15/spains-vineyards-destroy-record-harvest-as-wine-sales-crash

Buzby, J. C., Wells, H. F., & Hyman, J. (2014). *The Estimated Amount, Value and Calories of 599 Postharvest Food Losses at the Retail and Consumer Levels in the United States*. USDA 600 Economic Research Service. Retrieved October 18, 2021, from https://www.ers.usda.gov/media/1282296/eib121.pdf

Cervera, A., & de Arri, Y. O. (2020). *The coronavirus crisis in Spain's wine industry*. Retrieved October 15, 2021, from https://www.spanishwinelover.com/learn-432-the-coronavirus-crisis-in-spains-wine-industry

Clements, L. (2020). *Coronavirus outbreak 'worse than wartime' for dairy farmers forced to dump milk. Farmers have had no choice but to pour milk down the drain as tankers fail turn up to collect it*. Retrieved October 15, 2021, from https://www.walesonline.co.uk/news/wales-news/coronavirus-milk-farmers-wales-freshways-18048204

Coldiretti-SWG. (2011). *Italiani e alimentazione nel tempo della crisi indagine Coldiretti/SWG*. Retrieved October 15, 2021, from https:// www.napol i.coldi retti. it/itali ani-e-alime ntazi one-nel-tempo della crisi indag ineco ldire ttisw gotto bre20 11.aspx?KeyPu b=GP_CD_NAPOL I_HOME%7CCD_NAPOL I_HOME&Cod_Ogget to=30584 835&subsk intyp e=Detail

CSCP (Collaborating Centre on Sustainable Consumption and Production GmbH). (2021). *HandelsforumRLV. Dialogforum des Groß- und Einzelhandels zur Reduzierung von Lebensmittelverschwendung. Zu gut für die Tonne.* Stand der Umsetzung der Beteiligungserklärung. Zwischenbericht 2021. Retrieved October 14, 2021, from https://www.scp-centre.org/wp-content/uploads/2021/02/Dialogue-Forum_Interim-Report.pdf

Cullen, M. T. (2020). *COVID-19 and the risk to food supply chains: How to respond?* FAO. doi:10.4060/ca8388en

EC (European Commission). (2020). *Communication From the Commission to the European Parliament, the Council, the European Economic and Social Committee and the Committee of the Regions. A Farm to Fork Strategy for a Fair, Healthy and Environmentally-Friendly Food System.* COM(2020) 381 Final. Retrieved October 14, 2021, from https://www.seldia.eu/images/pdf/CELEX_52011DC0206_EN_TXT.pdf

Ellison, B., McFadden, B., Rickard, B., & Wilson, N. (2020). *Food Loss and Waste in the United States during COVID-19. CAST Commentary: Economic Impacts of COVID-19 on Food and Agricultural Markets.* Retrieved October 11, 2021, from https://www.cast-science.org/publication/economic-impacts-of-covid-19-on-food-and-agricultural-markets/

Ellisson, B., & Kalaitzandonakes, M. (2020). Food Waste and Covid-19: Impacts along the Supply Chain. *Farmdoc Daily, 10*, 164. Retrieved October 17, 2021, from https://farmdocdaily.illinois.edu/2020/09/food-waste-and-covid-19-impacts-along-the-supply-chain.html

Fanelli, R. M., & Di Florio, A. (2016). Domestic food waste, gap in times of crisis. *Italian Review of Agricultural Economics, 71*(2), 111–125.

FAO (Food and Agriculture Organization of the United Nations). (2013). Food wastage footprint: Impact on natural resources. Summary report. Rome: FAO.

FAO (Food and Agriculture Organization of the United Nations). (2015). *Regional Strategic Framework—Reducing Food Losses and Waste in the Near East & North Africa Region.* FAO.

FAO (Food and Agriculture Organization of the United Nations). (2020a). *COVID-19 causes havoc to supply chains for fresh fruits and vegetables.* Retrieved October 17, 2021, from https://reliefweb.int/report/ukraine/covid-19-causes-havoc-supply-chains-fresh-fruits-and-vegetables-enruuk

FAO (Food and Agriculture Organization of the United Nations). (2020b). *COVID-19 and the risk to food supply chains: How to respond? COVID-19 and the risk to food supply chains: How to respond?* Retrieved October 17, 2021, from https://www.fao.org/documents/card/en/c/ca8388en/

Fei, S., & Ni, J. (2020). *Local food systems and COVID-19: A look into China's responses.* Retrieved October 24, 2021, from https://www.fao.org/in-action/food-for-cities-programme/news/detail/en/c/1270350/

Financial Express Online. (2020). *Kisan Rath Mobile App: Centre launches new app to help farmers during coronavirus lockdown.* Retrieved October 28, 2021, from https://www.financialexpress.com/industry/technology/kisan-rath-mobile-app-features-benefits-of-app-to-help-farmers-during-coronavirus-lockdown/

Fleetwood, J. (2020). Social justice, food loss, and the sustainable development goals in the Era of COVID-19. *Sustainability, 12*(12), 5027. doi:10.3390u12125027

Folke, C., Jansson, Å., Rockström, J., Olsson, P., Carpenter, S. R., Chapin, F. S. III, Crépin, A.-S., Daily, G., Danell, K., Ebbesson, J., Elmqvist, T., Galaz, V., Moberg, F., Nilsson, M., Österblom, H., Ostrom, E., Persson, Å., Peterson, G., Polasky, S., ... Westley, F. (2011). Reconnecting to the biosphere. *Ambio*, *40*(7), 719–738. doi:10.100713280-011-0184-y PMID:22338712

Fredriksson, A., & Liljestrand, K. (2015). Capturing food logistics: A literature review and research agenda. *International Journal of Logistics Research and Applications*, *18*(1), 16–34. doi:10.1080/13675567.2014.944887

Geels, F. W. (2002). Technological transitions as evolutionary reconfiguration processes: A multi-level perspective and a case-study. *Research Policy*, *31*(8-9), 1257–1274. doi:10.1016/S0048-7333(02)00062-8

Gillard, R., Gouldson, A., Paavola, J., & Van Alstine, J. (2016). Transformational responses to climate change: Beyond a systems perspective of social change in mitigation and adaptation. *Wiley Interdisciplinary Reviews: Climate Change*, *7*(2), 251–265. doi:10.1002/wcc.384

Global Cycling Network. (2020). *The Bicycle Couriers Of Lockdown | Making Quarantine Better With Bikes*. Retrieved October 27, 2021, from https://www.youtube.com/watch?v=zoGn-2hatNo

Goldstein, J., Hazy, J. K., & Silberstang, J. (2010). A complexity science model of social innovation in social enterprise. *Journal of Social Entrepreneurship*, *1*(1), 101–125. doi:10.1080/19420671003629763

Graz. (2021). *Förderprojekt GrazLog*. Retrieved October 29, 2021, from https://www.graz.at/cms/beitrag/10320838/8709900/#

Grist. (2013). *These women deliver food from farm to table by bike, in minutes*. Retrieved October 27, 2021, from https://grist.org/food/these-women-deliver-food-from-farm-to-table-by-bike-in-minutes/

Gullickson, G. (2020). *How COVID-19 is Accelerating Online Agricultural Commerce*. Retrieved October 21, 2021, from https://www.agriculture.com/farm-management/finances-accounting/how-covid-19-is-accelerating-online-agricultural-commerce

Gunders, D. (2012). *Wasted: How America is Losing Up to 40 Percent of Its Food from Farm to Fork to Landfill*. Natural Resources Defense Council Issue Paper #12-06-B. Retrieved October 15, 2021, from https://www.nrdc.org/sites/default/files/wasted-food-IP.pdf

Gustavsson, J., Dederberg, C., & Sonesson, U. (2011). *Global food losses and food waste*. Food and Agriculture Organization of the United Nations. Retrieved October 12, 2021, from https://www.fao.org/3/a-i2697e.pdf

Hannan, M. A., Begum, R. A., Al-Shetwi, A. Q., Ker, P. J., Al Mamun, M. A., Hussain, A., Basri, H., & Mahlia, T. M. I. (2020). Waste collection route optimisation model for linking cost saving and emission reduction to achieve sustainable development goals. *Sustainable Cities and Society*, *62*, 102393. doi:10.1016/j.scs.2020.102393

Harper, J. (2020). *Asia's fishermen and farmers go digital during virus*. Retrieved October 24, 2021, from https://www.bbc.com/news/business-52767227

Hobbs, J. E. (2020). Food Supply Chains during the COVID-19 Pandemic. *Canadian Journal of Agricultural Economics/Revue Canadienne d'agroeconomie, 68*, 171-176. doi:10.1111/cjag.12237

Hobson, K. (2020). The limits of the loops: Critical environmental politics and the Circular Economy. *Environmental Politics, 30*(1-2), 161–179. doi:10.1080/09644016.2020.1816052

Horta, P. M., Matos, J., & Mendes, L. L. (2020). Digital food environment during the coronavirus disease 2019 (COVID-19) pandemic in Brazil: An analysis of food advertising in an online food delivery platform. *British Journal of Nutrition*, 1–6. doi:10.1017/S0007114520004560

Industry Europe. (2020). *The robots delivering food during coronavirus lockdown*. Retrieved October 28, 2021, from https://industryeurope.com/sectors/technology-innovation/the-robots-delivering-food-during-coronavirus-lockdown/

Institutions of Mechanical Engineers. (2013). *Global Food Waste Not, Want Not*. Retrieved October 16, 2021, from http://www.campaignforrealfarming.org/wp-content/uploads/2013/01/IME-Global-Food-Report.pdf

Jagtap, S., Bader, F., Gracia-Gracia, G., Trollmann, H., Fadiji, T., & Salonitis, K. (2021). Food Logistics 4.0: Opportunities and Challenges. *Logistics, 5*(2). Retrieved October 27, 2021, from https://www.mdpi.com/2305-6290/5/1/2

Jeffery, A., & Newburger, E. (2020). *Wasted Milk, Euthanized Livestock: Photos Show How Coronavirus has Devastated US Agriculture*. CNBC. Retrieved October 28, 2021, from https://www.cnbc.com/2020/05/02/coronavirus-devastates-agriculture-dumped-milk-euthanized-livestock.html

Jörissen, J., Prieler, C., & Bräutigam, K.-R. (2015). Food Waste Generation at Household Level: Results of a Survey among Employees of Two European Research Centers in Italy and Germany. *Sustainability, 2015*(7), 2695–2715. doi:10.3390u7032695

Jribi, S., Ismail, H. B., Doggui, D., & Debbabi, H. (2020). COVID-19 virus outbreak lockdown: What impacts on household food wastage? *Environment, Development and Sustainability*, *22*(5), 3939–3955. Advance online publication. doi:10.100710668-020-00740-y PMID:32837271

Kader, A. A. (2005). Increasing food availability by reducing postharvest losses of fresh produce. *International Postharvest Symposium*, *682*, 2169-2176. 10.17660/ActaHortic.2005.682.296

Kim, H. M., & Laskowski, M. (2018). Toward an ontology-driven blockchain design for supply-chain provenance. *Intelligent Systems in Accounting, Finance & Management*, *25*(1), 18–27. Retrieved October 29, 2021, from. doi:10.1002/isaf.1424

Korhonen, J., Nuur, C., Feldmann, A., & Seyoum, E. B. (2018). Circular economy as an essentially contested concept. *Journal of Cleaner Production*, *175*, 544–522. Retrieved October 17, 2021, from. doi:10.1016/j.jclepro.2017.12.111

Lattanzi, A. (2020). *Food delivery platforms revolutionizing the market during COVID-19: Why is regulation lagging behind?* Retrieved October 18, 2021, from https://www.ifis.org/blog/food-delivery-platforms-covid-19

Leesa-Nguanusk, S. (2020). *Covid-19: Thailand eateries banking on delivery apps, social media to survive lockdown*. Retrieved October 27, 2021, from https://www.thestar.com.my/tech/tech-news/2020/04/21/covid-19-thailand-eateries-banking-on-delivery-apps-social-media-to-survive-lockdown

Lemaire, A., & Limbourg, S. (2020). How can food loss and waste management achieve sustainable development goals? *Journal of Cleaner Production*, *234*, 1221–1234. doi:10.1016/j.jclepro.2019.06.226

Lumineau, F., & Henderson, J. E. (2012). The Influence of Relational Experience and Contractual Governance on the Negotiation Strategy in Buyer–supplier Disputes. *Journal of Operations Management*, *30*(5), 382–395. doi:10.1016/j.jom.2012.03.005

Lyndhurst, B. (2007). *Food behaviour consumer research—Findings from the quantitative survey*. Briefing Paper. WRAP.

Mambondiyani, A. (2020). *"It's lucrative": Zimbabwe's farmers turn to social media to stop the rot*. Retrieved October 28, 2021, from https://africanarguments.org/2020/04/its-lucrative-zimbabwes-farmers-turn-to-social-media-to-stop-the-rot/

Martinengo, M. C. (2014). Household food waste and consumer culture: Reflections on Italian behaviour. *Journal of Nutritional Ecology and Food Research*, *2*(1), 73–77. doi:10.1166/jnef.2014.1062

Meyer, D. S., & Staggenborg, S. (1996). Movements, counter movements, and the structure of political opportunity. *American Journal of Sociology*, *101*(6), 1628–1660. doi:10.1086/230869

Minor, T., Astill, G., Raszap Skorbiansky, S., Thornsbury, S., Buzby, J., Hitaj, C., Kantor, L., Kuchler, F., Ellison, B., Misra, A., Richards, T., Roe, B., & Wilson, N. (2020). *Economic Drivers of Food Loss at the Farm and Pre-Retail Sectors: A Look at the Produce Supply Chain in the United States*. U.S. Department of Agriculture – Economic Research Service, Economic Information Bulletin #216.

Mitchell, M. (2020). *COVID 19 is compounding the world's food waste problem*. Retrieved October 15, 2021, from https://farrellymitchell.com/covid-19-leads-to-the-problem-of-food-waste/

MM-Redaktion. (2020). *Weinbranche auf Mallorca leidet unter der Coronakrise*. Retrieved October 15, 2021, from https://www.mallorcamagazin.com/nachrichten/wirtschaft/2020/07/21/82253/weinbranche-auf-mallorca-leidet-unter-der-coronakrise.html

Mohammed, A., Goli, V. S. N. S., & Singh, D. N. (2020). Discussion on 'Challenges, opportunities, and innovations for effective solid waste management during and post COVID-19 pandemic. *Resources, Conservation and Recycling*, *164*, 105175. doi:10.1016/j.resconrec.2020.105175

Moore, M.-L., Tjornbo, O., Enfors, E., Knapp, C., Hodbod, J., Baggio, J. A., Norström, A., Olsson, P., & Biggs, D. (2014). Studying the complexity of change: Toward an analytical framework for understanding deliberate social-ecological transformations. *Ecology and Society*, *19*(4), 54. Retrieved October 27, 2021, from. doi:10.5751/ES-06966-190454

NdemezoE.NdikubwimanaJ. B.DukundeA. (2018). Determinants of capacity utilization of food and beverage manufacturing firms in Rwanda: do tax incentives matter? SSRN, 1-21. doi:10.2139/ssrn.3217757

Niewiadomski, P. (2020). Corporate maturity desiderata in the face of the COVID-19 pandemic – The digital plane of logistics microfoundations. *Logforum*, *16*(4), 503–519. doi:10.17270/J.LOG.2020.495

O'Brien, K. (2012). Global environmental change II: From adaptation to deliberate transformation. *Progress in Human Geography*, *36*(5), 667–676. doi:10.1177/0309132511425767

OECD. (2020). *COVID-19 and international trade: Issues and actions*. Retrieved October 22, 2021, from https://www.oecd.org/coronavirus/policy-responses/covid-19-andinternational-trade-issues-and-actions-494da2fa/

OLIO. (n.d.). *Join the #1 free sharing app*. https://olioex.com/

Olsson, P., Folke, C., & Hughes, T. P. (2008). Navigating the transition to ecosystem-based management of the Great Barrier Reef, Australia. *Proceedings of the National Academy of Sciences of the United States of America*, *105*(28), 9489–9494. doi:10.1073/pnas.0706905105 PMID:18621698

Padilla, K. (2020). *Responding to Food Waste Challenges from COVID-19. 05/13/20*. Retrieved October 16, 2021, from https://foodminds.com/food-thoughts/food-thoughts-items/responding-to-food-waste-challenges-from-covid-19/

Paganini, N., Adinata, K., Buthelezi, N., Harris, D., Lemke, S., Luis, A., Koppelin, J., Karriem, A., Ncube, F., Nervi Aguirre, E., Ramba, T., Raimundo, I., Sulejmanović, N., Swanby, H., Tevera, D., & Stöber, S. (2020). Growing and Eating Food during the COVID-19 Pandemic: Farmers' Perspectives on Local Food System Resilience to Shocks in Southern Africa and Indonesia. *Sustainability*, *2020*(12), 8556. doi:10.3390u12208556

Pappalardo, G., Cerroni, S., Nayga, R. M. Jr, & Yang, W. (2020). Impact of Covid-19 on Household Food Waste: The Case of Italy. *Frontiers in Nutrition*, *7*, 585090. doi:10.3389/fnut.2020.585090 PMID:33344492

Parfitt, J., Macnaughton, S., & Barthel, M. (2010). *Food Waste within Food Supply Chains: Quantification and Potential for Change to 2050*. doi:10.1098/rstb.2010.0126

Park, S. E., Marshall, N. A., Jakku, E., Dowd, A. M., Howden, S. M., Mendham, E., & Fleming, A. (2012). Informing adaptation responses to climate change through theories of transformation. *Global Environmental Change*, *22*(1), 115–126. doi:10.1016/j.gloenvcha.2011.10.003

Parshina-Kottas, Y., Buchanana, L., Aufrichtig, A., & Corkery, M. (2020). Take a Look at How Covid-19 is Changing Meatpacking Plants. *The New York Times*. Retrieved October 15, 2021, from https://www.nytimes.com/interactive/2020/06/08/us/meat-processing-plants-coronavirus.html

Pestle Analysis. (2020). *Using Big Data to Optimize Routing for Trucking-Based Shipping and Logistics*. Retrieved October 25, 2021, from https://pestleanalysis.com/using-big-data-to-optimize-routing-for-trucking-based-shipping-and-logistics/

Pieroni, M. P. P., McAloone, T. C., & Pigosso, D. C. A. (2019). Business model innovation for circular economy and sustainability: A review of approaches. *Journal of Cleaner Production*, *215*, 198–216. doi:10.1016/j.jclepro.2019.01.036

Polansek, T., & Huffstutter, P. J. (2020). Piglets Aborted, Chickens Gassed as Pandemic Slams Meat Sector. *Reuters*. Retrieved October 14, 2021, from https://www.reuters.com/article/us-health-coronavirus-livestock-insight-idUSKCN2292YS

Reddy, V. R., Singh, S. K., & Anbumozhi, V. (2016). Food supply chain disruption due to natural disasters: entities, risks, and strategies for resilience. Economic Research Institute for ASEAN and East Asia, 1-36.

Reynold, M. (2020). Supply Chains Race to Match Shifting COVID-19 Consumer Behavior. *Packaging World*. Retrieved October 16, 2021, from https://www.packworld.com/ covid-19/article/21132561/supply-chains-race-to-match-shifting-covid19-consumer-behavior

Richards, T. (2020). *Food Service versus Retail: COVID-19 Impacts. CAST Commentary: Economic Impacts of COVID-19 on Food and Agricultural Markets*. Retrieved October 23, 2021, from https://www.cast-science.org/publication/economic-impacts-of-covid-19-on-food-and-agricultural-markets/

Robarts, S. (2016). *Volvo's Robot Refuse Collectors ROAR into Life*. Retrieved October 27, 2021, from https://newatlas.com/volvo-robot-based-autonomous-refuse-handling-project-test/42042/

Roos, G., & Agarwal, R. (2015). Services Innovation in a Circular Economy. In The Handbook of Service Innovation (pp. 501-520). Springer. doi:10.1007/978-1-4471-6590-3_23

Rubinstein, P. (2020). *Why grocery shelves won't be empty for long*. Retrieved October 18, 2021, from https://www.bbc.com/worklife/article/20200401-covid-19-why-we-wont-run-out-of-food-during-coronavirus

Saghiri, S. S., Bernon, M., Bourlakis, M., & Wilding, R. (2018). Omni-channel logistics special issue. *International Journal of Physical Distribution & Logistics Management, 48*(4), 362–364. doi:10.1108/IJPDLM-05-2018-361

Schmidt, C. (2021). *UC 3.4 Intelligent fruit logistics*. Presentation at IoF2020 Farm to Fork Final Event.

Schott, A. B. S., & Andersson, T. (2015). Food waste minimization from a lifecycle perspective. *Journal of Environmental Management, 147*(1), 219–226. Retrieved October 18, 2021, from. doi:10.1016/j.jenvman.2014.07.048 PMID:25264296

Shafiee-Jood, M., & Cai, X. (2016). Reducing food loss and waste to enhance food security and environmental sustainability. *Environmental Science & Technology, 50*(16), 8432–8443. doi:10.1021/acs.est.6b01993 PMID:27428555

Sharma, H. B., Vanapalli, K. R., Cheela, V. R. S., Ved Prakash, R., Jaglan, A. K., Dubey, B., Goel, S., & Bhattacharya, J. (2020). Challenges, opportunities, and innovations for effective solid waste management during and post COVID-19 pandemic. *Resources, Conservation and Recycling, 162*, 105052. doi:10.1016/j.resconrec.2020.105052 PMID:32834486

Smith, A., Stirling, A., & Berkhout, F. (2005). The governance of sustainable socio-technical transitions. *Research Policy, 34*(10), 1491–1510. doi:10.1016/j.respol.2005.07.005

Stenmarck, A., Jensen, C. M., Quested, T., & Moates, G. (2000). *Estimates of European food waste levels*. Technical report from FUSIONS project. doi:10.13140/rg.2.1.4658.4721

Stenmarck, A., Jensen, C. M., Quested, T., & Moates, G. (2016). *Estimates of European food waste levels*. Retrieved October 11, 2021, from http://www.eu-fusions.org/phocadownload/Publications/Estimates%20of%20European%20food%20waste%20levels.pdf

Swamidass, P. M. (Ed.). (2000). Seven "rights" of logistics. In Encyclopedia of Production and Manufacturing Management (p. 684). Boston, MA: Springer. doi:10.1007/1-4020-0612-8_871

Szabó-Bódi, B., Kasza, G., & Szakos, D. (2018). Assessment of household food waste in Hungary. *British Food Journal, 120*(3), 625–638. Advance online publication. doi:10.1108/BFJ-04-2017-0255

Taylor, D., Pritchard, A., Dhuan, D., & Mirshra, S. (2020). *What's behind the empty grocery shelves*. Retrieved October 14, 2021, from https://www.scmr.com/article/whats_behind_the_empty_grocery_shelves

Teigiserova, D. A., Hamelin, L., & Thomsen, M. (2019). Towards transparent valorization of food surplus, waste and loss: Clarifying definitions, food waste hierarchy, and role in the circular economy. *The Science of the Total Environment*, *706*, 136033. doi:10.1016/j.scitotenv.2019.136033 PMID:31855638

The Economic Times. (2020a). *Flipkart preparing to start hyperlocal delivery services: Sources. The service will be available via the Flipkart app, and initially, deliveries will be done from local warehouses and select shops*. Retrieved October 27, 2021, from https://retail.economictimes.indiatimes.com/news/e-commerce/e-tailing/flipkart-preparing-to-start-hyperlocal-delivery-services-sources/76416609

The Economic Times. (2020b). *Amazon, Flipkart to increase warehouses*. Retrieved October 27, 2021, from https://economictimes.indiatimes.com/industry/services/retail/amazon-flipkart-to-increase-warehouses/articleshow/75523490.cms?from=mdr

Too Good To Go International. (2020). *Too Good To Go. Rettet Essen hilf unserem Planeten*. Retrieved October 28, 2021, from https://toogoodtogo.at/de-at?utm_medium=Search&utm_source=Google&utm_campaign=AT_B2C_Paid_Marketing_Search_Google_Brand&gclid=CjwKCAjwjbCDBhAwEiwAiudBy1eD2AaJSzVbr-0UfFLiOe5qQvE3GwySN57aR3xJLiMZ4BeH-_41YxoC7UgQAvD_BwE

United Nations. (2015). *Transforming our Wold: The 2030 Agenda for Sustainable Development*. Retrieved October 12, 2021, from https://sdgs.un.org/publications/transforming-our-world-2030-agenda-sustainable-development-17981

United Nations Environment Programme. (2015). *Global Waste Management Outlook*. Retrieved October 15, 2021, from https://www.unep.org/resources/report/global-waste-management-outlook

U.S. Department of Agriculture (USDA). (2020). *USDA Farmers to Families Food Box*. Retrieved October 19, 2021, from https://www.ams.usda.gov/selling-food-to-usda/farmers-to-families-food-box

Van Hilten, M., Adema, H., Nuhoff-Isakhanyan, G., & Otte, H. (2020). *D4.6: Validation of user acceptability in IOF2020 use cases*. Retrieved October 21, 2021, from https://www.iof2020.eu/deliverables/d4.6-validation-of-user-acceptability-of-iof2020-use-cases.pdf

Velocity Fietskoeriers. (2014). *Delivery of vegetables by bike*. Retrieved October 22, 2021, from http://cargobikefestival.blogspot.com/2014/02/delivery-of-vegetables-by-bike.html

Verdouw, C. N., Beulens, A. J. M., & van der Vorst, J. G. A. J. (2013a). Virtualisation of floricultural supply chains: A review from an Internet of Things perspective. *Computers and Electronics in Agriculture*, *99*(1), 160–175. doi:10.1016/j.compag.2013.09.006

Verdouw, C. N., Sundmaeker, H., Meyer, F., Wolfert, J., & Verhoosel, J. (2013b). Smart Agri-Food Logistics: Requirements for the Future Internet. In Dynamics in Logistics. Lecture Notes in Logistics. Springer. doi:10.1007/978-3-642-35966-8_20

Vincent, K. (2017). *Transformational adaptation: A review of examples from 4 deltas to inform the design of DECCMA's Adaptation Policy Trajectories*. DECCMA Working Paper, Deltas, Vulnerability and Climate Change: Migration and Adaptation, IDRC Project Number 107642. Retrieved October 27, 2021, from https://generic.wordpress.soton.ac.uk/deccma/wp-content/uploads/sites/181/2017/12/Vincent_Transformational-adaptation-working-paper.pdf

VolvoGroup. (2016). *The ROAR project - robot and drone in collaboration for autonomous refuse handling*. Retrieved October 29, 2021, from https://www.youtube.com/watch?v=fNIV6Dcj29E

Wang, L., Törngren, M., & Onori, M. (2015). Current status and advancement of cyber-physical systems in manufacturing. *Journal of Manufacturing Systems*, *37*, 517–527. doi:10.1016/j.jmsy.2015.04.008

Wen, Z., Hu, S., De Clercq, D., Beck, M. B., Zhang, H., Fei, F., & Lui, J. (2018). Design, implementation, and evaluation of an Internet of Things (IoT) network system for restaurant food waste management. *Waste Management*, *73*, 26-38. Retrieved October 27, 2021, from https://www.sciencedirect.com/science/article/abs/pii/S0956053X17309376

Westley, F. R., Tjornbo, O., Schultz, L., Olsson, P., Folke, C., Crona, B., & Bodin, Ö. (2013). A theory of transformative agency in linked social-ecological systems. *Ecology and Society*, *18*(3), 27. Retrieved October 21, 2021, from. doi:10.5751/ES-05072-180327

Westley, F. R., Zimmerman, B., & Patton, M. Q. (2006). *Getting to maybe: how the world is changed.* Vintage Canada.

WFP (World Food Programme). (2009). *Hunger and markets*. Earthscan.

Williamson, O. E. (1999). *The Mechanisms of Governance*. Oxford University Press.

Wills, R., Mcglasson, B., Graham, D., & Joyce, D. (1998). *Postharvest an Introduction to the physiology and handling of fruits, vegetables and ornamentals* (4th ed.). UNSW Press.

Wilson, N. (1996). Supply chain management: A case study of a dedicated supply chain for bananas in the UK grocery market. *Supply Chain Management*, *1*(2), 28–35. doi:10.1108/13598549610155279

Wunderlich, S. M., & Martinez, N. M. (2018). Conserving natural resources through food loss reduction: Production and consumption stages of the food supply chain. *International Soil and Water Conservation Research*, *6*(4), 331–339. doi:10.1016/j.iswcr.2018.06.002

Yaffe-Bellany, D., & Corkery, M. (2020). Dumped Milk, Smashed Eggs, Plowed Vegetables: Food Waste of the Pandemic. *The New York Times*. Retrieved October 11, 2021, from https://www.nytimes.com/2020/04/11/business/coronavirus-destroying-food.html

Zhang, L., Luo, Y., Tao, F., Li, B. H., Ren, L., Zhang, X., Guo, H., Cheng, Y., Hu, A., & Liu, Y. (2014). Cloud manufacturing: A new manufacturing paradigm. *Enterprise Information Systems*, *8*(2), 167–187. doi:10.1080/17517575.2012.683812

Zhou, L., Zhang, L., & Fang, Y. (2020). Logistics service scheduling with manufacturing provider selection in cloud manufacturing. *Robotics and Computer-integrated Manufacturing*, *65*, 101914. doi:10.1016/j.rcim.2019.101914

## KEY TERMS AND DEFINITIONS

**Agri-Food Logistics:** In a general food chain sense, about how logistic providers or an actor of the chain move food from farm to bin and beyond.

**EU Farm to Fork (F2F):** In the framework of the European Green Deal, an overhaul of the European food system through the F2F strategy the European Commission has proposed. This strategy aims to make food systems fair, healthy and environmentally-friendly.

**FLW Chain:** A series of processes by which agricultural commodities for food production or food are grown or produced, sold, transported, and eventually consumed, i.e., the food chain. FWL is generated but can be avoided, collected, recycled, and reused. The FLW chain covers the stages from farm to bin and beyond.

**FLW Management:** The managerial actions and processes required to mitigate FLW from its inception to its final disposal or reuse.

**Food Supply Chain:** A route the food moves from the farmer to consumers. A food supply chain refers to the stages through which food travels from farm to bin. This covers production, processing, distribution, consumption, and disposal.

**Food Waste and Loss (FLW):** The decrease in mass (quantitative) or nutritional value (qualitative) of food—edible parts—throughout the supply chain that was intended for human consumption.

**Guidance Framework:** A methodology that provides best practice guidance on how to evaluate, select, and implement agri-food logistics in the supply chain in order to mitigate FLW not only in the time of a crisis.

**Mitigation of Day-to-Day FLW:** A process of elimination that involves reducing the amount of waste produced in society daily and helps eliminate the generation of harmful and persistent wastes, supporting the efforts to promote a more sustainable supply chain as well as society.

**Sustainable Development Goals:** The 17 Sustainable Development Goals (SDGs), also known as the Global Goals. The United Nations adopted these in 2015 as a universal call to action to end poverty, protect the planet, and ensure that by 2030 all people enjoy peace and prosperity.

**Zero-FLW:** A designing and managing products and processes to systematically avoid and eliminate the volume and toxicity of waste and materials, conserve and recover all resources, and not burn or bury them.

## ENDNOTES

1 For example, bananas are transported in temperature-controlled containers (at 13.5°C) to their ripening centers where the conditions are altered to secure ripening when the retailer requires stock (Wilson, 1996).

2 As a long-term innovation, omni-channel is a hybrid solution in which components from multi- and cross-channel merge in online retailing. Access to food is made available to the consumers via digital as well as classic channels. The omni concept presupposes a kind of convergence of all digital and physical touchpoints – whether retail stores, catalog, e-commerce (e.g., online or mobile app stores) or telephone sales. All sales channels can be used simultaneously. To apply the Latin term Omni (everything, whole, everyone) in a "commercial" setting, the product range, marketing and the channels themselves have to be configured centrally. On the one hand, the consumer has access to various sales channels, and on the other hand, all the touchpoints mentioned are controlled centrally from one point. Usually, this point is the webshop. This enables the consumer, for instance, to order online and pick up the goods in the store (in-store pick-up) or to buy in-store but get it delivered directly to home. (Saghiri, 2018).

# Section 5
# Global Issues

*Section 5 discusses the changes in and evolution of global supply chains from a macro perspective. The supply chain exists everywhere consumers are in the world, and the supply chains are evolving daily to meet consumer needs by changing their structure and management.*

# Chapter 12
# The Global Supply Chain Management System Involving the ASEAN Industrial Clusters

**Tetsuro Saisho**
*Former Gunma University, Japan*

## ABSTRACT

*In the ASEAN, as a national industrial policy, many industrial clusters, such as industrial parks, have been established, and the region is experiencing dynamic growth through foreign direct investment. In the industrial clusters of the ASEAN, attracting foreign companies has had a great economic spillover effect, including increased employment of workers and creation of demand in the region. In addition, among the ASEAN countries, especially Thailand and the neighboring CLMV nations, the construction of a global supply chain, with distribution systems such as the East-West Economic Corridor, North-South Economic Corridor, and Southern Economic Corridor, is increasing the countries' connectivity. The regional GSC with neighboring countries is an international business system based on collaboration between cross-border industrial clusters and other business entities, here involving the logistics systems of the ASEAN countries. In this study, the authors consider the current situation and issues regarding the cross-border GSC that Thailand is developing with its neighbors in the ASEAN.*

## INTRODUCTION

This chapter discusses the future potential of ASEAN in global supply chains. Infrastructure development and education systems have been enhanced in ASEAN countries, making them more attractive as investment destinations. The development of transportation networks among ASEAN countries has enabled activities within the supply chain to be coordinated and efficient.

Currently, all the ASEAN countries are welcoming Foreign Direct Investment (FDI)[1], developing dynamic economic activities and aggressive corporate behavior, and experiencing increasing vitality and regional development. One of the sources of the dynamic economic development is the emergence of industrial clusters such as industrial parks, export processing zones, special economic zones, special

DOI: 10.4018/978-1-7998-9800-9.ch012

economic zones, economic and technological development zones, high-tech parks, science parks, software parks, and IT parks (Saisho, 2021).

In addition, the logistics system connecting the ASEAN countries supports collaboration among the region's industrial clusters. The system itself utilizes land routes, such as the road networks of the North-South Economic Corridor, East-West Economic Corridor, and Southern Economic Corridor, for freight truck transportation, and the railway network for freight trains; marine routes, using port facilities such as the Laem Chabang port (Thailand), the Cai Mep Thi Vai port (Vietnam), and the Yangon port (Myanmar), for freight ships; and air routes, using the air freight network, for freight airplanes. A Global Supply Chain (GSC) is being constructed as an international business system that involves, among other things, the industrial clusters of the ASEAN logistics system (Saisho, 2019).

The GSC includes many companies in the industrial clusters of the respective countries, who concentrate on producing products based on their respective strengths, and products that are required but not produced by a given country are not an international division of labor acquired through trade. In the ASEAN context, the companies in the industrial clusters of each country collaborate and play a part in the process in the product manufacturing process. In addition, among the industrial clusters, a company's GSC is being built by utilizing public infrastructure such as logistics systems and One-Stop Services (OSS)[2], which support corporate activities. The OSS is designed so that all the administrative procedures necessary for industrial clusters can be completed in one procedure.

This paper will present an overview of the ASEAN logistics system, focusing on land route utilization (truck transportation) in Thailand. Then, we will consider the current situation and issues involved in company collaboration among the industrial clusters in neighboring countries in terms of the GSC as an international business system.

## BACKGROUND

In the ASEAN, the logistics system for connecting industrial clusters across national borders includes freight transportation by land route (trucks and trains), sea route (ships), and air route (airplanes) within and beyond the region (ADB, 2015). Truck transportation by land route has the advantages of short- and medium-distance transportation, transportation of a small amount of cargo, and ease in turning. However, there are also disadvantages, such as its unsuitability for mass transportation, the need to improve the road network, transportation time being affected by traffic congestion, and the possible need for transshipment of cargo when crossing national borders.

Rail transportation has the advantages of mass transportation, safe transportation, accurate transportation time, good fuel efficiency, and environmental friendliness. However, among its disadvantages, the regional railway network needs improvement and depends on the terrain, the operating time is fixed, the cost is high for short- and medium-distance transportation and small cargo volume, and the location and cost of cargo transshipment can pose problems.

Transportation by sea route (ship) has the advantages of being able to transport heavy and large-volume cargo, in large quantities and at low cost, over long distances. However, among its disadvantages are the high costs when the cargo volume is small, slow ship speed, restrictions on the navigation and berthing of the ships, and the need for further transportation from the port facility.

Transportation by air route (airplane) has the advantages of overwhelmingly fast cargo transportation speed, safe cargo transportation, a lower accident rate, and terrain-independent transportation. However,

*Figure 1. Conceptual Diagram of the ASEAN industrial cluster strategy and logistics system*

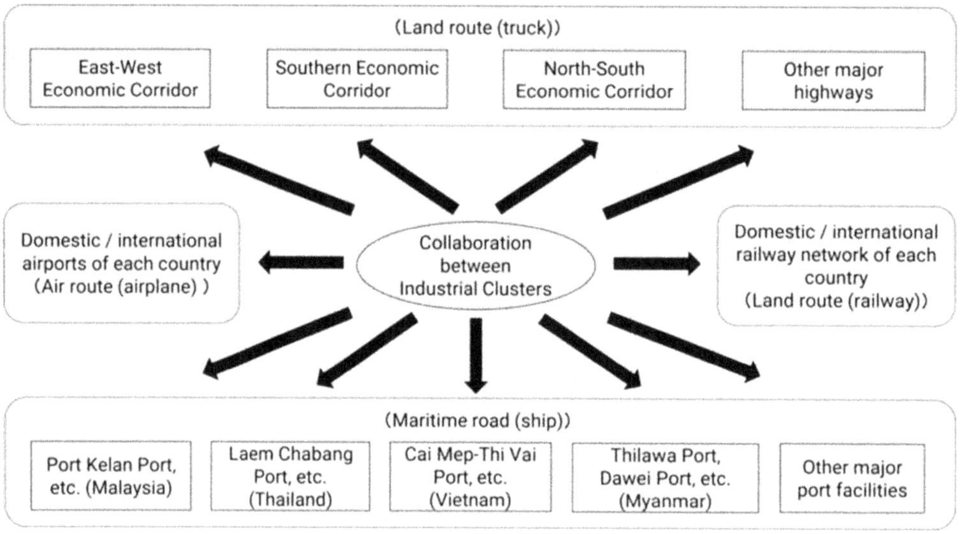


its disadvantages include its vulnerability to bad weather, high transportation costs, restrictions on the size and weight of cargo, and the need for additional transportation from the airport.

In the ASEAN, there are plans for land routes (railways) involving the Trans-Asian Railway and the ASEAN-Japan Logistics Project, which are cooperative systems that include third countries such as Japan, China, and South Korea. However, as an international business system, the rail-based cross-border freight transportation network has seen little development (Kawai, 2021).

On the other hand, in the ASEAN road network, pavement and bridges have been developed with the Official Development Assistance (ODA)[3] of nations such as Japan, and a cross-border freight transportation network has been developed. ASEAN transportation is mainly by land route (truck) because it is the most efficient means of short- and medium-distance transportation within the region. The network is principally defined by the North-South Economic Corridor (Kunming-Bangkok Expressway), the East-West Economic Corridor, and the Southern Economic Corridor (two routes)[4].

The following is an overview of the most important land routes in the ASEAN section of the GSC as a cross-border logistics system, with a focus on Thailand (Fig. 1).

The North-South Economic Corridor from China (Kunming, Yunnan Province) was completed in December 2013 with the completion of the 4th Thailand-Laos Friendship Bridge (International Mekong Bridge), which was constructed with the support of the Chinese and Thai governments (Fig. 1). In addition, a road connecting the four countries in Fig. 1 to Thailand (Bangkok) via Laos (Boten) and Thailand (Chiang Khong) has been opened (GMS, 2019) (Fig. 2).

In the East-West Economic Corridor, the Second Thai-Laos Friendship Bridge (connecting Mukdahan, Thailand and Savannakhet, Laos) has been completed with Japanese ODA financial support. ODA is roughly divided into bilateral and multilateral assistance (investment/contribution to international organizations), depending on its specific nature.

Bilateral assistance is essentially provided by three methods: "technical cooperation," "loan aid," and "grant aid," along with "other" methods such as dispatching volunteers. In December 2006, a road connecting Vietnam, Laos, and Thailand was opened. When the East-West Economic Corridor extends

*Figure 2. Overview of the ASEAN land route logistics system with a focus on Thailand*
*Source: GMS, 2019, Economic Corridors in the Greater Mekong Subregion)*

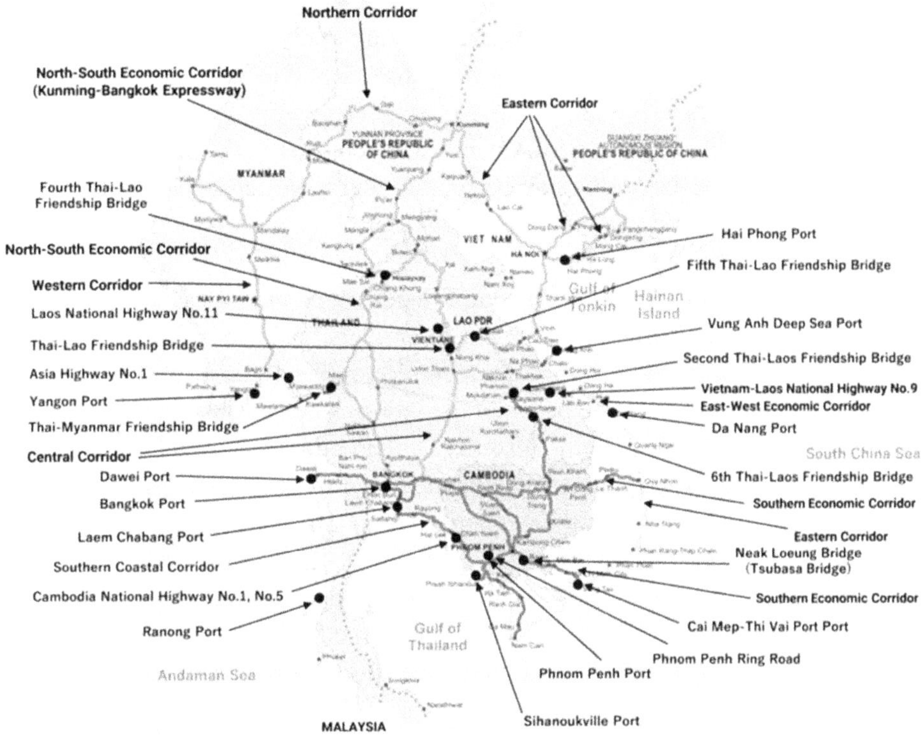


from Da Nang (Vietnam) to Mawlamyine (Myanmar), a distribution network will have been constructed for land freight transportation from the Pacific to the Indian Ocean.

In the Southern Economic Corridor, the Neak Loeung Bridge (Tsubasa Bridge, Kandal Province, Cambodia) has been completed with Japanese ODA financial support. In April 2015, a road connecting Vietnam, Cambodia, and Thailand in ASEAN was opened (GMS, 2019) (Fig. 2).

The coastal route (Southern Coastal Corridor), from Laem Chabang Port (Thailand) to Sihanoukville Port (Cambodia) and Nam Can, Camau Province (Southernmost Vietnam), is positioned as a secondary corridor. The Laem Chabang Port has excellent accessibility to the Khet Khlong Toei district of Bangkok, the capital of Thailand, and also functions as a river port that can efficiently and economically handle freight transportation from the port to inland regions. The Sihanoukville Port, the only open-sea port in Cambodia, is a deep-sea port with modern cargo processing facilities.

Among the other land-based (truck transportation) logistics systems are the Northern Corridor, Western Corridor, Eastern Corridor (two routes)[5], Central Corridor (two routes)[6], Northeast Corridor, North-South Corridor, etc. (GMS, 2019) (Fig. 2). In the ASEAN, the GSC involving neighboring countries has been principally constructed based on the main highways connecting the countries.

## THE ASEAN GLOBAL SUPPLY CHAIN AND INDUSTRIAL CLUSTERS

In today's global economy, the borders in the international business system are opening, including not only the developed countries in Europe and North America, but also developing countries in Asia, Africa, and Central and South America. Many countries are contributing to building the GSC and are constructing optimal production systems by developing corporate collaboration between industrial clusters across multiple borders.

Among the reasons for including the ASEAN industrial clusters in the development of the GSC system, an overall logistics system has been established, public infrastructure is provided, one-stop service is available, various incentives are available, labor costs are low, and risk management is possible for each element in the manufacturing process.

In the conventional industrial clusters, attracting overseas companies has had a great economic ripple effect in the region, such as increased employment of workers, expansion of the consumer market, increased demand for products, and extension to consumption-related industries. Construction of the GSC in the ASEAN will involve collaboration between the industrial clusters of each country.

Product creation is planned in Singapore, resources are procured from Laos and Cambodia, and parts are manufactured in Vietnam and imported to Thailand for assembly of the finished products (final products). The final products in Thailand are then exported to countries such as Japan, and an international business system has been realized.

In such a system, the location of the clusters is important, not only for the expansion of overseas companies but also for the construction of a GSC that crosses national borders (Krugman, 1991; Porter, 1998).

As a form of risk management for its own manufacturing industry, Thailand's part of the GSC not only provides resources with neighboring countries Laos and Cambodia, but also develops international business through the establishment of manufacturing bases in the industrial clusters along the Thai border with the two countries. A GSC-style network is constructed between these bases, and in the production process, the final products are manufactured at the optimal location, using the optimal materials, at the optimal manufacturing cost.

The ASEAN industrial cluster-based GSC is important for competition, cooperation, and collaboration at the corporate level, for competitiveness at the regional level, and for national-level industrial policy. Currently, the location advantage, connectivity, and network effects in the industrial clusters are highly important prerequisites for the success of the region's GSC.

With respect to connectivity[7], it is important to ensure ease of connection between a given country and another country or region, as well as ease of connection to things such as networks. With respect to network effects, it is important that the characteristics of a given product affect the number of users, the frequency of use, and the utility value obtained by using the product.

With an eye to the region as a whole, ASEAN Secretary-General Le Luong Min stated, on May 31, 2016, "We will promote cross-border infrastructure development and deepen the ASEAN Economic Community (AEC)[8]," acknowledging the importance of the ASEAN GSC (NKS, 2016).

The AEC was established on December 31, 2015, with the aim of expanding domestic demand, trade, and investment, by liberalizing the movement of people, goods, money, services, and investment in the ASEAN region and establishing region-wide standards.

In many cases, the ASEAN industrial clusters include internationally standardized public infrastructure such as roads, substations/power transmission facilities, water supply/sewage treatment facilities, and communication facilities such as telephone and internet information. In addition, port and customs clearance procedures are also routinely provided. Further, in order to enhance their competitive advantage, the ASEAN countries have established the OSS, which allows administrative procedures to be completed in one place and are provided as part of the public infrastructure.

Such public infrastructure has been established as a single-window system (SWS)[9], not only in the ASEAN countries but also in other countries (including developed countries) around the world. In an SWS, in order to strengthen the international competitiveness of one's own country, related ministries and agencies cooperate and collaborate; and by interconnecting multiple related information systems, multiple similar procedures can be performed simultaneously using a single data entry and transmission.

In recent years, the ASEAN industrial clusters have been trying to differentiate themselves based on their own unique characteristics; among these, the support of industry composition dedicated to small and medium-sized enterprises (SMEs), provision of small-scale space before full-scale entry, provision of back-office functions, exclusive use of Japanese small- and medium-sized enterprises, specialization in production for export, provision of import/export customs duty exemption and corporate income tax exemption, tax-protected cargo production, processing, and trading, and 24/7 customs services.

In addition, there are various forms of ASEAN industrial clusters, such as high-tech parks, science parks, software parks, and IT parks, which specialize in the introduction and application of advanced and cutting-edge technologies, human resource development, and the production of high-tech products.

In addition to the aforementioned features, the ASEAN land route (truck transportation) logistics system includes road maintenance in the international economic corridor, the bridge over the Mekong River, modernization of the border facilities, provision of mutual vehicle traffic licenses, simplification of the border procedures, and enhanced transit customs clearance procedures. Access and connectivity, such as the ease of connection between ASEAN countries and the ease of linking multiple industrial clusters, have improved dramatically.

In addition to truck transportation, there are railways for freight trains, sea routes for container freighters, and air routes for freight planes. In the future, the full implementation of the Cross Border Transportation Agreement (CBTA) in the Mekong region (Thailand, Cambodia, Laos, Myanmar, Vietnam) will further improve the efficiency and convenience of cross-border truck transportation; and in addition to the improvements in short- and medium-distance transportation, long-distance transportation to and from Europe and the United States is being developed.

Cross-border refers to bilateral or multilateral transport. Cross-border optimizes customer GSC by facilitating transportation, customs clearance, and transshipment, and shortening lead times. In addition to the conventional bilateral agreement, the GSC has created a CBTA on cross-border transportation. CBTA is an agreement on transportation, customs, immigration, and quarantine.

The specific CBTA includes (1) simplification of cross-border procedures, (2) Cross-border passenger transportation system, (3) Handling of international transit cargo, (4) Road vehicle standards that contribute to cross-border transportation, (5) Exchange of commercial transportation rights, (6) Infrastructure standards. The target countries of CBTA are the agreement of Laos, Thailand, and Vietnam in 1999, Cambodia in 2001, China in 2002, and Myanmar in 2003. In addition, all CBTA consents were signed by all member countries in March 2007.

# COOPERATION OF INDUSTRIAL CLUSTERS IN THE GLOBAL SUPPLY CHAIN

## Collaboration between Industrial Clusters through Global Supply Chains

In the ASEAN, Thailand and Vietnam are collaborating with Cambodia and Laos with respect to industrial clusters, and GSC construction is underway among the neighboring countries. In Thailand and Vietnam, wages are rising due to the expansion of many overseas companies, labor costs are rising, there are concerns about labor shortages, and the production process is being reviewed.

For example, the Board of Investment of Thailand (BOI)[10] is developing an industrial cluster strategy by establishing a border SEZ (Special Economic Zone)[11]. The BOI, which is under the jurisdiction of the Ministry of Industry of Thailand, was established as an operating window of the Industrial Incentive Law enacted in 1954. The BOI is engaged in activities such as licensing.

In Thailand, to aid in the recovery of the Thai economy after the impact of COVID-19, the BOI enacted the 2021 Investment Promotion Measures to promote large-scale investment projects in target industries (BOI, 2021); the application deadline is the last business day of 2021. Successful applicants will receive a 50% reduction in their corporate income tax for the next 5 years, in addition to the regular benefits for projects with an investment amount of 1 billion baht or more.

The SEZ is a region with special legal and administrative status (regarding, for example, subsidies and tax incentives) for economic development to promote FDI (Haseba. 2016). Unlike in a conventional SEZ, the BOI permits the employment of unskilled foreign workers in the border SEZ. In other words, taking advantage of the establishment of an SEZ on the Thai border, the employment of unskilled workers from Myanmar, Laos, and Cambodia is permitted.

As a result, industrial clusters have been developed along the border with neighboring Cambodia, Laos, and Myanmar, utilizing land routes (truck transportation) such as the East-West Economic Corridor and the Southern Economic Corridor to collaborate with the industrial clusters in Thailand.

In this Thai-based GSC, companies in the upstream process of the manufacturing industry have been established in the industrial clusters in Thailand, companies in the downstream process of the manufacturing industry have been established in the industrial clusters along the border, and inter-company collaboration is conducted (JETRO, 2015; GMS, 2019) (Fig. 2).

According to Thailand's industrial policy, in the industrial clusters in Thailand, a group of companies with high added value even in the manufacturing industry will focus on R&D[12], high-new technology[13], etc.; while, in the industrial clusters along the border with neighboring countries Cambodia, Laos, and Myanmar, a group of labor-intensive companies with cheap local labor supply will focus on simple assembly factories, etc. Thai companies will review the entire production process in collaboration with companies in neighboring Cambodia, Laos, and Myanmar, and build an international business system based on the regional GSC.

The GSC in Thailand and Laos will establish labor-intensive factories in the industrial cluster along the border in Laos, and the parts produced at the Laos factory will be exported to the mother factory in Thailand utilizing the land route. The mother factory, in an industrial cluster in Thailand, thus functions as a manufacturing base for high value-added products and produces final products. In other words, the Thai and neighboring countries' GSC will develop an international business system that links the industrial clusters of each country.

The following section focuses on the GSC involving collaboration among the industrial clusters that utilize the distribution system in Thailand and neighboring countries.

## The Global Supply Chain in Thailand and Laos

The first example is the GSC between industrial clusters straddling the border with neighboring Laos, using the East-West Economic Corridor in Thailand. The East-West Economic Corridor crosses the Indochina region from east to west, from central Vietnam to Myanmar (GMS, 2019) (Fig. 2).

This land route (truck transportation) is a road with a total length of about 1,500 km, and involves a logistics system that requires a 3 to 4-day journey to cover the entire route. Currently, the East-West Economic Corridor, being developed with financial support from Japan's ODA and the Asian Development Bank (ADB)[14], is greatly improving the efficiency of land transportation (ADB, 2015).

In the future, if the road to Mawlamyine (Myanmar) is improved, and the regional development and industrial clusters along the line progresses, this efficiency will be further enhanced. The East-West Economic Corridor crosses four countries on the Indochina Peninsula, connecting Da Nang (Vietnam), Suwannakhet (Laos), the Second Mekong Friendship Bridge, Mukdahan (Thailand), mountainous areas, and the port town of Mawlamyine (Myanmar).

An example of the collaboration in this context is the GSC between Thailand and the Savan-Seno special economic zone (Savan Park Savannakhet) located in Suwannakhet (southern Laos Area). In 2008, Savan Park Savannakhet (hereinafter, Savan Park) was established in Suwannakhet as an industrial cluster along the Thai-Laotian border. Jointly established in 2008 by Pacifica Streams Development (Malaysia) (70% stake) and the Ministry of Commerce and Industry of Laos (30% stake), Savan Park encompasses an area of 234 ha and is located about 3 km from the Thai border and about 5 km from Suwannakhet International Airport (Yamada, 2015; SPD, 2021).

Savan Park is developing a special economic zone by attracting FDI to Laos. FDI occurs when a company acquires a foreign company, or invests in production equipment in order to conduct business activities abroad. Laos enjoys a competitive advantage in that the Thai and Laotian languages are similar, and it is easy to dispatch and support Thailand engineers and managers in Laos. In addition, when entering Thailand or Vietnam by truck from Laos, transshipment is not required due to the bilateral agreement (Savan Logistics, 2016). Finally, Savan Park boasts abundant electricity, low electricity prices, investment incentives, and low labor and land costs.

Nikon Lao Co., Ltd. is an example of a Japanese company that has expanded into Savan Park along the border (in March 2013) (Nikon, 2013). Nikon Lao, which has a 99.99% stake in Nikon (Thailand) Co., Ltd., commenced operations in September 2013 and is responsible for part of the manufacturing process of the mother factory (digital single-lens reflex cameras) in Thailand (Ayutthaya). The establishment of such a factory in Laos not only reduces costs, but also enables risk diversification given the flood risk in Thailand.

Toyota Boshoku Lao Co., Ltd., which entered the market in April 2013, offers a further example of the expansion of Japanese companies into Savan Park (Toyota Boshoku, 2013). Toyota Boshoku Lao, which has a 90% stake in Toyota Boshoku Asia Co., Ltd. (Thailand), established a regional headquarters in the park and commenced operations as a satellite factory in May 2014, complementing the production by the mother plant (interior parts such as automobile seat covers) in Thailand (Laem Chabang) (Aderans, 2015).

Another example of the expansion of Japanese companies into Savan Park is Aderans Lao Co., Ltd., a local subsidiary of Aderans, which established a presence there in May 2014. Aderans Lao, which is wholly owned by the Japanese headquarters, began preparations for production at its own factory in Vientiane in May 2013, and began operating a temporary factory in the park using rental equipment in

September 2014. Then, in July 2015, the production of our own factory was started as the main factory. Aderans Lao complements the material and product logistics in Thailand (Buriram plant).

## The Global Supply Chain in Thailand and Cambodia

The second GSC example involves the industrial clusters straddling the border between Thailand and neighboring Cambodia, using the South Economic Corridors in Thailand. The Southern Economic Corridors (also known as the Second East-West Economic Corridors) cross the Mekong area of the Indochina region from east to west, from southern Vietnam to Myanmar (GMS, 2019) (Fig. 2).

This land route (truck transportation) is a road with a total length of about 1,000 km, and it takes two to three days to cross the Mekong area.

In the future, if the road to Dawei (Myanmar) is improved and the regional development and industrial clusters along with the line progress, the efficiency of the GSC will be further enhanced. The Southern Economic Corridors consist of a road that crosses four countries on the Indochina Peninsula, connecting Vung Tau (outer port of Ho Chi Minh, Vietnam), Moc Bai (Vietnam), Bavet (Cambodia), Neak Loeung Bridge (Tsubasa Bridge) (Cambodia), Phnom Penh (Cambodia), Poipet (Cambodia), Bangkok (Thailand), mountainous areas, and the port town of Dawei (Myanmar).

An example of collaboration in this context is the GSC involving the SANCO special economic zone (SANCO SEZ) located in Poipet (Cambodia). Established in 2012 as an industrial cluster along the Thai-Cambodian border, the SANCO SEZ has a total area of 67 ha and is located about 5 km from the Thai border. Cambodia's SEZ is a cutting-edge development (SPS, 2021), with the competitive advantage that there is no risk of flood damage because it is well above sea level.

In addition, the SANCO SEZ can use commercial facilities in neighboring Thailand, the border gate to neighboring Cambodia operates from early morning to midnight, and rapid movement is possible to major cities in the ASEAN countries. Among its other features, foreigners can lease land in the SEZ for 99 years, it has an investment incentive system, and labor and land costs are low.

An example of the expansion of Japanese companies into the area along the Thai-Cambodian border is Toyota Tsusho's Cambodian subsidiary (Techno Park Poipet Pvt. Co. Ltd.), which expanded into the SANCO SEZ in April 2015. Techno Park Poipet, which is wholly owned by the Japanese headquarters, was established in April 2015 and is developing techno park businesses in four countries (India, Thailand, China, and Indonesia) and strengthening its value chain in emerging countries (Toyota Tsusho, 2015).

A further example of the expansion of Japanese companies into the SANCO SEZ is the Cambodian subsidiary (NHK Spring (Cambodia) Co., Ltd.). Established by the Thai subsidiary of NHK Spring and entering the market in April 2016, NHK Spring (Cambodia) has a 75% stake in NHK Spring (Thailand) Co., Ltd. In April 2016, it began producing sewn parts for automobile seats, aiding in the optimization of the Thai-based production system in the Mekong region.

## The Global Supply Chain in Thailand and Myanmar

The third GSC example involves the industrial clusters straddling the Thai border with neighboring Myanmar, using the South Economic Corridors in Thailand. The Southern Economic Corridor has no roads on the Myanmar side from the western part of Bangkok (Thailand) to Kanchanaburi District, Phu Nam Ron (Thailand), and Dawei (Myanmar) (GMS, 2019) (Fig. 2).

Further, on this land route (rail transportation), there are some areas along the railway line where ethnic minorities in Myanmar have effective control. Though Governor Jirakiat Phumsawat of Kanchanaburi Province approved freight transportation between Thailand and Myanmar as of September 1, 2021, the logistics system to Dawei is almost non-functional (JMD, 2021).

The Dawei SEZ is about 600 km from Yangon (Myanmar), and about 160 km from the Thai border at Phu Nam Long, roughly 200 km from Bangkok (Thailand); however, Dawei is on the Andaman Sea, so if the road on the Myanmar side is improved, the Dawei SEZ can serve as a valuable export base from Thailand to India, the Middle East, and Africa.

An example of the collaboration, in this case, is the GSC involving the Dawei SEZ in Dawei (Myanmar), which was established in 2013 as an industrial cluster along the Thai border in the Dawei region. The Dawei SEZ is one of Myanmar's three special economic zones: the Kyaukpyu SEZ developed by China in the north, the Thilawa SEZ developed by Japan in the south, and the Dawei SEZ developed by Thailand in the south (Dawei SEZ, 2021). In May 2008, the Thai and Myanmar governments signed a basic agreement on the Dawei SEZ project, and Thailand private companies took the lead.

However, in June 2013, a Thailand company withdrew from the Dawei SEZ initiative due to difficulty in raising funds, and the development entity was transferred to the DDC company (Dawei Development Company Ltd.) which is a Special Purpose Vehicle (SPV)[15] funded by the Thailand and Myanmar governments. An SPV is an entity established when assets and receivables are securitized. In this case, there should be no capital relationship between the originator (the original holder of the securitized asset) and the SPV.

After this, the Dawei SEZ project was suspended due to political instability in Thailand. Then, in July 2015, a Memorandum of Intent (MoI)[16] was signed between the Government of Japan, the Government of Myanmar, and the Government of Thailand, for the development of the Dawei SEZ project. The MoI confirmed that Japan will participate in the SPV through the Japan International Cooperation Agency (JICA) or the Japan Bank for International Cooperation (JBIC) and that a preliminary commercialization survey will be conducted.

In addition, the MoI clearly states that appropriate measures will be taken with regard to environmental and social considerations in accordance with international standards. Based on the MoI, JBIC decided to invest in a DDC company in December 2015, and in 2016 Japan invested 800 million USD for joint development by the three countries (JBIC, 2015)[17]. In December 2020, JICA began investigating the Dawei Port project and its feasibility (JICA, 2020)[18]. In the future, the SEZ project will promote the development of the Dawei port through a process of strategic environmental assessment.

The Dawei SEZ is about 20 km from the center of Dawei and has a total area of 20,000 ha, including the industrial and harbor areas. The development plan for the Dawei SEZ is currently being implemented. In January 2021, Dawei SEZ development was terminated from a contract with a Thailand company because it was considered to have no financial capacity to continue the SEZ business due to continued development delays and default of financial obligations. In the future, through a loan from Thailand, a highway will be constructed between Dawei and the Thai border, which is scheduled to be completed in 2023.

## The Global Supply Chain in Other Area

The fourth GSC example involves the industrial clusters straddling the Thai-Laotian border, using the South Economic Corridors in Thailand. The Central Corridor runs from Cambodia's open-sea port city,

Sihanoukville, via Cambodia's capital, Phnom Penh, across Cambodia via Lao's Pakse, and crossing National Highway No. 13 along the border in Laos, Vientiane, the capital of Laos (GMS, 2019) (Fig. 2).

In Vientiane, along the Central Corridor, the Vientiane Logistics Park (VLP) has been established, an international logistics center near the Thai-Laotian border (Savan Logistics, 2016). Among other things, the VLP was created to alleviate congestion at the existing passenger railway Thanaleng Terminal Station, which is located near the border, and to alleviate a one-sided cargo problem (there is no cargo from Cambodia or Laos to Thailand), with one-way logistics, by managing container cargo in the border trade.

The Pakse-Japan SME SEZ (PJSEZ) was established along the central corridor in Pakse, the second largest city in Laos. The PJSEZ, Laos's first special economic zone for Japanese SMEs, is located in Champasak Province along the border between Thailand and Cambodia, about 770 km from Vientiane (PJSEZ, 2021).

An example of a Japanese company expanding into the PJSEZ is Daiwa Harness Lao Co., Ltd, a Lao subsidiary of Daiwa Sangyo Co., Ltd., which was established in June 2015, with factory operations commencing in December 2015. Daiwa Sangyo has transferred part of the harness process of its existing Thai mother factory (in Amatanacon Industrial Park) to the new factory in Laos. As a result, the Thai factory is focusing on the production of high value-added products such as light emitting diodes (LEDs) and harnesses with electronic boards.

The following is an example of a GSC that straddles the industrial cluster along the border between Thailand and neighboring Cambodia, using the Southern Coastal Corridor. In this case, it is possible to connect from Bangkok, Thailand, to Kamau, the border of Hartrec Changjiam, on the coast of Cambodia, and the southernmost city of Vietnam (GMS, 2019) (Fig. 2).

Koh Kong Province in Cambodia is a port area west of the capital Phnom Penh, facing the Gulf of Thailand. The Koh Kong special economic zone (KKSEZ) lies along the Southern Coastal Corridor (KKSEZ, 2021).

As an example of the expansion of Japanese companies into the KKSEZ, Yazaki (Cambodia) Products Co., Ltd., a Cambodian subsidiary of Yazaki Corporation, was established in 2011, with factory operations commencing in December 2012. Yazaki established a new wire harness plant in Koh Kong as a production base to complement the Thai factory, thereby relocating labor-intensive processes from the Chachoengsao Plant in Thailand and rising labor costs. Yazaki (Cambodia) products supply products to automobile manufacturers based in Thailand as a production base for automobile wire harnesses.

In this way, Thailand has developed the industrial clusters in areas along the border with neighboring Cambodia, Laos, and Myanmar by utilizing logistics systems such as the East-West Economic Corridor and the Southern Economic Corridor, and has developed a GSC based on its own industrial clusters.

In collaboration with the GSC across the Thai border, labor-intensive companies will be attracted to the industrial agglomeration of the neighboring countries (Laos, Cambodia, Myanmar); while, in the Thai industrial clusters, companies specializing in high value-added products are established, the regional GSC is constructed between those companies, and the international business system is developed.

## ISSUES INVOLVED IN THE ASEAN GLOBAL SUPPLY CHAIN

The ASEAN was established, with five original member countries (Thailand, Indonesia, Singapore, Philippines, Malaysia), by the 1967 Bangkok Declaration. After this, the number of ASEAN countries increased, and the organization is now composed of 10 Southeast Asian countries. On December 31,

2015, the ASEAN became the ASEAN Economic Community (AEC). Since then, it has shown high economic growth with the potential to become an "open growth center" in the world.

As aforementioned, on December 31, 2015, the AEC was established in the ASEAN. The 10 countries are now regional economic zones that promote the liberalization of people, goods, and services in the region (ASEAN, 2015a).

ACE almost eliminated tariffs on ASEAN6 (Thailand, Indonesia, Malaysia, Philippines, Singapore, Brunei) in 2010 and eliminated tariffs on CLMV (Cambodia, Laos, Myanmar, Vietnam) in 2015. Among its acts, in November 2018, the AEC signed the ASEAN Agreement on Electronic Commerce, and in October 2020, the ASEAN Trade in Services Agreement (ATISA), etc. Currently, the liberalization rate in the AEC is over 99%, the highest level in the world.

The border walls of the 10 ASEAN countries have become even lower due to the establishment of the AEC, the conclusion of various agreements, and the elimination of tariffs within the ASEAN region. As we have discussed, the amount of trade and physical distribution within the ASEAN region is increasing, along with the high economic growth of the AEC and ASEAN countries. The logistics systems for transportation by land routes (trucks and trains), sea routes (ships), and air routes (airplanes), which connect domestic and overseas industrial clusters, are being developed.

As aforementioned, the ASEAN logistics system is suitable for transportation with neighboring countries because truck transportation by land has the advantages of being able to transport with a small amount of cargo and having easy to turn. However, global companies developing business in the ASEAN must review the production process in the ASEAN region in order to improve management efficiency. Further corporate growth cannot be expected unless an international management system is constructed through collaboration among the industrial clusters utilizing the regional GSC with neighboring countries.

Although this collaboration has been steadily developing, some issues must be addressed in the international management system involving truck transportation. The first issue is related to infrastructure development for customs clearance operations at national borders; for example, in the use of the South Economic Corridors in Thailand, the customs clearance work must be expedited at the border gate with Cambodia. Every time a truck crosses this border, the customs activities on both sides require considerable time and effort because various procedures, such as cargo inspection, customs, and quarantine, are required.

Thus, for truck transportation, a One-Stop Border Post (OSBP) will be set up at Poipet (Cambodia) on the Thai border, the customs clearance service hours will be extended at Bavet (Cambodia) on the Vietnamese border, and a fast lane will be created on the road. The OSBP will integrate the border facilities of Vietnam and Cambodia into one entity, and/or a procedure office will be established in each country, which may be housed in a One-Stop Service Center (OSSC) in the industrial clusters of the two nations. In addition, the customs clearance service will extend the opening hours of the counter to 24 hours and streamline immigration procedures.

Overall, it is necessary to determine and introduce the optimal customs clearance operation method for the two neighboring countries; and with respect to infrastructure, for improved truck transportation, fast lanes such as high-speed lanes and overtaking lanes, will be installed on roads to alleviate traffic congestion.

The second issue is the digitization of various procedures at national borders and transparency in the application costs; for example, making import/export documents paperless in trade-related procedures within ASEAN, improving application costs for certificates of origin, creating plant protection and animal quarantine certificates, and eliminating opaque costs at the time of customs clearance. Paperless

ASEAN import/export documents will enable the creation of a single window of trade-related procedure digitization, which, in simplifying and streamlining trade-related procedures in each ASEAN country, will enable a variety of procedures to be completed with a single data entry and transmission.

The aim is to facilitate various procedures by handling trade procedures at a single general counter. By digitizing trade-related procedures in each country's single window, various operations can be linked, and a smooth import/export operation system can be constructed. There are differences in the single-window support in the various ASEAN countries, but in Cambodia, Laos, and Myanmar, domestic single window support is a priority.

By establishing single-window support among the ASEAN countries, it will be possible to eliminate paperless import/export documents, improve application costs for import/export documents at the time of customs clearance, and eliminate uncertain costs. Moreover, the information system will eventually be shared within the ASEAN, enabling the sharing of trade transaction data between related countries, simplifying global trade-related procedures, and expediting international logistics. For all these reasons, single-window support offers a promising tool for future ASEAN development.

In Laos, Cambodia, and Myanmar, there are problems of labor quality (workers typically only have education and knowledge at the elementary and junior high school graduation level) and labor mobility (workers often resign because they are not accustomed to working in factories, or after acquiring skills, etc.). In addition, the small size of the three countries presents challenges in terms of securing optimal workers, and there is a possibility of quantitative labor shortages in the future.

Finally, as described above, there are practical issues, not only in terms of GSC hardware such as infrastructure development, but also in terms of GSC operations, such as trade procedures, and the need for software simplification.

## FUTURE RESEARCH DIRECTION

The supply chain is a series of economic activities (procurement, production, distribution, sales, consumption, etc.) from producing a product to its consumption. The supply chain is also a management concept that began to be discussed in the United States in the 1980s. However, in modern times, when comparing the socio-economics and businesses of the 1980s, the information-oriented society and globalization are making dramatic progress. In today's society, economic activities that were unpredictable or unimaginable in the 1980s have been realized.

In the future, it is expected that the impact of economic activities on the supply chain due to the further evolution of the information society and globalization will become even greater. Therefore, it is essential to work on a wide range of global supply chains of economic activities across multiple cross-border organizations in the future supply chain, rather than a narrow range of economic activities in one company or group of companies.

## CONCLUSION

In the ASEAN countries, nation-building is being conducted with the aim of creating innovation, and many industrial clusters such as industrial parks, export processing zones, special economic zones, and high-tech parks have already been established. In these industrial clusters, through the promotion of the

GSC with neighboring countries, efforts are being made to create innovation for regional development and regional revitalization across national borders.

In Thailand, the logistics infrastructure is utilized for collaboration between industrial clusters established along the borders with neighboring countries; and a corporate strategy is emerging in which all the production processes are reviewed, and factories in neighboring countries such as Laos and Cambodia are responsible for simple processing and assembly, which are labor-intensive processes.

In developing the industrial clusters that utilize the ASEAN logistics infrastructure, companies and support organizations are being agglomerated and together constructing an international business system based on the regional GSC. The aim is to create innovation by strengthening the network relationships of the member countries' organizations and enhancing cross-border interaction (competition/cooperation).

To strengthen the network relationships, trade, customs, and customs clearance operations, which require import and export procedures on the departure and entry side of cross-border trade, will be integrated into a single window. Efforts must be made to shorten the residence time of goods that cross national borders and promote logistics by completing all the procedures at once.

Steady economic growth is seen in each ASEAN country, but there are issues regarding industrial cluster collaboration in the GSC; for example, delays in OSSC and OSBP efforts such as customs clearance procedures at borders. Although OSSC and OSBP efforts are being made in each ASEAN country, there are differences in the actual operations and progress. Moreover, there are issues in the customs clearance procedures at the borders, such as the operation of the CBTA (Cross Border Transportation Agreement), customs opening hours, weight restrictions, and high distribution costs.

Overall, there are a host of issues involved in the cooperation between the industrial clusters of the ASEAN countries. However, by establishing industrial clusters along the borders and utilizing the increasingly efficient distribution system such as the land routes (truck transportation), the member countries are working toward an international business system based on the regional GSC.

## ACKNOWLEDGMENT

This work was supported by JSPS KAKENHI Grant Number 19H01532.

## REFERENCES

ADB (Asian Development Bank). (2015). *Greater Mekong Subregion Economic Cooperation Program.* https://www.adb.org/sites/default/files/publication/29387/gms-ecp-overview-2015.pdf

Aderans Company Limited. (2015). *The Laos "Savannakhet Factory" main factory begins operations.* https://www.aderans.co.jp/news/detail/150727_01.html

BOI (Thailand Board of Investment). (2021). *Additional incentives for projects with an investment of THB 1 billion or more.* http://www.boi.go.th/upload/Tokyo210702/BOIMailMagazine_2021_5_StimulousMeasure.pdf

BOI (Thailand Board of Investment) Home Page. (2021). https://www.boi.go.th/en/index/

Dawei, S. E. Z. (Dawei special economic zone). (2020). *DSEZ MC received JICA December 18, 2020*. http://www.daweisez.gov.mm/news/dsez-mc-received-jica-18-dec-2020

Dawei, S. E. Z. (Dawei special economic zone). (2021). *Overview of the Dawei SEZ*. http://www.dawei-sez.gov.mm/content/overview-dawei-sez

GMS (Greater Mekong Subregion). (2019). *Economic Corridors in the Greater Mekong Subregion*. https://www.greatermekong.org/content/economic-corridors-in-the-greater-mekong-subregion

Haseba, J. (2016). Border SEZ as a pillar of investment attraction: Industrial policy of reshuffled cabinet (1). *The International Trade Public Bulletin*. https://www.jetro.go.jp/biznews/2016/01/c8aaec213765a950.html

JBIC (Japan Bank for International Cooperation) Home Page. (2021). https://www.jbic.go.jp/en/index.html

JBIC (Japan Bank for International Cooperation). (2015). *Concluded a shareholder agreement for the purpose of participating in an investment in the Dawei special economic zone Development Company of the Federal Republic of Myanmar*. https://www.jbic.go.jp/ja/information/press/press-2015/1215-44764.html

JETRO Phnom Penh Office. (2015). *Comparison of Cambodia-Laos special economic zones in the Thai Border Region*. https://www.jetro.go.jp/ext_images/world/reports/2014/7b3bacad38b0368a/kokkyo.pdf

JICA (Japan Bank for International Cooperation) Home Page. (2021). https://www.jica.go.jp/english/index.html

JMD (The Japan Maritime Daily). (2021). *Thailand / Myanmar resumes border traffic*. https://www.jmd.co.jp/article.php?no=270777

Kawai, H. (2021). *'Dream' or 'trap,' the end point of the "Chinese railway" expansion in Southeast Asia. International*. Nishi-Nippon Shimbun. Https://www.nishinippon.co.jp/item/n/778004/

KKSEZ (Koh Kong Special Economic Zone). (2021). *Welcome to the Koh Kong special economic zone*. https://kksez.com/

Krugman, P. R. (1991). *Geography and Trade*. MIT Press.

Logistics, S. (2016). *Savan Logistics is operating in the first Dry Port/ICD (Inland Container Depot) in Savannakhet, Lao P.D.R., Welcome to SAVAN Logistics*. http://www.savanlogistics.com/

Muramatsu, Y., & Nitta, Y. (2021). *Myanmar removes Thai builder from Indo-Pacific economic-zone project*. https://asia.nikkei.com/Economy/Myanmar-removes-Thai-builder-from-Indo-Pacific-economic-zone-project

NHK Spring Co. Ltd. (2015). *Notice regarding the establishment of a new sewing parts company in Cambodia, Thai subsidiary*. https://www.nhkspg.co.jp/news/release/pdfs/20150303_2.pdf

Nidec Corporation. (2012). *Notice of the establishment of a base plate manufacturing subsidiary*. https://www.nidec.com/-/media/www-nidec-com/corporate/news/2012/0528-01/120528-01.pdf

Nikon Corporation. (2013). *Establishment of a new factory in Laos*. https://www.nikon.co.jp/news/2013/0321_01.htm

NJS (Nikkan Jidousha Shinbun). (2021). *Daiwa Sangyo completes Laos factory for harness manufacturing base*. https://newspicks.com/news/1291286/body/?ref=company_SPD1ESW77DMR0S5A

NKS (Nihon Keizai Shimbun). (2016). *Cross-border infrastructure development*. Nihon Keizai Shimbun.

NKS (Nihon Keizai Shinbun). (2012). *Yazaki opens Cambodia factory to supplement production in Thailand*. https://www.nikkei.com/article/DGXNASDD170BC_X11C12A2TJ1000/

PJSEZ (Pakse-Japan SME SEZ). (2021). *The industrial park for exclusive use of the Japanese company*. http://pjsez.com/en/information/

Porter, M. E. (1998). *On Competition*. Harvard Business School Press.

Saisho, T. (2019). A Study on global supply chain management systems for mainland ASEAN: Case study of collaboration between industrial clusters using a logistics system. *Proceedings of ICLIE*, 117-122.

Saisho, T. (2021). *The Information and Communication Industry and Industrial Clusters in Asia*. Hakuto Shobo.

SPD (Savan Pacifica Development). (2021). *Savan Park Savannakhet*. http://www.savanpark. com/?page_id=1146&lang=ja

SPS (Sanco Poipet SEZ). (2021). *Sanco Investment*. http://www.sancosez.com/ja/

The ASEAN (Association of Southeast Asian Nations) Secretariat. (2015a). *ASEAN Economic Community*. https://asean.org/asean-economic-community/

The ASEAN (Association of Southeast Asian Nations) Secretariat. (2015b). *ASEAN 2025 at a Glance. A Community of Opportunities for All*. https://asean.org/asean-2025-at-a-glance/

Timetric. (2017). *MPWT-Vientiane Logistics Park-Laos-Project Profile*. https://www.marketresearch.com/Timetric-v3917/MPWT-Vientiane-Logistics-Park-Laos-11181862/

Toyota Boshoku Corporation. (2013). *Toyota Boshoku establishes first production base for automobile interior parts in Laos*. https://www.toyota-boshoku.com/jp/news/543.html

Toyota Tsusho Corporation. (2015). *First techno park project by a Japanese company in Poipet, Cambodia*. https://www.toyota-tsusho.com/press/detail/150331_002756.html

Vongsa, V. (2014). *The Vientiane Logistics Park*. https://www.mpwt.gov.la/attachments/article/877/Annex%206_IEE%20Preliminary%20Findginds_Mr%20Korn_Eng.pdf

Yamada, K. (2015). Development of Vita Park and Sawan Seno SEZ progresses: Looking for complementary development with neighboring countries in the border area. *The International Trade Public Bulletin (Current Business Brief Report)*. https://www.jetro.go.jp/biznews/2015/04/5525d02b1b198.html

Yamada, K. (2020), *Vientiane Logistics Park development begins. Business Brief Report*. https://www.jetro.go.jp/biznews/2020/07/efbe1fdffca6cf59.html

## KEY TERMS AND DEFINITIONS

**ASEAN (Association of South-East Asian Nations):** A regional intergovernmental organization of 10 Southeast Asian countries (Indonesia, Cambodia, Singapore, Thailand, Philippines, Brunei, Vietnam, Malaysia, Myanmar), it promotes intergovernmental cooperation and promotes economic, political, military, education, social culture, etc. integration between member states and other Asian countries.

**Country/Region Connectivity:** Connectivity is the ease of connecting multiple things, such as the ease of connection between one's own country and another country, region, or between industrial clusters, and the ease of connection to a network.

**Economic Corridor:** The idea is to collectively develop infrastructure such as roads and railroads so that people and goods can move actively across countries and borders. Aim to promote industry by thickening the distribution network and power supply network.

**Global Supply Chain:** The GSC includes many companies in the industrial clusters of the respective countries, who concentrate on producing products based on their respective strengths, and products that are required but not produced by a given country are not an international division of labor acquired through trade.

**Industrial Cluster Strategy:** Industry-academia-government organizations such as local companies, universities, research institutes, and industrial support organizations will build a wide-area network. Then, through cooperation among organizations, the creation of new industries and new businesses that utilize the strengths of the region by mutually utilizing technologies and know-how are desired.

**Logistics System:** Achieve smooth international transportation in countries and regions with adjacent borders. For a stable logistics system, an optimal transportation model by paying sufficient attention to the latest national circumstances, traffic regulations, and road conditions will be designed and built.

**One-Stop Service:** It is a service that allows people to complete all the necessary work at one business window for various management procedures.

**Single Window:** A system in which related ministries and agencies cooperate beyond the national borders to promote efficient operations. With a single window, people can perform multiple similar steps at the same time with a single input to the system.

**Special Economic Zone:** Special Economic Zone is a region that is given a special legal and administrative status for economic development such as subsidies and tax incentives.

## ENDNOTES

1 FDI (Foreign Direct Investment) is to invest capital in running a business in order to obtain permanent profits for foreign companies. There are two investments in FDI. The first is green field investment, which is an investment in the form of establishing a local subsidiary or subsidiary to create a local factory or sales channel from scratch. The second is an investment in the form of acquisitions of companies in the countries in which they invest, M&A of overseas companies, and cross-border M&A.

2 One-stop service (OSS) is a service that allows people to complete all the work required in one procedure in various administrative procedures.

3 ODA (Official Development Assistance) is the provision of funds and technology provided by the government or the implementing agency of the government to help the economic and social development and welfare of developing countries.

4 There are two routes in the Southern Economic Corridor. The first is the Bangkok-Phnom Penh route (via Thailand Aranyaprathet-Cambodia Poipet), which is mainly used on a commercial basis. The second is the route from Thailand Hartlake to Bangkok via Koh Kong, Cambodia to Phnom Penh, which is connected by a road along the Gulf of Thailand.

5 There are two routes in the Eastern Corridor. The first is the route from Nanning, the head of the Guangxi Zhuang Autonomous Region of China, to Hanoi via the Gulf of Tonkin coast (Nanning, Mong Cai, Hanoi). The second is the inland route between China and Vietnam, which connects Nanning, Dong Dang, and Hanoi.

6 There are two routes in the central corridor. The first is the Laos-Thailand-Cambodia route (Vientiane, Udon Thani, Nakhon Ratchasima, Laem Chabang Port), which is used for overseas imports and exports of Laos via Thailand. The second is the route within Laos. Laos-Thailand-Cambodia route (Vientiane, Thakhek, Savannakhet, Pakse, Shumliup, Phnom Penh, Sihanoukville port route, used for overseas import / export via Cambodia in Laos.

7 Connectivity is the ease of connecting multiple things, such as the ease of connection between one's own country and another country, region, or between industrial clusters, and the ease of connection to a network.

8 AEC (ASEAN Economic Community) was established on December 31, 2015, liberalized the movements of people, goods, money, services, and investment within the ASEAN (Association of South-East Asian Nations) region, and standardized them. At AEC, economic integration within the ASEAN region will be carried out to expand domestic demand, trade, and investment. For details on AEC, refer to the ASEAN website <https://asean.org/asean-economic-community/>.

9 In SWS (Single Window System), related ministries and agencies cooperate to connect and cooperate with each other in order to strengthen international competitiveness. With SWS, multiple similar procedures can be performed simultaneously by inputting and transmitting to the system once.

10 BOI (Board of Investment) was established as an operating window of the Industrial Incentive Law enacted in 1954 and is engaged in activities such as determining investment incentive measures in Thailand and licensing important investment projects. BOI has created the "2021 Investment Promotion Measures" to promote large-scale investment projects in order to recover the Thai economy affected by the new coronavirus (COVID-19). For details on BOI, refer to the Thailand Board of Investment website <https://www.boi.go.th/en/index/>.

11 SEZ (Special Economic Zone) is a region that is given a special legal and administrative status for economic development such as subsidies and tax incentives.

12 R&D (Research and development) is technical by investigating a specific target, searching for basic academic research and applied research according to the purpose, and testing technologies that will develop in the future. It is an activity to gain a great advantage.

13 High-New Industry is a high-tech industry that focuses on advanced and advanced technologies such as Computers, ICT(Information and Communication Technology), AI (Artificial Intelligence), RPA (Robotic Process Automation), rockets (Space Industry), Biotechnology, and Nanotechnology.

14 ADB (Asian Development Bank) is an international financial institution established for the purpose of promoting the economic development of developing countries in the Asia-Pacific region and reducing poverty. For details on ADB, refer to the bank website <https://asean.org/>.

15 SPV (Special Purpose Vehicle) is a business entity established when assets and receivables are securitized. This entity should not have a capital relationship between the originator (the original holder of the securitized asset) and the SPV.

16 At MoI (Memorandum of Intent), Japan will participate in investment through the Japan International Cooperation Agency (JICA) or Japan Bank for International Cooperation (JBIC), and conduct a preliminary commercialization survey for road consolidation projects. Has been confirmed. In addition, it is clearly stated that MoI will take appropriate measures in accordance with international standards regarding environmental and social considerations.

17 For details on JBIC, refer to the bank website <https://www.jbic.go.jp/en/index.html>.

18 For details on JICA, refer to the aid agency website <https://www.jica.go.jp/english/index.html>.

# Chapter 13
# Relocation Strategy of Production, Global Supply, and Value Chains

**José G. Vargas-Hernández**
https://orcid.org/0000-0003-0938-4197
*Tecnológico Mario Molina Unidad Zapopan, Mexico*

## ABSTRACT

*This chapter aims to critically analyze the implications that the national protectionist policies have on the global supply and value chains and the relocation of production. The analysis is based on the assumptions that the global economy is facing the possibility of decoupling of many trade connections and this trend favors deglobalization processes have long been promoted by populism, nationalism, and economic protectionism. It is concluded that global supply, production, and value chains, although being economically efficient, are no longer any more secure under national protectionist policies, and therefore, the relocation of production processes is mainly due to the increase in the level of income and wages of the developing countries that are the destination and which reduce the advantages to relocate.*

## INTRODUCTION

This chapter discusses the relocation of the global supply chain. Due to globalization, supply chains behave globally. Materials and products have been transferred and manufacturing facilities have been allocated globally. On the other, deglobalization has occurred many times. It is almost impossible for a company to control globalization and deglobalization trend. However, companies construct supply chains and change their structure globally according to internal and external factors.

The processes of economic globalization are in difficulties, showing a contraction in international trade flows in 2019, which are aggravated by the responses that companies have given to the health emergency. The outbreak of the coronavirus pandemic has immediate negative effects with a considerable impact on global trade, investment, and financial flows. Coronavirus is changing the way the world does business for bad or good. Business corporations and companies are being forced to rethink their

DOI: 10.4018/978-1-7998-9800-9.ch013

global value, production, and logistics chains, shaped to maximize efficiency and profits. Resilience, recovery, and adaptation are becoming relevant in the world economy (Javorcik, 2020).

This analysis shows expansive periods of free trade alternate with other periods in which protectionist measures and the relocation of production are part of a process that is called deglobalization and is characterized by a reduction in export growth that is compensated with increased consumption of the domestic market to defend national interests. Some developed economies have trade imbalances with negative effects on less developed countries.

The current environment of economic, social, political, and health instability has intensified the increase in the economic costs of transaction and coordination of the subsidiaries of multinational companies located in other international host territories, making relocation processes unviable, for which they have initiated processes of repression or de-globalization to return its production to the countries of origin. This situation has meant stagnation, and in some cases, a reversal in business strategy to deepen the globalization processes of companies (Meyer & Peng, 2016).

The level of economic integration in globalization processes is well advanced, as it has been shown that when production in some provinces of China is paralyzed, the supply of inputs to other companies from other nations has affected, a situation of vulnerability that has motivated deglobalization as a response that makes relocation more profitable with the repatriation of factories (Zhu et al., 2020).

This paper first makes a critical analysis of the national protectionist policies and its implications on the global supply and value chains and how these two factors determine the strategy of the relocation of production. Finally, a discussion is offered on these issues.

## BACKGROUND

### National Protectionism Policy

Protectionism has returned, and it will be having to think about it if it is wanted to reap all the benefits and implement this reasoned "deglobalization" that it called for and that now seems inevitable (Sapir, 2016). The term deglobalization was coined by Sapir (2011) to refer to the protectionism of countries that have a similar level of development and economic growth limited by the commercial and financial dimensions of globalization than through outsourcing and relocation processes of large companies, groups of production centers. Deglobalization processes are characterized by the recovery of the sovereignty of nations, reduction of their interdependence, implementation of automatic and protectionist policies to reduce economic and commercial relations.

In a protectionist policy, countries increase restrictions on the free flow of trade, finance, and people, reinforcing their national borders and are oriented towards deglobalization processes that threaten the internationalization of higher education, for example, which remains confined, although it is already advised to deepen the advancement of online education through platforms that reach all places, including the most remote places in the world (James, 2018). The concern about these changes is the depth in which they must occur to save and overcome the advances of globalization, so it can be considered that the advances will be different and different as it had been advancing before, although it is necessary that competition be promoted while cooperative and collaborative relationships are fostered.

Deglobalization is an inverse process to globalization that is manifested by the protectionist and regulatory economic and trade policies of the nation-states as well as the trade wars that are carried out between the great economic and commercial powers. To protect national production, domestic markets increase tariff barriers with the intensification of trade wars between western and eastern markets. What the health crisis has done is accelerate the process.

The international competition on economic systems in the world economy is reduced to economic structures and enterprises mechanisms of macroeconomic players supported by the strengthened functions of the state to stabilize macroeconomics, protect intellectual property rights, to ensure legality and enforcement of contracts, infrastructure provision, and other microeconomic policies to establish incentives and mechanisms for corporate governance, stimulating research and development, investments in human development. Protectionist, nationalist, and populist policies can be functional or dysfunctional depending on their correct design and implementation.

Some of the phenomena that disappointed the scope of the globalization economy were job insecurity and flexibility due to stagnant wages and rising unemployment. The far right has channeled discontent to promote protectionist measures. These situations have given rise to deglobalization processes through the implementation of protectionist economic policies. A greater presence of the State is necessary in the face of the challenges of economic growth, greater economic and social equality, social inclusion, environmental sustainability, protection of biodiversity and conservation of socio-ecosystems, the energetic and climate crisis, etc.

## History of National Protectionism Policy

During the winter war era from 1914 to 1945, from the outbreak of World War I until the end of World War II, globalization processes were in retreat from the first time, after a period of increased economic integration from 1870 until 1914 (Broadberry & Harrison, 2005). After the First World War, protectionism and nationalism were on the rise as international institutions and organizations weakened, but the economic depression deepened. After the year 1918, with the rise of nationalism, international organizations were weakened, an economic depression arose that drove national states to protective economic models.

The abandonment of global economic integration is an option for nation-states framed by a Keynesian scheme through the implementation of protectionist trade measures and maintaining democracy. These methods favored the economic growth of some developed countries that later embraced economic globalization (Rodrik, 2000 & 2007; Steinberg, 2007, p. 45). The countries that remained with borders closed to trade through protectionist and nationalist measures were imposed asymmetric trade conditions, as was the case with the colonies. When these nations achieved their independence, they could already take off in their economic and social development.

After the Second World War, a system of international governance institutions was established with the programs of the Marshall Plan, the Bretton Woods institutions, the United Nations (UN), and the General Agreement on Customs Tariffs (GATT) (Reinalda, 2009). During this period of globalization, retreatment and economic dislocation led to reduced integration, the Great Depression and protectionism as the solution. After World War II, and until the 1980s, new global institutions for economic cooperation were created and developed to promote economic integration and enable national economies to be opened to foreign markets (Spero & Hart, 1997). In 1989 the slow food movement was created to protect the consumption of local products, cultures, traditions, and gastronomic customs perceived as healthier and safer (Petrini, 2001). The movement aims to create awareness of decisions for food consumption and its origin.

During the international financial crisis of 2008 and 2009, the leaders of the most advanced economies managed adequately to avoid the trend of protectionist economic nationalism. The national state recovers functions that were taken from it and, together with international institutions, assumes responsibilities to protect national economies and societies. In 2017, China promoted globalization as a mechanism for economic integration, generating wealth and multilateral cooperation, while the United States promoted trade protectionism (Liu et al., 2018). Protectionist trade policies used as an instrument for multilateral and bilateral negotiations do not always result in benefits for the country that promotes them, as has been recently demonstrated in the case of the United States, which has encountered strong resistance from the trend of economic globalization processes.

## Modern National Protectionism Policy in North America

In 2018, many North American companies announced the relocation and transfer of their production plants back to the national territory. In 2019, the Kearney index detected a strategic trend in company production towards a greater weight of the "made in America" content of manufacturing production (Doh et al., 2021). In part, this was achieved by the warning that if they wanted to receive the protection of the American legal system, they should return the jobs. European countries grant aid through anti-crisis plans to their companies that disengage from tax havens.

Following North American policy, France encourages the repatriation of its companies, while Japan favors its companies that return from China with incentives. Nation-states have difficulty regulating the financialization that dominates the real economy and offshore strategies, as well as putting limits on the power of monopolies in the digital economy (Rasiah et al., 2010).

The unilateral discourses practiced by some powers attempt to control the world agenda of globalization processes through neo-protectionist mechanisms under the world economy revolving around a multipolarity. Geo-economics and geopolitical analyzes show a transition of leadership from the global economy to China. Now the United States plays the option of a more protectionist economy that drastically affects the economies that are more dependent on global trade. However, the slowdown in economic globalization began long before the pandemic, which has contributed to accelerating it by declining national economies.

The goal of the new United States government was to eliminate the trade deficit through the implementation of protectionist and nationalist fiscal policies, and started a trade war against its trading partners, but above all with China, its main competitor, but which had repercussions worldwide, because it drastically reduced world trade. The elimination of the deficit simply to date, has not been achieved, but also worsened and deepened. The coronavirus health crisis imposed a truce on the trade war that paralyzed the negotiations of trade relations. However, the largest producer of medical supplies is in China (Qin, 2020). With the health crisis, countries want to maintain their own economic activities and be in proximity through protectionism. Consistent with this, multinational companies plan to repatriate in reshoring part of their international production.

The world economy faced threats in its globalization process long before the 2020 health crisis, such as the growing challenge of trade wars and the protectionism of the economies of different national states with the implementation of a tariff war. The health crisis is the result of negative externalities of an interconnected world in globalization processes that are perceived to be linked to physical security in identity and economic spheres, whose responsibility to protect against risks has fallen more on the nation-state rather than on the international community.

## Economic Deglobalization Trend

The health crisis caused by the pandemic has accelerated the protectionist tendencies and the populist and nationalist policies of the nations and has caused tensions and trade wars in the face of the fall in international trade flows and foreign direct investment. The health crisis has accelerated and deepened this trend of economic deglobalization through protectionist actions, reduction of multilateral treaties, etc., with economic consequences that are legible, but uncertain and unpredictable (Didea & Ilie, 2020).

The protectionist tensions that lead to a trade war constitute a reconsideration in the opposite direction to the progress of trade liberalization. This situation that arises unilaterally resists the continued opening of markets and international economies to position itself as a closed economy, erodes economic, commercial, and political relations with its partners. In other words, the country that was the greatest promoter of economic globalization processes is now the greatest opponent of deepening economic, commercial, and financial relations.

The liberalization of regulations of local financial markets that protected the host countries from foreign investments allows MNES to have access to local natural resources and get actively involved in local markets. Because of this deregulation, the global FDI flows had increased regularly until 2000 and since then it had been falling until it reached a peak in 2007 (World Bank, 2016).

Now local governments have tried to implement different initiatives with protectionist measures against global markets since 2008, as ways to recover the economic growth of their economies, resulting in limitations to international trade. All these initiatives are strengthened to weaken the processes of economic globalization and cry out for deglobalization (Irwin, 2020). After the subprime crisis, citizens demand to governments for protection of their own interests against the globalization interest through the redesign and implementation of more protective economic and financial liberalization policies.

The processes of economic globalization are being pressured by isolationist positions that seek to deepen the self-sufficiency of national states to protect local interests over global interests. These changes in perspective have implications and effects on the harmonious development of people. The national state recovers relevant functions in this process of deglobalization for the financial rescue in the face of the economic debacle of important economic actors and agents, such as multinational companies and financial institutions (Napolitano, 2011). The new scheme is configured with less market and more state with a geopolitical reconfiguration of national borders evidenced in return to nationalist protectionism and more controls on cross-border financial transactions.

Factors such as technology-based automation, protectionist practices in national economies, rapid shipments, and deliveries, among many other factors, contribute to the acceleration of the processes of slowing down or reversing globalization. Rather, the concern is diverted towards how profound these changes that are already occurring will be, but above all in the way they are going to be managed. These trends are driven by rising wages in countries that previously offered low labor cost advantages, as well as protectionism in local economies.

The restrictive and protectionist economic policy measures that materialize in the deglobalization processes are, among the most common, the increase in tariff rates, the establishment of phytosanitary measures, cross-border labor restrictions, limitations on foreign investment, control of movements immigration, trade wars, etc. (Gaillard, 2020). As part of protectionist measures, importers raise their tariff barriers in response to the trade war.

Nation-states are receding, driven by protectionist trends due to falling global trade and investment flows driven by the health crisis. With the health crisis of the pandemic, the nation-states enact protectionist, deglobalizing economic policy measures that reduce and retract the advance of globalization processes, such as, for example, the closure of the border to commercial exchange activities and nationalist control of migratory movements of the population. Nation-states adopt nationalist, populist, and protective economic policies to recover their regulatory functions and fields of action in a gradual process of control of globalizing dynamics.

Trade protectionism is the relevant element of deglobalization for protecting the losers of globalization, assuring gains through imposing high rates of industrial and trade protection and imposing manufacturing tariffs (Findlay & O'Rourke, 2008, p. 401). Trade protectionism is a relevant action implemented in this deglobalization process. Deglobalization processes have repercussions that damage the economies that promote protectionist economic policies. The lack of leadership in the globalization processes makes it easier for each nation to reverse or at least slow down progress by adopting more protectionist measures.

National markets and economies are now less dependent on international markets and rely on the regulations of national economies to protect themselves. To exploit the advantages offered by the new environment, an emerging strategy has emerged that supports the resurgence of protection measures for national markets. The deglobalization of economic integration processes moves the center of gravity back from the market to the sustainable local market through a commercial policy and the use of fiscal, tariff, and quota mechanisms to protect the national production of transnational companies (IMCO, 2020). The uniformity and standardization of commercial regulations threaten regional and local development where the asymmetric is normal for self-protection.

Therefore, the protectionist attempt of an economy has a negative impact on national companies in such a way that the protectionist measures taken unilaterally by a country, and damages the competitiveness of its companies and, therefore, its own economy. It is the same multinational companies that promote the relocation of production, distribution, and consumption processes. Countries now attempt to relocate the production of goods within or near their national borders for the benefit of integrated regions through tariff protection measures.

The deglobalization process is supported by the promotion of protectionist measures and is characterized by export flows, investments, migratory movements, and technological innovation that are reduced or diminished, are reflected in political and economic decisions to orient themselves to domestic demand with measures with tariffs, cross-border restrictions and limitations on investment and foreign labor (Shavshukov & Zhuravleva, 2020).

Greater attention to domestic demand leads governments to reduce the growth of exports through direct or indirect protectionist measures. Countries alone are unlikely to oppose globalization given the omnipotence of global financial markets, so the alternative is to recur to the risks of trade wars more focused on national protectionism. National governments grant tax incentives that benefit protectionism and populism for the repatriation of manufacturing plants and investments. Manufacturing employment is likely to decline while most forms of services employments are likely to be heavily protected from internationalization, therefore avoiding anti-globalization backlashes focus more on improving the quality and provision.

The same powers that before spread the gospel of open market and free trade are the same that now predicate protectionism and support deglobalization markets. It has been said that the global economic and financial elites pursue the creation of a world government by centralizing order and power by protecting from enemies through a surveillance system based on traceability (Vanham, 2019)

Cultural globalization and an increase of human interactions have been the result of the economic, financial, and trade exchanges, contributing to the different values, traditions, customs, habits, etc., are being shared among local communities and other communities in such a way that it is homogenizing a world's culture. Local culture requires protection to maintain its uniqueness at a community level, environmental and development social movements and activists need the support of the nation-state to defend society to defend and protect society from the destructive capacities of economic globalization and global market to exploit the human and natural resources.

## MAIN FOCUS

The entire global economic structure is reeling from the health crisis of the pandemic. Governments of Nation-states and corporations are assessing the global market as a growing source of disruption of global value, production, and logistics chains, as well as the source of risk and competitive disadvantages. Local governments are retracting global policies of economic integration and are increasing the protectionist policies for the repatriation of manufacturers (Abdal & Ferreira, 2021). However, other national economies have already developed capabilities to become resilient, recovering, restructuring, and enhancing the new institutional governance emerging from the pandemic.

### Global Supply and Value Chain

Trade openness, economics, financial and commercial liberalization, information, and communication technology innovations facilitated the special and operational expansion of transnational and multinational corporations which in turn, contributed to altering the exchange of resources flows and supply chains between intra and inter firm as well as to a global power redistribution. Economic globalization processes accelerated the flow of goods through global supply chains and global trade (Kano et al., 2020).

The development of ICTs and the emergence of the Internet accelerated the processes of globalization with world communication in real time and, with financial digitization and the logistical development of supply and value chains, accelerated the scope of a global economy. Technological and scientific advances have intensified with economic globalization with the monopolistic emergence of digital companies that control the financialization of processes around global supply and value chains where BRICS countries have become the managers of changes in global competitiveness (Barykin et al., 2021).

The value chains as well as the supply chains of the companies in a global economy scenario are distributed throughout the world. Multinational and transnational corporations have established networks of supply chains, subcontractors, and logistics around the world. The networking-based global economy is formed by chains developed by a large group of shadow enterprises that are connected for economic activities across the boundaries of countries and makes meaningless the concept of distance and national borders.

In a competitive global market, the costs of the entire chain of supply, production, and consumption spread worldwide should be the lowest (Bello, 2013). However, globalization is based on the economies of scale and scope due to the location of production where is most efficient is over, while the concern is for the fragility of supply-chain diversification because their processes rely on each other to add their value.

The global production and distribution chains show the fragility of the high dependence on the processes of economic globalization to provide products and inputs to the economies that require them to continue their manufacturing processes. This failure in global production chains has exposed the weaknesses of national security and national industry, arguments that support protectionist positions, such as measures to guarantee supply in national markets. The national security policy acquires greater force by pressing for reversions in global production chains encouraged by supply decisions in local markets.

Starting in the 1990s, global production and value chains grew steadily. Since 2007, with the outbreak of the economic and financial crisis, the indicators of globalization processes show a trend of decrease in global production and supply chains due to a drop in demand from international markets and not so much to the structural changes. Since the financial crisis of 2008-2009, world trade has failed to maintain the level of world GDP due to the emergence of protectionist policies (WTO, 2021). Global economic, financial, health, and contingency crises such as natural disasters have a domino effect that has a greater impact on global production and value chains (FAO, 2021). An example is the tsunami in Japan in 2011 that affected global automobile production chains.

These stagnations in economic globalization processes have negative effects on the global economy due to the relocation of the production chain, although the reorientation may have some positive effects for certain national territories where some phases of this production chain can be carried out to take advantage of low labor costs. Reversing or slowing down the processes of economic globalization will mean changes in the practices and activities of multinational and transnational companies.

## Fragmentation of Global Supply Chain

In 2019 there is a high fragmentation of global supply chains, which is deepened by the 2020 health crisis. The ruptures of global supply chains produce a dislocation of production that produces in response to the withdrawal of companies located abroad for The Coronavirus has paralyzed the growth of global trade, which contributes to more than 60% of the domestic product world gross (Ellyat, 2021). This situation has been called deglobalization, aggravated by the health crisis, which has made interconnections more difficult for commercial practices between different countries.

The current scenario of the health crisis has affected the complex global supply and value chains of intermediate goods without being able to stop their fragmentation. This has shown that global supply chains are very vulnerable and complicated for companies to immediately redesign and redirect, which has accelerated de-globalization processes.

The critical situation of the health crisis has forced the space of global logistics and supply chains to be reduced to be replaced by shorter chains in such a way that the localities for the supply of raw materials and production of inputs or parts of a product must be shorter than the places where the final product is assembled (Shih, 2020). The health crisis has highlighted the limitations of global logistics and supply chains in sectors such as electronics, automotive, aeronautical, medical equipment, pharmaceutical products, textile industry, etc. The health crisis has broken global production chains.

The inability of the globalization processes to find a way out of the relocation of the production and supply chains, as well as the inability of the national industry in many countries to produce the required sanitary material, has complicated the economic scenario. The health crisis has exposed the dysfunctionality of global and multinational supply chains, placing excessively dependent companies at vulnerability (Baldwin & di Mauro, 2020). The health crisis has affected the global production chains of countries that are prone to international trade, although it is contradictory that it depends on corporate companies that originally relocated their production processes.

The dependence on imports of inputs for national production through supply chains, has been affected by the health crisis, so many nation-states have accelerated the processes of deglobalization by strengthening the production of inputs and operations in local spaces. Deglobalization processes imply having greater controls over commercial, financial, migration, travel flows, etc., which gives rise to retreats in the global supply and production chains.

Protecting and stimulating national food supply chains can help reduce the impact caused by the health crisis of the pandemic. Global supply and value chains have proven to be inoperative amid the health crisis (Bardt et al., 2021). Multinational corporations transferred their production operations to places where costs were lower, achieving supply through long global supply chains, which were suddenly interrupted during the Covid-19 health crisis, with serious threats to paralyze the production of certain essential products such as ago-food.

## Relocation of Production and Supply Chain

Deglobalization processes attempt to unlink local production from global supply chains to reorient production towards the internal market supported by movements in favor of food self-sufficiency and sovereignty based on domestic industrial and agricultural production, undertaken by economic policies and progressive commercials and not by right-wing nationalist governments that only serve the interests of the dominant ethnic and cultural group and displace minorities and immigrants.

With the emergence of the health crisis of the pandemic, countries have had to reconsider their supply chains and value of strategic production activities, as in the case of food production. For this reason, strategic production industries are a priority for national development, which is why they are maintained and strengthened with actions such as the development of local, flexible, and fast supply chains of value chains (Boiral et al., 2021).

Globalization undergoes profound changes with the crisis of the coronavirus pandemic and will not be as we knew it before in the modes of production, distribution, and consumption and in the global production, supply, and value chains. The dynamics of contemporary globalization processes have registered a strong interruption that calls into question the entire international economic system, disrupts global supply and value chains, as well as a slowdown in all economic sectors.

The continuity of the processes of economic globalization requires leading the mitigation of the negative impacts in the production and supply chains in the global economy based on the location in places where costs are lower. The priorities of the production, distribution, and consumption systems are changing their priorities through the location of supply chains as secure as possible rather than as economically as possible as was achieved during globalization (Ibn-Mohammed et al., 2021). The economic efficiencies of globalization processes are being highly questioned with the dysfunctionality of global supply chains that lead to more protectionist economic and fiscal policies.

## Deglobalization Process

Deglobalization is a period of slowdown and decline in international economic, commercial, financial, and people flows intensified by the coronavirus that has made companies rethink the risks of global supply chains that occur in remote locations. The economic phenomenon of deglobalization of the world economy is a period marked by a decline in commercial and financial flows, intensified by the coronavirus pandemic that has caused a rethinking of the risks of the global chain of supplies that come from geographically remote locations. Disruption of the supply chains of local companies dependent on a global system generates economic losses.

With the interruption of global production and supply chains, and due to perceived risks, production and consumption turn to alternative sources of inputs, goods, and services from local suppliers, passing the acquisition cost to second term Economic deglobalization. Witt (2019) considers the strategic policies that affect the political sustainability of multinational companies, the dynamic organizations of value chain specializations and the national context in which these decisions about strategies, structures, and behaviors are made. The breakdown of global supply chains has direct consequences on the profitability of many of these multinational companies.

The main cause that has given rise to the deglobalization processes, the slowdown in the growth of the global economy, the regression of global supply and value chains, and the increase in protectionism of local economies against multilateral processes, is the reduction of the concerns about external dependence on essential supplies (Abdal & Ferreira, 2021). The regression of global supply and value logistics chains go into regression processes for different causes, such as protectionism, wage increases, and the level of income reduce the advantages of countries that were the destination of relocations. If production is less delocalized, flows in global supply and value chains are reduced, along with the investments that accompany them.

The interruption of global supply chains and, therefore, of value is a consequence of the trade wars started by countries with deficiencies in commercial and financial exchanges. The Sino-US trade war is the landmark event for furthering the tendency of deglobalization with the disruption of the global supply chain and declining global trade flows in value and volume.

The trade wars coupled with the risks of the coronavirus have caused the blockage of global supply chains and international supplies. They have been shortening their global supply and value chains for several years now, because of trade wars, through the relocation of their plants, production processes, and the manufacture of their own components that came from distant locations and through the diversification of the origin of inputs and products. Companies around the world rethink their internationalization decisions as a reaction to dependence on global supply chains that distribute the production of products with the relocation of their plants and their production processes (Nandi et al., 2021). This situation has shown the vulnerability of companies due to their excessive dependence on these chains.

## Effect of Deglobalization

Deglobalization manifests itself in changes in production systems based on the locations where production is most efficient, leading to many logistical mismatches in supply chains and value in trade connections. The creation of alternative supply chains modifies the rules of globalization processes. For the United States, the intensity of globalization shows vulnerabilities, such as in situations where national economies depend on a single country for the supply of goods, which leads to the blockage of supply chains (Nandi et al., 2021).

Global supply chains are more complex in the production, distribution, and consumption of products that have had to be interrupted or reduced due to the lack of provision of essential components. Globalization is transformed to be different than it was before the pandemic and it is possible that the modes of production, distribution, and consumption are transformed due to changes in the global value, provision, and supply chains.

Destructuring the networks in which currently major strategic activities are included in supply chains, production, management, and distribution on a global scale are organized and interconnected in real time on a sophisticated information and communication system. Companies are moving away from just-in-time production systems to more secure supply chains. The reduction of global supply and value chains negatively affects commercial, financial, investment and people flow. The deglobalization processes are pressing the global production, provision, and value chains to change in organizational forms subject to local decisions.

Multinational companies are already reconsidering their logistics processes for the transport of goods that include socio-ecosystem concerns to try to shorten geographic distances and links in their global supply chains through the use and development of new technologies that reduce the costs and risks of production, increase quality, and respond more quickly to market demand. Multinational companies reconfigure global value chains to strengthen themselves in the face of shocks.

National economies are bounded together in globalization through the supply chains to achieve manufacturing efficiency and better prices in international trade. The flow of international business activities is retracted as global supply and supply chains are reconfigured, prioritizing production over economic efficiency. Business organizations are assessing the location of global supply chains relocating their production elsewhere, which is a globalization trend of natural churn and premises (Paul & Dhir, 2021). International trade replicates its operations while reconfiguring its supply chains sacrificing economic efficiencies in exchange for greater security in the provision of its inputs. International trade is territorially withdrawn to the nation through the reconfiguration of its production chains and supply, leading to importers raising tariff barriers.

Populist and nationalist nation-states have taken up this message, supported by political parties and social organizations to promote actions to deglobalize the economy that attempt to dismantle globalization through withdrawals of global value chains, repatriation of investments, and strategic relocation of Business.

Global supply chains are relocated, which implies the reorganization of production, distribution, and commercialization activities, reinforced with government policies, especially in sectors considered of national security. Returning plants to the country of origin can be more expensive, but in the current conditions of interrupted global supply chains, it turns out to be more productive and competitive due to savings in logistics risks, transportation, tariffs, etc. The reduction of dependence on the provision of supplies from other geographically distant locations through global chains of manufactured inputs has led to relocation or reshoring trends. Not only are the production sites relocated close to the markets, but also innovation, design, logistics, distribution, marketing activities, etc.

New technologies advance innovations in automation, robotization, artificial intelligence, internet of things, etc., which tend to replace the more routine and cheap labor, which implies that global supply and value chains reduce their importance with localized and robotic production.

The deglobalization trend converted into regional trade agreements allows economies to be fully integrated and to take advantage of regional and local value chains. From the crisis that economic globalization is going through, companies that have fewer global supply chains, more regional and therefore shorter with respect to assembly or marketing lines, will emerge strengthened, not necessarily from lower cost suppliers and with minimal inventory levels, which confirms deglobalization. The interruptions of the global supply chains forced people and companies to look for alternative local or regional sources of supply, even though they were more expensive.

The less advanced economies have seen their global value chains reduced with premature processes of deindustrialization, lower economic growth, a commodity boom that has given rise to the Dutch disease phenomenon, non-redistributive and regressive fiscal reforms with an increase in income levels of poverty and inequality. Countries are backtracking in their globalization advances and trying to avoid the continuity of outsourced production chains to maintain strategic production activities internally or as regionally as possible, with more flexible and faster local value chains.

The blockade of global supply chains represents the opportunity for Mexico to be the beneficiary due to its proximity to the North American market, as has been the case in the automotive, electronics, and aeronautical sectors. Without the supplies produced in Mexico by these industrial sectors, the manufacturing of finished products is interrupted. Deglobalization and the T-MEC favor the rapid integration of the sectors of the electrical, automotive, medical equipment, aeronautical, pharmaceutical, aeronautical industries, etc., to the supply chains of North American companies. Complementation among the member countries of the T-MEC facilitates regional integration processes and solves the problem of supply and logistics chains.

Risk assessment focuses on disturbances in production processes mainly due to supply chains of inputs that come from geographically distant locations, or other phenomena such as natural disasters, wars, etc. One of the risks that are run with deglobalization is derived from geopolitical and geoeconomics uncertainty and its impact on investments with repercussions on production levels for global supply chains, exports, and market volatility. Companies have reacted to the perception of risks through a strategy of geographic diversification of sources of supply and production that can affect global trade as production is relocated in the country itself.

The inability of the globalization processes to find a way out of the relocation of the production and supply chains, as well as the inability of the national industry in many countries to produce the required sanitary material, has complicated the economic scenario.

## SOLUTIONS AND RECOMMENDATIONS

In a free market system under the invisible hand, companies continue to track the location of their production, distribution, and consumption systems through offshoring or relocation decisions that mean benefits and cost efficiency. Tensions and trade wars accelerated the de-globalization processes under the premise of relocating the production and supply of resources from sources as close as possible, which confirms the trend towards open regionalism.

The processes of economic and financial de-globalization propose that local economies should be reoriented in short circuits towards production for local consumption, avoiding the relocation of companies that generate competition because they look for places where labor costs are lower, production standards and ecological are less restrictive, etc. On the other hand, foreign direct investment movements facilitate the relocation of production systems in global factories, taking advantage of the advantages offered by other national economies in cheap labor, more direct transport systems, the privatization of public companies, etc. The relocation of production is manifested in the flows of direct foreign investment (Grunwald & Flamm, 1985).

The relocation of production processes is mainly due to the increase in the level of income and wages of the developing countries that are the destination, which reduces the advantages to relocating. Delocalized production of companies motivated by lower production costs is returning to a closer place through relocation or reshoring processes. Discontent over the growing impoverishment of the working middle classes in the most developed countries, the precariousness of employment and labor benefits, and the loss of employment due to the relocation and flight of companies to locations where labor costs are lower. The advantages for relocating production, distribution, and consumption systems have been reduced due to an increase in the income and living standards of workers in the countries that were the destination of these relocations.

There are several reasons that are making the processes of economic globalization dysfunctional to the growth and development of some countries, such as the loss of their political and economic sovereignty, growth in unemployment due to the relocation of production, and the increase in automated systems and robotization, which also reduces relocations.

Companies have reacted to the perception of risks through a strategy of geographic diversification of sources of supply and production that can affect global trade as production is relocated in the country itself. Extraterritoriality characterizes economic globalization (Palomares, 2006, p. 30) because of the capacity that transnational companies must relocate production with geographic fragmentation. In such a way, this trend of regional proximity of production occurs, pointing to the relocation of production processes in countries that belong to the same economic region. The processes of regionalization of production are a trend in proximity to consumer markets that ensures the supply of resources, goods, and services in places to consumer markets to respond quickly and flexibly to demand through customization or product customization.

With globalization, companies become more dependent on the places from which the inputs and products necessary for production are provided, so national states are now offering incentives to their companies to return operations that they had relocated to other countries. The continuity of the processes of economic globalization currently marks a break in the breakdown of international economic relations that, although it attempts to relocate production, the competition for the attraction of talent, technology, and more advanced production capacity.

Relocation as a strategy of deglobalization processes has as immediate consequences the increase in labor costs due to differentials between nations, but also to the health crisis, with a tendency to reduce economic inequality. Another trend that accelerates because of relocation is robotization, which in times of pandemic is positive because it reduces the risks of contagion by eliminating or reducing face-to-face contacts. Another trend is the increase and consolidation of teleworking, with many implications for people's movements and the market for office space, parking lots, etc.

The increase in e-commerce is a trend that increases more with relocation and the health crisis of the pandemic. Pandemics have shown the risks that the globalized economy has under the logic of relocation of production to take advantage of lower costs that are then marketed in other regions of the world without establishing the pertinent health controls.

## FUTURE RESEARCH DIRECTIONS

Deglobalization processes and their implications on global supply chains remain a topic for future research, which can be presented in scenarios of their future development. A first scenario is one of the soft changes that do not modify the structures of international institutions but that focus on regulating distortions to free trade, as well as the conditions imposed on developing countries. The deconstruction of globalization processes, known as deglobalization, must be for a better reconstruction that truly integrates humanity through economic, political, and social change, and does not disintegrate. This change requires weakening the hegemony of the system of globalizing institutional powers, delegitimizing its ideology and its rules.

On the implications of digital technologies in supply chain values, international governance needs the potential transformation of information and communication technologies for the research and analysis of big data. The integration of the process of economic globalization requires the use of digital technologies for the world government function through the institutionalization, market, and global redistribution functions. The design and implementation of economic policies to promote the positive effects of the digital and political dimensions and eliminate the negative ones of economic globalization processes, enhance global governance and economic integration.

Another important issue to study in the future is the relocation of companies to places of production and local consumption. It is supported by protectionist regulations, recovery of customs fees on imported goods and services, control of capital transfers, levies on financial transactions.

Another topic to be considered for future research is the current deglobalization processes that show a clear subordination of emerging and less developed countries to powerful international financial interests, international organizations, and multinational companies. The construction of alternative integration processes requires national initiatives under a scheme different from the capitalist financial and transnational capital, not only at the economic and commercial level, which is supported by self-organization and self-management to satisfy social needs. These alternative processes of deglobalization have multiple economic, social, environmental, political, sociocultural, gender dimensions, etc. For the deglobalization alternatives to deepen their changes, they must acquire the character of anti-capitalism.

An analysis should be conducted on the difficulties for the processes of economic globalization to be completely reversed, after necessary adjustments that have slowed down progress to overcome the health crisis and the crisis of neoliberal financial capitalism. The construction of alternative integration processes requires national initiatives under a scheme different from the capitalist financial and transnational capital, not only at the economic and commercial level, which is supported by self-organization and self-management to satisfy social needs. These alternative processes of deglobalization have multiple economic, social, environmental, political, sociocultural, gender dimensions, etc.

## CONCLUSION

The post-pandemic world economy tends to be less globalized as it is rejected by national governments and populations to protect their national economies. The processes of economic globalization are deepening instead of a gradual process of deglobalization, under the argument of the principle of sovereignty with economic policies and measures that show a tendency towards a nationalist, protectionist, and populist retreat. The actions of national states and international organizations promoting globalization processes such as regional integration treaties for free trade tend to weaken the sovereignty of the states. This is somewhat paradoxical in its contradictory processes due to its origin of globalized localisms that have contributed to strengthening hierarchies and inequalities both between nations and between individuals. It creates victims who lack the protection of the state subject to their localities or force the state to abandon them.

The world order that has prevailed since the Second World War has been considered under the conception of linear processes of irreversible economic globalization and has undergone structural changes in the last ten years that require reconfiguration. This reconfiguration has been called a deglobalization stage and corresponds to a regression of global integration processes in the form of retractions in world trade and international financial investments carried out through nationalist, populist, and protectionist policies.

The movement of trade protectionism as a retreat from the processes of economic globalization with the renegotiation of trade agreements and trade wars was initiated by the United States. The trade war declared by the United States against China tries to weaken its strategic position in economic growth, cooperation, trade, finance, etc. The phenomenon of deglobalization is a popular political cause motivated by protectionist and reindustrializing economic forces.

The nation-states face great challenges to guarantee the protection of the minimum welfare of the citizens. Another consequence of the reversal of the global integration of production processes is the increase in costs and, therefore, consumer prices, which results in a drop in welfare. From an ethical perspective, deglobalization processes should give higher priority to values over interests, cooperative relationships over the competition, and community welfare over efficiency. From this same perspective, real economic thinking strengthens the values of social solidarity, justice, equity, and community to subordinate the action of the market.

Local economies must exercise fiscal and economic policy mechanisms for the protection of their own production, distribution, and consumption systems, as well as their socio-ecosystems from the subsidized importation of large transnational corporations that establish subsidized and artificial prices. A viable alternative as a sample is the emergence of large self-centered spaces that are constituted as poles of economic, political, social, cultural, and civilization power.

The new nationalist and protectionist sentiments that drive the decisions of the n countries have a high impact on migrant workers who seek better economic conditions and greater well-being for their families. Nation-states can prevent the flight of endogenous technological talent to other economies by creating institutional and instrumental frameworks for the establishment and protection of competitive advantages through reindustrialization processes.

## REFERENCES


Abdal, A., & Ferreira, D. M. (2021). Deglobalization, globalization, and the pandemic: Current impasses of the capitalist world-economy. *Journal of World-systems Research*, *27*(1), 202–230. doi:10.5195/jwsr.2021.1028

Baldwin, R., & di Mauro, B. W. (Eds.). (2020). *Economics in the time of COVID-19*. CEPR Press.

Bardt, H., Ezell, S., Flores, T., González, N., Hattingh, C., Randolph, S., & Bandini, C. (2021). *Global value chains after the COVID-19 Crisis*. Global Trade and Innovation Policy Alliance.

Barykin, S. E., Kapustina, I. V., Korchagina, E. V., Sergeev, S. M., Yadykin, V. K., Abdimomynova, A., & Stepanova, D. (2021). Digital logistics platforms in the BRICS countries: Comparative analysis and development prospects. *Sustainability*, *13*(20), 11228. doi:10.3390u132011228

Bello, W. (2013). *Capitalism's last stand? Deglobalization in the age of austerity*. Zed Books. doi:10.5040/9781350218895

Boiral, O., Brotherton, M.-C., Rivaud, L., & Guillaumie, L. (2021). Organizations' management of the COVID-19 pandemic: A scoping review of business articles. *Sustainability, 2021*(13), 3993. doi:10.3390u13073993

Broadberry, S., & Harrison, M. (2005). *The economics of World War I*. Cambridge University Press. doi:10.1017/CBO9780511497339

Didea, L., & Ilie, D. M. (2020). The State of emergency and the economic repercussions. A new "Avalanche" of Insolvencies. *J.L. & Admin. Sci, 89*(13).

Doh, J., Budhwar, P., & Wood, G. (2021). Long-term energy transitions and international business: Concepts, theory, methods, and a research agenda. *Journal of International Business Studies, 52*(5), 951–970. doi:10.105741267-021-00405-6 PMID:33716348

Ellyat, H. (2021). *Supply chain chaos is already hitting global growth. And it's about to get worse*. CNBC.

FAO. (2021). *The impact of disasters and crises on agriculture and food security*. Food and Agriculture Organization of United Nations.

Findlay, R., & O'Rourke, K. (2008). Power and Plenty: Trade, War, and the World Economy in the Second Millennium. Princeton University Press.

Gaillard, N. (2020). *Country risk. Subtitle the bane of foreign investors*. Springer., doi:10.1007/978-3-030-45788-4

Grunwald, J., & Flamm, K. (1985). *The global factory: Foreign assembly in international trade*. Brookings Institution.

Ibn-Mohammed, T., Mustapha, K. B., Godsell, J., Adamu, Z., Babatunde, K. A., Akintade, D. D., Acquaye, A., Fujii, H., Ndiaye, M. M., Yamoah, F. A., & Koh, S. C. L. (2021). A critical analysis of the impacts of COVID-19 on the global economy and ecosystems and opportunities for circular economy strategies. *Resources, Conservation and Recycling, 164*, 105169. Advance online publication. doi:10.1016/j.resconrec.2020.105169 PMID:32982059

IMCO. (2020). *Deglobalization. Implications for investors*. Oxford Economics.

Irwin, D. A. (2020). *The pandemic adds momentum to the deglobalization trend*. Peterson Institute for International Economics.

James, H. (2018). Deglobalization: The rise of disembedded unilateralism. *Annual Review of Financial Economics, 10*(1), 219–237. doi:10.1146/annurev-financial-110217-022625

Javorcik, B. (2020, Apr. 2). Coronavirus will change the way the world does business for good businesses will be forced to rethink their global value chains. *Financial Times.*

Kano, L., Tsang, E. W. K., & Yeung, H. (2020). Global value chains: A review of the multi-disciplinary literature. *Journal of International Business Studies, 51*(4), 577–622. doi:10.105741267-020-00304-2

Liu, W., Dunford, M., & Gao, B. A. (2018). Discursive construction of the belt and road initiative: From neo-liberal to inclusive globalization. *Journal of Geographical Sciences, 28*(9), 1199–1214. doi:10.100711442-018-1520-y

Meyer, K., & Peng, M. (2016). Theoretical foundations of emerging economy business research. *Journal of International Business Studies*, *47*(1), 3–22. doi:10.1057/jibs.2015.34

Nandi, S., Sarkis, J., Hervani, A. A., Helms, M. M. (2021). Redesigning supply chains using blockchain-Enabled circular economy and COVID-19 experiences. *Sustainable Production and Consumption*. . doi:10.1016/j.spc.2020.10.019

Napolitano, G. (2011, April). The two ways of global governance after the financial crisis: Multilateralism versus cooperation among governments. *International Journal of Constitutional Law*, *9*(2), 310–339. doi:10.1093/icon/mor038

Palomares, G. (2006). *Relaciones internacionales en el siglo XXI*. Tecnos.

Paul, J., & Dhir, S. (Eds.). (2021). *Globalization, deglobalization, and new paradigms in business*. Palgrave Macmillan. doi:10.1007/978-3-030-81584-4

Petrini, C. (2001). *Slow food, the case for taste*. Columbia University Press.

QinJ. Y. (2020). *WTO reform: Multilateral control over unilateral retaliation – Lessons from the US-China trade war.* Wayne State University Law School Research Paper No. 2020-73. https://ssrn.com/abstract=3654510 doi:10.2139/ssrn.3654510

Rasiah, R., Gammeltoft, P., & Jiang, Y. (2010). Home government policies for outward FDI from emerging economies: Lessons from Asia. *International Journal of Emerging Markets*, *5*(3/4), 333–357. doi:10.1108/17468801011058415

Reinalda, B. (2009). *Routledge history of international organizations: From 1815 to the present day*. Routledge. doi:10.4324/9780203876572

Rodrik, D. (2000). How far will international economic integration go? *The Journal of Economic Perspectives*, *14*(1), 177–186. doi:10.1257/jep.14.1.177

Rodrik, D. (2007). *One economics many recipes, globalization, institutions and economic growth*. Princeton University Press. doi:10.1515/9781400829354

Sapir, J. (2011). *La demondialisation*. Seuil.

Sapir, J. (2016). Jacques Sapir: Donald Trump, président de la démondialisation? *Le Figaro,* 10. https://www.lefigaro.fr/vox/monde/2016/11/10/31002-20161110ARTFIG00233-jacques-sapir-donald-trump-president-de-la-demondialisation.php

Shavshukov, V. M., & Zhuravleva, N. A. (2020). Global economy: New risks and leadership problems. *Int. J. Financial Stud*, *8*(1), 7. doi:10.3390/ijfs8010007

Shih, W. C. (2020). Global supply chain in a post-pandemic world. *Harvard Business Review*, (September-October), 2020.

Spero, J. E., & Hart, J. A. (1997). *The Politics of International Economic Relations*. Routledge., doi:10.4324/9781315006154

Steinberg, F. (2005). *Cooperación y conflicto en el Sistema comercial multilateral: La organización mundial de comercio como institución de gobernanza económica global.* Tesis Doctoral presentada en el Departamento de Análisis Económico: Teoría Económica e Historia Económica de la Facultada de Ciencias Económicas y Empresariales de la Universidad Autónoma de Madrid, España.

Vanham, P. (2019). *A brief history of globalization.* World Economic Forum.

Witt, M. A. (2019). De-globalization: Theories, predictions, and opportunities for international business research. *Journal of International Business Studies, 50*(7), 1053–1077. doi:10.105741267-019-00219-7

World Bank. (2016). *World Bank data.* http://data.worldbank.org/?display=default

WTO. (2021). *World trade report 2021. Economic resilience and trade.* World Trade Organization.

Zhu, G., Chou, M. C., & Tsai, C. W. (2020). Lessons learned from the COVID-19 pandemic exposing the shortcomings of current supply chain operations: A long-term prescriptive offering. *Sustainability, 12*(14), 5858. doi:10.3390u12145858

## ADDITIONAL READING

Antras, P. (2020). *Conceptual aspects of global value chains.* Discussion Paper. No. DP14191. Centre for Economic Policy Research.

Armando, E., Azevedo, A. C., Fischmann, A. A., & Costa Pereira, C. E. (2016). Business strategy and upgrading in global value chains: A multiple case study in Information Technology firms of Brazilian origin. *RAI Revista de Administração e Inovação, 13*(1), 39–47. doi:10.1016/j.rai.2016.01.002

Ferrantino, M., & Koten, E. E. (2019). *Understanding supply chain 4.0 and its potential impact on global value chains. Global Value Chain Development Report.* World Trade Organization.

Govindan, K., Mina, H., & Alavi, B. A. (2020). Decision support system for demand management in healthcare supply chains considering the epidemic outbreaks: A case study of coronavirus disease 2019 (COVID-19). *Transp. Res. E Logist. Transport Reviews, 138*, 101967. PMID:32382249

Hernández, V., & Pedersen, T. (2017). Global value chain configuration: A review and research agenda. *BRQ Business Research Quarterly, 20*(2), 137–150. doi:10.1016/j.brq.2016.11.001

Ivanov, D. (2020). Viable supply chain model: Integrating agility, resilience and sustainability perspectives. Lessons from and thinking beyond the COVID-19 pandemic. *Annals of Operations Research, 288*, 1–21. doi:10.100710479-020-03640-6 PMID:32836614

Ivanov, D., & Dolgui, A. (2020). Viability of intertwined supply networks: Extending the supply chain resilience angles towards survivability. A position paper motivated by COVID-19 outbreak. *International Journal of Production Research, 58*(10), 2904–2915. doi:10.1080/00207543.2020.1750727

Kano, L., Tsang, E. W. K., & Yeung, H. (2020). Global value chains: A review of the multi-disciplinary literature. *Journal of International Business Studies, 51*(4), 577–622. doi:10.105741267-020-00304-2

Kot, S., Haque, U. A., & Baloch, A. (2020). Supply chain management in smes: Global perspective. *Montenegrin J. Econ, 16*(1), 87–104. doi:10.14254/1800-5845/2020.16-1.6

Min, S., Zhang, X., & Li, G. (2020). A snapshot of food supply chain in Wuhan under the COVID-19 pandemic. *China Agricultural Economic Review, 12*(4), 689–704. doi:10.1108/CAER-04-2020-0056

Nagao, T., Ijuin, H., Yamada, T., Nagasawa, K., & Zhou, L. (2022). COVID-19 disruption strategy for redesigning global supply chain network across TPP countries. *Logistics., 6*(1), 2. doi:10.3390/logistics6010002

Pla-Barber, J., Villar, C., & Narula, R. (2021). Governance of global value chains after the Covid-19 pandemic: A new wave of regionalization? *BRQ Business Research Quarterly, 24*(3), 204–213. doi:10.1177/23409444211020761

Rodrik, D. (2018). *New technologies, global value chains, and the developing economies. Background Paper Series, No. 1.* Pathways for Prosperity Commission. doi:10.3386/w25164

Shi, D., Chen, Z., Marzena, H.-S., Razaque, L. A., & Zahid, R. M. (2021). The role of the global value chain in improving trade and the sustainable competitive advantage: Evidence from China's manufacturing industry. *Frontiers in Environmental Science, 9.* https://www.frontiersin.org/articles/10.3389/fenvs.2021.779295/full

World Trade Organization. (2021). *Global value chain development report 2021 beyond production.* Asian Development Bank., doi:10.22617/TCS210400-2

## KEY TERMS AND DEFINITIONS

**Deglobalization:** The slow-down or reverse of globalization. A political project opposed to neoliberal globalization. In the first definition, the term describes how global flows of trade, investment, and migration can decline.

**Global Supply Chain:** A set of activities, facilities, and means of distribution throughout the world necessary to carry out the entire sales process of a product. This is from the search for raw materials, their subsequent transformation, and their transportation and delivery to the final consumer anywhere in the world.

**Production Chain:** A system made up of people and companies related to each other by a succession of production operations.

**Protectionism:** A commercial policy established by a government that aims to protect the national industry against foreign competition with the application of tariffs or any other type of import restriction.

**Relocation of Production:** The international displacement of a production structure.

**Value Chains:** A theoretical model that graphs and allows to describe the activities of an organization to generate value to the end customer and to it.

# Chapter 14
# Evolutional Characteristics of the Global Supply Chain in Various Industries

**Yanghua Zhou**
*Edogawa University, Japan*

## ABSTRACT

*In this chapter, a literature review and abstract analysis is conducted on the evolutional characteristics of the global supply chain in various industries of the developed country of Japan and the emerging economy of China, respectively. It finds that in both countries, with the advancement of Industry 4.0, high-tech approaches, such as big data, AI, and DX, are gradually being utilized in the GSC. These approaches greatly contribute to its improvement in terms of efficiency, performance, and anti-risk capabilities. In addition, reducing costs and raising efficiency are effective measures for optimizing the GSC. Specifically, warehouse integration, positioning of warehouses, matching and sharing consumers' needs with both suppliers and agencies, further informatization and visualization of goods, innovative packing methods, reducing container numbers, and storage points are worth considering. A common SC platform and better SC resilience are expected. Other specific measures are also discussed.*

## INTRODUCTION

This chapter discusses the characteristics of global supply chains based on a literature review and cases from Asia. The supply chain (SC) is a crucial aspect of company management. The SC includes the entire process, from material supply to after-service. In this process, not only material and products are considered, but information and money are also the objectives of management (Bowersox, D. J., & Closs, 1996; Chopra, 2015). From the perspective of the resource-based view and competitive advantage, the SC has a significant strategic influence on a company's performance and social image.

The global SC (GSC) of a multinational corporation (MNC) refers to material imports, managing overseas factories, product exports, and interaction with foreign countries. The GSC has a broader range, including international business and cross-cultural management. Free On Board (FOB) is the main

DOI: 10.4018/978-1-7998-9800-9.ch014

style of the SC in the USA. Meanwhile, the cost insurance and freight (CIF) style is adopted in most cases in Japan (Kurosu & Iwama, 2017). However, there is an increasing number of MNCs in Japan, and they need to conduct business with foreign consumers, foreign companies, or overseas subsidiaries. Consequently, they face GSC-related strategies and issues. During the coronavirus disease (COVID-19) pandemic crisis, Komatsu of Japan stabilized its GSC because of its reasonable global logistics distribution. During this crisis, many Japanese factories and manufacturers had to reduce working hours or stop work altogether. However, Komatsu managed to deploy materials and parts from its overseas logistics base, which contributed to its survival during this crisis.

Sun, Fu, & Jiang (2020) conducted an empirical study on the degree of SC concentration and overinvestment based on the data (2008–2017) of Chinese listed companies. According to Sun et al. (2020), the relationship between supplier and client has positive and negative impacts on a company. The concentration of the SC has a reverse U-shaped relationship with overinvestment. Further group tests show that this relationship is more evident in private enterprises and when the degree of industry prosperity is relatively low. Hence, SCs are important for companies in both developed and developing economies.

The GSC in both developed countries and emerging economies is experiencing a revolution. However, the progress in and characteristics of various industries are different. Srinivasan et al. (2021) proposed a typology of SC types, strategies, and people management according to product complexity and environmental uncertainty (Table 1). Hence, this chapter aims to identify its evolutionary features across diverse industries in Japan and China through an analysis of the literature.

## BACKGROUND

With the influence of globalization in developed countries such as Japan, many transformations have occurred in the SC. Artificial intelligence (AI) has been used to control automatic program systems in many manufacturing factories. Meanwhile, robots are fully used to deliver postal matters or work in factories to handle parts of the products. Drones are also utilized to manage farm production systems. Moreover, many industries are conducting digital transformation (DX) to control and coordinate digital data management systems. Overall, the progress in DX and AI in GSCs is a universal phenomenon in various industries. Additionally, the green SC is at a high level in Japan. A green SC means that the idea of environmental protection and resource conservation is implemented across the entire SC (Meng, Li, Yin, & Li, 2021). However, some distinctiveness still exists among these industries (e.g., technology, human resources, local and international standards, infrastructure, monopoly problems in container harbors, customs duties, barriers, and obstacles in trading; Kurosu & Iwama, 2017).

In developing countries such as China, some problems in logistics remain, which have an impact on the globalization process of the country's SC management, such as road infrastructure, quality improvement and cost reduction of logistics, safety management systems of food and medicine, standardization and professionalization of logistics, and personal networks related to business habits (Kurosu & Iwama, 2017).

## GSC INNOVATION OF JAPANESE MNCS

The term "supply chain" has been used for nearly 40 years in academic and practical business contexts. During this period, the SC business has changed significantly owing to the changing economic situa-

*Table 1. Typology of SC types, strategies, and people management*

| . | Low product complexity | High product complexity |
|---|---|---|
| High environment uncertainty | *Adoptive SC* | *Involvedly innovative SC* |
| | Examples: Computer system manufacturers, Fashion apparel | Examples: Electric vehicle manufacturers |
| | Strategy: Leagile SC strategy | Strategy: Agile SC strategy |
| | SC relationships: focused on information exchange and contractual flexibility | SC relationships: strategic relationships |
| | Culture: innovative | Culture: affiliative |
| | Leadership style: coaching | Leadership style: affiliative |
| Low environment uncertainty | *Efficient SC* | *Integrative SC* |
| | Examples: Manufacturers of standardized everyday use products such as sugar, toilet paper, soap, etc. | Examples: Aircraft, automobile, machine tool manufactures, smartphones |
| | Strategy: Planning-based SC strategy | Strategy: Lean SC strategy |
| | SC relationships: operational linkages/transactional relationship | SC relationships: focus on asset-based integrative relationships |
| | Culture: market | Culture: perfectionist |
| | Leadership style: authoritative | Leadership style: democratic |

Source: (Srinivasan et al., 2021).

tion and the development of other businesses in various countries. In Japan, GSCs have also played a significant role in the international business of MNCs. This section introduces the innovation of the GSC of Japanese MNCs in recent years.

## Motor Industry (Toyota Motor Thailand)

Toyota Motor Thailand (TMT) was established in Bangkok in 1962 (Wikipedia, 2022). It has developed well over the past 50 years in many fields. Its GSC also achieved good performance and contributed to the entire company's development, especially during the financial crisis of 1997.

One of the most distinctive features of the SC of TMT is the subcontract between this transnational corporation and local small- and middle-sized enterprises (SMEs) (Kuriyama, 2017). With this type of subcontract, small-sized suppliers can provide innovative parts rapidly to product makers, which contributes well to the entire SC of this industry. Under this subcontract, small-sized suppliers frequently communicate with large transnational corporations to discuss what should be adjusted and how they are realized. As Thailand has many types of small-sized suppliers, such as Toyota-owned Japanese joint ventures, non-Japanese joint ventures, and pure Thai firms, these suppliers are able to innovate in terms of technology, functions, and designs of the parts (Kuriyama, 2017). This increases the attractiveness of the final products of TMT, a transnational corporation. TMT gives the entrance authority to SMEs to its innovation center and corporate training programs and then mentors programs to develop SMEs in both quality management and future improvement. It also offers managerial and technician consultations with SMEs (Kuriyama, 2017).

TMT formed a supplier association in Thailand, where suppliers can participate in training programs and learn how to manage and improve cost-and quality-related issues. This technique helps foster the support of the supplier industry and is quite useful for the upgrade of the local SC (Kuriyama, 2017). It also has a positive trickle-down effect on small firm development, the emergence of auto parts suppliers, and the creation of industrial clusters. Additionally, during the financial crisis in 1997, TMT provided increased capital to maintain the minimal operation of the local SC, which succeeded in ensuring that the entire industry survived and the SC was more resilient.

In addition to technical assistance, to maintain the normal operation of the SC, TMT provided co-operation on human resource development, such as technology-related training for local employees, so that they could master the necessary technology rapidly. Sometimes, the company assigns staff to SMEs.

With the partnership of supplier association and assistance in human resource management, TMT succeeded in building long-term cooperation relationships with suppliers, contributing to the smooth operation of the local SC.

## Household Appliance Industry

In the household appliance industry, because of yen appreciation and changes in promotion channels, the overseas production rate increased from 2004. However, due to competition in the international market, an increasing number of white goods from developing countries entered the international market. Their prices are not as high as those of developed countries, and their quality is decent. Hence, they have gained consumer attention, and this created a significant loss to several famous Japanese home appliance makers. To address this situation of financial deficit, many solutions and strategies have been considered in terms of many facets of management, including logistics.

To reduce logistics costs, Toshiba conducted a series of transformations (Kurosu & Iwama, 2017). First, it decreased the number of domestic distribution bases to two: one in the eastern area and the other in the western area. The company also reduces import container drayage costs. Second, it changes its transport model in logistics. Previously, the white goods of Toshiba were delivered from the manufacturer to electronics retail stores. However, after this transformation, home appliances were sent from the manufacturer to logistics centers of every mass retailer, thereby also decreasing the cost of delivery to some extent. Third, Toshiba placed its overseas distribution hub in Guangdong province, China, the main production base of Toshiba. At that time, the reservation costs of goods in Guangdong province were reasonable. This also contributes to the cost transformation of the company. Fourth, the company adopted mixed sending to reduce the number of containers for transportation. Specifically, washing machines and microwave ovens were placed on the upper space of refrigerators to conserve space efficiently and to reduce the number of containers further. Moreover, Toshiba adjusted and modified the packing volume of goods to reduce the number of containers. Fifth, to realize workload reduction and quality improvement, the company conducted a unitization measure on small-sized household appliances during the transportation process. Thus, man-hours can be reduced, and logistics quality can be increased. Another effective method to ensure the quality of transportation is to simplify package printing to avoid being rubbed during long-term transportation in a container.

## Logistics Industry

With globalization, many changes and innovations have also occurred in the logistics industry in Japan. This industry includes many world-famous companies, such as Amazon, Yamato, Sagawa, and Mitsui-Soko. This results in an increasing need for warehouses and other logistics facilities because of

*Figure 1. The transition of e-commerce market size (Trillion Dollars)*
*Source: (Nagasawa, 2018)*

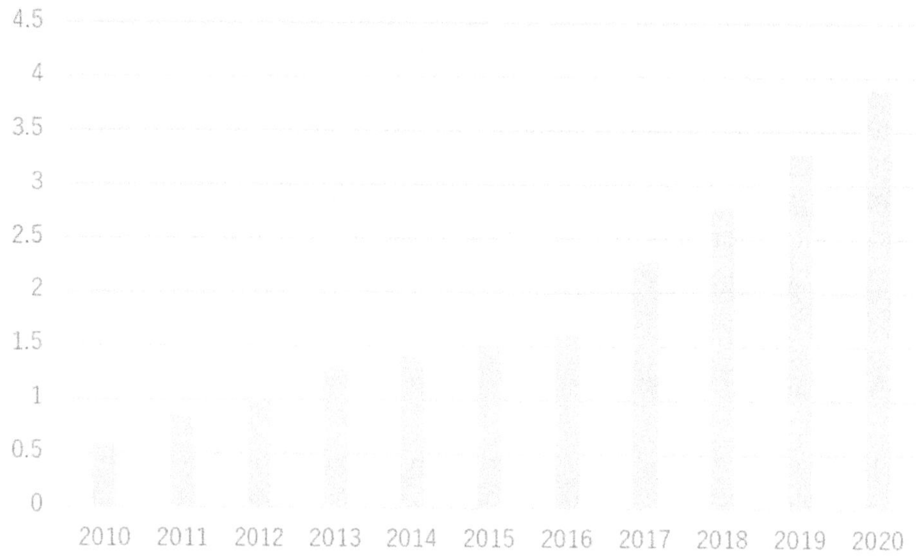


e-commerce and third-party logistics (3PL) (Nagasawa, 2018). Figures 1 and 2 show recent transitions. Figure 3 represents the diffusion rate of e-commerce in USA, Japan, and UK. To meet the needs of clients and consumers, logistics companies are considering the development of logistics facilities and expanding or rebuilding warehouses to deposit more goods. In particular, rebuilding old logistics facilities is necessary because most current logistics facilities were built around 40 years ago in Japan. Earthquake resistance standards have changed recently, and thus the need for more logistics facilities with updated standards is increasing. However, the needs of some products change with season or weather, such as cold drinks and furniture. It is well known that, in summer, people need more cold drinks, but in winter, these needs reduce drastically. Similarly, new employees typically enter companies in April, so house-moving is necessary. Thus, buying or selling furniture is at a higher level in this month than in other months. Considering these quantity changes of goods, the period when many warehouses are empty, which brings loss to logistics companies, can be easily determined. Hence, these warehouses should be fully used to reduce management costs. This creates a new business idea of sharing warehouses and rental-type logistics facilities. When goods need to be reduced and warehouses are not used fully, these warehouses may be rented by companies or individuals for other uses. This is a type of innovation in the logistics industry.

In addition, with the development of high technologies, robotics, AI, and Internet of Things (IoT) are used in the logistics industry to move goods, control management systems, and other facets. An example is the recent automatic delivery systems of Yamato at train stations. In 2017, auto-stores were used in warehouses to deposit commodities (Nagasawa, 2018). The transformation of Industry 4.0 contributes to the realization of logistics 4.0 (Table 2): Advanced logistics facilities and management styles.

Additionally, logistics facility providers consider how to utilize warehouses and business continuity plans to help clients increase the effectiveness of their business (Nagasawa, 2018). Presumably, an increasing number of robots will work in warehouses to move cargo; hence, floor precision should be increased. In this manner, another result of innovation in this industry will be the functional change of logistics facilities. Hence, innovation in the logistics industry includes rebuilding warehouses, increasing rental-styled warehouses, and changing the function of logistics facilities.

*Figure 2. The expanding of 3-PL market (Billion Yen)*
*Source: (Nagasawa, 2018)*

*Figure 3. The diffusion rate of e-commerce in 3 countries (%)*
*Source: (Nagasawa, 2018).*

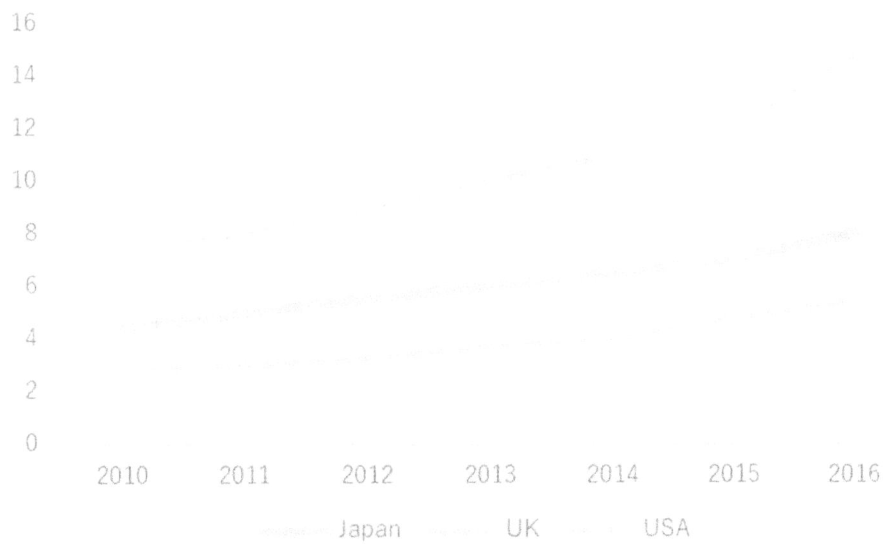

*Table 2. Logistics 4.0*

| | | **Provided value** | **>Specific cases** |
|---|---|---|---|
| Connect | 1. Cyber physical systems | >Structuralize the connection of systems. Raise the entire quality and function<br>>Increase the connection of systems, ensure the functions, streamline the entirety to reduce costs | >Modulization |
| | 2. New quality connectivity | >Connect real and virtual to reduce manufacturing time drastically<br>>Raise quality by faithful and real reproduction of virtual development | >Virtual simulation |
| Replace | 3. Smart robot and machine | >Decreasing producing time through automation advancement<br>>Deceasing the consumable materials through processing innovation | >3D printer |
| | 4. Energy efficiency and decentralization | >Protect environment better through utilizing fuel efficiently and introducing recyclable energy<br>>Reduce costs through the reduction of consumable fuel | >Electrification<br>>Energy management |
| | 5Virtual industrialization | >Reduce costs by introducing virtual construction<br>>Reduce the improving fee through early detection of problems virtually | >Virtual factory |
| Create | 6. Big data | >Reduce investment fee through highly accurate future analysis<br>>Reduce development fee through rapid and precise analysis on client needs | >Automatic operation, Predictive maintenance<br>>Various car service |
| 7. Artificial intelligence | | >Faster business innovation through the advancing of AI and Industry 4.0 | |

Source: (Nagasawa, 2018, translated by the author).

## Marine Transport Industry

In the marine transport industry, with the effect of globalization, transport needs and the quantity of merchandise are also increasing. In the early 1990s, many makers in developed countries actively used logistics services for a short time. However, in the middle of the 1990s, this logistics service style gradually became unable to satisfy the expanding marketing needs. Therefore, integration or alliances in logistics became necessary to realize the increasing frequency of larger container ship arrangements (Kurosu & Iwama, 2017). According to Kurosu and Iwama (2017), issues for future innovation in this industry include the generation of larger container ships, mechanicalizing of cargo handling, speed raising of shipping, and reducing fuel costs. To address these issues, technological innovation is necessary in terms of ship-making. Additionally, some other issues exist, such as reducing the burden on the environment by decreasing the emission of greenhouse gases generated by ship fuel, building social systems, or developing machines to support the decision-making of crews.

According to Kurosu and Iwama (2017), a company is almost impossible to accomplish an SC business only by itself. This is because the most important aspect of SCs is matching and sharing the needs of individual consumers or companies. Based on this concept, container shipping and international air companies have realized code-sharing for a period of time. Similarly, Yamato, a logistics company in Japan, has utilized the free space of local buses and electric trams. This is a matching and sharing in an early stage. The generation of alliances, shared logistics centers, and shared delivery of a common industry will increase in the future. This phenomenon will also occur in the e-commerce and household appliance industries (Kurosu & Iwama, 2017). Additionally, cooperating with various industries during the peak and slack seasons is a good strategy to use logistics resources fully. Consequently, both a platform and an ecosystem should be developed with the gradually increasing matching and sharing needs of GSCs.

## Air Transport Industry

Compared with marine transport, air transport is fast, safe, timely, and stable in temperature. The main cargo products for air transport are semiconductors, precision machinery, game machines, computers, and liquid crystal panels. With technological innovation in these products, air transport needs to provide better transport services. Furthermore, as a prospective market, Cool Japan and medication-related products, such as perishable goods and new medicines, are likely to be transported by air (Kurosu & Iwama, 2017).

## International Medical Industry

Japan has provided substantial capital assistance to the healthcare industry to better contribute to the international medical industry. Furthermore, it is considered to facilitate the international medical industry from other fields, including logistics. Professionals in this industry are studying how to improve business quality following international standards and manage risk from globalization. As the top international company in Japan's logistics, Yamato is attempting to build a total SC to meet the increasing needs of international healthcare.

## Insurance Industry

Meanwhile, the insurance system in the GSC is a significant issue and has an important influence on risk management, cargo price decisions, and transportation costs. In the international trading business, the processes of GSCs are influenced not only by the weather or fire but also by war and strikes in local regions. Hence, the insurance fee setting system and conditions must be improved with the changing environment. Before the Iraq War, the insurance fee for oil was 5% of its price, but after the war began, the insurance fee changed to 2% (40 times more). Further, the premium was 0.03% of the ship's price before the war, and it became 12 times more after the war (Kurosu and Iwama, 2017). Therefore, war has a significant impact on the insurance fee setting.

## Issues in Other Facets

To develop better GSC systems, innovation in the following aspects is necessary: optimization of the SC, organization transformation, human resource development, technology improvement in AI and information management improvement for IoT, coordination between local and international standards, addressing monopoly problems in container harbors, customs duties, barriers and obstacles in trading, and strengthening the functions of export base (Kurosu & Iwama, 2017).

Maximizing profits and reducing costs are important because they significantly influence a company's management. Hence, companies are introducing software, such as enterprise resource planning and SC planning, to perform the material and parts-related calculations (Kurosu & Iwama, 2017). With technology development, AI has also been adopted to strengthen and accomplish this control process. However, optimization in a certain period does not imply that perfectness can be maintained in the long term. Sometimes, a semi-optimal solution is the best option. Thus, the optimization issue really requires wisdom. GSCs are conducted in a multicultural environment. Therefore, understanding local culture and business habits and building a "glocal" organization are crucial. Additionally, implementing organizational transformation in corporate culture and organizational structure is necessary to better adapt to the global environment. With the globalization of business and logistics, human resources with global mindsets and professional skills in terms of the GSC, such as excellent pilots to drive drones, are increasingly needed (Kurosu & Iwama, 2017). Human resource development is a difficult issue in the logistics industry. Developing such elites for their exceptional performance in GSCs and other fields of international business requires a large amount of time and money. Professionals who have satisfactory and long SC experiences are able to participate in higher education at universities. Specifically, they are required to attend lectures in university classes or research conferences or even become professors in universities. Meanwhile, students in the academic world will understand and utilize abstract theories and knowledge better and deeper when hearing experiences from the real workplace. This contributes significantly to their positive work performance after graduation. Generally, people are in the times of an aging society, and labor is lacking. Therefore, man-hours and labor loads must be managed more efficiently to ensure work time and comfort for staff in the logistics industry.

With the development of AI, an AI system can better control the delivery process. The current place of goods or cargo can be tracked from the shared AI system, which ensures the safety and convenience of management.

Nissan is a world-famous multinational company in the automobile industry. One of its standardizations is to unify the container's size in Asia and Europe. To ensure seamless logistics, it is important that the container be used in domestic and foreign countries (Kurosu & Iwama, 2017).

According to statistics data from 2012 (Kurosu & Iwama, 2017), in the container shipping market, the Maersk Line of Denmark has the highest share at 15%. The market share of MSCs in Switzerland is 13%, that of France's CMA - CGM (COMPANIE MARITIME D'AFFERTMENT'- COMPANIE GENERAL MARITIME) is 8%, and other companies in other countries have only 4% (Nippon Yusen, 2021). Evidently, monopoly problems exist in container harbors. The interest balance in various countries must be considered as well. In the GSC, some barriers in customs procedure, barriers to entry of market, information and transport infrastructure hurt efficiency. In different countries, these factors are at various levels of development. To make the GSC operate more smoothly, the governments of these countries should improve related systems and rules so that customs procedures and barriers to entry become clear.

## Analysis Results

From the above literature review and analysis, it is evident that most industries in Japan are utilizing DX, AI, standardization, and green SC, especially in the manufacturing and logistics industries. Long-term cooperation with suppliers and agencies can reduce transaction costs between the two parties (Williamson,1979). Their GSCs are intelligent and operate at a relatively high level. However, some are still required to implement standardization with overseas countries, actualize the visualization SC, and create a digital SC to resist global crises. Sharing and integrating SCs is one of the most important innovation objectives for most industries. Almost every industry is attempting to optimize GSC to reduce costs and increase efficiency, as a quick response is an attractive quality of GSC. Under the COVID-19 crisis, an increasing number of industries have started respecting the significance of SC resilience in resisting risk.

Considering the evolutionary characteristics of various industries (Table 3), the logistics industry has utilized the current high-tech industry 4.0 (AI, IoT, robotics, auto-stores, etc.) to improve the GSC.

*Table 3. GSC innovation issues in various industries of Japan*

| Industries | Innovation issues |
|---|---|
| Motor industry | subcontract between this transnational corporation and local small- and middle-sized enterprises; supplier association; **HR development**; long-term cooperation relationships with suppliers. |
| Household appliance industry | decreased the number of domestic distribution bases; reduces import; container drayage cost; changes its transport model in logistics; placed its overseas distribution hub in Guangdong; mixed sending to reduce the number of containers; unitization measure on small-sized household appliances; **matching and sharing**; |
| Logistics industry | expanding or rebuilding warehouses; **sharing** warehouses and rental-type logistics facilities; **robotics, AI, and IoT; auto-stores;** business continuity plans |
| Marine transport industry | integration or alliances in logistics; larger container ships, mechanicalizing of cargo handling, speed raising of shipping, and reducing fuel costs; technological innovation; decreasing the emission of greenhouse gases; building social systems, or developing machines to support the decision-making of crews; optimization; **matching and sharing** the needs of individual consumers or companies |
| Air transport industry | better transport services; Cool Japan and medication-related products |
| International medical industry | substantial capital assistance; improve business quality in accordance with international standards and manage risk from globalization; customs and operation of logistics |
| Insurance industry | insurance fee setting system and conditions must be improved with the changing environment |
| e-commerce | **matching and sharing** the needs of individual consumers or companies; |
| Issues in other facets | organization transformation, human resource development, technology improvement in AI and information management improvement for IoT, coordination between local and international standards, addressing monopoly problems in container harbors, customs duties, barriers and obstacles in trading, and strengthening the functions of export base |

The manufacturing industry (e.g., Toyota Motor Thailand) implemented human resource development planning. The marine transport, e-commerce, household appliance, and logistics industries have a common vision of matching and sharing consumers' needs to improve the efficiency of the SC.

## GSC INNOVATION IN CHINA

In Asia, compared with the standardization of logistics infrastructure and seamless logistics in Europe and the USA, some problems regarding the customs and operation of logistics remain (Kurosu & Iwama, 2017). GSCs are influenced by many factors, such as the diverse facets of international business management, including the economic situation, political stability, and foreign exchange of fluctuation. In Asia, the functions and management of these facets need to be improved, especially the export base.

Hu and Tang (2021) conducted empirical research on Chinese listed companies (2009–2019) to analyze the influence of SC relationships on bank loans. Then, the higher the concentration degree of suppliers, the bigger the bank loan scale. Likewise, the higher the degree of concentration of clients, the bigger the bank loan scale. In industries with higher development and intensive competition, the concentration degree of both suppliers and clients is higher, and the significance of the bank loan scale is stronger. Other scholars are also researching the effect of SCs on supply chain finance (SCF). Hence, we can understand that the SCs of various industries impact company performance and even the development of diverse industries in China. In the next section, we consider the SC innovation situation in different industries in China and their effects.

## Automobile Industry

According to Le (2020), from January to February 2020, the sales volume of automobiles in China has reduced by 84%. Until March 2020, the loss of stop production was more than 1,200,000 vehicles. This has had a considerable impact on employment, suppliers, and the entire GSC. Because of COVID-19, many suppliers and product agencies have to shorten their working hours or even stop their schedules and work plans. Meanwhile, the needs of consumers also changed sharply, making it more difficult to manage the SC. Companies must consider more and better solutions in terms of information, materials, and capital management. As the crucial business partners of China, companies in the Japanese and Korean automobile industries suffered critical damage due to this virus crisis. Consequently, companies importing and exporting products from China faced significant losses. Hence, the positioning and strategies of the GSC, including cost control, performance improvement, and risk aversion, require deeper consideration. Some top companies in the Chinese automobile industry and logistics, such as SAIC (Shanghai Automobile Industry Corporation), Jingdong, and Shunfeng, attempt DX in management control (Le, 2020).

Automobile logistics include stock, transportation, and safekeeping. It connects makers, agents, retailers, and consumers and is an important process in automobile sales. According to Cui (2021), Chinese automobile logistics still has some stock management, delivery transportation, and information management problems. Liang (2020) states that the Chinese automobile industry's logistics have some problems in terms of corporate social responsibility, such as a relatively high turnover rate because of overtime work, environmental problems, and business competition, causing authority damage to consumers. Stability control is important for stock management. Some companies have a poor ability to manage the stability of consumers' needs, leading to high-level costs. There are mainly three stock management styles in China: a timely management model, a milk-run method, and supply hub pickup cargo management (Zhang, 2021). Under these stock management models, some problems, such as different quality of suppliers, unutilized information of logistics, target conflicts of logistics, and relatively low efficiency of cooperation among automobile makers, remain. Most automobile companies have built their own delivery systems regarding delivery transportation, which incur high costs and cause differing standards. From the GSC perspective, innovations for these issues include facilitating the development of 3PL, improving stock management, building an AI management platform, and developing contained transportation processes (Cui, 2021).

## Household Appliance Industry

In 2019, the revenue of the home appliance industry in China increased by 4.31% from that of the previous year (Zhao & Dai, 2020). The online product sales volume maintained an increasing trend although the retail industry's market needs downturn. In 2020, the COVID-19 pandemic had a negative impact on many industries, but its influence on the household appliance industry did not last long. Currently, the production and sales activities of this industry are recovering gradually. Haier, the top white goods maker in China, has been in the overseas market since 2002, including in Japan and Thailand. In global competition, the innovation and revolution in this industry is to control cost, improve efficiency, and foster adequate human resources with new technology and logistics capabilities (Zhao & Dai, 2020).

In recent years, more and more Chinese companies in this industry have adopted the M&A strategy to obtain business resources. Increasing M&A cases made it necessary for companies to actualize SC integration and cooperation. One path to actualizing this integration is the cooperation of business processes. This cooperation mechanism refers to the integration of information and logistics, using Enterprise Resource Planning (ERP), Manufacturing Execution Systems (MES), Advanced Planning and Scheduling (APS), and other systems for data sharing, effective decision making, and avoiding the bullwhip effect from incorrect information or operations (Zhao & Dai, 2020). Suppliers, manufacturers, and retailers should understand each other's situation, including the stock structure and sales status.

Another task for logistics in this industry is green SC. It refers to minimizing the influence of the entire SC on the outside environment, from obtaining materials, machining, packing, and transportation to utilizing and scrapping it. In 2015, the Chinese government promulgated the policy "Made in China 2025" to protect the environment, and in 2017, the standard system of household appliance SC management was introduced in China (Zhao & Dai, 2020). Thereafter, several green SC model companies were selected as the best examples for other companies to follow. In the medical industry, improving green SC and informatization are also important evolutionary tasks (Li, 2020; Jiang & Wang, 2021).

A digital SC is also an important objective for many logistics managers. The evolutionary target of it is the increased value in customer experience, service, the entire SC process, and the challenge of human resources (Zhao & Dai, 2020). With the development and advancement of digital technology, the customer expectations of SCs have increased exponentially. These needs should be satisfied by increasing the value of the consumer experience when they use logistics services.

Generally, the digital transformation of logistics in China lags behind that of developed countries. In 2017, the Chinese government published a guiding policy on digital transformation, emphasizing the vision of SC development. Zhao and Dai (2020) state that to actualize the digital SC, the following aspects are important: operation system transformation, AI, analysis technology, and 5G technology. Besides AI, higher analysis methods present another significant technology that can hasten the evolution of the SC. It has the merit of higher expectation ability, optimization of transportation, improving product tracking, and analyzing product returns. Combining this analysis technology with AI will be an effective expansion strategy and the result is expected to be significant (Zhao & Dai, 2020). Furthermore, 5G provides internet speeds that are 100 times faster than that of 4G. This can be utilized in automatic control, cargo tracking, transportation management, and others.

In the home industry, companies are also conducting SC-related innovation. As in other industries, visualization management and SC information systems, such as ERP, MES, warehouse management systems, and transportation management systems, are being developed and must be optimized (Qiu & Li, 2020). Many companies have adopted automatic warehouse solutions. Another revolutionary direction in this industry is the logistics network distribution of the SC. SC network distribution refers to the reasonable arrangement of suppliers, factories, regional warehouses, and hubs. Its objective is to satisfy consumer expectations, reduce costs, increase logistics speed, and strengthen anti-risk capabilities on a global scale. Furthermore, it can utilize and manage the running capital of logistics more effectively. Thus, the core competencies of a company can be built gradually.

Zhou et al. (2020) introduced the application of Handle identity resolution technology in the SC of the home appliance industry. This technology aims to improve the sharing and identity functions of products during the whole logistics process by giving white goods certain codes. Using this code, a product can be easily identified and tracked. If suppliers, manufacturers, and users provide this code, they can share the product information throughout the entire SC. This makes it easier to manage and control the SC and greatly reduces management costs. Even while producing and stocking a product, the code can be used for quick identification and to verify whether the product is in stock. This can help prevent human errors.

## Food Industry

In the food industry in China, the green SC is one of the most important evolutionary innovation tasks. It includes every logistics process, including the primary production process, food production and processing, logistics, sales, and food scrap (Cai & Jiang, 2021). Green supplier management is also important in the green SC. When selecting green suppliers, companies should do so based on a series of evaluation standards in terms of environmental management, cleanliness evaluation systems, compliance degree with environmental protection laws, and how environmental pollution is dealt with. Additionally, these standards must be adjusted according to the suppliers' category. For agriculture suppliers, the factors of irrigation level and the reasonable usage of resources are important. For sales agents, standards such as energy-saving lamps, refrigeration, and air conditioning are more relevant.

Cai and Jiang (2021) also suggest that informatization is a necessary approach for Chinese green SC management. The core corporation in the SC owns and controls the management software used to control critical products and contact partner information. They share this software with suppliers to enable them to enter product information into the system, such as places where the plants were cultivated, the quality of the soil environment, chemical fertilizers used, and sewage eluent. The core company then releases this information to the public or related partners. Meanwhile, the core company categorizes the suppliers into different levels, evaluates them, and consequently selects the best ones based on their degree of compliance with environmental protections. Companies also use system information to assess the product life cycle and link the evaluation results with the relevant suppliers. With this information on the product packaging, consumers can identify and select what they want most effectively. Such data may also be combined with other company data to be used in other related routine businesses.

Another significant innovation in the food industry is cold chain logistics. Currently, in China, aspects related to cold chain logistics-related aspects need improvement in areas such as technology, equipment and facilities, professional talent development, market planning, management, and services. This industry requires a very high level of transportation conditions. Temperature and humidity must be controlled strictly so that food quality is not impacted during this process (Cai & Jiang, 2021).

Xu, Sheng, and Wu (2021) introduced a case of SC evolution named "EC Dingdong (Getting Groceries by Dingdong)." This is an application software that can be installed on both mobile phones and computers. Using it, consumers can buy fresh vegetables and other food ingredients through the Internet. The fastest speed of the service is only 29 min from order to delivery. Lowson, King, and Hunter (2010) state that quick responses possess a number of strategic components, such as the alignment of organizational activity to demand, resource configuration, and primacy of information. Currently, the number of active users on this application is more than 1,500,000, and its daily order form has been over 200,000 (Xu et. al, 2021). The business started in 2017, and in 2021, it submitted its application documents for listing on the US stock exchange (Dingdong, 2021). Its competitive advantage is the positioning of its logistics warehouses. It takes advantage of big data and combines users' home addresses with nearby warehouses so that goods can be delivered as soon as possible. In warehouses, cold conditions are provided to ensure that food, vegetables, and other fresh commodities are well preserved. These warehouses have the capacity needed to fulfill the needs of consumers within a 1.5 km radius, ensuring that during the delivery process, goods are under cold SC conditions.

## Energy Industry

In the electric power industry, the COVID-19 pandemic created a lot of barriers in terms of electric power production, transportation, storage, and consumption (Yun et al., 2021). Specifically, suppliers have had to reduce working hours or stop production, causing a wide range of delays in taking delivery. This problem also occurred in the capital chain aspect. According to Yun et al. (2021), the inventory and delivery period had to be changed backward because of the unscheduled production progress. Hence, capital turnover became slower, and in some serious cases, capital rupture or worse occurred as a result. This provided SCF businesses with an opportunity. In SCF, 3PL companies provide financial services to companies that lack capital. Hence, SCF contributes to risk resistance for companies in the same SC.

In 2020, the Chinese government introduced the policy guideline of "Carbon Peak Carbon Neutralization" to control carbon dioxide emissions at the peak value and gradually reduce CO2 emissions with effective neutralization reactions with gases from trees in forests (Mnw, 2021[REMOVED HYPERLINK FIELD]). Under this guideline, logistics experts consider building better green SCs, especially in the energy industry. Some companies plan to develop energy accumulation and hydrogen energy technology (Zhang, 2021). Therefore, a revolution in this industry includes risk resistance through SCF, information management, digital transformation, intelligence, and carbon reduction.

## Fast-Moving Consumer Goods Industry

In the fast-moving consumer goods industry, sharing is an effective solution to facilitate the optimization of the SC (Zhao & Wang, 2021). Fast-moving consumer goods refer to basic living products, such as soft drinks, beer, and seasonings. During delivery, these goods are transferred from one vehicle to another several times, which accounts for the considerable transportation cost and increases the risk of damage to the goods. Through an interview with the "Yuanda Logistics" company in Yangzhou, Zhao and Wang suggest the effectiveness of palletized transportation for improving coordination among suppliers, retailers, and consumers. It helps to reduce costs and increase effectiveness. Using the standardized Loscam pallet in transportation throughout the logistics process, Yuanda succeeded in reducing the time taken to change pallets, thus decreasing damage to goods and reducing employee recruitment requirements. This case shows us the significance of standardization in the current SC in China. This is what we should actualize in the near future for GSCs in emerging economies.

## Steel Industry

In the steel industry, companies are also considering solutions to improve the green SC and reduce risk. Chen, Li, Ping, and Du (2020) conducted a case study on Magang (a famous Chinese steel company). They state that this industry encounters risks from the market, natural environment, external economic situation, and supply and demand of internal factors. They suggest that Magang put together an emergency response team to make the whole logistics process systematic and actualize it so that in case of a crisis, it is possible to deal with things smoothly. They also respect the importance of information management and emphasize the necessity to establish an apparent information platform. According to their study, Magang's technology is not at the leadership level in international business. It is necessary to improve their technology and equipment to fill this gap and better contribute to the green SC.

## New Retail Industry

With the development of technology and business, "new retail" has emerged as a popular concept of style consumption. It refers to the online and offline integration of retail business. Using a questionnaire survey of 180 consumers in the retail industry, Shi, Wang, and Yuan (2020) analyzed the influence of consumer experience on the SC optimization in this industry. They found that consumer experience has an impact on SC optimization from the aspects of consumer preference, consuming experience, and degree of consumer satisfaction. They proposed several measures to optimize the SC across four facets: production, retail, big data, and logistics. They suggest that flexible production and individualized service will raise the degree of consumer satisfaction. Another effective measure is to combine the online e-commerce and offline channels, following and accumulating consumer data during the entire consuming process, interacting with consumers in a timely manner, identifying their decision changes, and promptly providing them with individualized advice.

## Petrochemical Industry

Regarding the petrochemical industry, Pang (2020) states that some problems exist in this industry in China, although its SC is relatively sound. For instance, products are not that advanced, costs are high, there is homogenized competition, and profits decrease gradually.

According to Pang (2020), the COVID-19 pandemic has caused the following problems in the Chinese petrochemicals industry. A sudden stop in logistics has led to high storage volumes in the industry, slow capital turnover, and obstructed sales. More and more people stayed at home, leading to a sharp decrease in gasoline consumption. Compared with the same period in the previous year, consumption was reduced by 80%. The import of materials (gas and oil) also became difficult because many international flights were stopped, which has had a serious negative impact on the development of related industries. Exports of petrochemical products, such as plastic and fertilizer, also suffered because of this crisis, which resulted in substantial risks to export-oriented enterprises. Foreign direct investment has also been obstructed because COVID-19 remains a serious threat overseas.

To address these problems, Pang (2020) proposed several solutions and advice. First, intellectualization is an effective way to strengthen the anti-risk capabilities of this industry. Second, actualizing the diversity of purchasing sources and channels facilitates the improvement of the resilience of this industry's GSC. Third, technological innovations, such as blockchain technology, are effective strategies for developing an efficient information chain among suppliers, manufacturers, and clients. Fourth, if companies in this industry are able to build special emergency response systems in terms of customs, transportation logistics, international coordination, etc., this measure may strengthen the risk resistance ability of this industry's GSC in the event of a global crisis. Fifth, business environment optimization and improvements in trading stability are necessary. Sixth, a country-based common service platform for the SC is needed so that business standards can be shared and complied with across various industries. Moreover, to innovate and improve the quality of the GSC, a global risk prediction system is crucial for companies with logistics needs.

## Tobacco Industry

In China's tobacco industry, the systemic improvement of the green SC is being implemented. The suppliers have been divided into three grades according to their index evaluation results. The indices for evaluation include five aspects: environmental protection and performance, the level of clear industry production, energy management and conservation, the effect of green performance improvement, and the green influence of the SC. A total of 20 companies participated in this project and created 85 green performance improvement schemes. Of them, 76 had been implemented by 2018, leading to substantial conservation of materials and energy, as well as the creation of economic revenue (Li, Ma, Zhang, & Xu, 2020).

## Information Communication Technology (ICT) Industry

Regarding the ICT industry, an intelligent SC collaboration system is being built. Using the diamond model, smile curve, and Supply Chain Synergy Theory, Yin and Wang (2020) conducted a case study on a communication operator, company A, introducing the successful effect of its "integrated warehouse" model on SC improvement. Shapiro (2000) also stated that supply chain management required integrated planning. An integrated warehouse is the result of the integration of the logistics and ICT industries. It refers to a warehouse that is set near the manufacturing location. Manufacturers and logistics companies build warehouses that become special production pre-position warehouses in ICT. In this industry, there are around 200 manufactures, most of which are located in Shenzhen and Dongguan in Guangdong province. Some problems exist between these manufacturers and logistics companies in terms of supply, management, material, and technology. To resolve these problems, they have considered cooperating with each other and building integrated warehouses. As Ballow (1998) stated, inventories are essential for logistics management.

Compared to the traditional operation model, the innovative integration model has some advantages (Yin & Wang, 2020). It is more efficient and intelligent; it raises the degree of client satisfaction and, with the storage integration of manufacturing and logistics companies. Hence, it can shorten the SC to a single warehouse point, further reducing operation time. New technology, such as intelligent prediction, 3D simulation, GPS, and mobile phone applications, actualizes a seamless connection in the operation processes. As an evolution of this integration warehouse model, experts are attempting to realize product life cycle management by giving a specific intelligent code to every product, allowing it to be identified and followed during the entire logistics process.

## Building Materials Industry

In the building materials industry, the Chinese government and companies are building an evaluation index system of a green SC (Meng et. al, 2021). In the Chinese automobile industry, the green SC level of various companies is different. Although only a few corporations have developed a green SC, companies in this industry have achieved some progress toward this objective. In the electronic appliance industry, the recycling and reuse of old materials and products is a weakness in the green SC (Meng et. al, 2021). The disposal of harmful materials is a crucial issue that should be examined by experts in this field. The development of a green SC in the Chinese textile industry is lagging behind that of other industries (Meng et. al, 2021). Many companies in this industry release abundant wastewater into public areas, which must be controlled more effectively.

### Analysis Results

Based on the literature and an analysis of the innovations needed in the Chinese SC, we find some advanced and successful evolution cases in terms of technology and logistics strategies, as well as management, such as the pre-position warehouse in Dingdong E-Commerce and the integrated warehouse in the ICT industry. A few companies are utilizing advanced technology such as AI and 5G to implement DX, informatization, and optimize GSC. Some companies are building evaluation index systems to control environmental pollution problems. However, building an effective green SC is a common goal for the entire SC field in China. The level of standardization and globalization of the Chinese SC still needs improvement. Furthermore, a common SC platform, a healthy environment, and corporate social responsibility (CSR) are also required. Additionally, systematic and policy support from the Chinese government is another essential factor in improving the GSC.

Regarding the characteristics of various industries (Table 4), the automobile, home appliance, and energy industries are conducting DX to improve the GSC. The steel and petrochemical industries are performing technological innovation. The automobile, household appliance, food, energy, chemical, and steel industries are information management to actualize visualization operations. The automobile and household appliance industries emphasize cost reduction and efficiency raising. The automobile, household appliance, and new retail industries respect consumer experience to a large extent. The food industry is making great efforts to build a cold chain to satisfy consumer expectations. The household appliance industry is attempting to foster adequate human resources for better service and management. Under the COVID-19 crisis, GSC resilience and risk aversion are expected in almost all industries. As mentioned above, almost all industries are attempting to build or improve green SCs and contribute to CSR. Most industries are also expecting the GSC operational standardization and cooperation platform. Some industries take full advantage of SCF to change their capital running situation.

## FUTURE RESEARCH DIRECTIONS

In China, evaluation index systems for green SC, CSR, and SDG, operational standardization, and common cooperation platforms are crucial for diverse logistics departments. To build a better cold chain in the Chinese food industry, temperature controlling machines, equipment, and transportation vehicles need technological innovation, new management styles, and distinct cognition. Currently, country policies and systems in China are incomplete in multiple diverse facets, which creates obstacles for business management and globalization. In such an environment, business transactions incur more costs in terms of time, money, information, human resources, and material. From the perspective of transaction cost and neo-institutional economics, institutional changes will be an economic situation. Hence, the Chinese government may conduct policy and system innovation on logistics and GSC to create more and better support related departments and corporations, such as country-level logistics cooperation platforms and relatively effective financial systems to generate better SCF.

Another important implication of this chapter is human resource development. According to the analysis results of this chapter, only the household appliance industry is attempting to foster adequate

*Table 4. GSC innovation issues in various industries of China*

| Industries | Innovation issues |
|---|---|
| Auto Mobile Industry | **DX**; positioning and strategies of the GSC, including **cost control**, performance improvement, and **risk** aversion; CSR; Stability control of consumers' needs; different quality of suppliers, **information** management of logistics, target conflicts of logistics, and relatively low efficiency of cooperation among automobile makers; ununified **standards**; facilitating the development of 3PL, improving stock management, building an **AI** management **platform**, and developing contained transportation processes |
| Household appliance industry | control **cost**, improve efficiency, foster adequate **human resources**; integration of **information** and logistics; data **sharing**, effective decision making, and avoiding the bullwhip effect; **green SC**; **AI, analysis technology**, and **5G** technology; **visualization** management; automatic warehouse; logistics network distribution; **DX**; **consumers' experience**; Handle identity resolution technology |
| Food industry | **green SC**; evaluation standards; **informatization**; cold chain logistics; warehouses near users; |
| Energy industry | **SCF**; **information** management, **DX**, intelligence, and low carbon |
| Fast-moving consumer goods industry | **sharing**; optimization of SC; **standardized** pallet |
| Steel industry | improve **green SC** and reduce **risk**; **Emergency** Response Team; apparent **information** platform; improve **technology** and machine equipment |
| Building materials industry | evaluation index system of **green SC** |
| New Retail industry | **Consumers' experience**; **optimization** of SC |
| Petrochemical industry | intellectualization; diversity of purchase sources and channels; **resilience** of global supply chain; **technology** innovation; **emergency** response system; business environment optimization and trading stability improvement; country-level common service platform of SC; global **risk** prediction system |
| Tobacco industry | Index evaluation system for **green SC** |
| ICT industry | integrated **warehouse**, intelligent prediction, 3D simulation, **GPS**, and mobile phone applications, **seamless** connection |
| Medical industry | **green SC** and **informatization** |

human resources for better service and management, although several other industries lack professional human resources in logistics and GSC. Regarding the relationship between human resource management and SC, many scholars conduct studies on this topic. Mutsuddi (2012) states that the SC function of human resource practice is because it is the supplier of human resources for a company. Lengnick-Hall et al. (2013) proposed adaptive, exporting, and integrative approaches to human resource system design based on the various relationship types of SC partners. Similarly, Srinivasan et al. (2021) proposed coaching, affiliative, authoritative, and democratic leadership styles of human resource management for four types of SC strategies: leagile, agile, planning-based, and lean SC strategies. These leadership types and SC strategies are determined by the degree of product complexity and environmental uncertainty in various industries. According to the literature, human resources positively influence SC integration in the context of omni-channel retailing (Song, Shi & Song, 2020; Jena & Ghadge, 2021). Therefore, it is preferable to develop various types of human resources based on different industrial characteristics. SC professionals with good leadership skills and other competencies are expected. Similarly, other facets of GSC innovation may be considered based on diverse industrial features.

In this chapter, we mainly collected data from the literature and conducted analyses based on the secondary data. In the future, interviews with representative companies and persons in charge can be conducted to gain more detailed and deep insights. Future research could also gain more data from other industries that are not included in this chapter to make our opinions more respective. We are also attempting to conduct a questionnaire survey and obtain more data to conduct statistical analysis and make our conclusion more persuasive, and propose better suggestions toward the progress of the GSC for various industries. Additionally, we hope to find out the reasons for the different characteristics of various industries and the determining factors.

## CONCLUSION

In this chapter, a literature review and abstract analysis are conducted on the GSC evolution of various industries in the developed country of Japan and the emerging economy of China. In both countries, with the advancing of Industry 4.0, high-tech approaches, such as big data, AI, and DX, are gradually being utilized in the GSC, and greatly contribute to its improvement in terms of efficiency, performance, and anti-risk capabilities. In specific industries, the progress of the GSC and the levels of standardization are different. A common SC platform facilitates the growth of the GSC. Moreover, the progress of the GSC and the level of standardization in the developed country of Japan is much more advanced than that in the emerging economy of China. In Japan, long-term cooperation with suppliers and agencies can reduce transaction costs between the two parties. However, strengthening the resilience of the SC against world crises is a common vision for every industry. Furthermore, with the advancing of informatization and DX, GSC professionals and managers should try to protect privacy and pay attention to the safety of data of clients. As stated in previous research, various industries in China crucially need an evaluation index system so that a country-level green SC can be built smoothly. In accordance with the Chinese government's policy of "Carbon peak carbon neutralization," companies will focus more on the environment and consider the sustainable development goals (SDG) more specifically.

Additionally, based on the analysis results and findings in this chapter, reducing costs and raising efficiency are effective measures to optimize the GSC. Specifically, high tech, warehouse integration, positioning of warehouses, matching and sharing consumers' needs with both suppliers and agencies, further informatization and visualization of goods, innovative packing methods, reducing container numbers, and storage points are worthy of consideration.

## REFERENCES

Ballow, R. H. (1998). *Business Logistics Management: Planning, Organizing, and Controlling the Supply Chain* (3rd ed.). Prentice Hall.

Bowersox, D. J., & Closs, D. J. (1996). *Logistical management: The integrated supply chain process.* McGraw-Hill College.

Cai, Y., & Jiang, T. (2021). Feature Analysis and Implementation Approach of Green Supply Chain Management in Food Industry. *Supply Chain Management*, *4*, 48–56.

Chen, J., Li, Y., Ping, M., & Du, W. (2020). Risk management of green supply chain in steel industry—Magang group as an example. *Logistics Sci-Tech*, *10*, 121–125.

China Green Supply Chain Union. (2019). *Development Report of China Green Supply Chain.* Author.

Chopra. S., & Meindl, P. (2015). *Supply chain management: strategy, planning, and operation*. Pearson.

Cui, H. (2021). Study on logistics management optimization of China automobile industry—from the perspective of supply chain. *China Storage & Transport Magazine*, *2*, 123-124.

Dingdong. (2021). *Index*. Retrieved from https://www.100.me/home/index/

Gao, Q. (2020). The Application of Supply Chain in Food Industry. *Food Technology*, *11*, 170–171.

Jena, S. K., & Ghadge, A. (2021). An integrated supply chain - human resource management approach for improved supply chain performance. *International Journal of Logistics Management*, *32*(3), 918–941. doi:10.1108/IJLM-03-2020-0151

Jiang, S., & Wang, C. (2021). Study on Performance Indicator System of Green Supply Chain in Pharmaceutical Industry. *China Pharmacy*, *32*(16), 1932–1937.

Kuriyama, N. (2017). *Japanese human resource management: Labour-management relations and supply chain challenges in Asia*. Palgrave Macmillan. doi:10.1007/978-3-319-43053-9

Kurosu, S., & Iwama, M. (2017). *Global supply chain logistics*. Hakutoshobo.

Le, D. (2020). Study on supply chain digital transformation dynamics in automobile industry after coronavirus pandemic crisis. *China Logistics and Purchase*, *15*, 38–39.

Lengnick-Hall, M. L., Lengnick-Hall, C. A., & Rigsbee, C. M. (2013). Strategic human resource management and supply chain orientation. *Human Resource Management Review*, *23*(4), 366–377. doi:10.1016/j.hrmr.2012.07.002

Li, F., Ma, Y., Zhang, X., & Xu, H. (2020). Study on the Environmental Management of Green Supply Chain of Tobacco Industry in Yunnan. *Environment Science Survey*, *39*(5), 31–37.

Li, K., Jin, Y., & Liu, L. (2021). Analysis of Building Supply Chain Data in Automobile Industry. *Automobile and Parts*, *1*, 69-71.

Li, L. (2020). Research on the Current Situation and Supply Chain Management Mode of Chinese Medicine E-Commerce. *Logistics Engineering and Management*, *42*(5), 90-91.

Liang, Y. (2020). Analysis on Social Responsibility of Supply Chain Management in Automobile Industry. *Technology and Economic Guide*, *28*(30), 226–227.

Lowson, B., King, K., & Hunter, A. (2010). *Quick response: Managing the supply chain to meet consumer demand*. Wiley.

Meng, X., Li, J., Yin, J., & Li, W. (2021). Study on Management Assessment Index System of Green Supply Chain in Building Material Industry. *China Cement*, *4*, 64–68.

MNW. (2021). *What does carbon peaking and carbon neutrality mean? When was carbon neutrality proposed?* Retrieved from http://www.mnw.cn/news/cj/2373822.html

Mutsuddi, I. (2012). Supply Chain Management for Effective People Management: Issues and Challenges, *The IUP. Journal of Operations Management*, *11*(4), 53–65.

Nagasawa, S. (2018). *Reality of logistics supply chain management*. Koyoshobo.

Nippon Yusen Research Group. (2021). *Top 20 companies in the world's largest shipping company*. Retrieved from https://www.mlit.go.jp/common/001013342.pdf

Pang, G. (2020). What's the Influence of coronavirus pandemic crisis on Petrochemical Industry under the Global Crisis. *China Petroleum and Chemical Industry*, *5*, 4–9.

Qiu, F., & Li, Z. (2020). Model Innovation and Logistics Revolution of Supply Chain in Household Appliance Industry. *Supply Chain Technology and Application*, *9*, 88–92.

Shapiro, J. F. (2000). *Modeling the supply chain*. Duxbury Press.

Shi, Y., Wang, C., & Yuan, X. (2020). Research on the Influence of Consumer Experience on Supply Chain Optimization under New Retail: Based on the Survey of New Retail Industry in Nanjing. *Business Economics (Cleveland, Ohio)*, *8*, 14–16.

Song, S., Shi, X., & Song, G. (2020). Supply chain integration in omni-channel retailing: A human resource management perspective. *International Journal of Physical Distribution & Logistics Management*, *50*(1), 101–121. doi:10.1108/IJPDLM-04-2019-0115

Srinivasan, M., Hamdani, M., & Ma, S. (2021). Four supply chain management systems: From supply chain strategies to human resource management. *Business Horizons*, *64*(2), 249–260. doi:10.1016/j.bushor.2020.11.006

Sun, F., Fu, Q., & Jiang, S. (2020). Concentration degree of supply chain, Heterogeneity of property rights, and over-investment. *Finance and Accounting Monthly*, *18*, 15–23.

Wikipedia. (2022). *Toyota Motor Thailand*. Retrieved from https://en.wikipedia.org/wiki/Toyota_Motor_Thailand

Williamson, O. E. (1979). Transaction cost economics: The governance of contractual relations. *The Journal of Law & Economics*, *22*(2), 233–261. doi:10.1086/466942

Xu, Y., Sheng, J., & Wu, X. (2021). Facilitating Development of Fresh E-Commerce by Supply Chain Innovation and Value Chain Upgrading- the case of Dingdong. *Economic & Trade Update*, *7*, 14–17.

Yin, W., & Wang, L. (2020). Research and Practice of ICT Industry Smart Supply Chain Collaboration System. *Supply Chain Management*, *12*, 77–81.

Yun, C., Liu, K., Chen, Q., & Xu, S. (2021). The influence of coronavirus pandemic crisis on supply chain of electric power industry. *Modern Business Trade Industry*, *19*, 15–16.

Zhang, G. (2021). Analysis on optimization strategy of multi-tier stock of supply chain in automobile industry of China. *China Logistics and Purchase*, *8*, 73–74.

Zhang, H. (2021). Building green and intelligent supply chain of electric power industry under target 3060. *Industry Dynamics*, 17-19.

Zhao, J., & Wang, Y. (2021). Yuanda Logistics: facilitating the optimization of supply chain by sharing in fast consuming goods industry. *Logistics Technology and Application*, *5*, 94-96.

Zhao, L., & Dai, Q. (2020). Discussion on the Current Situation and Trends of Supply Chain Development in Home Appliance Industry. *Supply Chain Management*, *10*, 72–87.

Zhou, Z., Ren, T., Zhang, Z., Sun, M., Deng, Y., Liu, H., Wang, Y., & Zhang, D. (2020). The Application Research on Identity Resolution in Home Appliance Industry Industrial Internet—Appliance of Identity Resolution in Home Appliance Supply Chain. *Application Research*, *11*, 42–47.

## ADDITIONAL READING

Bowersox, D. J., & Closs, D. J. (1996). *Logistical management: The integrated supply chain process*. McGraw-Hill College.

Chopra. S., & Meindl, P. (2015). *Supply chain management: strategy, planning, and operation*. Pearson.

Lowson, B., King, K., & Hunter, A. (2010). *Quick response: Managing the supply chain to meet consumer demand*. Wiley.

Shapiro, J. F. (2000). *Modeling the supply chain*. Duxbury Press.

Williamson, O. E. (1979). Transaction cost economics: The governance of contractual relations. *The Journal of Law & Economics*, *22*, 233–261.

## KEY TERMS AND DEFINITIONS

**Agile Supply Chain:** A supply chain that can respond quickly to customer needs. It can soon supply plenty of products according to the demand and develop new products based on the customer needs.

**Carbon Peak Carbon Neutralization:** The policy guideline of China government to control carbon dioxide emissions at the peak value and reduce CO2 emissions with effective neutralization reactions with gases from trees in forests gradually.

**Consumers' Experience:** The experience of consumers during the process of selecting or purchasing goods. It is also called UX (User Experience), and DX helps companies analyze and improve customers' experiences.

**DX:** A digital transformation in terms of data storage and process management, etc. With the advancing of IT technology, companies are introducing this transformation to raise efficiency and performance.

**Green Supply Chain:** A supply chain that implements the idea of environmental protection and resource conservation across the entire supply chain.

**Leagile Supply Chain:** A supply chain that achieves that is lean and agile. It is well planned and well managed to fulfill customer orders efficiently and responsively.

**Lean Supply Chain:** A supply chain with minimal stocks within an entire supply chain. Cooperation and information sharing within a supply chain are the keys to smooth operations.

**Matching and Sharing:** An operational approach of sharing the needs of individual consumers or companies with suppliers and agencies to raise the efficiency of the supply chain.

**Plan-Based Supply Chain:** A supply chain attaching planned Supply chain strategy. It is formed to realize a plan that aims at the ideal flow and stock of materials, products, information, and services across the supply chain.

**Supply Chain Finance:** The financial service provided by finance institutes to raise the competitive advantage of SC, reduce costs, and improve the financial situation, etc.

# Compilation of References


Abdal, A., & Ferreira, D. M. (2021). Deglobalization, globalization, and the pandemic: Current impasses of the capitalist world-economy. *Journal of World-systems Research*, *27*(1), 202–230. doi:10.5195/jwsr.2021.1028

Abeliotis, K., Lasaridi, K., & Chroni, C. (2014). Attitudes & behaviour of Greek households regarding food waste prevention. *Waste Management & Research*, *32*(3), 237–240. doi:10.1177/0734242X14521681 PMID:24525671

Abernathy, W. J., Clark, K. B., & Kantrow, A. M. (1983). *Industrial renaissance*. Basic Books.

Aday, S., & Aday, M. S. (2020). Impact of COVID-19 on the food supply chain. *Food Quality and Safety*, *4*(4), 167–180. doi:10.1093/fqsafe/fyaa024

ADB (Asian Development Bank). (2015). *Greater Mekong Subregion Economic Cooperation Program*. https://www.adb.org/sites/default/files/publication/29387/gms-ecp-overview-2015.pdf

Aderans Company Limited. (2015). *The Laos "Savannakhet Factory" main factory begins operations*. https://www.aderans.co.jp/news/detail/150727_01.html

Akademie, D. W. (2020). *Dutch flower industry hit hard by the pandemic*. Retrieved October 14, 2021, from https://www.dw.com/en/dutch-flower-industry-hit-hard-by-the-pandemic/av-55714834

Aldaco, R., Hoehn, D., Laso, J., Margallo, M., Ruiz-Salmón, J., Cristobal, J., Kahhat, R., Villanueva-Rey, P., Bala, A., Batlle-Bayer, L., Fullana-i-Palmer, P., Irabien, A., & Vazquez-Rowe, I. (2020). Food waste management during the COVID-19 outbreak: A holistic climate, economic and nutritional approach. *The Science of the Total Environment*, *742*, 140524. Advance online publication. doi:10.1016/j.scitotenv.2020.140524 PMID:32619842

All Japan Coffee Association. (n.d.). *Monthly data*. https://coffee.ajca.or.jp/english/monthlydata/

All Japan Coffee Association. (n.d.). *World coffee consumption*. https://coffee.ajca.or.jp/english/consumption/

Amazon Annual Report 1997-2020. (n.d.). https://ir.aboutamazon.com/annual-reports-proxies-and-shareholder-letters/default.aspx

Amazon Web Services Inc. (2021). https://pages.awscloud.com/EMEA-Data- Flywheel.html?nc1=f_ls

Amicarelli, V., & Bux, C. (2020). Food waste in Italian households during the Covid-19 pandemic: a self-reporting approach. *Food Sec*. doi:10.1007/s12571-020-01121-z

Anonymous. (1997). Salaried man dai 439 wa boom no urade [Salaried worker episode 439, Behind the boom]. *Nihon Keizai Shimbun*.

Anonymous. (1997). Tamagotchi koukoku senndennhi zero de suta-to sita Tamagotchi ga kokomade ureta riyuu [Tamagotchi The reason why Tamagotchi was sold a lot Without advertising]. *Senden Kaigi*, *44*(6), 28–32.

Apiumhub. (2021). *Top 11 Waste Apps Available on IOS and Android.* Retrieved October 13, 2021, from https://apiumhub.com/tech-blog-barcelona/top-food-waste-apps/

Appelbaum, E., & Gaby-Biegle, J. (2020). *Spilt Milk: COVID-19 and the Dangers of Dairy Industry Consolidation.* Working Paper, 134. Retrieved October 15, 2021, from https://www.ineteconomics.org/uploads/papers/WP_134-Appelbaum-and-Gaby-Biegel.pdf

Arianina, K., & Morris, P. (2020). *COVID-19 Export Restrictions Threaten Global Food Supply.* Retrieved October 16, 2021, from https://www.law360.com/articles/1275290/covid-19-export-restrictions-threaten-global-food-supply

Armstrong & Associates Inc. (2020). *Rising Tide: The Rapid Growth of E-Commerce Logistics, 3PL Solutions, Last-Mile Delivery, and the Dominance of Amazon.* Armstrong and Associates Inc. https://www.prnewswire.com/news-releases/rising-tide-the-rapid-growth-of-e-commerce-logistics-3pl-solutions-last-mile-delivery-and-the-dominance-of-amazon-301137811.html

Asanaga, M. (2013). *Seven & I HLDGS. 9 chou en kigyou no himitsu - sekai saikyou omnichannel heno chousen* [Seven & i HLDGS. The secret of a 9 trillion yen company - Challenge to the World's Strongest Omnichannel]. Nikkei Business Publications.

Aschemann-Witzel, J., De Hooge, I., Amani, P., Becl-Larsen, T., & Osstindjer, M. (2015). Consumer-Related Food Waste: Causes and Potential for Action. *Sustainability, 7*(6), 6457–6477. doi:10.3390u7066457

Aschemann-Witzel, J., Haagen Jensen, J., Haagen Jensen, M., & Kulikovskaja, V. (2017). Consumer behaviour towards price-reduced suboptimal foods in the supermarket and the relation to food waste in households. *Appetite, 116*(1), 246–258. doi:10.1016/j.appet.2017.05.013 PMID:28487247

Askew, K. (2020). *Life in lockdown: Coronavirus prompts half of French consumers to reappraise "value" of food.* Retrieved October 24, 2021, from https://www.foodnavigator.com/Article/2020/05/29/Life-in-lockdown-Coronavirus-prompts-halfof-French-consumers-to-reappraise-value-of-food

Avey, T. (2013). *The caffeinated history of coffee. History of coffee-the history kitchen-PBS Food.* https://www.pbs.org/food/the-history-kitchen/history-coffee/

Azadnia, A. H., Saman, M. Z. M., & Wong, K. Y. (2015). Sustainable supplier selection and order lot-sizing: An integrated multi-objective decision-making process. *International Journal of Production Research, 53*(2), 383–408. doi:10.1080/00207543.2014.935827

Baldwin, R., & di Mauro, B. W. (Eds.). (2020). *Economics in the time of COVID-19.* CEPR Press.

Baležentis, A., & Baležentis, T. (2011). An innovative multi-criteria supplier selection based on two-tuple MULTIMOORA and hybrid data. *Economic Computation and Economic Cybernetics Studies and Research, 45*(2), 37–56.

Ballou, R. H. (1992). *Business logistics management.* Prentice-Hall.

Ballou, R. H. (1992). *Business Logistics Management.* Prentice-Hall.

Ballow, R. H. (1998). *Business Logistics Management: Planning, Organizing, and Controlling the Supply Chain* (3rd ed.). Prentice Hall.

Bardt, H., Ezell, S., Flores, T., González, N., Hattingh, C., Randolph, S., & Bandini, C. (2021). *Global value chains after the COVID-19 Crisis.* Global Trade and Innovation Policy Alliance.

Barykin, S. E., Kapustina, I. V., Korchagina, E. V., Sergeev, S. M., Yadykin, V. K., Abdimomynova, A., & Stepanova, D. (2021). Digital logistics platforms in the BRICS countries: Comparative analysis and development prospects. *Sustainability, 13*(20), 11228. doi:10.3390u132011228

Bashiri, M., Tjahjono, B., Lazell, J., Ferreira, J., & Perdana, T. (2021). The dynamics of sustainability risks in the global coffee supply chain: A case of Indonesia–UK. *Sustainability, 13*(2), 589. doi:10.3390u13020589

Bel, J.-B., & Marengo, P. (2020). *The impact of the COVID-19 pandemic on municipal waste management systems. Results and analysis of a survey carried out by ACR+ between July and October 2021. CR+.* Retrieved October 29, 2021, from https://acrplus.org/images/technical-reports/2021_ACR_Impact_COVID-19_pandemic_on_municipal_waste_management_systems.pdf

Bello, W. (2013). *Capitalism's last stand? Deglobalization in the age of austerity.* Zed Books. doi:10.5040/9781350218895

Berg, N., & Knights, M. (2019). *Amazon: How the world's most relentless retailer will continue to revolutionize commerce.* Kogan Page.

Berman, J. (2019, Dec.). Amazon's shipping and logistics spend remains in lockstep with expectations. *Logistics Management,* 12-13. https://www.logisticsmgmt.com/article/amazons_shipping_and_logistics_spend_remains_in_lockstep_with_expectations

Bicycle Dutch. (2020). *More food deliveries by bicycle in the Corona crisis.* Retrieved October 24, 2021, from https://bicycledutch.wordpress.com/2020/05/27/more-food-deliveries-by-bicycle-in-the-corona-crisis/

Bishop, T. (2017). Amazon Bringing Echo and Alexa to 80 Additional Countries in Major Global Expansion. *GeekWire.* https://www.geekwire.com/2017/amazon-bringing-echo-alexa-80-additional-countries-major-global-expansion/

BizVibe. (2020). *Top 10 coffee brands in the world 2020, Top coffee brands, Global coffee market factsheet.* https://blog.bizvibe.com/blog/top-10-coffee-brands

Blanchard, B. S., & Fabrycky, W. J. (1998). *Systems Engineering and Analysis* (3rd ed.). Prentice-Hall.

Bocken, N., Short, S., Rana, P., & Evans, S. (2013). A value mapping tool for sustainable business modelling. *Corporate Governance, 13*(5), 482–497. doi:10.1108/CG-06-2013-0078

BOI (Thailand Board of Investment) Home Page. (2021). https://www.boi.go.th/en/index/

BOI (Thailand Board of Investment). (2021). *Additional incentives for projects with an investment of THB 1 billion or more.* http://www.boi.go.th/upload/Tokyo210702/BOIMailMagazine_2021_5_StimulousMeasure.pdf

Boiral, O., Brotherton, M.-C., Rivaud, L., & Guillaumie, L. (2021). Organizations' management of the COVID-19 pandemic: A scoping review of business articles. *Sustainability, 2021*(13), 3993. doi:10.3390u13073993

Bowersox, J., & Cioss, D. J. (1996). *Logistical management.* McGraw-Hill.

Bowersox, J., & CIoss, D. J. (1996). *Logistical management.* McGraw-Hill.

Bowersox, D. J., & Closs, D. J. (1996). *Logistical management: The integrated supply chain process.* McGraw-Hill College.

Brant, R. (2011). *One Click: Jeff Bezos and the Rise of Amazon.com.* Portfolio.

Broadberry, S., & Harrison, M. (2005). *The economics of World War I.* Cambridge University Press. doi:10.1017/CBO9780511497339

Burgen, S. (2020). *Spain's vineyards destroy record harvest as wine sales crash.* Retrieved October 14, 2021, from https://www.theguardian.com/food/2020/aug/15/spains-vineyards-destroy-record-harvest-as-wine-sales-crash

Buzby, J. C., Wells, H. F., & Hyman, J. (2014). *The Estimated Amount, Value and Calories of 599 Postharvest Food Losses at the Retail and Consumer Levels in the United States*. USDA 600 Economic Research Service. Retrieved October 18, 2021, from https://www.ers.usda.gov/media/1282296/eib121.pdf

Cai, Y., & Jiang, T. (2021). Feature Analysis and Implementation Approach of Green Supply Chain Management in Food Industry. *Supply Chain Management*, *4*, 48–56.

Canalys. (2021). *United States cloud services market Q1 2021*. https://www.canalys.com/newsroom/united-states-cloud-infrastructure-q1-2021

Cervera, A., & de Arri, Y. O. (2020). *The coronavirus crisis in Spain's wine industry*. Retrieved October 15, 2021, from https://www.spanishwinelover.com/learn-432-the-coronavirus-crisis-in-spains-wine-industry

Chao, C., Scheuing, E.E., & Ruch, W.A. (1993). Purchasing performance evaluation: An investigation of different perspectives. *International Journal of Purchasing and Materials Management Summer, 29*(3), 33–39.

Charan, R., & Yang, J. (2019). *The Amazon Management System*. Ideapress.

Chen, H., & Xiao, X. P. Z. (2011). China's coffee industry situation and development measures. *Tropical Agricultural Engineering*, (23), 42.

Chen, J., Li, Y., Ping, M., & Du, W. (2020). Risk management of green supply chain in steel industry—Magang group as an example. *Logistics Sci-Tech*, *10*, 121–125.

Cheraghi, S. H., Dadashzadeh, M., & Subramanian, M. (2011). Critical success factors for supplier selection: An update. *Journal of Applied Business Research*, *20*(2). doi:10.19030/jabr.v20i2.2209

China Green Supply Chain Union. (2019). *Development Report of China Green Supply Chain*. Author.

Chopra. S., & Meindl, P. (2015). *Supply chain management: strategy, planning, and operation*. Pearson.

Chopra, S., & Meindl, P. (2007). *Supply Chain Management: Strategy, Planning & Operations* (3rd ed.). Pearson Education.

Christopher, M. (2005), *Logistics and Supply Chain Management: Creating Value-Adding Networks* (3rd ed.). Financial Times Prentice Hall.

Christopher, M. (2016). *Logistics and supply chain management* (5th ed.). Financial Times Publishing.

Cieśla, M. (2016). Aluminium supplier selection for the automotive parts manufacturer. *Metalurgija*, *55*(2), 237–240.

Clements, L. (2020). *Coronavirus outbreak 'worse than wartime' for dairy farmers forced to dump milk. Farmers have had no choice but to pour milk down the drain as tankers fail turn up to collect it*. Retrieved October 15, 2021, from https://www.walesonline.co.uk/news/wales-news/coronavirus-milk-farmers-wales-freshways-18048204

Coffee.org tm. (2021). *20 Interesting coffee facts*. https://coffee.org/blogs/news/20-interesting-coffee-facts?

Coldiretti-SWG. (2011). *Italiani e alimentazione nel tempo della crisi indagine Coldiretti/SWG*. Retrieved October 15, 2021, from https:// www.napol i.coldi retti. it/itali ani-e-alime ntazi one-nel-tempo della crisi indag ineco ldire ttisw gotto bre20 11.aspx?KeyPu b=GP_CD_NAPOL I_HOME%7CCD_NAPOL I_HOME&Cod_Ogget to=30584 835&subsk intyp e=Detail

Coniato, F., Ronchi, F., Luzzini, D., & Brivio, O. (2015). Total cost of ownership along the supply chain: A model applied to the tinting industry. *Production Planning and Control*, *26*(6), 427–437. doi:10.1080/09537287.2014.918285

Consortium for Advanced Management International (CAM-I). (1990). *The CAM-I ABC model-AKA The CAM-I cross*. https://www.cam-i.org/docs/Toolkit_CAM-I_Cross.pdf

Corbett, C. J., Blackbum, J. D., & Van Wassenhove, N. (1999). Partnerships to improve supply chains. *Sloan Management Review*, *40*(4), 71–82.

Council, S. C. (2010). Supply-chain operations reference-model. *Overview of SCOR Version*, *10*, 7-8.

CSCP (Collaborating Centre on Sustainable Consumption and Production GmbH). (2021). *HandelsforumRLV. Dialogforum des Groß- und Einzelhandels zur Reduzierung von Lebensmittelverschwendung. Zu gut für die Tonne.* Stand der Umsetzung der Beteiligungserklärung. Zwischenbericht 2021. Retrieved October 14, 2021, from https://www.scp-centre.org/wp-content/uploads/2021/02/Dialogue-Forum_Interim-Report.pdf

Cui, H. (2021). Study on logistics management optimization of China automobile industry—from the perspective of supply chain. *China Storage & Transport Magazine*, *2*, 123-124.

Cullen, J. (2009). *Supply Chain Management Accounting*. The Society of Management Accountants of Canada, the American Institute of Certified Public Accountants and The Chartered Institute of Management Accountants. http://www.cimaglobal.com/documents/importeddocuments/cid_mag_supply_chain_aug09.pdf

Cullen, M. T. (2020). *COVID-19 and the risk to food supply chains: How to respond?* FAO. doi:10.4060/ca8388en

David, S., Philip, K., & Edith, S. (2000). *Designing and managing the Supply Chain*. McGraw-Hill Companies.

Dawei, S. E. Z. (Dawei special economic zone). (2020). *DSEZ MC received JICA December 18, 2020*. http://www.daweisez.gov.mm/news/dsez-mc-received-jica-18-dec-2020

Dawei, S. E. Z. (Dawei special economic zone). (2021). *Overview of the Dawei SEZ*. http://www.daweisez.gov.mm/content/overview-dawei-sez

Didea, L., & Ilie, D. M. (2020). The State of emergency and the economic repercussions. A new "Avalanche" of Insolvencies. *J.L. & Admin. Sci*, *89*(13).

Diep, C. (2021). *Convenience store numbers in Japan 2011-2020*. Retrieved November 23, 2021, from https://www.statista.com/statistics/810901/japan-convenience-store-numbers/

Dimitrios, V., & Eleftherios, I. (2005). A System Dynamics Modeling Framework for the Strategic Supply Chain Management of Food Chains. *Journal of Food Engineering*, *70*(3), 351–364. doi:10.1016/j.jfoodeng.2004.06.030

Dingdong. (2021). *Index*. Retrieved from https://www.100.me/home/index/

District Roasters. (2019). *Types of coffee beans and what sets them apart*. https://districtroasters.com/blogs/news/types-of-coffee-beans

Doh, J., Budhwar, P., & Wood, G. (2021). Long-term energy transitions and international business: Concepts, theory, methods, and a research agenda. *Journal of International Business Studies*, *52*(5), 951–970. doi:10.105741267-021-00405-6 PMID:33716348

Dornier, P. P., Ernst, R., Fender, M., & Kouvelis, P. (2008). *Global operations and logistics: Text and cases*. John Wiley & Sons.

Douglas, M. L., & Martha, C. C. (2000). Issues in Supply Chain Management. *Industrial Marketing Management*, *29*(1), 65–83. doi:10.1016/S0019-8501(99)00113-3

Dweiri, F., Kumar, S., Khan, S. A., & Jain, V. (2016). Designing an integrated AHP based decision support system for supplier selection in automotive industry. *Expert Systems with Applications*, *62*, 273–283. doi:10.1016/j.eswa.2016.06.030

EC (European Commission). (2020). *Communication From the Commission to the European Parliament, the Council, the European Economic and Social Committee and the Committee of the Regions. A Farm to Fork Strategy for a Fair, Healthy and Environmentally-Friendly Food System.* COM(2020) 381 Final. Retrieved October 14, 2021, from https://www.seldia.eu/images/pdf/CELEX_52011DC0206_EN_TXT.pdf

Ellison, B., McFadden, B., Rickard, B., & Wilson, N. (2020). *Food Loss and Waste in the United States during COVID-19. CAST Commentary: Economic Impacts of COVID-19 on Food and Agricultural Markets.* Retrieved October 11, 2021, from https://www.cast-science.org/publication/economic-impacts-of-covid-19-on-food-and-agricultural-markets/

Ellisson, B., & Kalaitzandonakes, M. (2020). Food Waste and Covid-19: Impacts along the Supply Chain. *Farmdoc Daily, 10*, 164. Retrieved October 17, 2021, from https://farmdocdaily.illinois.edu/2020/09/food-waste-and-covid-19-impacts-along-the-supply-chain.html

Ellyat, H. (2021). *Supply chain chaos is already hitting global growth. And it's about to get worse.* CNBC.

Espresso & Coffee Guide. (2012). *Coffee history / 1650-1700.* https://espressocoffeeguide.com/all-about-coffee-2/worlds-best-history-of-coffee/coffee-history-1650-1700/

Estampe, D., Lamouri, S., Paris, J. L., & Brahim-Djelloul, S. (2013). A framework for analysing supply chain performance evaluation models. *International Journal of Production Economics, 142*(2), 247–258. doi:10.1016/j.ijpe.2010.11.024

EUR-Lex. (2000). *End-of life vehicles Directive 2000/53/EC.* Retrieved April 5, 2022, from https://eur-lex.europa.eu/legal-content/EN/TXT/?uri=celex%3A32000L0053

EUR-Lex. (2006). *Reach Regulation (EC) No 1907/2006.* Retrieved April 5, 2022, from https://eur-lex.europa.eu/legal-content/en/ALL/?uri=CELEX%3A32006R1907

EUR-Lex. (2017). *EU Regulation, 2017*(821). Retrieved April 5, 2022, from https://eur-lex.europa.eu/legal-content/EN/TXT/?uri=celex%3A32017R0821

Fanelli, R. M., & Di Florio, A. (2016). Domestic food waste, gap in times of crisis. *Italian Review of Agricultural Economics, 71*(2), 111–125.

FAO (Food and Agriculture Organization of the United Nations). (2013). Food wastage footprint: Impact on natural resources. Summary report. Rome: FAO.

FAO (Food and Agriculture Organization of the United Nations). (2015). *Regional Strategic Framework—Reducing Food Losses and Waste in the Near East & North Africa Region.* FAO.

FAO (Food and Agriculture Organization of the United Nations). (2020a). *COVID-19 causes havoc to supply chains for fresh fruits and vegetables.* Retrieved October 17, 2021, from https://reliefweb.int/report/ukraine/covid-19-causes-havoc-supply-chains-fresh-fruits-and-vegetables-enruuk

FAO (Food and Agriculture Organization of the United Nations). (2020b). *COVID-19 and the risk to food supply chains: How to respond? COVID-19 and the risk to food supply chains: How to respond?* Retrieved October 17, 2021, from https://www.fao.org/documents/card/en/c/ca8388en/

FAO. (2021). *The impact of disasters and crises on agriculture and food security.* Food and Agriculture Organization of United Nations.

Fei, S., & Ni, J. (2020). *Local food systems and COVID-19: A look into China's responses.* Retrieved October 24, 2021, from https://www.fao.org/in-action/food-for-cities-programme/news/detail/en/c/1270350/

Financial Express Online. (2020). *Kisan Rath Mobile App: Centre launches new app to help farmers during coronavirus lockdown.* Retrieved October 28, 2021, from https://www.financialexpress.com/industry/technology/kisan-rath-mobile-app-features-benefits-of-app-to-help-farmers-during-coronavirus-lockdown/

Findlay, R., & O'Rourke, K. (2008). Power and Plenty: Trade, War, and the World Economy in the Second Millennium. Princeton University Press.

Fisher, M. L. (1997). What is the right supply chain for your product? *Harvard Business Review, 1997*(March-April), 105–1156.

Fleetwood, J. (2020). Social justice, food loss, and the sustainable development goals in the Era of COVID-19. *Sustainability, 12*(12), 5027. doi:10.3390u12125027

Folke, C., Jansson, Å., Rockström, J., Olsson, P., Carpenter, S. R., Chapin, F. S. III, Crépin, A.-S., Daily, G., Danell, K., Ebbesson, J., Elmqvist, T., Galaz, V., Moberg, F., Nilsson, M., Österblom, H., Ostrom, E., Persson, Å., Peterson, G., Polasky, S., ... Westley, F. (2011). Reconnecting to the biosphere. *Ambio, 40*(7), 719–738. doi:10.100713280-011-0184-y PMID:22338712

Fontela, E., & Gabus, A. (1976). Current perceptions of the world problematique. In *World Modeling: A Dialogue.* North-Holland Publishing Company.

Fratus, M. (2019). *The Boston tea party: How coffee became the official morning beverage of America, Coffee or die magazine.* https://coffeeordie.com/boston-tea-party-history/

Fredriksson, A., & Liljestrand, K. (2015). Capturing food logistics: A literature review and research agenda. *International Journal of Logistics Research and Applications, 18*(1), 16–34. doi:10.1080/13675567.2014.944887

Fukushima, M. (1998). *Supply Chain keiei kakumei* [Revolution of SCM]. Nihonkeizaishimbumsha.

Gaillard, N. (2020). *Country risk. Subtitle the bane of foreign investors.* Springer., doi:10.1007/978-3-030-45788-4

Gao, Q. (2020). The Application of Supply Chain in Food Industry. *Food Technology, 11*, 170–171.

Gartner, Inc. (2020). *Worldwide Public Cloud Services End-User Spending Forecast.* https://www.gartner.com/en/newsroom/press-releases/2020-11-17-gartner-forecasts-worldwide-public-cloud-end-user-spending-to-grow-18-percent-in-2021

Geels, F. W. (2002). Technological transitions as evolutionary reconfiguration processes: A multi-level perspective and a case-study. *Research Policy, 31*(8-9), 1257–1274. doi:10.1016/S0048-7333(02)00062-8

Ghodsypour, S. H., & O'Brien, C. (1998). A decision support system for supplier selection using an integrated analytic hierarchy process and linear programming. *International Journal of Production Economics, 56*, 199–212. doi:10.1016/S0925-5273(97)00009-1

Gillard, R., Gouldson, A., Paavola, J., & Van Alstine, J. (2016). Transformational responses to climate change: Beyond a systems perspective of social change in mitigation and adaptation. *Wiley Interdisciplinary Reviews: Climate Change, 7*(2), 251–265. doi:10.1002/wcc.384

Global Cycling Network. (2020). *The Bicycle Couriers Of Lockdown | Making Quarantine Better With Bikes.* Retrieved October 27, 2021, from https://www.youtube.com/watch?v=zoGn-2hatNo

GMS (Greater Mekong Subregion). (2019). *Economic Corridors in the Greater Mekong Subregion.* https://www.greatermekong.org/content/economic-corridors-in-the-greater-mekong-subregion

Goldstein, J., Hazy, J. K., & Silberstang, J. (2010). A complexity science model of social innovation in social enterprise. *Journal of Social Entrepreneurship, 1*(1), 101–125. doi:10.1080/19420671003629763

Govindan, K., Rajendran, S., Sarkis, J., & Murugesan, P. (2015). Multi criteria decision making approaches for green supplier evaluation and selection: A literature review. *Journal of Cleaner Production, 98*, 66–83. doi:10.1016/j.jclepro.2013.06.046

Graz. (2021). *Förderprojekt GrazLog*. Retrieved October 29, 2021, from https://www.graz.at/cms/beitrag/10320838/8709900/#

Grist. (2013). *These women deliver food from farm to table by bike, in minutes*. Retrieved October 27, 2021, from https://grist.org/food/these-women-deliver-food-from-farm-to-table-by-bike-in-minutes/

Grunwald, J., & Flamm, K. (1985). *The global factory: Foreign assembly in international trade*. Brookings Institution.

Gullickson, G. (2020). *How COVID-19 is Accelerating Online Agricultural Commerce*. Retrieved October 21, 2021, from https://www.agriculture.com/farm-management/finances-accounting/how-covid-19-is-accelerating-online-agricultural-commerce

Gunders, D. (2012). *Wasted: How America is Losing Up to 40 Percent of Its Food from Farm to Fork to Landfill*. Natural Resources Defense Council Issue Paper #12-06-B. Retrieved October 15, 2021, from https://www.nrdc.org/sites/default/files/wasted-food-IP.pdf

Gustavsson, J., Dederberg, C., & Sonesson, U. (2011). *Global food losses and food waste*. Food and Agriculture Organization of the United Nations. Retrieved October 12, 2021, from https://www.fao.org/3/a-i2697e.pdf

Hannan, M. A., Begum, R. A., Al-Shetwi, A. Q., Ker, P. J., Al Mamun, M. A., Hussain, A., Basri, H., & Mahlia, T. M. I. (2020). Waste collection route optimisation model for linking cost saving and emission reduction to achieve sustainable development goals. *Sustainable Cities and Society, 62*, 102393. doi:10.1016/j.scs.2020.102393

Hara, T. (2021). Gaishyoku sangyo no Supply Chain Management [Supply chain management in restaurant industry]. *Shogakukenkyusyu, 54*, 237–256.

Harper, J. (2020). *Asia's fishermen and farmers go digital during virus*. Retrieved October 24, 2021, from https://www.bbc.com/news/business-52767227

Haseba, J. (2016). Border SEZ as a pillar of investment attraction: Industrial policy of reshuffled cabinet (1). *The International Trade Public Bulletin*. https://www.jetro.go.jp/biznews/2016/01/c8aaec213765a950.html

Hatakeyama, H. (2011). Jidoshasangyo niokeru sapuraiya tono kankyotorikumi – Nissan jidosha wo chushin ni [The environmental action with the supplier in the Japanese automotive industry: Case study on Nissan Motor]. *Journal of Sustainable Management, 11*(1).

Hatakeyama, H. (2014). Nihon jidoshasangyo niokeru seihinganyukagakubusshitsukanri – unyomen deno torikumi nitsuite [The management of chemical substances in products in the Japanese automotive industry: Focusing on the operational aspect]. In Hiroshima Papers on Society and Culture (Vol. 13). Hiroshima University Graduate School of Integrated Arts and Sciences.

Higuchi, T, & Troutt, M. D. (2008). *Life cycle management in Supply Chains*. Idea Group.

Higuchi, T. (2018). *Supply Chain ga umidasu kyosoyuii* [Competetive advantage generated by supply chain]. Tyu-oukeizaisya.

Higuchi, T. (2018). *Supply Chain ga umidasu kyousou yuui* [Competitive Advantage Created by Supply Chain]. Chuokeizai-sha.

Higuchi, T. (2016). Fusion of Short-term and Long-term SCM Strategies -The Case of Seven Eleven Japan. *Third International Workshop on Successful Supply Chain Management.*

Higuchi, T., & Troutt, M. D. (2004). Dynamic simulation of the supply chain for a short life cycle product - Lessons from the Tamagotchi case. *Computers & Operations Research*, *3*(7), 1097–1114. doi:10.1016/S0305-0548(03)00067-4

History of Beverage. (2014). *George Washington inventor of instant coffee process*. https://www.beveragehistory.com/2014/10/george-washington-inventor-of-instant.html

Hobbs, J. E. (2020). Food Supply Chains during the COVID-19 Pandemic. *Canadian Journal of Agricultural Economics/ Revue Canadienne d'agroeconomie, 68*, 171-176. doi:10.1111/cjag.12237

Hobson, K. (2020). The limits of the loops: Critical environmental politics and the Circular Economy. *Environmental Politics*, *30*(1-2), 161–179. doi:10.1080/09644016.2020.1816052

Honda Motor Co. Ltd. (2018a). *Honda gurin purchasing gaidorain* [Honda Green Purchasing Guidelines]. https://www.honda.co.jp/sustainability/supply-chain/pdf/green-guideline.pdf

Honda Motor Co. Ltd. (2018b). *Honda sapuraiya sasutenabiriti gaidorain* [Honda Supplier Sustainability Guidelines]. https://www.honda.co.jp/sustainability/supply-chain/pdf/supplier-sustainability-guidelines.pdf

Horta, P. M., Matos, J., & Mendes, L. L. (2020). Digital food environment during the coronavirus disease 2019 (COVID-19) pandemic in Brazil: An analysis of food advertising in an online food delivery platform. *British Journal of Nutrition*, 1–6. doi:10.1017/S0007114520004560

Huang, J. D., & Hu, M. H. (2013). Two-stage solution approach for supplier selection: A case study in a Taiwan automotive industry. *International Journal of Computer Integrated Manufacturing*, *26*(3), 237–251. doi:10.1080/0951192X.2012.685762

Ibn-Mohammed, T., Mustapha, K. B., Godsell, J., Adamu, Z., Babatunde, K. A., Akintade, D. D., Acquaye, A., Fujii, H., Ndiaye, M. M., Yamoah, F. A., & Koh, S. C. L. (2021). A critical analysis of the impacts of COVID-19 on the global economy and ecosystems and opportunities for circular economy strategies. *Resources, Conservation and Recycling*, *164*, 105169. Advance online publication. doi:10.1016/j.resconrec.2020.105169 PMID:32982059

IHS Automotive Data Center. (2017). Global light vehicle production summary. *IHS Automotive.* Available at https://www.ihs.com/pdf/IHS-Automotive-Global-Summary-Production-LVP-12-16_222719110913052132.pdf

Imaoka, Z. (1998). *Kigyo syu-eki wo ageru shikake supply chain management* [Increasing profit by SCM]. Kogyo-tyousakai.

IMCO. (2020). *Deglobalization. Implications for investors*. Oxford Economics.

Industry Europe. (2020). *The robots delivering food during coronavirus lockdown.* Retrieved October 28, 2021, from https://industryeurope.com/sectors/technology-innovation/the-robots-delivering-food-during-coronavirus-lockdown/

Institutions of Mechanical Engineers. (2013). *Global Food Waste Not, Want Not.* Retrieved October 16, 2021, from http://www.campaignforrealfarming.org/wp-content/uploads/2013/01/IME-Global-Food-Report.pdf

International Coffee Organization. (n.d.). *Historical data on the global coffee trade.* https://www.ico.org/new_historical.asp?section=Statistics

International Coffee Organization. (n.d.). *Trade statistics tables.* https://www.ico.org/trade_statistics.asp?section=Statistics

International Organization for Standardization. (2017). *ISO 20400 Sustainable Procurement.* Author.

Irwin, D. A. (2020). *The pandemic adds momentum to the deglobalization trend.* Peterson Institute for International Economics.

ISO SR Domestic Committee. (2011). *Nihongoyaku ISO26000:2010 - shakaitekisekinin ni kansuru tebiki* [ISO26000:2010—Guidance on social responsibility]. Japanese Standards Association.

Iwata, H. (2003). The Relationship between Activity-Based Costing and Theory of Constraints. *The Journal of Cost Accounting Research, 27*(2), 89–98.

Jacobides, M. G., MacDuffie, J. P., & Tae, C. J. (2015). Agency, structure, and the dominance of OEMs: Change and stability in the automotive sector. *Strategic Management Journal.*

Jagtap, S., Bader, F., Gracia-Gracia, G., Trollmann, H., Fadiji, T., & Salonitis, K. (2021). Food Logistics 4.0: Opportunities and Challenges. *Logistics, 5*(2). Retrieved October 27, 2021, from https://www.mdpi.com/2305-6290/5/1/2

James, H. (2018). Deglobalization: The rise of disembedded unilateralism. *Annual Review of Financial Economics, 10*(1), 219–237. doi:10.1146/annurev-financial-110217-022625

Japan Auto Parts Industries Association. (2010a). *CSR gaidobukku* [CSR Guidebook]. https://www.japia.or.jp/files/user/japia/work/csrbcp/csr/CSR_H22guidebook.pdf

Japan Auto Parts Industries Association. (2010b). *CSR chiekkushito* [CSR Check Sheet]. https://www.japia.or.jp/files/user/japia/work/csrbcp/csr/CSR_H22check.pdf

Japan Auto Parts Industries Association. (2017a). *JAPIA kankyojohoshi* [Activity of Environmental Management Committee] (Vol. 1). https://www.japia.or.jp/files/user/japia/work/kankyo/EMC_vol1_20170926.pdf

Japan Auto Parts Industries Association. (2017b). *JAPIA kankyojohoshi* [Activity of Environmental Management Committee] (Vol. 2). https://www.japia.or.jp/files/user/japia/work/kankyo/EMC_vol2_20180206.pdf

Japan Auto Parts Industries Association. (2018). *JAPIA kankyojohoshi* [Activity of Environmental Management Committee] (Vol. 3). https://www.japia.or.jp/files/user/japia/work/kankyo/EMC_vol3_20180928.pdf

Japan Auto Parts Industries Association. (2020). *JAPIA kankyojohoshi* [Activity of Environmental Management Committee] (Vol. 7). https://www.japia.or.jp/files/user/japia/work/kankyo/EMC_vol7_20210216.pdf

Japan Auto Parts Industries Association. (2021a). *Jigyokeikakusho* [Business Plan FY2021]. https://www.japia.or.jp/files/user/japia/japia/R3keikaku.pdf

Japan Auto Parts Industries Association. (2021b). *Konfurikutomineraru chosashiryo* [Conflict Minerals Survey Data]. https://www.jama.or.jp/c_minerals/index.html

Japan Electronics and Information Technology Industries Association. (2018). *Study Group on Conflict Minerals Purchasing.* Retrieved November 19, 2021, from https://www.jeita.or.jp/japanese/pickup/category/180802-02.html

Japan Food Service Association. (2020). https://jfnet.or.jp

Japan Institute of Logistics Systems. (2021). *FY2021 Logistics Cost Survey Report (Preliminary Version) (Japanese only).* https://www1.logistics.or.jp/(2022.2.14 access)

Javorcik, B. (2020, Apr. 2). Coronavirus will change the way the world does business for good businesses will be forced to rethink their global value chains. *Financial Times.*

JBIC (Japan Bank for International Cooperation) Home Page. (2021). https://www.jbic.go.jp/en/index.html

JBIC (Japan Bank for International Cooperation). (2015). *Concluded a shareholder agreement for the purpose of participating in an investment in the Dawei special economic zone Development Company of the Federal Republic of Myanmar.* https://www.jbic.go.jp/ja/information/press/press-2015/1215-44764.html

Jeffery, A., & Newburger, E. (2020). *Wasted Milk, Euthanized Livestock: Photos Show How Coronavirus has Devastated US Agriculture.* CNBC. Retrieved October 28, 2021, from https://www.cnbc.com/2020/05/02/coronavirus-devastates-agriculture-dumped-milk-euthanized-livestock.html

Jena, S. K., & Ghadge, A. (2021). An integrated supply chain - human resource management approach for improved supply chain performance. *International Journal of Logistics Management, 32*(3), 918–941. doi:10.1108/IJLM-03-2020-0151

Jeremy, F. S. (2006). *Modeling the supply chain.* Cengage Learning.

JETRO Phnom Penh Office. (2015). *Comparison of Cambodia-Laos special economic zones in the Thai Border Region.* https://www.jetro.go.jp/ext_images/world/reports/2014/7b3bacad38b0368a/kokkyo.pdf

Jiang, S., & Wang, C. (2021). Study on Performance Indicator System of Green Supply Chain in Pharmaceutical Industry. *China Pharmacy, 32*(16), 1932–1937.

JICA (Japan Bank for International Cooperation) Home Page. (2021). https://www.jica.go.jp/english/index.html

JMD (The Japan Maritime Daily). (2021). *Thailand / Myanmar resumes border traffic.* https://www.jmd.co.jp/article.php?no=270777

Joe's Garage Coffee. (2021). *Coffee trends to watch in 2021.* https://joesgaragecoffee.com/blog/coffee-trends/

John, G. (2017). *Strategic supply chain alignment.* Routledge.

Jörissen, J., Prieler, C., & Bräutigam, K.-R. (2015). Food Waste Generation at Household Level: Results of a Survey among Employees of Two European Research Centers in Italy and Germany. *Sustainability, 2015*(7), 2695–2715. doi:10.3390u7032695

Jribi, S., Ismail, H. B., Doggui, D., & Debbabi, H. (2020). COVID-19 virus outbreak lockdown: What impacts on household food wastage? *Environment, Development and Sustainability, 22*(5), 3939–3955. Advance online publication. doi:10.100710668-020-00740-y PMID:32837271

Kader, A. A. (2005). Increasing food availability by reducing postharvest losses of fresh produce. *International Postharvest Symposium, 682*, 2169-2176. 10.17660/ActaHortic.2005.682.296

Kakeda, Y., & Sumiya, H. (2009). *Gendai no kouri ryuutsuu* [Modern Retail Distribution]. Chuokeizai-sha.

Kano, L., Tsang, E. W. K., & Yeung, H. (2020). Global value chains: A review of the multi-disciplinary literature. *Journal of International Business Studies, 51*(4), 577–622. doi:10.105741267-020-00304-2

Kawabe, N. (2003). *Sebun-irebun no Keieishi* [A Business History of Seven-Eleven]. Yuhikaku Publishing. Retrieved October 11, 2021, from https://www.city.koto.lg.jp/

Kawai, H. (2021). *'Dream' or 'trap,' the end point of the "Chinese railway" expansion in Southeast Asia. International.* Nishi-Nippon Shimbun. Https://www.nishinippon.co.jp/item/n/778004/

Keskin, G. A. (2015). Using integrated fuzzy DEMATEL and fuzzy C: Means algorithm for supplier evaluation and selection. *International Journal of Production Research, 53*(12), 3586–3602. doi:10.1080/00207543.2014.980461

Kim, H. M., & Laskowski, M. (2018). Toward an ontology-driven blockchain design for supply-chain provenance. *Intelligent Systems in Accounting, Finance & Management, 25*(1), 18–27. Retrieved October 29, 2021, from. doi:10.1002/isaf.1424

Kittichotsatsawat, Y., Jangkrajarng, V., & Tippayawong, K. Y. (2021). Enhancing Coffee Supply Chain towards Sustainable Growth with Big Data and Modern Agricultural Technologies. *Sustainability, 13*(8), 4593. doi:10.3390u13084593

KKSEZ (Koh Kong Special Economic Zone). (2021). *Welcome to the Koh Kong special economic zone*. https://kksez.com/

Koffee Retail. (2021). *Life begins after coffee*. https://koffeeretail.com/

Korhonen, J., Nuur, C., Feldmann, A., & Seyoum, E. B. (2018). Circular economy as an essentially contested concept. *Journal of Cleaner Production, 175*, 544–522. Retrieved October 17, 2021, from. doi:10.1016/j.jclepro.2017.12.111

Krugman, P. R. (1991). *Geography and Trade*. MIT Press.

Kuriyama, N. (2017). *Japanese human resource management: Labour-management relations and supply chain challenges in Asia*. Palgrave Macmillan. doi:10.1007/978-3-319-43053-9

Kurokawa, F. (2017). *Jidoshasangyono ESGsenryaku* [ESG Strategies for the Automotive Industry]. Chuokeizai-Sha Holdings, Inc.

Kurosu, S., & Iwama, M. (2017). *Global supply chain logistics*. Hakutoshobo.

Lattanzi, A. (2020). *Food delivery platforms revolutionizing the market during COVID-19: Why is regulation lagging behind?* Retrieved October 18, 2021, from https://www.ifis.org/blog/food-delivery-platforms-covid-19

Le, D. (2020). Study on supply chain digital transformation dynamics in automobile industry after coronavirus pandemic crisis. *China Logistics and Purchase, 15*, 38–39.

Lee, H., Padmanabhan, V., & Whang, S. (1997a). The bullwhip effect in supply chains. *Sloan Management Review, 38*(3), 93–102.

Lee, H., Padmanabhan, V., & Whang, S. (1997b). Information distortion in a supply chain: *The bullwhip effect. Management Science, 73*(4), 546–558. doi:10.1287/mnsc.43.4.546

Leesa-Nguanusk, S. (2020). *Covid-19: Thailand eateries banking on delivery apps, social media to survive lockdown*. Retrieved October 27, 2021, from https://www.thestar.com.my/tech/tech-news/2020/04/21/covid-19-thailand-eateries-banking-on-delivery-apps-social-media-to-survive-lockdown

LEHOANGDIEPTHAO. (2021). *Thoi quen uong ca phe cua nguoi Viet thay doi ra sao?* [How have Vietnamese people's coffee-drinking habits changed?]. https://lehoangdiepthao.com/thoi-quen-uong-ca-phe-cua-nguoi-viet-thay-doi-ra-sao/

Lemaire, A., & Limbourg, S. (2020). How can food loss and waste management achieve sustainable development goals? *Journal of Cleaner Production, 234*, 1221–1234. doi:10.1016/j.jclepro.2019.06.226

Lengnick-Hall, M. L., Lengnick-Hall, C. A., & Rigsbee, C. M. (2013). Strategic human resource management and supply chain orientation. *Human Resource Management Review, 23*(4), 366–377. doi:10.1016/j.hrmr.2012.07.002

Li, K., Jin, Y., & Liu, L. (2021). Analysis of Building Supply Chain Data in Automobile Industry. *Automobile and Parts, 1*, 69-71.

Li, L. (2020). Research on the Current Situation and Supply Chain Management Mode of Chinese Medicine E-Commerce. *Logistics Engineering and Management, 42*(5), 90-91.

Liang, Y. (2020). Analysis on Social Responsibility of Supply Chain Management in Automobile Industry. *Technology and Economic Guide, 28*(30), 226–227.

Li, C. W., & Tzeng, G. H. (2009). Identification of a threshold value for the DEMATEL method using the maximum mean de-entropy algorithm to find critical services provided by a semiconductor intellectual property mall. *Expert Systems with Applications*, *36*(6), 9891–9898. doi:10.1016/j.eswa.2009.01.073

Li, F., Ma, Y., Zhang, X., & Xu, H. (2020). Study on the Environmental Management of Green Supply Chain of Tobacco Industry in Yunnan. *Environment Science Survey*, *39*(5), 31–37.

Liker, J. K. (2016). Striving for Excellence. *The Routledge Companion to Lean Management, 9*. Available at https://books.google.com.tw/books?hl=zh-TW&lr=&id=kDolDwAAQBAJ&oi=fnd&pg=PA9&dq=Liker,+J.+K.+(2016).+Striving+for+Excellence.+The+Routledge+Companion+to+Lean+Management,+9.+&ots=w92Z0Wq7AE&sig=cZHL0JX2ZI6zYo2swMey7LGYwag&redir_esc=y#v=onepage&q&f=true

Liu, W., Dunford, M., & Gao, B. A. (2018). Discursive construction of the belt and road initiative: From neo-liberal to inclusive globalization. *Journal of Geographical Sciences*, *28*(9), 1199–1214. doi:10.100711442-018-1520-y

Logistics, S. (2016). *Savan Logistics is operating in the first Dry Port/ICD (Inland Container Depot) in Savannakhet, Lao P.D.R., Welcome to SAVAN Logistics*. http://www.savanlogistics.com/

Lowson, B., King, R., & Hunter, A. (2010). *Quick Response: Managing the Supply Chain to Meet Consumer Demand*. John Wiley & Sons.

Lowson, B., King, K., & Hunter, A. (2010). *Quick response: Managing the supply chain to meet consumer demand*. Wiley.

Lowson, B., King, R., & Hunter, A. (1999). *Quick response*. Wiley.

Lumineau, F., & Henderson, J. E. (2012). The Influence of Relational Experience and Contractual Governance on the Negotiation Strategy in Buyer–supplier Disputes. *Journal of Operations Management*, *30*(5), 382–395. doi:10.1016/j.jom.2012.03.005

Lyndhurst, B. (2007). *Food behaviour consumer research—Findings from the quantitative survey*. Briefing Paper. WRAP.

Mambondiyani, A. (2020). *"It's lucrative": Zimbabwe's farmers turn to social media to stop the rot*. Retrieved October 28, 2021, from https://africanarguments.org/2020/04/its-lucrative-zimbabwes-farmers-turn-to-social-media-to-stop-the-rot/

Martinengo, M. C. (2014). Household food waste and consumer culture: Reflections on Italian behaviour. *Journal of Nutritional Ecology and Food Research*, *2*(1), 73–77. doi:10.1166/jnef.2014.1062

Mawson, E., & Fearne, A. (1996). Purchasing strategies and decision-making processes in the food service industry: A case study of UK restaurant chains. *Supply Chain Management*, *1*(3), 34–41. doi:10.1108/13598549610155305

Meng, X., Li, J., Yin, J., & Li, W. (2021). Study on Management Assessment Index System of Green Supply Chain in Building Material Industry. *China Cement*, *4*, 64–68.

Meyer, D. S., & Staggenborg, S. (1996). Movements, counter movements, and the structure of political opportunity. *American Journal of Sociology*, *101*(6), 1628–1660. doi:10.1086/230869

Meyer, K., & Peng, M. (2016). Theoretical foundations of emerging economy business research. *Journal of International Business Studies*, *47*(1), 3–22. doi:10.1057/jibs.2015.34

Michihata, M. (2010). Food service sangyo no syokuzai kaihatsu supply chain no Kochiku [Development of supply chain for foodstuff in food service industry]. *Kanko-gakukennkyu*, *9*, 103–115.

Minor, T., Astill, G., Raszap Skorbiansky, S., Thornsbury, S., Buzby, J., Hitaj, C., Kantor, L., Kuchler, F., Ellison, B., Misra, A., Richards, T., Roe, B., & Wilson, N. (2020). *Economic Drivers of Food Loss at the Farm and Pre-Retail Sectors: A Look at the Produce Supply Chain in the United States.* U.S. Department of Agriculture – Economic Research Service, Economic Information Bulletin #216.

Mitchell, M. (2020). *COVID 19 is compounding the world's food waste problem.* Retrieved October 15, 2021, from https://farrellymitchell.com/covid-19-leads-to-the-problem-of-food-waste/

Mizoue, Y. (2001). *Mujirushi syo-hin VS Uniqlo* [Muji vs. Uniqulo]. Paru syuppan.

MM-Redaktion. (2020). *Weinbranche auf Mallorca leidet unter der Coronakrise.* Retrieved October 15, 2021, from https://www.mallorcamagazin.com/nachrichten/wirtschaft/2020/07/21/82253/weinbranche-auf-mallorca-leidet-unter-der-coronakrise.html

MNW. (2021). *What does carbon peaking and carbon neutrality mean? When was carbon neutrality proposed?* Retrieved from http://www.mnw.cn/news/cj/2373822.html

Mohammed, A., Goli, V. S. N. S., & Singh, D. N. (2020). Discussion on 'Challenges, opportunities, and innovations for effective solid waste management during and post COVID-19 pandemic. *Resources, Conservation and Recycling, 164*, 105175. doi:10.1016/j.resconrec.2020.105175

Moore, M.-L., Tjornbo, O., Enfors, E., Knapp, C., Hodbod, J., Baggio, J. A., Norström, A., Olsson, P., & Biggs, D. (2014). Studying the complexity of change: Toward an analytical framework for understanding deliberate social-ecological transformations. *Ecology and Society, 19*(4), 54. Retrieved October 27, 2021, from. doi:10.5751/ES-06966-190454

Morris, J. (2019). *Coffea: A global history.* Reaktion Books.

Muramatsu, Y., & Nitta, Y. (2021). *Myanmar removes Thai builder from Indo-Pacific economic-zone project.* https://asia.nikkei.com/Economy/Myanmar-removes-Thai-builder-from-Indo-Pacific-economic-zone-project

Mutsuddi, I. (2012). Supply Chain Management for Effective People Management: Issues and Challenges, *The IUP. Journal of Operations Management, 11*(4), 53–65.

MWPVL International. (2021). *Amazon Global Supply Chain and Fulfillment Center. Network.* MWPVL International. https://www.mwpvl.com/html/amazon_com.html

Nagasawa, S. (2018). *Reality of logistics supply chain management.* Koyoshobo.

Nandi, S., Sarkis, J., Hervani, A. A., Helms, M. M. (2021). Redesigning supply chains using blockchain-Enabled circular economy and COVID-19 experiences. *Sustainable Production and Consumption.* . doi:10.1016/j.spc.2020.10.019

Napolitano, G. (2011, April). The two ways of global governance after the financial crisis: Multilateralism versus cooperation among governments. *International Journal of Constitutional Law, 9*(2), 310–339. doi:10.1093/icon/mor038

Naruke, M. (2018). *Amazon sekai saisendan no senryaku ga wakaru.* Daiyamondosya.

NdemezoE.NdikubwimanaJ. B.DukundeA. (2018). Determinants of capacity utilization of food and beverage manufacturing firms in Rwanda: do tax incentives matter? SSRN, 1-21. doi:10.2139/ssrn.3217757

Negishi, K. (2019). Nihon jidoshamekano CSR to jizokukanonakaihatsumokuhyo ni kansuru yobiteki kosatsu [Japanese Automobile Manufacturer's Corporate Responsibility and Sustainable Development Goals]. In Corporate Research Reports, (34). Chuo University Institute of Business Research.

Nemoto, T. (2000). Dejitaru jidai ni okeru hikari to kage (jou) [Light and shadow of a big Hit product in the digital era]. *Chushou Kigyou to Kumiai, 55*(8), 4–8.

News Picks. (n.d.). https://newspicks.com

Nguyen, G. T., & Sarker, T. (2018). Sustainable coffee supply chain management: A case study in Buon Me Thuot City, Daklak, Vietnam. *International Journal of Corporate Social Responsibility*, *3*(1), 1. doi:10.118640991-017-0024-x

NHK Spring Co. Ltd. (2015). *Notice regarding the establishment of a new sewing parts company in Cambodia, Thai subsidiary*. https://www.nhkspg.co.jp/news/release/pdfs/20150303_2.pdf

Nidec Corporation. (2012). *Notice of the establishment of a base plate manufacturing subsidiary*. https://www.nidec.com/-/media/www-nidec-com/corporate/news/2012/0528-01/120528-01.pdf

Niewiadomski, P. (2020). Corporate maturity desiderata in the face of the COVID-19 pandemic – The digital plane of logistics microfoundations. *Logforum*, *16*(4), 503–519. doi:10.17270/J.LOG.2020.495

Nikon Corporation. (2013). *Establishment of a new factory in Laos*. https://www.nikon.co.jp/news/2013/0321_01.htm

Nippon Yusen Research Group. (2021). *Top 20 companies in the world's largest shipping company*. Retrieved from https://www.mlit.go.jp/common/001013342.pdf

Nishizawa, O. (1999). *Logistics Cost*. Hakuto shobo.

Nissan Motor Co. Ltd. (2020). *Gurobarukobutsuchotatsunikansuru hoshin* [Nissan Minerals Sourcing Policy]. https://www.nissanglobal.com/JP/DOCUMENT/PDF/SR/Minerals_Sourcing_Policy_j.pdf

Nissan Motor Co. Ltd. (2021). *Nissan gurinchotatsu gaidorain* [Nissan Green Purchasing Guidelines]. https://www.nissanglobal.com/JP/DOCUMENT/PDF/SR/Nissan_Green_Purchasing_Guildeline_2021_j.pdf

NJS (Nikkan Jidousha Shinbun). (2021). *Daiwa Sangyo completes Laos factory for harness manufacturing base*. https://newspicks.com/news/1291286/body/?ref=company_SPD1ESW77DMR0S5A

NKS (Nihon Keizai Shimbun). (2016). *Cross-border infrastructure development*. Nihon Keizai Shimbun.

NKS (Nihon Keizai Shinbun). (2012). *Yazaki opens Cambodia factory to supplement production in Thailand*. https://www.nikkei.com/article/DGXNASDD170BC_X11C12A2TJ1000/

O'Brien, K. (2012). Global environmental change II: From adaptation to deliberate transformation. *Progress in Human Geography*, *36*(5), 667–676. doi:10.1177/0309132511425767

OECD. (2020). *COVID-19 and international trade: Issues and actions*. Retrieved October 22, 2021, from https://www.oecd.org/coronavirus/policy-responses/covid-19-andinternational-trade-issues-and-actions-494da2fa/

OLIO. (n.d.). *Join the #1 free sharing app*. https://olioex.com/

Olsson, P., Folke, C., & Hughes, T. P. (2008). Navigating the transition to ecosystem-based management of the Great Barrier Reef, Australia. *Proceedings of the National Academy of Sciences of the United States of America*, *105*(28), 9489–9494. doi:10.1073/pnas.0706905105 PMID:18621698

Padilla, K. (2020). *Responding to Food Waste Challenges from COVID-19. 05/13/20*. Retrieved October 16, 2021, from https://foodminds.com/food-thoughts/food-thoughts-items/responding-to-food-waste-challenges-from-covid-19/

Paganini, N., Adinata, K., Buthelezi, N., Harris, D., Lemke, S., Luis, A., Koppelin, J., Karriem, A., Ncube, F., Nervi Aguirre, E., Ramba, T., Raimundo, I., Sulejmanović, N., Swanby, H., Tevera, D., & Stöber, S. (2020). Growing and Eating Food during the COVID-19 Pandemic: Farmers' Perspectives on Local Food System Resilience to Shocks in Southern Africa and Indonesia. *Sustainability*, *2020*(12), 8556. doi:10.3390u12208556

Pai, P. (2015). Top 10 largest car companies in the world. *Tharawat Magazine*. Available at http://www.tharawat-magazine.com/facts/10-largest-car-companies/#gs.PbvLurI

Paich, M., & Sterman, J. D. (1993). Boom, bust, and failures to learn in experimental markets. *Management Science*, *39*(12), 1439–1458. doi:10.1287/mnsc.39.12.1439

Palomares, G. (2006). *Relaciones internacionales en el siglo XXI*. Tecnos.

Pang, G. (2020). What's the Influence of coronavirus pandemic crisis on Petrochemical Industry under the Global Crisis. *China Petroleum and Chemical Industry*, *5*, 4–9.

Pappalardo, G., Cerroni, S., Nayga, R. M. Jr, & Yang, W. (2020). Impact of Covid-19 on Household Food Waste: The Case of Italy. *Frontiers in Nutrition*, *7*, 585090. doi:10.3389/fnut.2020.585090 PMID:33344492

Parfitt, J., Macnaughton, S., & Barthel, M. (2010). *Food Waste within Food Supply Chains: Quantification and Potential for Change to 2050*. doi:10.1098/rstb.2010.0126

Park, S. E., Marshall, N. A., Jakku, E., Dowd, A. M., Howden, S. M., Mendham, E., & Fleming, A. (2012). Informing adaptation responses to climate change through theories of transformation. *Global Environmental Change*, *22*(1), 115–126. doi:10.1016/j.gloenvcha.2011.10.003

Parshina-Kottas, Y., Buchanana, L., Aufrichtig, A., & Corkery, M. (2020). Take a Look at How Covid-19 is Changing Meatpacking Plants. *The New York Times*. Retrieved October 15, 2021, from https://www.nytimes.com/interactive/2020/06/08/us/meat-processing-plants-coronavirus.html

Paul, J., & Dhir, S. (Eds.). (2021). *Globalization, deglobalization, and new paradigms in business*. Palgrave Macmillan. doi:10.1007/978-3-030-81584-4

Pestle Analysis. (2020). *Using Big Data to Optimize Routing for Trucking-Based Shipping and Logistics*. Retrieved October 25, 2021, from https://pestleanalysis.com/using-big-data-to-optimize-routing-for-trucking-based-shipping-and-logistics/

Petrini, C. (2001). *Slow food, the case for taste*. Columbia University Press.

Pettersson, A. I., & Segerstedt, A. (2013). Measuring Supply Chain Cost. *International Journal of Production Economics*, *143*(2), 357–363. doi:10.1016/j.ijpe.2012.03.012

Pieroni, M. P. P., McAloone, T. C., & Pigosso, D. C. A. (2019). Business model innovation for circular economy and sustainability: A review of approaches. *Journal of Cleaner Production*, *215*, 198–216. doi:10.1016/j.jclepro.2019.01.036

PJSEZ (Pakse-Japan SME SEZ). (2021). *The industrial park for exclusive use of the Japanese company*. http://pjsez.com/en/information/

Polansek, T., & Huffstutter, P. J. (2020). Piglets Aborted, Chickens Gassed as Pandemic Slams Meat Sector. *Reuters*. Retrieved October 14, 2021, from https://www.reuters.com/article/us-health-coronavirus-livestock-insight-idUSKCN2292YS

Porter, M. E. (1998). *On Competition*. Harvard Business School Press.

QinJ. Y. (2020). *WTO reform: Multilateral control over unilateral retaliation – Lessons from the US-China trade war*. Wayne State University Law School Research Paper No. 2020-73. https://ssrn.com/abstract=3654510 doi:10.2139/ssrn.3654510

Qiu, F., & Li, Z. (2020). Model Innovation and Logistics Revolution of Supply Chain in Household Appliance Industry. *Supply Chain Technology and Application*, *9*, 88–92.

Rahman, S., & Wu, Y. C. J. (2011). Logistics outsourcing in China: The manufacturer-cum-supplier perspective. *Supply Chain Management*, *16*(6), 462–473. doi:10.1108/13598541111171156

Rajesh, G., & Malliga, P. (2013). Supplier selection based on AHP QFD methodology. *Procedia Engineering*, *64*, 1283–1292. doi:10.1016/j.proeng.2013.09.209

Rasiah, R., Gammeltoft, P., & Jiang, Y. (2010). Home government policies for outward FDI from emerging economies: Lessons from Asia. *International Journal of Emerging Markets*, *5*(3/4), 333–357. doi:10.1108/17468801011058415

Rattanavijit, S., Somboonwiwat, T., & Khompatraporn, C. (2015). Analysis of Causal Competitive Factors of Thai Iron and Steel Supply Chain by DEMATEL Method. In *Industrial Engineering* (pp. 541–550). Management Science and Applications. Available at https://link.springer.com/content/pdf/10.1007%2F978-3-662-47200-2.pdf

Reddy, V. R., Singh, S. K., & Anbumozhi, V. (2016). Food supply chain disruption due to natural disasters: entities, risks, and strategies for resilience. Economic Research Institute for ASEAN and East Asia, 1-36.

Reinalda, B. (2009). *Routledge history of international organizations: From 1815 to the present day*. Routledge. doi:10.4324/9780203876572

Renault Nissan Purchasing Organization. (2015). *Runo Nissan sapuraiya CSR gaidorain* [Renault Nissan Corporate Social Responsibility Guidelines for Suppliers]. https://www.nissanglobal.com/JP/DOCUMENT/PDF/SR/CSR_Alliance_Guidelines.pdf

Reynold, M. (2020). Supply Chains Race to Match Shifting COVID-19 Consumer Behavior. *Packaging World*. Retrieved October 16, 2021, from https://www.packworld.com/ covid-19/article/21132561/supply-chains-race-to-match-shifting-covid19-consumer-behavior

Richards, T. (2020). *Food Service versus Retail: COVID-19 Impacts. CAST Commentary: Economic Impacts of COVID-19 on Food and Agricultural Markets*. Retrieved October 23, 2021, from https://www.cast-science.org/publication/economic-impacts-of-covid-19-on-food-and-agricultural-markets/

Robarts, S. (2016). *Volvo's Robot Refuse Collectors ROAR into Life*. Retrieved October 27, 2021, from https://newatlas.com/volvo-robot-based-autonomous-refuse-handling-project-test/42042/

Robert, B. H., & Ernest, L. N. (1999). *Introduction to supply chain management*. Prentice-Hall.

Rodrigue, J. (2020, October). The distribution network of Amazon and the footprint of freight digitalization. *Journal of Transport Geography*, *88*, 1–28. doi:10.1016/j.jtrangeo.2020.102825 PMID:32834678

Rodrik, D. (2000). How far will international economic integration go? *The Journal of Economic Perspectives*, *14*(1), 177–186. doi:10.1257/jep.14.1.177

Rodrik, D. (2007). *One economics many recipes, globalization, institutions and economic growth*. Princeton University Press. doi:10.1515/9781400829354

Roos, G., & Agarwal, R. (2015). Services Innovation in a Circular Economy. In The Handbook of Service Innovation (pp. 501-520). Springer. doi:10.1007/978-1-4471-6590-3_23

Rubinstein, P. (2020). *Why grocery shelves won't be empty for long*. Retrieved October 18, 2021, from https://www.bbc.com/worklife/article/20200401-covid-19-why-we-wont-run-out-of-food-during-coronavirus

Saaty, T. L. (1980). The Analytic Hierarchy Process. McGraw-Hill.

Saghiri, S. S., Bernon, M., Bourlakis, M., & Wilding, R. (2018). Omni-channel logistics special issue. *International Journal of Physical Distribution & Logistics Management*, *48*(4), 362–364. doi:10.1108/IJPDLM-05-2018-361

Saisho, T. (2019). A Study on global supply chain management systems for mainland ASEAN: Case study of collaboration between industrial clusters using a logistics system. *Proceedings of ICLIE*, 117-122.

Saisho, T. (2021). *The Information and Communication Industry and Industrial Clusters in Asia*. Hakuto Shobo.

Saito, M. (2021). *Amazon's Logistics Strategy in the E-Commerce Era* (Vol. 47). The Studies. In Economics and Trade.

SAIZERIYA Co. (n.d.). https://www.saizeriya.co.jp

Sakuma, T. (2006). *Toyota no CSRsenryaku - sekaikara sonkeisareru kigyono keiei* [Toyota CSR Strategy]. Japan Productivity Center.

Sakuma, T. (2008). *CSRsenryaku no hoteishiki - hondato rikcohno chidosetsu keiei* [Copernican CSR Management]. Japan Productivity Center.

Sapir, J. (2016). Jacques Sapir: Donald Trump, président de la démondialisation? *Le Figaro*, 10. https://www.lefigaro.fr/vox/monde/2016/11/10/31002-20161110ARTFIG00233-jacques-sapir-donald-trump-president-de-la-demondialisation.php

Sapir, J. (2011). *La demondialisation*. Seuil.

Sato, T. (2008). *Building Private Brand in Retail Marketing: Cooperation and specialization of The Hassyakai, Journal of Nippon-Keiei-Shindan-Gakkai*. Seven-Eleven Japan Co., Ltd. Retrieved October 27, 2021, from https://www.sej.co.jp/company/

Satou, M. (2021). *Amazon siki kawaritudukeru tikara* [Continuous Improvement by Amazon]. Daiwasyobou.

Schmidt, C. (2021). *UC 3.4 Intelligent fruit logistics*. Presentation at IoF2020 Farm to Fork Final Event.

Schott, A. B. S., & Andersson, T. (2015). Food waste minimization from a lifecycle perspective. *Journal of Environmental Management*, *147*(1), 219–226. Retrieved October 18, 2021, from. doi:10.1016/j.jenvman.2014.07.048 PMID:25264296

Schumpeter, J. A. (1949). *The theory of economic development. Harvard University Press*. Translated by Redvers Opie from Germany.

Seven Bank. (n.d.). Retrieved November 8, 2021, from https://www.sevenbank.co.jp/

Seven-i HLDGs. Co., Ltd. (2016). *Corporate outline*. Retrieved November 27, 2021, from https://www.7andi.com/library/dbps_data/_template_/_res/ir/library/co/pdf/2017_05.pdf

Shafiee-Jood, M., & Cai, X. (2016). Reducing food loss and waste to enhance food security and environmental sustainability. *Environmental Science & Technology*, *50*(16), 8432–8443. doi:10.1021/acs.est.6b01993 PMID:27428555

Shapiro, J.F. (2000). *Modeling the Supply Chain*. Duxbury Thomson Learning.

Shapiro. (2006). *Modeling the Supply Chain*. Brooks/Cole.

Sharma, H. B., Vanapalli, K. R., Cheela, V. R. S., Ved Prakash, R., Jaglan, A. K., Dubey, B., Goel, S., & Bhattacharya, J. (2020). Challenges, opportunities, and innovations for effective solid waste management during and post COVID-19 pandemic. *Resources, Conservation and Recycling*, *162*, 105052. doi:10.1016/j.resconrec.2020.105052 PMID:32834486

Shavshukov, V. M., & Zhuravleva, N. A. (2020). Global economy: New risks and leadership problems. *Int. J. Financial Stud*, *8*(1), 7. doi:10.3390/ijfs8010007

Shih, W. C. (2020). Global supply chain in a post-pandemic world. *Harvard Business Review*, (September-October), 2020.

Shimura, Y. (1998). *ERP/Supply Chain Seiko no himitsu* [The secret of ERP/supply chain]. Kogyo-tyousakai.

Shinoda, Y. (2013). *Sebun-irebun no Butsuryuu kenkyuu kokunai saidai no tenpomou wo musubu sekai saikyou rojisuthikusu no subete* [A Study of Seven-Eleven's Logistics -All about the World's Strongest Logistics Connecting Japan's Largest Store Network]. The Shogyokai Publishing.

Shinoda, Y. (2015). *Sebun-irebun no Hacchuuryoku* [Seven-Eleven's Ordering Capability]. The Shogyokai Publishing.

Shi, Y., Wang, C., & Yuan, X. (2020). Research on the Influence of Consumer Experience on Supply Chain Optimization under New Retail: Based on the Survey of New Retail Industry in Nanjing. *Business Economics (Cleveland, Ohio), 8*, 14–16.

Shogaki, Y. (2020). *Saizeriya oishii kara ureru no de ha nai ureteiruno ga oishisii nda* [Saizeriya is popular and the menu is delicious]. Nikkei BP.

Smith, A., Stirling, A., & Berkhout, F. (2005). The governance of sustainable socio-technical transitions. *Research Policy, 34*(10), 1491–1510. doi:10.1016/j.respol.2005.07.005

Song, S., Shi, X., & Song, G. (2020). Supply chain integration in omni-channel retailing: A human resource management perspective. *International Journal of Physical Distribution & Logistics Management, 50*(1), 101–121. doi:10.1108/IJPDLM-04-2019-0115

SPD (Savan Pacifica Development). (2021). *Savan Park Savannakhet*. http://www.savanpark. com/?page_id=1146&lang=ja

Spero, J. E., & Hart, J. A. (1997). *The Politics of International Economic Relations*. Routledge., doi:10.4324/9781315006154

SPS (Sanco Poipet SEZ). (2021). *Sanco Investment*. http://www.sancosez.com/ja/

Srinivasan, M., Hamdani, M., & Ma, S. (2021). Four supply chain management systems: From supply chain strategies to human resource management. *Business Horizons, 64*(2), 249–260. doi:10.1016/j.bushor.2020.11.006

Stadtler, H. (2015). Supply chain management: An overview. *Supply chain management and advanced planning*, 3-28. Available at https://link.springer.com/content/pdf/10.1007%2F978-3-642-55309-7.pdf

Steinberg, F. (2005). *Cooperación y conflicto en el Sistema comercial multilateral: La organización mundial de comercio como institución de gobernanza económica global*. Tesis Doctoral presentada en el Departamento de Análisis Económico: Teoría Económica e Historia Económica de la Facultada de Ciencias Económicas y Empresariales de la Universidad Autónoma de Madrid, España.

Stenmarck, A., Jensen, C. M., Quested, T., & Moates, G. (2000). *Estimates of European food waste levels*. Technical report from FUSIONS project. doi:10.13140/rg.2.1.4658.4721

Stenmarck, A., Jensen, C. M., Quested, T., & Moates, G. (2016). *Estimates of European food waste levels*. Retrieved October 11, 2021, from http://www.eu-fusions.org/phocadownload/Publications/Estimates%20of%20European%20food%20waste%20levels.pdf

Stone, B. (2013). *The Everything Store*. Back Bay Books Press.

Stone, B. (2021). *Amazon Unbound*. Simon & Schuster Inc.

Sudbury, A. W., & Hutchinson, E. B. (2016). A Cost Analysis of Amazon Prime Air (Drone Delivery). *The Journal of Economic Education, 16*, 1–12.

Suga, K., & Ishida, H. (2008). *Nissanno CSRsenryaku - seichoto shinraini motozuku jizokukanoseino keiei* [Nissan CSR Strategy]. Japan Productivity Center.

Sultana, I., Ahmed, I., & Azeem, A. (2015). An integrated approach for multiple criteria supplier selection combining Fuzzy Delphi, Fuzzy AHP & Fuzzy TOPSIS. *Journal of Intelligent & Fuzzy Systems*, *29*(4), 1273–1287.

Sumrit, D., & Anuntavoranich, P. (2013). Using DEMATEL method to analyze the causal relations on technological innovation capability evaluation factors in Thai technology-based firms. *Int Trans J Eng Manag Appl Sci Technol*, *4*(2), 81-103.

Sun, F., Fu, Q., & Jiang, S. (2020). Concentration degree of supply chain, Heterogeneity of property rights, and over-investment. *Finance and Accounting Monthly*, *18*, 15–23.

Sunil, C., & Peter, M. (2014). *Supply chain management: Strategy, planning, and operation*. Pearson.

Suzuki, T. (2012). *Zukai Ninki gaisyoku ten no rieki no dashikata* [Profitability of popular restaurant]. Ko-dansya.

Swamidass, P. M. (Ed.). (2000). Seven "rights" of logistics. In Encyclopedia of Production and Manufacturing Management (p. 684). Boston, MA: Springer. doi:10.1007/1-4020-0612-8_871

Szabó-Bódi, B., Kasza, G., & Szakos, D. (2018). Assessment of household food waste in Hungary. *British Food Journal*, *120*(3), 625–638. Advance online publication. doi:10.1108/BFJ-04-2017-0255

Taguchi, F. (2019). Ryutsu inobesyon kenkyu amazon no seityoukatei to kyousouyuui no gensen [A Study on Innovation in the Distribution: The Secret of Growth of Amazon]. *Business Review of the Senshu University.*, *108*, 41–76.

Taiwan Industrial Fastener Institute. (2016). *The Republic of China (Taiwan) Import/Export Statistical Data*. Available at http://www.fasteners.org.tw/Default.aspx?tabindex=8&tabid=11

Tanaka, M. (1997). Tamagotchi kaihatsu no kiseki wo ou [Following the development process of Tamagotchi]. *Nikkei Electronics*, *686*, 131–134.

Taylor, D., Pritchard, A., Dhuan, D., & Mirshra, S. (2020). *What's behind the empty grocery shelves*. Retrieved October 14, 2021, from https://www.scmr.com/article/whats_behind_the_empty_grocery_shelves

Taylor, R. (2018) Amazon Embraces the Gig Economy: Small Business Risk or Game-Changing Opportunity? *Forbes*. https://www.forbes.com/sites/forbestechcouncil/2018/09/04/amazon-embraces-the-gig-economy-small-business-risk-or-game-changing-opportunity/?sh=18c5d0897e63

Teigiserova, D. A., Hamelin, L., & Thomsen, M. (2019). Towards transparent valorization of food surplus, waste and loss: Clarifying definitions, food waste hierarchy, and role in the circular economy. *The Science of the Total Environment*, *706*, 136033. doi:10.1016/j.scitotenv.2019.136033 PMID:31855638

The ASEAN (Association of Southeast Asian Nations) Secretariat. (2015a). *ASEAN Economic Community*. https://asean.org/asean-economic-community/

The ASEAN (Association of Southeast Asian Nations) Secretariat. (2015b). *ASEAN 2025 at a Glance. A Community of Opportunities for All*. https://asean.org/asean-2025-at-a-glance/

The Economic Times. (2020a). *Flipkart preparing to start hyperlocal delivery services: Sources. The service will be available via the Flipkart app, and initially, deliveries will be done from local warehouses and select shops*. Retrieved October 27, 2021, from https://retail.economictimes.indiatimes.com/news/e-commerce/e-tailing/flipkart-preparing-to-start-hyperlocal-delivery-services-sources/76416609

The Economic Times. (2020b). *Amazon, Flipkart to increase warehouses*. Retrieved October 27, 2021, from https://economictimes.indiatimes.com/industry/services/retail/amazon-flipkart-to-increase-warehouses/articleshow/75523490.cms?from=mdr

Themido, I., Arantes, A., Fernandes, C., & Guedes, A. P. (2000). Logistics Costs Case Study-An ABC Approach. *The Journal of the Operational Research Society, 51*(10), 1148–1157.

Timetric. (2017). *MPWT-Vientiane Logistics Park-Laos-Project Profile*. https://www.marketresearch.com/Timetric-v3917/MPWT-Vientiane-Logistics-Park-Laos-11181862/

Too Good To Go International. (2020). *Too Good To Go. Rettet Essen hilf unserem Planeten.* Retrieved October 28, 2021, from https://toogoodtogo.at/de-at?utm_medium=Search&utm_source=Google&utm_campaign=AT_B2C_Paid_Marketing_Search_Google_Brand&gclid=CjwKCAjwjbCDBhAwEiwAiudBy1eD2AaJSzVbr-0UfFLiOe5qQvE3GwyS-N57aR3xJLiMZ4BeH-_41YxoC7UgQAvD_BwE

Toyota Boshoku Corporation. (2013). *Toyota Boshoku establishes first production base for automobile interior parts in Laos*. https://www.toyota-boshoku.com/jp/news/543.html

Toyota Motor Corporation. (2012). *Shiiresaki CSR gaidorain* [Toyota Supplier CSR Guidelines]. https://global.toyota/pages/global_toyota/sustainability/csr/gri/supplier_csr_jp.pdf

Toyota Motor Corporation. (2016). *Gurinchotatsu gaidorain* [Toyota Green Purchasing Guidelines]. https://global.toyota/pages/global_toyota/sustainability/esg/toyota_green_purchasing_guidelines_jp.pdf

Toyota Tsusho Corporation. (2015). *First techno park project by a Japanese company in Poipet, Cambodia*. https://www.toyota-tsusho.com/press/detail/150331_002756.html

U.S. Department of Agriculture (USDA). (2020). *USDA Farmers to Families Food Box*. Retrieved October 19, 2021, from https://www.ams.usda.gov/selling-food-to-usda/farmers-to-families-food-box

Umezawa, S. (2020). *Konbini Chain Shinka Shi* [History of Convenience Store Chains]. Eastpress.

United Nations Environment Programme. (2015). *Global Waste Management Outlook*. Retrieved October 15, 2021, from https://www.unep.org/resources/report/global-waste-management-outlook

United Nations. (2015). *Transforming our Wold: The 2030 Agenda for Sustainable Development*. Retrieved October 12, 2021, from https://sdgs.un.org/publications/transforming-our-world-2030-agenda-sustainable-development-17981

Unleashed Software. (2021). *The key coffee industry trends for 2022 & beyond*. https://www.unleashedsoftware.com/blog/the-key-coffee-industry-trends-for-2021-beyond

Urban Bean Coffee. (2020). *The most interesting coffee statistics*. https://urbanbeancoffee.com/coffee/usa-coffee-statistics/

Urban Bean Coffee. (2021). *Arabica vs. robusta: The ultimate guide - urban bean coffee*. http://urbanbeancoffee.com>coffee>arabica-vs-robusta/

Van Hilten, M., Adema, H., Nuhoff-Isakhanyan, G., & Otte, H. (2020). *D4.6: Validation of user acceptability in IOF2020 use cases*. Retrieved October 21, 2021, from https://www.iof2020.eu/deliverables/d4.6-validation-of-user-acceptability-of-iof2020-use-cases.pdf

Vanham, P. (2019). *A brief history of globalization*. World Economic Forum.

Velocity Fietskoeriers. (2014). *Delivery of vegetables by bike*. Retrieved October 22, 2021, from http://cargobikefestival.blogspot.com/2014/02/delivery-of-vegetables-by-bike.html

Verdouw, C. N., Sundmaeker, H., Meyer, F., Wolfert, J., & Verhoosel, J. (2013b). Smart Agri-Food Logistics: Requirements for the Future Internet. In Dynamics in Logistics. Lecture Notes in Logistics. Springer. doi:10.1007/978-3-642-35966-8_20

Verdouw, C. N., Beulens, A. J. M., & van der Vorst, J. G. A. J. (2013a). Virtualisation of floricultural supply chains: A review from an Internet of Things perspective. *Computers and Electronics in Agriculture*, *99*(1), 160–175. doi:10.1016/j.compag.2013.09.006

Vietnam Coffee Cocoa Association (VICOFA). (n.d.). *Country coffee profile: Vietnam*. http://www.vicofa.org.vn/country-coffee-profile-vietnam-bid385.html

Vincent, K. (2017). *Transformational adaptation: A review of examples from 4 deltas to inform the design of DECCMA's Adaptation Policy Trajectories*. DECCMA Working Paper, Deltas, Vulnerability and Climate Change: Migration and Adaptation, IDRC Project Number 107642. Retrieved October 27, 2021, from https://generic.wordpress.soton.ac.uk/deccma/wp-content/uploads/sites/181/2017/12/Vincent_Transformational-adaptation-working-paper.pdf

VolvoGroup. (2016). *The ROAR project - robot and drone in collaboration for autonomous refuse handling*. Retrieved October 29, 2021, from https://www.youtube.com/watch?v=fNIV6Dcj29E

Vongsa, V. (2014). *The Vientiane Logistics Park*. https://www.mpwt.gov.la/attachments/article/877/Annex%206_IEE%20Preliminary%20Findginds_Mr%20Korn_Eng.pdf

Vujanović, D., Momčilović, V., Bojović, N., & Papić, V. (2012). Evaluation of vehicle fleet maintenance management indicators by application of DEMATEL and ANP. *Expert Systems with Applications*, *39*(12), 10552–10563. doi:10.1016/j.eswa.2012.02.159

Wang, H., Potter, A., & Naim, M. (2011). Evaluation of postponement in the soluble coffee supply chain: A case study. *International Journal of Production Economics*, *131*(1), 355–3564. doi:10.1016/j.ijpe.2010.08.015

Wang, L., Törngren, M., & Onori, M. (2015). Current status and advancement of cyber-physical systems in manufacturing. *Journal of Manufacturing Systems*, *37*, 517–527. doi:10.1016/j.jmsy.2015.04.008

Weber, C. A., & Current, J. R. (1993). A multiobjective approach to vendor selection. *European Journal of Operational Research*, *68*(2), 173–184. doi:10.1016/0377-2217(93)90301-3

Wei, S., Zhang, J., & Li, Z. (1997). A supplier-selecting system using a neural network. In *Intelligent Processing Systems, 1997. ICIPS'97. 1997 IEEE International Conference on Intelligent Processing Systems*. IEEE.

Wen, Z., Hu, S., De Clercq, D., Beck, M. B., Zhang, H., Fei, F., & Lui, J. (2018). Design, implementation, and evaluation of an Internet of Things (IoT) network system for restaurant food waste management. *Waste Management, 73*, 26-38. Retrieved October 27, 2021, from https://www.sciencedirect.com/science/article/abs/pii/S0956053X17309376

Westley, F. R., Tjornbo, O., Schultz, L., Olsson, P., Folke, C., Crona, B., & Bodin, Ö. (2013). A theory of transformative agency in linked social-ecological systems. *Ecology and Society*, *18*(3), 27. Retrieved October 21, 2021, from. doi:10.5751/ES-05072-180327

Westley, F. R., Zimmerman, B., & Patton, M. Q. (2006). *Getting to maybe: how the world is changed*. Vintage Canada.

WFP (World Food Programme). (2009). *Hunger and markets*. Earthscan.

Wikipedia. (2022). *Toyota Motor Thailand*. Retrieved from https://en.wikipedia.org/wiki/Toyota_Motor_Thailand

Williamson, O. E. (1979). Transaction cost economics: The governance of contractual relations. *The Journal of Law & Economics*, *22*(2), 233–261. doi:10.1086/466942

Williamson, O. E. (1999). *The Mechanisms of Governance*. Oxford University Press.

Wills, R., Mcglasson, B., Graham, D., & Joyce, D. (1998). *Postharvest an Introduction to the physiology and handling of fruits, vegetables and ornamentals* (4[th] ed.). UNSW Press.

Wilson, N. (1996). Supply chain management: A case study of a dedicated supply chain for bananas in the UK grocery market. *Supply Chain Management*, *1*(2), 28–35. doi:10.1108/13598549610155279

Witt, M. A. (2019). De-globalization: Theories, predictions, and opportunities for international business research. *Journal of International Business Studies*, *50*(7), 1053–1077. doi:10.105741267-019-00219-7

World Bank. (2016). *World Bank data*. http://data.worldbank.org/?display=default

WTO. (2021). *World trade report 2021. Economic resilience and trade*. World Trade Organization.

Wunderlich, S. M., & Martinez, N. M. (2018). Conserving natural resources through food loss reduction: Production and consumption stages of the food supply chain. *International Soil and Water Conservation Research*, *6*(4), 331–339. doi:10.1016/j.iswcr.2018.06.002

Wu, W. W. (2008). Choosing knowledge management strategies by using a combined ANP and DEMATEL approach. *Expert Systems with Applications*, *35*(3), 828–835. doi:10.1016/j.eswa.2007.07.025

Wu, Y. C. J., Huang, S. K., Goh, M., & Hsieh, Y. J. (2013). Global logistics management curriculum: Perspective from practitioners in Taiwan. *Supply Chain Management*, *18*(4), 376–388. doi:10.1108/SCM-04-2012-0145

Wu, Y. C., Lin, B. W., Shih, C., & Chen, C. J. (2013). Communicating and prioritizing science and technology policy using AHP. *Innovation*, *15*(4), 437–451. doi:10.5172/impp.2013.15.4.437

Xu, Y., Sheng, J., & Wu, X. (2021). Facilitating Development of Fresh E-Commerce by Supply Chain Innovation and Value Chain Upgrading- the case of Dingdong. *Economic & Trade Update*, *7*, 14–17.

Yaffe-Bellany, D., & Corkery, M. (2020). Dumped Milk, Smashed Eggs, Plowed Vegetables: Food Waste of the Pandemic. *The New York Times*. Retrieved October 11, 2021, from https://www.nytimes.com/2020/04/11/business/coronavirus-destroying-food.html

Yahagi, T. (1994). *Konbiniensu sutoa shisutemu no kakushinsei* [Innovations in Convenience Store Systems]. Nikkei.

Yamada, K. (2015). Development of Vita Park and Sawan Seno SEZ progresses: Looking for complementary development with neighboring countries in the border area. *The International Trade Public Bulletin (Current Business Brief Report)*. https://www.jetro.go.jp/biznews/2015/04/5525d02b1b198.html

Yamada, K. (2020), *Vientiane Logistics Park development begins. Business Brief Report*. https://www.jetro.go.jp/biznews/2020/07/efbe1fdffca6cf59.html

Yamagata, M. (1998). Keiki teimei no genzai, AM sanngyou no genntenn ni tachimodori, aratana asobi no kouchiku wo Pokemon ya Tamagotchi nado no dai boom wo kanngaeru [Under the economic downturn, review the big boom of Pokemon, Tamagotchi, et al. to create new entertainment in the amusement industry]. *Amusement Industry*, *27*(1), 204–205.

Yang, Y. P. O., Shieh, H. M., Leu, J. D., & Tzeng, G. H. (2008). A novel hybrid MCDM model combined with DEMATEL and ANP with applications. *International Journal of Operations Research*, *5*(3), 160-168.

Yang, Y. P. O., Shieh, H. M., & Tzeng, G. H. (2013). A VIKOR technique based on DEMATEL and ANP for information security risk control assessment. *Information Sciences*, *232*, 482–500. doi:10.1016/j.ins.2011.09.012

Yin, W., & Wang, L. (2020). Research and Practice of ICT Industry Smart Supply Chain Collaboration System. *Supply Chain Management*, *12*, 77–81.

Yokoi, A. (1997). *Tamagotchi no tannjouki* [Birth record of Tamagotchi™]. KK Best Sellers.

Yun, C., Liu, K., Chen, Q., & Xu, S. (2021). The influence of coronavirus pandemic crisis on supply chain of electric power industry. *Modern Business Trade Industry*, *19*, 15–16.

Zhang, H. (2021). Building green and intelligent supply chain of electric power industry under target 3060. *Industry Dynamics*, 17-19.

Zhang, G. (2021). Analysis on optimization strategy of multi-tier stock of supply chain in automobile industry of China. *China Logistics and Purchase*, *8*, 73–74.

Zhang, J. (2006). The origin, development, spread, and drinking culture of coffee. *Chinese Agricultural History*, (25), 22–29.

Zhang, L., Luo, Y., Tao, F., Li, B. H., Ren, L., Zhang, X., Guo, H., Cheng, Y., Hu, A., & Liu, Y. (2014). Cloud manufacturing: A new manufacturing paradigm. *Enterprise Information Systems*, *8*(2), 167–187. doi:10.1080/17517575.2012.683812

Zhao, J., & Wang, Y. (2021). Yuanda Logistics: facilitating the optimization of supply chain by sharing in fast consuming goods industry. *Logistics Technology and Application*, *5*, 94-96.

Zhao, L., & Dai, Q. (2020). Discussion on the Current Situation and Trends of Supply Chain Development in Home Appliance Industry. *Supply Chain Management*, *10*, 72–87.

Zhou, L., Zhang, L., & Fang, Y. (2020). Logistics service scheduling with manufacturing provider selection in cloud manufacturing. *Robotics and Computer-integrated Manufacturing*, *65*, 101914. doi:10.1016/j.rcim.2019.101914

Zhou, Z., Ren, T., Zhang, Z., Sun, M., Deng, Y., Liu, H., Wang, Y., & Zhang, D. (2020). The Application Research on Identity Resolution in Home Appliance Industry Industrial Internet—Appliance of Identity Resolution in Home Appliance Supply Chain. *Application Research*, *11*, 42–47.

Zhu, G., Chou, M. C., & Tsai, C. W. (2020). Lessons learned from the COVID-19 pandemic exposing the shortcomings of current supply chain operations: A long-term prescriptive offering. *Sustainability*, *12*(14), 5858. doi:10.3390u12145858

# About the Contributors

**Toru Higuchi** is a Ph.D. in Business Administration and a Professor at Tokyo Seitoku University. His major is Business Logistics and Supply Chain Management.

* * *

**Noureddin Driouech** is an Agricultural Engineer specialized in Phytopathology. He got a Master of Science degree in Plant biotechnologies, and holds a PhD in Environmental Sciences, design and management of sustainable Mediterranean cropping systems at Tuscia University- Viterbo (Italy). His scientific interest focuses on educational, alumni networking and follow-up research studies, innovation in education/ training in sustainable agriculture, agri-foods sector, and food system. He is the authors of more than 80 scientific papers/articles, 2 chapters publications and 1 book. a member the UC Berkeley Environmental Leadership Program (ELP 2006-2016) Network and various International Conference Scientific Committees. He operated as an International expert/agent in various EU, Mediterranean and Balkan countries, Albania, Croatia, Bosnia, Egypt, France, Morocco, Poland, Tunisia, Serbia, Spain and Syria. He speaks Arabic, French, English and Italian.

**Hiromu Hatakeyama**, Ph.D., is associate Professor, Faculty of Business Administration, Sakushin Gakuin University (Japan). His main research focus is on the coordination of CSR measures in the supply chain of the Japanese automotive industry.

**Yukun Huang** is a Graduate School student at Sakushin Gakuin University and studies SCM under Prof. Higuchi.

**Matthew James Lamb** is a Teacher at the TGM Technical College, Vienna and an International Project Manager at the Polymer and Environmental Centre, LKT-TGM. His main focus is deeply rooted in lifelong learning for regional sustainable development at the European and international level. His key areas of expertise lie in network coordination for lifelong learning, waste management, Local Agenda 21 and international course development.

**Gary Mason** is a president of Japanese & Spanish Translation and a master of martial arts.

**Hitomi Nakagawa** is an associate professor at the Faculty of Business Management, Sakushin Gakuin University.

**Linh Nguyen** is a Graduate School of Management at Sakushin Gakuin University and studies SCM under Prof. Higuchi.

**Erika Quendler** is a researcher at the Federal Institute of Agricultural Economics, Rural and Mountain Research. She holds a PhD in Agricultural Economics from the University of Natural Resources and Life Sciences in Vienna. Her main research interests are sustainable development, quality of life, resilience, digital transformation, family farm and young farmer issues as well as farm holiday, value chain and economic accounts for agriculture. She has published several scientific papers and participated in many scientific international conferences.

**Tetsuro Saisho** is a former Professor, Faculty of Social and Information Studies, Gunma University, Part-time Lecturer, Faculty of Commerce, Waseda University. He obtained his Aoyama Gakuin University Graduate School of International Political Economics, Department of International Business, Master of Business Administration (MBA) (Japan) in 1993, and Nagasaki University Graduate School of Economics, Department of Economics and Business Policy, Master of Economics (Japan) in 1997. He also has a Chuo University Graduate School of Science and Engineering, Department of Information Engineering, Doctoral Program, Ph.D. (Engineering) (Japan) in 2002. He has also previously been a researcher at the Telecommunication Advancement Organization (TAO), now the National Institute of Information and Communications Technology (NICT). He has published numerous research papers and academic books on a wide range of business and information themes. His Field of Study on Management Information, Information Strategy, Information Security, Information Systems, Industrial Cluster. Currently, he is a director of the Director of JSIM (Japan Society for Information and Management), Director of JSPM (Japan Society for Production Management), Director of Tohren (International Federation of East Asian Management Associations) Japan, Councilor of JSAAM (Japan Scholarly Association for Asian Management).

**Yu-Shan Su** is a distinguished professor at National Taiwan Normal University, Taipei, Taiwan. Her research interests are innovation management in the high-tech industry. Dr. Su serves as an Associate Editor of Technological Forecasting and Social Change, and a member of editorial board of IEEE Transactions on Engineering Management. She has published in Research Policy, IEEE Transactions on Engineering Management, Journal of Innovation & Knowledge, Technological Forecasting and Social Change, R&D Management, Computers in Human Behaviour, Journal of World Business, Asia Pacific Journal of Management, Management Decision, International Journal of Technology Management, Journal of Organizational Change Management, International Journal of Innovation and Technology Management, Tsinghua Business Review, Sun Yet-Sen Management Review. Her book "Routledge Companion to Technology Management: Next Steps" edited with T. Daim, M. Dabić is published by Routledge Taylor & Francis Group in 2022. Her book "Innovation Management: Winning the Competitive Advantage in the Globe" edited with J. Chen and G. Zheng was published by Bestwise Publisher in Chinese in 2015.

**José G. Vargas-Hernández**, M.B.A., Ph.D., Member of the National System of Researchers of Mexico and a research professor at Posgraduate and research Department, Tecnológico Mario Molina Unidad Zapopan,. Professor Vargas-Hernández has a Ph. D. in Public Administration and a Ph.D. in Organizational Economics. He has undertaken studies in Organisational Behaviour and has a Master of Business Administration, published four books and more than 200 papers in international journals and reviews (some translated to English, French, German, Portuguese, Farsi, Chinese, etc.) and more than 300 essays in national journals and reviews. He has obtained several international Awards and recognition.

**Tien-Shou Wang** currently retired from Maclean-Fogg International Taiwan (MFI-TW). He had worked for MFI-TW as the General Manager around 16 years. His main works related to the Supply Chain Management (SCM) and International Procurement. Before MFI-TW, he was the plant manager of ESUSE Auto Parts, the Operational Manager of Ericsson Taiwan, the System Equipment Engineer of AT&T Taiwan and the CAD/CAM Engineer for Matsushita (Panasonic) Taiwan. He graduated in Master degree in Engineering at National Taiwan Normal University in 2017.

**Yang Zhengguang** is a Ph. D candidate at the Graduate School of Management in Sakushin Gakuin University and studies SCM under Prof. Higuchi.

# Index


1-Click 148, 151-153, 155, 163, 166

## A

Activity-Based Costing (ABC) 29, 43
Activity-Based Management (ABM) 29, 43
Agile Supply Chain 299
agri-food logistics 215-218, 222-223, 225-228, 236-238
Amazon 148-167, 236, 281
Amazon Marketplace 166
Amazon S3 (Amazon Simple Storage Service) 166
American 43, 48, 68-71, 73-78, 81-90, 93, 150, 174, 177, 184, 212, 233, 262, 270
American automotive companies 75, 88, 93
an evaluation model 68, 70, 77, 90
ASEAN (Association of South-East Asian Nations) 256-257
automotive companies 46, 68-71, 73, 75-79, 82, 88-90, 93-94
automotive industry 46, 62, 66, 69, 71, 75, 85, 90-98, 105-107, 109-111, 113
Automotive OEM Company 94
AWS 148, 158-164, 167

## B

BANDAI 115-124, 127-130, 132
Book Return System 141, 147
boom and bust 115, 118, 120, 123-124, 127-128, 130, 132
bottled coffee 169, 176, 181, 190
bullwhip effect 115, 117-118, 130-132, 289
business logistics 1-5, 22, 27, 39, 42, 131, 227, 296

## C

café 169, 183, 192, 195
canned coffee 169, 172, 174-175, 180-181, 193
Car Company 94
Carbon Peak Carbon Neutralization 291, 296, 299
case 1-2, 7-8, 16, 31, 36-38, 41-43, 46, 48, 53, 58-61, 66-68, 89, 92, 102, 110-113, 115, 118-119, 121, 123-124, 131-133, 136-137, 141-142, 145-146, 148-149, 153, 156, 166, 169, 171, 177, 179, 182, 184, 190-192, 194-195, 197, 201, 207, 211, 213, 217, 226, 234, 237, 249-250, 255, 261-262, 267, 270, 275-276, 290-291, 293, 298
central kitchen 194, 196, 205-207, 210, 212-214
chemical substances 96-98, 100, 103, 105-108, 110, 113
chemical substances in products 96-98, 103, 106-108, 110, 113
China 18, 54, 57-60, 64-65, 68-70, 75, 77, 92-93, 105-107, 120, 184-186, 190-191, 209, 230, 242, 245, 248-249, 257, 260, 262, 273, 277-279, 281, 287-299
click and mortar 152, 163, 167
coffee beverage 169, 174, 180, 193
Coffee House 169, 177, 179, 193
coffee shop 169, 174, 178, 189, 193
Coffee Shop Chain 169
cold chain 194, 209-213, 290, 294
company group 1, 22
conflict minerals 96-98, 102-103, 105, 108, 110, 113
cost management 24-25, 27, 29, 35, 39-42
COVID-19 pandemic 215-219, 221-222, 225, 227-229, 231, 233-235, 274, 276-277, 288, 291-292
CSR 95-97, 101, 103-105, 107-113, 294

## D

deglobalization 259-261, 263-264, 266-275, 277
Delivery by Temperature Zone 138
developing countries 55, 190, 216, 219, 223, 244, 257-259, 270-271, 279, 281
dominant strategy 136, 139, 142
drip coffee 169, 173-176, 179-181, 184, 186, 189-190, 192-193
drone 148, 160, 165-166, 237

DX 278-279, 286, 288, 294, 296, 299

## E

Economic Corridor 240-243, 245-248, 250, 256-257
ecosystem 100, 157, 164, 167, 285
EU Farm to Fork (F2F) 216, 238
European 16, 53-54, 68-71, 73, 75-78, 80, 82, 84-90, 93-94, 97-98, 105-106, 112-113, 221, 230, 232, 235, 238, 262
European automotive companies 75, 88, 94
EV 46-47, 53-66
exhaust gas fraud 46, 65

## F

FBA (Fulfillment by Amazon) 167
FCV 54-55, 59, 61
Fixed Cost 147
FLW chain 215, 226-228, 238
FLW chain management 215
FLW management 217, 222, 224-225, 227, 238
Fly Wheel 148
food loss and waste 215-216, 230, 232, 235
food supply chain 211, 217-220, 228, 234, 237-238, 277
Food Waste and Loss (FLW) 238
franchise chain 133, 136
fulfillment 3, 35, 44, 122, 125, 148, 156-159, 164, 166-167

## G

Global Supply Chain 71, 78, 80, 82, 84, 166, 194, 240-241, 244, 246-250, 255-256, 259, 266, 268, 275, 277-278, 297
globalization 71, 73, 112, 211, 252, 259-279, 281, 284-286, 294
Green Purchasing 98-99, 101, 110-111, 113
Green Supply Chain 296-297, 299
GSC 240-253, 256, 278-280, 285-288, 292, 294-296
guidance framework 217, 222-223, 225, 227-228, 238

## H

High-mix Low-volume Inventory 133
HV 54

## I

IaaS (Infrastructure as a Service) 167
IMDS 106-107, 113
industrial cluster 240, 242, 246-250, 253, 256
industrial cluster strategy 242, 246, 256
Industrial Engineering 92, 206, 213
industry association 95-96, 109
information distortion 115, 118, 123, 128-132
innovation 12-18, 23, 61, 73, 75, 93, 145, 148-149, 166, 169, 173, 215-216, 218, 222-223, 227, 231, 234-235, 238, 252-253, 264, 269, 273, 278-280, 282-290, 294-295, 298
instant coffee 169-172, 174-180, 182, 184-185, 189-191, 193
international business system 240-242, 244, 246, 250, 253
ISO 26000 95, 97, 112-113
Italian restaurant 201, 209

## J

Japan 1, 24-26, 43, 46, 48, 50-51, 53, 58-61, 64, 66-67, 69-70, 73, 77-78, 82, 94-96, 98, 101-107, 109-112, 115-116, 120, 128, 133-148, 165, 169, 174, 179-181, 184, 189-191, 194-198, 201, 203-204, 208-209, 213, 240, 242, 244, 247, 249, 254, 258, 262, 266, 278-282, 284-288, 296
Japanese automotive companies 46, 68-71, 73, 75-76, 78, 82, 88-90, 94
Japanese automotive industry 46, 66, 95-97, 106-107, 109-111
Japanese foodservice industry 194
JAPIA 95-96, 101-110, 112
Just-in-TIME (JIT) 47, 67

## K

KEIRETSU 46-53, 55-59, 61, 64, 66-67, 109, 130
KEIRETSU transaction 46-49

## L

Last One Mile 148, 160, 164-165, 167
LCA (Life Cycle Assessment) 113
Leagile Supply Chain 299
Lean Supply Chain 299
life cycle 22, 24, 37-38, 41, 44, 54, 100, 103, 113, 116, 119, 124, 130-131, 290, 293
Life Cycle Cost (LCC) 37, 44
light vehicle 59-60, 67, 92
Location Creation 206, 213
Logistic cost 44
logistic solution 215
logistics 1-5, 10, 22, 24-31, 33, 35-39, 41-44, 71, 91-93,

131-133, 136-137, 140-142, 146, 148, 156-158, 164-167, 194, 197, 200, 207, 209, 212, 214-218, 222-223, 225-228, 231-238, 240-245, 247-256, 260, 265-266, 268-270, 273, 277-279, 281-298
logistics costs 24-25, 27-29, 31, 35-36, 38, 41-44, 142, 164, 209, 281
logistics system 3, 25, 227-228, 240-245, 247, 249, 251, 255-256

## M

management accounting 24, 26, 41-43
Management Principles 202, 206, 214
Manufacture and Direct Sales 194, 207
Marketplace 148, 156-158, 164, 166
matching and sharing 278, 284-285, 287, 296, 299
Mitigation of Day-to-Day FLW 238
modularization 52, 75
multi-echelon system 115, 117, 132, 189
Multinational Corporations 265, 267, 278

## O

Oden 141, 147
OEM 73, 94
One-Stop Service 244, 251, 256
Opening up Parts Trading 67
opportunity loss 35, 140, 147

## P

person-hour productivity 203, 206, 214
PHV 54
physical distribution 1-2, 22-23, 26-27, 44, 235, 251, 298
Plan-Based Supply Chain 300
platform 58, 153-154, 156-157, 159, 162, 166, 200, 214, 232, 278, 285, 288, 291-292, 294, 296
Point of Sales 14, 123, 128, 133
POS 14, 123, 128, 135, 142, 147
Process Innovation 13-14, 23, 169, 173
Product Innovation 1, 13-14, 16-18, 23, 73, 169
Production Chain 266, 277
production chains 259, 265-267, 269-270
protectionism 259-264, 268, 273, 277
protectionist policies 259-260, 265-266, 273
Pull Operation 1, 23
Push Operation 1, 23
pyramid type 46, 49

## Q

QR (Quick Response) 47, 67

## R

relocation of production 259-260, 264, 267, 270-271, 277
reorganization of KEIRETSU 46, 58
resilience 215, 217, 223, 225, 234, 260, 276, 278, 286, 292, 294, 296
ROA 195, 214

## S

Saizeriya 194-214
SCM 1, 5, 10, 21-22, 39, 47, 65, 115, 120, 124-127, 130, 133, 145-146, 169, 171, 186, 194-197, 200-201, 211-214, 216
shortage game 115, 118, 124, 126-127, 132
single operation 196, 211, 214
single window 252-253, 256-257
Small-lot High-frequency Delivery 133
SPA 194, 196-197, 200, 206, 208-209, 212, 214
special economic zone 246-248, 250, 254, 256-257
SPFB 197, 206-207, 209-210, 212, 214
supplier 7, 49, 64, 66, 68, 70-79, 84, 86, 89-93, 100-101, 106-107, 110-113, 122, 143, 147, 150, 211, 233, 279-281, 290, 295
Supplier Power 143, 147
supplier selection 68, 70-71, 75-79, 84, 89-93
supply chain 1-14, 16, 21-26, 29, 37-44, 46-49, 51, 55, 59, 61, 63, 67, 71, 78, 80-87, 91-101, 103, 105-109, 111, 113, 115, 117-118, 121, 123, 125, 127-133, 145-146, 149, 157, 164, 166, 169-172, 179, 187, 190-192, 194-197, 199-201, 206-208, 210-223, 225-228, 230, 233-234, 237-238, 240-241, 244, 246-250, 252, 255-256, 259, 266-268, 272, 274-279, 287, 293, 296-300
Supply Chain Finance 287, 300
supply chain management 1, 3, 6, 10, 23-24, 26, 39-43, 47, 63, 71, 91-93, 95, 101, 109, 111, 117, 133, 146, 171, 190, 192, 194, 201, 211-213, 216, 237, 240, 255, 277, 293, 296-299
supply chain profitability 24-25, 38, 40, 42, 44, 129
supply chain strategy 1, 10, 12, 23, 169, 187, 190, 300
sustainability 96, 101, 109-113, 191, 221, 223, 225, 229-230, 232, 234-235, 261, 268, 273-274, 276
sustainable development goals 111, 230-232, 238, 296

## T

Tamagotchi™ 115-124, 127-132
Taspo Card 147
Tier-1 Fasteners Suppliers 94
Tier-2 Fasteners Suppliers 94
Total Cost of Ownership (TCO) 36, 44
trade-offs 35-36
transformation 46, 59, 61, 64, 74, 215-217, 222-225, 227-228, 233-234, 272, 277, 279, 281-282, 285-286, 289, 291, 297, 299

## U

Ultra-Compact Mobility 60, 67

## V

value chains 259-260, 265-270, 273-274, 276-277
Voluntary Chain 147

## Z

Zero-FLW 218, 238

www.ingramcontent.com/pod-product-compliance
Lightning Source LLC
LaVergne TN
LVHW060419300926
849162LV00006B/1469
*9781799898009*